Electronic Health Records

Understanding and Using Computerized Medical Records

SECOND EDITION

Richard Gartee

Pearson

Boston　Columbus　Indianapolis　New York　San Francisco　Upper Saddle River　Amsterdam
Cape Town　Dubai　London　Madrid　Milan　Munich　Paris　Montreal　Toronto
Delhi　Mexico City　Sao Paulo　Sydney　Hong Kong　Seoul　Singapore　Taipei　Tokyo

Publisher: Julie Levin Alexander
Publisher's Assistant: Regina Bruno
Editor-in-Chief: Mark Cohen
Executive Editor: John Goucher
Associate Editor: Bronwen Glowacki
Editorial Assistant: Mary Ellen Ruitenberg
Developmental Editor: Jill Rembetski, Triple SSS Press Media Development
Director of Marketing: David Gesell
Senior Marketing Manager: Katrin Beacom
Marketing Specialist: Michael Sirinides
Marketing Assistant: Crystal Gonzalez
Managing Production Editor: Patrick Walsh
Production Liaison: Julie Boddorf
Production Editor: Peggy Kellar
Senior Media Editor: Amy Peltier
Media Project Manager: Lorena Cerisano
Manufacturing Manager: Alan Fischer
Senior Art Director: Maria Guglielmo
Interior Designer: Solid State Graphics
Cover Designer: Rachael Cronin
Cover Photo: iStockphoto
Composition: Aptara®, Inc.
Printing and Binding: Courier Kendallville
Cover Printer: Lehigh-Phoenix

CPT-4® is a registered trademark of the American Medical Association
EXCEL®, Windows 2000®, Windows XP®, Windows Vista®, and Windows 7® are a registered trademarks of Microsoft Corporation
Google™ is a trademark of Google, Inc.
ICNP® is a registered trademark of the International Council of Nurses
IMPAC is a trademark of IMPAC Medical Systems, Inc.
IQmark™ is a trademark of Midmark Diagnostics Group
LOINC® is a registered trademark of the Regenstrief Institute
Lotus 1-2-3® is a registered trademark of International Business Machines, Corp.
MEDCIN® is a registered trademark of Medicomp Systems, Inc.
The Medical Manager, Intergy, and OmniDoc™ are trademarks of Sage Software Healthcare, Inc.
NextGen® is a registered trademark of NextGen Healthcare Information Systems, Inc.
pcAnywhere™ is a trademark of Symantec Corporation
SNOMED® and SNOMED CT® are registered trademarks of the College of American Pathologists
UMLS® and Unified Medical Language System® are registered trademarks of the National Library of Medicine
WebMD, WebMD Health, and Medscape are trademarks of WebMD, Inc.
All trademarks used in this book are the property of their respective owners.

Copyright © 2011, 2007 by Pearson Education, Inc., Upper Saddle River, New Jersey 07458.
Pearson Prentice Hall. All rights reserved. Printed in the United States of America. This publication is protected by Copyright and permission should be obtained from the publisher prior to any prohibited reproduction, storage in a retrieval system, or transmission in any form or by any means, electronic, mechanical, photocopying, recording, or likewise. For information regarding permission(s), write to: Rights and Permissions Department.

Library of Congress Cataloging-in-Publication Data available upon request.

10 9 8 7 6 5 4 3

www.pearsonhighered.com

ISBN 10: 0-13-249976-2
ISBN 13: 978-0-13-249976-7

For Hayley and RJ

Contents

Preface xiii
Learning Made Easy xvi
About the Author xx
Acknowledgments xxi
Reviewers xxiii

Chapter 1 — Electronic Health Records—An Overview 1

Evolution of Electronic Health Records 1
Institute of Medicine (IOM) 2
Computer-based Patient Record Institute (CPRI) 4
Health Insurance Portability and Accountability Act (HIPAA) 4
EHR Defined 4

Social Forces Driving EHR Adoption 5
Health Safety 5
Health Costs 5
Changing Society 6
Critical Thinking Exercise 1: EHR News 6

Government Response 6
Office of National Coordinator for Health Information Technology 7
Strategic Framework 7
GOAL 1: INFORM CLINICAL PRACTICE 7
GOAL 2: INTERCONNECT CLINICIANS 7
GOAL 3: PERSONALIZE CARE 8
GOAL 4: IMPROVE POPULATION HEALTH 8
Federal Health IT Strategic Plan 2008–2012 8
GOAL 1: PATIENT-FOCUSED HEALTHCARE 8
GOAL 2: POPULATION HEALTH 8
The HITECH Act 9
Critical Thinking Exercise 2: Compare ONC and HITECH 9
Strategic Plan Update 2011–2015 10

Meaningful Use of a Certified EHR 10
Meaningful Use 11
ELIGIBLE PROFESSIONALS 11
ELIGIBLE HOSPITALS 12
Certified EHR 13
Clinical Quality Measures (CQM) 14

Why Electronic Health Records Are Important 14
Real-Life Story: Where's My Chart? 15
Critical Thinking Exercise 3: When the Chart Is Lacking 16

Flow of Clinical Information into the Chart 16
Workflow of an Office Using Paper Charts 16
Workflow of an Office Fully Using an EHR 18
Critical Thinking Exercise 4: Think About Workflow 21

Inpatient Charts versus Outpatient Charts 22

Documenting at the Point of Care 24
The Physical Clinic and Clinician Mobility 27
EHR on Computer Workstations 28
EHR on Laptop Computers 29
EHR on a Tablet PC 30
Speech Recognition 31

Chapter One Summary 32

Chapter 2: Functional EHR Systems 35

Format of Data Determines Potential Benefits 35
- EHR Data Formats 36
- Limitations of Certain Types of Data 36

Standard EHR Coding Systems 37
- Prominent EHR Code Sets 38
- SNOMED-CT 39
- SNOMED-CT Structure 39
- MEDCIN 40
- MEDCIN Structure 40
- LOINC 42
- UMLS 43
- Nursing Code Sets 43
- Clinical Care Classification System (CCC) 43
- NANDA-I 43
- NIC and NOC 43
- ICNP® 44
- Omaha System 44
- NMDS 44
- PNDS 45
- PCDS 45

Capturing and Recording EHR Data 45
- Digital Image Systems 45
- *Guided Exercise 5: Exploring a Document Imaging System* 46
- The Toolbar 48
- The Catalog Pane 48
- The Image Viewer Pane 51
- Item Details 51
- Image Tools 51
- Cataloging Images 51
- *Guided Exercise 6: Importing and Cataloging Images* 53
- Picture Archival and Communication System (PAC) 58
- Importing Text to the EHR 58
- Importing Coded EHR Data 59
- HL7 59
- DICOM 61
- CDISC 61
- Biomedical Devices 61
- Telemonitors 62
- RIHO 62
- Patient-Entered Data 63
- Provider-Entered Data 64
- *Real-Life Story: Enhancing Process Efficiency through Remote Access* 64

Functional Benefits from Codified Records 65
- Trend Analysis 65
- *Critical Thinking Exercise 7: Retrieving a Scanned Lab Report* 65
- Lab Report as Text Data 66
- Coded Lab Data 66
- Alerts 68
- Drug Utilization Review 69
- Formulary Alerts 70
- Other Types of Alerts 70
- Health Maintenance 72
- Preventive Care 72
- Immunizations 73
- Decision Support 73
- Meeting the IOM Definition of an EHR 74

Chapter Two Summary 74

Chapter 3: Learning Medical Record Software 77

Introducing the Medcin Student Edition 77
- About the Exercises in This Book 78

Understanding the Software 78
- EHR Login 78
- *Guided Exercise 8: Starting Up the Software* 78

Navigating the Screen 80
- *Guided Exercise 9: Exiting and Restarting the Software* 81

Guided Exercise 10: Using the Menu to Select a Patient 82

Guided Exercise 11: Navigating the Medcin Findings 84

Guided Exercise 12: Tabs on the Medcin Nomenclature Pane 87

Data Entry of Clinical Notes 87

Guided Exercise 13: Creating an Encounter 88

Guided Exercise 14: Recording Subjective Findings 91

Guided Exercise 15: Removing Findings 94

Guided Exercise 16: Recording More Specific Findings 95

Guided Exercise 17: Recording History Findings 96

Adding Details to the Findings 97

Guided Exercise 18: Recording a Value 98

Using Free Text 99

Guided Exercise 19: Adding Free Text 99

Guided Exercise 20: Recording Objective Findings 101

Guided Exercise 21: Setting the Result Field 101

Guided Exercise 22: Adding Detail to Recorded Findings 103

Guided Exercise 23: Adding Episode Detail to Findings 104

Guided Exercise 24: Recording the Assessment 105

Guided Exercise 25: Recording Treatment Plan and Physician Orders 105

Introduction to Using Forms 108

Guided Exercise 26: Recording the Chief Complaint 108

Guided Exercise 27: Recording Vital Signs 109

Visually Different Button Styles 112

Real-Life Story: Paperless in Less Than a Day 113

Chapter Three Summary 114

Chapter 4 — Increased Familiarity with the Software 118

Applying Your Knowledge 118

Creating Your First Patient Encounter Note 119

Guided Exercise 28: Documenting a Visit for Headaches 119

Guided Exercise 29: Printing the Encounter Note 130

Invoking the Print Dialog Window from the Toolbar 134

Documenting a Brief Patient Visit 134

Guided Exercise 30: Documenting a Visit for Common Cold 134

Real-Life Story: A Nurse's Notes 144

Critical Thinking Exercise 31: A Patient with Sinusitis 145

Chapter Four Summary 151

Chapter 5 — Data Entry at the Point of Care 152

Why Speed of Entry Is Important in the EHR 152

Lists and Forms Speed Data Entry 153

Shortcuts That Speed Documentation of Typical Cases 153

The Concept of Lists 154

Guided Exercise 32: Using an Adult URI List 155

Critical Thinking Exercise 33: Timed Experiment 167

The Concept of Forms 171

Comparison of Lists and Forms 171

Initial Intake Form for an Adult 173

Guided Exercise 34: Using Forms 173

LEFT AND RIGHT MOUSE BUTTONS 176

Customized Forms 184

Real-Life Story: How I Learned to Stop Worrying and Love Forms 186

Critical Thinking Exercise 35: Using a Form and a List 187

Chapter Five Summary 194

Chapter 6: Understanding Electronic Orders 196

The Importance of Electronic Orders and Results 196

Recording Orders in the Student Edition 197

Lab Orders and Reports 198

Comparison of Orders and Results Workflow 201

Workflow of Paper Lab Orders and Results 202

Workflow of Electronic Lab Orders and Results 203

Learning to Use the Search and Prompt Features 205

How Search Works 206

Guided Exercise 36: Using Search and Prompt 206

Guided Exercise 37: Ordering Diagnostic Tests 212

Radiology Orders and Reports 217

Critical Thinking Exercise 38: Ordering an X-Ray 218

Medication Orders 221

Written Prescriptions 221

Electronic Prescriptions 222

Closing The Loop on Safe Medication Administration 223

Guided Exercise 39: Writing Prescriptions in an EHR 224

Quick Access to Frequent Orders 230

Critical Thinking Exercise 40: Ordering Medications Using a Quick-Pick List 230

Real-Life Story: When Orders and Results Are Critical 234

Protocols Based on Diagnosis Codes 235

Introducing Diagnosis Codes 235

History of ICD-9-CM 236

Future Developments: ICD-10 237

ICD-9-CM and EHR Nomenclatures 238

Primary and Secondary Diagnoses 238

Multiple Diagnoses 238

The Rule-Out Diagnosis 239

Using Diagnosis to Find Orders and Treatments 239

Guided Exercise 41: Orders Based on Diagnosis 239

Guided Exercise 42: Multiple Diagnoses 245

Chapter Six Summary 251

Comprehensive Evaluation of Chapters 1–6 254

Part I—Written Exam 254

Part II—MyHealthProfessionsKit Questions 255

Part III—Hands-On Exercise 255

Critical Thinking Exercise 43: Examination of a Patient with Asthma 256

Chapter 7: Problem Lists, Results Management, and Trending 261

Longitudinal Patient Records to Manage Patients' Health 261

Understanding Problem Lists 262

Guided Exercise 44: Exploring Patient Management 263

Citing Previous Visits from Problem Lists 269

Guided Exercises 45: Following Up on a Problem **269**

Orders and Results Management **278**

Guided Exercise 46: Viewing Pending Orders and Lab Results **279**

Real-Life Story: Experiencing the Functional Benefits of an EHR **289**

Trending **290**

Using Graphs to View Trends of Lab Results **290**

Guided Exercise 47: Graphing Lab Results **290**

Guided Exercise 48: Graphing Vital Signs in the Chart **294**

Visual Aides to Engage Patients in Their Own Healthcare **297**

Critical Thinking Exercise 49: Graphing Total Cholesterol and Weight **297**

Chapter Seven Summary **298**

Chapter 8

Data Entry Using Flow Sheets and Anatomical Drawings   301

Learning to Use Flow Sheets **301**

Guided Exercise 50: Working with a Flow Sheet **302**

ABOUT THE FLOW SHEET VIEW **305**

Guided Exercise 51: Creating a Problem-Oriented Flow Sheet **316**

Use of Anatomical Drawings in the EHR **320**

Navigation by Body System **321**

Annotated Drawings as EHR Data **321**

Guided Exercise 52: Annotated Dermatology Exam **321**

Real-Life Story: First Patient Whose Life Was Saved By Expert System Software He Operated Himself **333**

Critical Thinking Exercise 53: Examination of a Patient with Pressure Sores **333**

Chapter Eight Summary **340**

Chapter 9

Using the EHR to Improve Patient Health   342

Prevention and Early Detection **342**

Pediatric Wellness Visits **343**

Guided Exercise 54: A Well-Baby Check-Up **343**

Understanding Growth Charts **352**

What Is a Percentile? **355**

Guided Exercise 55: Creating a Growth Chart **356**

Body Mass Index **358**

Guided Exercise 56: Graphing BMI **358**

Critical Thinking Exercise 57: Adult BMI Categories **360**

The Importance of Childhood Immunizations **360**

Guided Exercise 58: Reviewing and Ordering Vaccines **361**

IMMUNIZATION SCHEDULES FROM THE CDC **362**

Critical Thinking Exercise 59: Determine Your Adult Immunizations **368**

Patients' Involvement in Their Own Healthcare **368**

Patient-Entered Data Graphs **368**

Preventative Care Screening **370**

Real-Life Story: Quality Care for Pediatric and Adult Patients **371**

Chapter Nine Summary **373**

Chapter 10 — Privacy and Security of Health Records 375

Understanding HIPAA 375
Administrative Simplification Subsection 376

HIPAA Transactions and Code Sets 376
Eight HIPAA Transactions 376
Standard Code Sets 377

HIPAA Uniform Identifiers 377

HIPAA Privacy Rule 378
Privacy Policy 379
Consent 379
Modifying HIPAA Consent 381
Authorization 381
RESEARCH 383
RESEARCH EXCEPTIONS 383
MARKETING 383
Government Agencies 383
Minimum Necessary 384
Incidental Disclosures 384
Critical Thinking Exercise 60: What Is Required? 385
A Patient's Right To Know about Disclosures 385
Patient Access To Medical Records 385
Personal Representatives 386
Minor Children 387
Critical Thinking Exercise 61: Comparison of Privacy Policy 387
Business Associates 389
Civil And Criminal Penalties 390
Real-Life Story: The First HIPAA Privacy Case 391

HIPAA Security Rule 391
Why a Security Rule? 392
The Privacy Rule and Security Rule Compared 392

Security Standards 393
Implementation Specifications 393

Administrative Safeguards 394
Security Management Process 395
Assigned Security Responsibility 396
Workforce Security 396
Information Access Management 397
Security Awareness and Training 397
Security Incident Procedures 398
Contingency Plan 399
Evaluation 399
Business Associate Contracts and Other Arrangements 399
Real-Life Story: Contingency Plans Ensure Continued Ability to Deliver Care 400

Physical Safeguards 400
Facility Access Controls 401
Workstation Use 402
Workstation Security 402
Device And Media Controls 402

Technical Safeguards 402
Access Control 403
Audit Controls 404
Integrity 404
Person or Entity Authentication 404
Transmission Security 405

Organizational, Policies and Procedures, and Documentation Requirements 405
Organizational Requirements 406
Policies and Procedures 406
Documentation 406

Breach Notification Requirements 406
Individual Notice 407
Media Notice 407
Notice to the Secretary 408
Notification by a Business Associate 408

Electronic Signatures for Health Records 408
What Is an Electronic Signature and What Is Not? 408
How Digital Signatures Work 410
Some EHR Signatures Are Not True Electronic Signatures 411
The Future of Electronic Signatures 411
Critical Thinking Exercise 62: Your Electronic Signature 412

HIPAA Privacy, Security, and You 412

Chapter Ten Summary 412

Chapter 11: Using the Internet to Expedite Patient Care 417

The Impact of Technology 417

The Internet and the EHR 419

Decision Support Via the Web 420

Critical Thinking Exercise 63: Internet Medical Research 422

Integrating Decision Support 423

Understanding The Internet 424

Secure Internet Data 424

Remote EHR Access for the Provider 425

Practicing Medicine Online 426

Telemedicine 427

Teleradiology 428

Patient Entry of Symptoms and History 429

Workflow Using Patient-Entered Data 431

Internet Workflow 432

Improved Patient Information 432

Guided Exercise 64: Experiencing Patient-Entered HPI 434

Critical Thinking Exercise 65: Reviewing Patient-Entered Data 439

Provider-to-Patient E-Mail Communication 441

Secure Messaging 442

E-Visits 442

Workflow of an E-Visit 442

Real-Life Story: Using the Internet to Build a Patient-Centered Practice 444

Mayo Clinic Study of E-Visits 446

California Study 447

Guided Exercise 66: Patient Requests an E-Visit 447

Guided Exercise 67: Clinician Completes the E-Visit 451

Patient Access to Electronic Health Records 457

The Patient-Centered Medical Home 457

The Personal History Record 459

Critical Thinking Exercise 68: Researching the PHR 460

Chapter Eleven Summary 461

Chapter 12: EHR Coding and Reimbursement 464

The EHR and Reimbursement 464

EHR Helps Meet Government Mandates 465

Incentives and Penalties 465

HIPAA-Required Code Sets 466

Diagnosis Codes Justify Billing 466

CPT-4 and HCPCS Codes 467

Evaluation and Management (E&M) Codes 467

Four Levels of E&M Codes 468

How the Level of an E&M Code Is Determined 468

Undercoding 468

Accurate Coding 469

Using EHR Software to Understand E&M Codes 469

Guided Exercise 69: Calculating E&M Code from an Encounter 469

Problem Screening Checklist Window 472

Levels of Key Components 473

Key Component: History 474

Key Component: Examination 478

Key Component: Medical Decision Making 481

Determining the Level of Medical Decision Making 485

Other Components: Counseling, Coordination of Care, and Time 486

Putting It All Together 486

Evaluating Key Components 487

How Changes in Key Components Affect the E&M Code 488

Guided Exercise 70: Calculating E&M for a More Complex Visit 489

HISTORY 490

EXAMINATION 492

Contents xi

Medical Decision Making 495

Time 496

Critical Thinking Exercise 71: Understanding How Procedures Are Posted to the Billing System 499

Real-Life Story: A New Level of Efficiency in Addition to Improved E&M Coding 502

Guided Exercise 72: Counseling Over 50% of Face-to-Face Time 503

Factors That Affect the E&M Code Set 507

Guided Exercise 73: Exploring Other Factors of E&M Codes 508

Critical Thinking Exercise 74: Counseling an Established Patient 512

Chapter Twelve Summary 517

Comprehensive Evaluation of Chapters 7—12 519

Part I—Written Exam 519

Part II—Hands-On Exercise 520

Critical Thinking Exercise 75: Examination of a Patient with Arterial Disease 520

Part III—Internet Exercise 528

Critical Thinking Exercise 76: Patient Researches Medication 528

Glossary 530

Index 541

Acronyms 550

Preface

Introduction

When the first edition of this textbook was published, it predicted that electronic health records would be the "next big thing" in healthcare. Surely that has come to pass. Almost daily the media makes us aware that healthcare is making a transition from paper charts to electronic health records (EHR). Government incentive programs have increased the rate at which this is occurring and have set a target date of 2015 to complete the transition. The result is that everyone who works in healthcare—anyone who touches the paper chart—is going to need to understand and be able to use electronic health records.

For most of the healthcare workforce, the thought of that impending transition is scary. The purpose of this book is to build, through practical experience in the classroom, an understanding and a level of comfort with computerized medical records that can be applied directly in the clinical workplace.

This book was the first of its kind. EHR books available before its publication were oriented toward medical groups wishing to purchase an EHR system and inappropriate to the classroom. Instead, this book focused on the users of an EHR—doctors, nurses, medical assistants, physician assistants, and other medical office staff using an innovative "learn by doing" approach.

The new edition continues that mission, providing the learner with a thorough understanding of the EHR that is continuously reinforced by actual EHR experiences. Updated to reflect the latest rules, regulations, and innovations in EHR, this new edition has 50 percent more guided and critical thinking exercises. These hands-on exercises use real EHR software to transform theoretical EHR concepts into practical understanding.

The first edition has been adopted by schools nationwide and has helped prevent the anxiety and fear that medical staffs have of changing from paper to electronic records by allowing students to understand the history and use of EHR before they are exposed to it in the workplace. Using the combination of textbook and software, we are creating an educated clinical workforce that understands and is comfortable with computerized health records. It is my hope that practical application of this new edition will prepare you, the learner, for a bright future in healthcare.

The Development and Organization of the Text

This book is organized to provide learners with a comprehensive understanding of the history, theory, and functional benefits of Electronic Health Records. Each chapter builds on the knowledge acquired in previous chapters.

Chapter 1: Electronic Health Records—An Overview provides a foundation for student learning, introducing concepts and topics that are explained in depth in subsequent chapters. The chapter begins with a definition of Electronic Health Records, discusses why they are important, what forces in our society and what federal laws are driving their adoption. Illustrated scenarios compare the workflow of a medical office using paper charts versus one using electronic charts, and the differences between inpatient and outpatient settings. Additional topics include how a medical practice is changed by adoption of an EHR and what constitutes meaningful use of an EHR. The chapter is illustrated with numerous photos of medical personnel using different types of computers to document at the point of care.

Chapter 2: Functional EHR Systems explains that the format EHR data is stored in determines the potential uses of EHR data to improve patient care and safety. Chapter 2 describes the various forms of EHR data and the value of using standardized codes for that data. Guided exercises provide the students with an opportunity to explore a component found in most EHR systems—Document Imaging. Major EHR nomenclatures are discussed. The student not only achieves knowledge of EHR nomenclatures and their history, but also their importance in enabling different healthcare systems to exchange data. Functional benefits of an EHR such as trending changes in patients' health, generating medical alerts and decision support such the drug interaction checking feature of electronic prescription writing software are also covered.

Chapter 3: Learning Medical Record Software introduces the Medcin Student Edition software, which will be used for the remainder of the book. In a series of brief hands-on exercises, the student becomes familiar with EHR concepts, learns to navigate the software, and creates an actual encounter note.

Chapter 4: Increased Familiarity with the Software reinforces the student's computer skills with additional hands-on exercises. Students also learn how to save their work as printed encounters or output encounter notes to PDF or XPS files.

Chapter 5: Data Entry at the Point of Care stresses the importance of entering data at the time of the encounter, not after the fact. Students learn how to increase data entry speed by using EHR features of Lists and Forms.

Chapter 6: Understanding Electronic Orders introduces students to computerized order entry and electronic prescriptions that are now required in all certified EHR systems. The workflows of paper versus electronic order system are compared and "closed loop safe medication administration" is emphasized. Hands-on exercises are used for each feature. ICD-9-CM codes are introduced and compared with ICD-10, the future standard. Students continue to build EHR computer skills learning how to search the EHR nomenclature and prompt for diagnosis-based order protocols.

Chapter 7: Problem Lists, Results Management, and Trending expands on concepts introduced in Chapters 1–6. Hands-on exercises allow students to experiment with other methods of documenting the exam and introducing the concepts of patient management, problem lists, pending orders, and electronic results. Students gain firsthand experience trending changes in patients' health by learning to graph lab test results and vital signs.

Chapter 8: Data Entry Using Flow Sheets and Anatomical Drawings teaches the concept of flow sheets and provides students hands-on experiences using several types of flow sheets. Additionally, students learn to annotate medical illustrations electronically to document observations in the EHR and for patient education.

Chapter 9: Using the EHR to Improve Patient Health focuses on preventative care with hands-on exercises on pediatric wellness visits, immunizations, and preventative care screening. Students extend their understanding of trending by learning to create growth charts and to graph additional types of data.

Chapter 10: Privacy and Security of Health Records provides a thorough presentation of HIPAA privacy and security regulations that are of paramount concern in any medical setting. Critical thinking exercises help the learner put the material in context of their experiences. Chapter 10 also explains data encryption, electronic signatures, and how records are signed electronically. Because HIPAA rules apply to patient data stored and transmitted electronically, understanding the rules prepares students for Chapter 11, which focuses on the Internet.

Chapter 11: Using the Internet to Expedite Patient Care includes a thorough discussion of the Internet's impact on healthcare, the practice of medicine online, telemedicine, and teleradiology. Hands-on exercises include online medical research, data entry of symptoms and history using the Internet, and the newest innovation, E-visits. The chapter also covers what is necessary for secure patient–provider communications, the Patient-Centered Medical Home concept, and personal health records.

Chapter 12: EHR Coding and Reimbursement deals with the fact that providers get paid for the vast majority of their work by filing health insurance claims. Health plans require that the codes billed be supported by the encounter documentation. EHR systems help ensure the documentation matches the code. Using the EHR, this chapter takes a unique approach that helps the student understand the relationship of the encounter note to the Evaluation and Management codes. Hands-on exercises use visual and tactile methods to simplify complicated billing rules and explain how key components determine the billing code.

Learning Made Easy

A Unique Approach to Learning the Electronic Health Records

This textbook–software package introduces learners to the electronic health record (EHR) through practical applications and guided exercises. The textbook and Medcin Student Edition software combination provides a complete learning system. Chapters integrate the history, theory, and benefits of EHR with the opportunity to experience the EHR environment firsthand by completing guided exercises and critical thinking exercises using the Student Edition software. Each chapter builds on the knowledge acquired in previous chapters.

Applying Theory to Practice

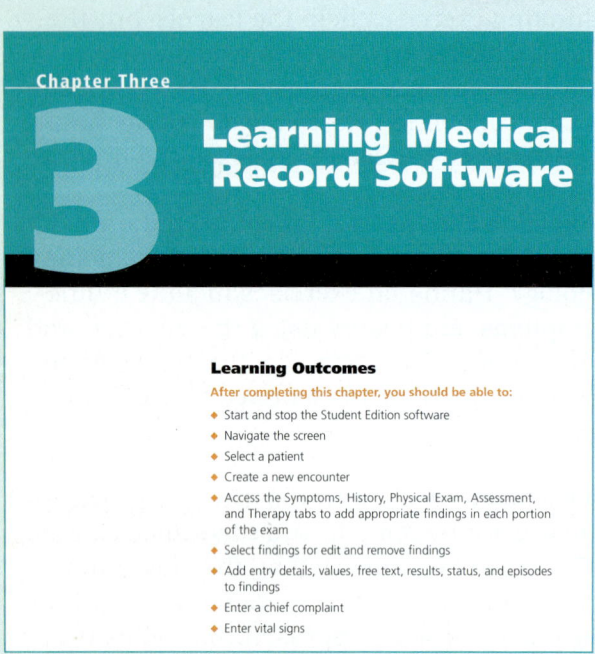

▲ **LEARNING OUTCOMES** Each chapter begins with a list of learning outcomes that highlight the key concepts contained in that chapter.

▼ **ACRONYMS** Acronyms and their definitions are provided in a quick reference.

Acronyms Used in This Book			
ABG	Arterial Blood Gas	ENT	Ears, Nose, Throat
ABN	Advance Beneficiary Notice	EPHI	Protected Health Information in Electronic form
ABN	Abnormal		
AHIMA	American Health Information Management Association	EPs	Eligible Professionals
		ER	Emergency Department or Emergency Room
AHRQ	Agency for Healthcare Research and Quality	FDA	Food and Drug Administration
AMA	Against Medical Advice	FEIN	Federal Employer Identification Number
ARRA	American Recovery and Reinvestment Act	FS Form	Flow Sheet (based on a) Form
BID	Twice Daily	FS Hx	Family and Social History
BIPAP	Bilevel Positive Airway Pressure	GI	Gastrointestinal
BMI	Body Mass Index	H&P	History and Physical
BMP	Basic Metabolic Panel	HAC	Hospital Acquired Condition
CAT	Computerized Axial Tomography	HCAHPS	Hospital Consumer Assessment Healthcare Providers and Systems
CBC	Complete Blood Count		
CC	Chief Complaint	HCPCS	Healthcare Common Procedure Coding System
CCC	Clinical Care Classification system		
CCHIT	Certification Commission for Healthcare Information Technology	HDL-C	High-Density Lipoprotein (cholesterol test)
		HEENT	Head, Eyes, Ears, Nose, (Mouth), and Throat
CCU	Critical Care Unit	HepB	Hepatitis B (vaccine)
CDC	Centers for Disease Control and Prevention	HHS	U.S. Department of Health and Human Services
CDISC	Clinical Data Interchange Standards Consortium	Hib	Haemophilus influenzae type B (vaccine)
		HIM	Health Information Management
CDR	Clinical Data Repository	HIMSS	Health Information Management Systems Society
CHF	Congestive Heart Failure		
CIR	Citywide Immunization Registry (New York City)	HIPAA	Health Insurance Portability and Accountability Act
CME	Continuing Medical Education	HITECH	Health Information Technology for Economic and Clinical Health
CMS	Centers for Medicare and Medicaid Services		
COB	Coordination of Benefits	HIV	Human Immunodeficiency Virus
CPOE	Computerized Provider Order Entry	HL7	Health Level 7
CPR	Cardio-Pulmonary Resuscitation	HPI	History of Present Illness
CPRI	Computer Based Patient Record Institute	Hx	History
CPT-4	Current Procedural Terminology, 4th Revision	ICD-9-CM	International Classification of Diseases, ninth revision, with clinical modifications
CRNA	Certified Registered Nurse Anesthesiologist		

Note

EHR

The acronym EHR is commonly used as shorthand for Electronic Health Records, and will be used in the remainder of this book.

◀ **NOTES** Note boxes found within the chapters explain key terms that are used within the text and provide additional information about the software.

▶ **ALERTS** Alert boxes found within the chapters caution or remind learners about information related to using the software.

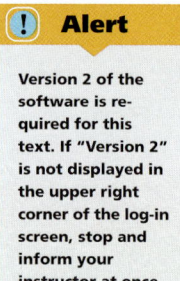

Alert

Version 2 of the software is required for this text. If "Version 2" is not displayed in the upper right corner of the log-in screen, stop and inform your instructor at once.

◀ **REAL-LIFE STORY** Each chapter features a Real-Life Story told by a doctor, nurse, administrator, physician assistant, or patient about their experiences with EHR. These vignettes help learners connect chapter content to real life in the clinic.

▶ **CHAPTER SUMMARY** Summaries at the end of each chapter synthesize key points for students and include a reference table of exercises that cover specific EHR skills.

Practice Opportunities

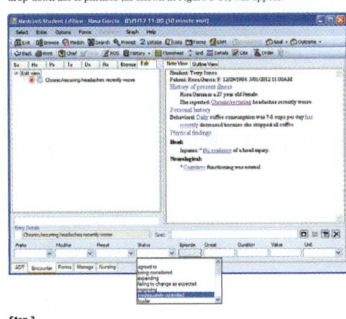

◀ **GUIDED EXERCISES** Guided hands-on exercises using a step-by-step approach allow the students to learn by doing. The companion Medcin® Student Edition software provides a computer experience similar to that of an actual medical facility.

▼ **CRITICAL THINKING EXERCISES** Hands-on critical thinking exercises challenge learners to extend what they have learned through their completion of the guided exercises by applying their knowledge in a new way.

▶ **TESTING YOUR KNOWLEDGE** Open-ended study questions at the end of each chapter allow learners to test their knowledge and think critically.

xvii

▶ **COMPREHENSIVE EVALUATION** Learners will test their mastery of the material through two comprehensive evaluations found at the midpoint and end of the text. Each evaluation includes a written exam and hands-on critical thinking exercises using the software and the Internet.

Visualizing the Electronic Health Record

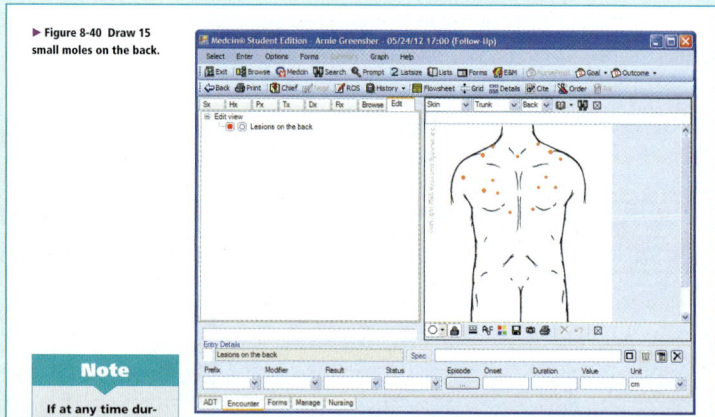

▶ Figure 8-40 Draw 15 small moles on the back.

▶ **SCREEN CAPTURES** Easy-to-follow, step-by-step screen captures of the computer screens from the Medcin software illustrate the steps of the exercise. They serve as a ready reference to help learners orient themselves and assess their progress as they master content.

▼ ▶ **FIGURES AND TABLES** Numerous figures throughout the text help learners visualize workflow scenarios and technical concepts. Photographs of healthcare providers using various types of EHR systems and medical devices make it easy to see the practical applicability in a medical office.

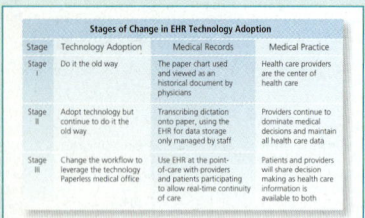

Figure 2-16 Nurse taking vital signs using Welch Allyn® Spot Vitals Signs®.

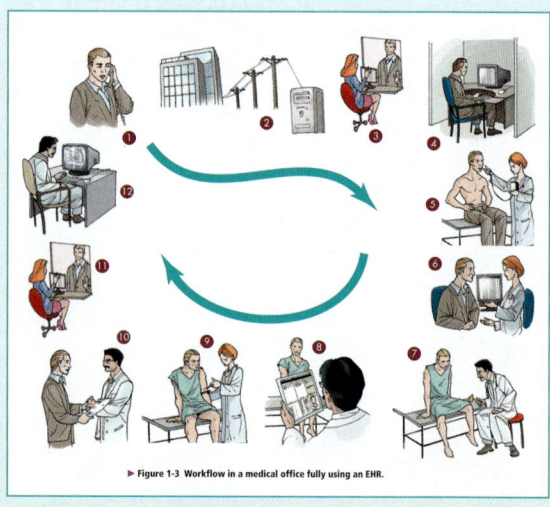

▶ Figure 1-3 Workflow in a medical office fully using an EHR.

The Medcin Student Edition Software

- The Medcin Student Edition contains the entire Medcin nomenclature used in professional EHR systems. Medcin is the licensed core technology in many prominent EHR systems. Because the leading EHR systems for medical offices use the Medcin nomenclature as the technology underlying commercial EHR systems, students in most cases may apply skills they acquire in this course directly to an EHR application in their office. Those systems may not be identical to the student software, but they will seem very familiar to someone who has completed this course.
- Hands-on exercises are short and have been designed to be completed in a normal class time.
- Multiuser software allows multiple students to work simultaneously and keeps each student's work separate.
- All work is printed and no exercise requires saving. This allows students from multiple classes to share the same computer and avoids complications caused by saving and backing up databases. Printouts or file output from the exercises automatically include the student's login name or student ID.
- The printers will use the standard Windows system, and any compatible printer should work.
- For distance learning, the software allows the student to "print" to a file that will output the exercise document into a file in either PDF or XPS format. The output file can then be e-mailed or given to the instructor, who may open and view the student's work with Adobe Reader or an ordinary web browser such as Microsoft Internet Explorer.
- All schools will receive Medcin Student Edition software they can install on the school network and computer lab workstations.
   Software may be installed in two ways: schools with networked computer labs can install a networked client/server system, or schools can install it locally on each student workstation.
- Students may download the individual workstation version and install it on their own (Windows-based) computer as well. This is ideal for distance learning students or those who wish to work outside the classroom.

Software Requirements

To complete the exercises in this book, you will need access to the Medcin Student Edition software. If you are taking this course in a classroom, the software will already be installed. If you are in a distance learning program or working independently, you will need to download and install the software on a computer running the Windows operating system. Directions to download and install the software are found on the MyHealthProfessionsKit web page, which is described on the inside cover of this book.

To complete the exercises in Chapters 2, 11, and both comprehensive evaluations, you will also need access to the Internet and a web browser.

Minimum Workstation Requirements

Processor: 200 mHz Pentium
Operating system: Windows XP, Windows Vista, Windows 7 (or later)
RAM: 64 megabytes (free, not counting OS)
Number of colors: 256 (8-bit color)
Display size (pixels per inch): 800×600 (1024×768 recommended)
Internet Explorer version 6 or later
Microsoft.Net Framework version 2.0 or later

You must have a mouse with at least two buttons that respectively perform the right and left click functions.

Notice

The Medcin Student Edition software is licensed only for educational purposes, to allow the student to perform exercises in the textbook.

By using this program, a healthcare provider agrees that this product is not intended to suggest or replace any medical decisions or actions with respect to the patient's medical care and that the sole and exclusive responsibility for determining the accuracy, completeness, or appropriateness of any diagnostic, clinical, billing, or other medical information provided by the program and any underlying clinical database resides solely with the healthcare provider. Licensor assumes no responsibility for how such materials are used and disclaims all warranties, whether expressed or implied, including any warranty as to the quality, accuracy, or suitability of this information and product for any particular purpose.

About the Author

Richard Gartee is the author of seven college textbooks on health information technology, computerized medical systems, managed care, and electronic health records. Before becoming a full-time author and consultant, Richard spent 20 years in the design, development, and implementation of the preeminent practice management and electronic health records systems.

Richard also served as a liaison to other companies in the medical computer industry as well as Blue Cross/Blue Shield, a U.S. Department of Commerce International Trade Mission, and various universities.

Richard is a current or past member of many of the professional organizations and national standards groups recommended in this book:

- American Health Information Management Association (AHIMA)
- Healthcare Information Management Systems Society (HIMSS)
- American National Standards Institute (ANSI) X12n Committee for Development of Electronic Claims Standards
- Health Level Seven (HL7) Committee for Development of Claims Attachment Standards
- Workgroup for Electronic Data Interchange (WEDI) Task Force for Development of Electronic Remittance Guidelines
- A faculty member/speaker at the Medical Records Institute International Electronic Health Records Conference (TEPR) for 12 years

Acknowledgments

This book was made possible by the contribution of many individuals and several of the most prominent commercial EHR vendors, whom I personally would like to thank and acknowledge here.

I first would like to thank Peter S. Goltra, David Lareau, and Roy Soltoff of Medicomp Systems, Inc.

> Peter S. Goltra is the father of the Medcin nomenclature. He is the founder and CEO of Medicomp Systems, which he established in 1978 to develop advanced documentation and diagnostic tools for use by physicians at the point of care. His honors include an award from the American Medical Informatics Association for contributions to the field of medical informatics.
>
> David Lareau is chief operating officer of Medicomp Systems, Inc. Before joining Medicomp in 1995, Mr. Lareau founded and served as CEO of a medical software and billing company and served as controller of one of the nation's largest distribution companies. In addition to his COO duties, David is the leading proponent of the Medcin nomenclature, having personally presented it to thousands of physicians, key EHR developers, and decision makers during his 15-year tenure.
>
> Roy Soltoff is the director of software development for Medicomp Systems. Mr. Soltoff has been involved in software development, starting with AT&T in 1964. He joined the Medicomp development staff in 1992 and has been responsible for significant advances in clinical user interface design.

The medical content and EHR theory of the textbook were greatly enhanced by my acquaintance with Dr. Allen R. Wenner, M.D., a physician, teacher, author, speaker, and expert on information technology, and with Dr. John Bachman, M.D., professor of family medicine at Mayo Clinic, Rochester, Minnesota. I would also like to thank Kimberly Freese Beal, M.D., and Sharyl Beal, R.N., for their advice on several of the exercises and Jim O'Connor, M.D., for his advice on asthma codes.

My special thanks go to the many individuals who shared firsthand experiences in real-life stories and allowed them to be used in this book. Their unique perspectives help the student understand the relationship of the conceptual to the practical. I would like to thank Richard A. Gartee, Michelle White (whose story was written by Julie DeSantis), Allen R. Wenner, M.D., Sharyl Beal, R.N., MSN, Michael Lukowski, M.D., Marney Thompson, R.N., Henry Palmer, M.D., Primetime Medical (who contributed the real-life story of Mr. John Gould), Alison Connelly, P.A., Tanya Townsend, CIO, Karen L. Smith, M.D., and Philip C. Yount, M.D.

I am also indebted to the following commercial EHR vendors for allowing their copyrighted work to be reprinted herein. In alphabetical order:

Allscripts, LLC; Carestream Health, Inc.; Digital Identification Solutions, LLC; EHS—Electronic Healthcare Systems; GE Healthcare, IMPAC Medical Systems;

McKesson, Inc. (Medisoft); Medfusion, Inc.; Medicomp Systems, Inc.; Midmark Diagnostics Group; NextGen Primetime Medical Software & Instant Medical History; WebMD, Inc., for the Medscape screen; and Welch Allyn.

Also thanks to Michael Lukowski, M.D. for allowing me to reproduce his GYN form; and Susan Majors at EHS—Electronic Healthcare Systems for contributing the pediatric forms for the well-child exercises in Chapter 9.

I would also like to acknowledge the help of all my editors who assisted me with this work.

Reviewers

I would like to thank the academic reviewers, who took time to review and comment on this book.

Second Edition

Shasta Bennett, BA, MS
Instructor
Olney Central College
Olney, IL

Robert James Campbell, EdD, CPEHR
Assistant Professor
East Carolina University
Greenville, NC

Kat Chappell, BS, CMA, AAMA
Program Coordinator and Instructor
Medical Assisting Department
Highline Community College
Des Moines, WA

Jennifer Duffey, MBA
Associate Campus Director
National American University
Independence Campus
Independence, MO

Brina Hollis, MHHS
Assistant Professor of Health Services Management
Chancellor University
Elyria, OH

Kevin Keehan
Dean of Academics/Director of Education
Southwestern College
Franklin, OH

Gregory Martinez, MS
Instructor
Wichita Technical Institute
Wichita, KS

Cindy Nivens, BS
Medical Office Administration, Program Coordinator
Forsyth Technical Community College
Winston Salem, NC

Luis Royer, MD, MHA
Director of Medical Assistant/Medical Billing and Coding
Sanford Brown Institute
Fort Lauderdale, FL

M. Beth Shanholtzer, MAEd, RHIA
Faculty, School of Health Sciences
Kaplan University
Martinsburg, WV

Lisa Stamper, RMA, AAS
Medical Assistant Program Director
Vatterott College—O'Fallon Campus
O'Fallon, MO

First Edition

Robin Berenson, ABD, MS, JCTC
Faculty
Spartanburg Technical College
Spartanburg, SC

Mary T. Boylston, RN EdD
Chair and Associate Professor
Department of Nursing
Eastern University
St. Davids, PA

Leah Grebner, RHIA, CCS
Director of Health
Midstate College
Peoria, IL

Bonnie Hemp, BS, RHIA, CPHQ
Chair, Health Information Technology
Owens Community College
Toledo, OH

Linda Scarborough, RN, CMA, CPC, BSM
Health Care Management Technology Program Director
Lanier Technical College
Oakwood, GA

Lynn G. Slack
Medical Programs
ICM School of Business & Medical Careers
Pittsburgh, PA

Marsha C. Steele, MEd, RHIA
Former Director, Health Information Technology
Henry Ford Community College
Dearborn, MI

Medcin Consulting Editors

Finally, I would like to recognize the work of the numerous doctors who consulted on the development of the Medcin nomenclature. These clinicians did not review the exercises in this book, but they did review the medical accuracy of the Medcin nomenclature that underlies this entire work. Therefore, I would like to acknowledge their work in the development and evolution of the knowledge base on which the Medcin Student Edition is based.

Medcin Consulting Editors

Robert G. Barone, MD
Clinical Assistant Professor of Ophthalmology
Cornell University Medical College;
Attending Surgeon, The New York Hospital
New York, NY

J. Gregory Cairncross, MD
Professor, Departments of Clinical Neurological Sciences and Oncology
University of Western Ontario and London Regional Cancer Centre
London, Ontario, Canada

Richard P. Cohen, MD
Clinical Associate Professor of Medicine
Cornell University Medical College;
Associate Attending Physician, The New York Hospital
New York, NY

Bradley A. Connor, MD
Clinical Assistant Professor of Medicine
Cornell University Medical College;
Adjunct Faculty, Rockefeller University;
Assistant Attending Physician, The New York Hospital
New York, NY

David R. Gastfriend, MD
Assistant Professor in Psychiatry
Harvard Medical School;
Director of Addiction Services
Massachusetts General Hospital
Boston, MA

Stephanie M. Heidelberg, MD
Medical Director, Adult, Older Adult Programs
American Day Treatment Centers, Fairfax, VA;
Psychiatrist, Adult Day Treatment Program,
Northwest Mental Health Center, Reston, VA

Edmund M. Herrold, MD, PhD
Associate Professor of Medicine
Director, Section of Biophysics and Biomechanics
Division of Cardiovascular Pathophysiology
Cornell University Medical College;
Associate Attending Physician, The New York Hospital
New York, NY

Allan N. Houghton, MD
Professor of Medicine and Immunology
Cornell University Medical College;
Chair, Immunology Program,
Memorial Sloan-Kettering Cancer Center
New York, NY

Ralph H. Hruban, MD
Associate Professor of Pathology
Associate Professor of Oncology
The Johns Hopkins School of Medicine;
Director, Division of Cardiovascular-Respiratory Pathology
The Johns Hopkins Hospital
Baltimore, MD

Mark Lachs, MD, MPH
Assistant Professor of Medicine
Cornell University Medical College;
Chief, Geriatrics Unit, Department of Medicine
The New York Hospital
New York, NY

Fredrick A. McCurdy, MD, PhD
Associate Professor of Pediatrics
Director of Pediatric Undergraduate Education
University of Nebraska College of Medicine
Omaha, NE

Paul F. Miskovitz, MD
Clinical Associate Professor of Medicine
Cornell University Medical College;
Associate Attending Physician
The New York Hospital, New York, NY

Preeti Pancholi, PhD
Staff Scientist, Department of Virology and Parasitology
Kimball Research Institute
New York Blood Center
New York, NY

Louis N. Pangaro, MD
Associate Professor, Clinical Medicine
Vice Chairman for Educational Programs,
Department of Medicine, Uniformed Services
University of The Health Sciences,
F. Edward Herbert School of Medicine
Bethesda, MD

Edward J. Parrish, MD, MS
Assistant Professor of Medicine
Cornell University Medical College;
Department of Medicine, Division of Rheumatology,
The New York Hospital, Hospital for Special Surgery
New York, NY

William B. Patterson, MD, MPH
Assistant Professor of Environmental Health
Boston University School of Public Health
Boston, MA;
President, New England Health Center
Wilmington, MA

David Posnett, MD
Associate Professor of Medicine
Cornell University Medical College;
Division of Immunology, Department of Medicine
The New York Hospital, New York, NY

Calvin W. Roberts, MD
Professor of Ophthalmology,
Cornell University Medical College
New York, NY

Ronald C. Silvestri, MD
Assistant Professor of Medicine
Harvard Medical School;
Director, Medical Intensive Care Unit
Deaconess Hospital
Boston, MA

Michael Thorpe, MD
Musculoskeletal Radiology Fellow
The Hospital for Special Surgery
New York, NY

Anshu Vashishtha, MD, PhD
Adjunct Faculty Member
Laboratory of Bacterial Pathogenesis and Immunology
The Rockefeller University;
Clinical Fellow in Allergy and Immunology,
The New York Hospital, New York, NY

H. Hallett Whitman, III, MD
Clinical Assistant Professor of Medicine
Cornell University Medical College;
Clinical Affiliate, Hypertension Center
The New York Hospital, New York, NY;
Attending Physician in Internal Medicine
  and Rheumatology
Summit Medical Group, Summit, NJ

E. David Wright, MD
Clinical Assistant Professor of Medicine
Department of Dermatology
University of Virginia Health Sciences Center
Charlottesville, VA;
Dermatology Associates, Inc.;
Attending Physician, Winchester Medical Center
Winchester, VA

Joseph Zibrak, MD
Assistant Professor of Medicine
Harvard Medical School;
Associate Chief of Pulmonary and Critical Care Medicine
Beth Israel Deaconess Medical Center
Boston, MA

Chapter One

Electronic Health Records—An Overview

Learning Outcomes

After completing this chapter, you should be able to:

- Define electronic health records
- Understand the core functions of an electronic health record as defined by the Institute of Medicine
- Discuss social forces that are driving the adoption of electronic health records
- Describe federal government strategies to promote electronic health record adoption
- Explain why electronic health records are important
- Describe the flow of medical information into the chart
- Compare the workflow of an office using paper charts with an office using an electronic health record
- Contrast inpatient and outpatient charts
- Explain why patient visits should be documented at the point of care
- Compare various types of electronic health record computers such as workstation, laptop, and Tablet PC

Evolution of Electronic Health Records

The idea of computerizing patients' medical records has been around for more than 30 years, but only in the past decade has it become widely adopted. Prior to the EHR, a patient's medical records consisted of handwritten notes, typed reports, and test results stored in a paper file system. Although paper medical records are still used in many healthcare facilities, the transition to electronic health records is underway.

> **Note**
>
> **EHR**
>
> The acronym EHR is commonly used as shorthand for Electronic Health Records, and will be used in the remainder of this book.

Beginning in 1991, the IOM (which stands for the Institute of Medicine of the National Academies) sponsored studies and created reports that led the way toward the concepts we have in place today for electronic health records. Originally, the IOM called them *computer-based patient records*.[1] During their evolution, the EHR have had many other names, including *electronic medical records*, *computerized medical records*, *longitudinal patient records*, and *electronic charts*. All of these names referred to essentially the same thing, which in 2003, the IOM renamed as the *electronic health records*, or EHR.

Institute of Medicine (IOM)

The IOM report[2] put forth a set of eight core functions that an EHR should be capable of performing:

Health information and data This function provides a defined data set that includes such items as medical and nursing diagnoses, a medication list, allergies, demographics, clinical narratives, and laboratory test results. Further, it provides improved access to information needed by care providers when they need it.

Result management Computerized results can be accessed more easily (than paper reports) by the provider at the time and place they are needed.

- Reduced lag time allows for quicker recognition and treatment of medical problems.
- The automated display of previous test results makes it possible to reduce redundant and additional testing.
- Having electronic results can allow for better interpretation and for easier detection of abnormalities, thereby ensuring appropriate follow-up.
- Access to electronic consults and patient consents can establish critical links and improve care coordination among multiple providers, as well as between provider and patient.

Order management Computerized provider order entry (CPOE) systems can improve workflow processes by eliminating lost orders and ambiguities caused by illegible handwriting, generating related orders automatically, monitoring for duplicate orders, and reducing the time required to fill orders.

- CPOE systems for medications reduce the number of errors in medication dose and frequency, drug allergies, and drug–drug interactions.
- The use of CPOE, in conjunction with an EHR, also improves clinician productivity.

Decision Support Computerized decision support systems include prevention, prescribing of drugs, diagnosis and management, and detection of adverse events and disease outbreaks.

- Computer reminders and prompts improve preventive practices in areas such as vaccinations, breast cancer screening, colorectal screening, and cardiovascular risk reduction.

Electronic communication and connectivity Electronic communication among care partners can enhance patient safety and quality of care, especially for patients who have multiple providers in multiple settings that must coordinate care plans.

- Electronic connectivity is essential in creating and populating EHR systems with data from laboratory, pharmacy, radiology, and other providers.

---

[1] Adapted from R. S. Dick and E. B. Steen, *The Computer-based Patient Record: An Essential Technology for Health Care* (Washington, DC: Institute of Medicine, National Academy Press, 1991, revised 1997, 2000).

[2] Ibid.

- ◆ Secure e-mail and web messaging have been shown to be effective in facilitating communication both among providers and with patients, thus allowing for greater continuity of care and more timely interventions.
- ◆ Automatic alerts to providers regarding abnormal laboratory results reduce the time until an appropriate treatment is ordered.
- ◆ Electronic communication is fundamental to the creation of an integrated health record, both within a setting and across settings and institutions.

Patient support Computer-based patient education has been found to be successful in improving control of chronic illnesses, such as diabetes, in primary care.

- ◆ Examples of home monitoring by patients using electronic devices include self-testing by patients with asthma (spirometry), glucose monitors for patients with diabetes, and Holter monitors for patients with heart conditions. Data from monitoring devices can be merged into the EHR, as shown in Figure 1-1.

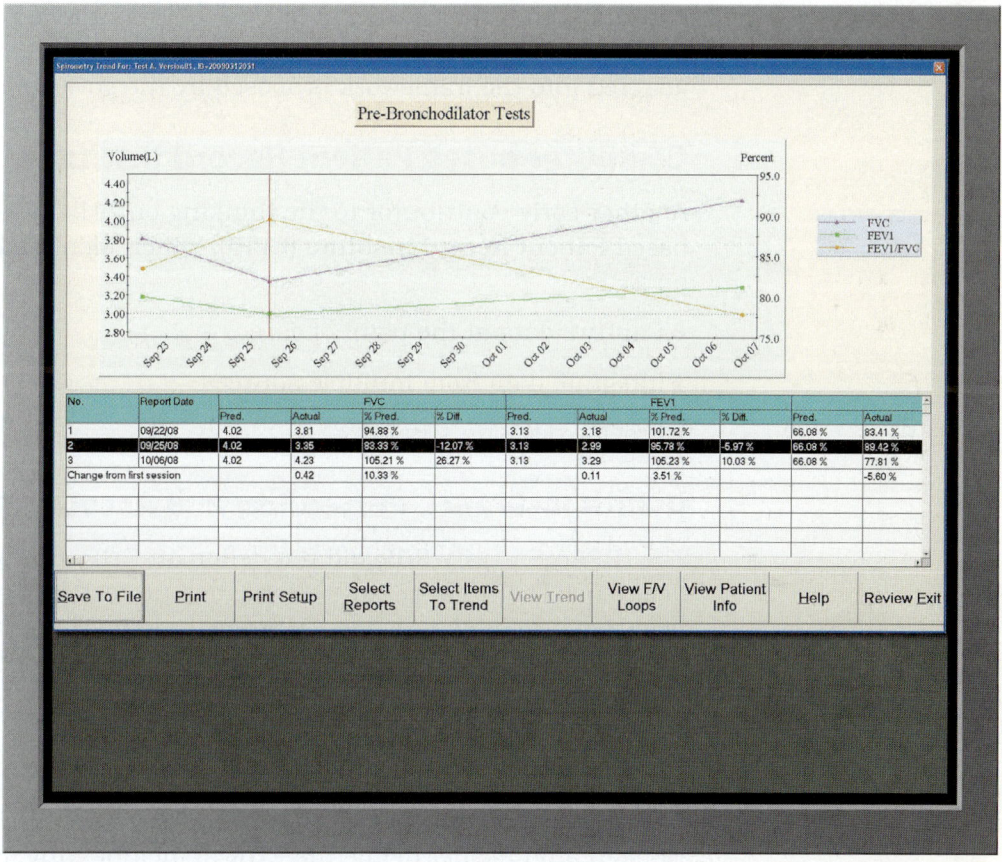

Courtesy of Midmark Diagnostics Group.

▶ Figure 1-1 Data from digital spirometer transfers to EHR.

Administrative processes and reporting Electronic scheduling systems increase the efficiency of healthcare organizations and provide better, timelier service to patients.

- ◆ Communication and content standards are important in the billing and claims management area.
- ◆ Electronic authorization and prior approvals can eliminate delays and confusion; immediate validation of insurance eligibility results in more timely payments and less paperwork.

- EHR data can be analyzed to identify patients who are potentially eligible for clinical trials, as well as candidates for chronic disease management programs.
- Reporting tools support drug recalls.

Reporting and population health Public and private sector reporting requirements at the federal, state, and local levels for patient safety and quality, as well as for public health, are more easily met with computerized data.

- Eliminates the labor-intensive and time-consuming abstraction of data from paper records and the errors that often occur in a manual process.
- Facilitates the reporting of key quality indicators used for the internal quality improvement efforts of many healthcare organizations.
- Improves public health surveillance and timely reporting of adverse reactions and disease outbreaks.

Later in this chapter, we will discuss initiatives by the U.S. government to encourage the development of healthcare information technology. It will become apparent how the IOM definitions of core functions influenced and were adapted into the framework proposed by the government.

Computer-based Patient Record Institute (CPRI)

Another early contributor to the thinking on EHR systems was the Computer-based Patient Record Institute (CPRI), which identified three key criteria for an EHR:

- Capture data at the point of care
- Integrate data from multiple sources
- Provide decision support

Health Insurance Portability and Accountability Act (HIPAA)

The HIPAA Security Rule did not define an EHR, but perhaps it broadened the definition. The Security Rule established protection for *all* personally identifiable health information stored in electronic format. Thus, everything about a patient stored in a healthcare provider's system is protected and treated as part of the patient's EHR.

EHR Defined

In *Electronic Health Records: Changing the Vision*, authors Murphy, Waters, Hanken, and Pfeiffer define the EHR to include "any information relating to the past, present or future physical/mental health, or condition of an individual which resides in electronic system(s) used to capture, transmit, receive, store, retrieve, link and manipulate multimedia data for the primary purpose of providing healthcare and health-related services."[3] The EHR can include dental health records as well.

The core functions defined by the IOM and CPRI suggest that the EHR is not just what data is stored, but what can be done with it. In the broadest sense, *Electronic Health Records are the portions of a patient's medical records that*

---

[3]Gretchen Murphy, Kathleen Waters, Mary A. Hanken, and Maureen Pfeiffer, eds., *Electronic Health Records: Changing the Vision* (Philadelphia: W. B. Saunders Company, 1999), 5.

are stored in a computer system as well as the functional benefits derived from having an electronic health record.

Social Forces Driving EHR Adoption

Visionary leaders in medical informatics have been making the case for the EHR for a long time. However, the combination of several important reports caught the public's attention and set in motion economic and political forces that are driving the transformation of our medical records systems.

Health Safety

The IOM published a report that stated the following: "Healthcare in the United States is not as safe as it should be—and can be. At least 44,000 people, and perhaps as many as 98,000 people, die in hospitals each year as a result of medical errors that could have been prevented, according to estimates from two major studies.

"Beyond their cost in human lives, preventable medical errors exact other significant tolls. They have been estimated to result in total costs (including the expense of additional care necessitated by the errors, lost income and household productivity, and disability) of between $17 billion and $29 billion per year in hospitals nationwide. Errors also are costly in terms of loss of trust in the healthcare system by patients and diminished satisfaction by both patients and health professionals.

"A variety of factors have contributed to the nation's epidemic of medical errors. One oft-cited problem arises from the decentralized and fragmented nature of the healthcare delivery system—or 'non-system,' to some observers. When patients see multiple providers in different settings, none of whom has access to complete information, it becomes easier for things to go wrong."[4]

These statements got the attention of the press and public. They also got the attention of 150 of the nation's largest employers.

Health Costs

Employers who sponsored employee health insurance programs had become frustrated by the increasing costs of health insurance benefits for which they had little or no say about the quality of care. Following the release of the IOM report, these employers formed the Leapfrog group.

A study by the Center for Information Technology Leadership found more than 130,000 life-threatening situations caused by adverse drug reactions alone. The study suggested that $44 billion could be saved annually by installing computerized physician order entry systems in ambulatory settings.

Leapfrog created a strategy that tied purchase of group health insurance benefits to quality care standards. It also promoted computerized provider order entry (CPOE) as a means of reducing errors.

---

[4]Linda T. Kohn, Janet M. Corrigan, and Molla S. Donaldson, eds., *To Err Is Human: Building a Safer Health System* (Washington, DC: Committee on Quality of Healthcare in America, Institute of Medicine, 1999).

Changing Society

Changes in the way we live have also made paper medical records outdated. In an increasingly mobile society, patients relocate and change doctors more frequently, thus needing to transfer their medical records from previous doctors to new ones. Additionally, many patients no longer have a single general practitioner who provides their total care. Increased specialization and the development of new methods of diagnostic and preventive medicine require the ability to share exam records among different specialists and testing facilities.

The Internet, one of the strongest forces for social change in the past decade, also affects healthcare. Consumers are becoming accustomed to being able to access very sensitive information securely over the web. They are beginning to ask, "If I can write checks and use Internet banking securely; if I can trade stocks and see my brokerage account; if I can check in for my airline flight and print my boarding passes; why can't I see my lab test result online?"

One solution is personal health records (PHR), secure web sites that allow patients to keep their own medical records online and enable them to control who has access. One advantage of an online PHR is that it is available everywhere. Wherever patients travel and need medical care, they can retrieve their own records using the Internet.

Another important aspect of the World Wide Web is patient accessibility to medical information and research. There are literally millions of health-related pieces of information on the web. Patients are arriving at their doctor's office armed with questions and sometimes answers. Medical information previously unavailable to the average consumer is now as easy to access as searching Google™ or WebMD®.

A small but growing number of medical offices are creating interactive web sites that actually allow the patient to request an appointment time or a prescription renewal. In a number of states it is even possible for patients and doctors to conduct the medical visit via the Internet. These are called "E-visits" and will be discussed further in Chapter 11.

Critical Thinking Exercise 1: EHR News

1. The topic of EHR is frequently in the news. Describe something you have read or seen on television about EHR.

Government Response

The response to the IOM report was swift and positive, within both the government and private sectors. Almost immediately, President Bill Clinton's administration issued an executive order instructing government agencies that conduct or oversee healthcare programs to implement proven techniques for reducing medical errors and creating a task force to find new strategies for reducing errors. Congress appropriated $50 million to the Agency for Healthcare Research and Quality (AHRQ) to support a variety of efforts targeted at reducing medical errors.

President George W. Bush followed through by establishing the Office of the National Coordinator for Health Information Technology (ONC), under the U.S. Department of Health and Human Services (HHS) to "develop, maintain, and direct the implementation of a strategic plan to guide the nationwide implementation of interoperable health information technology in both the public and private healthcare sectors that will reduce medical errors, improve quality, and produce greater value for healthcare expenditures."[5]

President Barack Obama identified the EHR as a priority for his administration and signed into law the Health Information Technology for Economic and Clinical Health (HITECH) Act. The act promotes the widespread adoption of EHR and authorizes Medicare incentive payments to doctors and hospitals using a certified EHR and eventually financial penalties for physicians and hospitals that do not.[6] Note that the HITECH Act is contained within the American Recovery and Reinvestment Act (ARRA), therefore you may see reference to it by the ARRA designation as well.

Office of National Coordinator for Health Information Technology

David J. Brailer, M.D., Ph.D., the first National Coordinator, acted quickly. Ten weeks after his appointment, the ONC delivered a framework for strategic action outlining 4 goals and 12 strategies for national adoption of health information technology.[7] The document outlined a vision for consumer-centric and information-rich healthcare derived from the widespread adoption of health information technology and set a 10-year time frame for that to happen.

Strategic Framework

The framework as first published listed four major goals and a corresponding set of strategies. These were:

Goal 1: Inform Clinical Practice This goal centered largely on efforts to bring EHR directly into clinical practice. The goal was to reduce medical errors and duplicative work, and enable clinicians to focus their efforts more directly on improved patient care. Three strategies for realizing this goal are:

- Strategy 1. Incentivize EHR adoption.
- Strategy 2. Reduce risk of EHR investment for clinicians who purchase EHR to reduce risk, failure, and partial use of EHR.
- Strategy 3. Promote EHR diffusion in rural and underserved areas.

Goal 2: Interconnect Clinicians Interconnecting clinicians allows information to be portable and to move with consumers from one point of care to another. This will require an interoperable infrastructure to help clinicians get access to critical healthcare information when their clinical or treatment decisions are being made. The three strategies for realizing this goal are:

- Strategy 1. Foster regional collaborations.
- Strategy 2. Develop a national health information network.
- Strategy 3. Coordinate federal health information systems.

---

[5]President George W. Bush, Executive Order #13335, April 27, 2004.
[6]H.R. 1 American Recovery and Reinvestment Act of 2009, Title XIII Health Information Technology for Economic and Clinical Health, February 17, 2009.
[7]*The Decade of Health Information Technology: Delivering Consumer-centric and Information-rich Healthcare* (Washington, DC: U.S. Department of Health and Human Services, July 21, 2004).

Goal 3: Personalize Care Consumer-centric information helps individuals manage their own wellness and assists with their personal healthcare decisions. The three strategies for realizing this goal are:

- Strategy 1. Encourage use of PHR.
- Strategy 2. Enhance informed consumer choice to select clinicians and institutions based on what they value, including but not limited to the quality of care that providers deliver.
- Strategy 3. Promote use of telehealth systems.

Goal 4: Improve Population Health Population health improvement by the collection of timely, accurate, and detailed clinical information to allow for the evaluation of healthcare delivery and the reporting of critical findings to public health officials, clinical trials and other research, and feedback to clinicians. Three strategies for realizing this goal are:

- Strategy 1. Unify public health surveillance architectures.
- Strategy 2. Streamline quality and health status monitoring.
- Strategy 3. Accelerate research and dissemination of evidence.

Federal Health IT Strategic Plan 2008–2012

In June of 2008, the ONC published an update to the strategic framework called the Federal Health IT Strategic Plan.[8] The plan had two goals, patient-focused healthcare and population health, with four objectives under each goal. The themes of privacy and security, interoperability, IT adoption, and collaborative governance recur across the goals, but they apply in very different ways to healthcare and population health.

Goal 1: Patient-focused Healthcare Enable the transformation to higher quality, more cost-efficient, patient-focused healthcare through electronic health information access and use by care providers, and by patients and their designees.

- Objective 1.1—Privacy and Security: Facilitate electronic exchange, access, and use of electronic health information while protecting the privacy and security of patients' health information.
- Objective 1.2—Interoperability: Enable the movement of electronic health information to where and when it is needed to support individual health and care needs.
- Objective 1.3—Adoption: Promote nationwide deployment of EHR and PHR that put information to use in support of health and care.
- Objective 1.4—Collaborative Governance: Establish mechanisms for multi-stakeholder priority setting and decision making to guide development of the nation's health IT infrastructure.

Goal 2: Population Health Enable the appropriate, authorized, and timely access and use of electronic health information to benefit public health, biomedical research, quality improvement, and emergency preparedness.

---

[8]*Federal Health IT Strategic Plan (ONC): 2008–2012* (Washington, DC: U.S. Department of Health and Human Services, Office of National Coordinator, June 3, 2008, pp. iii–iv).

- ◆ Objective 2.1—Privacy and Security: Advance privacy and security policies, principles, procedures, and protections for information access and use in population health.
- ◆ Objective 2.2—Interoperability: Enable the mobility of health information to support population-oriented uses.
- ◆ Objective 2.3—Adoption: Promote nationwide adoption of technologies and technical functions that will improve population and individual health.
- ◆ Objective 2.4—Collaborative Governance: Establish coordinated organizational processes supporting information use for population health.

Achievement of the eight objectives was tied to measurable outcomes, describing 43 strategies that needed to be done to achieve the objectives. Each strategy was associated with a milestone against which progress could be assessed. The plan included a set of illustrative actions to implement each strategy.

The HITECH Act

In passing the HITECH Act,[9] the federal government showed that it firmly believes in the benefits of using EHR. The act encourages the widespread adoption of EHR by authorizing Medicare to make incentive payments to doctors and hospitals that use a certified EHR. These incentives are intended to drive adoption of EHR in order to reach the goal of every American having a secure EHR. To achieve this vision of a transformed healthcare system that health information technology can facilitate, there are three critical short-term prerequisites:

- ◆ Clinicians and hospitals must acquire and implement certified EHR in a way that fully integrates these tools into the care delivery process.
- ◆ Technical, legal, and financial supports are needed to enable information to flow securely to wherever it is needed to support healthcare and population health.
- ◆ A skilled workforce is needed that can facilitate the implementation and support of EHR, exchange of health information among healthcare providers and public health authorities, and the redesign of workflows within the healthcare settings.

Providers that implement and have a meaningful use of a certified EHR prior to 2015 are eligible for incentives. This means that a practice adopting an EHR actually gets paid more than a practice continuing to use paper charts.

After 2015, Medicare will begin to administer financial penalties for physicians and hospitals that do not use a EHR. These will involve reducing the provider's payments by 1 percent per year for up to five years. By 2020, a provider still using paper charts will have payments reduced by 5 percent.

Critical Thinking Exercise 2: Compare ONC and HITECH

Compare the HITECH requirements with the goals and strategies of the original Strategic Framework discussed earlier.

---

[9]H.R. 1 American Recovery and Reinvestment Act of 2009, Title XIII Health Information Technology for Economic and Clinical Health, February 17, 2009.

Strategic Plan Update 2011–2015

The HITECH Act requires the ONC, in consultation with other appropriate federal agencies, to update the 2008–2012 Strategic Plan (discussed above). The 2008–2012 plan is intended "to guide the nationwide implementation of interoperable health information technology in both the public and private healthcare sectors that will reduce medical errors, improve quality, and produce greater value for healthcare expenditures."[10]

The HITECH Act requires that the update include specific objectives, milestones, and metrics with respect to the following:

1. The electronic exchange and use of health information and the enterprise integration of such information.

2. The use of an EHR for each person in the United States by 2014.

3. The incorporation of privacy and security protections for electronic exchange of an individual's individually identifiable health information.

4. Establishing security methods to ensure appropriate authorization and electronic authentication of health information and specifying technologies or methodologies for rendering health information unusable, unreadable, or indecipherable.

5. Specifying a framework for coordination and flow of recommendations and policies under this subtitle among the Secretary, the National Coordinator, the HIT Policy Committee, the HIT Standards Committee, and other health information exchanges and other relevant entities.

6. Methods to foster the public understanding of health information technology.

7. Strategies to enhance the use of health information technology in improving the quality of healthcare, reducing medical errors, reducing health disparities, improving public health, increasing prevention and coordination with community resources, and improving the continuity of care among healthcare settings.

8. Specific plans for ensuring that populations with unique needs, such as children, are appropriately addressed in the technology design, as appropriate, which may include technology that automates enrollment and retention for eligible individuals.

Meaningful Use of a Certified EHR

The HITECH act specifies the following three components of Meaningful Use:

1. Use of certified EHR in a meaningful manner

2. Use of certified EHR technology for electronic exchange of health information to improve quality of healthcare

3. Use of certified EHR technology to submit clinical quality measures (CQM) and other such measures selected by the Secretary of Health and Human Services

---

[10]*The ONC-Coordinated Federal Health IT Strategic Plan: 2008–2012* (Washington, DC: Office of National Coordinator for Health Information Technology, 2008).

The key terms here are *meaningful use* and *certified EHR*. What is meaningful use and what is a certified EHR?

Meaningful Use

CMS officially published the Electronic Health Record Incentive Program Final Rule July 28, 2010, which finalized the incentive program and defined the criteria for determining "meaningful use."[11]

Requirements for meaningful use incentive payments were implemented over a multiyear period, in three stages. Stage 1, spanning the years 2011 and 2012, set the baseline for electronic data capture and information sharing. Stage 2 (scheduled to begin in 2013) and Stage 3 (scheduled for 2015) will continue to expand on this baseline and be developed through future rule making.

The 2011–2012 meaningful use requirements include a "core" group of requirements that must be met, plus an additional five that providers choose from a list of ten. The requirements for hospital and eligible professionals differ.

Eligible Professionals
For Eligible Professionals (EPs), there are a total of 25 meaningful use objectives. Twenty of the objectives must be completed to qualify for an incentive payment. Fifteen are core objectives that are required, and the remaining 5 objectives may be chosen from the list on the right.

EPs Core Requirements (all 15 must be met)	Additional EPs Objectives (choose 5, at least one with asterisk*)
Computerized physician order entry (CPOE)	Drug-formulary checks
E-Prescribing	Incorporate clinical lab test results as structured data
Report ambulatory clinical quality measures	Generate lists of patients by specific conditions
Implement one clinical decision support rule	Send reminders to patients per patient preference for preventive/follow-up care
Provide patients with an electronic copy of their health information, upon request	Provide patients with timely electronic access to their health information
Provide clinical summaries for patients for each office visit	Use certified EHR technology to identify patient-specific education resources and provide to patient, if appropriate
Drug–drug and drug–allergy interaction checks	
Record demographics	Medication reconciliation
Maintain an up-to-date problem list of current and active diagnoses	Summary of care record for each transition of care/referrals

---

[11]*Electronic Health Record Incentive Program Final Rule* (Washington, DC: U.S. Department of Health and Human Services, Final Rule July 28, 2010, 42 CFR Parts 412, 413, 422, and 495).

Maintain active medication list

Maintain active medication allergy list

Record and chart changes in vital signs

Record smoking status for patients 13 years or older

Capability to exchange key clinical information among providers of care and patient-authorized entities electronically

Protect electronic health information

Capability to submit electronic data to immunization registries/systems*

Capability to provide electronic syndromic surveillance data to public health agencies*

Eligible Hospitals

For Hospitals, there are a total of 24 meaningful use objectives. Fourteen are core objectives that are required, and the remaining 5 objectives may be chosen from the list on the right.

Hospitals Core Requirements Additional Hospital Objectives

CPOE

Drug–drug and drug–allergy interaction checks

Record demographics

Implement one clinical decision support rule

Maintain up-to-date problem list of current and active diagnoses

Maintain active medication list

Maintain active medication allergy list

Record and chart changes in vital signs

Record smoking status for patients 13 years or older

Report hospital clinical quality measures to CMS or states

Provide patients with an electronic copy of their health information, upon request

Provide patients with an electronic copy of their discharge instructions at time of discharge, upon request

Capability to exchange key clinical information among providers of care and patient-authorized entities electronically

Protect electronic health information.

Additional Hospital Objectives (choose 5, at least one with asterisk*)

Drug-formulary checks

Record advanced directives for patients 65 years or older

Incorporate clinical lab test results as structured data

Generate lists of patients by specific conditions

Use certified EHR technology to identify patient-specific education resources and provide to patient, if appropriate

Medication reconciliation

Summary of care record for each transition of care/referrals

Capability to submit electronic data to immunization registries/systems*

Capability to provide electronic submission of reportable lab results to public health agencies*

Capability to provide electronic syndromic surveillance data to public health agencies*

Certified EHR

Under the CMS EHR incentive programs, eligible health care providers must adopt and meaningfully use a "certified EHR" that has been certified by an ONC Authorized Testing and Certification Body (ONC-ATCB). To synchronize the two regulations, the ONC published the Health Information Technology: Initial Set of Standards, Implementation Specifications, and Certification Criteria for Electronic Health Record Technology Final Rule[12] on the same date as the CMS Final Rule.

The ONC certification criteria represent the minimum capabilities an EHR needs to include and have properly implemented in order to achieve certification. They do not preclude developers from including additional capabilities that are not required for the purposes of certification.

Even before the HITECH Act, various leaders in health information technology recognized the need to create a credible authority for certification of EHR systems. Goal 1: Strategy 2 of the original Strategic Framework called for a mechanism to reduce the risk to providers adopting an EHR. The Certification Commission for Healthcare Information Technology (CCHIT®) was formed to do just that.

The history of CCHIT:

- 2004: organized by leading health information associations, the American Health Information Management Association (AHIMA), the Healthcare Information and Management Systems Society (HIMSS), and the National Alliance for Healthcare Information Technology, to examine and certify Health IT products.
- 2005: awarded a three-year contract by the HHS to develop certification criteria and an inspection process for EHR systems.
- 2006: began certifying ambulatory EHR systems.
- 2007: began certifying inpatient EHR systems.
- 2009: became an independent nonprofit organization.
- 2010: applied to become an ONC Authorized Testing and Certification Body.
- 2011: began usability testing for ambulatory EHR systems.

The CCHIT Certified® program is an independently developed certification that includes a rigorous inspection of an EHR's integrated functionality, interoperability, and security using criteria developed by CCHIT's broadly representative, expert work groups.

The CCHIT inspection process is based on real-life medical scenarios designed to test products rigorously against the complex needs of healthcare providers. As part of the process, successful use is verified at live sites.[13]

---

[12]*Electronic Health Record Incentive Program Final Rule* (Washington, DC: U.S. Department of Health and Human Services, 45 CFR Part 170; Final Rule, July 28, 2010).

[13]*CCHIT Certified® 2011 Certification Handbook* (Chicago, IL: Certification Commission for Health Information Technology, 2010).

The 2011 CCHIT certification criteria specifically align with those required to meet the ARRA/HITECH meaningful use criteria, with the intention that a provider using a CCHIT Certified EHR will be in compliance with eligibility requirements.

The ONC will recognize Authorized Testing and Certification Bodies in addition to CCHIT

Clinical Quality Measures (CQM)

CMS has specified a number of clinical quality measures for meaningful use. EPs must report on 3 required core or alternate core CQM and 3 additional CQM selected from a list of 38. Hospitals must report on 15 CQM.

To ensure EHR systems can support these CQM reporting requirements, ONC certification requires an EHR designed for an inpatient setting to be tested and certified to all of the clinical quality measures specified by CMS. An EHR designed for an ambulatory setting must be tested and certified as including at least 9 clinical quality measures specified by CMS—all six of the core (3 core and 3 alternate core) clinical quality measures specified, and at least 3 of the 38 additional measures. Of course EHR developers may include as many clinical quality measures above that requirement as they see fit.

Why Electronic Health Records Are Important

Historically, a patient's medical records consisted of handwritten notes, typed reports, and test results stored in a paper file system. A separate file folder was created and stored at each location where the patient was examined or treated. X-ray films and other radiology records typically were stored separately from the chart, even when they were created at the same medical office.

These are some of the drawbacks to paper records: Handwritten records often are abbreviated, cryptic, or illegible. When information is to be used by another medical practice, the charts must be copied and faxed or mailed to the other office. Even in one practice with multiple locations, the chart must be transported from one office to another when a patient is seen at a different location than usual. Paper records are not easily searchable. For example, if a practice is notified that all patients on a particular drug need to be contacted, the only way of finding those patients is literally to open every chart and look at the medications list.

Certainly, improved legibility, the ability to find, share, and search patient records are strong points for an EHR. There are additional benefits from an EHR that take the practice of medicine to levels that cannot be achieved with paper records. Four examples of this are: health maintenance, trend analysis, alerts, and decision support. These will be covered in more detail in Chapter 2.

However, there are the additional criteria. The IOM report calls for *electronic communication and connectivity among care partners* and the second goal of the

Real-Life Story

Where's My Chart?

A 63-year-old man went to his doctor's office in Kentucky complaining of chest pains and tightness in his chest. He was immediately transferred to the local hospital, where a stress test and cardiac catheterization confirmed he had had a heart attack. He was hospitalized overnight.

Early retirement from his stressful job as well as a regimen of exercise, diet, beta blockers, aspirin therapy, and other medications proved successful. He moved from Kentucky to Florida and tried unsuccessfully to have his medical records concerning the previous heart attack transferred to his new doctor in Florida. The ECG and stress tests were repeated in Florida. Finally, after two years, the records from Kentucky arrived.

In subsequent years, he moved twice more but, wiser now, he took copies of his medical records with him. He continued a normal and active life until age 77, when he slipped in his workshop and broke his right knee. With his leg in a cast he was less active; a blood clot formed and broke free.

Three weeks after he broke his knee, he went to the doctor's office with what he described as very severe flu symptoms, extreme fatigue, a bad cough, and sharp pains in his back when he moved or coughed. The doctor sent him to the emergency room, where he was diagnosed with a pulmonary embolism in the lower lobe of the right lung. He was hospitalized and put on a therapy of blood thinners.

At age 79, he was continuing to lead an active lifestyle, but he was experiencing occasional sharp brief chest pain and brief dizziness. His doctor scheduled a stress test and cardiac catheterization at a cardiac center connected to the hospital. A blockage was discovered and a double bypass surgery was performed at the same hospital. The patient tolerated the surgery well and recovered quickly.

However, one of the veins used in the bypass operation had been harvested from the leg that had the previous broken knee. Three weeks after he was discharged, he passed out and fell. He was taken by ambulance to the ER at the same hospital where he had had his surgery and where he had been hospitalized for the previous pulmonary embolism. Here is what happened:

- When the ambulance crew arrived at the house, they took a medical history from the patient and his wife. They gave him oxygen and transported him to the hospital.

- When the ambulance arrived at the hospital, the nurses and ER staff again took a medical history from the patient and patient's family.

- The patient's primary care physician had a complete medical history of the patient, including copies of his records dating back to his heart attack in Kentucky, but the hospital system was not connected with the physician's office system.

- The patient reported that he had just had surgery at the same hospital only three weeks before. The hospital system surely had his medical history, but the ER was on a different system and the ER doctors did not have access to the records.

- Although the ER was in the same hospital as the cardiac lab, the ER doctors did not have access to those records, either.

- The patient told the ER staff he thought the symptoms felt similar to his previous experience with a pulmonary embolism, but even though the ER was in the same hospital where the patient was hospitalized for a pulmonary embolism two years before, the ER doctors did not have access to the records from his past condition.

- A CAT scan was ordered based on patient history of the embolism provided by a family member, not his medical record.

- After waiting in the ER for 14 hours, he was hospitalized with two pulmonary embolisms, one in each lung.

Seven days later, the patient was discharged from the hospital. He has fully recovered and is doing fine.

This is not the story of poor medical care or a bad hospital. The hospital is affiliated with a major teaching hospital and is as good as or better than most. This is a story of the unfortunate state of medical records. Paper records are not accessible and can take months to transfer. The lack of timely copies of existing records often causes tests to be reordered or the obvious conditions to be overlooked. Electronic records are better, more accessible, but even the most sophisticated systems do not necessarily have the infrastructure in place to communicate with other EHR systems even in the same community or, as in this case, not even in the same facility!

ONC strategic framework is to *interconnect clinicians*. The need for EHR and better connectivity between EHR systems is examined in the Real-Life Story: Where's My Chart?

Critical Thinking Exercise 3: When the Chart Is Lacking

Read the Real-Life Story: Where's My Chart?

1. What are the dangers to the patient of a provider not having access to paper charts?
2. What is the likelihood of the second incident of the pulmonary embolism being overlooked?
3. How would the patient care be improved if the various EHR systems had been able to exchange patient records electronically?

Flow of Clinical Information into the Chart

Whether medical records are paper or electronic, the clinician's exam notes are usually documented in a defined structure organized into four components:

- Subjective
- Objective
- Assessment
- Plan

Charts in this format are referred to as SOAP notes; the acronym representing the first letter of the words *subjective, objective, assessment,* and *plan*. Guided Exercises throughout this book will follow the SOAP format.

However, the EHR requires not only computers and software, but also change in the way providers work. To understand this, let us compare the workflow in a medical office using paper charts with a medical office using an EHR system.

Workflow of an Office Using Paper Charts

Follow the arrows in Figure 1-2 as you read the following description of a workflow in a primary care medical practice using paper charts.

1. An established patient phones the doctor's office and schedules an appointment.
2. The night before the appointment, the patient charts are pulled from the medical record filing system and organized for the next day's patients.
3. On the day of the appointment, the patient arrives at the office and is asked to confirm that insurance and demographic information on file is correct.

    The patient is given a clipboard with a blank medical history form and asked to complete it. The form asks the reason for today's visit and asks

▶ Figure 1-2 Workflow in a medical office using paper charts.

the patient to report any previous history, any changes to medications, new allergies, and so on.

❹ Patient is moved to an exam room and is asked to wait.

Subjective—The patient is asked to describe in his or her own words what the problem is, what the symptoms are, and what he or she is experiencing.

A nurse reviews the form the patient completed, and may ask for more detail about the reason for the visit, which usually is called "the chief complaint." The nurse writes the chief complaint on a form that is placed at the front of the chart along with the updated patient form. The nurse takes the vital signs and records them on the form. Vital signs are "objective" data.

❺ The doctor or other healthcare provider enters the exam room and discusses the reason for the visit, reviews the symptoms and may add to the subjective portion of the note.

Chapter 1 | Electronic Health Records—An Overview

Objective—The clinician performs a physical exam and makes observations about what he or she finds.

Assessment—Applying his or her training to the subjective and objective findings, the clinician arrives at a decision of what might be the cause of the patient's condition, or what further tests might be necessary.

Plan of Treatment—The clinician prescribes a treatment, medication, or orders further tests. Perhaps a follow-up visit at a later date is recommended. A note will be made in the chart of each element of the plan.

6. If medications have been ordered, a handwritten prescription will be given to the patient or phoned to the pharmacy. A note of the prescription will be written in the patient's chart.

   The doctor marks one or more billing codes and one or more diagnosis codes on the chart and leaves the exam room.

7. If lab work has been ordered, a nurse, medical assistant, or phlebotomist will obtain the necessary specimen and send the order to the lab.

8. At many practices, the physician creates the exam note from memory, either handwriting in the chart or dictating the subjective, objective, assessment, plan, and treatment information.

9. When the patient is dressed, the patient will be escorted to the check-out area. The nurse or staff may give the patient education material or medication instructions.

   If x-rays or other diagnostic tests have been ordered at another facility, the office staff may call on behalf of the patient and schedule the tests.

   If a follow-up visit has been indicated, the patient will be scheduled for the next appointment.

10. The dictated notes are later transcribed and returned to the doctor to review before being permanently stored in the chart.

11. If lab, x-ray, or other diagnostic tests have been ordered, the results and reports are subsequently sent to the practice either by fax or on paper a number of days later. When received, they are filed in the patient's chart and the chart is sent to the clinician for review. They are reviewed by the physician, and then re-filed in the paper chart.

12. The paper chart is filed again. Note that the chart may have to be pulled and re-filed each time a new document, such as the transcription or lab report, was added, which required the doctor's review.

One obvious downside to paper charts is accessibility. If the patient chart is needed for a follow-up visit or by another provider, it is possible that it has not been returned to the file room while it is pending dictation or while the provider is reviewing test results.

Workflow of an Office Fully Using an EHR

Follow the arrows in Figure 1-3 as you read the following description of a workflow of a patient visit to an office that fully uses the electronic capabilities that are available in EHR systems today, including patient participation in the process and the capabilities of the Internet.

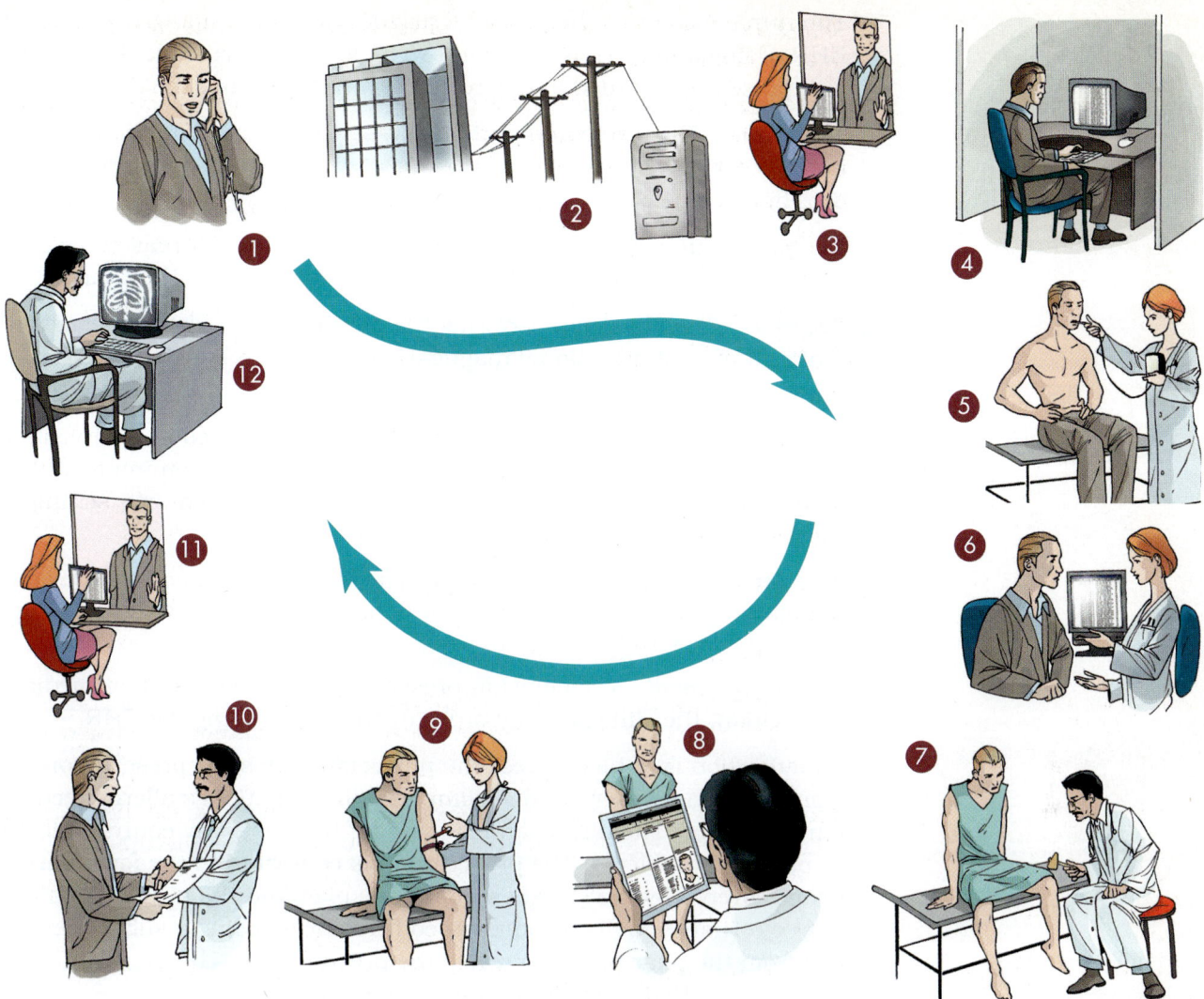

▶ Figure 1-3 Workflow in a medical office fully using an EHR.

❶ An established patient phones the doctor's office and schedules an appointment.

Internet alternative—Patients are increasingly able to request an appointment and receive a confirmation via the Internet.

❷ The night before the appointment, the medical office computer electronically verifies insurance eligibility for patients scheduled the next day.

❸ On the day of the appointment, the patient arrives at the office and is asked to confirm that the demographic information on file is still correct.

❹ A receptionist, nurse, or medical assistant asks the patient to complete a medical history and reason for today's visit using a computer in a private area of the waiting room. The patient completes a computer-guided questionnaire concerning his symptoms and medical history.

Internet alternative—Some medical practices allow patients to use the Internet to complete the history and symptom questionnaire before coming to the office.

❺ When the patient has completed the questionnaire, the system alerts the nurse that the patient is ready to move to an exam room.

Chapter 1 | Electronic Health Records—An Overview

The nurse measures the patient's height and weight and records it in the EHR. Using a modern device, vital signs for blood pressure, temperature, and pulse are recorded and wirelessly transferred into the EHR.

❻ **Subjective**—The nurse and patient review the patient-entered symptoms and history. Where necessary, the nurse edits the record to add clarification or refinement.

The physician enters the exam room and discusses the reason for the visit and reviews with the patient the information already in the chart.

❼ **Objective**—The physician performs the physical exam. The clinician typically makes a mental provisional diagnosis. This is used to select a list or template of findings to quickly record the physical exam in the EHR.

The EHR present a list of problems the patient reported in past visits that have not been resolved. The physician reviews each, examining additional body systems as necessary, and marks the improvement, worsening, or resolution of each problem.

Assessment—Applying his or her training to the subjective and objective findings, the clinician arrives at a decision of one or more diagnoses, and decides if further tests might be warranted.

❽ **Plan of treatment**—The clinician prescribes a treatment and/or medication; in addition, the clinician may order further tests using the EHR.

If medication is to be ordered, the physician writes the prescription electronically. The prescription is compared to the patient's allergy records and current drugs. The physician is advised if there are any contraindications or potential problems. The prescription is compared to the formulary of drugs covered by the patient's insurance plan and the physician is advised if an alternate drug is recommended (thereby avoiding a subsequent phone call from the pharmacist to revise the prescription). The prescription is then transmitted directly to the patient's pharmacy.

A built-in function of the EHR accurately calculates the correct evaluation and management code used for billing. The billing code is confirmed by the physician and automatically transferred to the billing system.

When the visit is complete, so is the exam note. The physician signs the note electronically at the conclusion of the visit.

❾ If lab work has been ordered, a nurse, medical assistant, or phlebotomist will obtain the necessary specimen and the order is sent electronically to the lab.

❿ **Patient education**—Because of the efficiency of the EHR system, the physician has more personal time with the patient for counseling or patient education. In many systems the provider can display and annotate pictures of body areas for patient education, and print them so that the patient can take them home.

When the patient is dressed, he or she is given patient education material, medication instructions, and a copy of the exam notes from the current visit. Allowing the patient to take away a written record of the visit enables better compliance with the doctor's plan of care and recommended treatments.

⓫ The patient is escorted to the checkout area.

If x-rays or other diagnostic tests have been ordered at another facility, the office staff may call on behalf of the patient and schedule the tests.

If a follow-up visit has been indicated, the patient will be scheduled for the next appointment.

⑫ If lab tests were ordered, the results are sent to the doctor electronically, are reviewed on screen, and automatically merged into the EHR.

If radiology or other diagnostic reports are sent to the practice electronically as text reports, they are imported into the EHR and can be reviewed by the physician.

Accessibility is not a problem in the EHR system because there is no chart to "re-file." Multiple providers can access the patient's chart, even simultaneously; for example, a physician could review the previous lab results before entering the exam room, even if the nurse was currently entering vital signs in the chart.

Critical Thinking Exercise 4: Think About Workflow

Having compared the two workflow scenarios, we see the immediate advantages of the EHR for the patient and clinician. Think about the workflow of the office that used paper charts (refer to Figure 1-2 if necessary.) Answer the following questions about the first workflow:

1. What was the nurse or physician doing at the time of the patient interaction?
2. Could they have recorded this data in a computer?
3. Could they have saved time later?
4. Could the data be entered by someone other than the person seeing the patient?

    The patient completed a form concerning any previous history, any changes to medications, new allergies, and so on.

5. Could the patient have used a computer, or could the form have been designed to be read by a computer?
6. Could the patient have completed the information before the visit?

    The nurse recorded various health measurements (vital signs) in the exam room.

7. Could the nurse have recorded the "chief complaint" or the vital signs in a computer instead of on a paper chart?
8. Were any of the instruments used capable of transferring their measurements to a computer system?

    During the physical exam, the physician made observations and an assessment. This was later dictated from memory, subsequently transcribed by a typist, and finally reviewed and signed by the physician.

9. Is the time it would take to record the observations and assessment in the exam comparable to the time it takes to dictate and review the transcribed notes later?

    The physician prescribed medications and ordered tests.

10. Would the time spent entering the prescriptions on a computer justify the benefits of electronic prescribing?
11. Are results available electronically from laboratories that the medical practice uses?

12. Would ordering a test electronically improve the matching of results to orders when the tests were completed?

Inpatient Charts versus Outpatient Charts

The previous figures illustrated the differences between two medical offices, one using a paper chart and another using an EHR. The differences between a hospital using a paper chart and a hospital fully using electronic records are even more significant. However, there are also differences in the type of chart each facility uses and overall workflow process. In this section we are going to compare both.

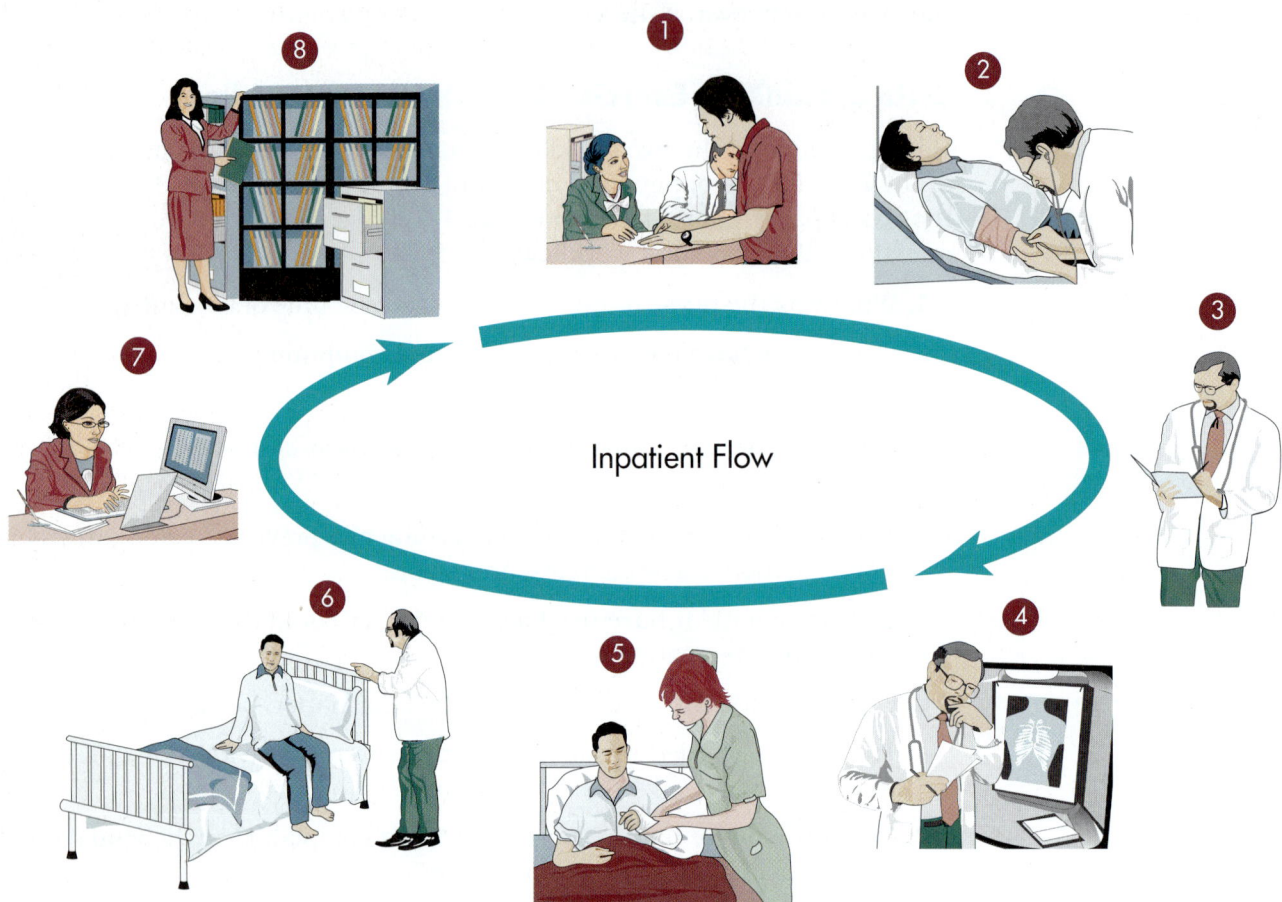

▶ Figure 1-4 Flow of an inpatient from admission through discharge.

Although some patients are admitted to the hospital through the emergency department or by transfer from another facility, most patient admissions begin in the registration department. As depicted in Figure 1-4, the steps involved in an inpatient admission and discharge include the following:

❶ When the patient arrives, patient demographic and insurance information is collected or updated, and an account is set up for the patient stay. Even if the patient has been an inpatient previously, a new account is created (although previous patients will use their existing medical record number).

❷ An admitting and/or attending doctor is assigned to the patient. A physician is required to perform a complete history and physical on an inpatient within 24 hours of the admission. In an outpatient facility, no such time limit is imposed on when or what type of physical is performed.

❸ The doctor orders tests, medications, and procedures.

❹ The doctor reviews the results of tests and diagnostic procedures when they are ready.

❺ Nurses provide most of the patient care, administer medications, take samples for tests, measure vital signs, perform nursing assessments and nursing interventions, and enter nursing notes into the chart.

❻ When a patient leaves an inpatient facility, there is also a formal discharge process. Normally, the physician performs a final examination of the patient and writes a discharge order. Discharge does not necessarily mean the patient goes home. Patients may be discharged to a skilled nursing facility or a rehabilitation facility for further care. Patients who leave without a doctor's order are discharged AMA (against medical advice).

❼ Following discharge, the Health Information Management (HIM) department examines the patient's chart to determine if it has any missing or unsigned documents (called chart deficiencies). When the chart is complete, it is sent to the billing department where the proper billing codes are assigned.

❽ In a facility using paper charts, the last step is to file the chart.

There are also several significant differences in the content and purpose of a patient chart used in an acute care facility and that used by a medical office: the amount of information gathered about each patient and the number of individuals who will need access to it. Figure 1-5 highlights some of the differences between inpatient and outpatient charts.

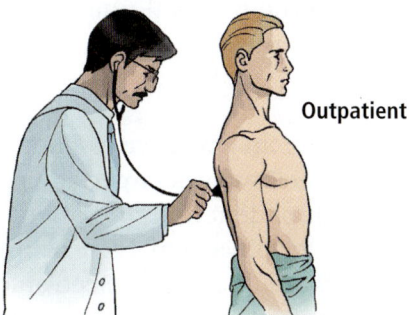
Outpatient

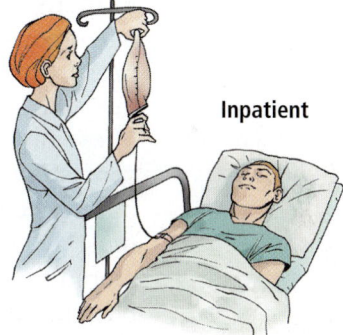
Inpatient

Most physician offices have a single chart for the patient. Notes for each visit, test results, and any other reports are added to the chart.	Most hospitals start a new chart each time a patient is admitted. Information from previous stays in the hospital is linked to the patient ID, but the current chart contains only information related to the current stay.
The quantity of data in an outpatient chart is relatively low by comparison.	The quantity of data in an inpatient chart is likely to be much larger. Vital signs are taken and nurses' notes are added numerous times per day; dietitians, respiratory therapists, and other providers add to the chart; there are typically many more orders for labs, medications, and so on.
The central element in the chart is the physician's exam note.	Physician exams tend to be brief; the main focus of the chart is the physician orders and nurse's notes indicating the patient's response.

▶ Figure 1-5 Contents typical of acute care versus ambulatory patient charts.

In an ambulatory setting such as a physician's office, the patient visits the physician's office a number of times over a period of months or years. Although items produced outside of each visit, such as lab results and consult reports, are also integrated into the patient's chart, the most important element of the outpatient chart is the doctor's notes about each visit. The clinician reviews previous notes on each subsequent visit using them to follow up on past ailments and to measure the patient's progress in managing chronic problems.

The medical chart is primarily used by the physician and nurse, but is also used briefly by the administrative staff to prepare billings following each visit. The focus of the chart is the longitudinal care of the patient. As such, it usually contains all records of the patient's visits and any reports or results received from other providers.

The inpatient chart, however, focuses on the treatment of a specific ailment or condition for which the patient was hospitalized. Data are gathered more frequently during the inpatient's stay, resulting in a substantially large amount of information gathered during a short period of time. In most hospitals, a new chart or medical record is started for each hospital stay. Although records from previous hospitalizations are available for reference, they are not incorporated into the current chart, except as described in the admitting physician's history and physical notes.

Because a large number of caregivers are involved with the patient's stay in an acute care facility, there are a larger number of individuals with a legitimate need to access a patient's record than in an ambulatory care setting. These caregivers include not only nurses and physicians, but other specialists that may consult on the case; radiologists, respiratory therapists, dietitians, and in many hospitals, even the hospital pharmacists have access to records when consulting with the ordering physicians about the medications being prescribed.

These differences between an acute care chart and a medical office chart are consistent whether the facility uses paper or electronic charts. However, another difference between the inpatient and outpatient EHR is the system itself. In most systems designed for physician's offices, the data typically is received and stored by the EHR software in a single electronic medical record system. Most hospitals have a large number of departments using computer systems from many different vendors. The hospital EHR may not necessarily merge the data from these systems into a single EHR. Often the hospital EHR allows the clinician to view data in these other systems through an interface but does not necessarily store the data in a single EHR.

Documenting at the Point of Care

A goal of using an EHR system is to improve the accuracy and completeness of the patient record. One way to achieve this is to record the information in the EHR at the time it is happening. This is called *point-of-care documentation*. In a physician's office, this means completing the SOAP note before the patient ever leaves the office. In an inpatient setting, this means that nurses enter vital signs and nursing notes at bedside, not at the end of their shift. Figure 1-6 shows a nurse entering notes while seeing the patient.

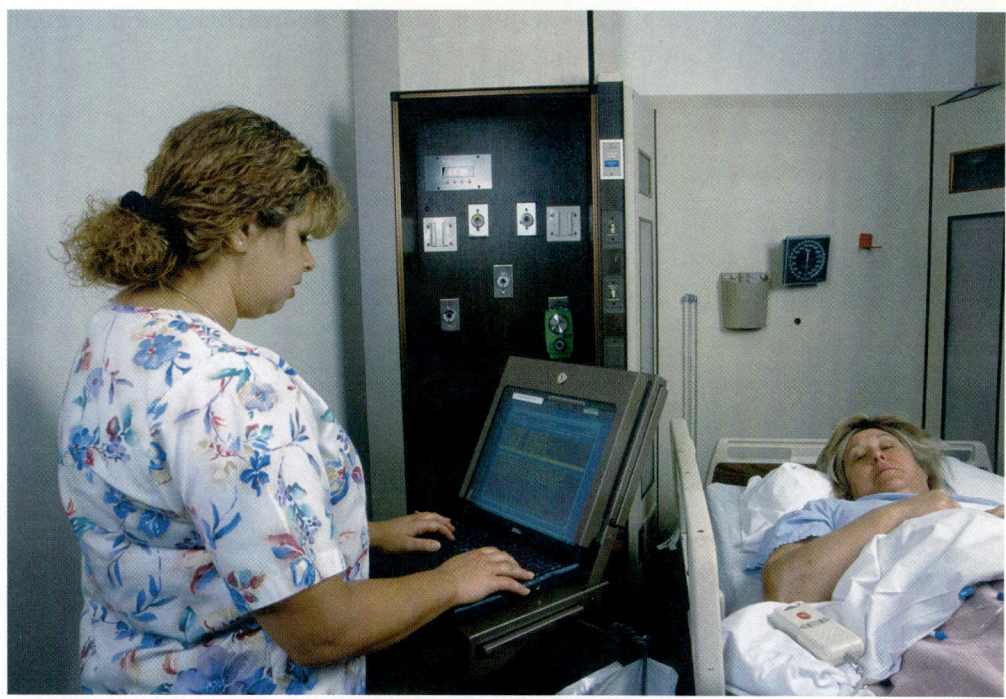

▶ **Figure 1-6 Nurse enters data at patient's bedside.**

Using a point-of-care EHR, when the visit is complete, the note is complete. The clinician can then provide not only patient education materials for patients to take home, but also can actually print a copy of the finished note. Giving patients a copy of the notes from that day's visit ensures that they will remember the key elements of their plan of treatment. They also will have a clearer understanding of their condition as well as information on any tests that may have been ordered or performed.

Leading physician experts on the EHR, Allen R. Wenner, an M.D. in Columbia, South Carolina, and John W. Bachman, an M.D., professor of Family Medicine at the Mayo Medical School in Rochester, Minnesota, wrote: "Documenting an encounter at the point of care is the most efficient method of practicing medicine because the physician completes the medical record at the time of a patient's visit. Dictation time is saved and the need for personal dictation aides is eliminated. Thus, point-of-care documentation is less expensive than traditional dictation with its associated high cost of transcription. In addition, the physician can sign the note immediately.

Patient care is improved because the patient can leave with a complete copy of the medical record, a step that stimulates compliance. The delivery process is improved with point-of-care documentation because referrals can be accomplished with full information available at the time that the referral is needed. For these benefits to occur, the clinical workflow changes to improve efficiency, increase data accuracy, and lower the overall cost of healthcare delivery."[14]

---

[14]Allen R. Wenner and John W. Bachman, "Transforming the Physician Practice: Interviewing Patients with a Computer, Chap. 26 in *Healthcare Information Management Systems: Cases, Strategies, and Solutions*, 3rd ed., ed. Marion J. Ball, Charlotte A. Weaver, and Joan M. Kiel, (New York: Springer Science+Business Media, Inc., 2004), 297–319. Copyright © 2004 Springer Science+Business Media, Inc., New York.

Dr. John Bachman, M.D., has formulated what he refers to as Bachman's Rule and Bachman's Law:

Bachman's Rule: "A patient who has a copy of a note is impressed by the fact that all the information they provided and were given is included for them to review. It also is useful in that it has immunizations prevention information and instructions. Outcome studies have shown it to be helpful in compliance and improvement of health; crossing the Quality Chasm."

Bachman's Law: "A clinician who gives a patient a copy of their note has all their work complete. Consequently there is no dictation, rework, signing, or any activity of maintaining the administrative workflow. This saves a great deal of money and means the workflow systems are extremely efficient."

Underscoring doctors Bachman and Wenner are the CMS regulations for meaningful use[15] which require eligible professionals to provide clinical summaries to patients each office visit.

The availability of information from the EHR during the patient visit is an invaluable tool in counseling and patient education. The clinician has access to graphs, medical images, test results, and anatomical drawings, all of which are useful in explaining something related to the patient's condition or to illustrate an upcoming procedure. Using a Tablet PC, the doctor in Figure 1-7 is able to access the results of the patient's most recent electrocardiogram wirelessly and explain them to the patient.

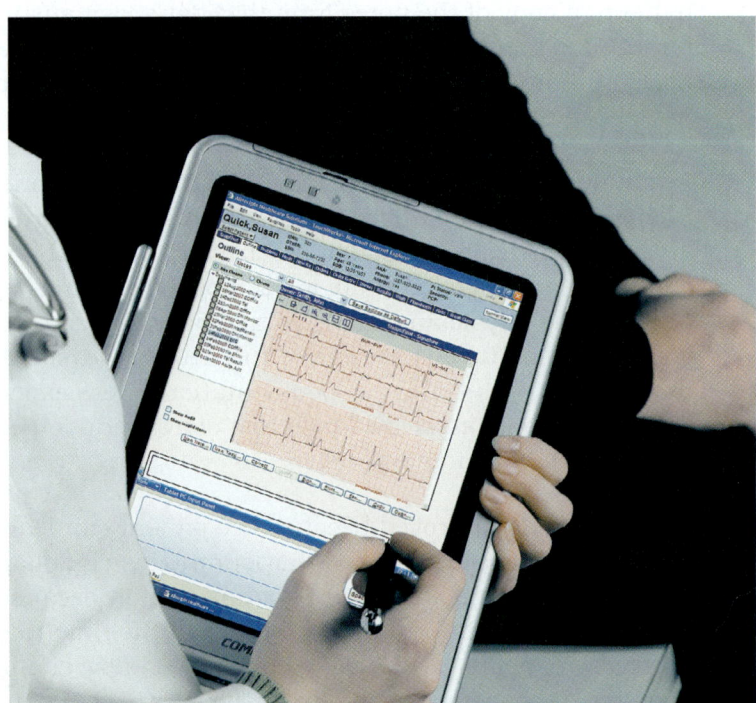

Courtesy of Allscripts, LLC.

▶ Figure 1-7 Using a Tablet PC, doctor discusses ECG results with patient.

---

[15]*Electronic Health Record Incentive Program Final Rule* (Washington, DC: U.S. Department of Health and Human Services, Final Rule July 28, 2010, 42 CFR Parts 412, 413, 422, and 495).

As stated earlier, adopting an EHR may change the way doctors work. Experience has shown that patients react favorably to the use of a computer during the exam, especially when they are part of the process, able to see the screen, and able to participate in the review of their information. However, Wenner and Bachman describe three types of patient–physician relationships[16]:

1. The doctor is paternalistic, telling the patient what to do.
2. The doctor gives the patient information and the patient decides what to do.
3. Patients and doctors share information to determine the best plan for given conditions.

Figure 1-8, provided by Dr. Wenner, lists the stages of change resulting from adoption of an EHR. Wenner and Bachman believe patients will help the physician when they are given some degree of control, as reflected in points 2 and 3.

Stages of Change in EHR Technology Adoption			
Stage	Technology Adoption	Medical Records	Medical Practice
Stage I	Do it the old way	The paper chart used and viewed as an historical document by physicians	Health care providers are the center of health care
Stage II	Adopt technology but continue to do it the old way	Transcribing dictation onto paper, using the EHR for data storage only managed by staff	Providers continue to dominate medical decisions and maintain all health care data
Stage III	Change the workflow to leverage the technology Paperless medical office	Use EHR at the point-of-care with providers and patients participating to allow real-time continuity of care	Patients and providers will share decision making as health care information is available to both

▶ Figure 1-8 Stages of change in EHR adoption.

The EHR system strives to improve patient healthcare by giving the provider and patient access to complete, up-to-date records of past and present conditions; it also enables the records to be used in ways that paper medical records could not. The sooner the data is entered, the sooner it is available for other providers and the patient. Chapters 2–12 will explore how data is entered in the EHR and focus on ways EHR systems speed up data entry, enabling clinicians to achieve point-of-care documentation in real time.

The Physical Clinic and Clinician Mobility

Let us examine how the office environment and the choice of computers, devices, and technologies can affect the successful adoption of an EHR. To quote Peter Gerloffs, Medical Director of Allscripts, a leading EHR vendor, "If physicians don't use it, nothing else matters." This means, of course, that the EHR has to be designed and deployed in a way that enables clinicians to make it a part of their workflow.

---

[16]Allen R. Wenner and John W. Bachman, "Transforming the Physician Practice: Interviewing Patients with a Computer, Chap. 26 in *Healthcare Information Management Systems: Cases, Strategies, and Solutions*, 3rd ed., ed. Marion J. Ball, Charlotte A. Weaver, and Joan M. Kiel, (New York: Springer Science+Business Media, Inc., 2004), 297–319. Copyright © 2004 Springer Science+Business Media, Inc., New York.

One consideration is how mobile the providers are when they are in the office.

1. Does a clinician have a preassigned set of exam rooms he or she always uses for patients or does the office have a number of rooms that are shared randomly by several providers throughout the day?
2. Is the clinician likely to complete the note and all orders when in the exam room, or do so on the way to the next room?
3. Where/when will the clinician review lab results, radiology reports, e-mail messages, prescription renewals, and so on: on the move throughout the day, at a desk in his or her office, or from home over the Internet?

The following discussion of various technologies and devices used in EHR solutions today will provide you with an idea of how these installations work in a medical office.

EHR on Computer Workstations

In most offices, you will find computer workstations in the billing, nursing, and lab areas, as shown in Figure 1-9. In some offices, you will find them in the exam room, and in a comparatively few offices you will find them in the waiting room or a subwaiting area for patients to use.

Computer workstations are cheap, reliable, dependable, and usually fixed in one location. You are probably working on one right now. They take up more space, requiring extra room for the keyboard and mouse. They are, however, easier for the IT department to manage and usually easier to upgrade when necessary.

Certainly workstations at fixed positions will be the right choice for some of the personnel who input data in your EHR. Whether they make sense at the point of care depends on how much free space you have in your exam rooms and if your providers want to finish up their exam notes before or after leaving the room. Most medical facilities were built long before anyone thought of putting computers in the exam rooms. Many exam rooms are already filled with supplies and equipment used for the exams and have only a small counter or writing area.

Courtesy of GE Healthcare.

▶ **Figure 1-9 Computer workstation connected to the wired local area network (LAN).**

Although workstations can pose a security risk in the exam room when left unattended, that is easily handled through any number of biometric, or smart card, and auto sign-off solutions. With these solutions, the screen blanks or the EHR software is logged off whenever an authorized user is not present. An ID badge or other device has a computer chip imbedded in it that can be detected by the workstation. Biometric solutions usually involve a pad on the keyboard or mouse that reads and authenticates a user's fingerprint. These will be discussed further in Chapter 10.

One final advantage of the workstation is that it can support a substantially higher screen resolution (finer picture) than any other device. This makes it the only viable choice for radiologists and others who "read" diagnostic quality images of x-rays, CAT scans, and so on.

Of course, the medical office EHR is actually on a network server somewhere else. Workstations and other devices are connected to the network. This can be done with cables that have been wired in the building walls or through "wireless" access points that connect to the network through high-frequency radio signals. One advantage of a workstation is that it is ideally suited to a wired network connection. These are usually much faster and less subject to failure.

EHR on Laptop Computers

A laptop computer, as shown in Figure 1-10, packages the screen, keyboard, mouse, and computer in one unit, about the size of an 8″ × 11″ notebook. In a medical office, these provide mobility for clinicians who want to stay connected and take their work from room to room.

Courtesy of Allscripts, LLC.
▶ **Figure 1-10** Laptop computers with Wi-Fi connectivity provide portability.

Although laptops can be connected to a wired network fairly easily, it is usually bothersome to have to plug the computer in and log on to the network each time you enter a room. For this reason, most laptops use a wireless standard called "Wi-Fi," which stands for "wireless fidelity," to connect to the network. Wi-Fi capability is standard on many laptop computers.

Wireless networking, however, works only for very short distances; therefore, it requires infrastructure in the medical facility. Transmitters and receivers called "access points" must be installed throughout the building in close enough proximity that the laptop (or other wireless device) can always find the radio signal.

There are some concerns that wireless access points can be used by unauthorized computers to enter the network, or that wireless transmissions containing EPHI (protected health information in electronic form) can be intercepted. However, medical systems installed by qualified installers use secure authentication and encryption techniques (these will be explained in Chapter 10). These technical safeguards effectively protect the EHR and patient data.

The real risk with laptop computers is that providers and clinical users will save protected health information (PHI) data to the laptop computer's hard drive. That data may then not be protected by the same safeguards used on the office network or built into the EHR system. Laptops also are more troublesome for the IT department to manage and update, and laptops eventually become obsolete because they have only limited capability for hardware upgrades.

Laptops have other issues as well. Typically they run on batteries. This means after 2 to 4 hours of use, the batteries need to be recharged. Although laptop computers have A/C adapters, most users do not like having to plug them in every time they come into a room. The small appearance of a laptop is deceptive. They typically weigh from 3.5 to 9 pounds; after carrying it all day, that weight feels quite heavy.

Being mobile, laptops also are more susceptible to being dropped, lost, or damaged. The keyboards are smaller and the built-in pointing devices that replace the mouse take some getting use to. However, laptops typically have high-resolution screens and will typically run any program that will run on a workstation.

One choice for facilities with limited counterspace in the exam rooms is to combine the laptop with a portable cart, as shown in Figure 1-11. The cart can be easily rolled from room to room and provides a stable and comfortable work area for the clinician. If the laptop has Wi-Fi connectivity, there is nothing to plug in. Also, if the batteries begin to run low, the A/C adapter-battery charger is usually right on the back of the cart. You also may have seen computer carts used on hospital floors where they are affectionately known as computers on wheels.

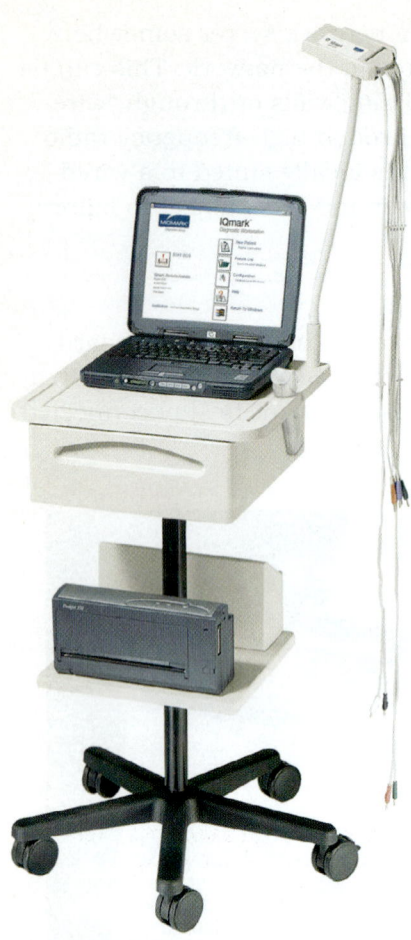

Courtesy of Midmark Diagnostics Group.
▶ **Figure 1-11 Laptop on computer cart.**

EHR on a Tablet PC

The Tablet PC offers the size and portability (and drawbacks) of a laptop computer. However, it offers one feature that many providers really like. Users can move and click the mouse by just touching the screen with a special stylus supplied with the Tablet PC. EHR systems that involve primarily opening lists and clicking findings with a mouse work well on a Tablet PC, as shown in Figure 1-12.

If 95 percent of the charting is done with a mouse, then a Tablet PC is ideal. However, a Tablet PC typically does not have a keyboard for touch typing. Most have a small area of the screen that can be used as a keyboard. Typing is done by clicking the mouse over each letter of the alphabet. This technique is serviceable for a word or two but painful for a clinician who uses a lot of free text.

To compensate for the lack of a keyboard, the Tablet PC has two other features. One is handwriting recognition, which allows you to hand print characters on the screen, and then a few seconds later it will convert them into typed characters. The other is speech recognition, which is built into the Tablet PC operating system. Spoken words are recorded and then processed with special software to produce a text note. Both of these features require you to train the computer

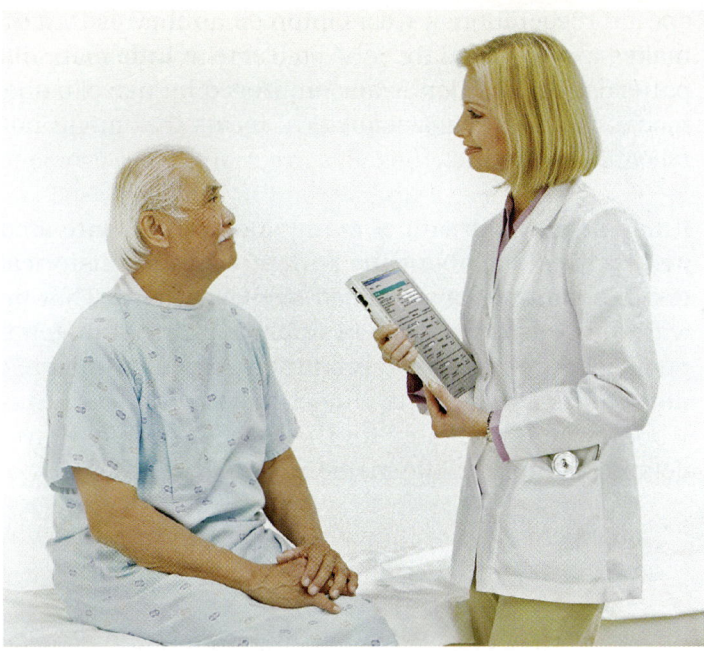

Courtesy of GE Healthcare.

▶ **Figure 1-12** Tablet PC uses a stylus instead of a mouse.

to recognize your handwriting or speech patterns. For some providers, these features work relatively well; others find that the error rate is too high.

Speech Recognition

Another useful computer tool for clinicians is speech recognition. Speech recognition software recognizes the patterns in your speech as words and turns them into text.

For specialties such as radiology and pathology, speech recognition is ideal as it allows providers to document their observations, while they use the mouse for a different application such as the manipulation of x-rays or diagnostic images. Modern voice recognition software can also recognize verbal commands to operate the software. This allows the radiologist or pathologist to select patients, open orders, save reports, zoom images, or change contrast without using his or her hands. Integration of speech recognition with an EHR can ensure the clinician's report is automatically tied to the patient chart.

In other specialties speech recognition is sometimes used to add free-text comments to findings in the codified medical record. This is especially popular with providers who use a Tablet PC. Having clinical dictation instantly and automatically transcribed by a computer reduces turn-around time and eliminates the cost of a transcription service.

Most people speak at least 160 words per minute but type fewer than 40 words a minute, so speech recognition should be a lot faster. Speech recognitions systems can achieve up to 99% accurate recognition, but most people seem to average about 95%. This means that a full-length dictation will have one or more errors that must be corrected. The time spent backing up and making corrections slows down the overall rate of efficiency. The good news is that speech recognition systems improve as they are used. Each time the speaker makes a correction, the system learns a little more about the speaker's voice patterns. Recognition is also improved by use of a special medical language model, which recognizes medical terms that might not be in a generic speech recognition product.

It has been the dream of many doctors to create a complete encounter note just by speaking about the patient visit, but historically that has produced a text note instead of a codified medical record. That problem has been overcome with the development of new applications that match the spoken text to Medcin nomenclature findings to produce a structured note. To learn how speech recognition works, read the technical explanation, *How Speech Recognition Software Works,* which is located on the Myhealthprofessionskit.com web site (access details provided on the inside cover).

Chapter One Summary

Electronic Health Records are the portions of a patient's medical records that are stored in a computer system as well as the functional benefits derived from having an electronic health record.

The IOM set forth eight core functions that an EHR should be capable of performing:

- **Health information and data** Provide improved access to information needed by care providers, using a defined data set that includes medical and nursing diagnoses, a medication list, allergies, demographics, clinical narratives, laboratory test results, and more.

- **Result management** Electronic results for better interpretation, quicker recognition and treatment of medical problems; reduces redundant testing and improves care coordination among multiple providers.

- **Order management** CPOE systems improve workflow, eliminate lost orders and ambiguities caused by illegible handwriting, monitor for duplicate orders, and reduce the time required to fill orders.

- **Decision support** Includes prevention, prescribing of drugs, diagnosis and management, and detection of adverse events and disease outbreaks.

  Computer reminders and prompts improve preventive practices in areas such as vaccinations, breast cancer screening, colorectal screening, and cardiovascular risk reduction.

- **Electronic communication and connectivity** Among care partners, enhances patient safety and quality of care, especially for patients who have multiple providers.

- **Patient support** For example, patient education and home monitoring by patients using electronic devices.

- **Administrative processes and reporting** Increases the efficiency of healthcare organizations and provide better, timelier service to patients.

- **Reporting and population health** Facilitates the reporting of key quality indicators and timely reporting of adverse reactions and disease outbreaks.

The CPRI identified three key criteria for an EHR:

- Capture data at the point of care
- Integrate data from multiple sources
- Provide decision support

The ONC created a strategic framework for achieving widespread adoption of EHR within 10 years. The framework was revised for 2008–2012, and again for 2011–2015.

The HITECH Act provides CMS incentives for providers to use a certified EHR.

ONC seeks to reduce the risk of EHR investment by establishing Authorized Testing and Certification Bodies to certify EHR systems.

A patient encounter document is organized into four components:

- Subjective
- Objective
- Assessment
- Plan

EHR systems strive to improve patient healthcare by giving the provider and patient access to complete, up-to-date records of past and present conditions.

Documenting at the point of care means the providers (clinicians, nurses, and medical assistants) record findings at the time of the encounter, not after they have left the patient.

Implementing an EHR requires changes in the way providers work. The choice of computers, devices, and technology can affect the successful adoption of an EHR. One aspect, how much space is available, may determine the type of device to use. The second aspect is the mobility of the clinicians. The third aspect is what type of clinician–patient interaction the clinicians hope to achieve. These factors determine how and where to use computers to achieve point-of-care EHR.

Each of the devices we discussed had advantages and disadvantages:

- Computer workstations are cheap, reliable, dependable, easier for the IT department to manage, and can be upgraded when necessary. But they take up more space and may not fit in the exam rooms.
- A laptop computer packages everything in a unit about the size of a notebook. They provide mobility for clinicians who want to take their work from room to room. But they require a wireless network to gain that mobility and they have limited battery life.
- The Tablet PC offers the size and portability of a laptop computer and users can move and click the mouse by just touching the screen with a special stylus. However, in tablet mode, it does not have a keyboard, so it is less desirable when there is a lot of keyboard input. It works well for EHR systems that primarily involve opening lists and clicking findings with a mouse. Similar to laptops, it requires a wireless network and has a limited battery life.
- Speech Recognition software can interpret the sound waves of speech and match them to vocabulary words, converting speech to text.

Testing Your Knowledge of Chapter 1

1. What does the acronym EHR stand for?
2. What is the definition of an EHR?
3. Explain the benefits of EHR over paper charts.
4. Describe what points of the workflow are different between offices using a paper and an electronic chart.
5. Name at least three forces driving the change to EHR.
6. What are the four goals of the Strategic Framework created by the Office of the National Coordinator for Health Information Technology?
7. Describe at least three differences between inpatient and outpatient EHR systems.
8. Explain why documenting at the point of care improves patient healthcare.
9. What is the HITECH Act?
10. What is the name of an organization that certifies EHR systems?
11. List the 3 styles of the physician-patient relationships described by Wenner and Bachman.
12. List the eight core functions that an EHR should be capable of performing.
13. List the three criteria of an EHR defined by CPRI.
14. What are the four defined sections in a SOAP note?
15. What three benefits of electronic results identified by the IOM report?

Chapter Two

Functional EHR Systems

Learning Outcomes

After completing this chapter, you should be able to:

- Compare different formats of EHR data
- Describe the importance of codified EHR
- Have an understanding of prominent EHR code sets such as SNOMED-CT, MEDCIN, LOINC, and CCC
- Explain different methods of capturing and recording EHR data
- Catalog and retrieve documents and images from a digital image system
- Discuss the exchange of data between EHR and other systems
- Discuss the benefits of patient-entered data
- Describe the functional benefits from a codified EHR
- Compare different formats of lab result data
- Discuss alert systems and drug utilization review
- Describe two important components of health maintenance
- Provide examples of EHR decision support

Format of Data Determines Potential Benefits

The ability to easily find, share, and search patient records makes an EHR superior to a paper record system. However, remember that Chapter 1 defined the EHR as the portions of the patient's medical record stored in the computer system *as well as the functional benefits derived from them.*

The IOM defined eight core functions that an EHR should be capable of performing.

Four of the *functional benefits* identified by the IOM are health maintenance, trend analysis, alerts, and decision support. The form in which the data is stored determines to what extent the computer can use the content of the EHR to provide additional functions that improve the quality of care.

This chapter will examine the forms in which EHR data is stored, explore how functional benefits are derived from it, and how data may be entered.

EHR Data Formats

The various ways in which medical records data are stored in the database may be broadly categorized into three forms:

Digital images

This form of EHR data can be retrieved and displayed by the computer, but a human is required to interpret the meaning of the content. This category may be subcategorized into:

> **Diagnostic images** such as digital x-rays, CAT scans, digital pathology, and even annotated drawings
>
> **Scanned documents** such as paper forms, old medical records, letters, or even sound files of dictated notes

Text files

The second type of data includes word processing files of transcribed exam notes and also text reports. It is principally obtained in the EHR by importing text files from outside sources.

Discrete data

This third form of stored information in an EHR is the easiest for the computer to use. It can be instantly searched, retrieved, and combined or reported in different ways. Discrete data in an EHR may be subcategorized into:

> **Fielded data** in which each piece of information is assigned its own position in a computer record called a "field." The meaning of the information is inferred from its position in the record. For example, a record of the patient's medical problem might look like this:
>
> "knee injury","20120331","improved","20120428"
>
> The fields in this example are surrounded by quotation marks. The computer would be programmed to look for the name of the problem in the first field, the date of onset in the second field, the status of the problem in the third field, and the date of the last exam in the fourth field.
>
> **Coded data** is fielded data that also contains codes in addition to or in place of descriptive text. Codes eliminate ambiguities about the clinician's meaning.
>
> A codified EHR record of the same knee problem might look like this:
>
> "8442", "knee injury","20120331","improved","20120428"

Limitations of Certain Types of Data

An EHR offers improved accessibility to patient records over a paper chart. That is certainly a functional benefit of any EHR regardless of the format of its data. However, to achieve its full functional benefits, the computer must be able to quickly and accurately identify the information contained within the records.

Digital image data can be retrieved and displayed by the computer, but a human is required to interpret the meaning of the content. Although this is beneficial for sharing diagnostic images, if the bulk of the EHR is simply scanned paper documents, only one or two of the IOM criteria defined in Chapter 1 are satisfied.

Text data are useful for doctors and nurses to read and can be searched by the computer for research purposes. However, text data is seldom used for generating alerts, trend analysis, decision support, or other real-time EHR functions, because the search capability is slow and the results often ambiguous.

Fielded data is the most common way to store information in computers and EHR systems. It is fast and efficient and uses very little storage space. However, unless the fielded data is also codified, the meaning of the data can be ambiguous.

Within medicine, many different terms are used to describe the same symptom, condition, or observation. Additionally, clinicians often use short abbreviations to document their observations in a patient chart. This makes it difficult for a computer to compare notes from one physician to another. For example, providers at two different clinics might record a knee injury problem differently:

Dr. 1: "twisted his knee"

Dr. 2: "knee sprain"

A search of medical records by the description "knee injury" might not find the records created by either clinician.

Coded data is when a code is stored in the medical record in addition to the text description—the record is then considered codified. The EHR system can instantly find and match the desired information by code regardless of the clinician's choice of words. A codified EHR is more useful than a text-based record because it precisely identifies the clinician's finding or treatment.

EHR data stored in a fielded, codified form adds significant value, but if the codes are not standard it will be difficult to exchange medical record data between different EHR systems or facilities. Remember, the exchange of data is one of the eight core functions defined by the IOM. Using a national standard code set instead of proprietary codes to codify the data will better enable the exchange of medical records among systems, improve the accuracy of the content, and open the door to the other functional benefits derived from having an electronic health record.

Standard EHR Coding Systems

EHR coding systems are called *nomenclatures*. EHR nomenclatures differ from other code sets and classification systems in that they are designed to codify the details and nuance of the patient–clinician encounter. EHR nomenclatures are different from billing code sets in this respect. For example, a procedure code used for billing an office visit does not describe what the clinician observed during the visit, just the type of visit and complexity of the exam. EHR nomenclatures need to have a lot more codes to describe the details of the exam; for this reason, they are said to be more *granular*. Two prominent nomenclatures for EHR records are SNOMED-CT® and MEDCIN®. Another prominent coding system, LOINC®, is used for lab results.

Unfortunately, many hospital systems use none of these standard systems, having instead developed internal coding schemes applicable only to their facilities. These work within the organization but create problems when trying to integrate other software or exchange data with other facilities. To create an EHR that is able to receive, create, and compare medical information from numerous sources, it is necessary to adopt a coding system that is used by other providers—in other words, a national standard.

Prominent EHR Code Sets

EHR nomenclatures have hundreds of thousands of codes to represent not only procedures and diseases but also the symptoms, observations, history, medications, and a myriad of other details. The level of granularity determines how fine a level of detail is represented by a code in the nomenclature.

However, too much granularity can make a code set difficult to use at the point of care. The point of care is when both the clinician and patient are present. Extremely granular code sets, called *reference terminologies*, are impractical for a clinician to use in an exam. Designed for data analysis, these code sets often are applied to the medical records after the fact for a specific research project.

To balance the need for granularity with the practical requirements of point of care documentation, EHR nomenclatures use the concept of *findings*, or codified observations, which are medically meaningful to the clinician. Although some systems of clinical vocabulary are just "data dictionaries" that are used to standardize medical terms, EHR nomenclatures precorrelate those terms into clinically relevant findings.

For example, a clinical vocabulary will have the terms *eye, arm, leg, chest, nostril, left, right, red, yellow, radiating, discharge,* and *pain*. These terms could be combined in many ways, some of them meaningless. Findings are less granular than individual terms but combine those terms in ways that are clinically relevant. For example, "chest pain radiating to the left arm" uses one coded finding to record five clinical terms as a meaningful symptom.

Findings are often linked to other findings, whereas codes in classification code sets are usually only related to the root code of the group that the code is in.

For example, the finding abdominal pain is related to more than 550 diagnosis codes, whereas a specific diagnosis code for peptic ulcer is not related to any other diagnosis code.

Conversely, in an EHR nomenclature the diagnostic finding of peptic ulcer is related to 168 other findings (one of which is abdominal pain).

Linked or indexed findings in an EHR nomenclature enable clinicians to quickly locate related symptoms, elements of the physical exam, assessments, and treatments when documenting the visit.

EHR users tend to locate findings by the description, not by the code. EHR nomenclature code numbers are typically invisible to the user.

A feature unique to EHR nomenclatures is that they often include internal cross-references to other standard code sets. These tables help the EHR to communicate with other systems. Code sets not designed for an EHR do not typically contain a map to other code sets with their structure.

The following sections will provide a brief history and purpose of several of the most prominent coding standards you are likely to encounter or use in an EHR.

SNOMED-CT SNOMED stands for Systematized Nomenclature of Medicine; CT stands for Clinical Terms. SNOMED-CT is a merger of SNOMED, a medical nomenclature developed by the College of American Pathologists, and the "Read Codes," developed by Dr. James Read for the National Health Service in the United Kingdom.

SNOMED-CT includes cross-references to map SNOMED-CT to other standard code sets, including those discussed below.

SNOMED-CT Structure The SNOMED-CT Core terminology contains over 364,400 healthcare *concepts*, organized into 18 hierarchical categories. The data structure of SNOMED-CT is complex. Concept names, descriptions, and synonyms number more than 984,000.

SNOMED Concepts have descriptions and Concept IDs (numeric codes). The concepts are arranged in the following hierarchies:

- Finding
- Disease
- Procedure and intervention
- Observable entity
- Body structure
- Organism
- Substance
- Pharmaceutical/biological product
- Specimen
- Physical object
- Physical force
- Events
- Environments and geographical locations
- Social context
- Context-dependent categories
- Staging and scales
- Attribute
- Qualifier value

SNOMED-CT has approximately 1,450,000 semantic relationships in the nomenclature. There are two types of relationships between SNOMED-CT concepts: *Is-A* relationships and *Attribute* relationships.

Is-A relationships connect concepts within a single hierarchy. For example, the disease concept Bronchial Pneumonia *Is-A* Pneumonia (also a disease concept).

Attribute relationships, however, connect concepts from two different hierarchies. For example, the disease concept Bronchial Pneumonia has the associated *Attribute* Inflammation (which is from a different hierarchy, morphology.)

MEDCIN MEDCIN is a medical nomenclature and knowledge base developed by Medicomp Systems, Inc., in collaboration with physicians on staff at Cornell, Harvard, Johns Hopkins, and other major medical centers. The purpose of the MEDCIN nomenclature and the intent of the design differentiate it from other coding standards. SNOMED-CT and other coding systems were designed to classify or index medical information for research or other purposes. MEDCIN was designed for point-of-care use by the clinician. MEDCIN is not just a list of medical terms, but rather a list of *findings* (clinical observations) that are medically meaningful to the clinician.

MEDCIN includes cross-references to map MEDCIN to SNOMED-CT as well as other standard code sets that will be discussed later in this book. These include: ICD-9-CM, CPT-4, LOINC, CCC, and RxNorm drug codes.

MEDCIN Structure The MEDCIN nomenclature consists of 277,000 clinical concepts or "findings" divided into six broad categories:

- Symptoms
- History
- Physical Examination
- Tests
- Diagnoses
- Therapy

MEDCIN differs from other EHR coding systems in that the nomenclature is not just a codified list of findings. The MEDCIN nomenclature is available in a "knowledge base" with a diagnostic index of more than 68 million links between clinically related findings. This "knowledge" enables an EHR system based on MEDCIN to quickly find other clinical "findings" that are likely to be needed; this in turn reduces the time it takes to create exam notes.

This difference means a physician selects less individual codes to complete the patient exam note. For example, SNOMED-CT has a code for "arm" and a code for "pain," MEDCIN has a "finding" for "arm pain." MEDCIN often has additional findings that infer important nuances, for example, the "finding" for "arm tenderness" might more accurately describe the patient's symptom than arm pain.

SNOMED-CT is often referred to as a "reference terminology." It provides very granular coding that normalizes data for research and reporting. Its structure provides millions of semantic links based on a term, word, or concept. Figure 2-1 shows the SNOMED-CT finding Asthma with its various Is-A relationships.

▶ **Figure 2-1** SNOMED-CT links for the term "Asthma."

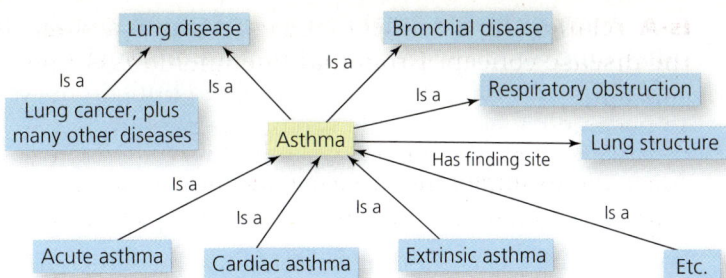

Figure 2-1 and Figure 2-2 compare the structure of SNOMED-CT and MEDCIN using the finding for asthma. As you can see from the comparison, the MEDCIN knowledge base relates asthma to 279 total direct links (only 70 are shown in Figure 2-2). Each of these has relevancy to point-of-care use for an asthma patient. SNOMED-CT links include obvious links to asthma but not directly to

▶ **Figure 2-2** MEDCIN links for the term "Asthma."

ASSESSMENT (53 total)
Asthma
+ 52 more findings

SYMPTOMS (66 total):
  Sinus pain
  Eyes itch
  Nasal discharge
  Chest tightness
  Feeling congested in the chest
  Difficulty breathing
  Recurrent episodes of difficulty breathing
  Awakening at night short of breath
  Cough
  Coughing up blood
  Wheezing
  Wheezing recurs intermittently
  + 54 more findings

PHYSICAL EXAM (52 total):
  Respiration rate
  Tachypnea
  Pulse rate
  Blood pressure
  Pulsus paradoxus
  Intranasal polyp
  Percussion low diaphragm
  Percussion hyperresonance
  Auscultation wheezing
  Auscultation prolonged expiratory time
  + 19 more findings

RELEVANT HISTORY (49 total):
  Prior use of cortiscosteroids for asthma
  Previous hospitilization for pulmonary problem
  Previous ER visit for pulmonary problem
  Protracted upper respiratory infection
  Exposure to cigarette smoke
  Exposure to dust mites
  Exposure to animal dander
  Exposure to roach antigen
  Recent contact with pets or other animals
  Smoking
  Symptoms recur seasonally
  History of sinusitis
  History of nasal polyps
  History of allergic rhinitis
  History of urticaria
  Family history of asthma
  Family history of hay fever
  Family history of status asthmaticus
  Family history of atopic eczematous dermatitis
  + 29 more findings

THERAPY (37 total):
  Environmental control measures
  Abstinence from smoking
  Avoid exposure to allergens
  Avoid exposure to triggers
  Antihistamines
  Anti-inflammatory inhaled steroids
  Anti-inflammatory steroids
  Antiasthmatics
  Bronchodilato
  + 28 more findings

TESTS (75 total):
  CBC
  WBC count
  Spirometry
  Pulse oximetry
  Chest x-ray
  + 70 more findings

Chapter 2 | Functional EHR Systems

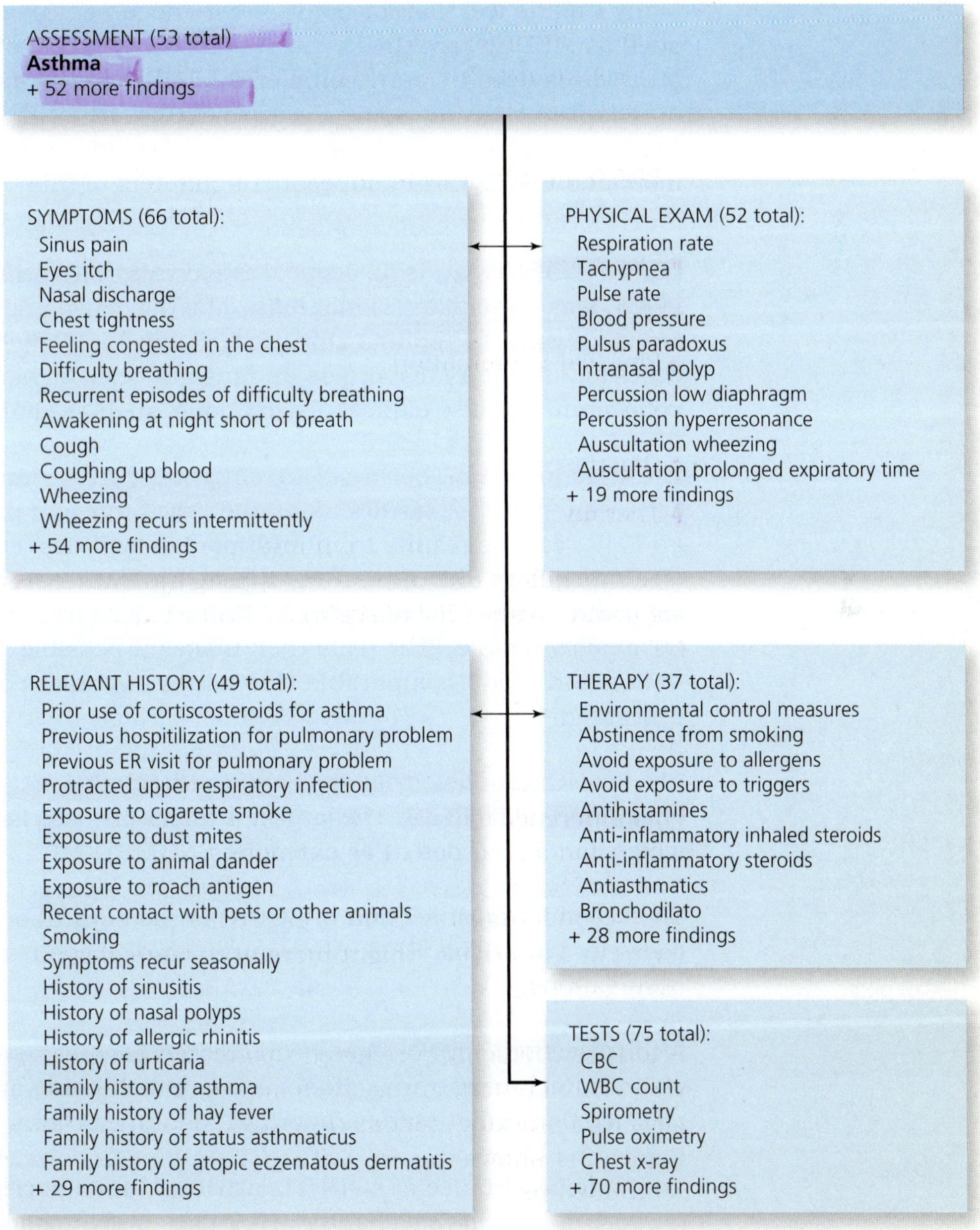

the symptoms, tests, or therapy. Links in Figure 2-1 also connect to lungs and other lung diseases not related to asthma. Such associations are sometimes useful when coding records for research but can make it difficult for the clinician to use such a system while seeing the patient.

The MEDCIN knowledge base also includes 600,000 synonyms for findings allowing a finding to be looked up by several different terms. The MEDCIN knowledge base includes each finding selected by the clinician into a readable narrative text. EHR applications using the MEDCIN nomenclature can store medical information as coded data elements and still generate readable exam notes from the same data.

An EHR system based on MEDCIN enables the clinician to select fewer individual codes and to quickly locate other clinical "findings" that are likely to be needed. This difference reduces the time it takes to create exam notes and allows a physician to complete the patient exam note at the time of the encounter.

Many experts feel that for point-of-care documentation medical nomenclatures such as MEDCIN are the key to successful adoption of an EHR by clinicians. MEDCIN is used in many commercial EHR systems as well as the Department of Defense CHCS II system. Because of this, MEDCIN has been selected as the EHR nomenclature for the student exercises in this textbook. You will learn more about MEDCIN in subsequent chapters of this book.

LOINC LOINC stands for Logical Observation Identifiers Names and Codes. LOINC was created and is maintained by the Regenstrief Institute, which is closely affiliated with the Indiana University School of Medicine. LOINC standardizes codes for laboratory test orders and results, such as blood hemoglobin and serum potassium, and also clinical observations, such as vital signs or EKG.

LOINC is important because currently most laboratories and other diagnostic services report test results using their own internal proprietary codes. When an EHR receives results from multiple lab facilities, comparing the results electronically is like comparing apples and oranges. LOINC provides a universal coding system for mapping laboratory tests and results to a common terminology in the EHR. This then makes it possible for a computer program to find and report comparable test values regardless of where the test was processed.

The LOINC terminology is divided into three portions: laboratory, clinical (nonlaboratory), and HIPAA. The largest number of codes is in the laboratory section, which contains codes in 14 categories.

The second largest section of LOINC is the clinical section, which includes codes for vital signs, EKG, ultrasound, cardiac echo, and many other clinical observations.

A third section of LOINC has been created to categorize codes for a HIPAA claims attachment transaction. Claims attachments are used to provide additional information to support an insurance claim.

The wide acceptance of LOINC is attributable in part to its adoption by HL7 (discussed later in this chapter). HL7 uses LOINC codes in its clinical messages.

UMLS UMLS stands for Unified Medical Language System®. It is maintained by the National Library of Medicine (NLM). Because students may find mention of UMLS elsewhere, it is included here. However, UMLS is not itself a medical terminology, but rather a resource of software tools and data created from many medical nomenclatures, including those described in this chapter. UMLS is described as a "meta-thesaurus." It can be used to retrieve and integrate biomedical information and provide cross-references among selected vocabularies.

Nursing Code Sets

Twelve standards for coded nursing languages are recognized by the American Nurses Association today for use in the assessment, diagnosis, intervention, and outcome of nursing care. Using a commonly understood codified structure enables nurses to create and communicate a patient plan of care that is evidence based, facilitates documentation of the practice of nursing in the EHR, and permits data sharing to improve patient care outcomes. This is not a comprehensive explanation of all 12 coding structures, but does represent some of those that may be found in EHR systems today.

Clinical Care Classification System (CCC) The Clinical Care Classification system (CCC) was developed by Virginia Saba at Georgetown University. It can be used to document patient care in hospitals, home health agencies, ambulatory care clinics, and other healthcare settings. Developed from government-funded research, it was originally known as the Home Health Care Classification system, but CCC is now considered applicable to clinical care as well as other healthcare services.

The CCC system provides standardized coding concepts for nursing diagnoses, outcomes, nursing interventions, and actions in two interrelated taxonomies. CCC defines 21 Care Components that provide a framework to interrelate the 182 CCC Nursing Diagnoses and 198 CCC Nursing Interventions.

The CCC system offers a unique approach to documenting the nursing process in an EHR by correlating the six steps of the CCC system with the six steps of the nursing process. The CCC codes have been integrated into the Medcin nomenclature used for this course, as well as UMLS, SNOMED-CT, and LOINC.

NANDA-I NANDA-I stands for the North American Nursing Diagnosis Association International. The NANDA-I Taxonomy is a system of classification of 206 Nursing Diagnosis that have been grouped into 13 domains of nursing practice. They offer a clearly understood language to enable the professional nurse to identify and prioritize nursing diagnosis to plan interventions that are based on best practice but individualized to the patient's responses to health problems or life processes. It is available in 11 international languages, is ISO and HL7 compatible, included in UMLS, and available in SNOMED-CT. This association's body of work facilitates all forms of nursing communications and guides the process of professional nursing practice for assessing and treating the nursing diagnosis. The NANDA-I taxonomy supports the development of EHR and enables the collection, retrieval, and analysis of nursing data to promote education, research, and evidence based standards of care.

NIC and NOC NIC stands for Nursing Interventions Classification. It is a code set designed for documenting nursing interventions in any clinical setting. NIC was first published in 1992 and is updated every four years. The system consists of numeric codes for 514 interventions, which are grouped into 30 classes and seven domains that span all nursing specialties. The seven domains are: Basic Physiological, Complex Physiological, Behavioral, Safety, Family, Health System, and Community. Their design is for use at the point of care to document care planning and nursing practices.

NOC stands for Nursing Outcomes Classification and includes a comprehensive list of nursing outcomes. It is used to document the effect of nursing interventions on patient progress. It can be used to measure the quality of care, cost efficiency, and progress of treatment. It is a structure of 330 numerically coded outcomes (311 individual, 10 family, and 9 community level outcomes). The NOC codes are grouped into 31 classes and seven domains corresponding to those identified in NIC.

NIC and NOC codes were developed in the University of Iowa, College of Nursing, and are owned by Elsevier Science.

ICNP® ICNP stands for International Classification for Nursing Practice. It is the result of a project by the International Council of Nurses, to create an organizing structure into which other nursing terminologies can be mapped. It was intended to facilitate the comparison of nursing data gathered from multiple systems. However, ICNP has evolved into a separate coding system attempting to unify other systems. It uses numeric codes to represent concepts in three areas—Nursing Phenomenon, Nursing Actions, and Outcomes, which are similar to the concepts of nursing diagnosis, interventions, and outcomes.

One factor that differentiates ICNP from other systems is that it has merged the two different taxonomies used for nursing diagnosis and nursing interventions into one classification, which can be used to represent diagnoses, interventions, and outcomes.

Omaha System The Omaha System is a standardized terminology recognized by the American Nurses Association as a standard language system to support nursing practice. It has been in development since the 1970s and is one of the oldest systems for nursing documentation. It often is used in community-based nursing such as visiting nursing associations. It is no longer under copyrights, but when used the terms and structure must be used as published. It is included in the U.S. Department of Health and Human Services interoperability standards for electronic health records, is integrated into LOINC and SNOMED-CT. It is recognized by HL7, congruent with ISO, and being mapped to the ICNP.

NMDS NMDS stands for Nursing Minimum Data Set. It was originally developed as the result of conferences held at the University of Illinois College of Nursing in Chicago in 1977 and at the University of Wisconsin—Milwaukee School of Nursing in 1985 in an attempt to define the minimum set of basic data elements for nursing use in the EHR. It has label and conceptual definitions of the essential, specific elements that are used on a regular basis by the majority of nurses in a variety of settings. The elements are arranged into three categories: nursing care, patient or client demographics, and service elements. NMDS is intended to standardize the collection of essential nursing data and can be used to capture nursing data for comparison of patient outcomes.

PNDS PNDS stands for Perioperative Nursing Data Set and was developed by the Association of Perioperative Registered Nurses in the early 1990s. Like other nursing systems, it codifies nursing diagnoses, interventions, and outcomes, but this system is focused on the special needs and level of detail required to document perioperative nursing.

PNDS is used by nurses in hospital perioperative settings to document the patient experience from preadmission to discharge. PNDS consists of 74 nursing diagnoses, 133 nursing interventions, and 28 nurse-sensitive patient outcomes. PNDS is incorporated into SNOMED-CT.

PCDS PCDS stands for Patient Care Data Set. PCDS was developed by Judy Ozbolt at the University of Virginia as a comprehensive catalog of terms used in patient care records at nine hospitals. PCDS was officially adopted as one of the standards by the American Nurses Association in 1998.

PCDS is different from the other classifications that have been previously described. Where CCC was based on home care nursing, the Omaha System on community-based nursing, and PNDS on perioperative needs, PCDS has a much stronger acute care origin. PCDS also includes terms for 363 problems, 311 goals, and 1357 patient care orders. PCDS is organized into 22 care components (the CCC components plus one as Immunology and Metabolism were divided into separate components). However, "the Patient Care Data Set has been developed primarily not as a classification system for clinical terms but as a data dictionary defining elements to be included in and abstracted from clinical information systems."[1]

Capturing and Recording EHR Data

The value of having an EHR is evident, but how does the data get into the EHR? Thus far we have discussed three forms of EHR data. In subsequent chapters of this book we will explore how healthcare providers (clinicians, nurses, and medical assistants) create codified EHR. But before we move on, let us briefly examine how digital image data and text file data are added to the EHR and used. We will also discuss additional sources of EHR data that can be imported directly into the system.

Digital Image Systems

As discussed previously, digital image data may be subcategorized into diagnostic images and scanned document images. Even with the implementation of a codified EHR, there will always be some paper documents. Obviously there are all the old paper charts of established patients, but there is also a continuing influx of referral letters and other medical documents from outside sources.

Many healthcare organizations choose to bring paper documents into the EHR as scanned images. Although document images do not offer all the benefits of a codified medical record, they do provide widespread accessibility and a means to include source documents for a complete electronic chart.

---

[1]Multiple Attributes for Patient Care Data: Toward a Multiaxial, Combinatorial Vocabulary, Judy G. Ozbolt, Ph.D., R.N., 1997.

Most document image systems have a computer program to associate various ID fields and keywords with scanned images. This is called *cataloging the image*. Catalog data adds the capability to search for the electronic document images in multiple ways.

Guided Exercise 5: Exploring a Document Imaging System

In this exercise you will experience how an imaging system works. You will need access to the Internet for this exercise. If you have not already done so, complete the student registration for the MyHealthProfessionsKit provided on the inside cover of this textbook.

Step 1

Start your web browser program and follow the steps listed inside the cover of this textbook to select a discipline, click on the book cover that matches this *Electronic Health Records* textbook, and log in.

When the welcome page is displayed, click on the link "**Activities and Exercises**" or select "Activities" from the drop-down list and click on the button labeled "Go."

Step 2

A menu on the right of the screen will list various activities and exercises. Locate and click on the link **Exercise 5**.

Information about the exercise will be displayed.

Locate and click the link "Click here to start the Document/Image System program."

A screen similar to Figure 2-3 will be displayed.

▶ **Figure 2-3 Document/Image System window.**

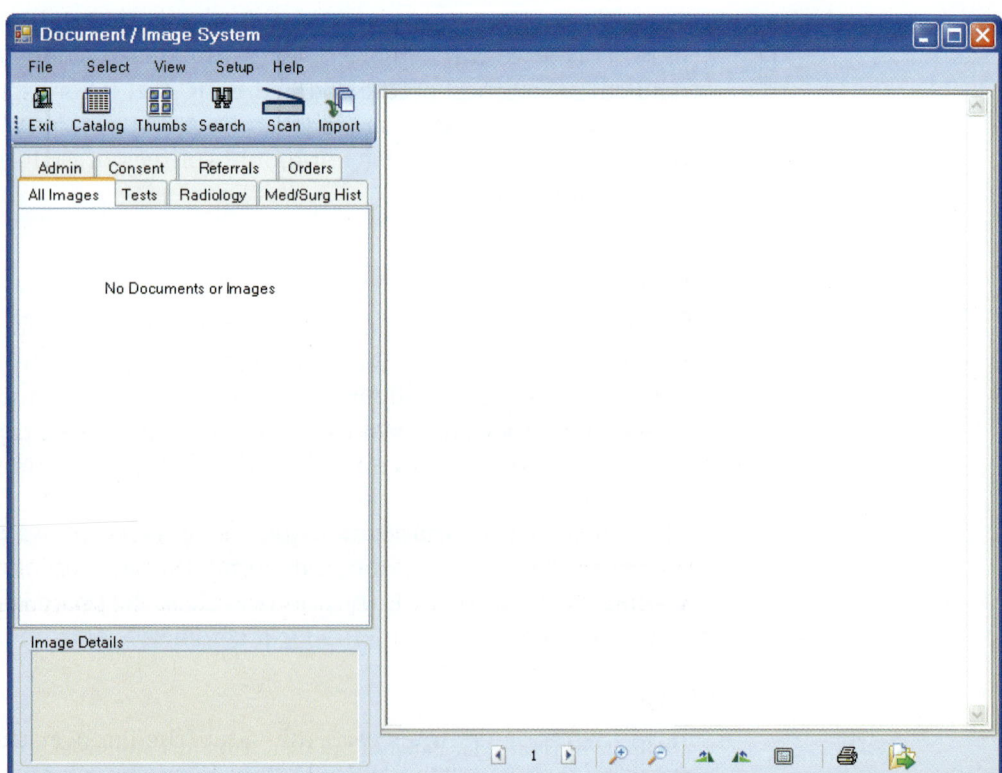

46   **Chapter 2** | Functional EHR Systems

The Document/Image System Window

As you proceed through the following steps, you will be introduced to names, functions, and components of the Document/Image System window. This program simulates many of the features typically found in an EHR document/image management system.

The Menu Bar At the top of the screen, the words "File," "Select," "View," "Setup," and "Help" are the menus of functions typically found in document image software. We call this the *Menu bar*. When you position the mouse over one of these words and click the mouse once, a list of functions will drop down below the word.

Once a menu list appears, clicking one of the items will invoke that function. Clicking the mouse anywhere except on the list will close the list. Certain items on the menu are displayed in gray text. These items are not available until a patient or document has been selected. The Setup and Help options are not available in this simulation.

Step 3

Position the mouse pointer over the word "Select" in the Menu bar at the top of the screen and click the mouse button once. A list of the Select menu functions will appear (see Figure 2-4).

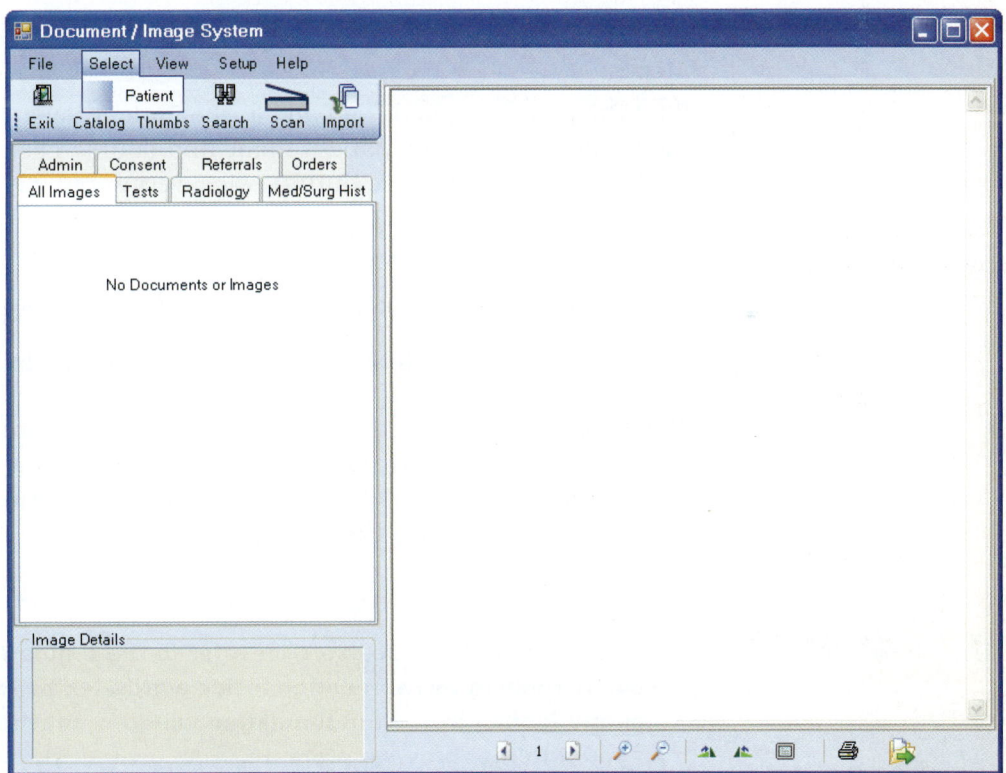

▶ Figure 2-4 Document/Image System after clicking the Select menu.

Step 4

Move the mouse pointer vertically down the list over the word "Patient" and click the mouse to invoke the Patient Selection window shown in Figure 2-5.

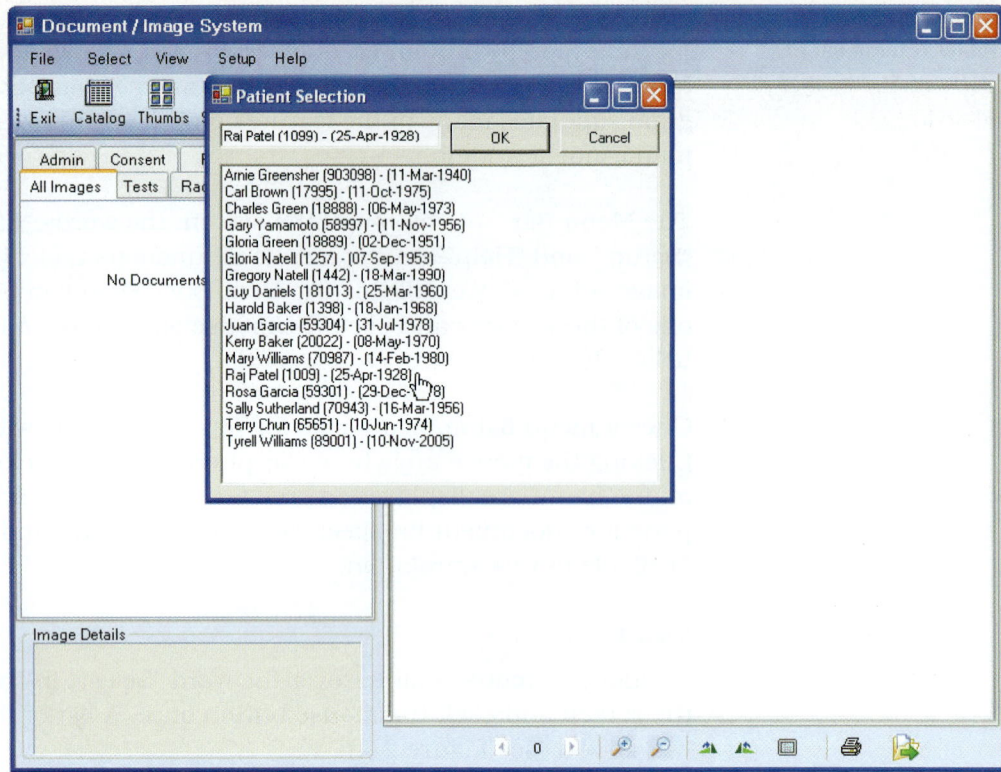

▶ **Figure 2-5** Selecting Raj Patel from the Patient Selection window.

Step 5

Find the patient named Raj Patel in the Patient Selection window. Position the mouse pointer over the patient name and double-click the mouse. (*Double-click* means to click the mouse button twice, very rapidly.)

Once a patient is selected, the patient's name, age, and sex are displayed in the title at the top of the window.

Compare your screen to Figure 2-6 as you read the following information:

The Toolbar Also located at the top of your screen are a row of icon buttons called a *Toolbar*. The purpose of the Toolbar is to allow quick access to commonly used functions. Most Windows programs feature a Toolbar, so you may already be familiar with the concept.

> **Alert** All instructions in these exercises refer to the simulation window. Because you are running this simulation inside a browser, be careful to use the Menu bar and Toolbar inside the simulation window, not the Menu bar or Toolbar of your Internet browser program.

The Catalog Pane The middle portion of the screen is divided into two window panes. The left pane (just below the Toolbar) is where a list of cataloged documents display once a patient is selected. At the top of the catalog pane there are

48   **Chapter 2** | Functional EHR Systems

▶ Figure 2-6 Left pane displays catalog list of documents and images for Raj Patel.

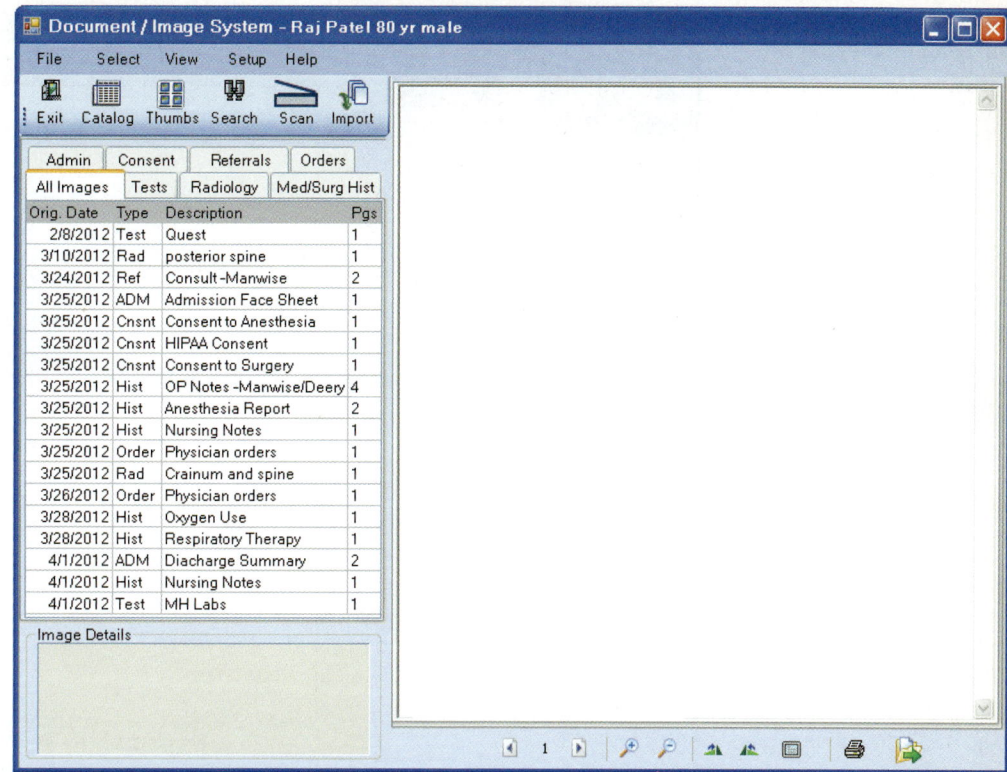

eight tabs. These look like tabs on file folders. The tabs are used to limit the list to images by category, making it easier to find a specific type of image quickly. The initial tab is "All Images," listed in date order.

Step 6

Locate the Toolbar in the Document/Image System window. The first icon is labeled "Exit" and it will close the simulation program and return you to the MyHealthprofessionskit page. Do not click it yet.

The next two buttons are used to change display of items in the Catalog pane from a list to thumbnails. Thumbnails are small versions of the document or image.

Position your mouse pointer over the "Thumbs" icon on the Toolbar (circled in Figure 2-7) and click your mouse.

Compare your screen to Figure 2-7.

Now position your mouse pointer over the "Catalog" icon on the Toolbar and click your mouse. Your screen should again resemble Figure 2-6.

Step 7

Locate the tab labeled "Med/Srg Hist" above the Catalog pane. Position your mouse pointer over it and click your mouse. The list should now be shorter as it is limited to items cataloged in the category of Medical/Surgical History.

Chapter 2 | Functional EHR Systems 49

▶ Figure 2-7 Catalog pane displaying thumbnails of images.

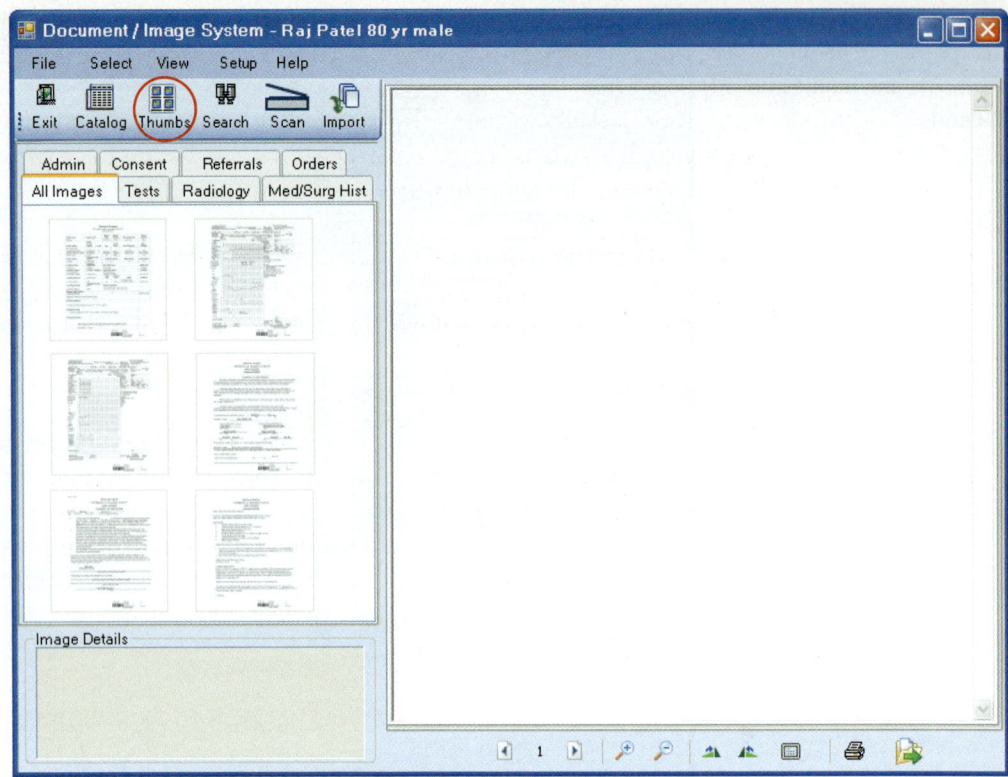

Step 8

Locate the catalog item "Anesthesia Report" and click on it. Compare your screen to Figure 2-8 as you read the following information.

▶ Figure 2-8 Catalog on Med/Srg tab, Anesthesia Report, displayed in Image Viewer pane.

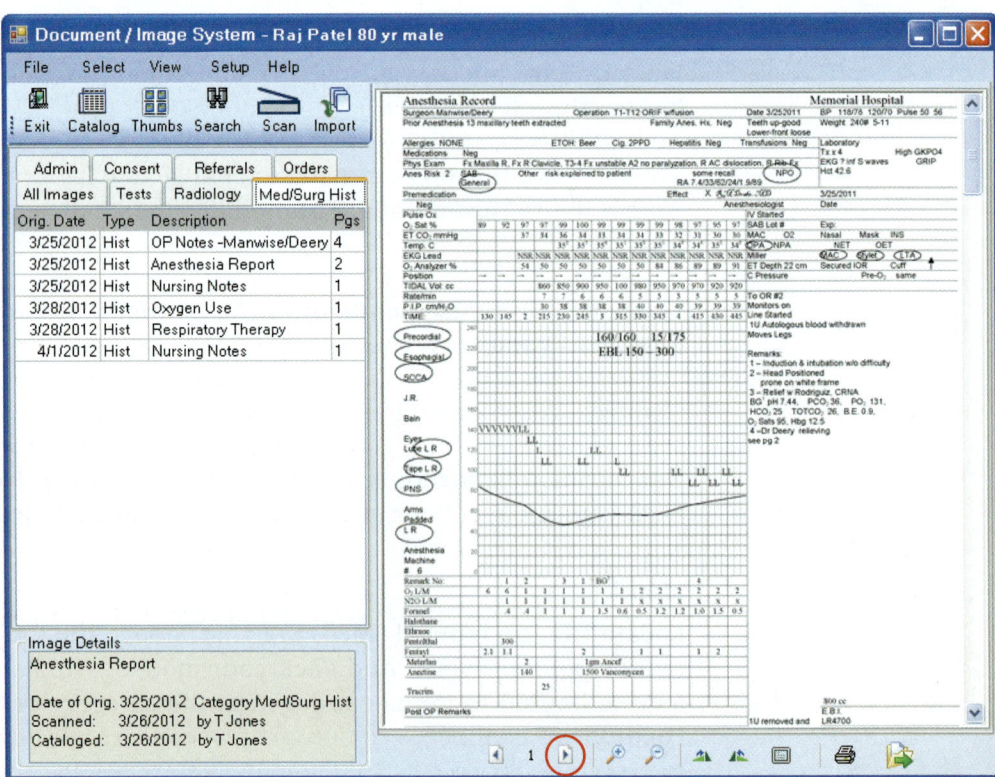

50   **Chapter 2** | Functional EHR Systems

The Image Viewer Pane The right pane of the window will dynamically display the corresponding image for a catalog entry that is clicked.

Item Details Just below the Catalog pane is a gray panel that displays information about a selected catalog item such as the user who scanned the document, relevant dates, and a longer description of the item.

Image Tools Just below the Image Viewer pane are a row of icon buttons used to change the displayed image. These include the ability to page through multipage documents, enlarge or reduce the displayed image.

Step 9

Locate the image tools buttons just below the viewer pane. The first three icons become active whenever a multipage document is selected. The Anesthesia Report has two pages. Locate and click on the Next page button (circled in red in Figure 2-8). The button displays the next page of a multipage document. The numeral between the two buttons is the page number currently displayed. Your screen should now display the second page of the report and the Image Tool should display the numeral two.

The Previous page button is the first icon in the image tools. Locate it and click on it. The image tool area should now display numeral one, and the image viewer should again display the first page of the report.

The next two icons resemble magnifying glasses. One includes a plus sign—this is the Zoom In tool; it enlarges the text in the viewer. The other magnifying glass has a minus sign—this is the Zoom Out tool; it reduces the enlarged view to show more of the page in the viewer.

Locate and click on the Zoom In icon to see how this works.

Cataloging Images

The process of scanning documents or importing scanned images into an image system includes not only capturing the image but tying it to the correct patient and entering data in the computer about the document such as the date, provider, type of image, and so on. This is called *cataloging the image*. Figure 2-10, shown later, is an example of an image catalog system.

Document images are scanned and cataloged into the EHR by many different people, including nurses, medical assistants, and personnel in the patient registration and Health Information Management departments. During scanning and cataloging, quality control is most important. Once a document has been scanned and cataloged, the original may be shipped to a remote storage facility or shredded. In either case, the original document may no longer be available for comparison. Although the scanned document image is stored safely on the computer, if it has been incorrectly cataloged it may not be easy to locate.

For the most part, the catalog data is entered by hand, but in some instances the image cataloging can be automated. Here are some examples of automated image cataloging:

Paper forms can include a barcode to identify catalog data; the scanning software interprets the barcode and automatically creates the catalog record. For example,

Memorial Hospital
876 Memory Ln, Anywhere, ID 83776
(208) 378-5555
CONSENT TO USE AND DISCLOSE HEALTH INFORMATION
for Treatment, Payment, or Healthcare operations

I understand that as part of my healthcare, Memorial Hospital originates and maintains health records describing my health history, symptoms, examination and test results, diagnoses, treatment, and any plans for future care or treatment. I understand that this information serves as:

- a basis for planning my care and treatment
- a means of communication among the many health professionals who contribute to my care
- a source of information for applying my diagnosis and surgical information to my bill
- a means by which a third-party payer can verify that services billed were actually provided
- and a tool for routine healthcare operations such as assessing quality and reviewing the competence of healthcare professionals

I understand and have been provided with a *Notice of Privacy Practices* that provides a more complete description of information uses and disclosures. I understand that I have the right to review the notice prior to signing this consent. I understand that Memorial Hospital reserves the right to change their notice and practices and prior to implementation will mail a copy of any revised notice to the address I've provided. I understand that I have the right to object to the use of my health information for directory purposes. I understand that I have the right to request restrictions as to how my health information may be used or disclosed to carry out treatment, payment, or healthcare operations and that Memorial Hospital is not required to agree to the restrictions requested. I understand that I may revoke this consent in writing, except to the extent that the hospital and its employees have already take action in reliance thereon.

I request the following restrictions to the use or disclosure of my health information:

Signature of Patient or Legal Representative Witness

Date Notice Effective Date or Version

__X__ Accepted _____ Denied

Signature: ___Raj Patel___   Date: ___3-24-2011___

Patient: Patel, Raj
Med Rec #: 837155

▶ **Figure 2-9 HIPAA Consent Form with barcode.**

Figure 2-9 shows a HIPAA authorization form that was printed for patient signature. The form includes a barcode identifying the patient, date, and document type, allowing automatic cataloging of the signed copy when it is scanned by the Document/Image System.

Another type of technology uses Optical Character Recognition (OCR) software to recognize text characters in images. Some document imaging systems can be programmed to find and use the text contained in the scanned document to populate the fields in the catalog records. Typically, only a few types of documents are processed this way, as each document type requires custom programming. However, when an organization images thousands of the same type of document, it can be worth it. For example, your bank keeps an image of the front and back of each check it processes. Because the account number and check number are in a consistent place at the bottom of the check, the bank computers can automatically catalog each image to the correct account as it is scanned.

Guided Exercise 6: Importing and Cataloging Images

In this exercise you will catalog a scanned report and 2 diagnostic images for a patient. You will need access to the Internet for this exercise.

Step 1

If you are still logged in from the previous exercise, proceed to Step 2; otherwise, start your web browser program and follow the steps listed inside the cover of this textbook to select a discipline, click on the book cover that matches this *Electronic Health Records* textbook, and log in.

When the welcome page is displayed, click on the link "**Activities and Exercises**" or select "Activities" from the drop-down list and click on the button labeled "Go."

Step 2

Locate and click on the link **Exercise 6**. Information about the exercise will be displayed.

Locate and click the link "Click here to start the Document/Image System program."

The document image system screen will be displayed. (Refer to Figure 2-3 for an example.)

Position your mouse pointer over the word "Select" in the Menu bar at the top of the screen and click the mouse button once.

Move the mouse pointer vertically down the list over the word "Patient" and click the mouse to invoke the Patient Selection window shown in Figure 2-10.

Step 3

Find the patient named **Sally Sutherland** in the Patient Selection window. Position the mouse pointer over the patient name and double-click the mouse.

Once a patient is selected, the patient's name, age, and sex are displayed in the title at the top of the window. The Catalog pane displays the message "No Documents or Images" because Sally has no documents or images in the catalog.

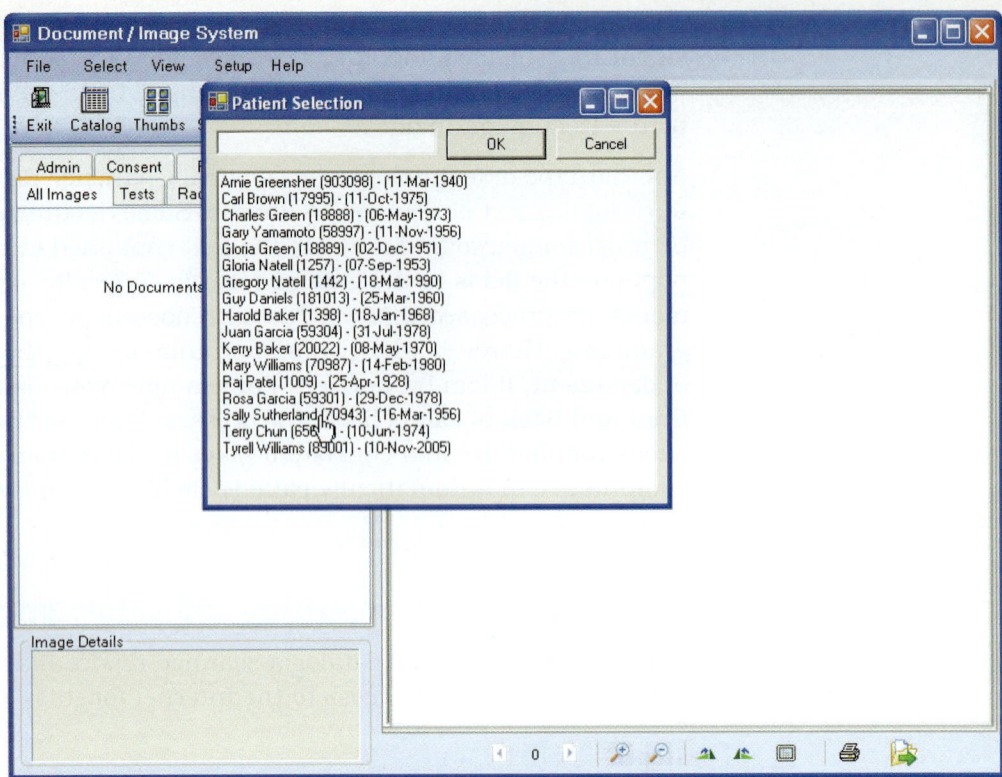

▶ Figure 2-10 Selecting Sally Sutherland from the Patient Selection window.

Step 4

Because you may not have a scanner connected to your computer, you are going to import a file that has already been scanned but not yet cataloged.

Locate and click on the Toolbar button labeled "Import".

The "Open Media File" window, displaying available files, will open. Compare your screen to Figure 2-11.

Step 5

Locate and click on the thumbnail image of the **radiologist report document** (suth70943rpt.tif).

Locate and click on the button labeled "Open."

Compare your screen to Figure 2-12.

Step 6

The imported file displays in the Image Viewer pane and data entry fields replace the catalog list. The fields shown in Figure 2-12 are the minimum for most Document/Image systems. The actual fields in a catalog record will differ by software vendor or medical facility.

The image you have imported should be the radiologist's report. The Catalog pane reminds you that it has not been saved into the patient's EHR.

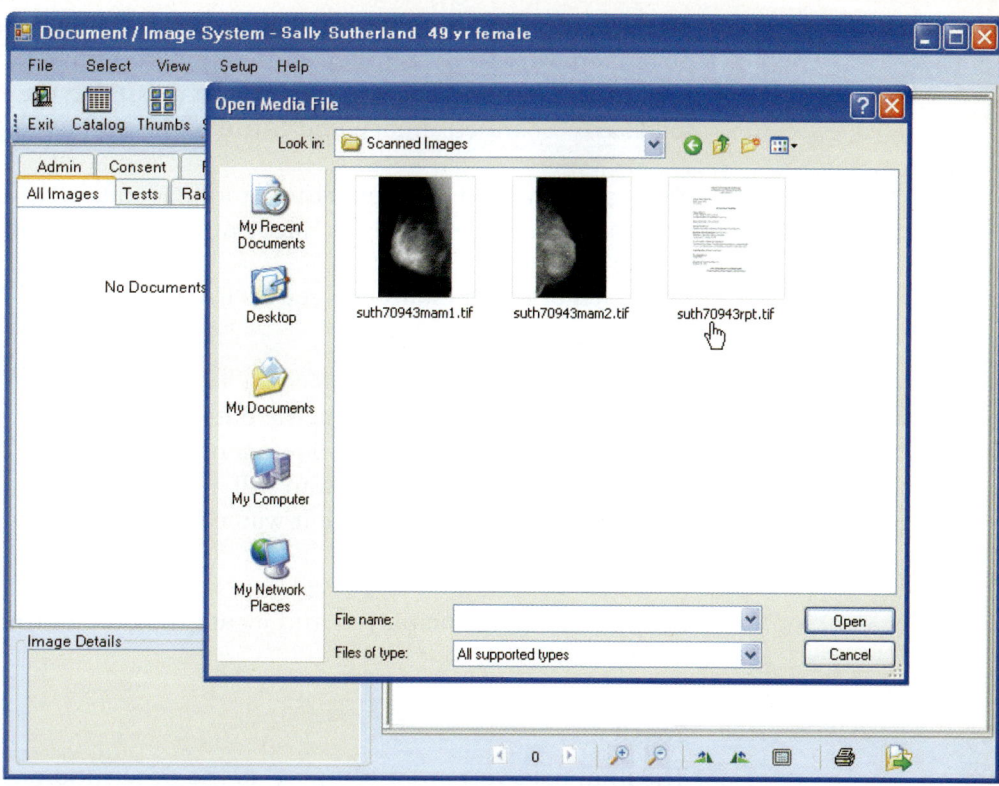

▶ Figure 2-11 Open Media window displays after the clicking Import icon.

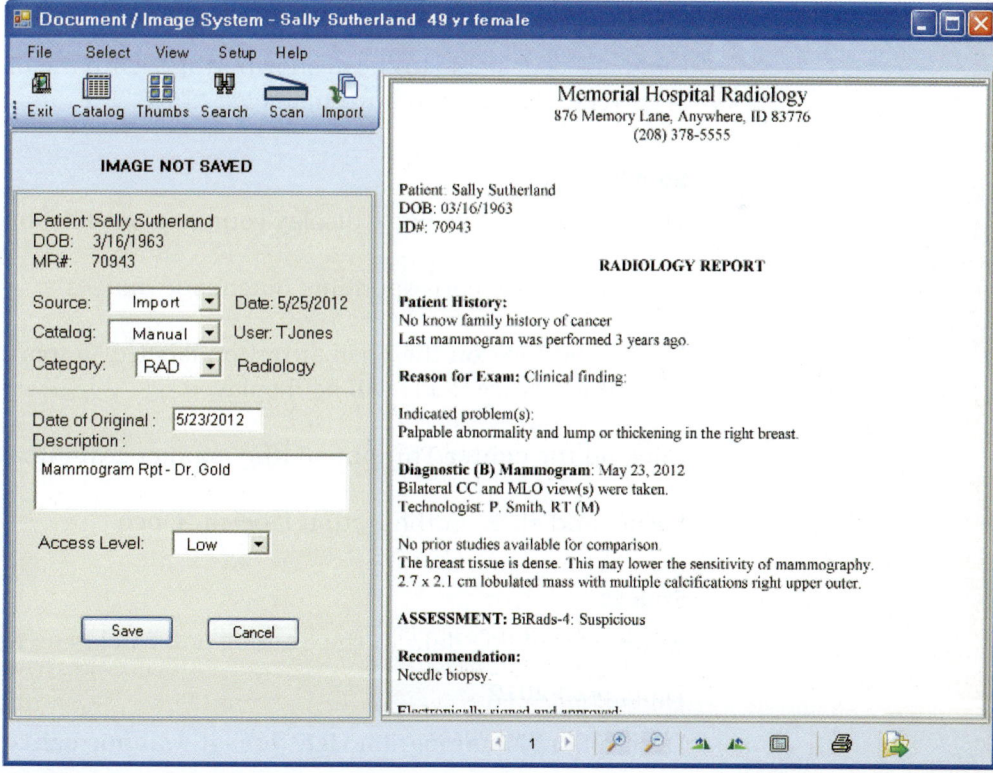

▶ Figure 2-12 Data entry fields in Catalog pane; Image Viewer displays imported Radiology report.

The first two fields in the catalog pane are determined automatically because the Document/Image System recognizes that you have imported the file and that you are performing a manual entry of the catalog data. Other options for these fields are "Scanned" image and "Automatic" cataloging (e.g., from a barcode).

The Category field uses short mnemonic codes to represent longer category names, for example, HIST for "Medical/Surgical History," or RAD for "Radiology."

The Category field is already set to "RAD."

Step 7

The first field you will enter is the date of the original document; this is for reference purposes, to locate a document by the date of the report, letter, surgery, and so on. Note that the system will automatically record other dates, such as the date of the scan, the date it was cataloged, and so forth. These other dates are used for audit purposes.

Look at the image displayed and locate the date of the report, May 23, 2012. Enter 5/23/2012.

Step 8

The final field you must complete is the description. Although the field can hold a lengthy description, only the first portion of it is displayed in the catalog list, which is used by others at the healthcare facility to find the document/image. Therefore, when cataloging documents and images, be sure to put the most important information at the beginning of the description. In this case, you will type: **Mammogram Rpt - Dr. Gold.**

Compare your fields to those shown in the left pane of Figure 2-12. If everything is correct, click on the button labeled "Save."

Step 9

The Catalog pane will now display your cataloged listing (as shown in Figure 2-13).

Now catalog the corresponding diagnostic images.

Locate and click on the Toolbar button labeled "Import." The Open Media window (shown in Figure 2-11) will be displayed.

Click on the **center** Thumbnail (the mammogram image "suth70943mam2.tif).

Locate and click on the button labeled "Open."

Step 10

Enter the catalog data in the Catalog entry fields as follows:

Date: 5/23/2012

Description: **Mammogram right breast w/abnormality**

Compare your screen to Figure 2-14. Click the button labeled "Save."

The Catalog pane will now display two listings.

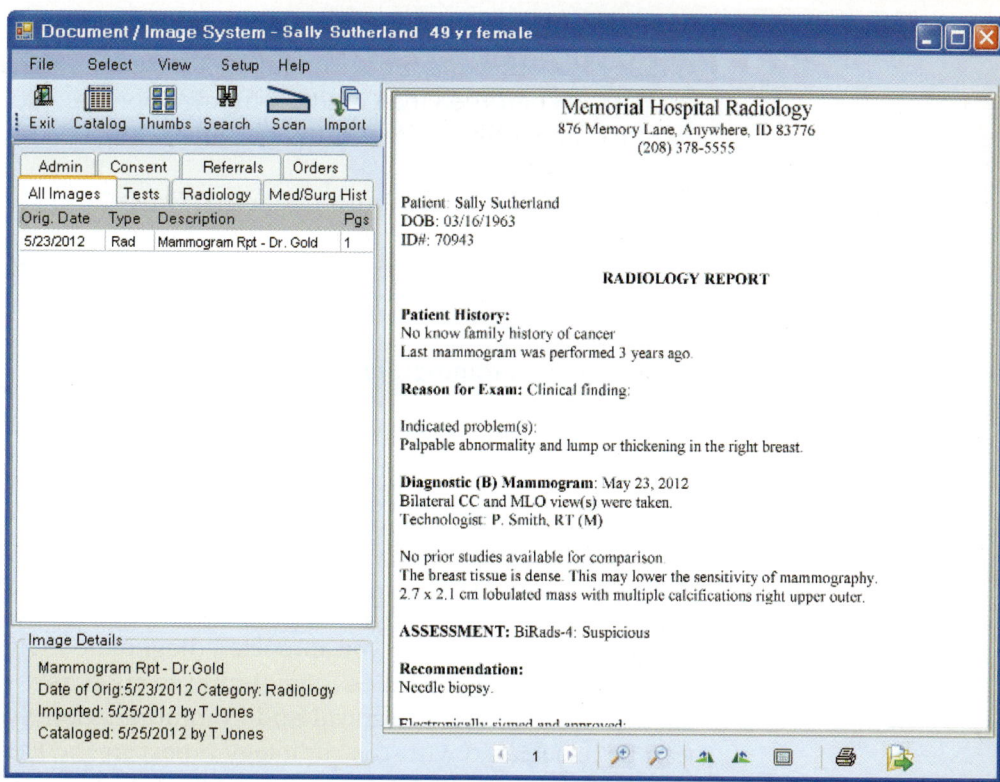

▶ Figure 2-13 Cataloged mammogram report.

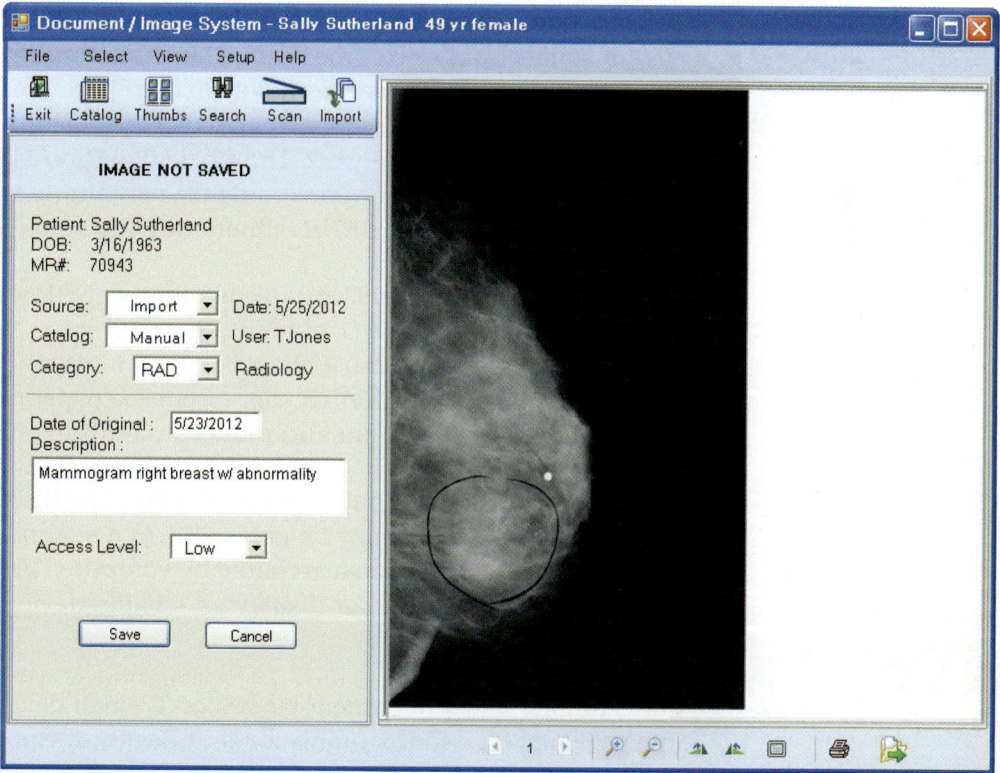

▶ Figure 2-14 Cataloged mammogram image.

Chapter 2 | Functional EHR Systems

Step 11

Catalog the other mammogram image by clicking the Toolbar button labeled "Import." When the Open Media window appears, click on the **left** Thumbnail (the mammogram image "suth70943mam1.tif).

Locate and click on the button labeled "Open."

Enter the catalog data in the Catalog entry fields as follows:

Date: **5/23/2012**

Description: **Mammogram left breast**

Click the button labeled "Save." The Catalog pane will now display three listings.

The exercise is concluded. You may exit and close your browser.

Picture Archival and Communication System (PAC)

In the previous exercise you imported diagnostic images (mammograms) into the EHR. At many facilities, digital images such as x-rays and CAT scans reside on a separate Picture Archival and Communication System (PAC). These images can be associated with the radiology report in the EHR and appear to be part of the EHR record, even though they are on a separate system. In those facilities, the diagnostic image is not actually imported into the EHR, but rather linked to the patient EHR record.

Importing Text to the EHR

The second form of data we discussed is text data—that is, data that consists of words, sentences, and paragraphs, but is not fielded data. Frequently this type of data comes from word processing files that result from transcribed dictation. A good example of this is the radiologist's report. A radiologist is a specialist who interprets diagnostic images. Radiologists often dictate their impressions of a study (as shown in Figure 2-15.) Their dictation is later typed by a medical transcriptionist. The word processing file containing the radiology report can be imported directly into the EHR, eliminating the steps of printing and scanning.

Similarly, a healthcare facility implementing an EHR will eventually need to bring old paper charts into the Document/Image system. If the facility has retained word processing files of transcribed dictation, importing them as EHR text records instead of scanning the printed pages from the paper chart increases the amount of the EHR that is text data and reduces the number of pages to be scanned.

Although imported text data are not codified like those created when clinicians enter actual data, they may be preferable to a scanned image for two reasons. First, the text records are searchable by computer. Second, text data can be dynamically reformatted for display on smaller devices such as mobile phones, images of scanned documents cannot.

For example, a text document viewed on a small device such as a mobile phone might display in a font suitable for that device. If the same document were a scanned image, it might be too small to read, thus requiring the clinician to zoom the image and making it cumbersome to read.

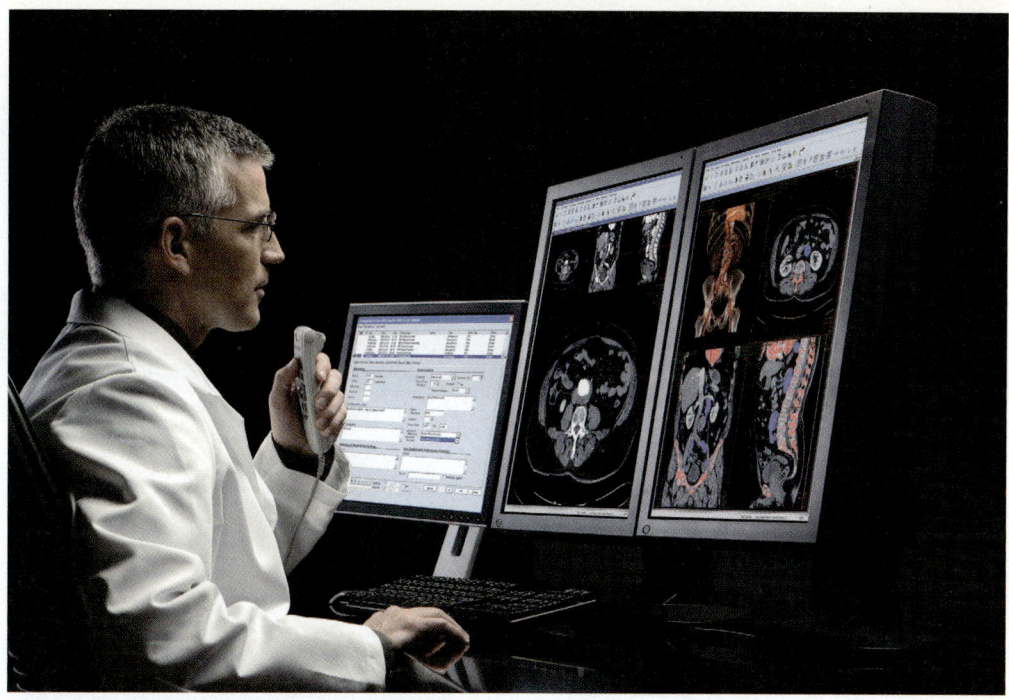

Photo provided courtesy of Carestream Health, Inc.

▶ **Figure 2-15 Radiologist dictates report while interpreting radiology study on a PAC system.**

Importing Coded EHR Data

As we have already learned, the very best for of EHR data is fielded, codified data. In addition to the coded data that will be created by the clinician using an EHR, many other sources of codified data can be imported. Importing coded data produces a better EHR and eliminates the need to re-key data or scan reports into the chart.

For example, electronic lab order and results systems can be interfaced to send the orders and merge test results directly into the patient's chart. The numerical data that makes up many lab results lends itself to trend analysis, graphs, and comparison with other tests. The ability to review and present results in this manner allows providers to see the immediate, tangible benefits of using an EHR and improves patient care.

Other sources of EHR data available for import into the EHR include vital signs when they are measured with modern electronic devices (as shown in Figure 2-16). Similarly, glucose monitors and Holter monitors are devices that gather and store data about the patient. Most of these medical devices have the ability to transfer the data they have collected to a computer.

When clinicians use the EHR to write prescriptions, the orders are also automatically recorded in the EHR as part of the workflow. This keeps a record of the patient's past prescriptions and makes renewing prescriptions much faster for the provider.

HL7   Health Level 7 (HL7) is a nonprofit organization and the leading messaging standard used by healthcare computer systems to exchange information. The organization is comprised of healthcare providers, institutions, government

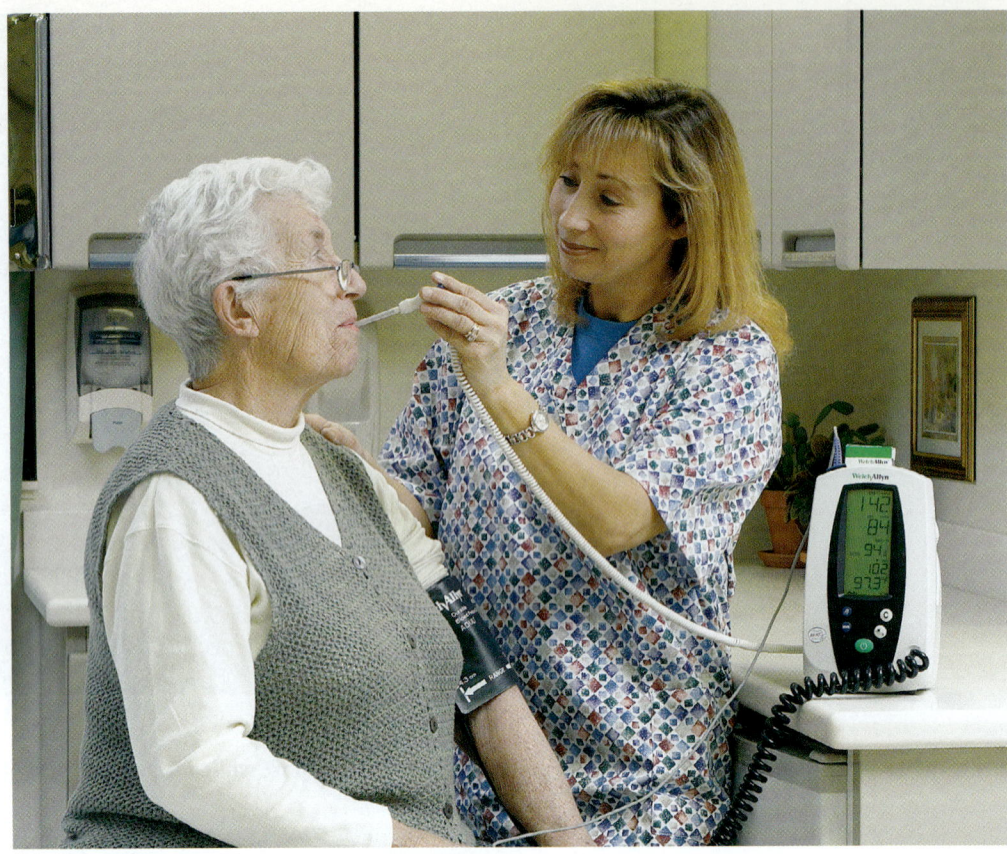

Courtesy of Welch Allyn.

▶ Figure 2-16 Nurse taking vital signs using Welch Allyn® Spot Vitals Signs®.

representatives, and software developers. HL7 uses a consensus process to arrive at specifications acceptable to every-one involved. The HL7 specifications are updated regularly and released as new versions.

Hospitals and other large healthcare organizations often have many different computer systems created by unrelated vendors. These systems generate various portions of the patient's medical data. HL7 is used to translate and interface that data into a main EHR system.

The simplest act of transferring patient information from the admissions office to the radiology department or hospital pharmacy would not be easy without HL7. If you work in a hospital, your hospital probably uses HL7. As a part of this course, it is not necessary to delve into the specific structure or flow of HL7 messages, but it is helpful to understand its advantages and limitations.

HL7 specifications are independent of any application or vendor; therefore, applications that can send and receive HL7 messages can potentially exchange information. That is its advantage and importance to an EHR system.

HL7 has been successful because it is very flexible both in its structure as well as its support for multiple coding standards. However, when a message is received the codes and terms used by the other system may not match those used by the EHR. That is its disadvantage.

To overcome this problem, segments of the HL7 message that contain coded data also contain an identifier indicating which coding standard is being used. A special computer program called an HL7 translator is used to match the codes in the message with the codes in the EHR. The translator also can reconcile differences between HL7 versions from multiple systems.

DICOM DICOM stands for Digital Imaging and Communications in Medicine. It is the standard used for medical images, such as digital x-rays, CT scans, MRIs, and ultrasound. Other uses include the images from angiography, endoscopy, laparoscopy, medical photography, and microscopy. It was created by the National Electrical Manufacturers Association and is the most widely used format for storing and sending diagnostic images.

DICOM is the standard for communication between diagnostic imaging equipment and the image processing software. The standard also defines the specification for a file that contains the actual digital image. A DICOM file includes a "header" that contains information about the image, dimensions, type of scan, image compression, and so on, as well as patient information such as ID number or name. DICOM compatible software is required to view the image.

CDISC A subgroup of HL7 is CDISC, which stands for Clinical Data Interchange Standards Consortium. CDISC originated as a special interest group of the Drug Information Association but became its own entity and formed an alliance with HL7. Although the focus of HL7 is to facilitate message standards for a broad range of healthcare, CDISC has a specific focus on clinical drug trials.

CDISC standards enable sponsors, vendors, and clinicians to acquire and exchange data used in clinical trials. Because the FDA is the agency to whom the final results are submitted, the standard is very focused on following the FDA requirements. However, the commitment of CDISC to HL7 will eventually make it easier to use EHR data in clinical trial studies. It is mentioned here because you may encounter CDISC if you work at a healthcare facility that participates in clinical trials.

Biomedical Devices Biomedical devices can output important and useful medical information that can be received and stored as data in the patient's EHR. However, the type of data and method of communicating between the device and EHR often are proprietary to the particular device. Therefore HL7 is often used to exchange demographic information between the device and the EHR system.

Still, the advantage of having the data in the EHR is so strong as to warrant the additional interfaces. Many of the patient monitoring, point-of-care testing, and biomedical devices in hospitals have the capability of exporting data to the EHR. Examples include instruments for measuring vital signs and cardiac and arterial blood gas monitors. Today, many of these devices have wired or wireless telemetry to transmit their information to nurses and into the EHR.

A similar capability is available in systems used in medical offices and for patient home monitoring such as the spirometer data shown in Chapter 1, Figure 1-1. Other examples include electrocardiograms, ultrasound, and the vital signs device shown earlier.

Telemonitors Many patients with chronic conditions are monitored at home using devices such as blood pressure monitors, glucose meters, and Holter monitors. Some of these devices store the readings and transfer the data to the doctor's system either by using a modem and phone line or by downloading from the device during a patient encounter. For blood pressure monitoring, if the device does not store the readings, the patient may keep a log, which is then entered into the patient's medical record at the doctor's office.

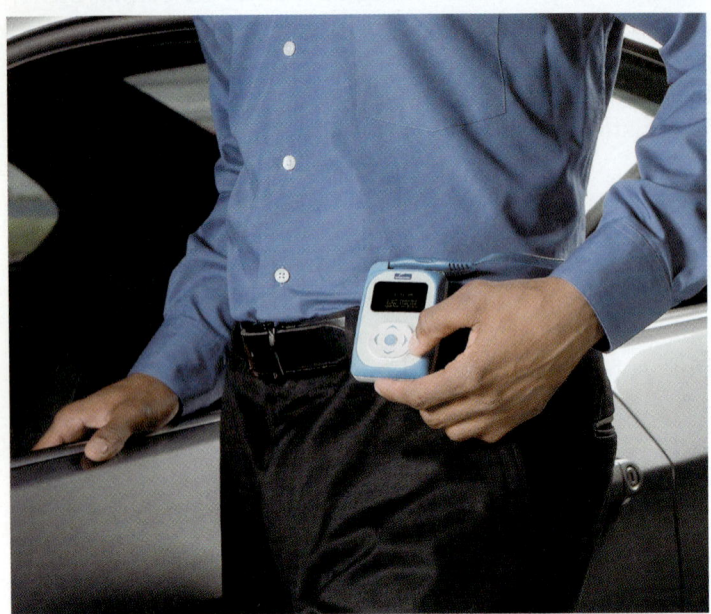

Courtesy of Midmark Diagnostics Group.

▶ **Figure 2-17** An IQholter™ worn by the patient gathers cardio data.

One example of a telemonitor is the Holter monitor, a device the patient wears for 24 to 72 hours to measure and record information about the patient's heart. The data is then transferred either remotely or in person to the doctor's computer, where it is reviewed. Figure 2-17 shows a patient wearing a Holter monitor.

When a patient is seen in a doctor's office, measurements of vital signs, a glucose test, or even an ECG reflect only the patient's condition at that particular time. The advantage of telemonitoring is that it allows the provider to study these values measured many times over the course of the patient's normal daily activity.

RHIO One of the issues discussed in Chapter 1 was that patients often no longer see a single doctor, so their records reside at many separate facilities. Regional Health Information Organizations (RHIO) and the Office of National Coordinator for Health Information Technology's development of a national health information network (NHIN) are both examples of projects to enable to electronic transfer of health records between providers.

Although it may take considerable time to create a true NHIN, many areas of the nation are attempting to create state or local versions. RHIO stands for regional health information organization. The Health Information Management Systems Society (HIMSS) defines a RHIO as a "neutral organization that adheres to a defined governance structure which is composed of and facilitates collaboration among the stakeholders in a given medical trading area, community or region through secure electronic health information exchange to advance the effective and efficient delivery of healthcare for individuals and communities."[2]

RHIOs encourage the exchange of a patient's health information across medical practices and facilities that are owned by different entities for the better well-

---

[2]Health Information Management Systems Society RHIO Federation Definitions Workgroup, http://himss.org.

being of the patient. The formation and operation of a RHIO must overcome numerous obstacles. These include technical, economic, and political issues:

Technical Interfacing systems from different vendors in a hospital is not an easy task, but at least it is managed by one Information Technology (IT) department and shares a common network. The level of difficulty becomes multiplied when unrelated hospitals and physician practices—each with numerous systems—attempt to translate data and share a common network.

Economic The translation of data from one system to another requires an interface engine and possibly a regional MPI (master person index). Who bears the cost of the networking, interface programming, and maintenance of the translation and MPI systems? Also, many RHIOs operate on a volunteer basis, but require a paid IT director, employed by the RHIO, not one of its members.

Political Some participants in the RHIO are business competitors who may be leery about what data is shared and whether it can be analyzed to reveal their patient or case mix, volume of business, and so on. Additionally, state laws may affect who can participate in the RHIO and whether members can be in bordering states.

Patient-Entered Data

Numerous studies have shown that patient data also can become a significant contributor to the EHR, for some of the following reasons:

- Only the patient has the information about what symptoms were present at the outset of the illness.
- Only the patient knows the outcome of medical treatment of those symptoms.
- The patient is also the source of past medical, family, and social history.
- Patient-entered data is a more accurate reflection of a patient's complaints.
- Patients who can review their histories are better prepared for the visit.

A computer program such as Instant Medical History™ developed by Dr. Allen Wenner, allows patients to enter their history and symptom information on a computer in the waiting room or via the Internet prior to the visit. This is the same symptom and history information that the nurse or clinician would have entered. Once the process is completed, the data is organized by the computer for the provider in a succinct and easy-to-read format that becomes the starting point for the encounter.

According to Dr. Allen Wenner, up to 67 percent of the nurse or clinician's time with the patient is spent entering the patient's symptoms into the visit documentation. Patient-entered data saves time and allows the triage nurse to focus on the review of the information with the patient rather than on the keying of data. Having a complete history in advance of the visit allows the clinician to ask fewer questions about the diagnosis and concentrate more on the effects of the illness on the patient. It also allows the clinician more time to discuss the treatment plan with the patient.

Real-Life Story

Enhancing Process Efficiency through Remote Access[3]

By Julie DeSantis

Hinsdale Hematology Oncology Associates, Ltd. (HHOA), of Hinsdale, Illinois, switched from traditional paper records to the advanced technology of wireless, mobile electronic medical records (EMR) from IMPAC Medical Systems. At HHOA, the result of implementing an EMR is improved patient and clinician satisfaction, an increased patient load, and an elevated level of process efficiency that has paid for itself within 2 years of implementation.

Michele White, practice administrator at HHOA, said that patient confidence improved with the use of advanced technology, such as PDAs and wireless laptop systems. "Our patients have noticed that our medical documentation is complete, up-to-date, and right at hand," she said. The patients have more confidence in our doctors, and have received more face-to-face interaction time during their visits, she said. "We have a high standard of care that we did not want to compromise, and with tablet PCs, wireless laptops, and the Siemens PDAs—we have everything we need to access lab reports, scheduling, and more."

HHOA provides services to 80–100 patients a day—an increase in patient load since installing IMPAC. With 12 busy exam rooms and only 6 physicians, they use IMPAC's online transcription and report management system to quickly and accurately document patient encounters and manage them online. In addition, HHOA uses a structured noting system for patient documentation within the EMR. All incoming lab results also are downloaded into the system via interface, and available from any laptop at the practice, ensuring the patient record is complete, up-to-date, and easily accessible to physicians and staff. "From an administrative and economic perspective, our mobile access to EMRs has meant that we did not need to purchase additional antivirus software and miscellaneous upgrades. We've saved a lot of money, while increasing efficiency, security, and reliability," White said.

For six years, HHOA used pcAnywhere™ in the physicians' homes to access the office. However, they have found remote access to the EMR from IMPAC to be faster, more reliable, and readily accessible from anywhere. There are six physicians on staff at HHOA, all with different technical knowledge, but "they are all comfortable with IMPAC's EMR," White explained. "They can get any reports they need and print right through the system when they are off-site."

[3]©2005 IMPAC Medical Systems, Inc. Used with permission.

Patients do not have access to the EHR, but use a separate program that is linked to the EHR. The patient-entered data is reviewed by the doctor or nurse during the exam and before being merged into the EHR. You will have an opportunity to explore this concept yourself in Chapter 11.

Provider-Entered Data

Finally, the surest source of reliable coded EHR data is that entered by the providers (doctor, nurse, and medical assistant) during the patient encounter using a standardized nomenclature. That process will be the subject of Chapters 3–12 of this book.

Functional Benefits from Codified Records

Because coded EHR data is nonambiguous, the computer can use it for trend analysis, alerts, health maintenance, decision support, orders and results, administrative processes, and population health reporting. We will now explore four of the functional benefits that can be derived from using a codified EHR.

Trend Analysis

In healthcare, laboratory tests are used to measure the level of certain components present in specimens taken from the patient. When the same test is performed over a period of time, changes in the results can indicate a *trend* in the patient's health.

With a paper chart, the clinician must page through the reports and mentally remember the values to compare them. When a health record is electronic, it is easier to compare data from different dates, tests, or events. When the data is fielded and coded, it is possible to generate graphs and reports that support trend analysis.

To experience the differences in forms of data, we will compare a patient's lab results that have been stored in each of the three data formats we discussed earlier in this chapter.

Critical Thinking Exercise 7: Retrieving a Scanned Lab Report

In this exercise you will use what you have learned in Guided Exercise 5 to locate information from a recent lab report for a patient.

Step 1

Log into the Document/Imaging simulation on the Myhealthprofessionskit web site as you did in Guided Exercise 5.

Step 2

Select patient **Raj Patel**.

Step 3

On **February 8, 2012**, the facility received the results of a lab test performed by **Quest** laboratories. The lab report was scanned and cataloged in Raj Patel's chart.

Locate the catalog entry for this lab report and click on it to display the report.

Step 4

When the report is displayed in the Image Viewer, locate the results for the test component "Triglycerides" and write down the value on a sheet of paper with your name and today's date.

You may need to use the Zoom In button to read the value accurately.

```
Raj Patel: M: 3/5/1932:

Doctor's Laboratory
3/10/2012 11:30AM

Tests
Blood Chemistry:                      Value              Normal Range
Total plasma cholesterol level        215 mg/dl          140 - 200
Plasma HDL cholesterol level          40 mg/dl           30 - 70
Plasma LDL cholesterol level          98 mg/dl           80 - 130
Total cholesterol/HDL ratio           5.4                4 - 6

Hematology:                           Value              Normal Range
INR                                   2.1                25 - 40
```

▶ **Figure 2-18** Text-based lab results.

Step 5

Close your browser window and give your paper to your instructor.

This is an example of data in the format of a digital image. As you can see, the lab data are present in the EHR, but requires a human to locate and read the data values.

Lab Report as Text Data If a lab results report was received as a text file, it might resemble Figure 2-18. The file could be imported into the EHR, but because the data is not fielded or codified, a computer might have difficulty accurately parsing the data in the report, but it could easily search text records and locate those that contained the word *cholesterol*. This could be useful to quickly locate records of previous tests containing the same word.

Coded Lab Data If the test result data is fielded and coded, the computer can find matching results in the data and generate a cumulative summary report or a graph, making it easier to compare test results from different times and dates.

The cumulative summary report shown in Figure 2-19 has three sections of results: blood gases, whole blood chemistries, and general chemistry. Within each section are the results from tests performed five different times; the date and time is printed above each column of data.

The report is read from left to right; each row contains the name of the test component followed by result values for each of the five times. The right two columns are informational; they contain the range of values considered normal for each particular test and the unit of measure.

A simple graphing tool can turn numeric data in the EHR into a powerful visual aid that would be impractical to create from a paper chart. Figure 2-20 provides an example of how data from multiple lab tests can be quickly extracted and graphed for the clinician. The value of the total cholesterol results over a three-month period of time is trended with the green line. The reference ranges of normal high (200) and low (140) values are shown in the graph as red and blue lines, respectively.

```
*************************************** Blood Gases ***************************************
DATE:           [------------------- 03/26/2012 -------------------] 03/25/2012
TIME:              2132         1920         1720         1506         1615       NORMAL       UNITS

pH-Arterial        7.30 L       7.36         7.38         7.47 H       7.48 H     7.35-7.45
PCO2-Arterial      47.4 H       41.1         38.3         34.8 L       33.0 L     35-45        mm Hg
PO2-Arterial       90.2         189.0 H      187.0 H      188.0 H      227.0 H    90-105       mm Hg
HCO3-Arterial      22.8         22.8         22.0         24.9         24.4       21-27        mEq/L
Base Excess-A                                              1.7          1.6       0-3          mEq/L
Base Deficit-A     3.2 H        1.9          2.3                                  0-3          mEq/L
O2 Sat Dir-A       96.0         99.3 H       99.5 H       99.6 H       99.9 H     95-99        % Saturation
O2 Content-A       15.9         15.3         14.6 L       10.3 L       14.4 L     15-17        vol %
Hemoglobin-BG      12.0         10.8         10.3         7.2          10.1                    g/dL
CarboxyHb-A        1.1 H        1.0 H        1.2 H        0.9          1.6 H      0.0-0.9      % Saturation
MetHb-A            0.9          0.4          0.7          0.4          0.8        0.0-0.9      % Saturation
FIO2                            .55          .56          0.54         .65                     %


*************************************** Whole Blood Chemistries ***************************************
DATE:           [----------------------03/26/2012----------------------] 03/25/2012
TIME:              2209         2132         1920         1720         1506         1615       NORMAL       UNITS

Sodium-WB                                    142          142          142          139        135-145      mEq/L
Potassium-WB       3.5                       3.3          3.0 L        2.9 L        2.7 L      3.3-4.6      mEq/L
Calcium Ionized                 1.21         1.05         0.99 L       1.07         1.08       1.05-1.30    mmol/L
Lactic Acid-WB                  1.3          0.8          1.1          0.8          0.5        0.3-1.5      mmol/L
Glucose-WB                      197 H        156 H        165 H        118 H        90         65-99        mg/dL
Hematocrit-WB                   37           34 L         32 L         22 L         31 L       36-46        %


*************************************** General Chemistry ***************************************
DATE:           04/01/2012 [---- 03/30/2012 ----] [---------- 03/29/12 ----------] 03/28/2012
TIME:              *0620        0653         0327         1835         0915         0532         2048       NORMAL       UNITS

Sodium             140                                                              143                     136-145      mmol/L
PotaSSium          2.7 L        3.0 L                     2.9 L        3.0 L        2.7 L                   3.3-5.1      mmol/L
Chloride           101                                                              100                     98-107       mmol/L
Carbon Dioxide     32 H                                                             36 H                    22-30        mmol/L
Urea Nitrogen      10                                                               7                       6-20         mg/dL
Creatinine         0.54                                                             0.60                    0.40-0.90    mg/dL
Glucose            115 H                                                            96                      65-99        mg/dL
Calcium            8.4                                                              8.0                     8.0-10.6     mg/dL
Magnesium          1.9                                                              2.3          1.8        1.5-2.8      mg/dL
Phosphorus Inorg   2.3 L                                                            2.8          1.8 L      2.7-4.5      mg/dL
CK Total                                     165                                                 273 H      30-170       U/L

--------------------------------------------------------------------------------------------------
     H=Abnormal High           L=Abnormal Low        H*=Critical High        L*=Critical Low
     Date Printed: 04/01/2012       Admit Date: 03/25/2012       Discharge Date: 04/01/2012
                                INPATIENT MEDICAL RECORDS COPY                     Page: 1
```

▶ **Figure 2-19 Cumulative summary lab report.**

The computer is able to generate this graph because the data is fielded and the different tests and components have unique codes. From all the possible tests a patient might have had, the computer can quickly find those coded as "total cholesterol." Using a graph, the clinician can easily see the trend of this patient's total cholesterol levels.

Trend analysis is not limited to lab test results. Graphs of patient weight loss or gain are used as patient education tools. Effects of medication can be measured by comparing changes in dosage to changes in blood pressure measurements. Flow sheets (shown later in Chapter 8) are another type of trend analysis tool.

▶ Figure 2-20 Graph of total cholesterol from codified lab results.

Alerts

One of the important reasons for the widespread adoption of EHR is the potential to reduce medical errors. Paper charts and even electronic charts that are principally scanned images depend on the clinician noticing a risk factor about the patient. However, when an EHR consists primarily of fielded and codified data using standard nomenclature, rules can be set up that allow the computer to do the monitoring.

Alert is the term used in an EHR for a message or reminder that is automatically generated by the system. Alerts are based on programmed rules that cause the EHR to alert the provider when two or more conditions are met. For example, an electronic prescription system generates an alert when two drugs known to have adverse interactions are prescribed for the same patient.

Alerts can be programmed for just about anything in the EHR. However, the most prevalent alert systems are those implemented with electronic prescription systems. Interactions between multiple prescription drugs, allergic reactions to certain classes of drugs, and patient health conditions that contraindicate certain drugs can all contribute to suffering, additional illness, and in extreme cases even death.

To prevent this, most physicians consult the patient medication list, allergy list, and the *Physicians' Desk Reference* (for interactions) before writing a prescription. As a further precaution, the pharmacy checks for drug conflicts and provides the patient with warning materials about the drug. When prescriptions are written electronically, however, the computer can quickly and efficiently check for drug safety and present the clinician with warnings, alerts, and explanatory

Courtesy of Allscripts, LLC.

▶ Figure 2-21 Electronic prescription DUR alert.

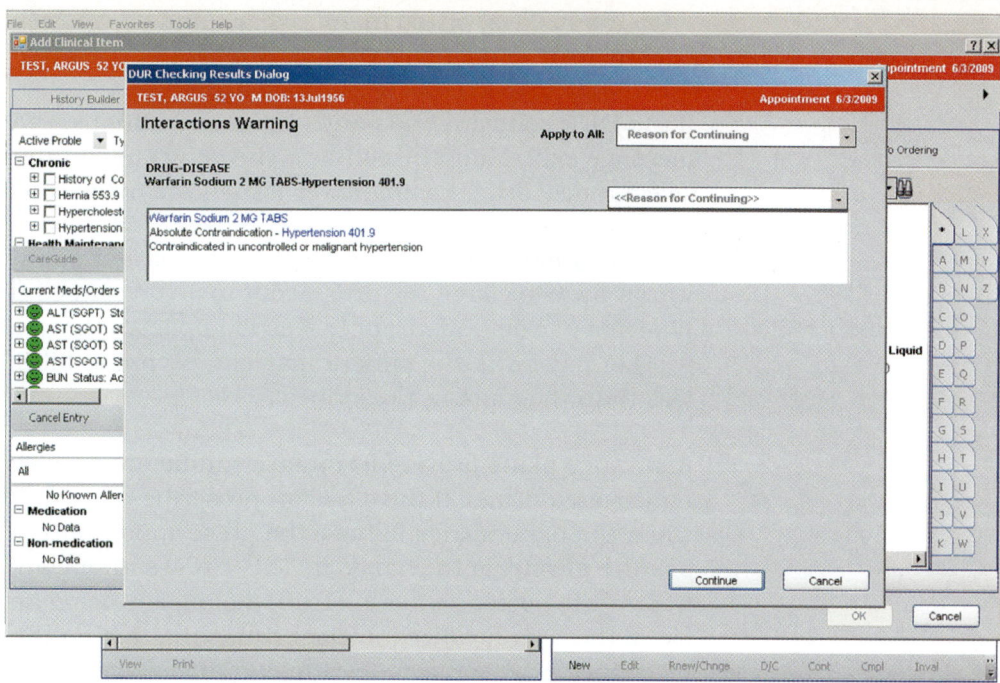

information about the risks of particular drugs. Figure 2-21 shows a clinical warning alert generated by the Allscripts EHR system. Let's take a closer look at how this process works.

Drug Utilization Review When the clinician writing an electronic prescription selects a drug and enters the Sig[4] information, the EHR system scans the patient chart for allergy information, past and current diagnoses, and a list of current medications. This information is then passed to a drug utilization review (DUR) program that compares the prescription to a database of most known drugs. The database includes prescription drugs as well as over-the-counter drugs, and even nutritional herb and vitamin supplements. The DUR program performs the following functions:

♦ The drug about to be prescribed is checked against the patient medication list to determine if there is a conflict with any drug the patient is already taking. Certain drugs remain in the body for a period of time after the patient has stopped taking it. This latency period is factored in as well.

♦ Ingredients that make up the drug are checked against the ingredients of current medications to see if they conflict or would hinder the effectiveness of the drug.

♦ Drugs are checked for duplicate therapy, which occurs when a patient is taking a different drug of the same class that would have the effect of an overdose.

♦ Allergy records are checked for food and drug allergies that would be aggravated by the new drug.

♦ Some drugs cannot be given to patients with certain medical conditions; the patient's diagnosis history is checked to see if such a situation would occur.

♦ A patient education alert is created when the drug might be affected by certain foods or alcohol interactions.

♦ If the Sig has been entered at the time of the DUR, then it is also checked to see if it matches recommended guidelines for the drug. Too much, too little,

---

[4]The term *Sig*, from the Latin *signa*, refers to the instructions for labeling a prescription.

too many days, or too many refills could cause overdosing, underdosing (causing it to be ineffective), or abuse.

If the DUR software finds any of these conditions, the clinician is given an alert message explaining the conflict. The clinician can then alter the prescription or select a new drug, having never issued the incorrect one.

Formulary Alerts Another type of alert found in many EHR prescription systems warns the clinician if the drug about to be prescribed is not covered by a patient's pharmacy benefit insurance. This is important because if a patient's insurance will not pay for it, the patient may choose not to fill the prescription or to take less than the amount prescribed.

Insurance plans provide formularies indicating preferred, nonpreferred, and noncovered drugs. If the clinician prescribes a drug that is not on the list, then when the patient tries to have the prescription filled, the pharmacy will call and ask the physician to change it. This causes an inconvenience to the patient and wastes the doctor's time. Instead, a clinician using an EHR can select from a list of therapeutically equivalent drugs that are on the formulary of the patient's insurance plan and avoid writing an incorrect prescription. Figure 2-22 shows an Allscripts Therapeutic Alternatives alert.

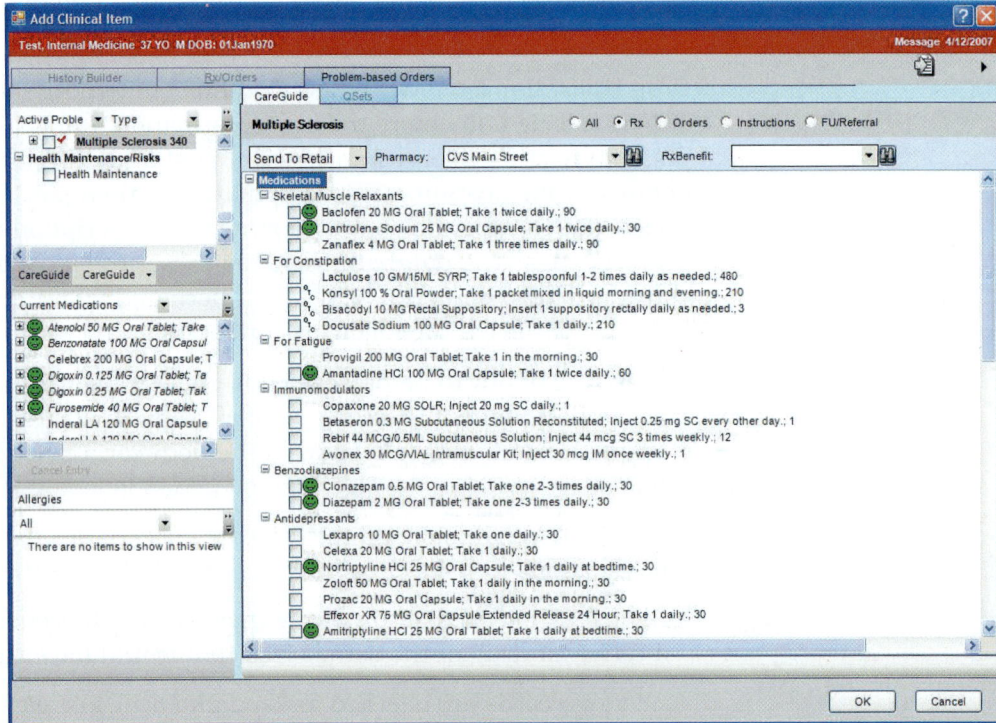

Courtesy of Allscripts, LLC.

▶ **Figure 2-22 Electronic prescription formulary alert.**

Other Types of Alerts Electronic lab order systems can provide alerts as well. For example, certain tests are not covered by Medicare. CMS requires that patients sign a waiver indicating that they were notified that a test would not be covered. The waiver is called an Advance Beneficiary Notice (ABN). When certain tests are ordered, the clinician is alerted if an ABN is required.

Another example is an alert that monitors changes in values of certain blood tests and pages a doctor whenever the value is outside of a certain range.

(A) **Notifier(s):**	
(B) **Patient Name:**	*(C)* **Identification Number:**

ADVANCE BENEFICIARY NOTICE OF NONCOVERAGE (ABN)

<u>**NOTE:**</u> If Medicare doesn't pay for *(D)*_____ below, you may have to pay.

Medicare does not pay for everything, even some care that you or your health care provider have good reason to think you need. We expect Medicare may not pay for the *(D)*_____ below.

*(D)*_____	*(E)* **Reason Medicare May Not Pay:**	*(F)* **Estimated Cost:**

WHAT YOU NEED TO DO NOW:
- Read this notice, so you can make an informed decision about your care.
- Ask us any questions that you may have after you finish reading.
- Choose an option below about whether to receive the *(D)*_____ listed above.
  Note: If you choose Option 1 or 2, we may help you to use any other insurance that you might have, but Medicare cannot require us to do this.

(G) **OPTIONS:** Check only one box. We cannot choose a box for you.
❏ **OPTION 1.** I want the *(D)*_____ listed above. You may ask to be paid now, but I also want Medicare billed for an official decision on payment, which is sent to me on a Medicare Summary Notice (MSN). I understand that if Medicare doesn't pay, I am responsible for payment, but **I can appeal to Medicare** by following the directions on the MSN. If Medicare does pay, you will refund any payments I made to you, less co-pays or deductibles.
❏ **OPTION 2.** I want the *(D)*_____ listed above, but do not bill Medicare. You may ask to be paid now as I am responsible for payment. **I cannot appeal if Medicare is not billed**.
❏ **OPTION 3.** I don't want the *(D)*_____ listed above. I understand with this choice I am **not** responsible for payment, and **I cannot appeal to see if Medicare would pay**.

(H) **Additional Information:**

This notice gives our opinion, not an official Medicare decision. If you have other questions on this notice or Medicare billing, call **1-800-MEDICARE** (1-800-633-4227/**TTY**: 1-877-486-2048).
Signing below means that you have received and understand this notice. You also receive a copy.

(I) **Signature:**	*(J)* **Date:**

According to the Paperwork Reduction Act of 1995, no persons are required to respond to a collection of information unless it displays a valid OMB control number. The valid OMB control number for this information collection is 0938-0566. The time required to complete this information collection is estimated to average 7 minutes per response, including the time to review instructions, search existing data resources, gather the data needed, and complete and review the information collection. If you have comments concerning the accuracy of the time estimate or suggestions for improving this form, please write to: CMS, 7500 Security Boulevard, Attn: PRA Reports Clearance Officer, Baltimore, Maryland 21244-1850.

Form CMS-R-131 (03/08)   Form Approved OMB No. 0938-0566

▶ Figure 2-23 Sample advance beneficiary notice form.

Alerts can be generated by nonactions as well. Task list systems can notify an administrator when medical items are not handled in a timely fashion. CPOE systems can generate alerts when results for a pending test order have not been received within the time frame normally required for that type of test.

Once an EHR system contains codified data, an alert system is just a matter of programming a rule to watch for a certain event or detect a finding with a value above or below the desired limit.

Health Maintenance

One of the best ways to maintain good health is to prevent disease, or if it occurs, to detect it early enough to be easily treated. Two important components of health maintenance are preventive care screening and immunizations.

Preventive Care The simplest example of health maintenance is a card or letter reminding the patient that it is time for a checkup. In a paper-based office, creating this reminder is a manual process. However, when a medical practice has electronic records, preventive screening can become more dynamic and sophisticated.

Health maintenance systems, also known as preventive care systems, can go beyond simple reminders for an annual checkup. When an EHR has codified data, it can be electronically compared to the recommendations of the U.S. Preventive Services Task Force (described further in Chapter 9).

Using a sophisticated set of rules, the EHR software compares the list of tests recommended for patients of a certain age and sex to previous test results stored in the EHR. It also calculates the time since the test was last performed and compares that to the recommended interval for repeat testing. A guideline unique to the patient is generated and displayed on the clinician's computer. Using

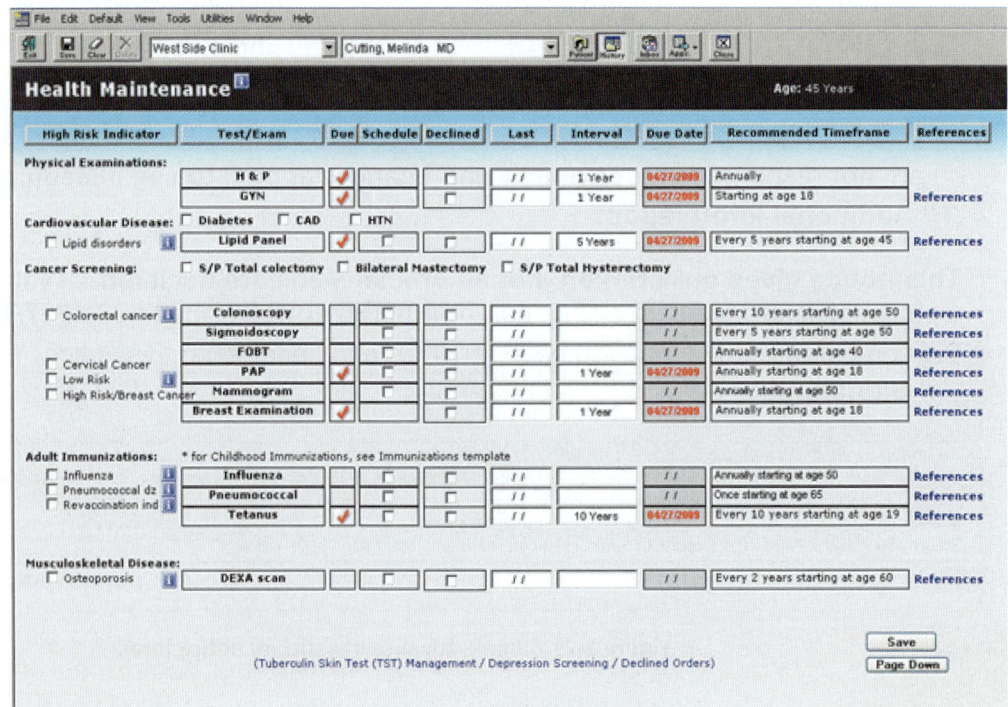

Courtesy of NextGen.

▶ Figure 2-24 Health Maintenance screen.

this information, the clinician can order tests, discuss important healthcare options, and recommend lifestyle changes to the patient at the point of care. Figure 2-24 shows the Health Maintenance screen from EHR vendor NextGen.

It would be difficult to create standardized rules for the preventive care system if the tests were not coded using a standardized coding system. Preventive care screening guidelines are not limited to lab tests; other examples include mammograms, hearing and vision screening, and certain elements of the physical examination.

Immunizations The other important component of preventive care is immunizations. Immunization slows down or stops disease outbreaks. Vaccines prevent disease in the people who receive them and protect those who come into contact with unvaccinated individuals.

Immunizations must be acquired over time. Vaccines cannot be given all at once. Several require repeated applications over a period of time, and some, such as the measles vaccine, cannot be given to children under the age of one year. Therefore, the CDC and state health departments have designed a schedule to immunize children and adolescents from birth through 18 years of age. The CDC also publishes a recommended immunization schedule for adults. Adult immunizations are different from those given to a child.

Using the codified data in an EHR, computers can compare a patient's immunization history with the CDC-recommended vaccines and intervals and identify which immunizations the patient needs. EHR systems can also scan the data and generate letters to send to patients who have not been in recently but may need to renew their immunizations.

Decision Support

Physicians are trained to analyze information from a patient's history, physical exams, and test results for a medical decision. They are also accustomed to researching the medical literature when faced with an unusual case. However, the quantity of information available to clinicians regarding conditions, disease management, protocols, case studies, and treatments far exceeds their available time to read it.

Decision support refers to the ability of EHR systems to store or quickly locate materials relevant to the findings of the current case. These might include defined protocols, results of case studies, or standard care guidelines prepared by specialists, medical societies, or government organizations.

Decision support is not about "artificial intelligence" replacing a physician with a computer; it is instead about providing help just when the clinician needs it. There are many examples of decision support systems, but let us look at four:

- ◆ **Prescriptions** Decision support can include the drug formularies mentioned earlier. Formularies can be used to look up drugs by name or therapeutic class. Electronic prescription systems provide decision support to the clinician by comparing alternative brands that are therapeutically equivalent. They can also provide information on costs, indications for use, treatment recommendations, dosage, guidelines, and prescribing information.

- ◆ **Medical references** Decision support systems can provide quick access to medical references directly from the EHR. This can make access to evidence-based guidelines or medical literature as easy as clicking on a link in the chart.

- ◆ **Protocols** Protocols are one form of decision support that can ultimately speed up documentation of the patient exam and improve patient care. Protocols are standard plans of therapy established for different conditions. With a decision support system, when a doctor has diagnosed a patient with a particular condition, the appropriate protocol appears on the EHR screen and all therapies are ordered with a click of the mouse.

- ◆ **Medication dosing** Many medications have serious side effects, some of which must be monitored by regular blood tests. When both the medications and lab results are stored in the EHR as codified data, it is possible for decision support software to compare changes in medication dosing with changes in the patient's test results. This assists the clinician in adjusting the patient's medication levels to obtain the maximum benefit to the patient.

Meeting the IOM Definition of an EHR

Each of the functional benefits we have discussed—trend analysis, alerts, health maintenance, and decision support—are products of EHR systems that store medical records as codified, fielded data. It is only when these functional benefits are added to the clinical practice that the EHR approaches the vision of the IOM and meets the CMS "meaningful use" criteria discussed in Chapter 1.

Chapter Two Summary

The IOM definition of an EHR went beyond a computer that just stores the patient's medical record to include *the functional benefits* derived from having an electronic health record. In this chapter we explored how the format that the data are stored in determines to what extent the data can be used to achieve that extended functionality.

The forms of EHR data are broadly categorized into three types:

1. Digital image data (provides increased accessibility)
2. Text-based data (provides accessibility and text search capability; can be displayed on different devices)
3. Discrete data, fielded and ideally codified (provides all of the above plus the capability to be used for trending, alerts, health maintenance, and data exchange)

Increased benefits of an EHR can be realized when the information is stored as codified data. In addition, codified EHR data that adheres to a national standard enables the exchange and comparison of medical information from other facilities.

A code set designed specifically to record medical observations is referred to as a clinical "nomenclature." Using an EHR nomenclature provides consistency in patient records and improves communication between different medical specialties.

EHR nomenclatures differ from other coding standards in several ways:

- EHR nomenclatures precorrelate individual terms into clinically relevant "findings" or codified observations that are medically meaningful to the clinician.

- Findings are often linked to other findings, which helps the clinician quickly locate associated information and shortens the time required to document the exam.

- EHR nomenclatures differ from billing codes in that EHR nomenclatures have many more codes used to describe the detail of the exam such as the symptoms, history, observations, and plan. Billing codes tend to represent simply that the service was rendered.

- Reference terminologies designed for research may codify each medical term, but these terms can combine in ways that are not clinically relevant; therefore, these nomenclatures are not easy to use at the point of care.

- EHR nomenclatures often include cross-references to other standard code sets. Coding systems not intended for EHR do not typically contain a map to other coding systems.

Several of the most prominent coding standards you are likely to encounter or use in an EHR were discussed in this chapter.

- SNOMED-CT is a medical nomenclature developed by the College of American Pathologists and United Kingdom's National Health Service.

- MEDCIN is a medical nomenclature and knowledge base used in many commercial EHR systems as well as the Department of Defense CHCS II system. MEDCIN differs from other EHR coding systems in that MEDCIN was designed for point-of-care use by the clinician, so that each "finding" represents a meaningful clinical observation or term. The MEDCIN findings are linked in a "knowledge base." This enables a clinician to quickly find other clinical "findings" that are likely to be needed. This difference means a physician selects fewer individual codes to complete the patient exam note.

- LOINC stands for Logical Observation Identifier Names and Codes. LOINC is an important clinical terminology for laboratory test orders and results. LOINC has become one of the standard code sets designated by the U.S. government for the electronic exchange of clinical health information.

- CCC stands for Clinical Classification Codes, a system of codes for nursing that is incorporated into other EHR nomenclatures, such as SNOMED-CT, MEDCIN, and LOINC.

EHR data may be captured in many ways:

- Scanning paper records
- Importing diagnostic images in digital format
- Importing text or word processing files
- Receiving data electronically from other systems using
  - HL7
  - DICOM
  - CDISK

- ◆ RHIO
- ◆ Biomedical devices
- ◆ Telemonitoring devices

◆ Patients may enter their own history and symptoms

◆ Providers record the EHR at the point-of-care

When EHR data is coded, it can be used for:

◆ Trend analysis, the comparison of multiple values or findings over a period of time

◆ Alerts, computer-prompted warnings such as a potential drug interaction or a lab result seriously above or below the expected range

◆ Health maintenance, which creates reminders of health screening, immunizations, and other preventive measures

◆ Decision support, systems to quickly locate materials relevant to the findings of the current case such as defined protocols, standard care guidelines, or medical research

Testing Your Knowledge of Chapter 2

1. Name three forms of EHR data.
2. Name at least two medical code sets considered national standards.
3. What is a nomenclature?
4. In an EHR, what is meant by the term "finding"?
5. Describe the difference between an EHR nomenclature and a billing code set.
6. What is one advantage of codified data over document imaged data?

Give examples for the following terms:

7. Trend analysis
8. Decision support
9. Alerts
10. Health maintenance
11. List at least two ways codified data in the EHR can be used to manage and prevent disease.
12. Name at least two benefits of having patients entering their own symptoms and history into the computer.
13. Name a type of decision support.
14. Name some advantages of electronic prescriptions.
15. What is HL7?

Chapter Three

Learning Medical Record Software

Learning Outcomes

After completing this chapter, you should be able to:

- Start and stop the Student Edition software
- Navigate the screen
- Select a patient
- Create a new encounter
- Access the Symptoms, History, Physical Exam, Assessment, and Therapy tabs to add appropriate findings in each portion of the exam
- Select findings for edit and remove findings
- Add entry details, values, free text, results, status, and episodes to findings
- Enter a chief complaint
- Enter vital signs

Introducing the Medcin Student Edition Software

In this chapter you will learn to document a patient encounter using Medcin, one of the standard EHR nomenclatures discussed in Chapter 2. Special Medcin Student Edition software has been created for you to use with this course. It is similar to many commercial software packages that use the Medcin knowledge base for their EHR nomenclature.

The Student Edition software allows you select findings for symptoms, history, physical examination, tests, diagnoses, and therapy to produce medical documents typical of the physician encounter notes created in a medical facility that uses an EHR. At the conclusion of certain exercises, you will print out your work and hand it in to your instructor.

Because the Student Edition is designed for the classroom, it will be different in some aspects from EHR systems you will encounter when working in a medical office or hospital. However, the concepts, skills, and familiarity with EHR systems you will acquire by practicing with the Student Edition software will transfer directly into the workplace.

About the Exercises in This Book

The purpose of the exercises is to teach EHR concepts by providing hands-on experience. Completing the exercises in this and subsequent chapters of the book using the software provided will give you practical experience in creating electronic health records. Each set of exercises is designed to illustrate an EHR concept and will result in a documented encounter note. Once you have mastered the basics, you will learn in subsequent chapters how to increase data entry speed through the use of forms, lists, and flow sheets. These capabilities are useful to document a patient visit during the encounter. Later, you also will learn how information from previous exams can be used during subsequent patient encounters.

The purpose of the exercises is to teach EHR concepts by providing hands-on experience. Although the clinical notes produced by the exercises are medically accurate, routine elements of a complete patient assessment that should normally be documented are frequently omitted from the exercise. This is done solely to facilitate completion of exercises in the allotted class time. Note that some exercises will ask you to document items that would normally be entered by a physician, physician assistant, or nurse practitioner. The reason for including these components in the exercises is to demonstrate additional aspects of the EHR.

Understanding the Software

The following series of exercises are designed to allow you to become familiar with the Student Edition software, the Medcin nomenclature, and the screen navigation controls. Do not worry if you cannot complete all of them in one class period.

EHR Login

In the next exercise you will learn to log in to the Student Edition software. Your student login is your name or student ID. In a healthcare facility your login will be unique and will provide a permanent record of your use of the system, recording which entries into the patient record were made by you. To protect the integrity of the patient's records and your liability for entries made under your "electronic signature," it is imperative that you use the correct log-in and log-off procedures required by the hospital or clinic. Electronic signatures are discussed more fully in Chapter 10.

Guided Exercise 8: Starting Up the Software

The Student Edition software should have been installed on your school's network computers or on your local workstation. If you are working on your own computer and have not already installed the Student Edition software, you must do so before you can proceed. See the inside cover of this book for information on downloading the Student Edition software.

▶ **Figure 3-1** The Medcin Student Edition icon.

▶ **Figure 3-2** Student Edition log-in screen.

Step 1

Turn on the computer and wait for the Windows operating system desktop to appear on the screen. If you are using a school computer, you may be required to log in to the school network first; if so, ask your instructor for the correct log-in procedure.

Step 2

Locate the Medcin icon shown in Figure 3-1. If you do not see it on the computer desktop screen, click on the Start Button, and look in Programs or All Programs for the program named "Medcin Student Edition."

Position the mouse pointer over the Medcin icon shown in Figure 3-1 and double-click the mouse button. This will display the Student Edition log-in screen shown in Figure 3-2.

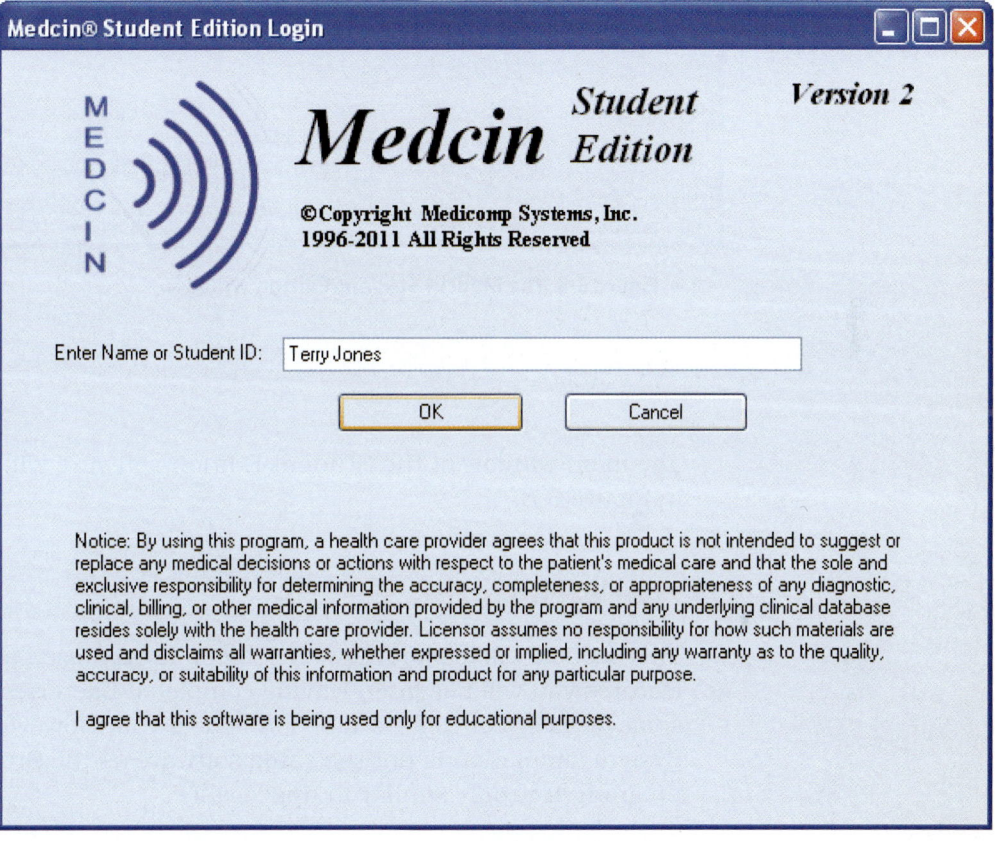

> ⚠ **Alert**
>
> Version 2 of the software is required for this text. If "Version 2" is not displayed in the upper right corner of the log-in screen, stop and inform your instructor at once.

Step 3

Figure 3-3 shows the Medcin Student Edition log-in screen. The screen contains one data entry field and two buttons. The field is used for either the student's name or the student ID, depending on the policy of the school. Confirm with your instructor whether you should use your name or student ID. In the example, the student's name is Terry Jones. Do not type Terry Jones in the field.

Type either your name or student ID into the field.

When your name or ID is exactly as you want it to be, position the mouse pointer over the button labeled "OK" and click the mouse.

The button labeled "Cancel" is used to cancel the log in and close the window.

Chapter 3 | Learning Medical Record Software

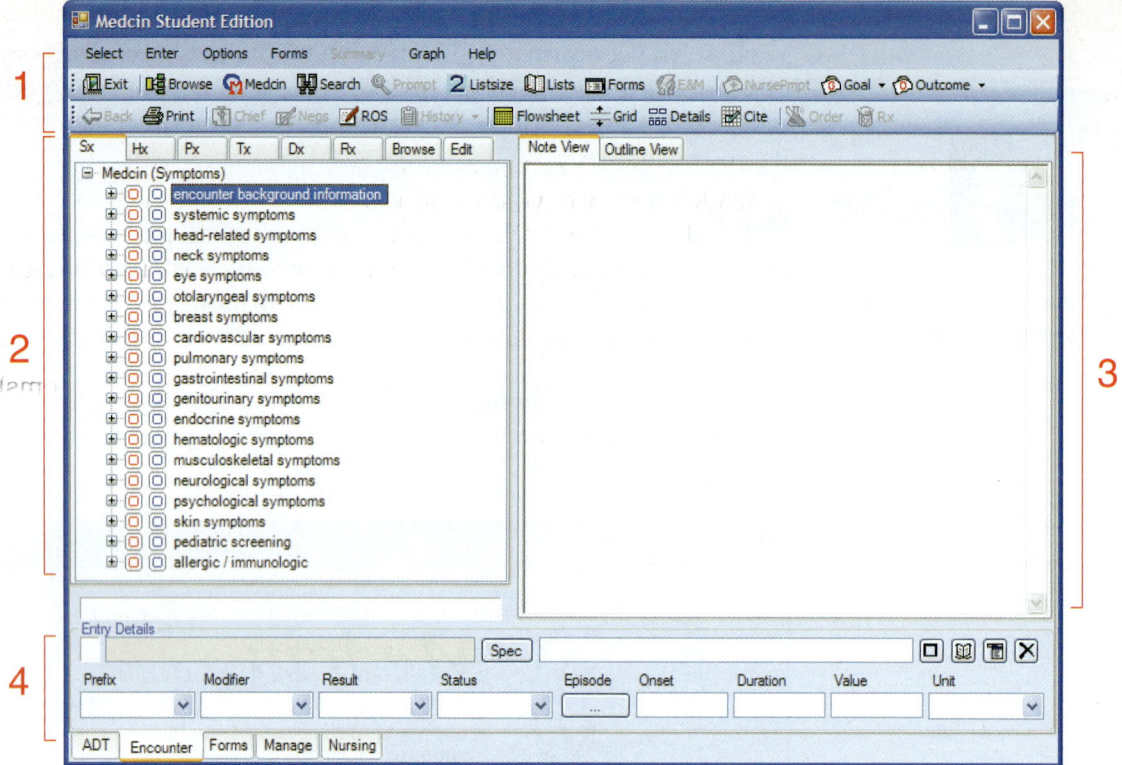

▶ Figure 3-3 The Medcin Student Edition window.

The main window of the Student Edition software will be displayed, as shown in Figure 3-3.

Navigating the Screen

This section will explain how the screen is organized and discuss some of the features you will use later. Having completed Exercises 5 through 7 in Chapter 2, some of these concepts will be familiar to you. However, the Document/Image System simulation is not the same software as the Student Edition software program. It is only similar in appearance.

The main window can be divided into four functional sections. These four sections interact with each other, as you will learn in this chapter. Refer to Figure 3-3 and locate each of the sections indicated by the red numerals 1–4.

Section 1: The Menu Bar and Toolbar At the top of the screen, the words "Select," "Enter," "Options, " "Forms," "Summary," "Graph," and "Help" are the menus of functions in the Student Edition software. As you learned in the previous chapter, when you position the mouse pointer over one of these words and click the mouse once, a list of functions will drop down below the word. Once a list appears, moving the mouse pointer vertically over the list will highlight each item. In the Student Edition, *highlight* refers to a colored rectangle that appears over an item. Clicking on the highlighted item will invoke that function. Clicking the mouse anywhere on the screen other than the list will close the list.

Also located at the top of your screen are two rows of icon buttons called a "Toolbar." The purpose of the Toolbar is to allow quick access to commonly used functions. Toolbar buttons will be identified later in the chapter, as you learn to use them.

Section 2: The Medcin Nomenclature Pane The middle portion of the screen is divided into two window panes. The left pane (shown in Figure 3-3 with the numeral 2) displays the Medcin nomenclature findings you will select from. In the next exercise, you will select a patient and learn to navigate the Medcin Nomenclature Pane.

At the top of the Nomenclature Pane there are eight tabs. These look like tabs on file folders. The first six of these are labeled: Sx (symptoms), Hx (history), Px (physical examination), Tx (tests), Dx (diagnosis, syndromes, and conditions), and Rx (therapy). The tabs are used to logically group the findings into six broad categories. Two additional tabs, labeled Browse and Edit, will be explained later as you use it the software.

Section 3: The Encounter View Pane The right pane of the window (shown in Figure 3-3 with the numeral 3) will dynamically display the encounter note as it is being created. When a healthcare professional selects a finding from the Nomenclature Pane, the finding and relevant accompanying text are recorded in the encounter note and displayed in the pane on the right.

Free text also may be entered through the software; it will appear in the Note View Pane as well. This will become clearer during subsequent exercises. Because you have not yet selected a patient or an encounter, the pane is empty at this time.

There are two tabs on the top of the right pane. The Note View tab displays the encounter note in SOAP format as you create it. The Outline View displays findings that have been selected as well as appropriate ICD-9-CM or CPT-4 codes.

Section 4: Entry Details for a Current Finding The bottom portion of the screen (shown in Figure 3-3 with the numeral 4) consists of two rows of fields that allow the user to add detail to any finding recorded in the right pane. Entry of data in these fields adds informational text to the finding in the encounter note, and in some cases modifies its meaning.

For example, a patient-reported symptom of "headaches" could be modified using the Entry Details field labeled "Status" to indicate the condition was "improving." The meaning of the finding could be altered completely by use of the Entry Details field labeled "Prefix" to indicate "family history of." This would indicate that the patient did not have this condition, but that it had been a problem for close relatives. Each of the fields in the details section of the screen will be covered in subsequent exercises in this book.

To actually see the interactions of the four sections of the screen, you need to select a patient and create a new encounter. Subsequent exercises will show you how, but first let us discuss exiting the software.

Guided Exercise 9: Exiting and Restarting the Software

There are three ways to exit the Student Edition software. In this exercise, you will practice exiting the software. You will then restart the program to continue with subsequent exercises.

At the top of your screen is a row of words called the Menu bar. Below it are two rows of buttons with icons, called the Toolbar. The first button in the

Toolbar is labeled "Exit"; its icon looks like an open door. If you click on the Exit button, the Student Edition program will end and the window will close.

In the upper right corner of the window are three buttons that are standard to all Windows programs. From left to right, these buttons minimize, maximize, and close the window. The close button is red, with a large X. If you click on the close button, the Student Edition program will end and the window will close.

A third way to close the program is explained next.

Step 1

The first word in the Menu bar is "Select." Position the mouse pointer over the word "Select" in the Menu bar at the top of the screen and click the mouse button once. A list of the functions on the Select menu will drop down.

You will notice some of the items in the menu are listed in black text and some of them are in gray. Menu items in gray text indicate a particular function is not applicable to the current state of the encounter note and are therefore not selectable. You may have noticed some of the buttons on the Toolbar also are gray; this is for the same reason.

Step 2

Move the mouse pointer vertically down the list until the Exit function is highlighted. Click the mouse on the word "Exit" to end the program.

Step 3

Start the Student Edition software again by repeating Exercise 8, and logging in.

> **Note**
>
> **In subsequent exercises, when you attempt to exit after entering some data, you will receive a warning that you have not printed the encounter. It is permissible to exit without printing** for this chapter only. **In all other chapters you must not exit without printing or you will lose your work.**

Guided Exercise 10: Using the Menu to Select a Patient

Once you are logged in, the first step in every encounter is to select the patient.

Step 1

Position the mouse pointer over the word "Select" in the Menu bar at the top of the screen and click the mouse button once. A list of the Select menu functions will appear (see Figure 3-4).

Step 2

Move the mouse pointer vertically down the list until Patient is highlighted. Click the mouse on the word "Patient" to invoke the Patient Selection window shown in Figure 3-5.

Step 3

The Student Edition Patient Selection window displays a list of all patients in the system, their last name, first name, patient ID number, and date of birth. A field at the top of the window allows you to type the patient's last name to quickly find someone in a large list.

▶ **Figure 3-4** Functions on the Select menu.

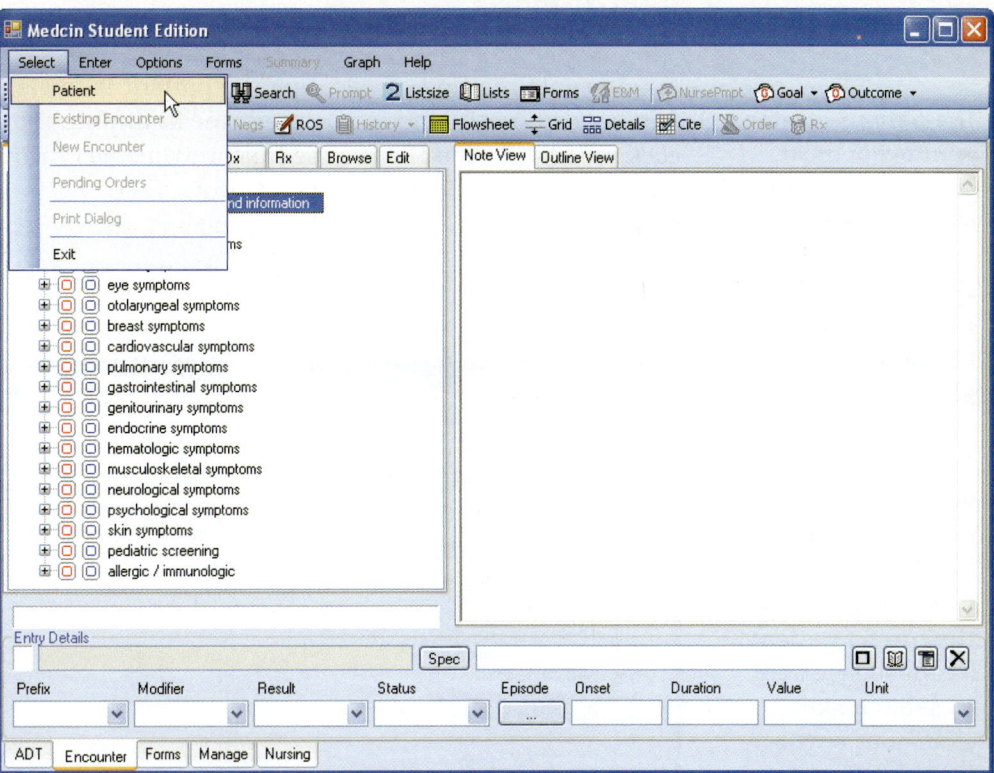

▶ **Figure 3-5** Selecting Rosa Garcia from the Patient Selection window.

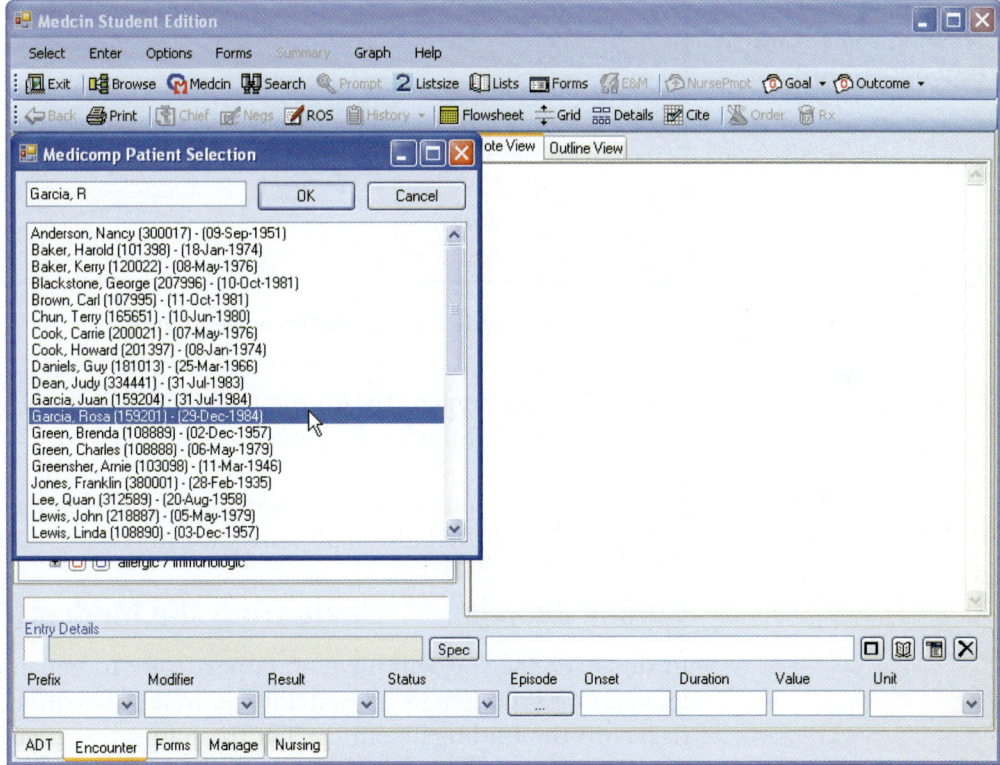

Find the patient named Rosa Garcia in the Patient Selection window by typing "Garcia, R" in the field. When you start typing the name, the first name beginning with a "G" will be highlighted; as you continue to type, the next alphabetical name will be highlighted. When "Rosa Garcia" is highlighted, click the OK button.

> **Note**
>
> The patient locator window in most commercial medical software will have additional ways to sort and search the patient list, and may display more information about each patient. Whenever you select a patient name from a list, it is imperative to verify that the correct patient has been selected to avoid making erroneous entries in the patient's record or making decisions while reviewing the wrong patient's record.

Clicking the Cancel button will close the window.

An alternate method of selecting the patient is to visually locate the patient's name, position the mouse pointer over it, and double-click the mouse. (*Double-click* means to click the mouse button twice, very rapidly.)

Step 4

Once a patient is selected, the patient's name is displayed in the title at the top of the window (see Figure 3-6).

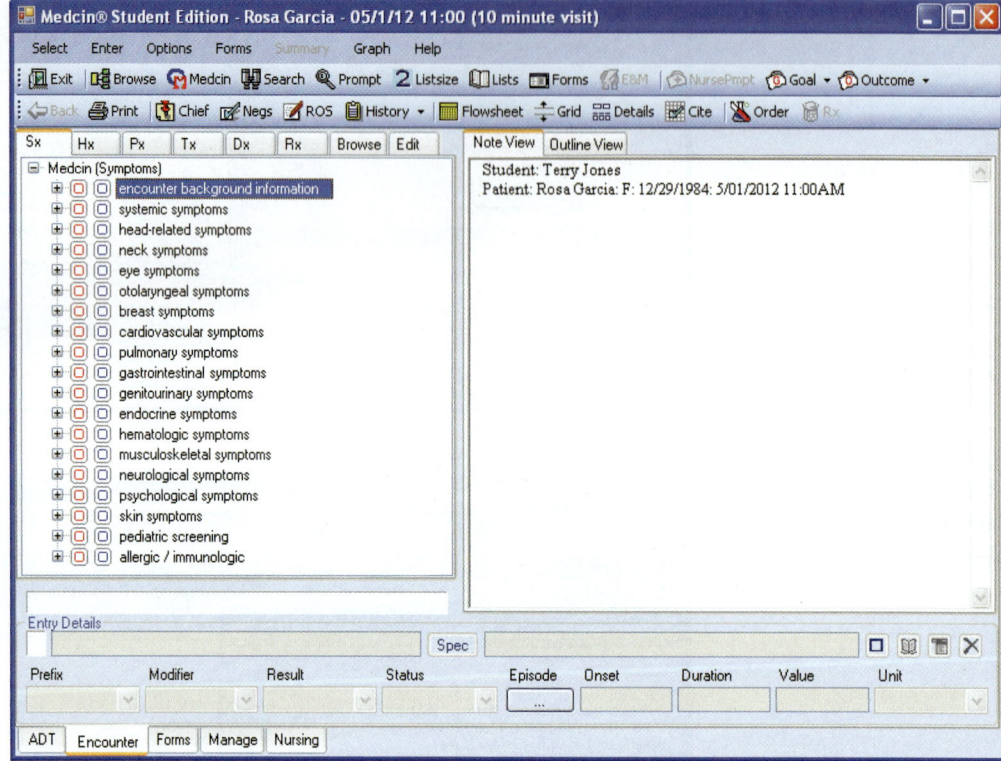

▶ **Figure 3-6** Left pane displays Medcin nomenclature.

The Medcin Nomenclature (in the left pane) becomes active and the first group of findings (symptoms) is displayed.

The right pane containing the encounter note is populated with the student's name or ID and the patient's name, sex, and date of birth.

Guided Exercise 11: Navigating the Medcin Findings

In this exercise you will have an opportunity to become familiar with one way to navigate the Medcin nomenclature. In a subsequent exercise, you will learn to record the findings from the left pane into the encounter note in the right pane. In this exercise, you will not yet record any findings.

Your screen should resemble Figure 3-6. If it does not, repeat Exercise 10.

Step 1

Look at the list of findings in the left pane. As mentioned earlier, the pane on the left of the screen is used to select findings to document the current patient encounter.

The Medcin Nomenclature consists of more than 277,000 findings with 68 million relationships. To make it easy to find what you are looking for, the tabs on the left of the pane categorize findings into six broad groups that follow the order of a typical exam.

Chapter 1 described the standard order of medical exams in a SOAP format. The six tabs on the left pane make it easy to document in that format as follows:

Subjective	Sx	Symptoms
	Hx	History
Objective	Px	Physical Exam
	Tx	Tests (performed)
Assessment	Dx	Diagnosis
Plan	Rx	Therapy, plan and tests (ordered)

In addition to the tabs, another feature that shortens the list of findings displayed in the nomenclature pane is to show only the main topics.

▶ **Figure 3-7** Buttons used in the Nomenclature Pane.

You will notice that most findings in the Medcin list are preceded by buttons. These are shown in Figure 3-7. The symbols on the buttons are a small plus sign, a larger button with a red circle, and a larger button with a blue circle.

The small plus sign indicates there are more specific findings hidden from view that are related to the finding displayed.

Step 2

Locate the finding "head-related symptoms" in the nomenclature symptoms list, as shown in Figure 3-8. Position the mouse pointer over the small plus symbol and click the mouse button once.

▶ **Figure 3-8** Locate the finding "head-related symptoms."

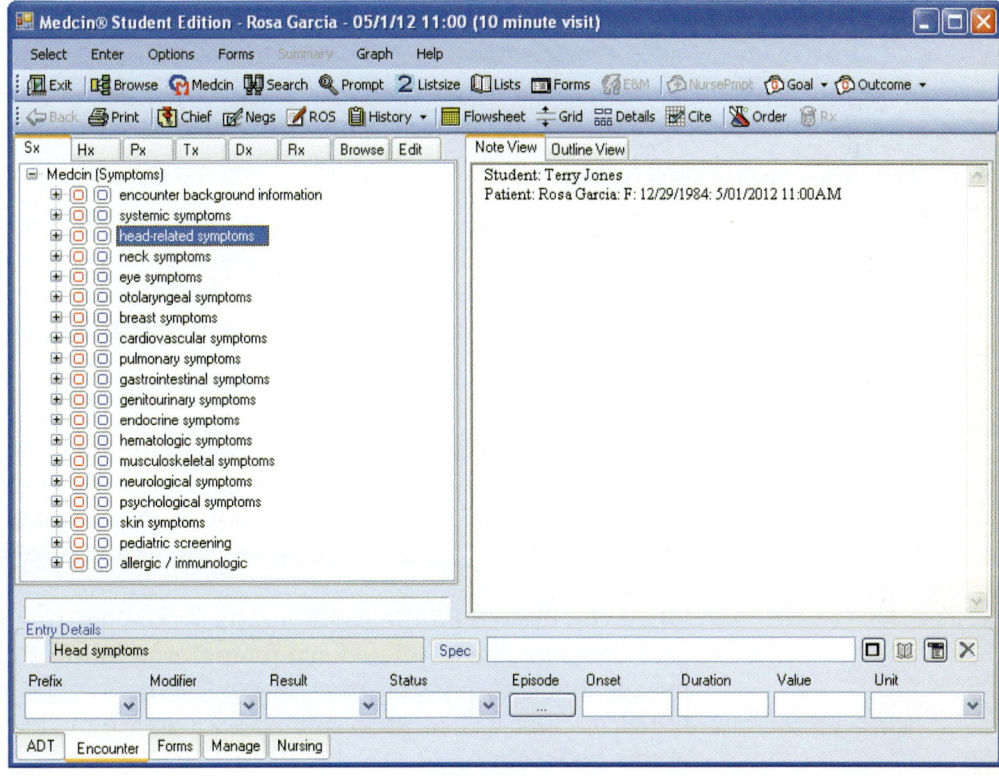

Chapter 3 | Learning Medical Record Software   85

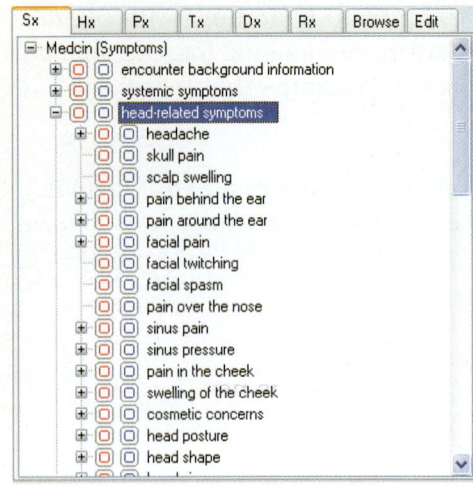

▶ **Figure 3-9** Expanded list of findings for head-related symptoms.

Compare the left pane of your screen with Figure 3-9. The list should have expanded to reveal many additional head-related findings. Notice that the findings under "head-related symptoms" are indented.

Notice also that some of the additional findings have small plus symbols as well—for example, "headache" and "pain behind the ear." This indicates that even more specific findings are available for those items. Conversely, findings such as "skull pain," and "scalp swelling" no longer have the small plus. This means that there are no more specific findings available for those items.

Step 3

Position the mouse pointer over the small plus symbol for the finding "headache" in the indented list, and click the mouse. The list expands further.

Position the mouse pointer over the small plus symbol for the finding "timing" indented under headache, and click the mouse. The list expands further.

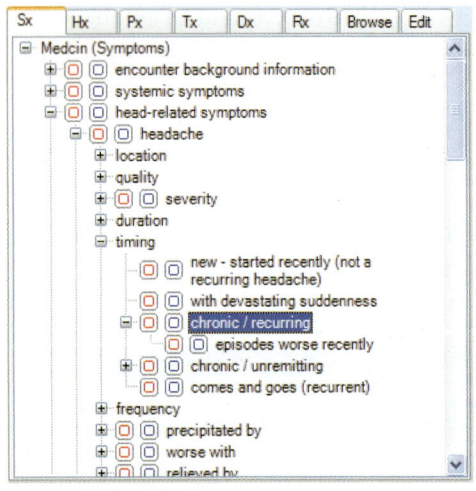

▶ **Figure 3-10** Fully expanded list of findings for headache.

Step 4

Notice that even the detailed the findings "chronic/recurring" and "chronic/unremitting" still have small plus symbols, indicating that further detailed findings are available.

Position the mouse pointer over the small plus symbol for the finding "chronic/recurring" and click the mouse. Compare your list to Figure 3-10.

This type of list is called a *tree* because each indention of the list represents smaller branches of the finding above it. Look again at Figure 3-10; notice how each new level is indented further than the one above it. You may already be familiar with this concept because it is used in many other computer programs, including the Windows operating system.

Each time you clicked on the small plus symbol next to a finding in steps 2–4, the list grew. The term we use for this is to say that "the tree has expanded." Also notice that a small minus sign replaced the small plus sign in the button next to the finding that has been expanded.

Step 5

Position the mouse pointer over the small minus symbol next to the finding "head-related symptoms" and click the mouse button again. The expanded list of various types of head-related symptom findings will again be hidden from view. Your screen should once again look like Figure 3-8.

When you clicked on the small minus symbol for the main finding, the number of findings for "head-related symptoms" was reduced back to one. The term we use for this is to say that "the view of the tree has been collapsed." These are the terms that will be used when working with Medcin lists for the remainder of this book.

Guided Exercise 12: Tabs on the Medcin Nomenclature Pane

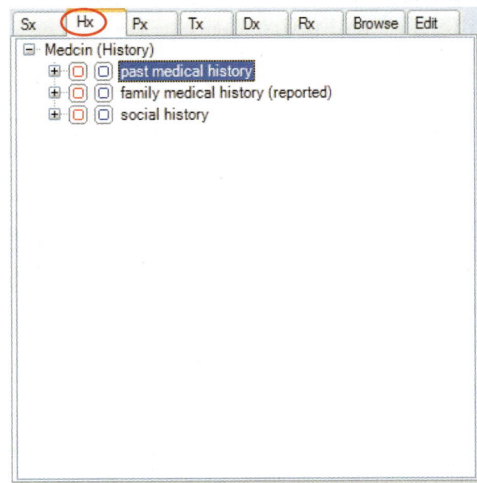

▶ Figure 3-11 The History tab (circled in red).

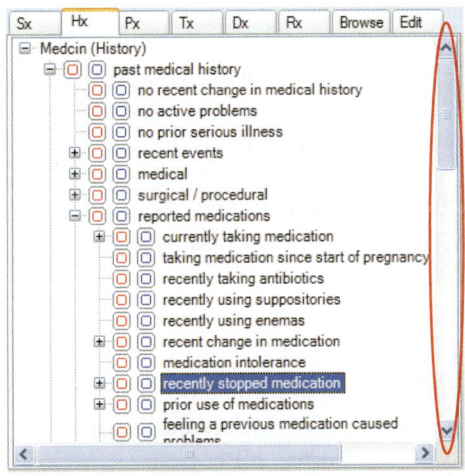

▶ Figure 3-12 Expanded past history (scroll bar is circled in red).

Step 1

Position the mouse pointer over the Hx Tab (circled in red in Figure 3-11) and click the mouse once.

The list will change to that shown in Figure 3-11. Notice that the currently selected tab has the appearance of being slightly raised from the others.

Step 2

Position the mouse pointer over the small plus next to "past medical history" and click the mouse button to expand the list.

Step 3

Position the mouse pointer over the small plus next to "reported medications" and click the mouse button to expand the list. Notice that this time there were too many findings to fit in the space allotted. A light blue scroll bar has appeared on the right side of the pane. You are probably familiar with the concept of scrolling a window.

Position the mouse pointer on the light blue scroll bar and hold the mouse button down while you drag the mouse in a downward motion. This action will scroll the list. Continue scrolling the list until you can see all the findings under "recently stopped medication," (highlighted in Figure 3-12). Click on the small plus sign next to the finding "recently stopped medication."

Step 4

Position the mouse pointer over the Sx tab and click the mouse once. The display will return to the previous list shown in Figure 3-8.

Step 5

Position the mouse pointer again over the Hx tab and click the mouse once. Notice the list is expanded as when you left it. In most cases, the software will remember how much of the expanded tree was displayed in each tab as well as what finding was highlighted. This feature allows the clinician to easily go back to a previous tab to add another finding, and then return to where he or she left off.

Step 6

Explore each of the remaining sections of the Medcin Nomenclature Pane, by clicking on each of the remaining tabs. Take a moment on each tab to look at the type of findings in each tab. Feel free to expand or collapse the list in any of the tabs.

Data Entry of Clinical Notes

The main purpose of the EHR software such as those systems based on Medcin is to document clinical notes in a codified electronic medical record. This is done by selecting the finding from the Medcin nomenclature list in the left pane of the window. The finding and accompanying text are automatically recorded in the encounter note displayed in the right pane of the window. (The note view portion of the screen is indicated by the numeral 3 in Figure 3-3.)

Information is also added to the clinical note by adding or modifying a finding using the Entry Details fields in the bottom portion of the window. (The Entry Details section is indicated in Figure 3-3 by the numeral 4.)

The following exercises are designed to let you explore the interactions of the four sections of the Student Edition window. During the course of these exercises, you will create your first clinical encounter note with the Medcin nomenclature.

Guided Exercise 13: Creating an Encounter

When a doctor, nurse, or other healthcare provider examines a patient in a facility or at home, it is commonly referred to as an *encounter*. Similarly, an outpatient visit to a provider in a medical office or clinic is also called an encounter. Clinical notes documenting the encounter are variously referred to as *exam notes*, *provider notes*, or *encounter notes*. Whatever term is used, the encounter note is a record of the findings of an examination that occurred on a specific date and time. Although a portion of the data may be recorded by the medical assistant, another portion by the nurse, and yet another by a doctor, one completed encounter note should encompass the entire visit. However, when the patient returns for another visit, a new encounter is created.

In any type of medical facility it is important to accurately record the date and time of the encounter. In this exercise, you will create a new encounter and learn how to set the date and time of the encounter.

Case Study

Exercises in this chapter concern a 27-year-old female patient who complains of headaches lasting for more than five days. She was previously consuming 7–8 cups of coffee a day and has recently stopped drinking all coffee.

Step 1

The name of the patient Rosa Garcia should be displayed at the top of the Medcin window. If it is not, repeat Guided Exercise 10.

The Select menu (which you have used previously) also has functions to select an existing encounter or create a new encounter. In this exercise, you will create a new encounter.

Position the mouse pointer over the word "Select" in the Menu bar, and click the mouse button. Move the mouse pointer vertically down the list until the item "New Encounter" is highlighted. Click the mouse button.

Step 2

When you create a new encounter, a window is invoked that allows you to set the date, time, and reason for the encounter. The month, day, year, and time will default to current date and time settings in your own computer. Today's month and year are displayed in the calendar on the window. Today's date is outlined in red. Days that occur in the previous and subsequent months are in gray text.

Because it is unlikely that you are doing this exercise on May 1, 2012, you will need to manually set the date and time as instructed in this exercise. The purpose of this exercise is to teach you how to set the date and time using the New Encounter window.

Setting the Date to May 1, 2012

Small gray buttons with left and right arrows are located at the top of the calendar window. Clicking the button with the right arrow advances the calendar one month for each click of the mouse. Clicking the button with the left arrow takes the calendar backward one month for each click. If you click on the year, the field will open and small up and down arrows will appear (as shown in Figure 3-13). Clicking on these arrow buttons will allow you to quickly change years without cycling through all the months.

▶ **Figure 3-13** Select New Encounter, set date/time May 1, 2012, 11:00 AM.

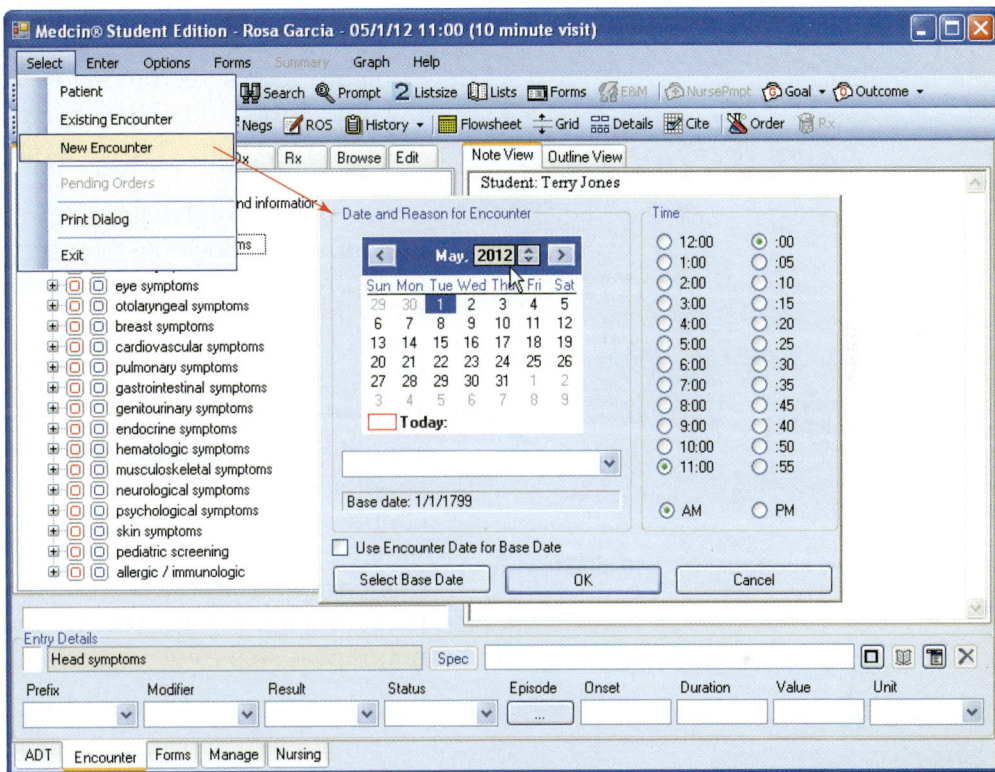

Click the buttons on the top of the calendar until the month **May** is displayed.

If the year 2012 is not currently displayed, click on the year to quickly modify it. Click the up or down arrow button to increase or decrease the year until 2012 is displayed.

Position the mouse pointer over day **1** and click the mouse button. The first day will be highlighted with a blue rectangle.

The time is indicated on the right side of the window by white circles that are filled in the center. For example, in Figure 3-13, the circles next to 11:00 and :00 and :AM are each filled, indicating the time of the encounter will be 11:00 AM.

Select the time by clicking your mouse in the circles next to **11:00** and **:00** and **:AM**. Each of the circles should become filled in.

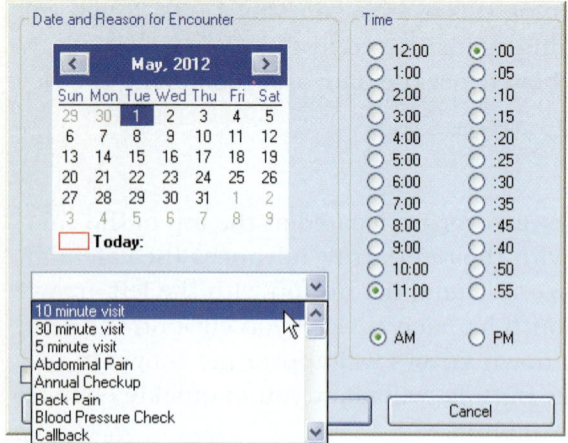

▶ **Figure 3-14** Select 10 minute visit from list of reasons for encounter.

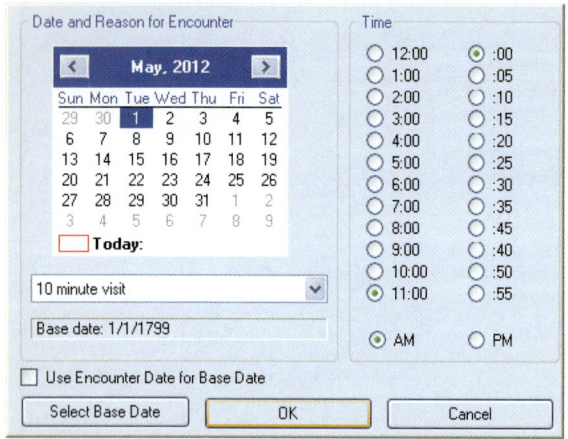

▶ **Figure 3-15** New encounter for a 10 minute visit, May 1, 2012, 11:00 AM.

Step 3

The reason for the encounter is also set in this window. The encounter Reason field is located just below the calendar. To view a list of reasons, position the mouse pointer over the button with the down arrow in the right side of the field, and click the mouse. A drop-down list of reasons will appear as shown in Figure 3-14.

In a previous exercise, you learned to scroll a list by holding the mouse button while dragging it down the scroll bar. Using the same technique, you can scroll the list of reasons. Highlight the reason "10 minute visit" by moving the mouse pointer over it. When the reason is highlighted, click the mouse button to select the reason.

Step 4

Compare your screen to Figure 3-15. Make certain you set the date, time, and reason correctly. If the date, time, or reason needs to be corrected repeat the previous steps.

Locate the button labeled OK in the bottom of the New Encounter window, position the mouse pointer over the OK button, and click the mouse. The "Date and Reason for Encounter" window will close.

Step 5

The encounter date, time, and reason "10 minute visit" should be displayed in the title of the window. The encounter date and time should be recorded in the encounter note in the right pane of the window.

Compare your screen with Figure 3-16; if your screen matches Figure 3-16, you are ready to proceed. If it does not, repeat steps 1–4.

Note

Tips for Completing the Exercises

The purpose of this chapter is to help you become familiar with the software and EHR concepts through guided exercises. You will not be able to complete all the exercises in this chapter in one class period.

However, in subsequent class periods, each time you resume work on this chapter you must repeat at least three steps:

1. Start the Medcin Student Edition software
2. Select the Patient Rosa Garcia
3. Create a New Encounter for a 10 minute visit, May 1, 2012 11:00 AM

In most cases, you will be able to continue with the next guided exercise without repeating preceding ones. When you continue without repeating prior exercises, the encounter note in the right pane of the window will not contain as much information as the figures printed in the textbook.

In Chapter 4 you will create and print an entire encounter note in one session.

▶ Figure 3-16 New encounter for Rosa Garcia.

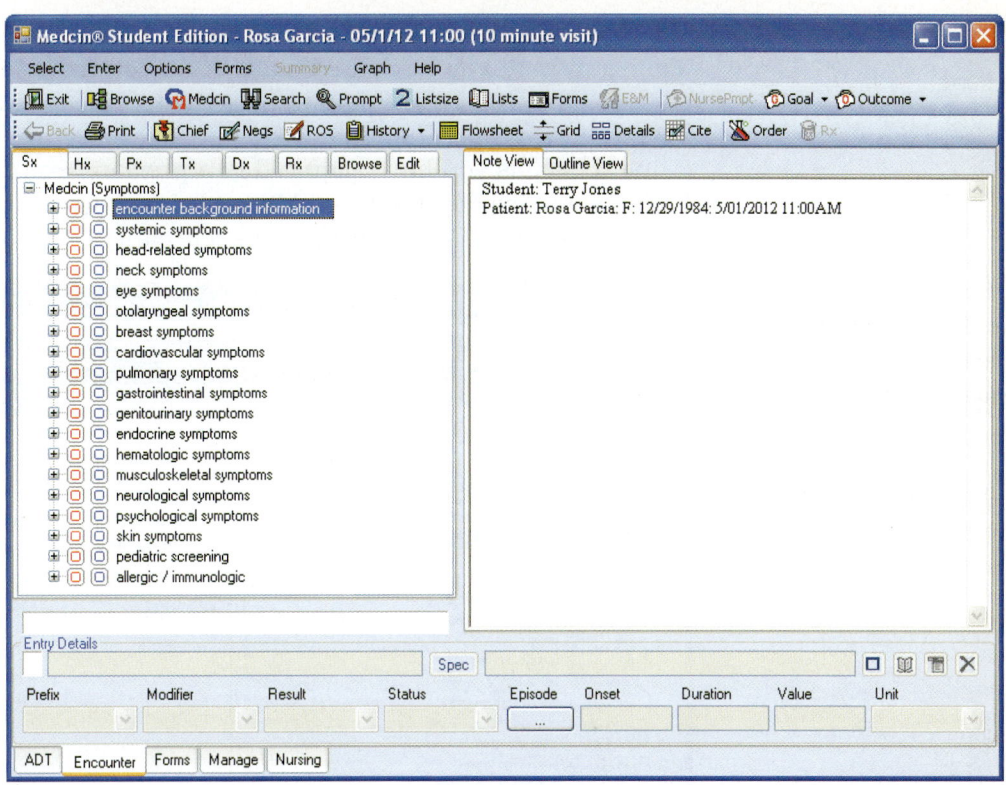

Guided Exercise 14: Recording Subjective Findings

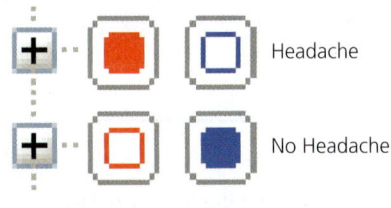

▶ Figure 3-17 Buttons adjacent to findings fill with color when selected.

Information is recorded in the encounter note by clicking the mouse on the red or blue buttons adjacent to each finding (shown enlarged in Figure 3-17). Clicking on a button with the red circle will record the finding as it appears in the list and fill in the red circle. Clicking on a button with the blue circle will record the finding in its opposite state and fill in the blue circle. For example, clicking on the button with the red circle next to "Headache" will record that the patient has a headache; clicking on the button with the blue circle will record that the patient has reported no headache.

When a finding is recorded in the encounter note on the right pane, the description of the finding in the left pane also changes to match the selected state. For example, the finding Headache becomes "No Headache" when the blue button is selected, as shown in Figure 3-17.

Because the description of the findings change when their buttons are clicked, instructions to click a red or blue button identify a finding by its description *before* it is selected, so that you can locate it in the nomenclature pane. Screen figures used for comparison show the description of a finding as it appears *after* being selected.

For the remainder of this book, the buttons used to select findings will simply be referred to as the red button or the blue button.

A finding can be highlighted (surrounded with a blue background) without selecting either the red or blue button by clicking on the description of the finding instead of the buttons. You will learn to highlight a finding later, in Exercise 21.

Chapter 3 | Learning Medical Record Software

Step 1

Make sure that you have the Sx tab in the left pane selected. If you are uncertain, position the mouse pointer over the Sx tab and click the mouse once.

Using the skills you have acquired in a previous exercise, navigate the list of findings and expand the tree of "head-related symptoms" until your list resembles the expanded tree shown in the left pane of Figure 3-18.

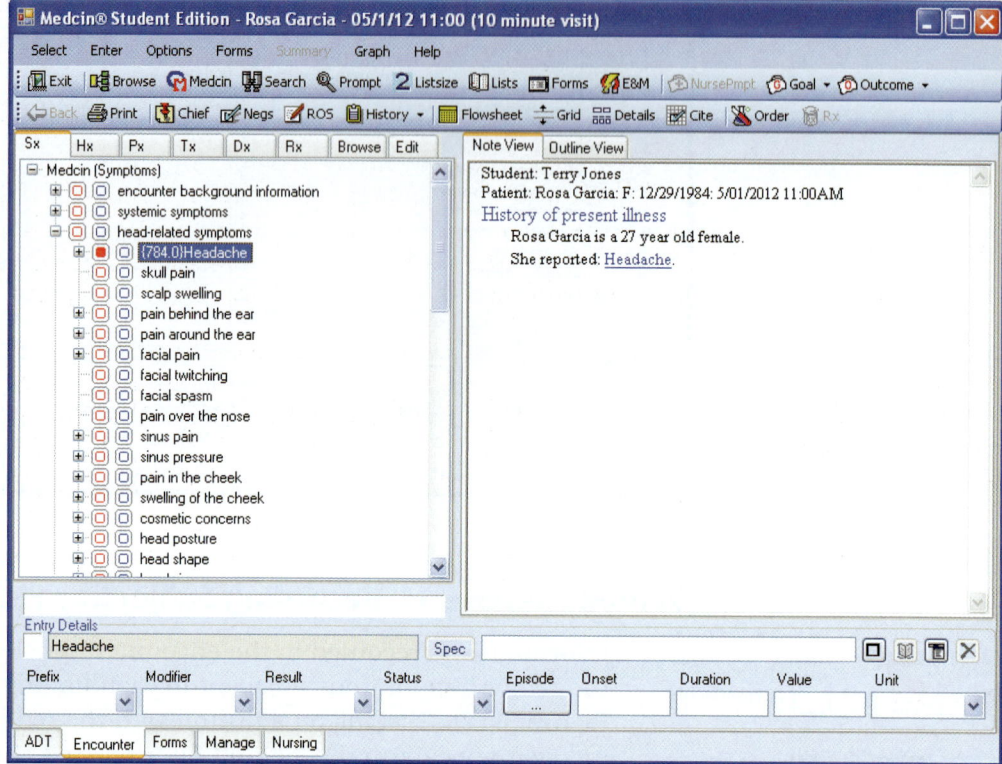

▶ Figure 3-18 Expanded tree for head-related symptoms—Headache finding selected.

Step 2

Position the mouse over the red button for the finding "Headache." Click the mouse button. Compare your screen to Figure 3-18.

The center of the button should turn red. This indicates that the finding has been selected. The word "Headache" should have also appeared on the right pane in the encounter note.

When you record the first subjective finding, a section title "History of Present Illness" is added to the encounter note as well. The history of present illness section also includes the patient's age on the date of the encounter.

Section titles are dynamically added or removed by the software based on the findings selected. Dynamically adding section titles only when they are needed creates a nice-looking encounter note without empty sections. For example, if tests are not performed, the right pane does not show an empty section called "Tests."

Step 3

To further explore the operation of the red and blue buttons, position the mouse over and then click on the blue button for headache instead. The center of the blue button should fill in and the red button should return to its previous (cleared) state. Also, the text in the encounter note and the finding description will both change to "No Headache."

Click on the red button to restore the finding back to "Headache." Make sure the button is red and the text in the encounter note again reads "Headache" before proceeding to step 4.

Step 4

EHR information should be as specific as possible. If the patient indicates that her headaches are chronic, you will want to select a more specific finding.

Click on the small plus next to Headaches to expand the tree. Locate the finding Chronic/Recurring and click on the red button.

Did the red button fill in? Did the text change in the encounter note?

Step 5

The patient further reports that her headaches have been getting worse.

Notice the small plus sign next to chronic/recurring, which indicates that there are more detailed findings available. Click on the plus sign to expand the tree.

Compare your screen to Figure 3-19.

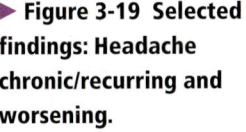

▶ **Figure 3-19** Selected findings: Headache chronic/recurring and worsening.

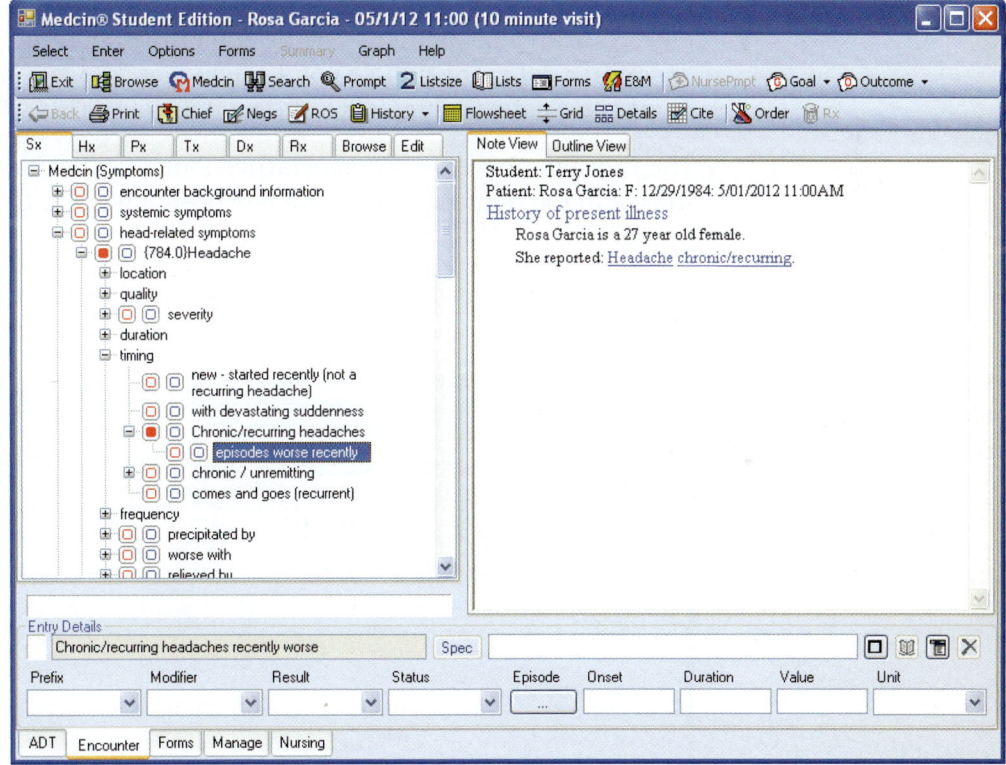

Step 6

In the expanded list for chronic/recurring, click the mouse on the red button for "episodes recently worse."

Notice that the software changes the description of findings when you click a red or blue button. In this case, the finding description changes to "chronic/recurring headaches recently worse." When the finding descriptions in the nomenclature pane become too long, they are displayed truncated with an ellipsis (three dots), which indicates there is more to the description than will fit in the left pane.

Guided Exercise 15: Removing Findings

In step 3 of the previous exercise, you learned that you could change the state or meaning of a finding that was already recorded by simply clicking your mouse on the opposite color button. In that example, clicking on the blue button changed "Headache" to "No Headache" and clicking on the red button changed it back to "Headache."

However, what if you accidentally clicked on the wrong finding? How would you undo it completely? In this exercise, you will learn how to remove findings from the encounter note.

Step 1

As mentioned previously, the left pane has two additional tabs, Browse and Edit. In this exercise, we are going to use the Edit tab.

Look at the encounter note displayed in the right pane. Notice that findings in the encounter note are underlined and the surrounding text is black. The section titles are blue and not underlined. You can click on underlined findings to edit them. You cannot click on section titles or the black text (i.e., you cannot click on text that is not underlined).

Move your mouse pointer over the underlined finding "with episodes" in the encounter note. The mouse pointer changes into the shape of a hand. While the hand is over the finding, click the mouse once. This will Edit the finding.

The Edit tab above the Nomenclature Pane has been automatically selected and the list in the Nomenclature Pane has been limited to the one finding being edited.

Step 2

Locate the button with an X in the lower right corner of the screen. (It is circled in red in Figure 3-20.) This is the Delete button, which is similar in

▶ **Figure 3-20** Edit mode with Delete finding button circled in red.

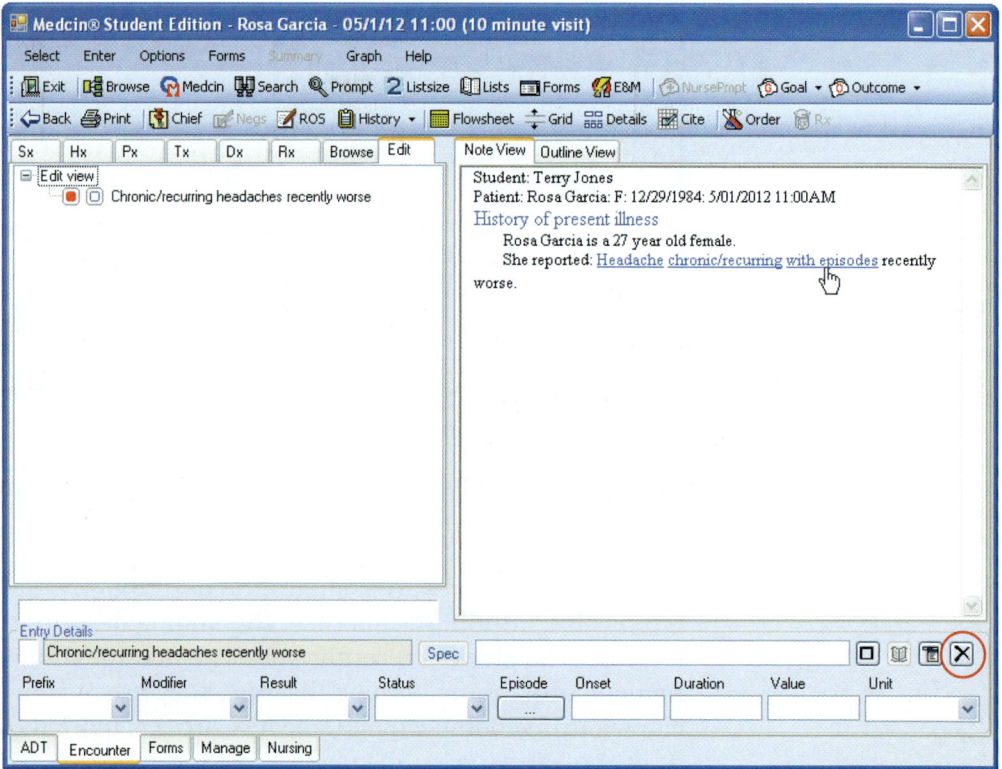

appearance to the Delete button used in word processors, e-mail, and many other Windows programs. Position your mouse pointer over the Delete button and click once.

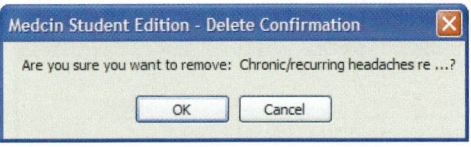

▶ Figure 3-21 Click OK to confirm removing the finding.

A small window called a "dialogue" will appear (as shown in Figure 3-21). The dialogue is asking you to confirm your intention to remove the finding from the encounter note.

Note this procedure only removes the finding from the patient's current encounter note. Findings will not be deleted from the Medcin nomenclature or other patient encounters by this procedure.

Click on the OK button.

The finding "with episodes" and the text "recently worse" will be removed from the encounter note. The left pane will remain on the Edit tab. This is normal.

Step 3

Practice removing findings by repeating steps 1 and 2 for each of the other two findings: headaches and chronic/recurring. The order that you remove them does not matter.

When you remove the last finding in a section, the section title will be removed automatically. In this case, "History of Present Illness" and "Rosa Garcia is a 27 year old female" were removed.

Step 4

Restore the Medcin Nomenclature list to the left pane by positioning the mouse over the Sx tab and clicking once. This will redisplay the Medcin nomenclature.

Guided Exercise 16: Recording More Specific Findings

In a previous exercise, you recorded a patient's symptom of chronic/recurring headaches by selecting three different findings from the list. There is nothing wrong with doing it that way if the natural flow of the exam progresses in that manner. For example, the patient reports having headaches. The clinician asks if they are recurring, and the patient says "yes." The clinician adds the finding, but then patient also mentions that the headaches are getting worse. The clinician then adds the finding "worse."

However, if you have all of the information before selecting the finding, you can simply select the most specific finding and Medcin will add the surrounding text. In this exercise, you will record all three pieces of information about the patient's symptom by clicking only one finding.

Step 1

If your screen does not currently resemble Figure 3-16, repeat the necessary steps to select a patient, select a new encounter, and then select the Sx tab.

Expand the tree view of "head-related symptoms," "headache," chronic/recurring (clicking on small plus signs) until you can see the full list shown in Figure 3-22.

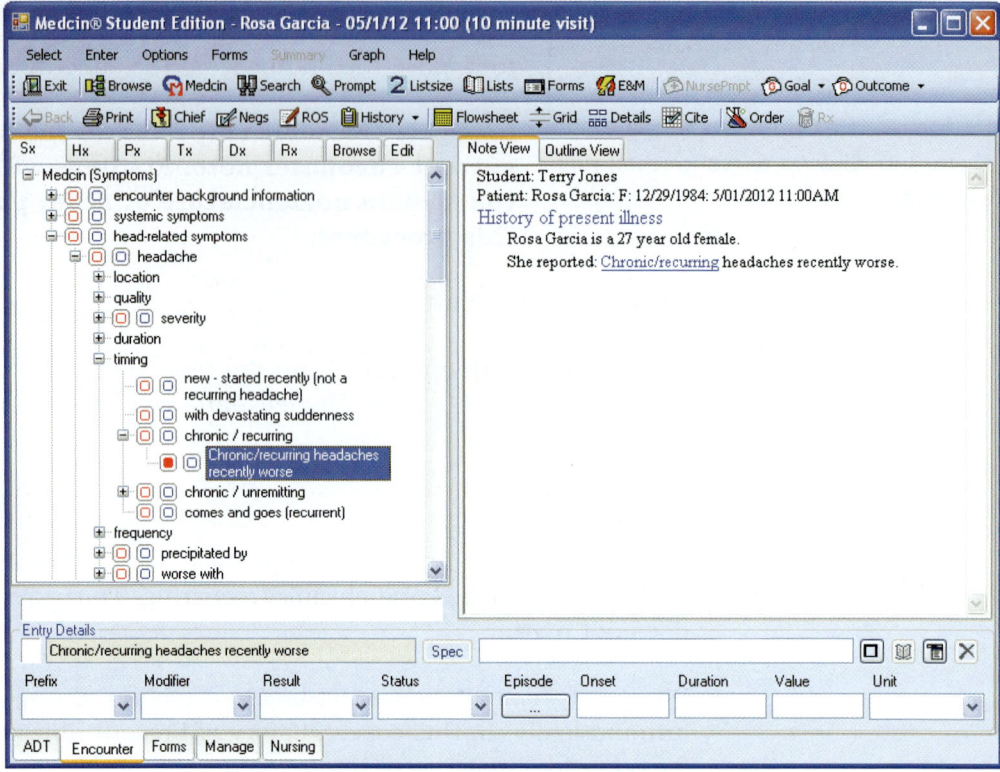

▶ **Figure 3-22** Chronic/recurring headaches recently worse.

Step 2

Position the mouse pointer over the red button for the finding "episodes recently worse" (indented under "chronic/recurring") and click the mouse.

Compare your screen with Figure 3-22. Did the red button fill in?

Compare the text of the encounter note in Figure 3-22 with the text in Figure 3-20. The two notes are different but medically equivalent. Additionally, in the codified EHR, Medcin has taken care of relating the underlying codes.

In the real-world application of electronic medical records, speed of input is important. Use whichever technique accurately documents the exam in the least amount of time. There is no reason to go back and delete the findings as we did in the previous exercise when they are correct. However, when an entire symptom or observation can be documented by selecting a single finding, do so, as you have in this exercise. The purpose of Guided Exercise 15 was to teach you how to remove findings when necessary.

Guided Exercise 17: Recording History Findings

The History tab is used to record the patient's past medical, surgical, family, and social history.

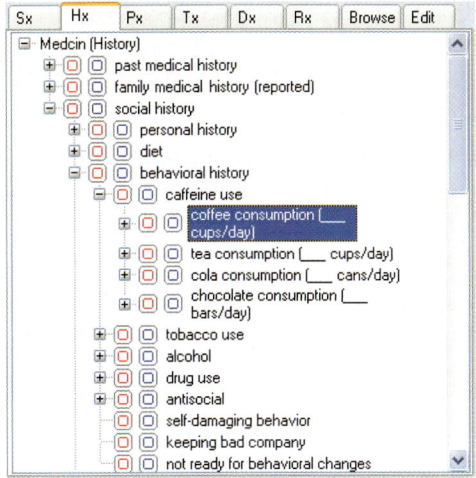

▶ Figure 3-23 Hx list—coffee consumption.

Step 1

Position the mouse pointer over the Hx tab and click the mouse once.

Step 2

Using the skills you have acquired in previous exercises, navigate the Medcin list and expand the tree by clicking on the small plus signs next to "social history," "behavioral history," and "caffeine use." The left pane of the window should resemble Figure 3-23.

Step 3

Position the mouse over the red button next to the finding "coffee consumption (—cups/day)." Click the mouse button. The center of the button should turn red and "Behavioral: Daily coffee consumption" should appear in the encounter note pane on the right pane.

Compare your screen to Figure 3-24. Note that two new titles were added as well: Personal history and Behavioral.

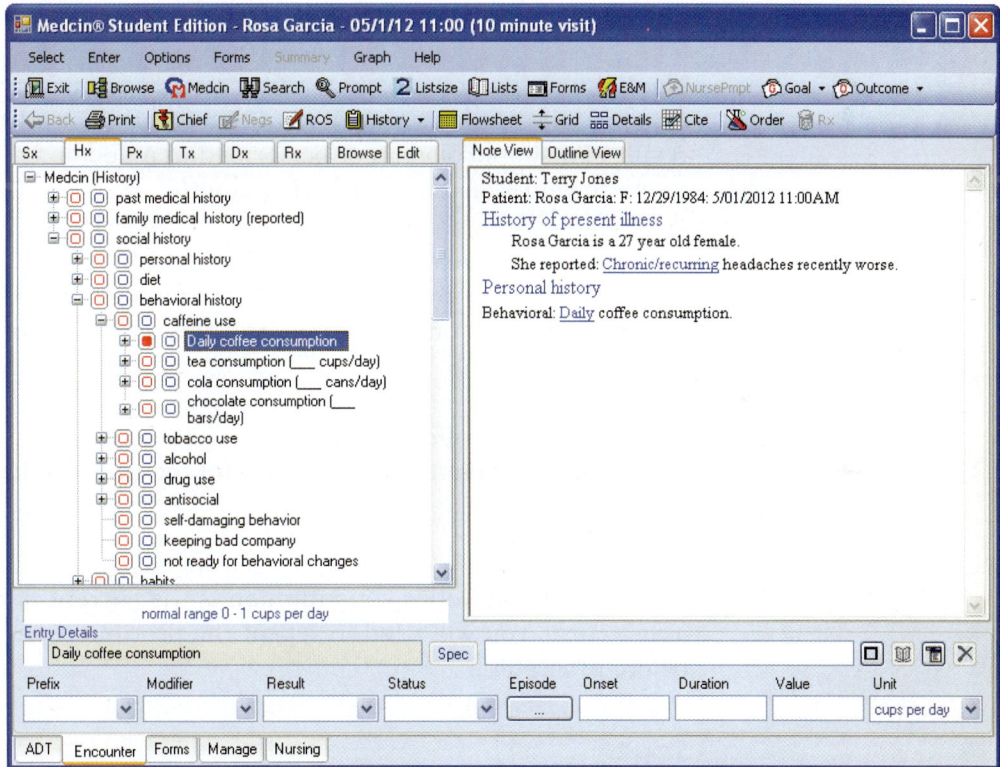

▶ Figure 3-24 Daily coffee consumption.

Adding Details to the Findings

In addition to the narrative text that the software automatically generates, you also can add further clarification to the encounter note using Entry Details fields.

Chapter 3 | Learning Medical Record Software   97

The section labeled "Entry Details" is located at the bottom of your screen. It was indicated in Figure 3-3 with the numeral 4. The Entry Details section consists of two rows of white boxes. These are the Entry Details fields.

The first row of fields contains the description of the currently highlighted finding, a note field for adding free-text about the current finding, and four buttons. You have already used the delete button (with the X) in a previous exercise. We will discuss and use the two other buttons in later exercises.

The second row contains the following fields: prefix, modifier, result, status, episode, onset, duration, value, and unit.

All of the fields in the Entry Details section apply to a single finding, the one currently selected or highlighted.

In the following exercises you will learn to use the Entry Details fields. Notice the Entry Details fields as you select findings. In some cases, Medcin will automatically set one or more of the fields; other times you will set the field yourself.

Guided Exercise 18: Recording a Value

The Value field can be used to enter a value about any type of finding. For example, the patient's weight could be entered for a finding of weight, or the result of a simple blood test performed in a doctor's office could be entered as a numeric value for the finding Hematocrit.

The Unit field is related to the Value field in that it describes the unit of measure for the value. In the two previous examples, the unit for weight would be pounds or kilograms, and the unit for the Hematocrit would be percent.

In this exercise, coffee consumption is measured in cups. So the value will be the number the patient consumed and the unit would be "cups per day."

Step 1

Make sure Daily Coffee consumption is the current finding. If you are beginning a new class, you will need to repeat the previous exercise to add the finding before proceeding.

Step 2

Locate the Value and Unit fields in the Entry Details section at the bottom of the screen. Notice that the Unit field already contains the words "cups per day."

Click your mouse in the Value field and type "**7–8**" and then press the Enter key on your keyboard.

Compare your screen with Figure 3-25. The text in the encounter note should now read: "Behavioral: Daily coffee consumption was 7-8 cups per day."

▶ Figure 3-25 Recording the value 7-8 and unit cups per day.

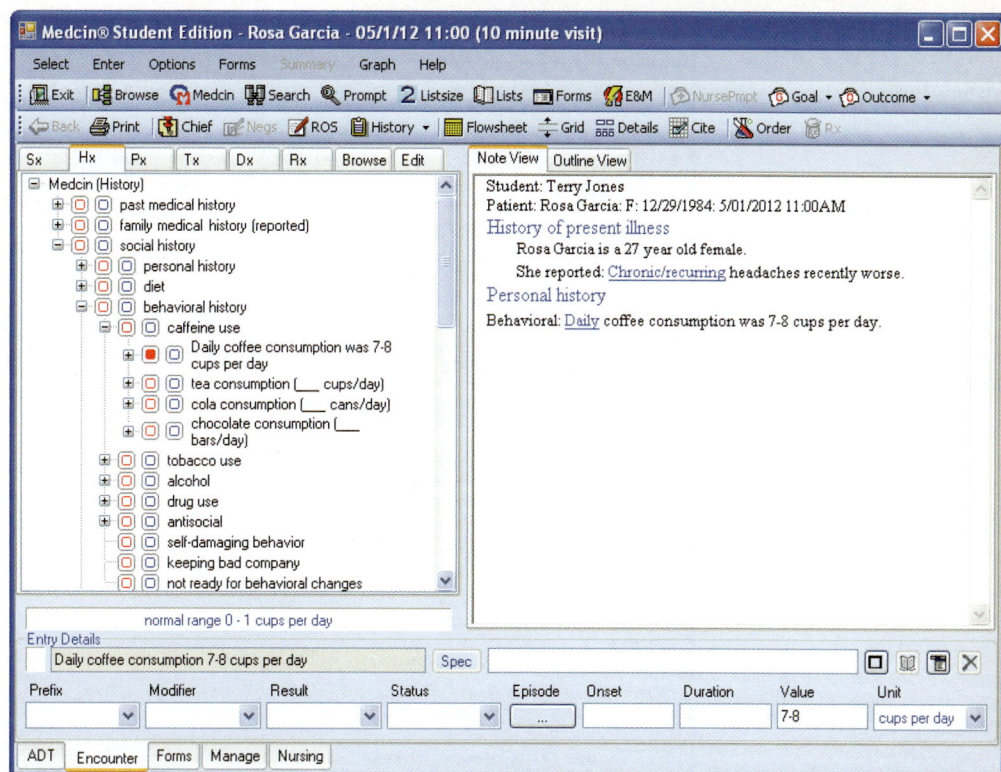

Using Free Text

In this exercise you will learn how to add your own text into the note. The term for this is "free text," meaning that the text is not codified and might contain anything.

In contrast, the other Entry Details fields (Prefix, Modifier, Result, Status, Episode, Onset, Duration, Value, and Unit) are stored as fielded data. This has the advantage of producing a uniform, searchable EHR throughout the medical practice.

Ideally the less free text used in the EHR the better. Still, there are many times when free text is appropriate—for example, adding a nuance to a finding that extends its meaning or entering text that more accurately portrays the patient's own words.

Guided Exercise 19: Adding Free Text

In this exercise, the patient reports she has recently stopped drinking coffee. If you are beginning a new class, you will need to repeat the two previous exercises to add the finding before proceeding.

Step 1

Click on the small plus sign next to Daily coffee consumption to expand the list of findings.

Locate the finding "recently decreased" and click the mouse on the red button. Compare your screen to Figure 3-26.

Step 2

Look at the Entry Details section at the bottom of your screen. There are two long fields in the first row. The gray field on the left contains the description

Chapter 3 | Learning Medical Record Software 99

▶ **Figure 3-26** Patient reported decreased coffee consumption.

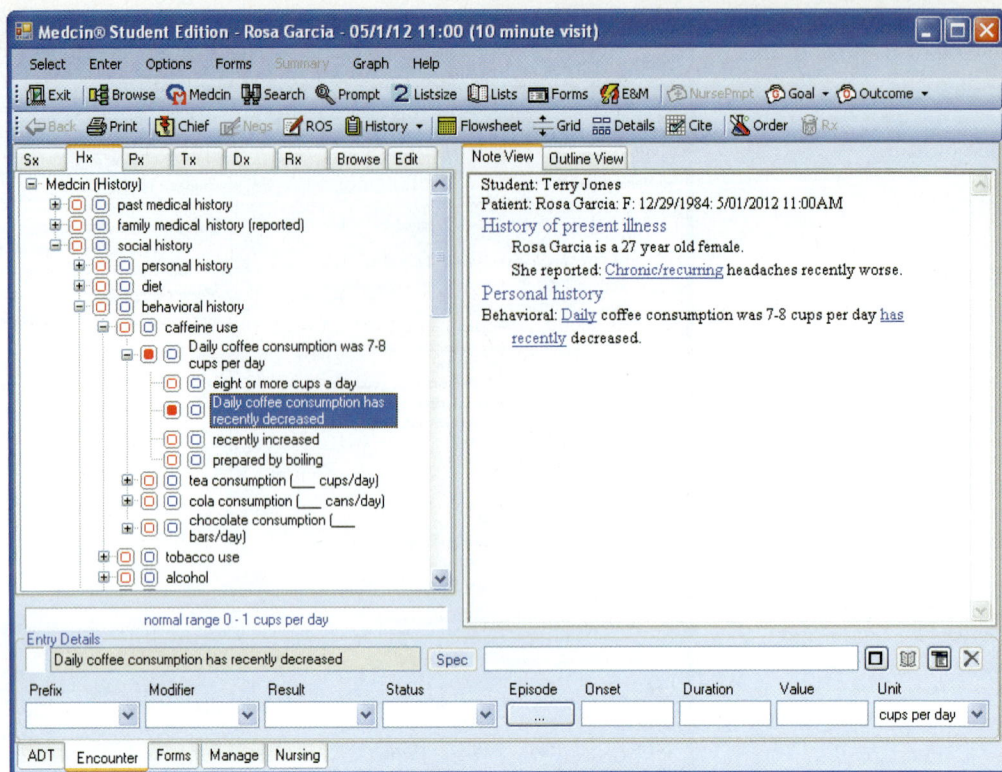

that appears in the note and cannot be directly edited; the field on the right is used to add free text to the currently selected finding.

Click your mouse in the free-text field. Type **"because she stopped all coffee"** in the field and then press the Enter key on your keyboard. Compare your screen with Figure 3-27.

▶ **Figure 3-27** Behavioral history with additional free text.

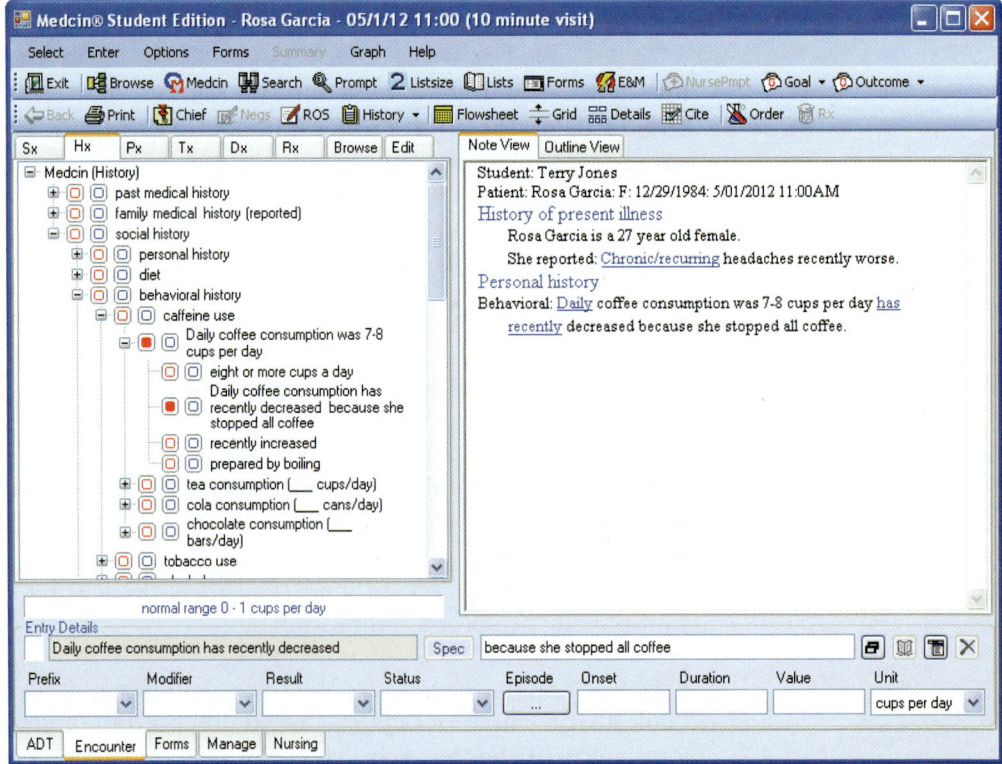

Guided Exercise 20: Recording Objective Findings

The Px tab is used to record the observations and results of the clinician's physical examination of the patient as well as measurements and vital signs recorded during the course of the encounter.

Step 1

Position the mouse pointer over the Px tab and click the mouse once. The Physical Examination list will be displayed. Notice that the list is organized by body systems, essentially in the order you would perform a head-to-toe exam.

Step 2

Click on the small plus sign next to "Head" to expand the list. Locate the finding "Exam for evidence of injury" and click the mouse on the blue button. Compare your screen to Figure 3-28. The blue button should be filled in and the text "No evidence of a head injury" should be recorded in the encounter note pane.

▶ Figure 3-28 No evidence of head injury.

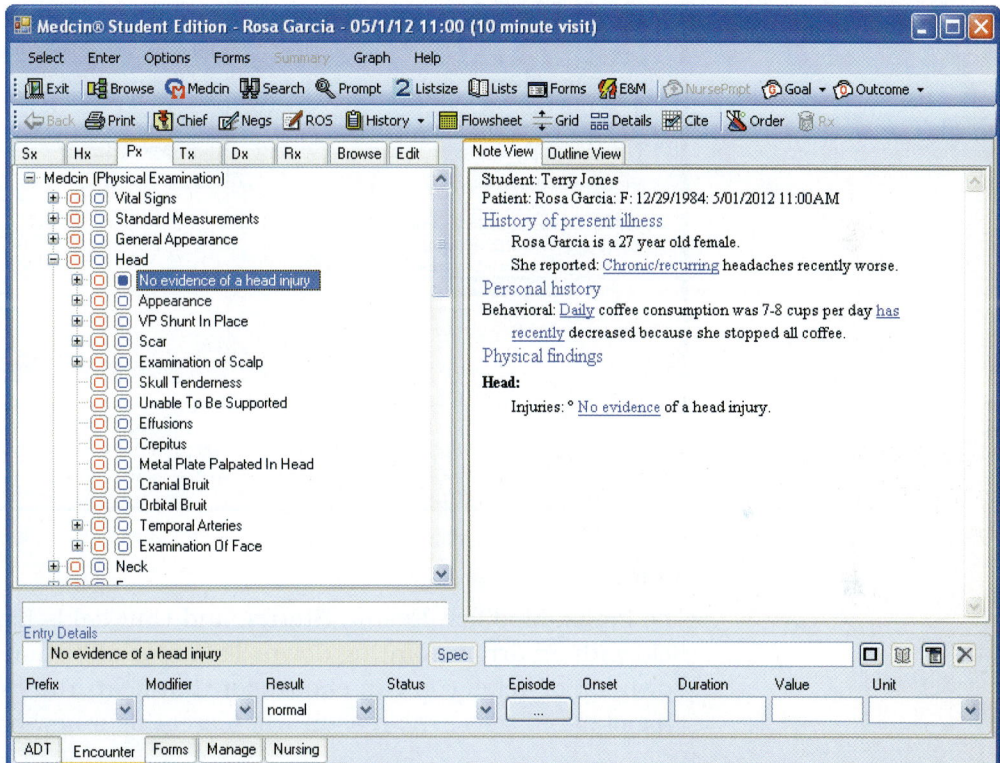

Step 3

Look at the Entry Details field for Result. It was previously blank but now contains the word "normal." This is an example of how the EHR software can set the field for you based on the assumption that it is normal not to have a head injury.

Guided Exercise 21: Setting the Result Field

As mentioned earlier, the software can set Entry Detail fields automatically (as in the previous exercise) or you can set the field. In this exercise you will learn how to highlight a finding and how to set the Result field.

Chapter 3 | Learning Medical Record Software

Step 1

Using the mouse, scroll the list of physical examination findings until you see "Neurological System." Expand the list by clicking on the small plus sign next to Neurological System.

Step 2

Locate the finding "Cognitive Functions" and highlight the finding by clicking your mouse on the description (not on the red or blue buttons). Compare your screen to Figure 3-29.

▶ Figure 3-29 Neurological/Cognitive Functioning finding.

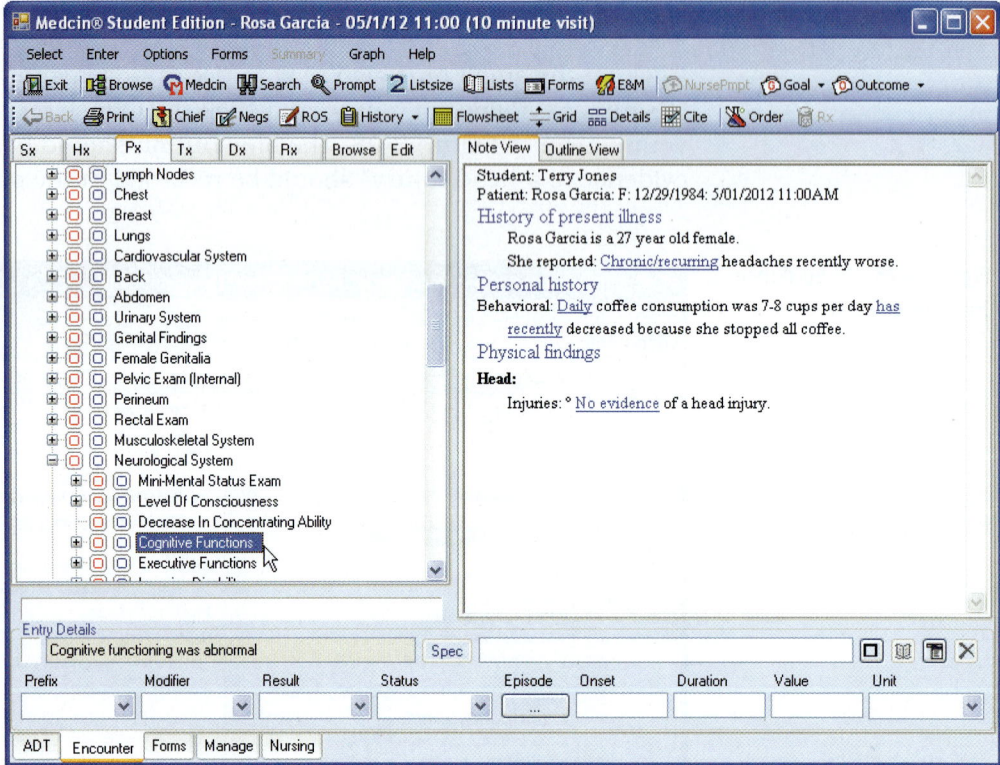

Step 3

The Prefix, Modifier, Result, Status, and Unit fields have buttons next to the field with an arrow pointing down. This type of button indicates there is a drop-down list of items you can choose for that field. You have previously used this type of list to select the reason when creating a new encounter.

Locate the Result field in the Entry Details section at the bottom of the screen. Click your mouse on the button with the down arrow in the field. A drop-down list of choices (as shown in Figure 3-30) will appear. Do not be concerned if the position of a drop-down list differs from the figures in this book. Drop-down lists may appear either above or below a field, depending on the screen settings of each computer.

▶ Figure 3-30 Drop-down list for Result field.

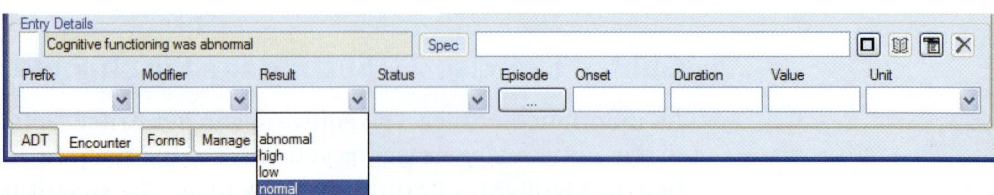

> **Note**
>
> The first item in each drop-down list is a blank. The blank is selected whenever you want to clear the Entry Details fields Prefix, Modifier, Result, Status, or Unit.

Position your mouse pointer on the result "normal" and click the mouse button. The field will display the word "normal," the blue button will have automatically been selected, and the encounter note will read "Cognitive functioning was normal."

Guided Exercise 22: Adding Detail to Recorded Findings

EHR software must be very flexible because additional observations or information from the patient could necessitate going back to any section at any time. In this exercise, you will add status information to the patient's reported symptom.

Step 1

Select the finding for Edit by moving your mouse pointer over the underlined words "Chronic/recurring" headache in the right pane. When the mouse pointer changes to a hand, click the mouse button. The Px tab in the left pane should be replaced by the Edit tab. This step of the procedure is the same one you used in Guided Exercise 15: Removing Findings.

Chronic/recurring headache is now the current finding.

Step 2

Locate the Status field in the Entry Details section at the bottom of the screen. Click your mouse on the button with the down arrow in the status field. A drop-down list of phrases (as shown in Figure 3-31) will appear.

▶ Figure 3-31 Drop-down list for Status field.

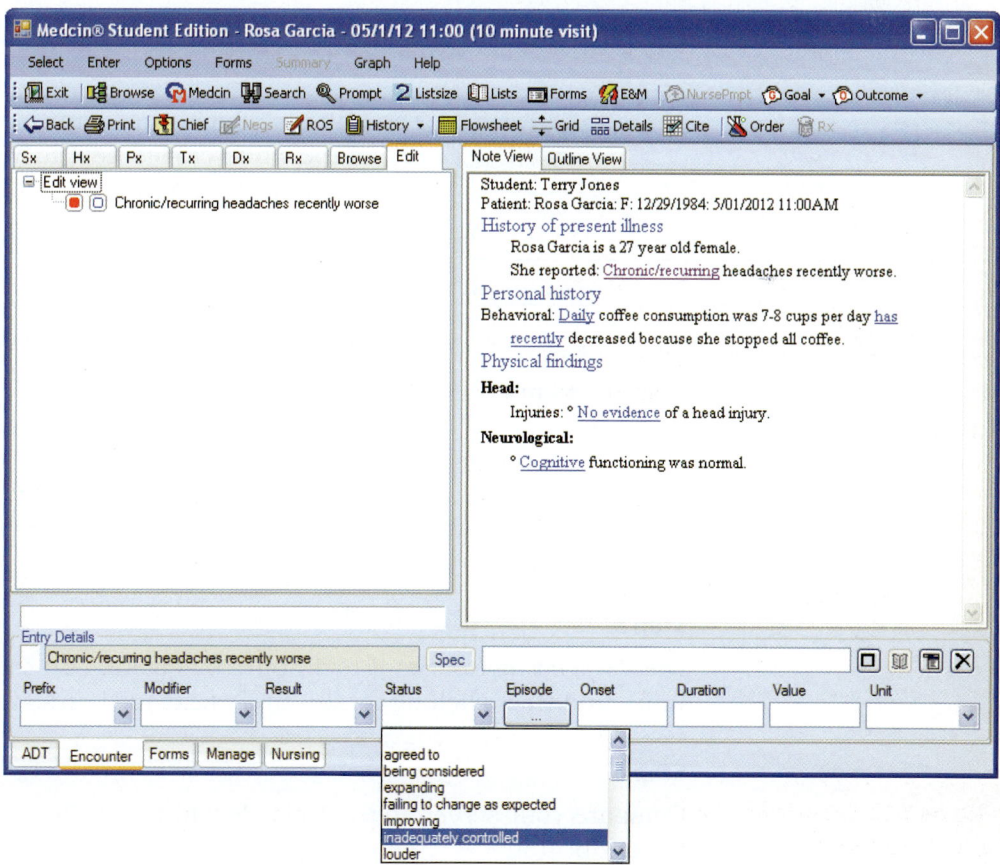

Step 3

Position your mouse pointer on the status "inadequately controlled" and click the mouse button. The field will display a portion of the phrase, and the text in

Chapter 3 | Learning Medical Record Software

the encounter note will change to "Chronic/recurring headaches recently worse which is inadequately controlled."

Guided Exercise 23: Adding Episode Detail to Findings

In addition to drop-down lists, another method of input is used to enter frequency or interval data. In this exercise, you will add information about the frequency of the patient's headaches.

Step 1

The finding "Chronic/recurring" headache should still be selected for edit. If it is not, then repeat step 1 of the previous exercise.

Step 2

Locate the label "Episode" in the Entry Details section at the bottom of your screen. The Episode button located below the label has an ellipsis (three dots) on it. Click your mouse on the Episode button.

The Episode window shown in Figure 3-32 will be invoked. It is used to record information about the intervals and repetitions at which findings occur.

The numeric value of a field in the Episode window is increased or decreased by clicking on the up or down arrow buttons next to the numeric field. The arrow buttons are circled in Figure 3-32.

The units in which time is measured are set by clicking on one of the white circles next to Minutes, Hours, Days, Weeks, Months, or Years.

Step 3

Locate "Occurring from." Set it to 1 day by clicking on the up arrow button once and then clicking on the circle next to Days.

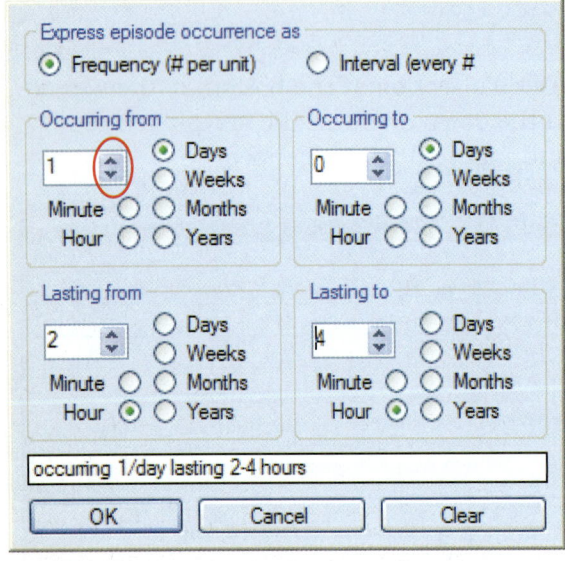

▶ **Figure 3-32 Episode window (numeric controls circled in red).**

Step 4

Locate "Lasting from." Set it to 2 hours by clicking on the up arrow button twice and then clicking on the circle next to Hours.

Step 5

Locate "Lasting to." Set it to 4 hours by clicking on the up arrow button four times and then clicking on the circle next to Hours.

Step 6

Compare your screen to the Episode window in Figure 3-32, and then click on the OK button.

Look at the encounter note in the right pane. Does the text read "Chronic/recurring headaches recently worse occurring 1/day lasting 2–4 hours which is inadequately controlled"?

Guided Exercise 24: Recording the Assessment

The assessment is the clinician's diagnosis of the patient's problem or condition. This exercise will give you further experience in navigating and expanding the *tree* of findings.

Step 1

Position your mouse pointer on the tab "Dx" and click the mouse. The Diagnosis, Syndromes, and Conditions list should be displayed in the left pane of the window.

Step 2

Scroll the list downward until you see "Neurologic Disorders" (highlighted in Figure 3-33.) Click on the small plus sign to expand the list.

Locate "Headache Syndromes" in the list and click on the small plus sign.

Step 3

Scroll the list further downward until you see "Benign syndromes" (highlighted in Figure 3-34) and then click on the small plus sign.

Step 4

Scroll the list further downward until you see "Drug-induced headache" and then click on the small plus sign.

Step 5

Scroll the list further downward until you see "Vasoconstrictor withdrawal headache" and then click on the small plus sign.

The fully expanded list of findings is shown in Figure 3-35.

Step 6

Position your mouse pointer on the red button next to "From caffeine" and click the mouse. Compare your screen to Figure 3-35. The finding "Vasoconstrictor withdrawal headache from caffeine" should be recorded in the encounter note under a new heading: "Assessment."

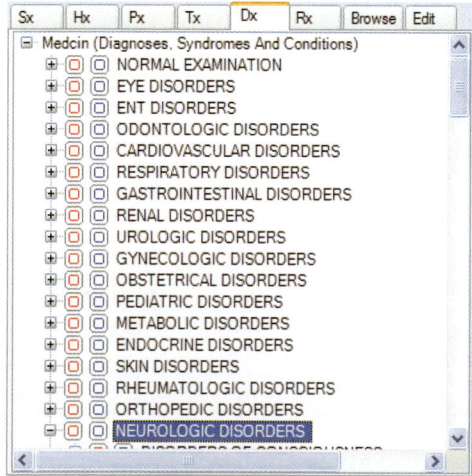

▶ **Figure 3-33** Dx tab with Neurologic Disorders highlighted.

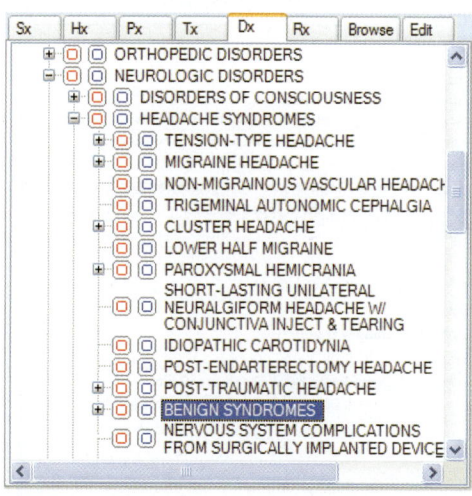

▶ **Figure 3-34** Dx tab scrolled to Benign syndromes.

Guided Exercise 25: Recording Treatment Plan and Physician Orders

In Exercise 19, you added free text to a specific finding. Medcin also has several special findings that are used as anchors for general free-text entry.

Additionally, when you have more than a few words of free text to enter, a larger window may be useful as well. In this exercise, you will add a free-text finding and enter information through a special free-text window.

Step 1

Position the mouse pointer on the Rx tab and click the mouse button. The Medcin Therapy list will be displayed.

Chapter 3 | Learning Medical Record Software   **105**

▶ Figure 3-35 Dx tab—assessment: withdrawal headache from caffeine.

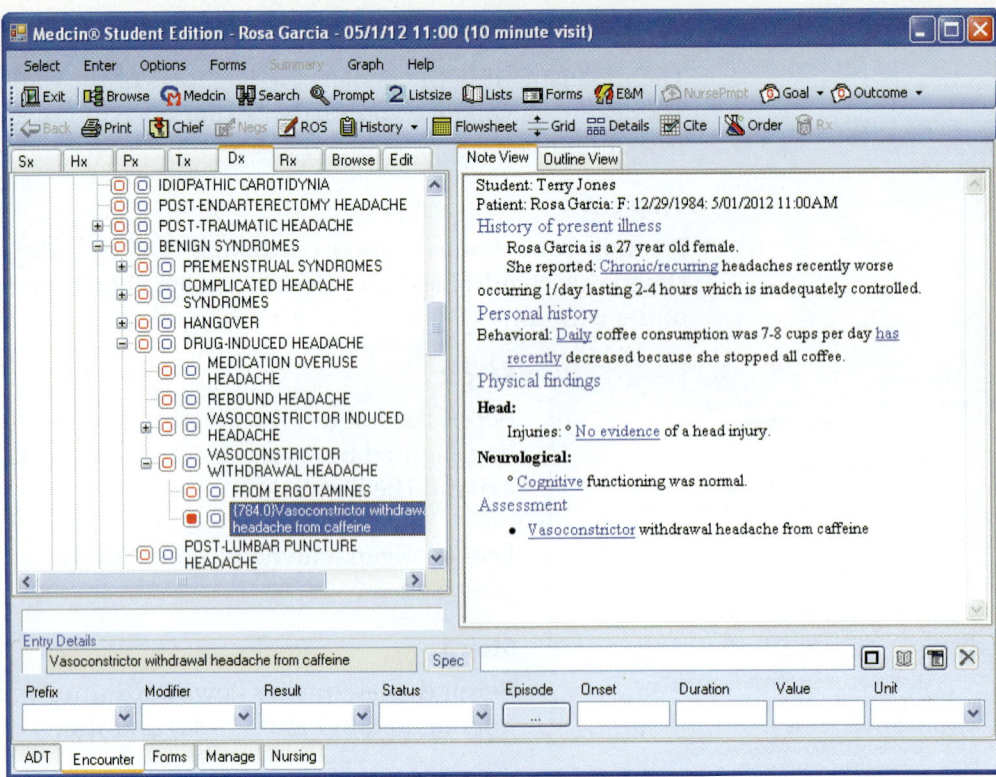

▶ Figure 3-36 Free-text finding (highlighted) on Rx tab.

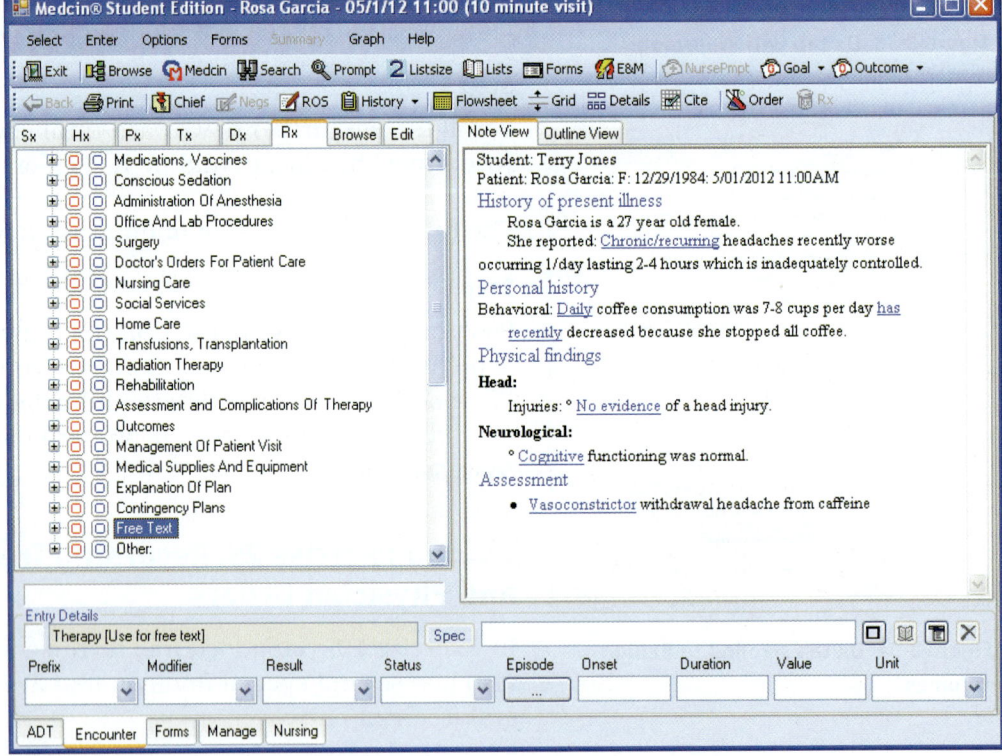

Step 2

This time, instead of typing free text into the Entry Details field, you will invoke a small window used for adding and editing finding notes.

Scroll to the bottom of the list, then locate and highlight the finding labeled "Free Text" as shown in Figure 3-36. Do not click a red or blue button.

Step 3

In the lower right corner of your screen are four buttons. You used the delete button (with the X) in previous exercises. In this exercise you will use the Finding Note button, which is circled in red in Figure 3-37.

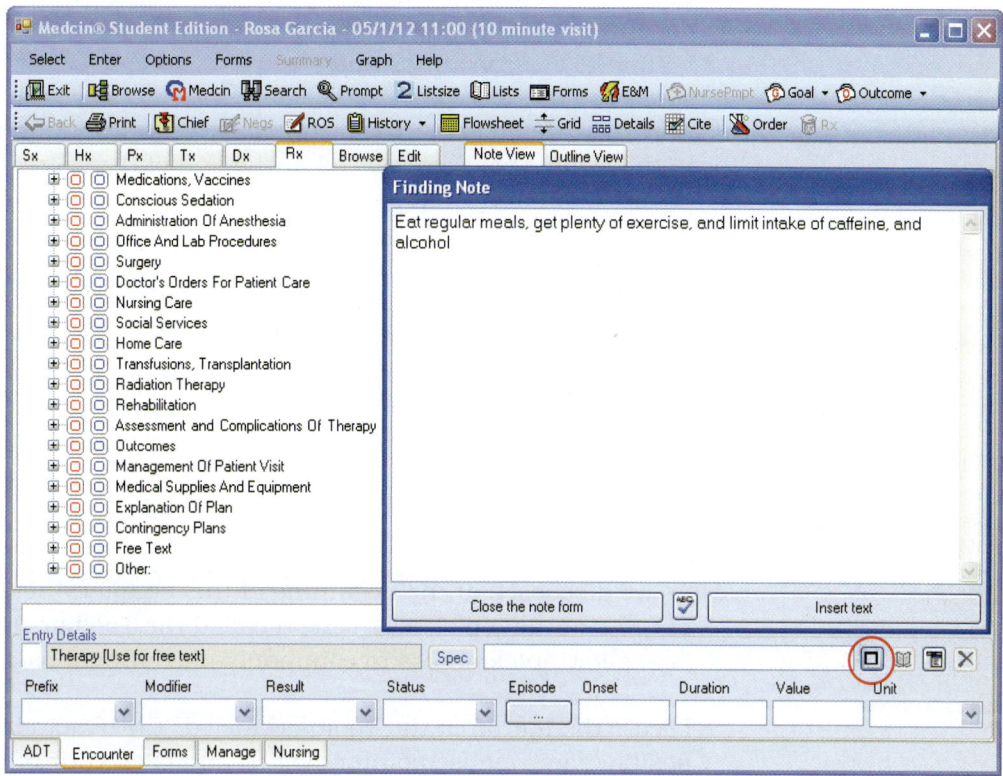

▶ **Figure 3-37** Finding note window used for free text (button circled in red).

Position your mouse pointer on the Finding Note button and click the mouse. A small Finding Note window will be invoked, as shown in Figure 3-37.

Step 4

There are several advantages to entering free text in this window as opposed to in the free-text field in the Entry Details section.

1. The area in the window is larger than the free-text field, making it easier to type a longer note.
2. The window includes a spell checker (the "abc" button in the center of the finding note window).
3. The Insert text feature allows frequently used text to be stored inserted as free text whenever appropriate, saving time typing.

Type the following text into the Finding Note window:

"Eat regular meals, get plenty of exercise, and limit intake of caffeine, and alcohol"

When you have finished, click your mouse on the button labeled "Close the note form." This will add your text to the encounter note under a new section title "Therapy."

Chapter 3 | Learning Medical Record Software   **107**

Introduction to Using Forms

You may have noticed in the previous exercise that the finding note window was called a *form*. Forms make it convenient to enter findings or free text without locating and selecting the finding from the nomenclature. When a form is used, the information is automatically recorded in the proper section of the encounter note. In the following two exercises, you will use forms to add information to the encounter note.

Normally, the items in the next two exercises would have been recorded early in the exam; they were placed at the end of the exercises only because of the organization of the chapter.

Guided Exercise 26: Recording the Chief Complaint

Typically, the first thing recorded in the exam is a description of the patient's reason for the encounter. This is called the "Chief complaint." You could locate the finding "Chief complaint" and then enter a free-text note, but because Chief complaint is a standard part of every exam, it is more efficient to provide a form for text entry.

Step 1

As we discussed at the beginning of this chapter, there are two rows of icon buttons at the top of your screen called the Toolbar. The purpose of the Toolbar is to allow quick access to commonly used functions.

Locate the button in the Toolbar labeled "Chief" (circled in Figure 3-38), position your mouse pointer over it, and click your mouse.

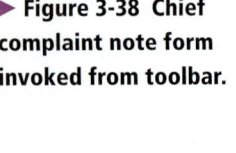

▶ Figure 3-38 Chief complaint note form invoked from toolbar.

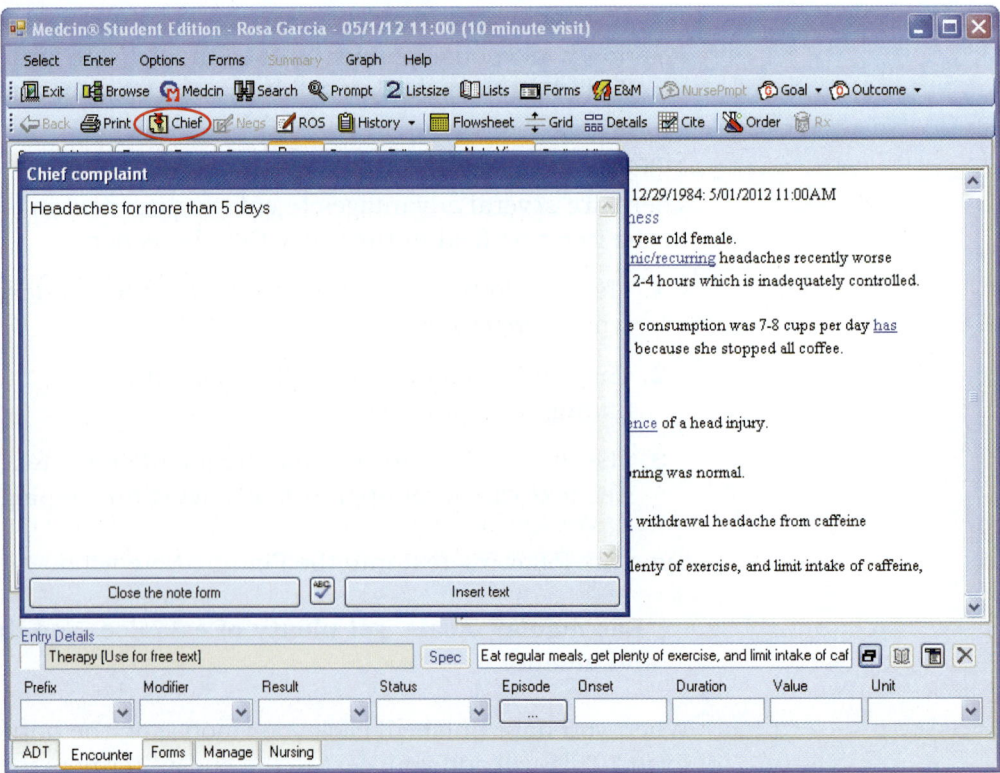

Step 2

The Chief complaint window will be invoked. This window looks similar to the finding note window in the previous exercise except that when you close the note form, instead of just recording free text, it will automatically associate the text with the finding "Chief complaint."

Step 3

Type the following text into the finding note window: "**Headaches for more than 5 days.**"

When you have finished, compare your screen to Figure 3-38.

Position your mouse on the button labeled "Close the note form" and click the mouse. This will add a new section to the encounter note titled "Chief complaint" followed by the text you typed.

Guided Exercise 27: Recording Vital Signs

Forms are not limited to free text. Many findings can be included on one form, and the form can contain specific Entry Details fields such as Result, Status, Value, and Unit.

A form is frequently used to record Vital Signs (routine measurements of the body taken at nearly every patient encounter). As you will see in this exercise, it is more efficient to enter numerical data using a form than to locate and select findings one at a time and then enter data in the value field for each.

Step 1

At the very bottom of the screen are five tabs labeled "ADT," "Encounter," "Forms," "Manage," and "Nursing." All forms except the small free-text boxes used in previous exercises are accessed from the Forms tab.

Position your mouse pointer over the tab labeled "Forms" (circled in red at the bottom of Figure 3-39) and click the mouse.

When the tab changes the familiar Encounter view of the Student Edition will be replaced with an Outline View of the headings that have findings in your encounter note. The Outline View presents the headings as icons of file folders, with small plus signs preceding them. If you click on the small plus signs next to the folders, the tree will expand to show the findings recorded in the encounter under that heading. The Outline View will also show the ICD-9-CM and CPT-4 codes for relevant findings. Those codes will be discussed in Chapter 12.

Because you may not have performed all of the previous exercises in a single class period, your Outline View may not have as much detail as shown in Figure 3-39.

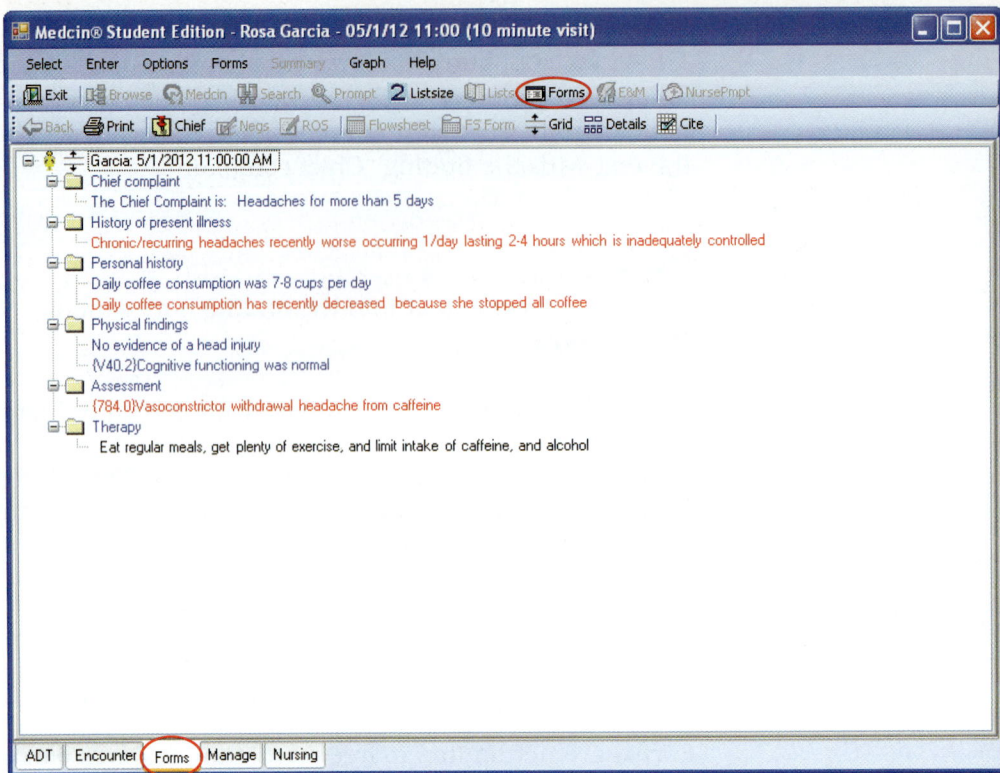

▶ **Figure 3-39** Forms tab and forms button (both circled in red).

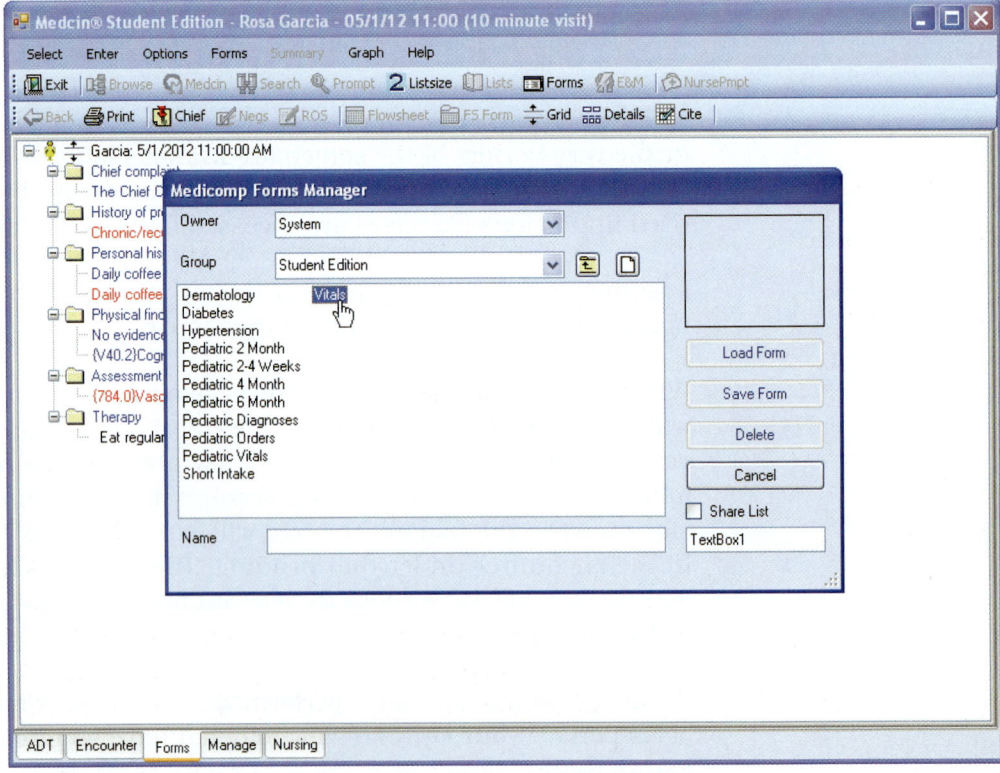

▶ **Figure 3-40** Select Vitals from the list in the Forms Manager window.

Step 2

Locate and click on the button labeled "Forms" in the top row of the Toolbar at the top of your screen. (The button is circled in red in Figure 3-39.) This will invoke the Forms Manager window shown in Figure 3-40. The Forms Manager lists forms used in the Student Edition.

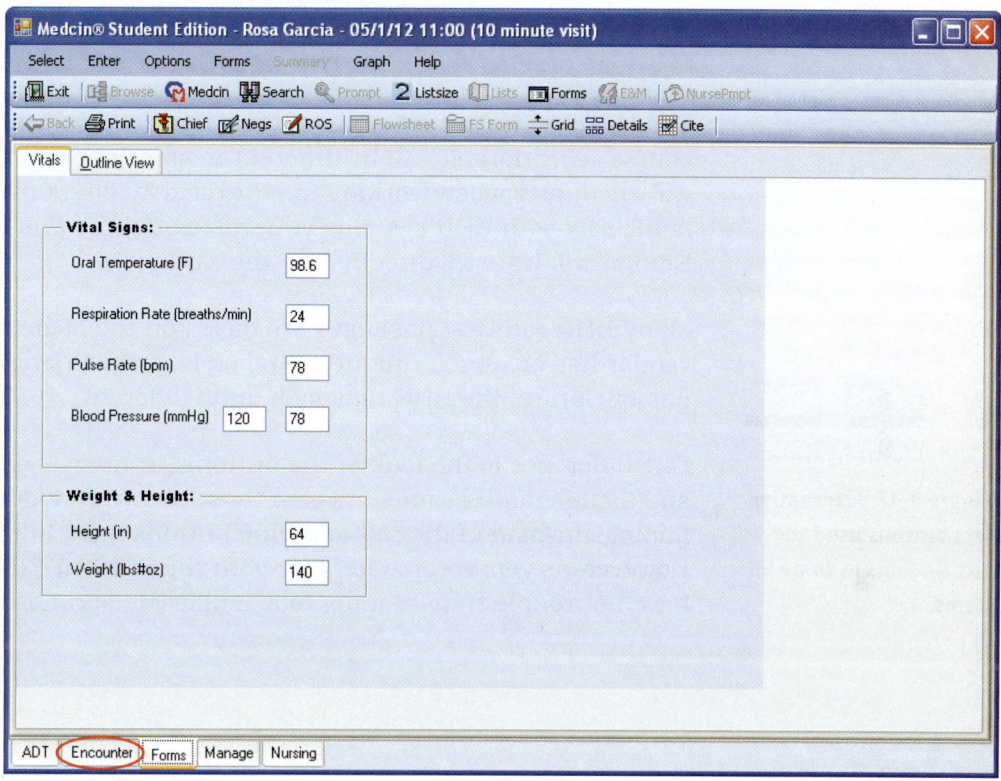

▶ **Figure 3-41** Vital Signs Form for Rosa Garcia.

> **Note**
>
> Systolic and Diastolic blood pressure readings are entered in two separate fields. Omit the "/" character when entering Blood pressure (BP) in the form.

Locate and click on the form labeled "Vitals" in the Form Manager window as shown in Figure 3-40. This should open the form shown in Figure 3-41.

Enter Ms. Garcia's vital signs into the corresponding fields. They are as follows:

Temperature:	**98.6**
Respiration:	**24**
Pulse:	**78**
BP	**120/78**
Height:	**64**
Weight:	**140**

When you have entered all of the vital signs, compare your screen to Figure 3-41 and then click your mouse on the Encounter tab (circled in red) at the bottom of the screen.

The vital signs information will now be recorded in the encounter note on the right pane under the Physical Findings section.

Chapter 3 | Learning Medical Record Software 111

Step 3

Look at the results of the Vital Signs entry as they appear in the encounter note. Also notice that there is a tab on top of the right pane labeled "Outline View." This tab will display the same outline in the right pane, as was displayed on the Forms tab.

When you have finished looking at the note, exit the Student Edition software.

Visually Different Button Styles

The Medcin Student Edition software has been specially created for this course. Therefore, it will be different in some aspects from EHR systems you will encounter when working in a medical facility, but the concepts, skills, and familiarity with EHR systems you will acquire by practicing with the Student Edition will transfer directly into the workplace.

Many EHR software packages are based on the Medcin Nomenclature. Each vendor has created a unique visual style, and although they share a common nomenclature, the EHR may look quite different.

▶ **Figure 3-42 Alternative Select buttons used to select findings in some EHR systems.**

One difference is the look of the buttons. In many systems, a large plus sign and a large minus sign similar to those shown in Figure 3-42 are used to select findings instead of the red and blue buttons used in the Student Edition. However, as you become familiar with the Student Edition software, you should have no trouble transitioning to a similar Medcin-based EHR in your job.

Real-Life Story

Paperless in Less Than a Day

By Allen R. Wenner, M.D.[1]

Dr. Wenner is a practicing physician in Columbia, South Carolina, and a well-known expert on electronic health records.

The schedule was full. It was going to be a busy day. I had awakened two hours early that morning fearing this day. Because of delays in hardware installation and software updating, instead of installing the paperless system during our least busy time in December, we were forced to begin an electronic medical record in January, our busiest time of the year.

I knew there would be problems with a staff adjusting to the new workflow of a paperless environment, but the time had come to go to an electronic medical record or drown in the paper while being accused of Medicare fraud. There were many within the organization who did not believe it is possible to eliminate the majority of the paper in a medical office or comply with new CMS documentation guidelines. I feared that we might get behind in the heavy patient schedule and the electronic medical record project would fail. If patients waited needlessly, the hope of converting to electronic medical records at this time would be lost. The project was already a year beyond my scheduled plan, so time was running out.

Because the project was to involve only a third of the clinic's patients, only brief training of three employees was completed. The training had occurred during breaks on the previous day and was not well structured. It was anticipated that we would see only a few patients in the paperless environment the first day.

The change from paper chart to an electronic chart requires some familiarity with the software, but no amount of touching the keys can approximate the sensation when the patient arrives for care. As a sick patient begins his history, and the examination begins, the software cannot interfere.

The most difficult part of electronic medical record software is the new capability of software. Having multiple windows open in an electronic chart is like seeing several things at once. This is a stark contrast to the familiar one or two sheets that can be viewed in the paper record. Arranging the multiple windows in a way that is most appropriate for one's use in a real clinical examination requires time to think about and experience. On the first day of my actual use, the lack of familiarity with this new capability caused a decrease in my productivity as the information overwhelmed me. I felt lost at times not knowing what to do next. Disorientation is to be expected with any change this dramatic in the work process. All physicians will have difficulty making this leap as just I did that first morning. I felt lost and bewildered. I felt the same uncertainty I first felt as a second-year medical student when I walked for the first time alone into an exam room with a live patient.

Before I arrived in the exam room, each patient completed a medical interview on the computer (described further in Chapter 11). I entered the room and the clinical examination began. Having a documented medical history on each patient is like having a medical student examine the patient before you enter the room. It makes the job of gathering the data easier, faster, and better than having to do it entirely yourself. As I sat down, both the patient and I recognized a new format of the office visit—a triangle of the patient, the doctor, and the computer. As I confirmed the history and briefly edited the data that the patient had entered, the subjective note was completed without me dictating a word. Over half of my documentation was totally finished before I started the physical examination. Unhurried, for the first time I could ask my patients open-ended questions about how their illness was affecting their life. I could see quickly that when all the pieces of the computer-based paperless patient medical record functioned together, this would be a new world of healthcare delivery.

Next I examined the patient. I entered the objective data for the physical examination in a documentation-by-exception fashion using hot keys. It was clear that this system was far faster, more complete, and better than any written or the dictated method that I had ever used. Again, everything was complete by the end of the exam with no dictation.

Subsequently, I noticed on the computer screen was the appointment schedule online in real time. I had never seen it before. I never knew how many patients were actually waiting to see me, what time they had arrived, and why they were coming. It was immediately apparent that having the schedule of patients and their presenting complaints was helpful to the workflow. As patients arrived, I had the ability to order tests and procedures in advance of seeing them. This hastened workflow and saved the patient waiting time. Throat cultures were taken of all patients presenting with sore throats. I could look at the names and complaints of familiar patients and order studies from another exam room. This increased my efficiency.

---

[1] Allen R. Wenner M.D., Primetime Medical, Inc.

The other remarkable part of the first morning was a consistency in the presentation of data. The nursing staff checked the vital signs and medications in a uniform fashion. Heretofore, because of any changes in staff necessitated by a large organization, sometimes information was omitted or documented differently in the paper format by various staff members. The computerized format made everything the same. Because the medications were located in a consistent place on the screen, medication review was easier. This increased productivity slightly.

Laboratory, therapeutic, and radiological ordering were next in the workflow. Software streamlined this process and productivity was again enhanced. Electronic prescription writing was faster than any paper equivalent. Coding was frustrating. Coding is a process that is normally performed by the front office staff. Provider coding will enhance coding accuracy. Provider coding is a necessity to avoid rejected insurance claims and to prevent accusations of fraud under Medicare law. Diagnosis coding was difficult because ICD-9-CM does not have practicing physicians in mind as its user. Procedural coding seemed easier, yet still more trouble than writing a five-digit number or circling a superbill entry. I slowed down coding. My neck began to hurt as I realized that I had the keyboard at the wrong height and the mouse was on the wrong side.

I felt lost at many times during the first day, even if only for a moment. Despite my computer skills, I could not remember where I was within the office visit. It was a horrible feeling of not only trying to determine what was wrong with the patient, but also trying to document it appropriately without a scrap of paper. Although the first day was only to be for practice, I had to have the documentation for the legal medical record and I was no longer dictating.

In an electronic system, disposition, instructions, patient education, and referral are all different. The process is markedly different yet more complete. A learning curve is required.

We were late going to lunch as we tried to get the last patients through the system. The first morning we had had a 10% loss of efficiency, but I had expected much worse. At lunch the staff discussed what was happening to other employees. Soon they began to check in our afternoon patients because we missed most of our lunch. Throughout the afternoon minor delays occurred as the originally trained staff members began to show other employees how the system worked. The technical support staff graciously taught other staff how to use the system in brief lessons. Twice the anticipated number used the system by the first afternoon. Less hectic patient flow in the afternoon allowed for more comfort with the software.

Adequate on-site technical support prevented any hardware failures until the last hour, when a computer failure prevented data entry. Aside from that computer hiccup, the day went surprisingly well. Nobody was abandoned in the waiting room unseen for hours. No patient was left in an exam room asleep. No patient departed without a prescription. Indeed, most were given a patient education handout. Patients were favorably impressed that they could see their medical record appearing before their eyes.

The day had gone much better than I had anticipated. My neck hurt as I arrived home. I self-diagnosed a job-related injury from twisting toward the screen on my ill-positioned stool. I denied that my neck pain was tension from the stress of taking a medical office paperless in less than a day. I knew how the Wright brothers felt a hundred years ago. I went to bed early, contemplating the day, knowing we would never go back again. We had left the world of the paper medical record forever.

The advantage of the system is clear. The paperwork is finished at the time the patient leaves the exam room. Patient education is possible. The software assures full documentation of the visit as it is happening. But the most amazing part of it all was that I spent 100% of my day sitting next to my patients. I never left them once!

Chapter Three Summary

In this chapter you have learned about the Student Edition software: the menus and Toolbar, the Nomenclature Pane, the Note View Pane, the Entry Detail fields, as well as the Chief complaint, Free-text Note, the Outline View, and Vital Signs forms.

As you continue through the course, you can refer to the Guided Exercises in this chapter when you need to remember how to perform a particular task.

Task	Guided Exercise(s)	Page #
Starting up and exiting the software	8 and 9	78 and 81
Select a patient	10	82
Navigating Medcin findings and tabs	11 and 12	84 and 87
Creating an new encounter. Setting the date, time, and reason for encounter	13	88
Recording findings		
Subjective findings	14	91
History findings	17	96
Objective findings	20	101
Assessment	24	105
Treatment plan	25	105
Removing findings or selecting findings for edit	15	94
Adding details to the findings		
Adding a value	18	98
Adding free text	19	99
Setting the Result field	21	101
Adding detail to current findings	22	103
Adding episode detail to findings	23	104
Adding free text using the Finding Note window	25	105
Using the Chief complaint form	26	108
Forms tab, Forms Manager, and the Vital Signs form	27	109

EHR software allows clinicians to document the patient exam by selecting findings for symptoms, history, physical examination, tests, diagnoses, and therapy.

The Medcin Student Edition software has been specially created for this course. Therefore it will be different in some aspects from EHR systems you will encounter when working in a medical office, but the concepts, skills, and familiarity with EHR systems that you will acquire by practicing with the Student Edition will transfer directly into the workplace.

To more easily understand the Student Edition software, we divided the screen into four sections and discussed each of them.

1. **The Menu bar and Toolbar** are located at the top of the window.

    The menus are Select, Enter, Options, Forms, Summary, Graph, and Help. Within these are lists of functions in the Student Edition software.

    You select a menu item by positioning the mouse pointer over one of these words and click the mouse once; a list of functions will drop-down below the word. Moving the mouse pointer vertically down the list will highlight each item. Clicking on the highlighted item will invoke that function. Clicking the mouse anywhere on the screen other than the list will close the list.

In the Student Edition, *highlight* means a colored rectangle appears over an item or a button on the Toolbar changes color.

The Toolbar is also located at the top of your screen. It consists of two rows of buttons, each containing a small picture called an icon, and a brief label. The purpose of the Toolbar is to allow quick access to commonly used functions. Clicking on a button in the Toolbar invokes a function or feature. The Exit, Chief, and Forms buttons on the Toolbar were used in this chapter.

2. **The Medcin Nomenclature Pane** is located in the left pane of the window.

    The left pane displays the lists of Medcin findings from which you choose when documenting a patient exam. On the top of the nomenclature pane there are eight tabs. These look like tabs on file folders. Six of the tabs, labeled Sx (symptoms), Hx (history), Px (physical examination), Tx (tests), Dx (diagnosis, syndromes, and conditions), and Rx (therapy or plan) are used to logically group the findings into six broad categories. An additional tab labeled Edit is used when Editing a finding that has already been selected. The Browse tab was not covered in this chapter.

3. **The Encounter View Pane** is located in the right pane of the window. It has two tabs labeled Note View and Outline View. When the clinician selects a finding from the Medcin nomenclature list in the left pane, the text for that finding will display in the right pane.

    The Note View tab dynamically displays the findings accompanied by narrative text automatically generated by Medcin. Titles for the sections of the note are also added dynamically as findings are selected.

    The Outline View displays findings that have been selected and appropriate ICD-9-CM or CPT-4 codes. The extra narrative text is omitted in the Outline View.

4. **The Entry Details** fields are located at the bottom portion of the screen. The Entry Details section consists of two rows of fields and four buttons that affect only the currently selected finding. Using the Entry Details features, the user can add detail or free text to the finding, or remove a finding from the encounter note.

    The first row has two fields and four buttons. The first field displays the finding description as it appears in the text. The field cannot be directly edited. The second field may be used to add short free text to notes to the finding.

    The four buttons are also located in the first row of fields. The first button invokes the Find Note window, which makes it easier to enter longer free-text notes and includes a spell checker. The second and third buttons were not covered in this chapter. The fourth button deletes the current finding from the encounter note (but not from the nomenclature).

    The fields in the second row are Prefix, Modifier, Result, Status, an Episode button, Onset, Duration, Value, and Unit. The fields add informational text to the finding in the encounter note, and in some cases modifies its meaning. The advantage of these fields over free text is that they allow the EHR to store the status, result, and the like as fielded data that can be used later, which free-text entries do not.

Documenting the Encounter

The first step in every encounter is to select the patient, then open an existing encounter or create a new encounter. In this chapter you learned to select patients and create new encounters.

It is important when creating new encounters to use the exact date, time, and reason given in the exercise.

Selecting patients, encounters, adding chief complaint, notes, and selecting forms open small windows that close when the user is finished.

The left pane displays lists of Medcin findings in a *tree* structure where small plus signs indicate more detailed findings are available. Clicking on the button with the small plus sign expands the list further like branches on a tree. When the tree is expanded, the button changes from a small plus sign to a small minus sign. If the button with the small minus sign is clicked, the expanded list collapses to its previous size.

Findings are selected by clicking on buttons with red or blue circles in them located next to each finding. When a finding is selected, circles in the button become filled with red or blue and the finding is displayed in the encounter note. The solid colors in the buttons help you quickly identify which findings have already been selected. Generally, the red button records that a patient has the condition described in the finding. Clicking the blue button generally records that a patient did not have the symptom or the condition described in the finding. The description of the finding in the left pane also changes when a red or blue button is clicked.

Testing Your Knowledge of Chapter 3

You may run the Medcin Student Edition software and use your mouse on the screen to answer the following questions:

1. Which menu did you use to select the patient?
2. Which menu did you use to start a New Encounter?
3. Where did you set the label "10 minute visit," which appeared in the title of the window?

The tabs on the left pane of Medcin findings have medical abbreviations. Write the meaning of each of the following:

4. Sx _____
5. Hx _____
6. Px _____
7. Tx _____
8. Dx _____
9. Rx _____
10. What was the patient's chief complaint?
11. How long had she been having headaches?
12. What was the clinical assessment (her diagnosis)?
13. How did you invoke the Vital Signs window?
14. How do you remove a finding?
15. How did you invoke the Chief complaint window?

Chapter Four

Increased Familiarity with the Software

Learning Outcomes

After completing this chapter, you should be able to:

- Create a new encounter
- Document a patient visit
- Print a copy of the completed encounter note

Applying Your Knowledge

In this chapter, you will practice documenting patient visits using the Student Edition software. One of the goals in this chapter is to increase your familiarity with the software and thereby increase your speed of data entry. Another is to learn how to print your work. You will learn how to use the print function in Exercise 29.

It is important to remember is that the Student Edition software does **not** save your entries to the patient's permanent medical record; therefore, you will **keep a record of your work by printing it**. Whereas in the previous chapter you could stop exercises at any point, in this chapter it is important to complete the entire exercise and print out your work before stopping. You cannot stop and then resume an exercise where you left off. You can print the encounter note at any time and as often as you like while practicing your exercises. However, remember not to quit or exit the program **until you are sure the encounter note has printed**. Once you exit, you will lose your work.

In Chapter 3, you learned the basic layout of the screen and the concepts of creating an encounter note, adding findings, editing findings, and adding details to findings. Detailed instructions for scrolling and navigating the lists, which were provided in the previous chapter, should no longer be necessary. From this point forward, simplified instructions will guide you in areas where you are already familiar with the program. Also, red or blue circles will be printed in the text as a visual cue to indicate whether to click on a red or blue button to select a finding.

Exercises in this chapter are intended to provide conceptual learning experiences with the software. The encounter notes you will produce will be similar to documents you would create in a medical office. However, they are not intended to represent full and complete medical exams.

Creating Your First Patient Encounter Note

In Guided Exercise 28, you will apply what you have learned in Chapter 3 to document Rosa Garcia's visit. In Guided Exercise 29, you will learn to print out your work to hand in to your instructor. You must complete both exercises in a single session. Do not begin Guided Exercise 28 unless you have enough class time remaining to complete both exercises.

Guided Exercise 28: Documenting a Visit for Headaches

The exercise is similar, but not identical to, the cumulative exercises in Chapter 3.

Case Study

Rosa Garcia is a 27-year-old female who visits her doctor's office complaining of headaches for the last five days. She was a heavy coffee drinker who recently stopped all coffee.

Step 1

If you have not already done so, start the Student Edition software.

Locate the Medcin icon shown in Chapter 3, Figure 3-1. If you do not see it on the computer desktop, click on the Start button, and look in Programs or All Programs for the program named Medcin Student Edition.

Step 2

When the Student Edition login screen is displayed, type into the field either your name or student ID.

When your name or ID is exactly as you want it to be, position the mouse pointer over the button labeled "OK," and click the mouse. The Student Edition software window will be displayed.

Step 3

Position the mouse pointer over the word *Select* in the menu at the top of the screen and click the mouse button once. A list of the Select menu options will appear.

Click the mouse on the word *Patient* to invoke the Patient Selection window shown in Figure 4-1.

Locate and click on the patient named **Rosa Garcia**.

Step 4

Again, position the mouse pointer over the word *Select*, and click the mouse button. Move the mouse pointer vertically down the list until the item New Encounter is highlighted. Click the mouse button.

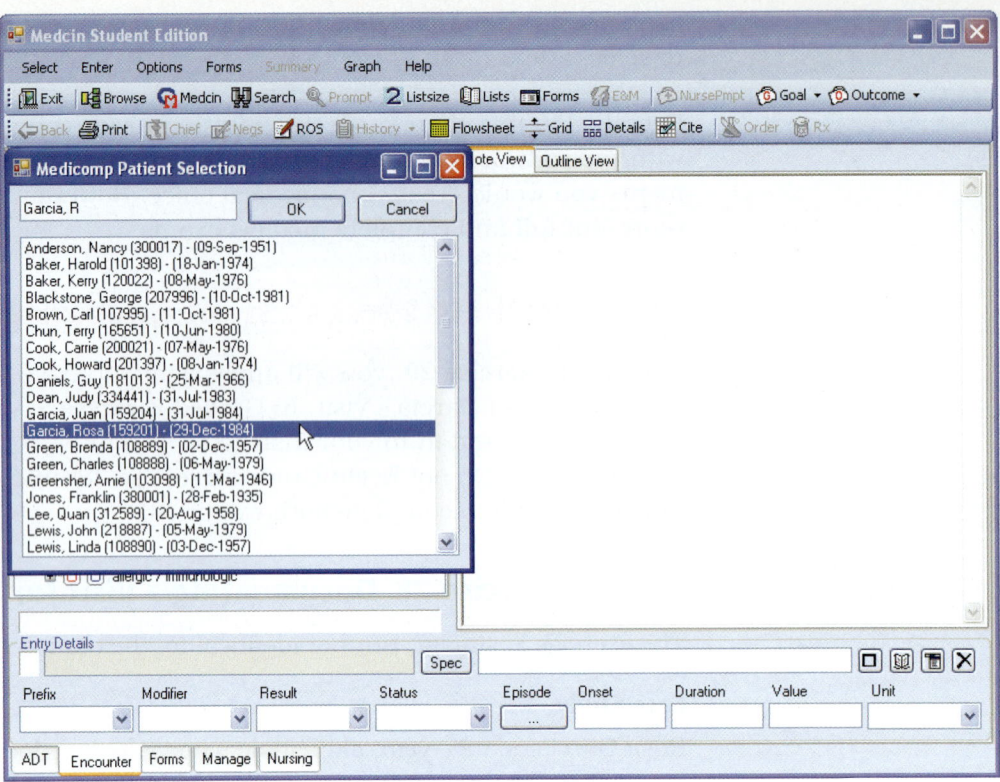

▶ Figure 4-1 Select Rosa Garcia from Patient Selection window.

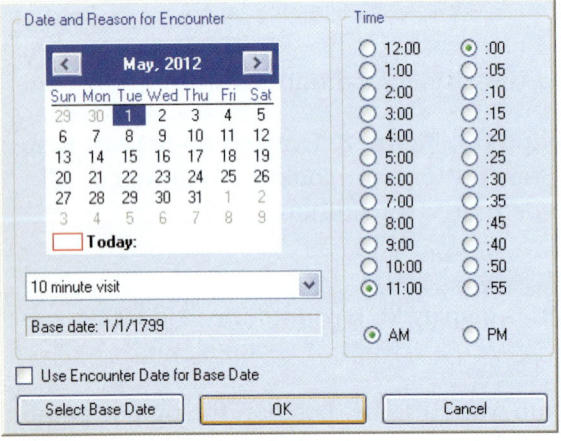

▶ Figure 4-2 New encounter for a 10-minute visit.

Using what you have learned in previous chapters, select the reason **10 minute visit** from the drop-down list.

You do not have to set the date or time for this exercise; you may use the current date. However, be certain to set the encounter reason correctly.

Compare the Reason field on your screen to Figure 4-2 before clicking on the OK button.

The left pane should now display the Medcin Symptoms list and the right pane should display your student ID and Rosa Garcia's information. Before proceeding, confirm that the patient, and the reason for the visit displayed in the title of the window are all correct.

Note

The software calculates the patient's age based on the encounter date. In any exercise where you use today's date instead of the date in the book, the date of the encounter and the age of the patient will differ from the screen figures in the book. Except for the date and age, you should ensure your work matches the figures.

Step 5

Enter the Chief complaint by locating the button in the Toolbar labeled "Chief" and clicking on it.

The Chief complaint window will open; type: "**Headaches for more than 5 days.**"

120 Chapter 4 | Increased Familiarity with the Software

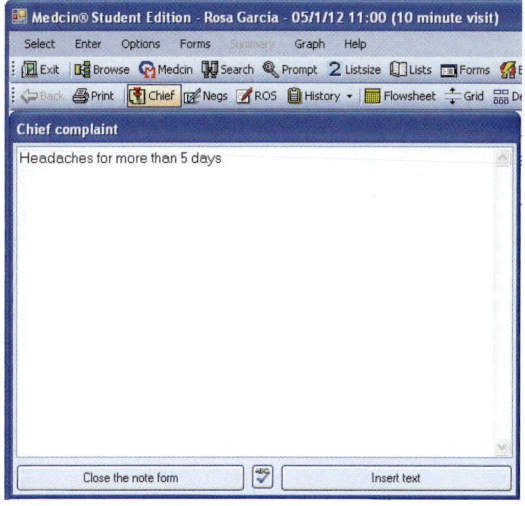

▶ Figure 4-3 Chief complaint: Headaches more than 5 days.

Compare your screen to Figure 4-3. If it is correct, click the button labeled "Close the note form."

Step 6

Make sure that you have the Sx tab in the left pane selected. If you are uncertain, position the mouse pointer over the Sx tab and click the mouse once. Using the skills you have acquired in previous chapters, navigate the list of findings.

Locate and expand the tree of head-related symptoms:

Click on the small plus sign next to "head-related symptoms"

Click on the small plus sign next to "headache"

Click on the small plus sign next to "timing"

Click on the small plus sign next to "chronic/recurring"

Locate and click on the red button next to the following finding:

- (red button) episodes worse recently

Compare your screen to Figure 4-4.

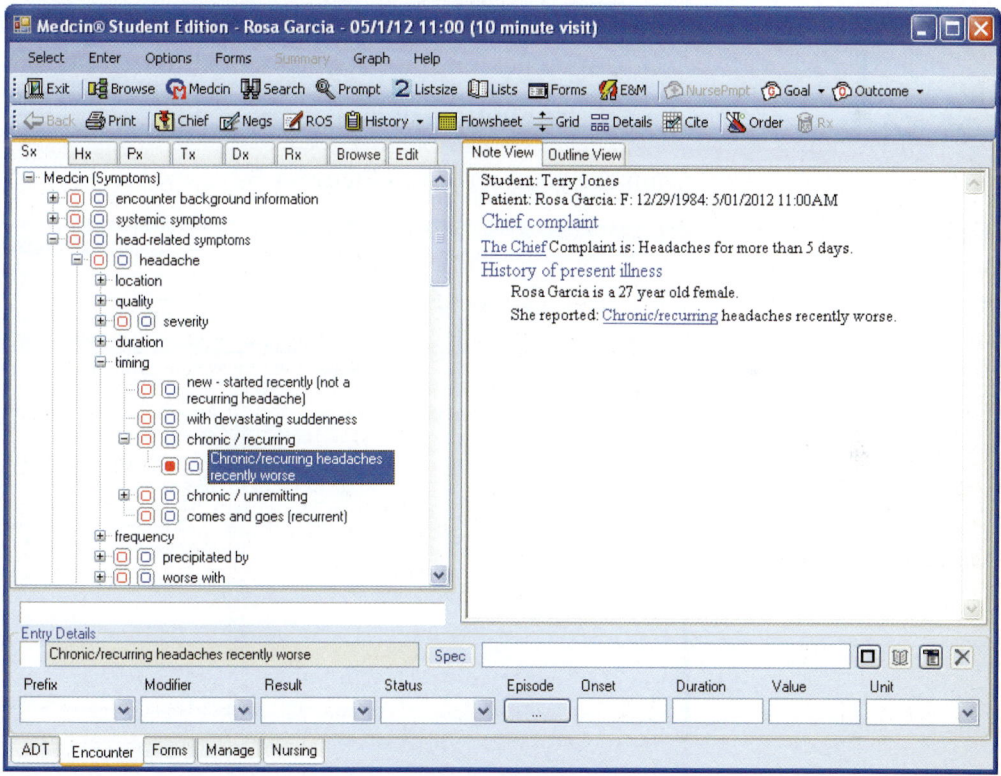

▶ Figure 4-4 Sx tab—Chronic/recurring headaches recently worse.

Step 7

Add information about the episodes of Ms. Garcia's headaches by scrolling the nomenclature pane to show more of the findings under the expanded the tree of headache symptoms:

Locate and click on the small plus sign next to "frequency"

Chapter 4 | Increased Familiarity with the Software 121

▶ **Figure 4-5** Set frequency to daily.

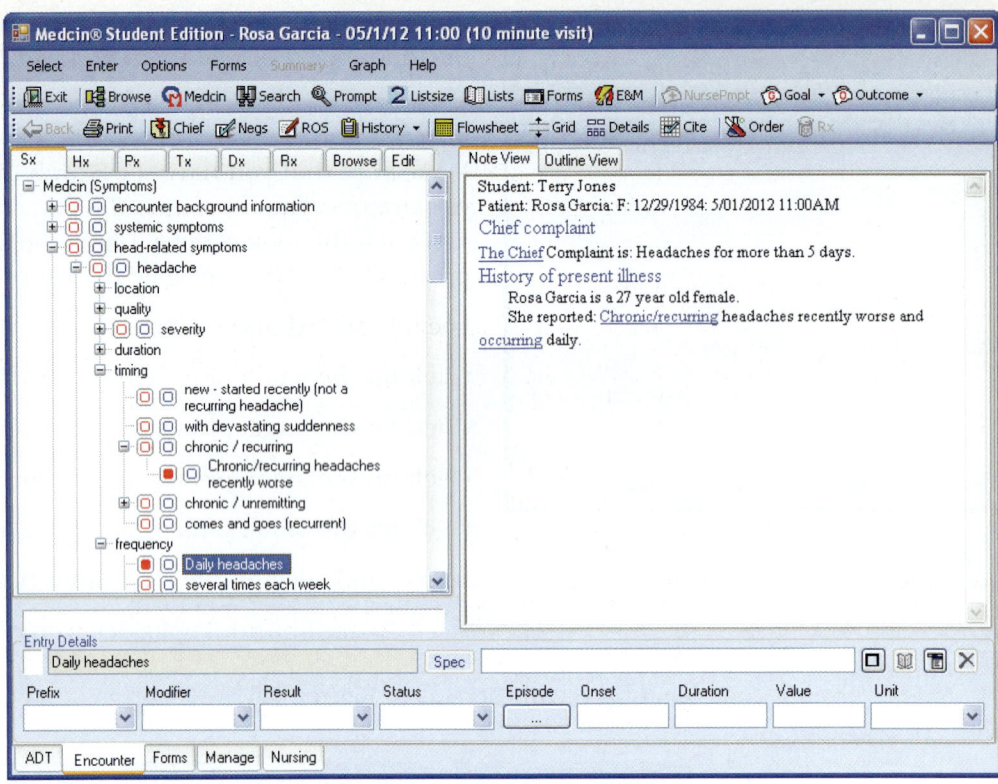

Locate and click on the red button next to the following finding:

- (red button) daily

Compare your screen to Figure 4-5.

▶ **Figure 4-6** Select "inadequately controlled" from the Status drop-down list.

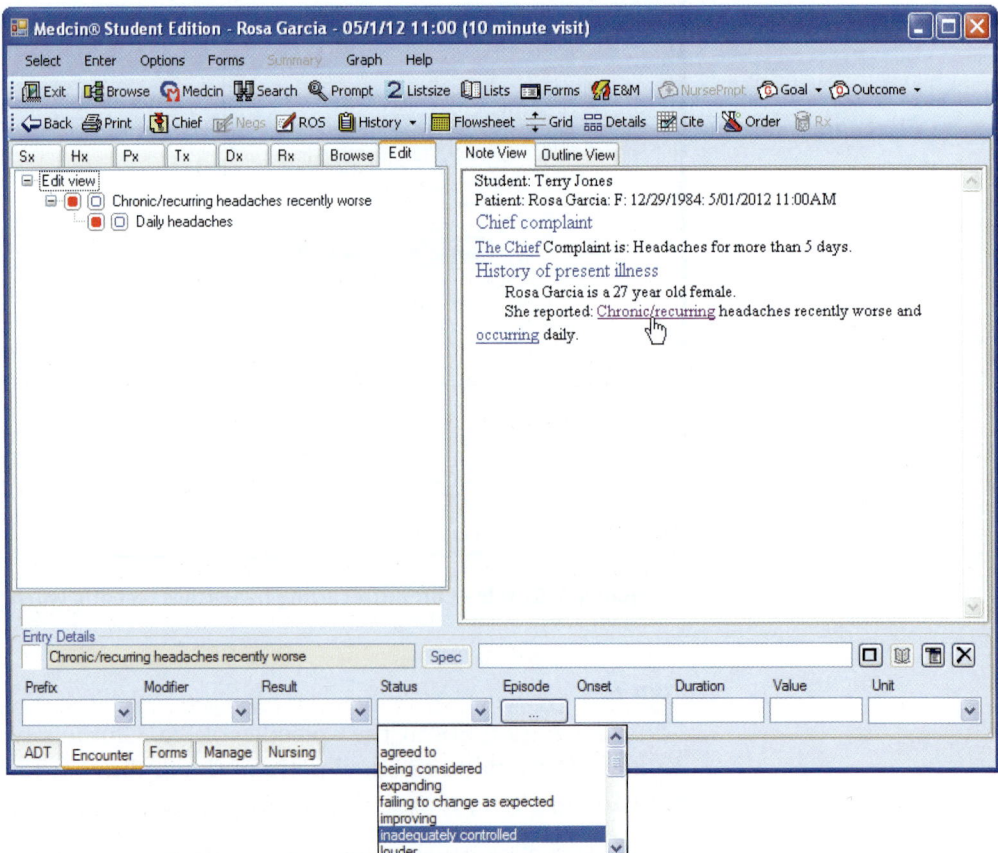

122   Chapter 4 | Increased Familiarity with the Software

Step 8

Select the finding "Chronic/recurring" for edit by moving your mouse pointer over the words *Chronic/recurring* headache in the encounter note pane. When the mouse pointer changes to a hand, click the mouse button. The Sx tab in the left pane should be replaced by the Edit tab with "Chronic/recurring headaches recently worse" as the current finding.

Step 9

Locate the Status field in the Entry Details section at the bottom of the screen. Click your mouse on the button with the down arrow in the status field. A drop-down list of status phrases (as shown in Figure 4-6) will appear.

Position your mouse pointer on the status "inadequately controlled" and click the mouse button.

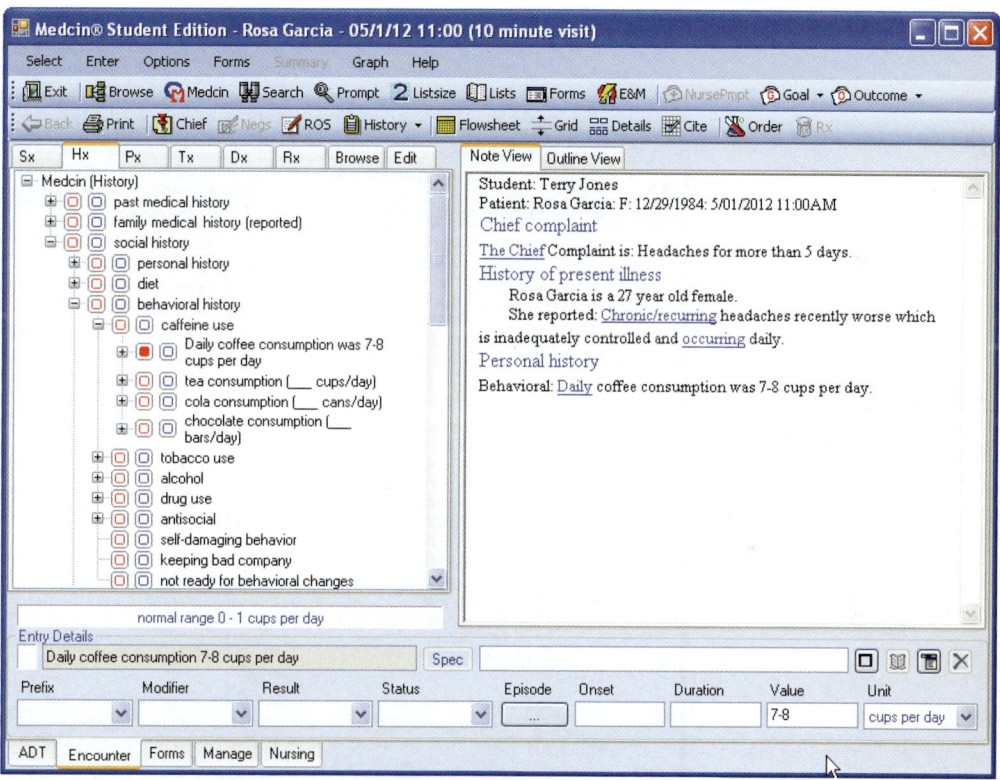

▶ Figure 4-7 Social history—Daily coffee consumption was 7-8 cups.

Step 10

Position the mouse pointer over the Hx tab and click the mouse once.

Expand the social history tree by locating and clicking on the small plus sign next to "social history."

Click on the small plus sign next to "behavioral history."

Click on the small plus sign next to "caffeine use."

Locate and click on the red button next to the following finding:

- (red button) "coffee consumption (cups/day)"

Chapter 4 | Increased Familiarity with the Software **123**

Step 11

Locate the Value and Unit fields in the Entry Details section at the bottom of the screen. Notice that the Unit field already contains the words "cups per day."

Click your mouse on the Value field and type the numerals **7-8**.

Press the Enter key on your keyboard.

Compare your screen to Figure 4-7.

Step 12

In the left pane, click on the small plus sign next to "Daily coffee consumption was 7-8 cups per day." This will expand the tree.

Locate and click on the red button next to the following finding:

- (red button) "recently decreased"

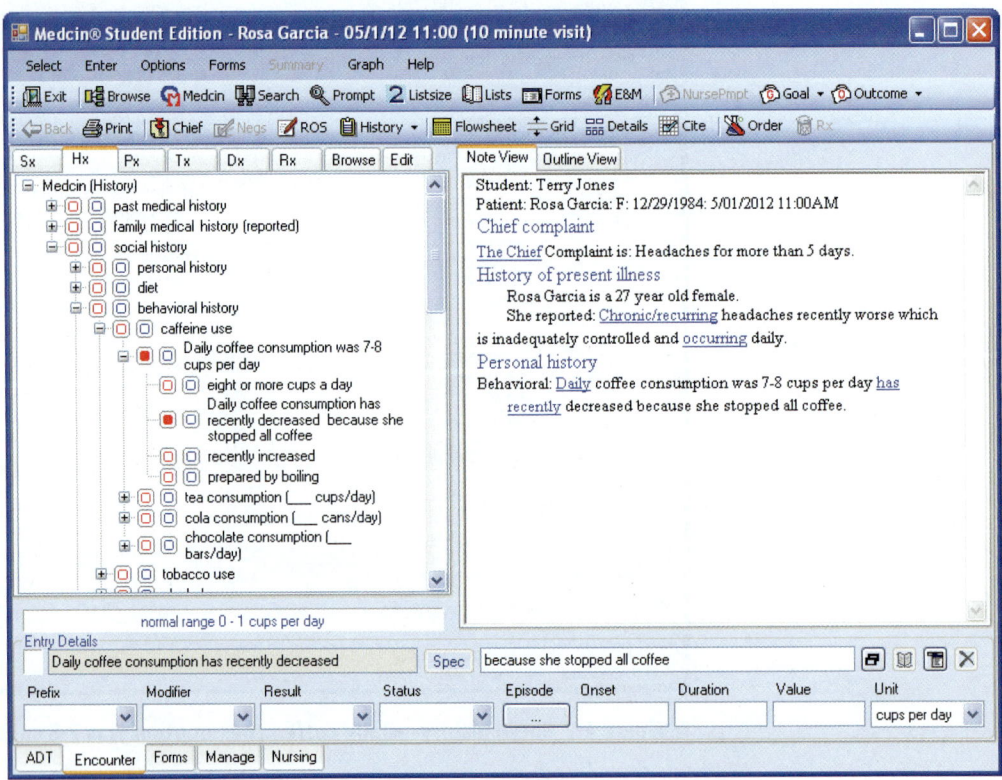

▶ Figure 4-8 Caffeine recently decreased because she stopped all coffee.

Step 13

Locate the free-text field in the first row of the Entry Details section, under the right pane.

Click your mouse in the free-text field. Type **"because she stopped all coffee"** in the field and then press the Enter key on your keyboard. Compare your screen with Figure 4-8.

124 Chapter 4 | Increased Familiarity with the Software

Step 14

Locate and click on the button labeled "Forms" in the top row of the Toolbar. The tabs at the bottom screen will automatically change to the Form tab. The Forms Manager window will be invoked.

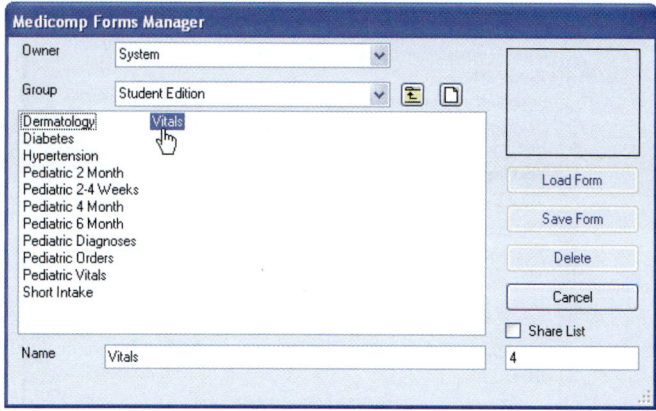

Locate and double-click on the form labeled "Vitals," as shown in Figure 4-9.

Step 15

Enter Ms. Garcia's vital signs into the corresponding fields as follows:

Temperature:	98.6
Respiration:	24
Pulse:	78
BP	120/78
Height:	64
Weight:	140

▶ Figure 4-9 Select vitals from Forms Manager.

When you have entered all of the vital signs, compare your screen to Figure 4-10 and then click your mouse on the Encounter tab at the bottom of the screen.

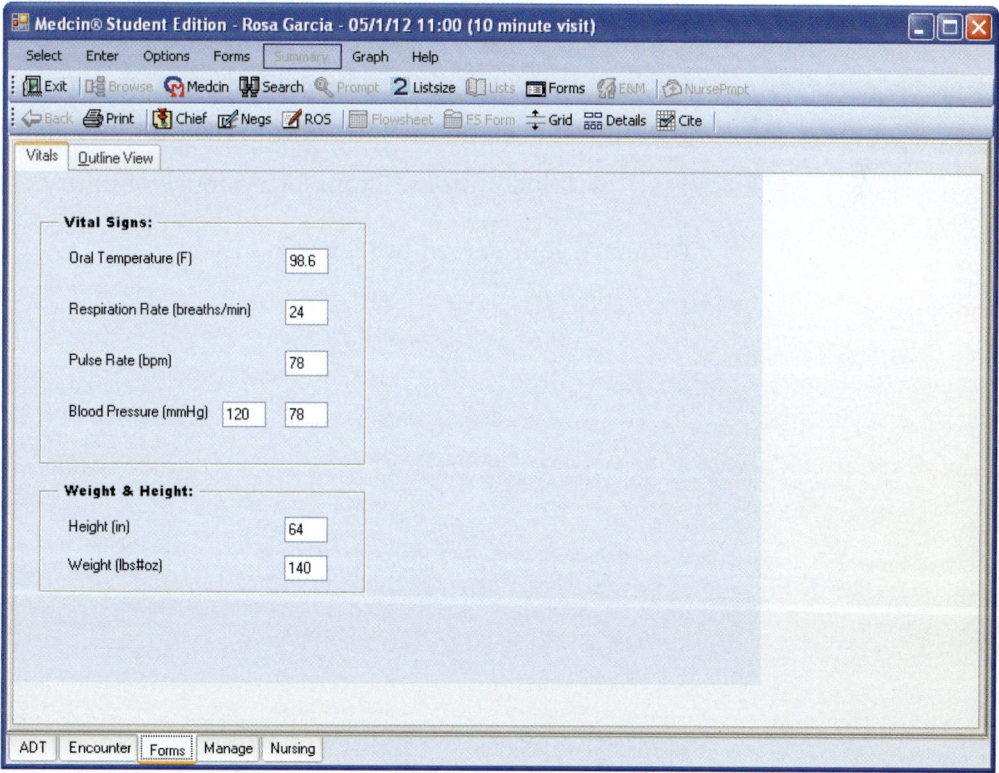

▶ Figure 4-10 Information for Rosa Garcia entered in Vitals form.

Chapter 4 | Increased Familiarity with the Software   **125**

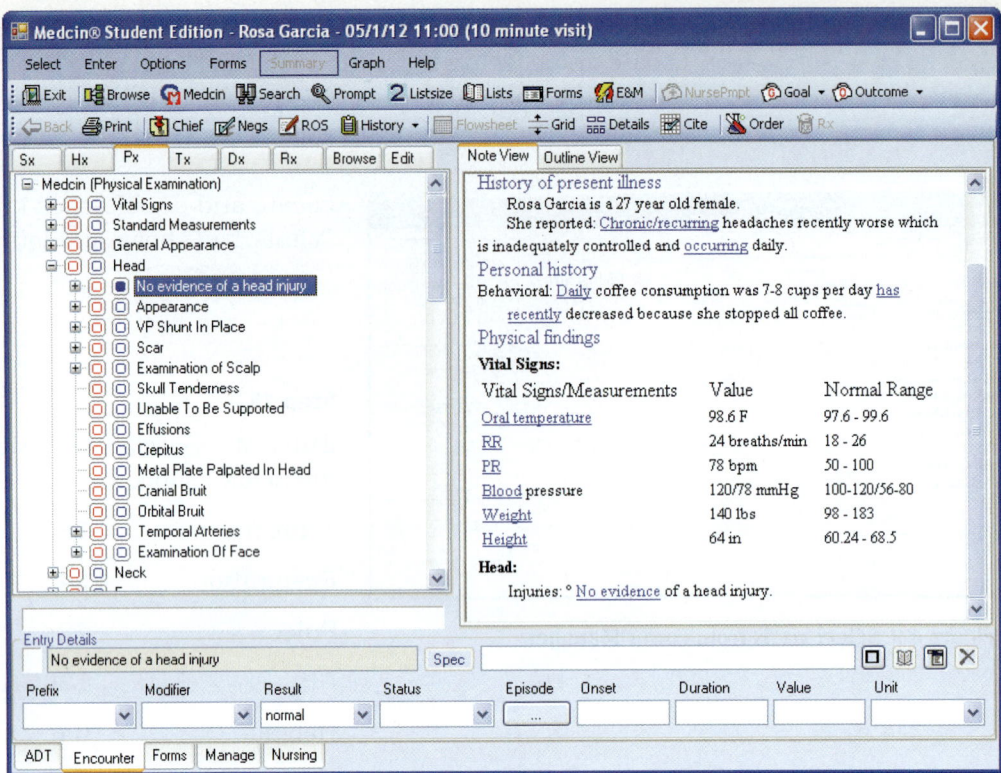

▶ Figure 4-11 Px tab—No evidence of head injury.

Step 16

Position the mouse pointer over the Px tab and click the mouse once. Notice that the vital signs information has been recorded in the encounter note under the Physical Findings section.

Click on the small plus sign next to "Head" to expand the list.

Locate and click on the blue button next to the following finding:

- (blue button) "Exam for evidence of injury".

Compare your screen to Figure 4-11.

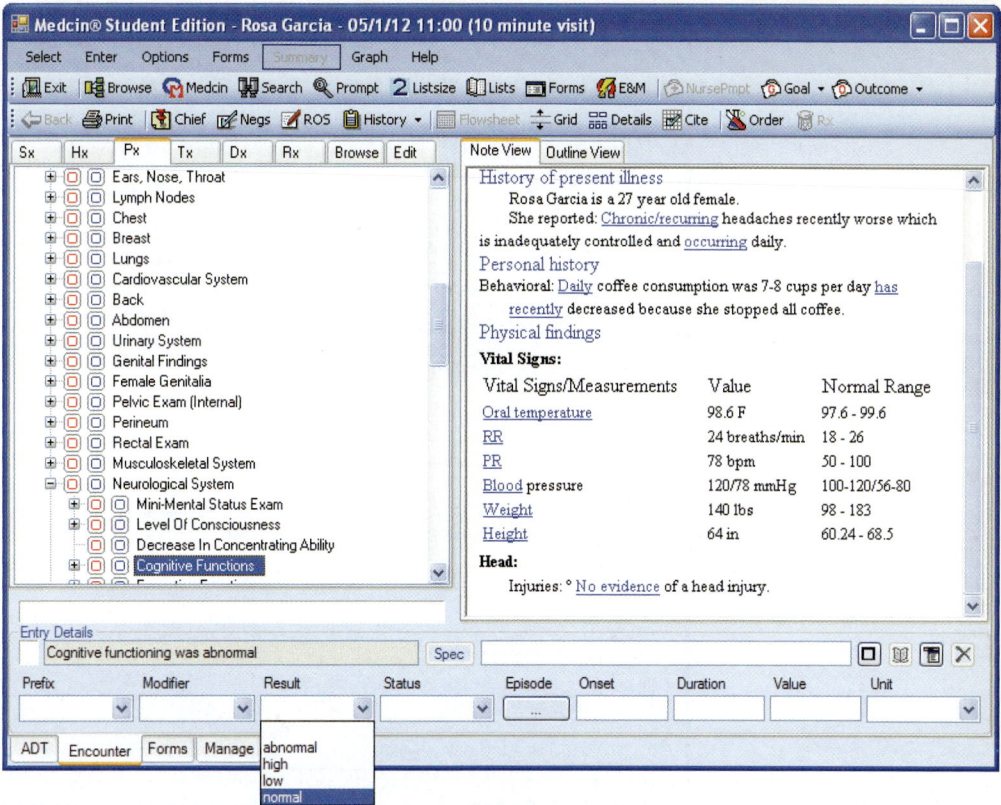

▶ Figure 4-12 Setting cognitive functions to normal.

Step 17

Using the mouse, scroll the list of physical examination findings until you see Neurological System. Expand the list by clicking on the small plus sign next to "Neurological System."

Locate and highlight the finding "Cognitive Functions" by clicking your mouse on the description. Do not click either the red or blue button.

Locate the Result field in the Entry Details section at the bottom of the screen. Click your mouse on the down arrow button within the Result field. A drop-down list will appear (as shown in Figure 4-12).

Position your mouse pointer on the result "normal" and click the mouse button. The result field will display the word "normal," the button next to the finding should be blue, and the text in the encounter note should read "Cognitive functioning was normal."

Chapter 4 | Increased Familiarity with the Software

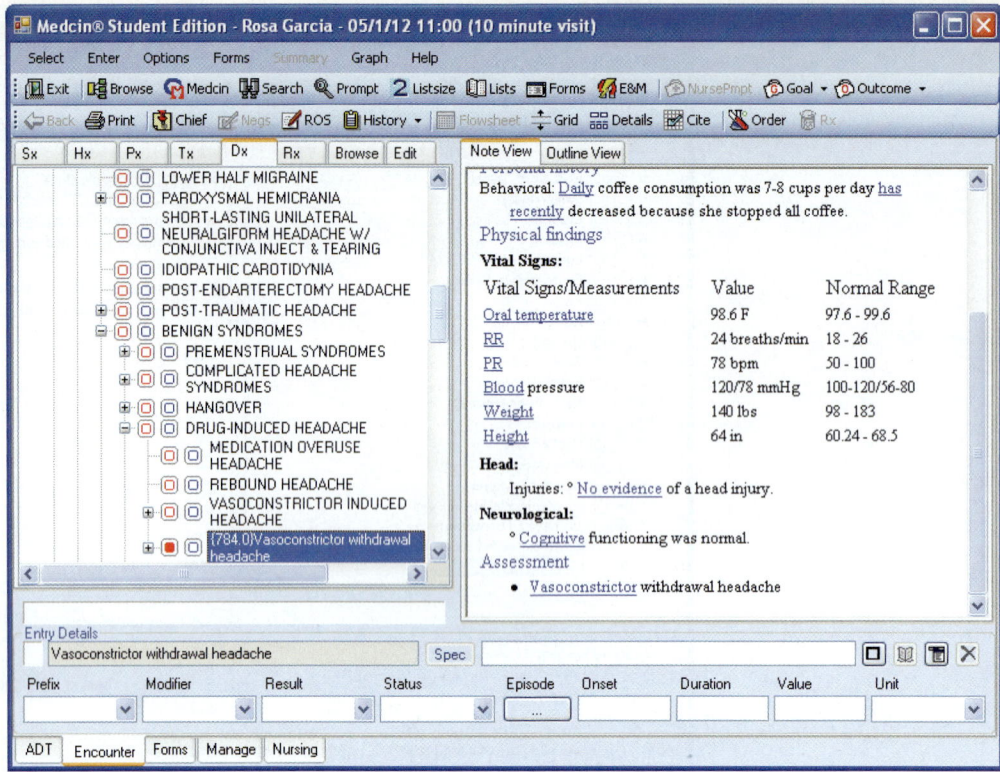

▶ Figure 4-13 Dx tab—Assessment: withdrawal headache from caffeine.

Step 18

Position your mouse pointer on the "Dx" tab and click the mouse. The Diagnosis, Syndromes, and Conditions list should be displayed in the left pane of the window.

Scroll the list downward until you see "Neurologic Disorders." Click on the small plus sign to expand the list.

Locate "Headache Syndromes" in the list and click on the small plus sign.

Scroll the list further downward until you see "Benign syndromes" and then click on the small plus sign.

Scroll the list further downward until you see "Drug-induced headache" and then click on the small plus sign.

Scroll the list further downward until you see "Vasoconstrictor withdrawal headache" and then click on the small plus sign.

Locate and click on the red button next to the following finding:

- (red button) "from caffeine"

Compare your screen to Figure 4-13. The finding "Vasoconstrictor withdrawal headache from caffeine" should be recorded in the encounter note under a new heading: "Assessment."

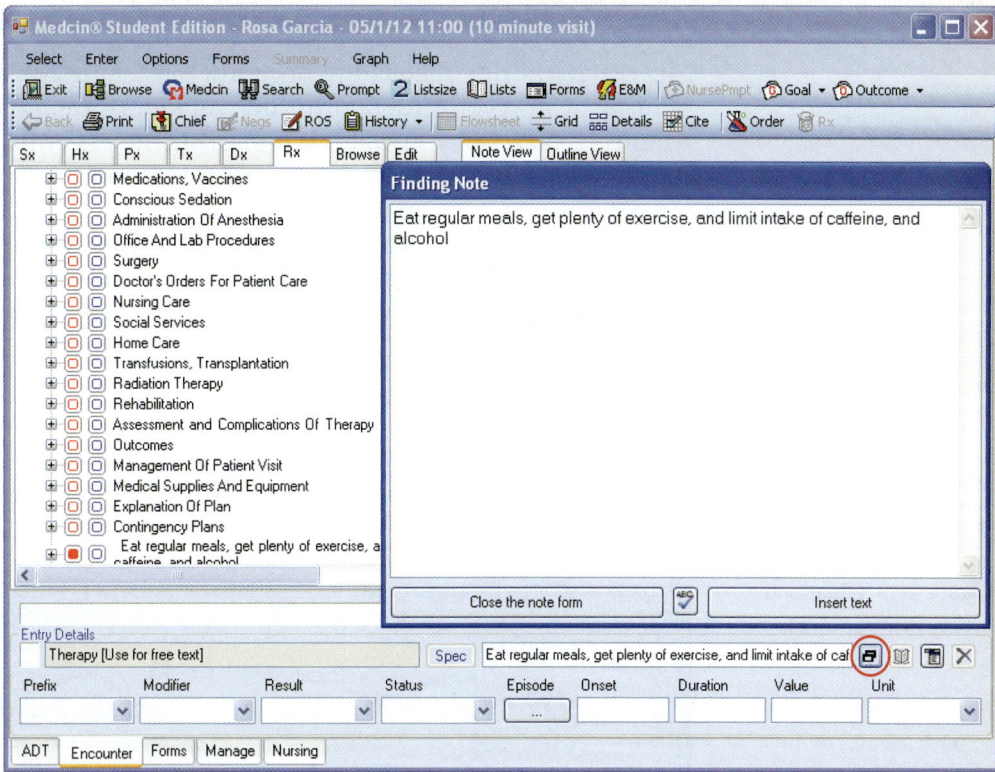

▶ Figure 4-14 Rx tab—free-text therapy note.

Step 19

Position the mouse pointer on the Rx tab and click the mouse button. The Medcin Therapy list will be displayed.

Scroll the list until you see "Free Text," then and click on the red button next to the finding:

- ● (red button) "Free Text"

Locate and click on the Finding Note button in the lower right corner of your screen (circled in red in Figure 4-14). A small Finding Note window will be invoked.

Type the following text into the Finding Note window: "**Eat regular meals, get plenty of exercise, and limit intake of caffeine, and alcohol.**"

When you have finished, compare your Finding Note window to the one shown in Figure 4-14. If it is correct, click your mouse on the button labeled "Close the note form." This will add your text to the encounter note.

You have now successfully created your first complete encounter note. However, do not stop or close the program until you complete the following exercise.

Chapter 4 | Increased Familiarity with the Software

Guided Exercise 29: Printing the Encounter Note

The Student Edition software does **not** save your entries to the patient's permanent medical record; therefore, you will **keep a record of your work by printing it.** In this exercise, you will learn to print the encounter note. You will be asked to give your finished printout to your instructor.

You can use either of two methods to print your work, sending the output to a printer or to a file. The method you will use will be based on the policy of your school. Your instructor will tell you which to use. The choice of printer or file is selected from the Print Dialog window.

Step 20

Position your mouse pointer over the menu item Select at the top of the screen and click your mouse button. A list of the Select menu functions will appear (see Figure 4-15).

▶ Figure 4-15 File menu showing print options.

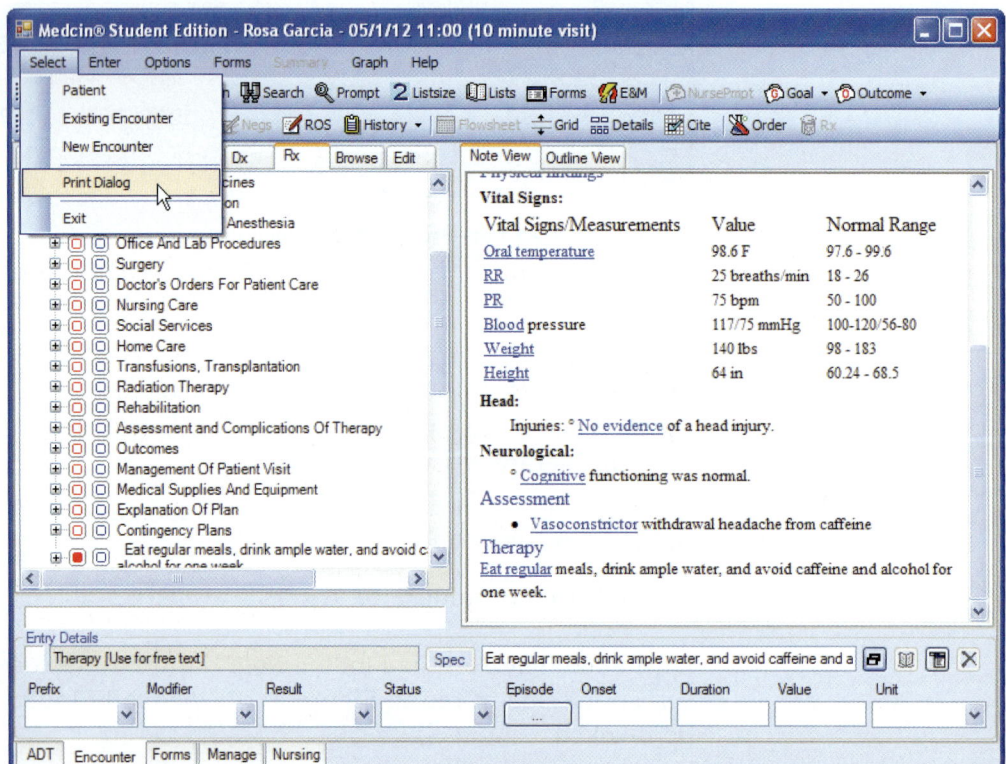

Move the mouse pointer vertically down the list until Print Dialog is highlighted and then click the mouse button. The Print Data window (shown in Figure 4-16) will be invoked.

The two panes on the left of the Print Data window list items that are available for printing. A check box selects the items you wish to print. If the box next to "Current Encounter" does not have a check mark, position your mouse pointer over it and click the mouse button. A check mark should appear in the box.

The right pane displays a preview of what is to be printed.

Located below the right pane are two rows of buttons. Those of interest to us are as follows:

▶ Figure 4-16 Print Dialog window.

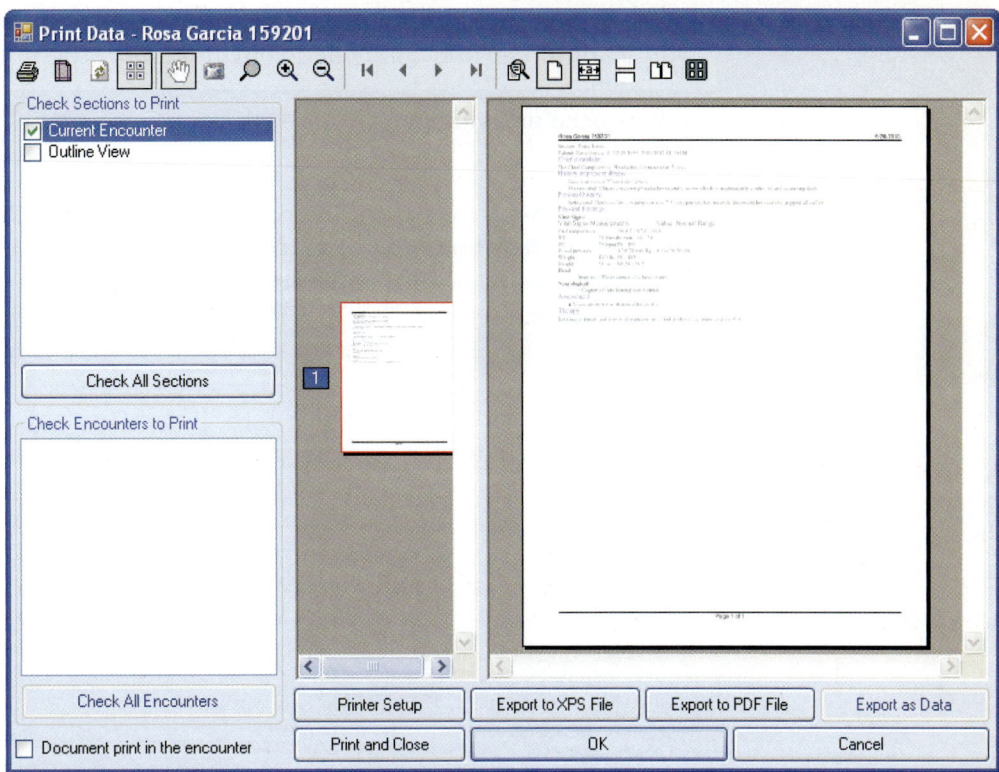

Print and Close	Prints the items selected with check marks to a local or networked printer. This produces a paper copy you can hand in to your instructor.
Export to XPS File	Outputs the items selected with check marks to a file on your local computer. The file can be copied to a disk or flash drive, or e-mailed to your instructor. The XPS file is a Microsoft file that can be viewed with Internet Explorer.
Export to PDF File	Outputs the items selected with check marks to a file on your local computer. The file can be copied to a disk or flash drive, or e-mailed to your instructor. The PDF file is a file that can be viewed with Adobe Acrobat Reader®.

Your instructor will tell you which method is appropriate for your class.

Step 21 Print a Paper Copy of the Encounter Note

If the instructor wants you to export a file, skip this step and proceed to step 22.

If the instructor wants you to print out a paper copy, locate the button labeled "Print and Close" and click the mouse.

Depending on how your computer is set up, an additional print window from the operating system may appear. Figure 4-17 shows an example. Yours may be different, but if you

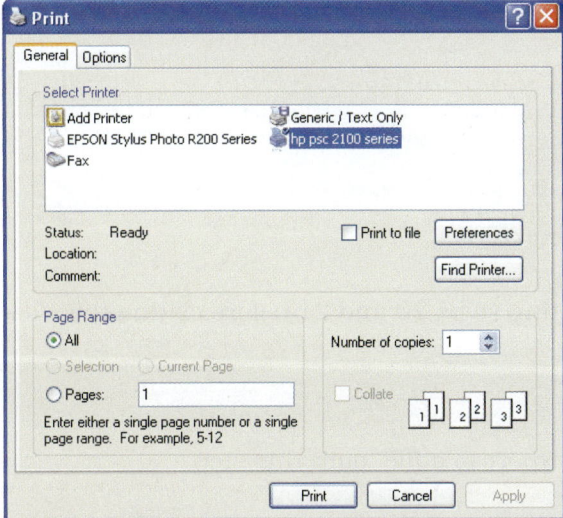

▶ Figure 4-17 Additional print window from operating system.

Chapter 4 | Increased Familiarity with the Software   131

see a printer dialog similar to this, verify that the printer name is the printer you want to use and then click your mouse on the button labeled "Print."

If you need assistance printing, ask your instructor.

 **Alert** Some printers may close the print window before the printing has even started. Therefore, do not exit the Student Edition program or go on to another exercise until you have your printout in hand. You could lose your work.

Compare your printout to Figure 4-18. If there are any differences (other than the date and patient age), review the previous steps in the exercise and find your error.

```
Rosa Garcia                                                              Page 1 of 1

Student: your name or ID here
Patient: Rosa Garcia: F: 12/29/1984: 5/01/2012 11:00AM
Chief complaint
The Chief Complaint is: Headaches for more than 5 days.
History of present illness
     Rosa Garcia is a 27 year old female.
She reported: Chronic/recurring headaches recently worse which is inadequately controlled
and occurring daily.
Personal history
Behavioral: Daily coffee consumption was 7-8 cups per day has recently decreased because
she stopped all coffee.
Physical findings
Vital signs:
Vital Signs/Measurements                    Value                    Normal Range
Oral temperature                            98.6 F                   97.6 - 99.6
RR                                          24 breaths/min           18 - 26
PR                                          78 bpm                   50 - 100
Blood pressure                              120/78 mmHg              100-120/56-80
Weight                                      140 lbs                  98 - 183
Height                                      64 in                    60.24 - 68.5
Head:
Injuries: ° No evidence of a head injury.
Neurological:
          ° Congnitive functioning was normal.
Assessment
       • Vasoconstrictor withdrawal headache from caffeine
Therapy
Eat regular meals, get plenty of exercise, and limit intake of caffeine, and alcohol.
```

▶ **Figure 4-18** Printed encounter note for Rosa Garcia.

You may print extra copies by repeating steps 20 and 21 before exiting the Student Edition software.

Step 22 Print to a File

Unless the instructor wants you to export to a file, omit this step.

To export to a file instead of printing to paper, click mouse pointer on the appropriate button (either Export to XPS File or Export to PDF File as directed by your instructor.)

The action of either button is to create a file on your computer in the directory named My Documents. The file name will include the student name or ID you entered when you logged in plus the date and time. The file name ends in either "XPS" or "PDF."

When the file has been successfully created, a confirmation similar to Figure 4-19 will be displayed.

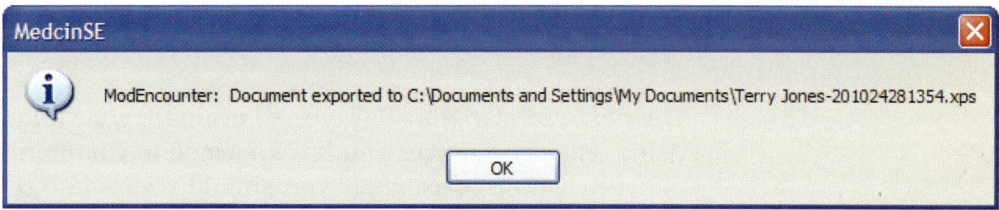

▶ **Figure 4-19** Export to file confirmation.

Write down the file name shown in the dialog box, then click on the OK button.

Once the file has been created, you can copy it to a disk or e-mail it, as directed by your instructor. Use the computer operating system to locate the file on your computer. It will be located in the directory named "My Documents." Follow your instructor's directions for handing in your file.

The instructor can view or print the student XPS file using Internet Explorer as shown in Figure 4-20. The instructor can view or print the student PDF file using Adobe Acrobat Reader (not shown).

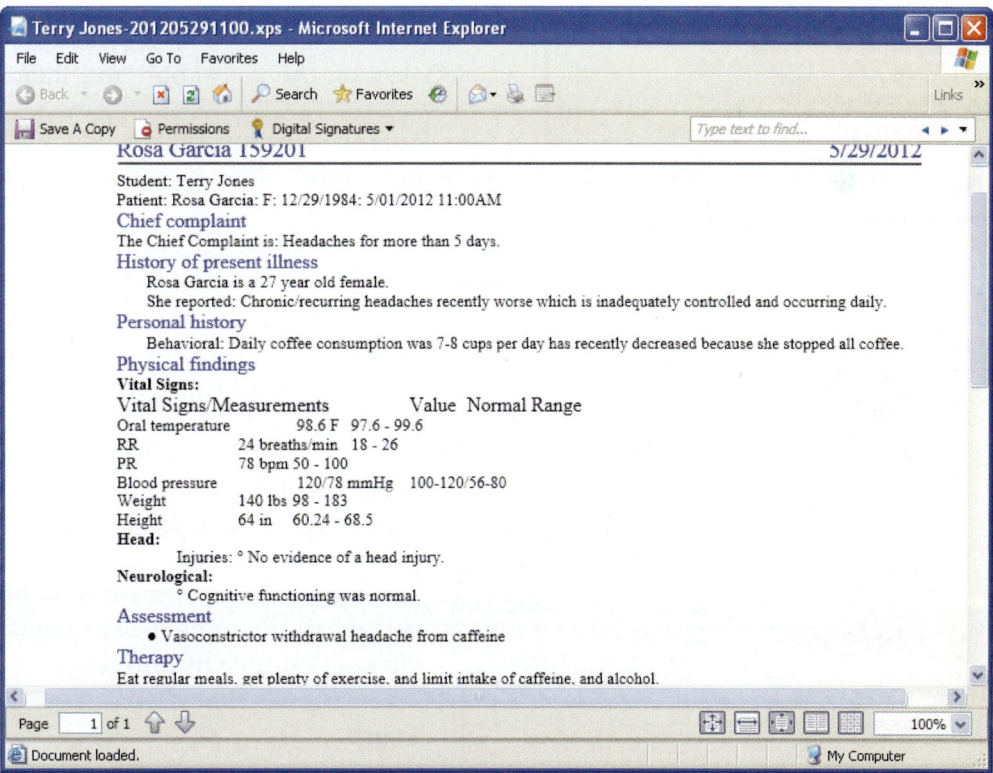

▶ **Figure 4-20** Student XPS file displayed with Internet Explorer.

Chapter 4 | Increased Familiarity with the Software

Invoking the Print Dialog Window from the Toolbar

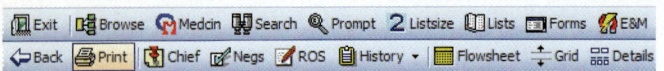

▶ Figure 4-21 Print button on Toolbar (highlighted).

Another way to invoke the Print Dialog window is by clicking the button labeled "Print" on the Toolbar at the top of your screen (highlighted orange in Figure 4-21). You can print out or export copies of the encounter note as frequently as you like, and at anytime during an exercise.

Documenting a Brief Patient Visit

The next exercise will allow you to evaluate your knowledge of the software by using only the features you have learned in Chapters 3 and 4. If you have any difficulty with this exercise, you should review and repeat the exercises in Chapter 3 before continuing with this chapter.

Guided Exercise 30: Documenting a Visit for Common Cold

Using what you have learned so far, document Mr. Baker's brief exam.

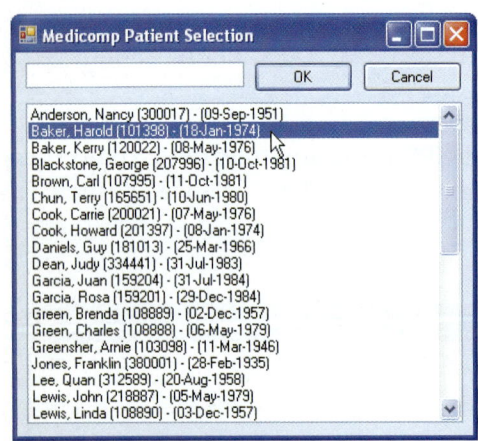

▶ Figure 4-22 Selecting Harold Baker from the Patient Selection window.

Case Study

Patient Harold Baker feels like he has caught some sort of "bug." Like many patients who have a cold, he wants to see his doctor, and so the medical office has scheduled a brief 10-minute office visit for him.

Step 1

If you have not already done so, start the Student Edition software.

Click Select on the Menu bar, and then click Patient.

In the Patient Selection window (shown in Figure 4-22), visually locate and double click on patient **Harold Baker**.

Alternatively, you can always type the patient's *last name, first name* in the field at the top of the window as you did in Chapter 3.

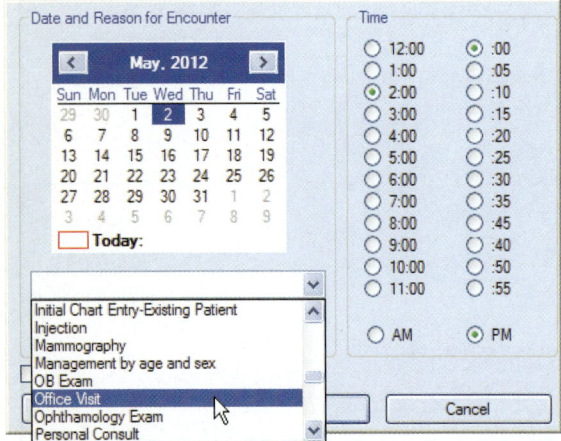

▶ Figure 4-23 New encounter for an office visit.

Step 2

Click Select on the Menu bar, and then click New Encounter.

Scroll the drop-down list to locate the reason **Office visit**, as shown in Figure 4-23, and then click on it.

You may use the current date for this exercise, but be certain that you have selected the correct reason before clicking on the OK button.

Step 3

Enter the Chief complaint by locating the button in the Toolbar labeled "Chief" and clicking on it.

134 Chapter 4 | Increased Familiarity with the Software

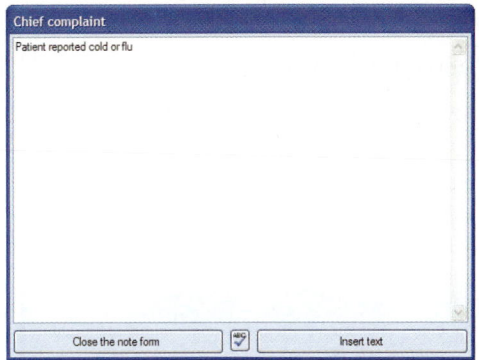

▶ Figure 4-24 Chief complaint dialog for patient reported cold or flu.

In the dialog window that will open, type "**Patient reported cold or flu.**"

Compare your screen to Figure 4-24 before clicking on the button labeled "Close the note form."

Step 4

The patient reports a headache, runny nose, and sneezing. Enter the patient's symptoms using the list of findings on the Sx tab.

Expand the tree of Medcin findings.

Locate and click on the small plus sign next to "head-related symptoms."

Locate and click on the red button next to the following finding:

● (red button) Headache

Compare your screen to Figure 4-25.

▶ Figure 4-25 Symptom—Headache.

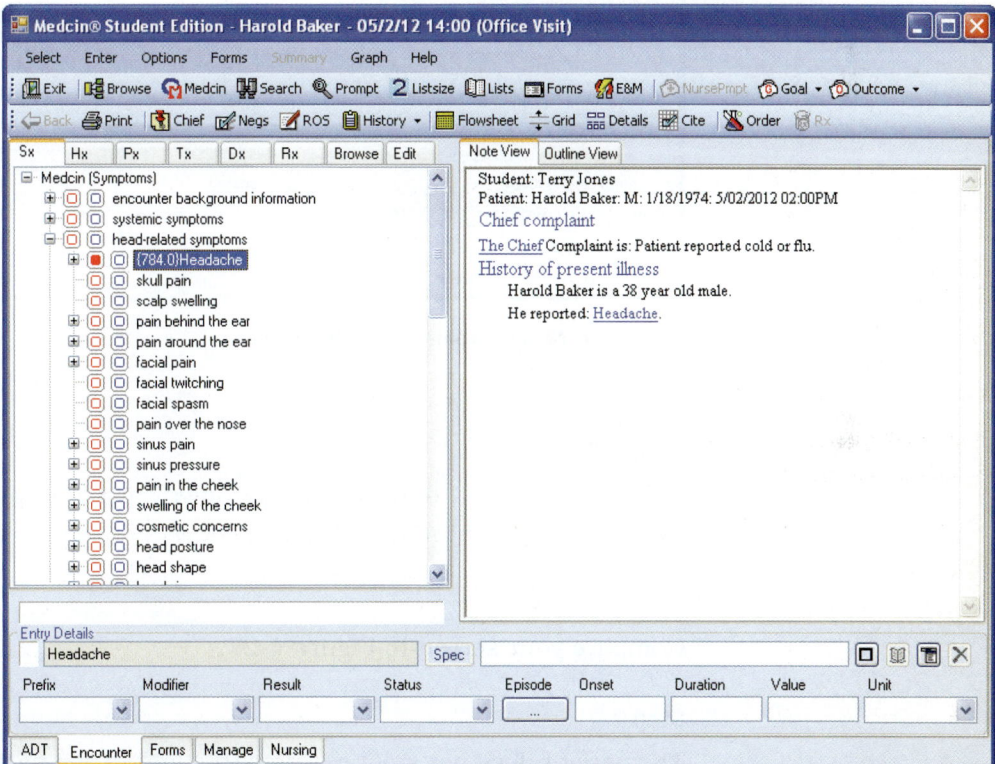

Step 5

Scroll the list of Sx findings downward to locate "otolaryngeal symptoms."

Click on the small plus sign next to "otolaryngeal symptoms."

Expand the tree of findings further.

Locate and click on the small plus sign next to "nose."

Chapter 4 | Increased Familiarity with the Software

Locate and click on the small plus sign next to "nasal discharge."

Locate and click on the red button for the following finding:

- (red button) watery

Compare your screen to Figure 4-26.

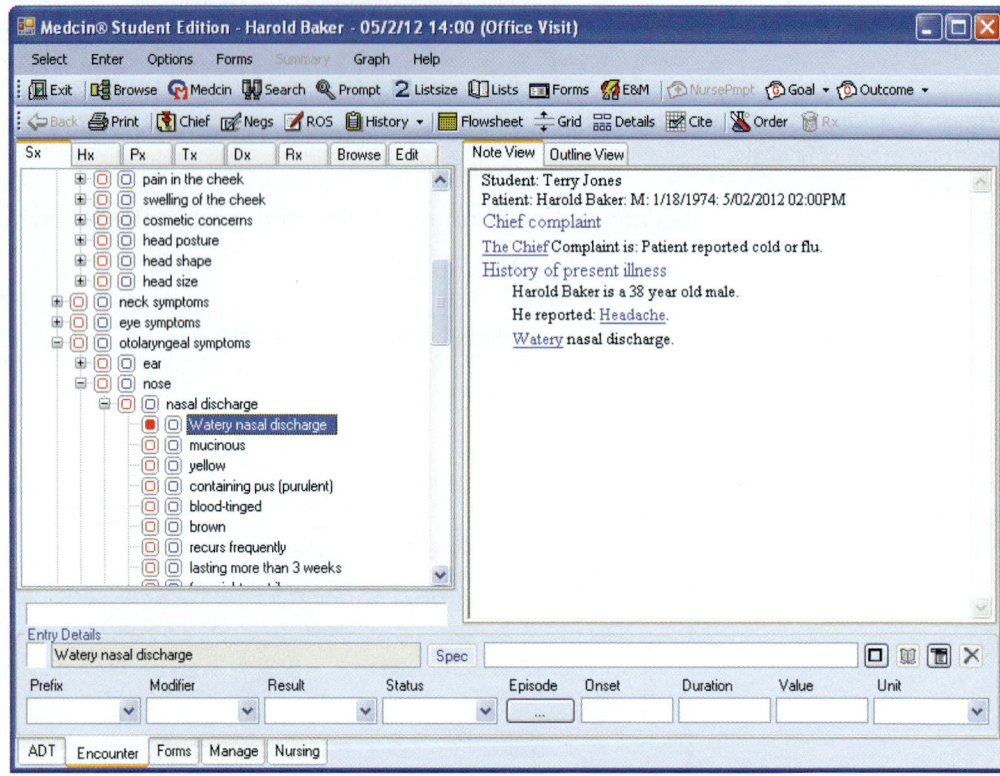

▶ Figure 4-26 Symptom—Nasal discharge.

Step 6

Scroll the list of Sx findings further downward to locate and click on the red button for the following finding:

- (red button) Sneezing

Compare your screen to Figure 4-27.

Step 7

The patient does not smoke. Enter this fact in the patient's history.

Click on the Hx tab.

Expand the tree of Medcin findings.

Locate and click on the small plus sign next to "social history."

Locate and click on the small plus sign next to "behavioral history."

Locate and click on the blue button next to the following finding:

- (blue button) Tobacco use

▶ Figure 4-27 Symptom—Sneezing.

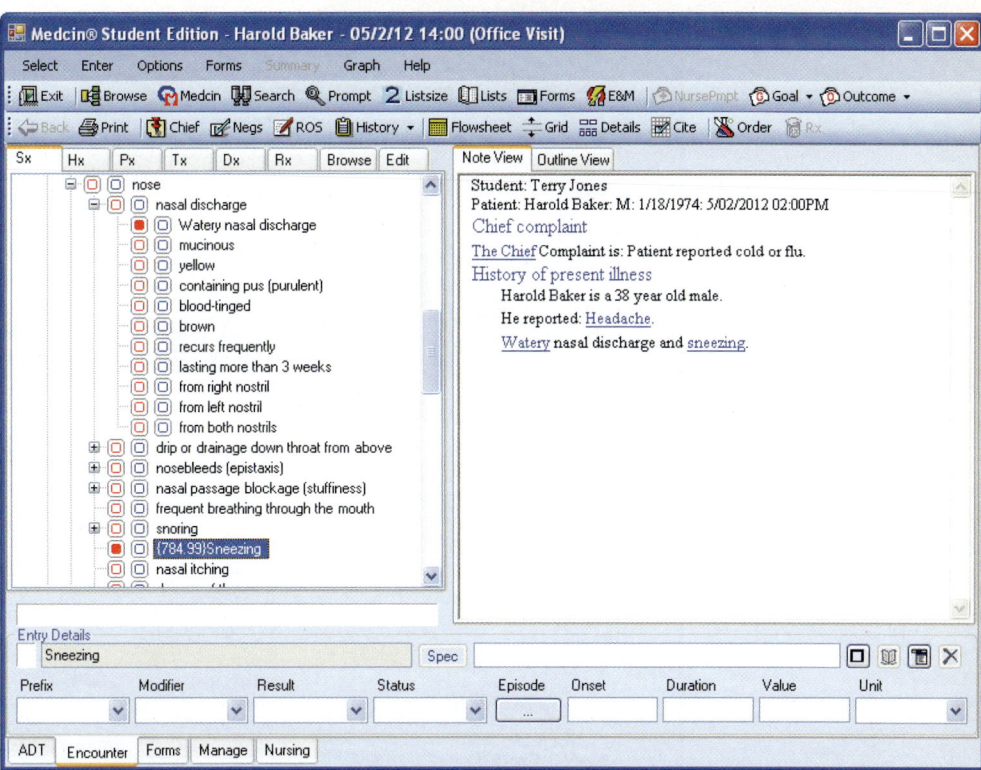

▶ Figure 4-28 History—No tobacco use.

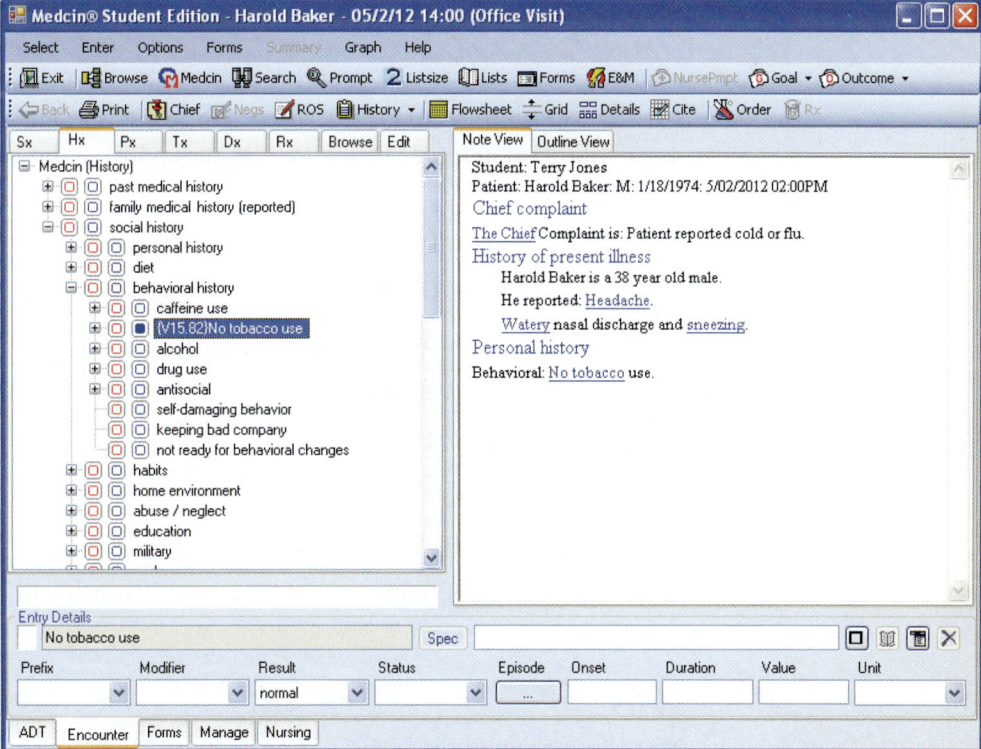

The description will change to "No tobacco use."

Compare your screen to Figure 4-28.

Step 8

Locate and click on the button labeled "Forms" in the top row of the Toolbar. The tabs at the bottom of the screen will automatically change to the Form tab and the Forms Manager window will be invoked.

Chapter 4 | Increased Familiarity with the Software

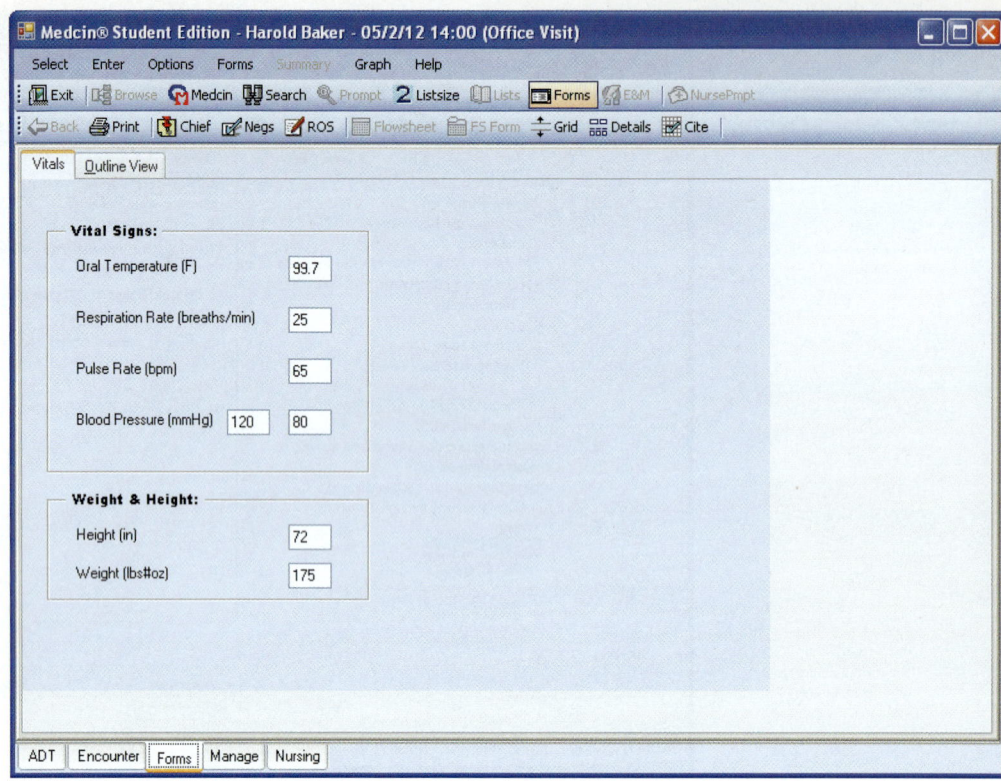

▶ Figure 4-29 Vital Signs form.

Locate and double-click on the form labeled "Vitals." The form shown in Figure 4-29 will be displayed. Enter Mr. Baker's vital signs in the corresponding fields as follows:

Temperature: 99.7

Respiration: 25

Pulse: 65

BP: 120/80

Height: 72

Weight: 175

When you have entered all of the vital signs, compare your screen to Figure 4-29 and then click your mouse on the Encounter tab at the bottom of the screen.

Step 9

The clinician examines the patient's head, eyes, ears, nose, inside of mouth, and lungs.

Begin recording the Physical Examination by clicking on the Px tab.

Locate and click on the small plus sign next to "Head."

Locate and click on the blue button next to the following finding:

- (blue button) Exam for evidence of injury

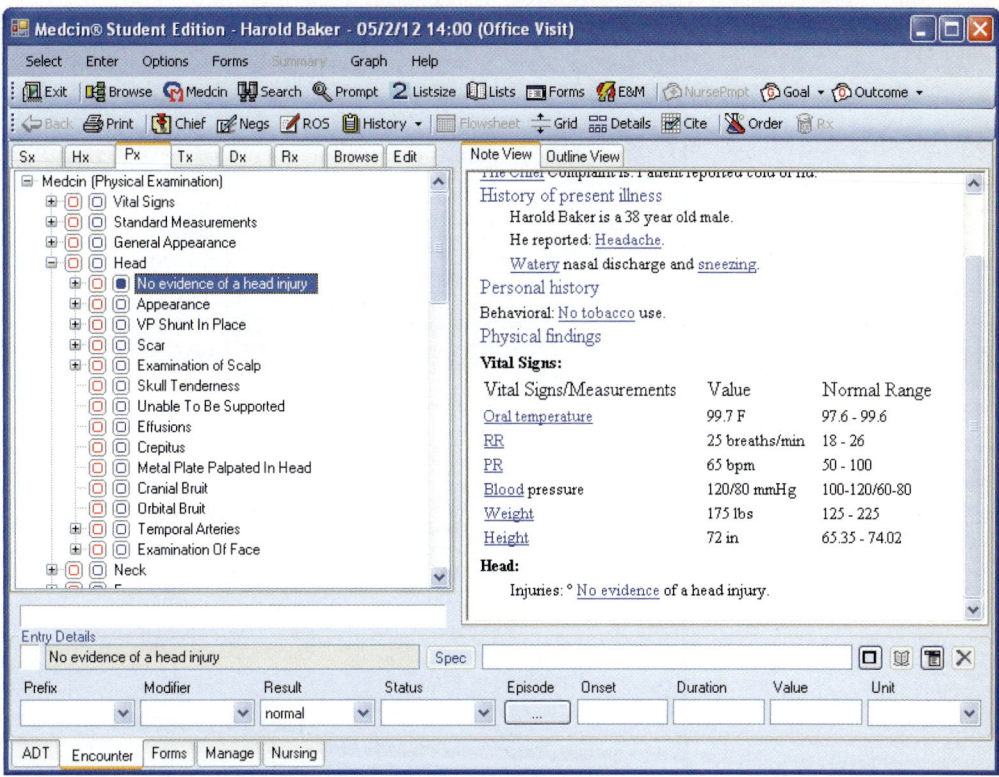

▶ Figure 4-30 Physical Exam—No evidence of head injury.

The description will change to "No evidence of injury." Compare your screen to Figure 4-30.

Step 10

Scroll the list of Physical findings downward to locate "Eyes."

Locate and click on the blue button for the following finding:

- (blue button) Eyes

Expand the tree of findings further.

Locate and click on the small plus sign next to "Ears, Nose, and Throat."

Locate and click on the small plus sign next to "Nose."

Locate and click on the buttons indicated for the following findings:

- (blue button) Ears
- (red button) Nasal Discharge
- (blue button) Sinus tenderness
- (blue button) Upper airway

Compare your screen to Figure 4-31.

▶ **Figure 4-31** Physical Exam—Eyes, ears, and nose.

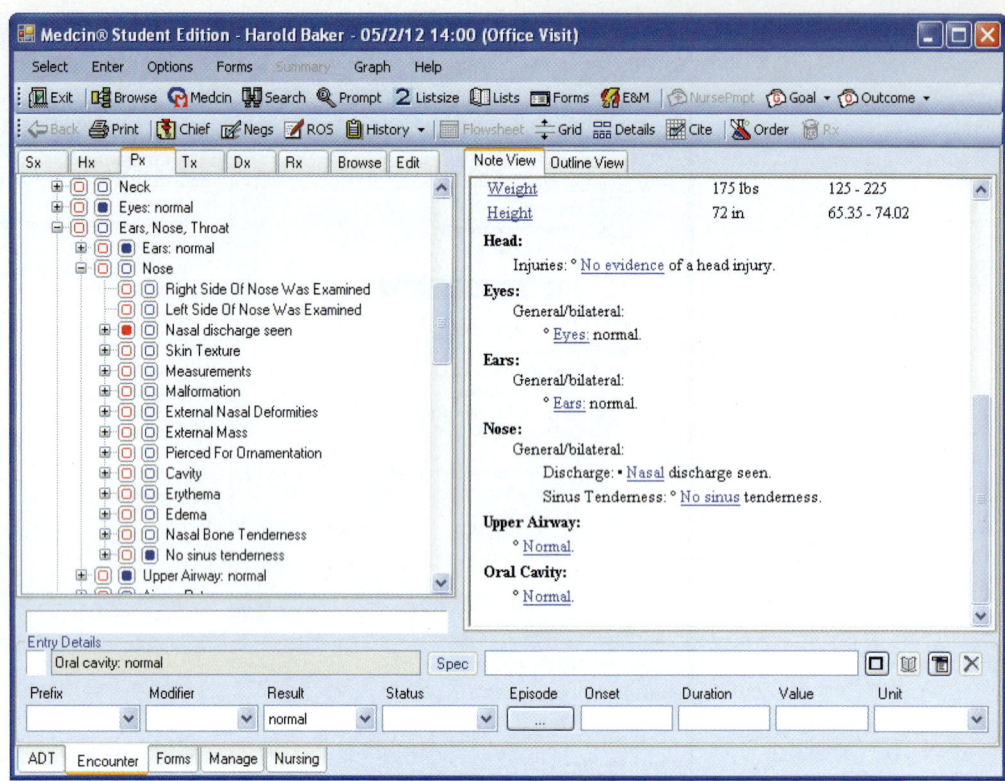

▶ **Figure 4-32** Physical Exam—Throat and lungs.

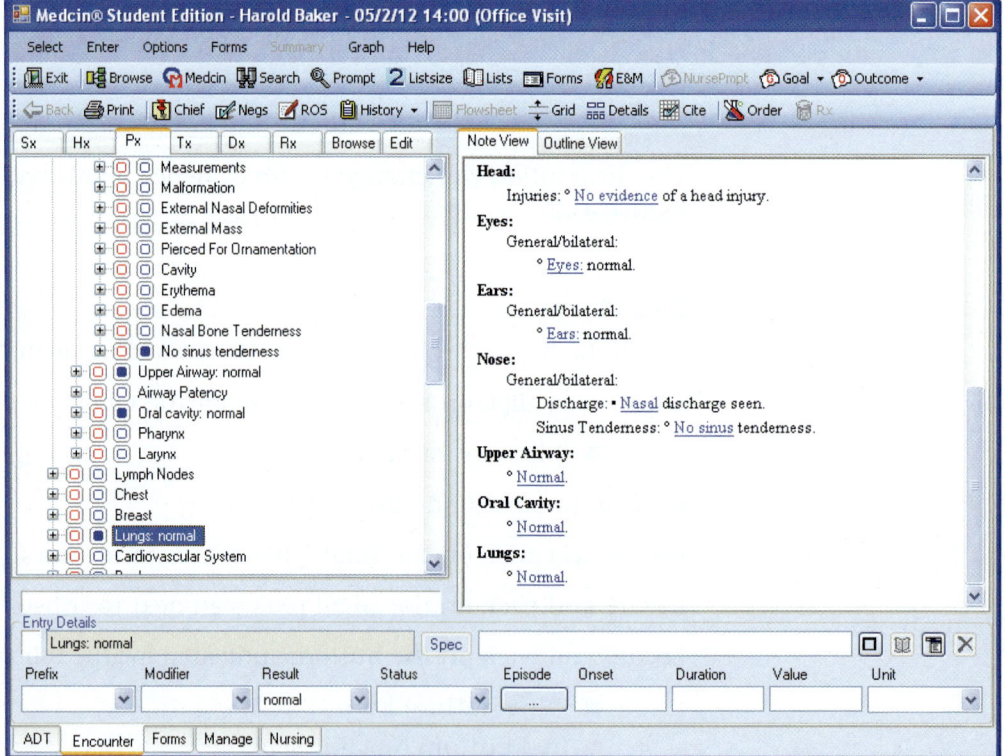

Step 11

Scroll the list of Physical findings further downward to locate "Lungs."

Locate and click on the blue buttons for the following findings:

- (blue button) Oral cavity
- (blue button) Lungs

Compare your screen to Figure 4-32.

Step 12

The clinician concludes the patient has a common cold, and tells him to rest and drink plenty of fluids.

Record the Assessment by clicking on the Dx tab.

Expand the tree of findings.

Locate and click on the small plus sign next to "ENT Disorders."

Locate and click on the small plus sign next to "Nose."

Locate and click on the red button for the following finding:

- (red button) Common cold

Compare your screen to Figure 4-33.

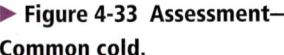

Figure 4-33 Assessment—Common cold.

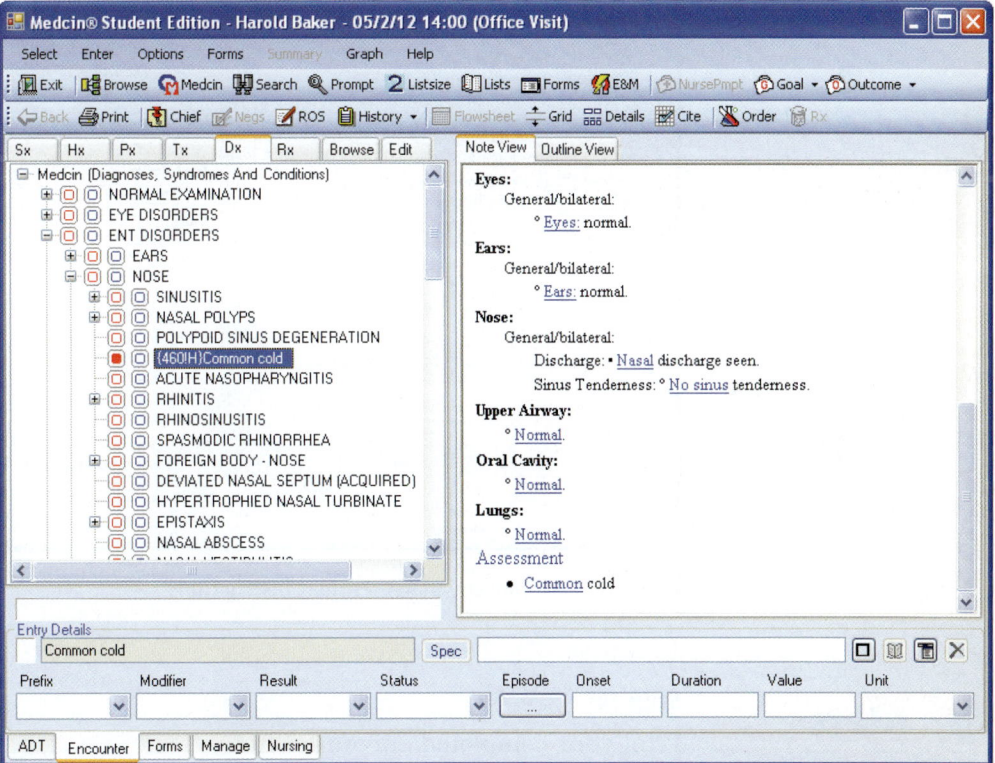

Step 13

Record the Plan by clicking on the Rx tab.

Expand the tree of findings.

Locate and click on the small plus sign next to "Basic Management Procedures and Services."

Scroll the list downward until you locate "Nutrition and Hydration Services," then click on the small plus sign next to it.

Chapter 4 | Increased Familiarity with the Software

Locate and click on the red button for the following finding:

- (red button) Fluids

Expand the tree of findings further.

Locate and click on the small plus sign next to "Education and Instructions."

Locate and click on the small plus sign next to "Instructions for Patient."

Locate and click on the red button for the following finding:

- (red button) Bed rest

Compare your screen to Figure 4-34.

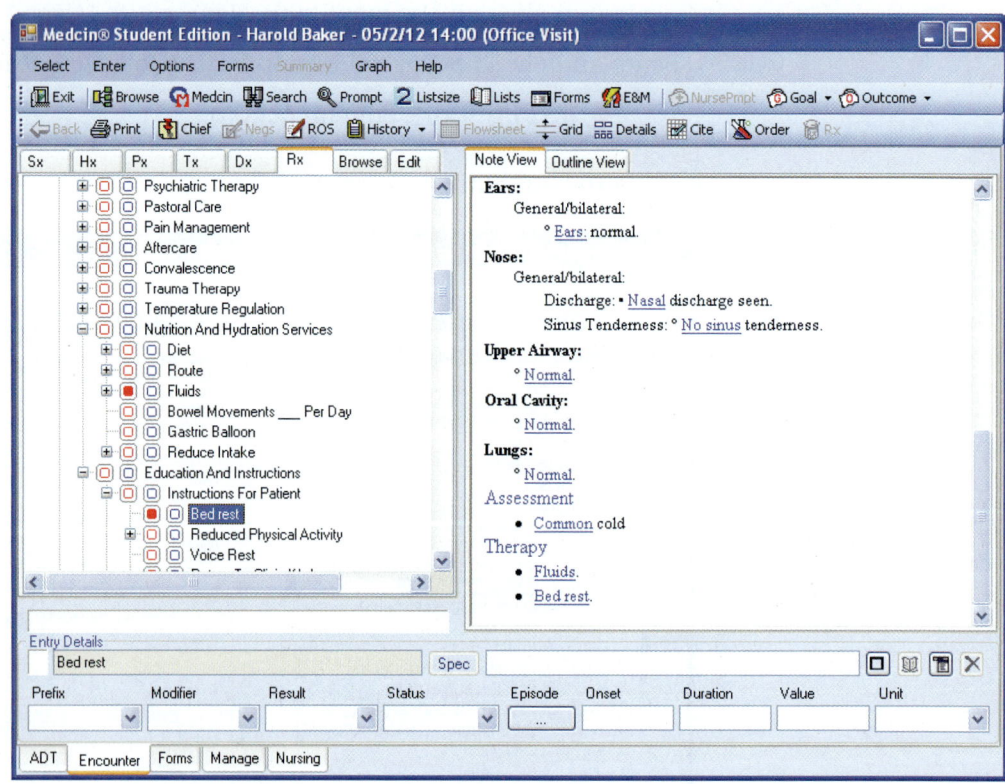

▶ Figure 4-34 Therapy plan—Patient instructions.

Do not close or exit the encounter until you have a printed copy in your hand. You will lose your work if you exit before printing.

Step 14

Print your completed encounter note.

Click on the Print button on the Toolbar at the top of your screen to invoke the Print Data window.

Look at the upper left pane of the window. If the box next to "Current Encounter" does not have a check mark, position your mouse pointer over it and click the mouse button. A check mark should appear in the box.

Click on either the button labeled "Print and Close," or "Export to XPS File," or "Export to PDF File," as directed by your instructor.

142 Chapter 4 | Increased Familiarity with the Software

Compare your printout or file output to Figure 4-35. If it is correct, hand it in to your instructor. If there are any differences (other than the date and patient age), review the previous steps in the exercise and find your error.

```
Harold Baker                                                    Page 1 of 1

Student: your name or ID here
Patient: Harold Baker: M: 1/18/1974: 5/02/2012 02:00PM
Chief complaint
The Chief Complaint is: Patient reported cold or flu.
History of present illness
     Harold Baker is a 38 year old male.
He reported: Headache.
Watery nasal discharge and sneezing.
Personal history
Behavioral: No tobacco use.
Physical findings
Vital signs:
Vital Signs/Measurements            Value              Normal Range
Oral temperature                    99.7 F             97.6 - 99.6
RR                                  25 breaths/min     18 - 26
PR                                  65 bpm             50 - 100
Blood pressure                      120/80 mmHg        100-120/60-80
Weight                              175 lbs            125 - 225
Height                              72 in              65.35 - 74.02
Head:
Injuries: ° No evidence of a head injury.
Eyes:
General/bilateral:
    ° Eyes: normal.
Ears:
General/bilateral:
    ° Ears: normal.
Nose:
General/bilateral:
Discharge: • Nasal discharge seen.
Sinus Tenderness: ° No sinus tenderness.
Upper Airway:
         ° Normal.
Oral Cavity:
         ° Normal.
Lungs:
    ° Normal.
Assessment
   • Common cold
Therapy
   • Fluids.
   • Bed rest.
```

▶ **Figure 4-35** Printed encounter note for Howard Baker.

Once you have successfully completed this exercise, you should be comfortable with the general process of locating findings and expanding the tree to view additional findings. Future exercises in this book will instruct you to expand the tree by listing multiple findings for which you will click the small plus signs.

Real-Life Story

A Nurse's Notes

By Sharyl Beal, RN

Sharyl Beal is a registered nurse with a master's degree in nursing and a subspecialty in nursing informatics. Sharyl has over 35 years nursing experience. She served as a nurse and a department head for 16 years before becoming a clinical systems analyst at a 500-bed hospital in the Midwest where she was involved in creating and implementing electronic medical records for the nursing and ancillary departments, as well as training the nurses and doctors to use the clinical systems. She currently serves as a project manager for the Clinical Information Systems department and is co-author of the book, Electronic Health Records and Nursing.

Our hospital has successfully transitioned all nursing units to computerized patient charts. We rolled it out very slowly, one unit at a time, taking three years to implement all the areas. Today, all inpatient units are online, including our behavioral health units. We do not print nursing reports—everyone works online. These are some of my experiences and observations from this project.

We did med/surg first because it is the broadest definition and fits the majority of patients. When that model was in operation, we went to the next unit and asked, "With this as a model, what do we need to do to make it work for you?" We did a fair amount of redesign as we added units, but sometimes they were minor changes like adding descriptors that had not been necessary for another unit.

The first thing we did for all departments was to spend considerable time flowcharting all their processes; how they get their patients, how they communicate about their patients, with whom, what it looks like. We created a "life in the day of" scenario for every skill level in the unit; then we designed their charting based on their patient population.

The last unit to go online was Behavioral Health. Behavioral Health was challenging because this department's charts contain more abstract observations describing mental reactions, emotional reactions, and so on. But the most problematic unit was the Obstetrics (OB) Department.

OB charting is not difficult, but it is very meticulous. Our OB Department had a lot of rules and regulations about what had to be charted and how it was to be worded. The hospital legal department had to review all of our designs before the nurses could begin using them; they then reviewed samples of what was actually being documented once the department went online. We had to do some redesign to let the nurses better describe things, but we finally got it to everyone's satisfaction.

That was our design process; implementation was another matter. Our methodology of bringing one unit online at a time allowed us to provide plenty of support when the unit went online. I think that was key. Clinical Informatics personnel were scheduled in shifts that overlapped the nursing shifts. We were in the unit, with the nurses, 24 hours a day for the first two weeks. Whenever new users were struggling, someone was right at their elbow to calmly guide them through, to make sure they were successful. Even with that level of support, there were some concerns that remained constant through the last unit of the rollout.

Nurses are very accustomed to being in control, confident in their expertise and their skills; when their department becomes computerized, all of a sudden everything they know has to be translated through the limitations of a computer. The most common reaction when we rolled out charting into a new unit was that the nurses were extremely apprehensive their first day of charting. The universal complaint was that they could not sleep the night before.

My experience was that at the end of the first day they were still not feeling good about it, but when they came back the second day they had figured out how to get through it and they had very few questions. By the third day, they were usually doing very well. They still did not feel confident about finding the information, but they knew they could do it.

The nurses' biggest fear was that they would spend all their time taking care of the computer instead of their patients. They verbalized that idea for months afterwards, but that really is not reality. Research has repeatedly shown that nurses spend 50 to 70% of their time documenting. In short, nurses already spend an enormous amount of their work life documenting, but it takes them a long time to feel like they are spending less time on the computer than on their patients.

The real issue was that they felt like they were cut off from the information; they could not just flip open a chart and see what they were looking for. They had to remember how to find it and that was time out of their day. I have had them cry; I have had them yell, venting their frustration. But the good part was that they were all in the same boat together, so their peers readily understood what they were going through because they were all going through it together.

The nurses who had the easiest time transitioning were nurses who were accustomed to taking the time to write everything down as they went through their workday. The majority of nurses do not do that. Most nurses have notes stuffed in their pockets and tons of information in their head. They tend to store it up and write it all down when they come back from lunch at the end of their shift. When they try to follow that same model with a computer, but they are not yet comfortable with the computer; it is twice as hard because they have a lot to remember and they have to figure out what to do with it. Nurses who normally charted as their day progressed did not have to remember as much so they seem to learn faster.

In nursing school students have to chart as it happens—instructors insist on it. This meant that nurses who just came out of nursing school had an advantage because they came to the job with good habits. Additionally, most of the new nurses grew up with computers and were more familiar with them.

We found that the ancillary departments—respiratory therapy, physical therapy, dietary, and so on—were also easy to implement. Their documentation is much more concrete, limited in its focus, so it was much easier to adapt from paper to computer. They were almost self-sufficient from the very beginning.

The doctors, however, were another story. You have to spend time up front making sure the doctors can get the information, and most doctors cannot give up enough time in their day to learn a computer. The nurses trained for 8 hours for the computer but the doctors only for about 15 minutes. We balanced this by trying to be attentive to any doctor who came on the floor. We would often say, "Let me help you find the information. The nurses are now charting on the computer. As of today you are not going to find that information on a piece of paper." We don't print anything. The doctors have adapted to the readily available information so well that on the rare occasion when we have downtime, it is usually the physicians who are the most upset.

One thing I think is important is for the nursing leadership to dedicate time to learning the system so its members are fully on board with why the switch to computers is happening and what the benefits are. Then when their staff is apprehensive or when the physicians are frustrated because the nurses have not charted, there is reinforcement from the management that computerized charting is an expectation.

This point was illustrated in two of the units we rolled out. In one unit, the leadership was very computer savvy and expected the staff to do well. Leadership members held reinforcing in-service programs every 10 days and they would have us talk about specific areas where they thought their staff was weak in charting. Because the nurse manager was so proactive, that whole area adapted very easily and as a result the physicians adapted very easily.

In another unit where the nurse manager was not very computer savvy, the manager's apprehension reinforced that of the staff. For that reason, our team found it to support them. Although this unit has been online for long time, there is still a core group of nurses who just do not understand it, because their leaders do not require them to do it.

One final benefit of an involved leadership is that it results in better charting. When we did the first units, the implementation team spent a lot of time reading the documentation for quality, seeing if the nurses forgot to chart something, and so on. However, as the rollout continued throughout the hospital, the implementation team could not really spend a lot of time reviewing. You really need the people who know the patient population of the unit, the leaders, the managers, or supervisors to be spending some time each day randomly selecting charts created by their nurses, reading them, and helping their nurses understand if they are not doing it thoroughly enough. This not only improves the quality of the charts but also helps the staff get better at it quickly.

Critical Thinking Exercise 31: A Patient with Sinusitis

This exercise will help you evaluate how well you can use the Student Edition software to create an encounter note. The exercise provides step-by-step instructions, but does not provide screen figures for reference. The exercises in Chapter 3 covered each feature used in this exercise. If you have difficulty at any step during this exercise, refer to the Chapter 3 Summary, where a table lists each feature and the corresponding exercise for that feature.

Case Study

Patient Charles Green has been experiencing stuffy sinus pain. The medical office has scheduled a brief office visit for him to see the nurse practitioner. Using what you have learned so far, document Mr. Green's brief exam.

Step 1

If you have not already done so, start the Student Edition software.

Click Select on the Menu bar, and then click Patient.

In the Patient Selection window, locate and click on **Charles Green**.

Step 2

Click Select on the Menu bar, and then click New Encounter.

Select the reason **Office visit** from the drop-down list.

Make sure you have selected the reason correctly. You may use the current date for this exercise.

Step 3

Enter the Chief complaint by locating the button in the Toolbar labeled "Chief" and clicking on it. In the dialog window which will open, type "**Stuffy sinus**."

Click on the button labeled "Close the note form."

Step 4

The patient reports a sinus pain, stuffy nose, and nasal discharge. Enter the patient's symptoms using the list of findings on the Sx tab.

Locate "Head-related symptoms" and click on the small plus sign next to it to expand the tree of Medcin findings.

Locate and click on the red button next to the following finding:

- (red button) Sinus pain

Step 5

Scroll the list of Sx findings downward to locate "otolaryngeal symptoms."

Expand the tree by clicking on the small plus sign next to "otolaryngeal symptoms."

Locate and click on the small plus sign next to "nose" to expand the tree of findings further.

Locate and click on the red buttons for the following findings:

- (red button) nasal discharge
- (red button) nasal passage blockage (stuffiness)

Step 6

The patient reports smoking a pack of cigarettes a day. Enter this fact in the patient's history.

Click on the Hx tab.

Locate and click on the small plus sign next to "social history."

Locate and click on the small plus sign next to "behavioral history."

Locate and click on the small plus sign next to "Tobacco use."

Locate and click on the small plus sign next to "current smoker."

Locate and click on the red button next to the following finding:

- (red button) cigarettes

Step 7

Locate the **value** field in the Entry Details section at the bottom of the screen.

Type **1** in the field and press the Enter key.

The description will change to "Cigarette smoking 1 pack(s)/day."

Step 8

Enter the patient's vital signs using the Vitals form.

Locate and click on the button labeled "Forms" in the Toolbar at the top of your screen to invoke the Forms Manager window.

Locate and click on the Form name "Vitals" in the list.

Enter Mr. Green's vital signs in the corresponding fields as follows:

Temperature:	**96.7**
Respiration:	**27**
Pulse:	**67**
BP:	**120/88**
Height:	**68**
Weight:	**177**

When you have entered all of the vital signs, click your mouse on the Encounter tab at the bottom of the screen.

Step 9

The nurse practitioner examines the patient's head, eyes, ears, nose, inside of mouth, and lungs.

Begin recording the Physical Examination by clicking on the Px tab.

Locate and click on the small plus sign next to "Head."

Locate and click on the blue button next to the following finding:

- (blue button) Exam for evidence of injury

The description will change to "No evidence of injury."

Step 10

Scroll the list of Physical findings downward to locate "Eyes."

Locate and click on the blue button for the following finding:

- (blue button) Eyes

Locate and click on the small plus sign next to "Ears, Nose, and Throat."

Locate and click on the small plus sign next to "nose."

Locate and click on the buttons indicated for the following findings:

- (blue button) Ears
- (red button) Nasal Discharge
- (red button) Sinus tenderness
- (blue button) Oral cavity
- (blue button) Pharynx

Step 11

Scroll the list of Physical findings further downward to locate and click on the small plus sign next to "Lungs."

Locate and click on the blue button for the following finding:

- (blue button) Percussion

Step 12

The nurse practitioner concludes the patient has acute sinusitis that is already improving.

Record the Assessment by clicking on the Dx tab.

Locate and click on the small plus sign next to "ENT Disorders."

Locate and click on the small plus sign next to "Nose."

Locate and click on the small plus sign next to "Sinusitis."

Locate and click on the red button for the following finding:

- (red button) Acute

Step 13

Locate the **status** field in the Entry Details section at the bottom of the screen. Click your mouse on the button with the down arrow in the field. A drop-down list of choices will appear.

Locate and click on the status: **improving**.

The assessment will change to read: "Acute sinusitis which is improving"

Step 14

The nurse advises Mr. Green to continue taking over-the-counter antihistamines, drink plenty of fluids, and to abstain from smoking.

Record the Plan by clicking on the Rx tab.

Locate and click on the small plus sign next to "Basic Management Procedures and Services."

Scroll the list downward until you locate "Nutrition and Hydration Services," then click on the small plus sign next to it.

Locate and click on the red button for the following finding:

- (red button) Fluids

Scroll the list downward until you locate "Education and Instructions," then click on the small plus sign next to it.

Locate and click on the small plus sign next to "Instructions to Patient."

Locate and click on the red button for the following finding:

- (red button) Abstinence from smoking

Scroll the list downward until you locate "Medications and vaccines," then click on the small plus sign next to it.

Locate and highlight the medicine **Antihistamines** (do not click the red or blue button.)

Locate the **prefix** field in the Entry Details section at the bottom of the screen. Click your mouse on the button with the down arrow in the field. A drop-down list of choices will appear.

Locate and click on the status: **continue**.

Locate the **free-text** field in the Entry Details section at the bottom of the screen. (It is located just above the button labeled Episode.)

Type **OTC** in the field and press the enter key. OTC means over-the-counter.

The description should now read "Continue antihistamines OTC."

Do not close or exit the encounter until you have a printed copy in your hand. You will lose your work if you exit before printing.

Step 15

Print your completed encounter note.

Click on the Print button on the Toolbar at the top of your screen to invoke the Print Data window.

Be certain there is a check mark in the box next to "Current Encounter" and then click on either the appropriate button to print or export a file, as directed by your instructor.

Charles Green Page 1 of 1

Student: your name or ID here
Patient: Charles Green: M: 5/06/1979: 5/03/2012 02:15PM
Chief complaint
The Chief Complaint is: Stuffy sinus.
History of present illness
    Charles Green is a 32 year old male.
He reported: Sinus pain.
Nasal discharge and nasal passage blockage.
Personal history
Behavioral: Cigarette smoking 1 pack(s)/day.
Physical findings
Vital signs:

Vital Signs/Measurements	Value	Normal Range
Oral temperature	96.7 F	97.6 - 99.6
RR	27 breaths/min	18 - 26
PR	67 bpm	50 - 100
Blood pressure	120/88 mmHg	100-120/60-80
Weight	177 lbs	125 - 225
Height	68 in	65.35 - 74.02

Head:
Injuries: ° No evidence of a head injury.
Eyes:
General/bilateral:
    ° Eyes: normal.
Ears:
General/bilateral:
    ° Ears: normal.
Nose:
General/bilateral:
Discharge: • Nasal discharge seen.
Sinus Tenderness: • Tenderness of sinuses.
Oral Cavity:
    ° Normal.
Pharynx:
    ° Normal.
Lungs:
    ° Chest was normal to percussion.
Assessment
  • Acute sinusitis which is improving
Therapy
  • Fluids.
  • Continue antihistamines OTC.
Counseling/Education
  • Abstinence from smoking

▶ **Figure 4-36** Printed encounter note for Charles Green.

Compare your printout or exported file to Figure 4-36. If it is correct, hand it in to your instructor. If there are any differences (other than the date and patient age), review the previous steps in the exercise and find your error.

Chapter Four Summary

In this chapter you have performed exercises intended to increase your familiarity with the Student Edition software and thereby increase your speed of data entry. You have also learned to print out encounter notes or export them as files. You can print the encounter note at any time and as often as you like while practicing your exercises. However, remember not to quit or exit the program **until you are sure the encounter note has printed**. Once you exit, you will lose your work.

As you continue through the course, you can refer to the Guided Exercise 29 in this chapter if you need to remember how to print or export a file. You can also repeat any of the exercises in this chapter to increase your skills using the software. You should not proceed with the remainder of the text until you can perform the exercises in this chapter with ease.

In these and many subsequent exercises you are permitted to use the current date instead of setting it to a specific date. Remember when you do that, the date of the encounter and the patient's age will differ from the samples printed in the book. However, all of the other items in your printout or file should match the figures in the book.

Task	Guided Exercise(s)	Page #
Printing or exporting an XPS or PDF file of the encounter note	29	130

Testing Your Knowledge of Chapter 4

1. Why is it important to print your work before exiting?
2. What does the Export PDF button do?
3. How many cups of coffee per day had Rosa Garcia been drinking before she quit?
4. How long had Rosa Garcia been having headaches?
5. What Entry Details field was used to record that Rosa's headaches were inadequately controlled?
6. How long was Harold's office visit scheduled for?
7. Which of Harold Baker's symptoms did you record under otolaryngeal symptoms?
8. Does Harold smoke?
9. Did Harold report sinus pain or tenderness?
10. What was the doctor's assessment (diagnosis) of Harold's condition?
11. What was the doctor's plan (Rx) for Harold Baker?
12. What was Charles Green's chief complaint?
13. On what tab did you record that he smoked?
14. What does the acronym OTC stand for?
15. You should have produced three narrative documents of patient encounters, which you printed. If you have not already done so, hand it in to your instructor with this test. The printed encounter notes will count as a portion of your grade.

Chapter Five

Data Entry at the Point of Care

Learning Outcomes

After completing this chapter, you should be able to:

- Load and use Lists of Findings to speed up data entry
- Describe Review of Systems
- Change symptoms from History of Present Illness to Review of Systems
- Know how to quickly record "pertinent negatives"
- Understand and use Forms
- Use Lists and Forms together

Why Speed of Entry Is Important in the EHR

A recent survey of nurses conducted by Jackson Healthcare[1] found that nurses in a hospital setting spent 25 percent of their time on indirect patient care activities. The report stated that the majority of that time was spent on documentation. In Chapter 2, EHR expert Dr. Allen Wenner estimated that in a medical office, up to 67% of the nurse or clinician's time with the patient is spent entering the patient's symptoms into the visit documentation.

There is no question that symptoms, history, orders, observations, assessments, and all other aspects of patient care must be documented. The accuracy of documentation and efficiency of workflow can be improved by documenting at the time of the encounter, not after the clinician has left the patient. Previous chapters have referred to this as "point-of-care" or "real-time: data entry—that is, to document the visit completely before the patient ever leaves the office.

---

[1]Jackson Healthcare, "Hospital Nurses Study 2010 Summary of Findings," Jackson Healthcare, LLC, Alpharetta, GA, 2010.

Speed of entry is important because the less time it takes to record the provider's notes, the more time a provider has available for patient care. Real-time data entry is important because the chart is always up-to-date. Accuracy is improved because nothing is forgotten. Documenting at the point of care allows the nurse to ask the patient to elaborate or clarify any point of concern. Best of all, when the provider leaves the patient's room, the notes are done. No longer will the doctor or nurse spend the final hours of every day finishing up "paperwork." Most importantly, health information about the patient is available for other caregivers instead of in the provider's memory or dictation system.

To document in real time, a provider must be able to quickly navigate and enter findings. To help the clinician accomplish this, an EHR needs to present the finding the provider needs when it is needed. In this chapter we are going to look at several approaches EHR vendors use to help the healthcare professional accomplish that.

Lists and Forms Speed Data Entry

As you have seen from the exercises in the previous chapters, completely documenting the encounter could take quite a bit of time. Those exercises documented relatively simple encounters with findings that were fairly easy to locate. However, patient's often have multiple problems, more complex history and symptoms. Is there a faster way to find what you are looking for than just scrolling the navigation list and expanding the trees? Yes!

EHR vendors work constantly with EHR users to devise means to locate and present findings when they are most likely needed. The Student Edition software provides examples of a few of the ways EHR systems do this. In this chapter, you will learn about two features that help a doctor, nurse, or medical assistant enter data more quickly. These are Lists and Forms.

Lists and Forms are two approaches to point-of-care data entry that are used extensively in nearly every EHR system. These are templates to display findings that a provider uses most frequently for typical cases so that the encounter can be documented with minimal navigation or searching.

Shortcuts That Speed Documentation of Typical Cases

Both inpatient and outpatient facilities see a lot of patients with similar conditions. There are several reasons for this:

- The top 10 diseases cause the highest proportion of patients to be hospitalized.
- Geographic location may cause a facility to see more cases of a particular nature than similar facilities in another region.
- There can be seasonal increases of certain illnesses such as influenza and other upper respiratory infections.
- The specialty of the clinic or hospital may focus on a single type of disease or patient. For example, an oncology center sees only cancer patients, or a children's hospital focuses on children's diseases.

- In outpatient clinics the specialty of the physician often means patients are seeing them for similar reasons. For example, a pulmonary specialist sees primarily respiratory cases, nephrologists see patients with kidney problems, and a pediatric clinic sees children.

- Nurses tend to need the same sort of findings to document the admission and create care plans for patients with similar conditions.

Facilities have discovered that for similar cases, clinicians tend to perform the same type of exam, look for the same findings, order the same tests, and prescribe from a short list of treatments recommended for the condition. Therefore, it is logical to create shorter, quicker methods of entering the data. This is frequently based on the admitting diagnosis or type of ailment.

The Concept of Lists

You may not have heard the term *Lists* used in the context of an EHR, but the concept should be very familiar to you because you have been scrolling and navigating the list of findings since Chapter 3. Now, imagine that you are a pediatrician who treats many children with earaches (otitus media) and that each time the patient's chief complaint was an earache the system could magically present the findings that you typically used to document the visit. That is the idea behind lists. Of course, lists do not magically appear. They are created by clinicians and their assistants for the many types of exams and conditions seen at their practice. However, the time spent making each list is saved again and again when subsequent patients are seen for the same or similar reasons.

The advantage of using these short lists is that they are used just like browsing the full Medcin Nomenclature except that only the desired subset is shown. The list can (and usually does) contain findings in every tab. This means that time savings are realized all the way through the exam. If only certain therapies or certain drugs are used for a particular condition, then when the clinician clicks the mouse on the Rx tab, only those items are shown. When using a list, if there is a finding that is needed but is not on the list, the provider can instantly switch to the full hierarchy of Medcin findings and then back to the list.

Although lists are sometimes limited to one particular condition such as otitis media, this is not a rule; it is a convenience factor because shorter lists mean less scrolling. Lists are flexible and can contain as many findings as necessary to document a typical visit.

With some types of symptoms the assessment could be one of several possible diagnoses. For example, adult upper respiratory infections could be the result of rhinitis, sinusitis, or bronchitis. Therefore, a list with more findings reduces the possibility that the provider will need to switch to browsing the full nomenclature.

A good example of a multiple diagnosis type of list is the one used for the next exercise. During the cold and flu season, medical clinics and primary care physicians often see many patients with URI (an acronym for upper respiratory infection). Therefore, a list of findings for adults presenting with symptoms of URI can speed up the documentation process considerably.

Over time, practices should create lists for any medical condition that is seen regularly. This will speed up entry of all routine exams and increase adoption of the EHR by clinicians in the practice. If clinicians differ in how they would document a particular exam, they should create personal copies of the list and tailor it to their style of medicine.

Guided Exercise 32: Using an Adult URI List

During the cold and flu season, medical offices often see many patients with upper respiratory infections. Therefore, a list of findings for adults presenting with symptoms of URI can really speed up the documentation process. In this exercise, you will learn to use the List feature as well as several additional buttons on the Toolbar.

Case Study

Kerry Baker comes to the office complaining of sinus pain, stuffiness, and a runny nose. She says she has caught her husband's "bug." The medical practice has created a List of Medcin findings to use for this type of visit. They have named it Adult URI.

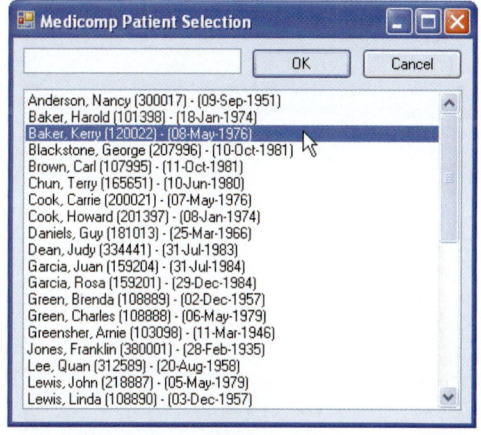

▶ Figure 5-1 Selecting Kerry Baker from the Patient Selection window.

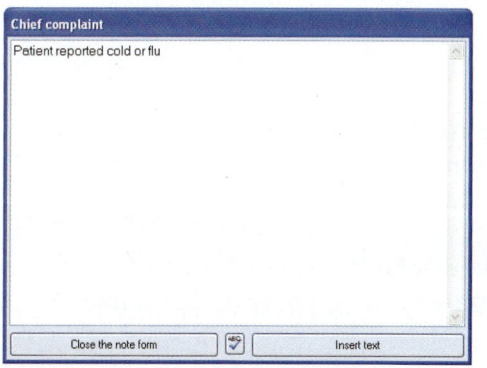

▶ Figure 5-2 Chief complaint dialog for patient-reported cold or flu.

Step 1

If you have not already done so, start the Student Edition software.

Click Select on the Menu bar, and then click Patient.

In the Patient Selection window, locate and click on **Kerry Baker** as shown in Figure 5-1.

Step 2

Click Select on the Menu bar, and then click New Encounter.

Use the current date and time. Select the reason **10 Minute Visit**. Click on the OK button.

Step 3

Enter the Chief complaint by locating the button in the Toolbar labeled "Chief" and clicking on it.

In the dialog window that will open, type "**Patient reported cold or flu**."

Compare your screen to Figure 5-2 before clicking on the button labeled "Close the note form."

Step 4

In this exercise, begin the visit by taking Kerry's vital signs.

Use the form labeled "Vitals," which you will select from the Forms Manager, as you have in previous exercises.

Chapter 5 | Data Entry at the Point of Care

Enter Kerry's vital signs in the corresponding fields on the Form as follows:

Temperature: **99**

Respiration: **16**

Pulse: **78**

BP: **120/80**

Height: **60**

Weight: **100**

When you have finished, compare your screen to Figure 5-3 and, when it is correct, click on the Encounter tab at the bottom of the screen.

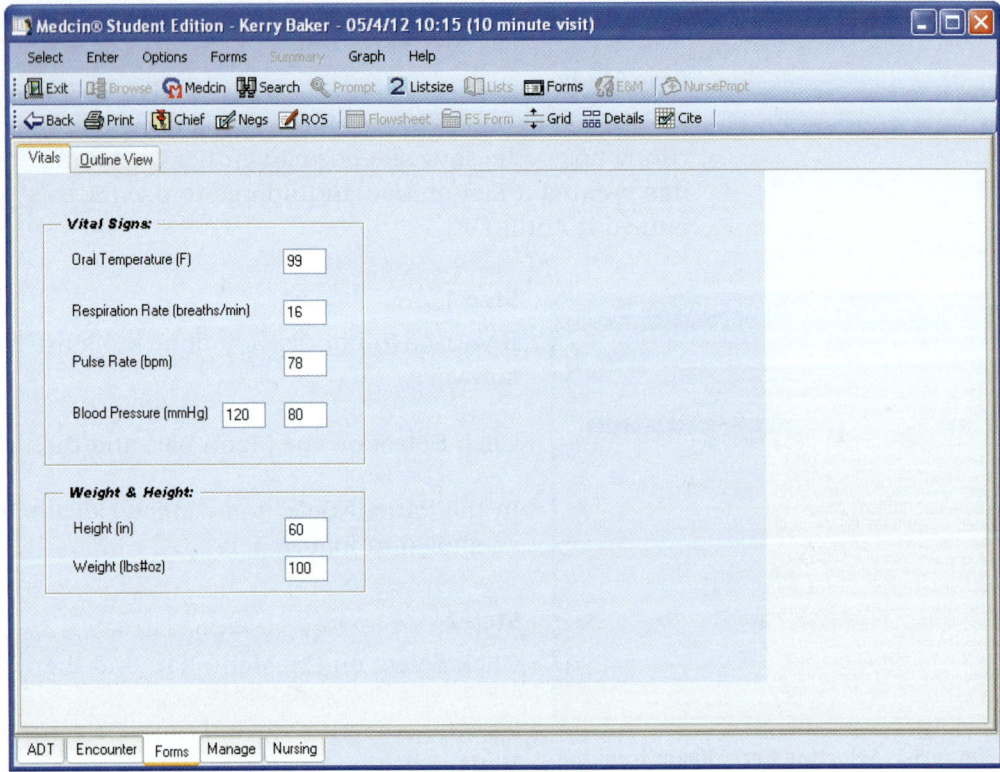

▶ **Figure 5-3 Vital Signs form for Kerry Baker.**

Step 5

As the patient reported cold or flu symptoms, we will use a List created for this type of exam.

Locate and click on the Lists button in the Toolbar at the top of your screen (highlighted orange in Figure 5-4). The icon resembles an open book. The List Manager window will be invoked.

The List Manager displays the various Lists available to providers in the practice. Two fields at the top of the screen organize the display of List names, filtering them by Owner and Group.

As we discussed earlier in this section, clinicians also can create personal copies of Lists customized to their style of practice. The Owner field allows the

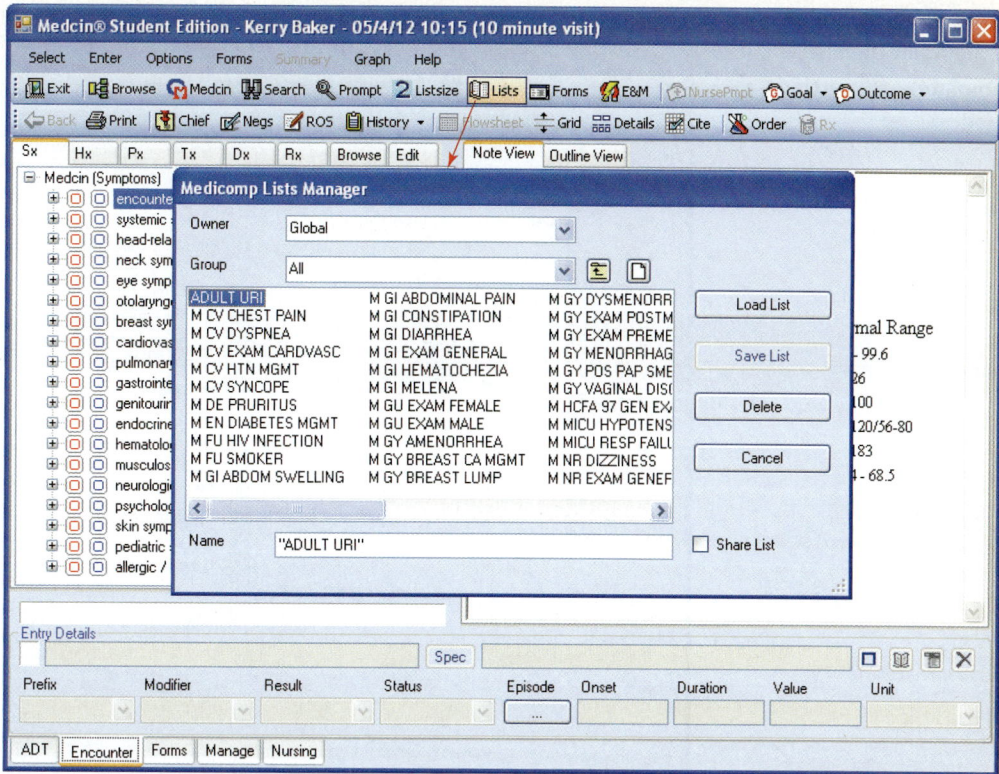

► Figure 5-4 Select Adult URI from Lists Manager window (invoked by Lists button).

clinician to quickly find their customized Lists by changing the field from "Global" to "Personal."

Lists also can be assigned to Groups, which helps to organize them by body system, disease, type of exam, or any other criteria the practice desires. The Group field allows a user to quickly find a list by limiting the display to a desired group. Note that the Student Edition has two groups, "All" and "Student Edition."

Locate and highlight the list named Adult URI, which is the first list in the window. Click your mouse on the button labeled "Load List."

Step 6

Notice that the normal display of the Medcin Nomenclature in the left pane has been replaced with a list of symptoms that patients with upper respiratory infections are likely to report. Notice that the title of the first line "Templates (Symptoms)" indicates that the findings are limited by a List (referred to in the left pane as a Template). You will also notice a special HPI button next to each finding—this will be explained in a moment.

Locate and click on the following symptom findings:
- (red button) sinus pain
- (red button) nasal discharge
- (red button) nasal passage blockage (stuffiness)

▶ Figure 5-5 Symptoms on the Adult URI List (Template)—HPI circled in red.

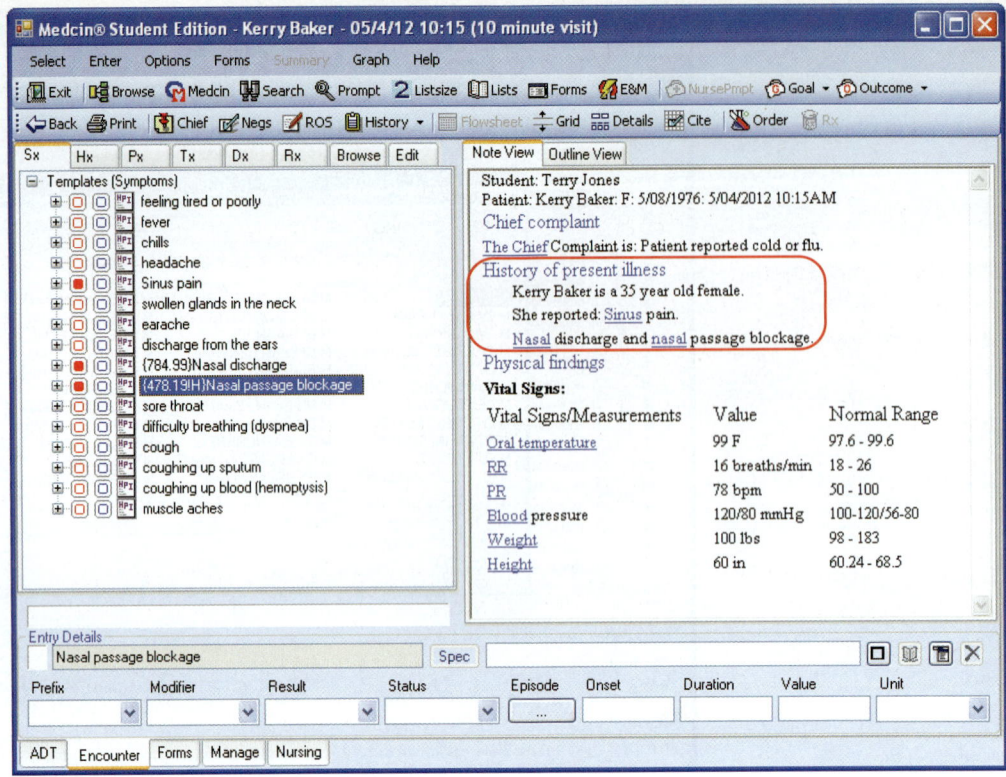

Compare your screen to Figure 5-5. Before proceeding, notice that Symptoms reported by the patient have been documented in "History of Present Illness," or "HPI" (circled in red in Figure 5-5).

Step 7

Review of Systems (ROS) is a way of organizing an exam by body systems starting from the head down. You may be familiar with the body systems from anatomy and physiology or other medical classes. The body systems in a standard ROS are:

- Constitutional symptoms
- HEENT (head, eyes, ears, nose, mouth, throat)
- Cardiovascular
- Respiratory
- Gastrointestinal
- Genitourinary
- Musculoskeletal
- Integumentary (skin and/or breast)
- Neurological
- Psychiatric
- Endocrine
- Hematologic/lymphatic
- Allergic/immunologic

Typically, a provider will document the symptoms directly related to the Chief complaint in the HPI. The remainder of the symptoms review is to rule out other causes. It is typically documented in a ROS.

In Chapter 12 you will learn about the CMS coding guidelines used to determine the correct Evaluation and Management code for billing. Because the CMS guidelines have specific rules for counting ROS body systems, it is not advisable to group all symptoms in the HPI.

▶ Figure 5-6 Auto Negative (Neg) and Review of Systems (ROS) buttons.

The Toolbar at the top of your screen has a button that can be used to change the way symptom findings are grouped from HPI into a ROS. The button on the right in Figure 5-6, labeled "ROS," toggles between on and off. When you click on the ROS button so that it changes from blue to orange, this indicates that the ROS grouping is on. If you click on the button again, it will change back to its original color. This indicates that the ROS grouping is off.

Locate and click on the ROS button. It will turn orange as shown in Figure 5-7. When you click on symptom findings while the ROS button is orange, the symptoms selected will be placed in the Review of Systems group.

▶ Figure 5-7 Symptom: No Headache in Review of systems group (circled in red).

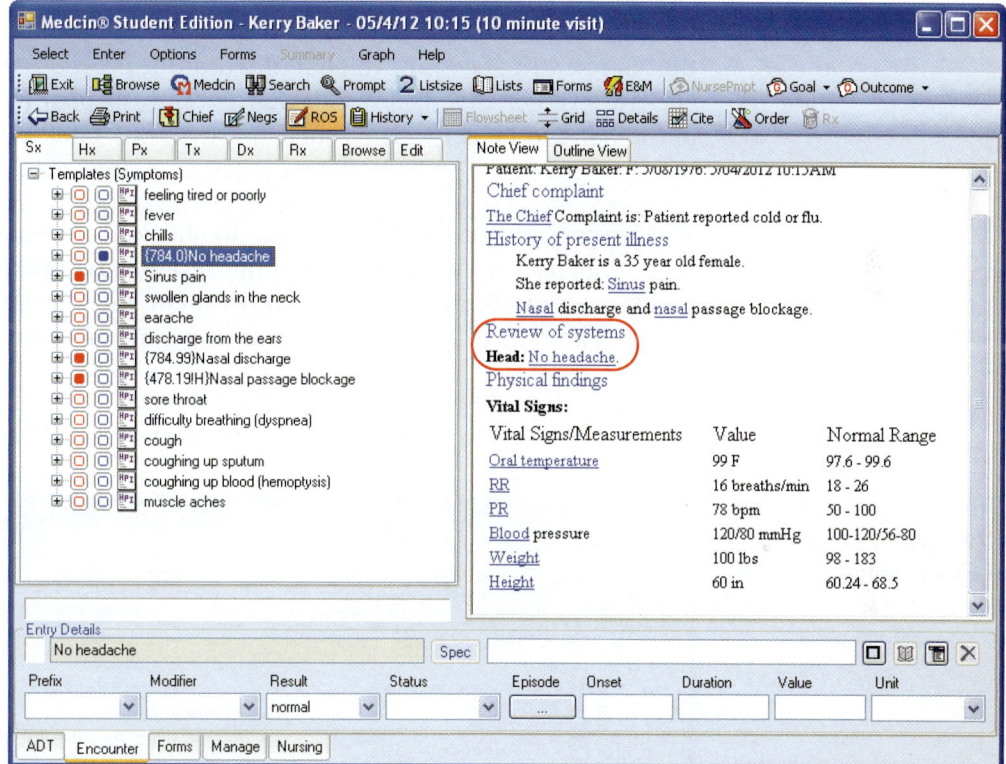

Step 8

Verify the ROS button is orange, then locate and click on the following finding:

- (blue button) headache

Compare your screen to Figure 5-7. Notice that the finding "No headache" was placed in a new group "Review of systems" that was created in the note (shown circled in red).

The small HPI button next to each finding in the Nomenclature Pane is used to switch an individual finding from HPI to ROS without using the ROS button on the Toolbar. You will not be using the button on the individual findings until later in this exercise.

Chapter 5 | Data Entry at the Point of Care   159

The differences between the actions of these two buttons are as follows:

- The ROS button on the Toolbar applies to all Symptoms selected while the button is on (orange).

- The HPI/ROS button on an individual finding affects only the selected finding and only affects it when the toolbar ROS button is off (blue).

- The HPI/ROS button on individual findings is only available on the Sx tab, and only when a List is loaded.

- The ROS button on the Toolbar is available anytime you are on the Sx tab.

Step 9

Frequently, most of the symptoms in the ROS will be negative, as they were not reported by the patient in the HPI. Using a List such as Adult URI, you could quickly go down the list clicking a blue button on each of the remaining findings. However, that would still be a lot of mouse clicks.

Fortunately, the Toolbar has another button, labeled "Negs" for "Auto Negatives," that is used to speed up the documentation process. When the clinician has clicked a red or blue button for all the relevant positive findings, the remainder of the list can be set to the "normals" with one click on the "Negs" button on the Toolbar. (It is the button on the left in Figure 5-6.)

The purpose of Auto Negatives is not to shortcut the exam process but to speed up the documentation of the encounter. Clinicians find they can review systems much more quickly than they can document each finding. The Auto Negatives feature allows providers to document this portion of the encounter in fewer clicks.

The Auto Negative feature selects the "normal" button (usually the blue button) for all displayed findings that are not already set. The user can modify any

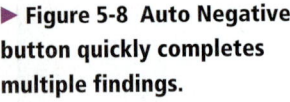

▶ **Figure 5-8** Auto Negative button quickly completes multiple findings.

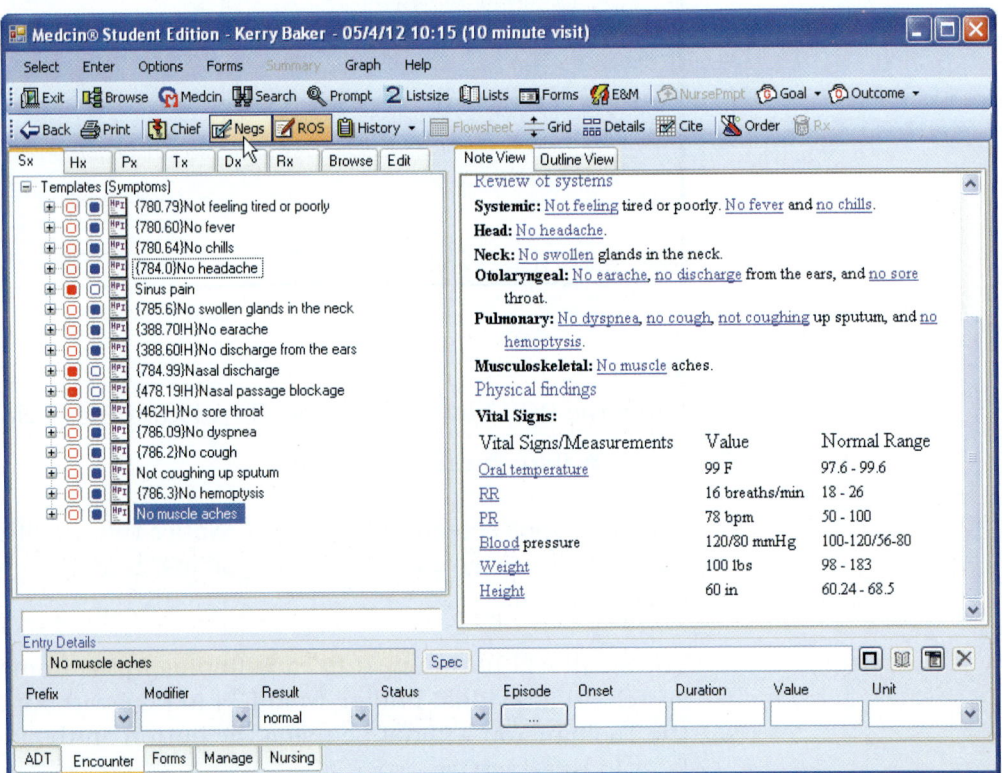

finding after the process is finished. Because all the findings displayed in the current tab are automatically selected, the Auto Negative feature works best with Lists or Forms because the List is already limited to findings the clinician would normally use in a particular type of encounter.

Locate and click on the button labeled "Negs" in the Toolbar at the top of your screen. The icon resembles a box with a teal check mark. The Negs button is highlighted in Figure 5-8.

All symptoms that have not previously been selected have automatically had their blue buttons selected. Notice how quickly the documentation process was completed.

Compare the encounter notes on your screen with Figure 5-8. (You may need to scroll the right pane upward to see the full effect.) Notice that the three findings with red buttons were not altered.

The Auto Negative function will record the findings according to the state of the ROS button. Because the ROS button was orange, the additional symptoms were recorded in the Review of Symptoms group, not the HPI group.

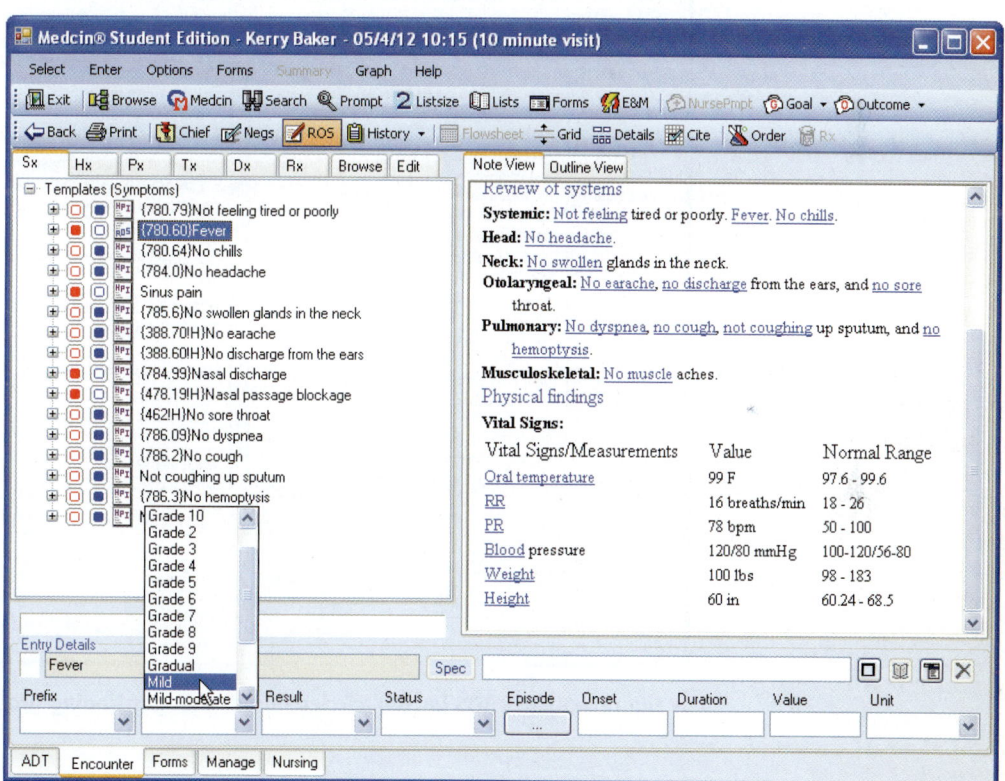

▶ Figure 5-9 Modifying the finding "No Fever."

Step 10

Although all unselected symptoms findings were set by the Auto Negative feature, they can be changed by the user at any time during the exam. Kerry mentions that she has had a mild fever. You note that Ms. Baker's temperature is 99°F. Therefore, you will change the finding.

Locate and click on the following finding:

- (red button) No fever

Chapter 5 | Data Entry at the Point of Care   **161**

This will change the button from blue to red and the description will change to "Fever." With the finding still highlighted, locate the Entry Details field "Modifier" and click your mouse on the down arrow button to display a drop-down list (as shown in Figure 5-9). Scroll the list of modifiers until you locate the word "**Mild**," then click on it.

Step 11

As this is a symptom reported by the patient, you will also want to change "Fever" from ROS to HPI.

Locate and click on the ROS button on the Toolbar, to turn it off. The button should no longer be orange.

Locate the finding of "Fever" in the Nomenclature Pane and click the small HPI button next to it. The button is circled in Figure 5-10.

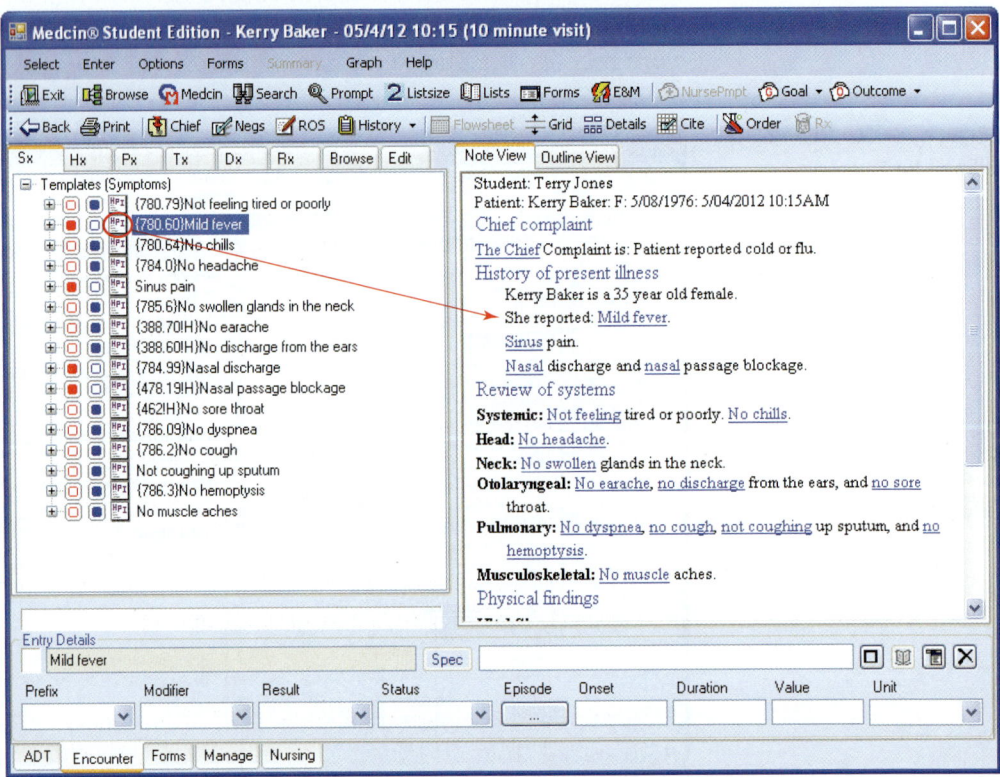

▶ **Figure 5-10** HPI/ROS button (circled in red) changes finding group.

Look at the button. Did it change? Look at the encounter note. Did "Mild Fever" move from the Review of systems group to the History of present illness group?

If "Mild Fever" did not change groups, repeat step 11, being certain that the ROS button on the Toolbar is off (blue).

Step 12

Next, click on the Hx tab to enter the patient's history. Note that the "Negs" button is grayed out. This is because the Auto Negative function is only available on the Sx (Symptoms) and Px (Physical Exam) tabs.

You will recall from previous exercises how many items are typically in the Hx tab, but, because you are using a list, only those items related to Adult URI are displayed. This makes navigation of the list quicker because the list is shorter. Locate and click on the buttons indicated for the following History findings.

- (red button) recent upper respiratory infection (URI)
- (blue button) allergies
- (blue button) taking medications
- (blue button) current smoker

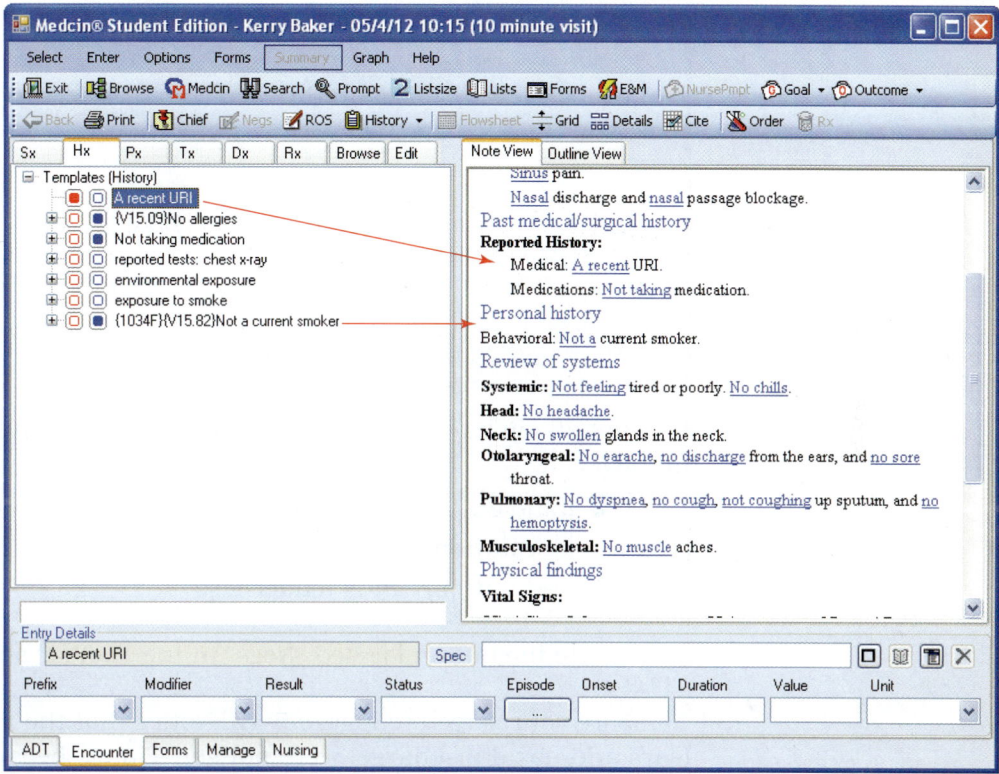

▶ Figure 5-11 Two different history groups from List.

Compare your left pane to Figure 5-11. If it is correct, scroll the encounter note (right pane) upward far enough to see both groups of history. Note that even though the findings were listed together in the left pane, they were actually from three different history groups: Past Medical History, Social (Behavioral) History, and Allergies. Note that Allergy findings are in their own group at the very bottom of the note.

This is an example of how lists can present together findings that are normally located very far apart in the expanded tree.

Step 13

Click on the Px tab to document the physical exam. Note that the "Negs" button in the Toolbar that was grayed out in the previous tab is again available when you are on this tab. The Negs button is available only on the Sx and Px tabs.

Chapter 5 | Data Entry at the Point of Care 163

▶ Figure 5-12 Physical exam completed using Neg button (highlighted).

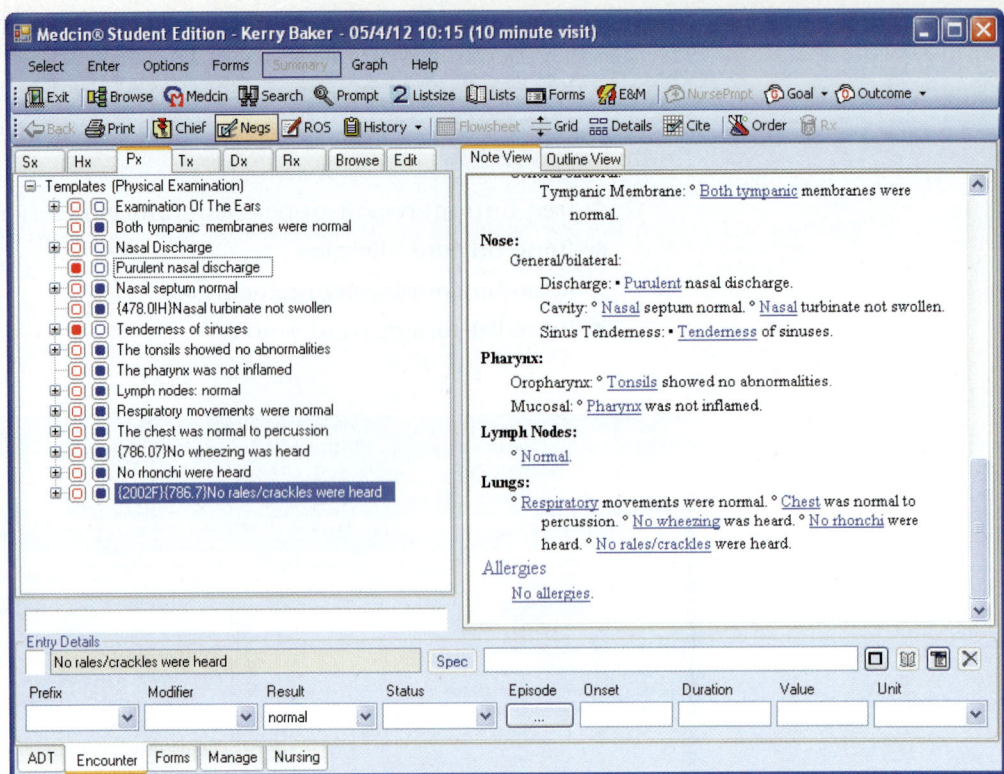

Locate and click on the buttons indicated for the following Physical Exam findings.

- (blue button) Both tympanic membranes were examined
- (red button) Nasal discharge purulent
- (red button) Sinus tenderness

Now locate the button labeled "Negs" in the Toolbar and click it once.

Compare your screen to Figure 5-12. Notice that the first and third findings (ears and nasal discharge) were not set. This is because the Auto Negative feature correctly determined that the tympanic membrane finding was an examination of the ears, and the purulent discharge finding was a refinement of the nasal discharge finding.

Step 14

The clinician has determined that the patient has acute sinusitis. Click on the Dx tab and notice that the Adult URI list contains only diagnoses that the clinic has decided are likely to present for this type of condition.

Locate and click on the following finding:

- (red button) Sinusitis Acute

Compare your screen to Figure 5-13.

Step 15

Click on the Rx tab and again appreciate the fact that the tab contains only types of treatments that the practice is likely to prescribe for an adult URI. The clinician is going to order fluids and a cool mist vaporizer.

▶ Figure 5-13 Assessment—acute sinusitis.

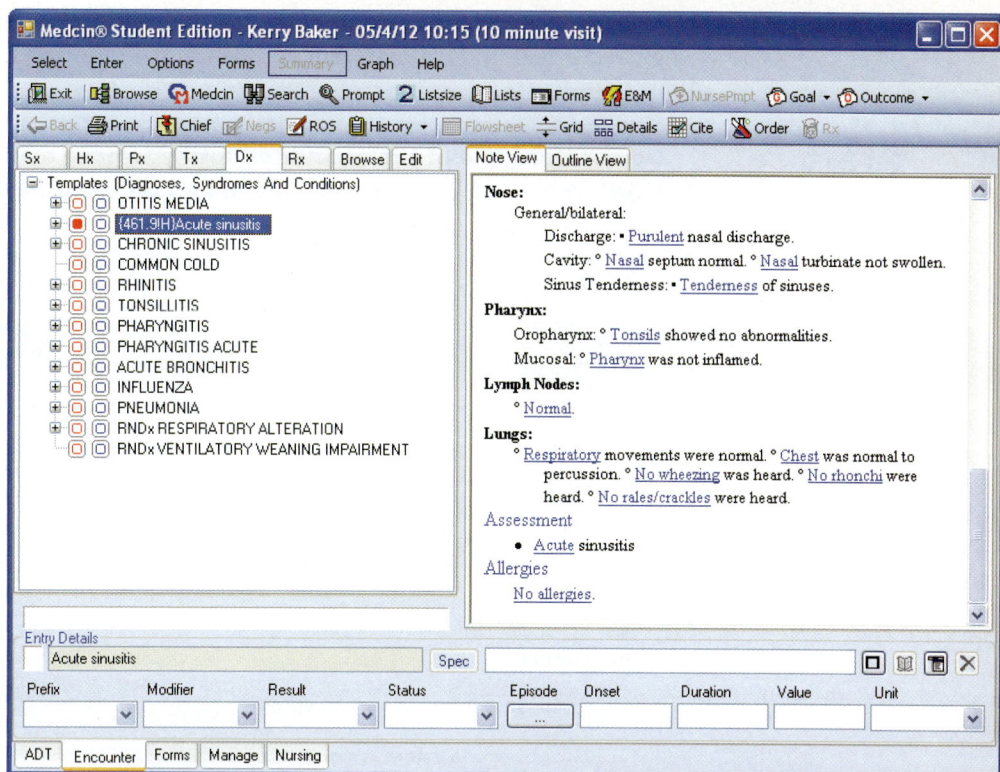

▶ Figure 5-14 Orders for Kerry Baker.

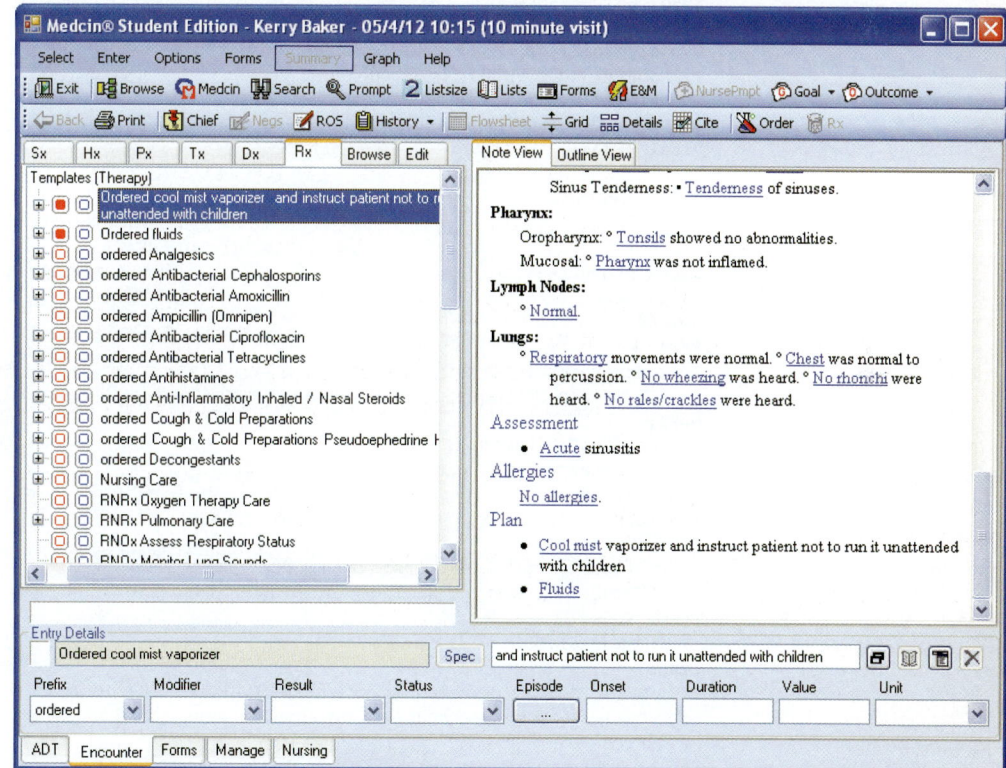

Locate and click on the following findings:
- (red button) ordered cool mist vaporizer
- (red button) ordered fluids

Compare your screen to Figure 5-14.

In this exercise you learned to use the List feature as well as the ROS and Auto Negative buttons. You also learned to use the Modifier field and the individual ROS/HPI button.

>  **Alert** Do not close or exit the encounter until you have a printed copy in your hand. *You will lose your work if you exit before printing.*

```
Kerry Baker

Student: your name or ID here
Patient: Kerry Baker: F: 5/08/1976: 5/04/2012 10:15AM
```
Chief complaint
The Chief Complaint is: Patient reported cold or flu.
History of present illness
    Kerry Baker is a 35 year old female.
    She reported: Mild fever.
    Sinus pain.
    Nasal discharge and nasal passage blockage.
Past medical/surgical history
Reported History:
    Medical: A recent URI.
    Medications: Not taking medication.
Personal history
    Behavioral: Not a current smoker.
Review of systems
Systemic: Not feeling tired or poorly. No chills.
Head: No headache.
Neck: No swollen glands in the neck.
Otolaryngeal: No earache, no discharge from the ears, and no sore throat.
Pulmonary: No dyspnea, no cough, not coughing up sputum, and no hemoptysis.
Musculoskeletal: No muscle aches.
Physical findings
Vital Signs:

Vital Signs/Measurements	Value	Normal Range
Oral temperature	99 F	97.6 - 99.6
RR	16 breaths/min	18 - 26
PR	78 bpm	50 - 100
Blood pressure	120/80 mmHg	100-120/56-80
Weight	100 lbs	98 - 183
Height	60 in	60.24 - 68.5

Ears:
    General/bilateral:
    Tympanic Membrane: ° Both tympanic membranes were normal.
Nose:
    General/bilateral:
    Discharge: • Purulent nasal discharge.
    Cavity: ° Nasal septum normal. ° Nasal turbinate not swollen.
    Sinus Tenderness: • Tenderness of sinuses.
Pharynx:
    Oropharynx: ° Tonsils showed no abnormalities.
    Mucosal: ° Pharynx was not inflamed.
Lymph Nodes:
    ° Normal.
Lungs:
    ° Respiratory movements were normal. ° Chest was normal to percussion.
    ° No wheezing was heard. ° No rhonchi were heard. ° No rales/crackles were heard.
Assessment
    • Acute sinusitis
Allergies
    No allergies.
Plan
    • Cool mist vaporizer and instruct patient not to run it unattended with children
    • Fluids

▶ **Figure 5-15** Printed encounter note for Kerry Baker.

Step 16

Click on the Print button on the Toolbar at the top of your screen to invoke the Print Data window.

Be certain there is a check mark in the box next to Current Encounter and then click on the appropriate button to either print or export a file, as directed by your instructor.

Compare your printout or file output to Figure 5-15. If it is correct, hand it in to your instructor. If there are any differences (other than the date or patient's age), review the previous steps in the exercise and find your error.

Critical Thinking Exercise 33: Timed Experiment

Now that you have learned that the Lists and Auto Negative feature can help you enter EHR data more quickly, prove it to yourself with this exercise.

Case Study

In Chapter 4, you documented a visit for an adult URI for Kerry's husband Harold. In this exercise he is returning as his condition has not improved. You are going to document a visit very similar to his previous visit, but this time using what you have learned about lists.

Step 1

Look at the clock and write down the current time.

If you have not already done so, start the Student Edition software.

Click Select on the Menu bar, and then click Patient.

In the Patient Selection window, locate and click on **Harold Baker**.

Step 2

Click Select on the Menu bar, and then click New Encounter.

Select the reason **10 Minute Visit** from the drop-down list.

Make sure you have selected the reason correctly. You may use the current date for this exercise.

Step 3

Enter the Chief complaint by locating the button in the Toolbar labeled "Chief" and clicking on it.

In the dialog window that will open, type "**Return visit for cold**."

Click on the button labeled "Close the note form."

Step 4

Click on the Forms button on the Toolbar to invoke the Forms Manager window.

Select the form labeled "Vitals." Enter Harold's vital signs in the corresponding fields on the Form as follows:

Temperature:	**99.7**
Respiration:	**25**
Pulse:	**65**
BP:	**120/80**
Height:	**72**
Weight:	**175**

When you have finished, click on the Encounter tab at the bottom of the screen.

Step 5

Locate and click on the Lists button in the Toolbar at the top of your screen (highlighted orange in Figure 5-4). The List Manager window will be invoked.

Locate and highlight the list named Adult URI. Click your mouse on the button labeled "Load List."

Step 6

Verify that the first line of the Medcin Nomenclature in the left pane reads: "Templates (Symptoms)."

Locate and click on the following symptom findings:

- (red button) headache
- (red button) sinus pain
- (red button) nasal discharge
- (red button) nasal passage blockage (stuffiness)

Step 7

Expand the list of findings by clicking the small plus sign next to "Cough."

Locate and click on the following symptom findings:

- (red button) while lying down
- (red button) worse at night

Step 8

Harold's vital signs show a mild fever.

Locate a click on the following symptom finding:

- (red button) fever

Modify the finding "Fever" by clicking the down arrow in the Entry Details field "Modifier" to display a drop-down list. Scroll the list of modifiers until you locate the word "**Mild**," then click on it.

The description should change to "Mild fever."

Step 9

Locate and click on the ROS button on the Toolbar. The ROS button should change color from blue to orange.

Verify the ROS button is orange, then locate and click on the button labeled "Negs" in the Toolbar at the top of your screen. (The Negs button was shown highlighted in Figure 5-8.)

Step 10

Click on the Hx tab to enter the patient's history. Locate and click on the buttons indicated for the following History findings:

- (red button) recent upper respiratory infection (URI)
- (blue button) allergies
- (blue button) taking medications
- (blue button) current smoker

Step 11

Click on the Px tab to document the physical exam.

Locate and click on the buttons indicated for the following Physical Exam findings:

- (blue button) Both tympanic membranes were examined
- (red button) Nasal Discharge
- (red button) Nasal discharge purulent
- (red button) Sinus tenderness

Step 12

Now locate the button labeled "Negs" in the Toolbar and click it once.

Step 13

The clinician has determined that Harold has acute sinusitis.

Click on the Dx tab and then locate and click on the following finding:

- (red button) Sinusitis Acute

Step 14

The clinician is going to order fluids and a cool mist vaporizer.

Click on the Rx tab and then locate and click on the following finding:

- (red button) ordered cool mist vaporizer
- (red button) ordered fluids

Step 15

Look at the clock and write down the time you completed the encounter note.

Were you surprised how quickly you completed the complete encounter note?

Step 16

Click on the Print button on the Toolbar at the top of your screen to invoke the Print Data window.

Be certain there is a check mark in the box next to "Current Encounter," and then click on the appropriate button to either print or export a file, as directed by your instructor.

Alert

Do not close or exit the encounter until you have a printed copy in your hand. *You will lose your work if you exit before printing.*

Chapter 5 | Data Entry at the Point of Care

Compare your printout or file output to Figure 5-16. If there are any differences (other than the date or patient's age), review the previous steps in the exercise and find your error. If you are printing your work, write your start and stop time on your printed encounter note and hand it in to your instructor.

Harold Baker

Student: your name or ID here
Patient: Harold Baker: M: 1/18/1974: 5/07/2012 03:00AM
Chief complaint
The Chief Complaint is: Return visit for cold.
History of present illness
    Harold Baker is a 38 year old male.
    He reported: Mild fever.
    Headache and sinus pain.
    Nasal discharge and nasal passage blockage.
    Cough while lying down worse at nigth.
Past medical/surgical history
Reported History:
    Medical: A recent URI.
    Medications: Not taking medication.
Personal history
    Behavioral: Not a current smoker.
Review of systems
Systemic: Not feeling tired or poorly. No chills.
Neck: No swollen glands in the neck.
Otolaryngeal: No earache, no discharge from the ears, and no sore throat.
Pulmonary: No dyspnea, not coughing up sputum, and no hemoptysis.
Musculoskeletal: No muscle aches.
Physical findings
Vital Signs:

Vital Signs/Measurements	Value	Normal Range
Oral temperature	99.7 F	97.6 - 99.6
RR	25 breaths/min	18 - 26
PR	65 bpm	50 - 100
Blood pressure	120/80 mmHg	100-120/60-80
Weight	175 lbs	125 - 225
Height	72 in	65.35 - 74.02

Ears:
    General/bilateral:
    Tympanic Membrane: ° Both tympanic membranes were normal.
Nose:
    General/bilateral:
    Discharge: • Nasal discharge seen. • Purulent nasal discharge.
    Cavity: ° Nasal septum normal. ° Nasal turbinate not swollen.
    Sinus Tenderness: • Tenderness of sinuses.
Pharynx:
    Oropharynx: ° Tonsils showed no abnormalities.
    Mucosal: ° Pharynx was not inflamed.
Lymph Nodes:
    ° Normal.
Lungs:
    ° Respiratory movements were normal. ° Chest was normal to percussion. ° No wheezing was heard. ° No rhonchi were heard. ° No rale/crackles were heard.
Assessment
    • Acute sinusitis
Allergies
    No allergies.
Plan
    • Cool mist vaporizer and instruct patient not to run it unattended with children
    • Fluids

▶ Figure 5-16 Printed encounter note for Harold Baker's follow-up visit.

The Concept of Forms

In this chapter, you experienced the use of lists dynamically created by the search and prompt features and the value in using predesigned lists for specific types of exams such as Adult URI. The other type of template that can speed up data entry is called a Form. You already have worked briefly with Forms, because the Vital Signs screen is actually a form.

Forms are templates that display a desired group of findings in a consistent position every time. Forms enable quick entry of positive and negative findings, as well as Entry Details field data such as value or results.

The Vitals Signs form is a good example. You could enter Vitals on the Encounter Px tab by locating and clicking on individual findings on the Px tab, then repositioning your mouse at the bottom of the screen, then entering the value and unit of measurement for each vital sign. This would obviously be a time-consuming way to do it. As you have already experienced, vitals are much easier to enter using the Vitals form on which all the necessary findings are arranged with the value fields ready for data entry and the unit of measurement fields preset.

The Vitals form is only a very small example of what can be done with forms. Complete multipage forms can be created that make it fast and easy to document standard types of exams.

Comparison of Lists and Forms

The value of lists is that they are dynamic and expand as necessary. A side effect of this is that sometimes findings do not appear on the screen, because they are in the nonexpanded portion of the tree, or the user must scroll the List to find them.

Forms, however, are static. Findings have a fixed position on the form and will remain in that location every time the form is used.

Lists arrange findings in the appropriate tab (Sx, Hx, Px, Tx, Dx, and Rx), but this means that clinicians must change tabs as they work through the encounter. This is not a limitation with forms. The form designer is free to put any finding anywhere on the form. This allows each form to be designed to allow the quickest entry of data for a particular type of encounter. For example, if a nurse or medical assistant routinely enters the Chief complaint and records the patient's symptoms at the same time she or he takes the vital signs, these could all be placed on one page of the form, even though the findings will appear in three different sections of the note.

Forms offer many additional features to the designer. These include check boxes, drop-down lists, and most of the fields in the Entry Details section. Free-text boxes in a form can be pre-assigned to a finding; therefore, they do not require the user to locate a free-text finding to record comments.

The Forms designer has the option to require entry of data for certain findings before the form can be closed.

Memorial Hospital
Anytown, USA

Date: _____
Patient Name: _____
Date of Birth: _____
☐ Male ☐ Female
Race: _____

What is the reason you are here today?
_____

Please check any of the following conditions which you have had

General
☐ Serious Infections
  (e.g. pneumonia)
☐ Diabetes Mellitus
☐ Rheumatic fever
☐ HIV Infection
☐ Cancer

Cardiovascular
☐ High Blood Pressure
☐ Congestive Heart failure
☐ Heart Murmur
☐ Heart Valve Disease
☐ Angina
☐ Heart Attack
☐ High Cholesterol
☐ Abnormal Heart Rhythm
☐ Blood Clot in Veins
☐ Blocked Arteries in Neck
☐ Blocked Arteries in Legs

HEENT
☐ Glaucoma
☐ Allergies "hay fever"
☐ Frequent Ear Infections
☐ Frequent Sinus Infections

Respiratory
☐ Asthma
☐ Emphysema
☐ Blood Colt in Lungs
☐ Sleep Apnea

Musculoskeletal / Extremities
☐ Osteoporosis
☐ Rheumatoid Arthritis
☐ Degenerative Joint Disease
☐ Fibrmyalgia
☐ Neck Pain (herniated disk)
☐ Back Pain (herniated disc)

GI/GU
☐ Stomach Ulcers
☐ Ulcerative Colitis
☐ Crohns Disease
☐ Bleeding from Intestines
☐ Diverticulitis
☐ Colon Polyps
☐ Irritable Bowel Disease
☐ Hepatitis
☐ Cirrhosis of the liver
☐ Liver Failure
☐ Pancreatitis
☐ Gallstones
☐ Kidney Stones
☐ Kidney Failure
☐ Prostate Disease
☐ Endometriosis
☐ Sex Transmitted Infection

Lymphatic / Hematologic
☐ Thyroid Goiter
☐ Over Active Thyroid
☐ Under Active Thyroid
☐ Transfusions
☐ Anemia

Skin / Breast
☐ Acne
☐ Eczema
☐ Psoriasis
☐ Fibrocystic Breast Disease

Neurological / Psychiatric
☐ Chronic Vertigo (Meniere's)
☐ Peripheral Nerve Disease
☐ Migraine Headaches
☐ Stroke
☐ Multiple Sclerosis
☐ Depression
☐ Anxiety

Please check any of the following major illnesses in your family members:

☐ Tuberculosis
☐ Emphysema
☐ Heart Disease
☐ High Blood Pressure
☐ Osteoporosis

☐ Diabetes Mellitus
☐ Thyroid Disease
☐ Anemia
☐ Hemophilia
☐ Other _____

☐ Kidney Disease
☐ Epilepsy
☐ Neurological Disorder
☐ Liver Disease
☐ Other _____

☐ Breast Cancer
☐ Ovarian Cancer
☐ Colon Cancer
☐ Prostate Cancer
☐ Other _____

If you have had surgery please indicate the year:

Year	Surgery	Year	Surgery	Year	Surgery	Year	Surgery
___	Angioplasty	___	Colonoscopy	___	Neurosurgery	___	Tubal ligation
___	Appendectomy	___	Coronary Bypass	___	Sinus Surgery	___	C-Section
___	Back or Neck Surgery	___	Ear Surgery	___	Stomach Surgery	___	Hysterectomy
___	Bladder Surgery	___	Gallbladder	___	Thyroid Surgery	___	Ovary Removed
___	Carotid Artery Surgery	___	Hip Surgery	___	Tonsillectomy	___	Breast Surgery
___	Carpal Tunnel Surgery	___	Inguinal Hernia	___	Trauma Related Surgery	___	Thyroid Surgery
___	Chest/lung Surgery	___	Knee Surgery	___	Vascular Surgery	___	Other

Please indicate when you had the following preventative services:

Date	Immunizations	Date	Tests	Date	Tests / Exams	Date	Tests / Exams
___	Flu Vaccine	___	Chest X-ray	___	Colon Cancer Stool Test	___	Breast Exam
___	Hepatitis Vaccine	___	EKG	___	Flexible Sigmoidoscopy, Rectal Exam	___	Mammogram
___	Pneumonia Vaccine	___	Echocardiogram	___		___	Pap Smear
___	Tetanus Booster	___	Stress Test	___	Barium Enema	___	Bone Density Test
___	Other	___	Cardiac Angiogram	___	Prostate Cancer Blood Test	___	Date of last Physical Exam

Personal Habits

Tobacco
☐ Never
☐ Previous user
☐ Current user
packs per day _____

Alcohol
☐ Never
☐ Previous user
☐ Current user
drinks per day _____

Caffeine
☐ Never
☐ Previous user
☐ Current user
cups per day _____

Illicit Drugs
☐ Never
☐ Previous user
☐ Current user

▶ Figure 5-17 Sample Intake Form from a paper chart.

Initial Intake Form for an Adult

The intake form used in the following exercise provides an example of different designs and features that are possible with forms. These include the unique ability to record two types of history at once, the Auto Negative feature, and other features you will explore during the exercise.

Figure 5-17 is an example of a form that might be found in a medical facility that uses paper medical records. You have probably seen a similar form at your own doctor's office. As you complete the following exercise, notice the similarities to the design of the EHR form. Electronic forms are one of the easiest ways to use an EHR.

Guided Exercise 34: Using Forms

In this exercise, you will use an EHR form to record symptoms, history, and a physical exam. The EHR form, in this case, has been abridged to shorten the time it takes a student to complete the exercise; a full version of the form as it is used in a medical office would have much more detail. A short intake form might be used by a nurse or medical assistant for prescreening.

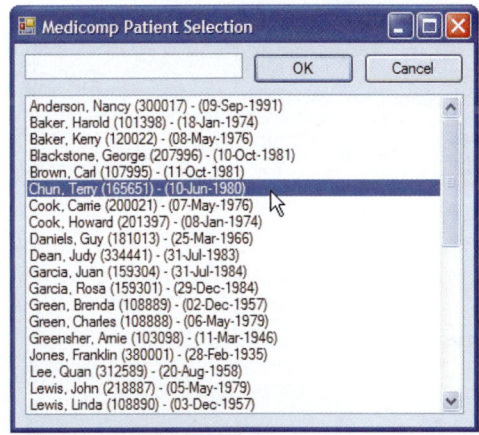

▶ **Figure 5-18** Selecting Terry Chun from the Patient Selection window.

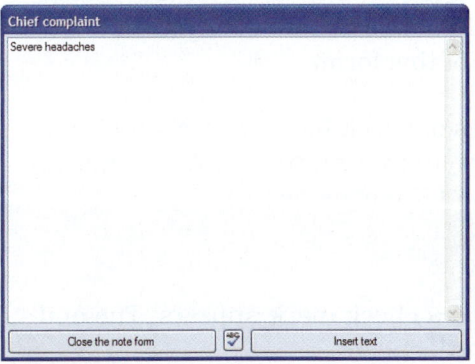

▶ **Figure 5-19** Chief complaint "Severe headaches."

Case Study

Terry Chun is a 31-year-old female complaining of an excruciating headache lasting greater than one week. She is being admitted for status migrainous.

Step 1

If you have not already done so, start the Student Edition software.

Click Select on the Menu bar, and then click Patient.

In the Patient Selection window, locate and click on **Terry Chun** as shown in Figure 5-18.

Step 2

Click Select on the Menu bar again, and then click New Encounter.

Use the current date and time. Select the reason **Headaches** from the drop-down list. Click on the OK button.

Step 3

Enter the Chief complaint by locating the button in the Toolbar labeled "Chief" and clicking on it.

In the dialog window that opens, type "**Severe headaches**."

Compare your screen to Figure 5-19 before clicking on the button labeled "Close the vote form."

Chapter 5 | Data Entry at the Point of Care **173**

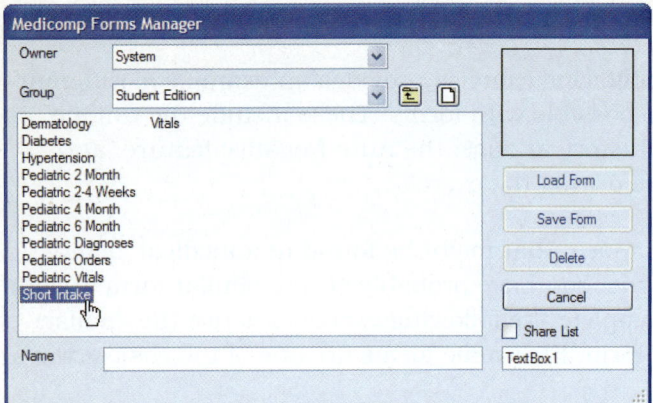

Step 4

Click on the Forms button in the Toolbar at the top of the screen.

In the Forms Manager window, select the Form labeled "Short Intake," as shown in Figure 5-20. The Short Intake form shown in Figure 5-21 will be displayed.

Step 5

Compare your screen to Figure 5-21. Take a few minutes to study the form on your screen.

▶ Figure 5-20 Select Short Intake in Forms Manager window.

▶ Figure 5-21 Short Intake Form—Review of Symptoms tab.

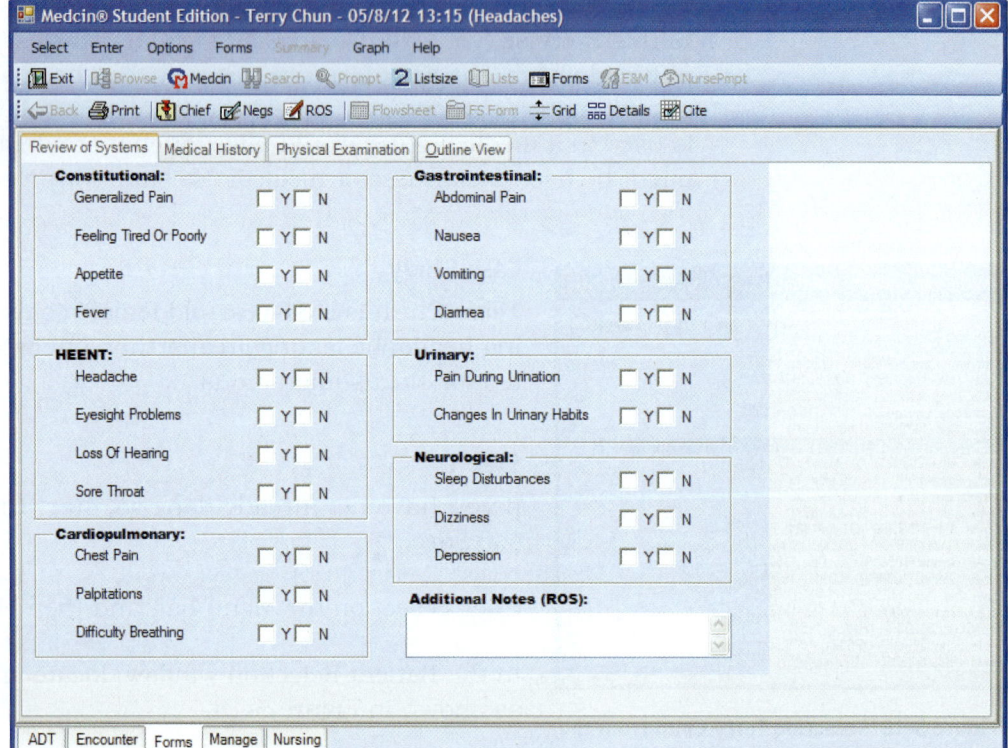

Note that at the top of the form there are tabs, labeled "Review of Systems," "Medical History," "Physical Examination," and "Outline View." This form has three pages on which you may enter data. In subsequent steps, you will use each of these pages to explore the features of this form.

Probably what you first noticed are columns of check boxes with Y and N next to them. This is very similar to a paper form and very intuitive. With almost no training, people understand Y means yes and N means no.

Check boxes work very simply, here is how:

✓ If you click your mouse on an empty box, a check mark appears. The finding will be recorded in the patient's record.

✓ If you change your mind and click in the opposite box, the check mark moves to the box you just clicked.

174   Chapter 5 | Data Entry at the Point of Care

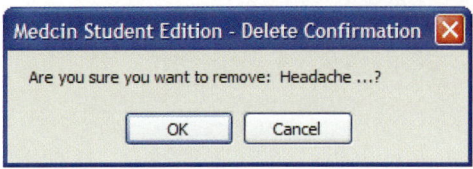

▶ **Figure 5-22** Confirmation that you want to remove a finding.

✓ If you did not want either box checked, click on whichever box already has the check mark and you will be asked to confirm that you want the finding removed (as shown in Figure 5-22).

Step 6

On the Review of Symptoms tab, if you put a check in the Y box, it means that the patient has that symptom. If you put check in the N box, this means that the patient does not have that symptom.

Practice using the check boxes with the finding of Headache, which is located in the section of the form labeled "HEENT." Remember, HEENT stands for head, eyes, ears, nose and throat.

Locate the finding of Headache and click in the check box next to the letter **Y**.

Now click the mouse in the check box next to the letter **N**. Did the check mark move?

Although you cannot see the encounter note at this moment, you just changed the note from the "headache" to "No headache."

Click the mouse again in the same box that already has the check mark in it; this should be next to the letter **N**. The confirmation message shown in Figure 5-22 should appear. Click on the OK button. Both check boxes should now be empty.

Remember, even though the form looks different than the Encounter tab, you really are adding and removing findings on the patient note when you work with the form.

Step 7

The patient reports that she has headaches, vision problems, nausea, vomiting, and trouble sleeping.

▶ **Figure 5-23** Recording Headache and Sleep Disturbances.

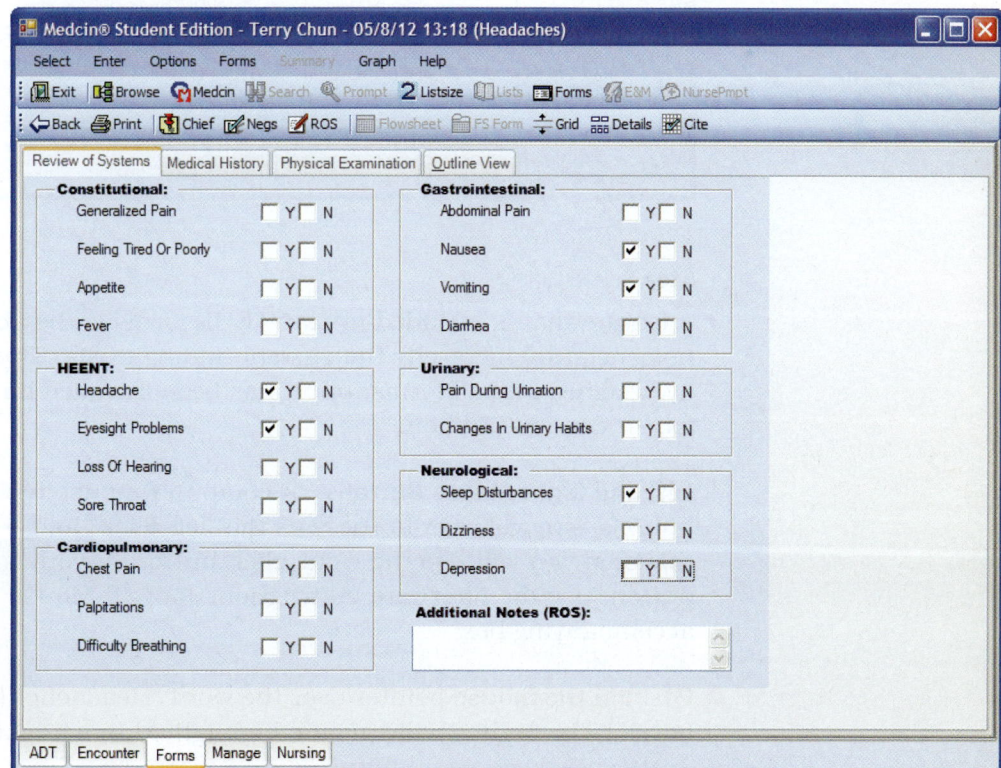

Chapter 5 | Data Entry at the Point of Care

Locate and click in the check box next to the letter **Y** for the following findings:

- ✓ **Y** Headache
- ✓ **Y** Eyesight Problems
- ✓ **Y** Nausea
- ✓ **Y** Vomiting
- ✓ **Y** Sleep Disturbance

Compare your screen to Figure 5-23.

▶ **Figure 5-24** Nomenclature Pane displaying tree of current finding.

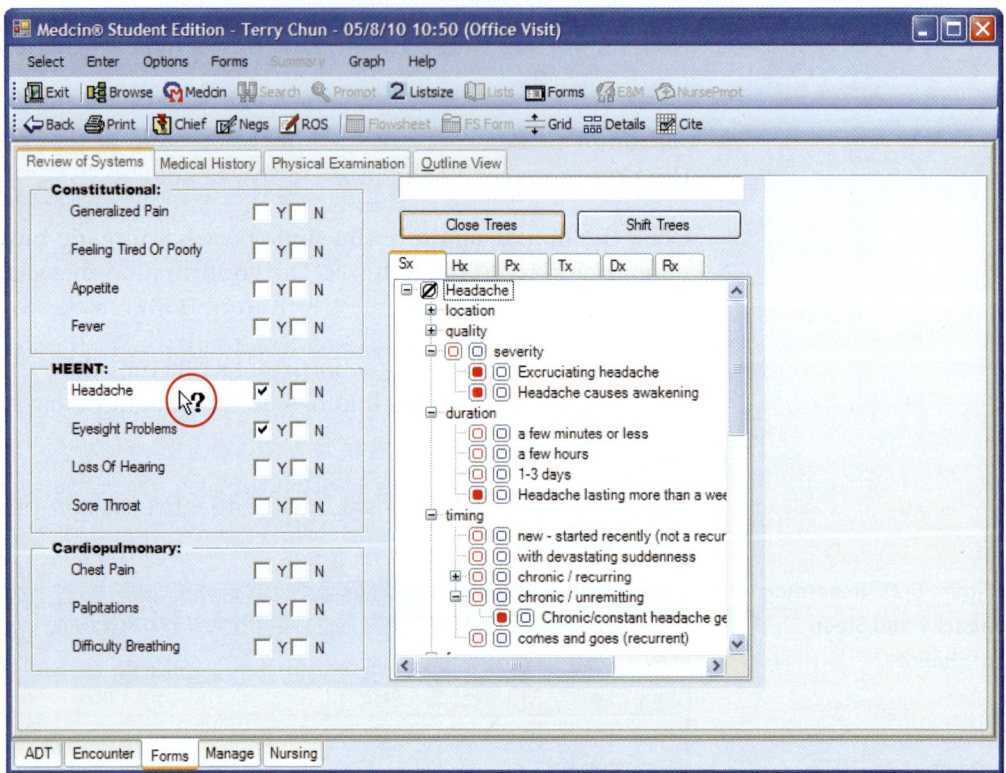

Step 8

A feature that is included in many EHR forms is the ability to see where in the nomenclature hierarchy the current finding exists. This feature is not necessarily designed into all forms, but it has been included on the Short Intake form for the Student Edition.

Left and Right Mouse Buttons A computer mouse typically has at least two buttons—we will refer to these as the "left-click" and "right-click" buttons. In this step you will use the right-click button. If your mouse has only one button, use the Alternate Instructions for Left Mouse Button provided in the accompanying box.

Position the mouse pointer over the word "Headache" (not over the Y/N check boxes.) The finding will become highlighted in white and the mouse pointer

> **Note** — **Alternate Instructions for Left Mouse Button**
>
> An alternative to using the right mouse button to open the Nomenclature Pane in a form is to click the left button of your mouse on the finding name "Headache" (not over the Y/N check boxes).
>
> When you see the check boxes outlined with a rectangle (as shown in Figure 5-25), then move your mouse pointer to the Toolbar and locate and click on the button labeled "Browse." A small pane of Medcin findings will open in the middle of the form and should be positioned in the tree on the finding "Headache." Continue with the remainder of step 8.
>
> ▶ Figure 5-25 Check boxes outlined with a rectangle.

will change shape to include a question mark. When your mouse pointer looks like the one circled in red in Figure 5-24, click the **right-click button** on your mouse. A small pane of Medcin findings will open in the middle of the form.

The Nomenclature Pane shows the highlighted finding in context of the Medcin tree structure. When the Nomenclature Pane is displayed, you can expand the tree structure as well as select additional or different findings.

One reason for invoking the Medcin tree is to locate a more specific finding. In the previous step you recorded the finding "Headache," but the patient elaborates further.

Expand the tree for "Headache by clicking on the small plus sign next to "Severity," "Duration," "Timing," and "Chronic/Unremitting."

Locate and click on the following findings in the expanded tree:

- (red button) excruciating - worse I've ever had
- (red button) causing awakening
- (red button) more than a week
- (red button) getting progressively worse

The button labeled "Close Trees" closes the pane to restore your view of the entire form.

Click on the button labeled "Close Trees" (shown in Figure 5-24 outlined in orange).

Step 9

The Auto Negative button, which you learned to use in Exercise 32, also can be enabled in Forms. This feature allows you to complete Form pages quickly whenever most of the answers are "No" or "Normal."

▶ Figure 5-26 Auto Negative in a form.

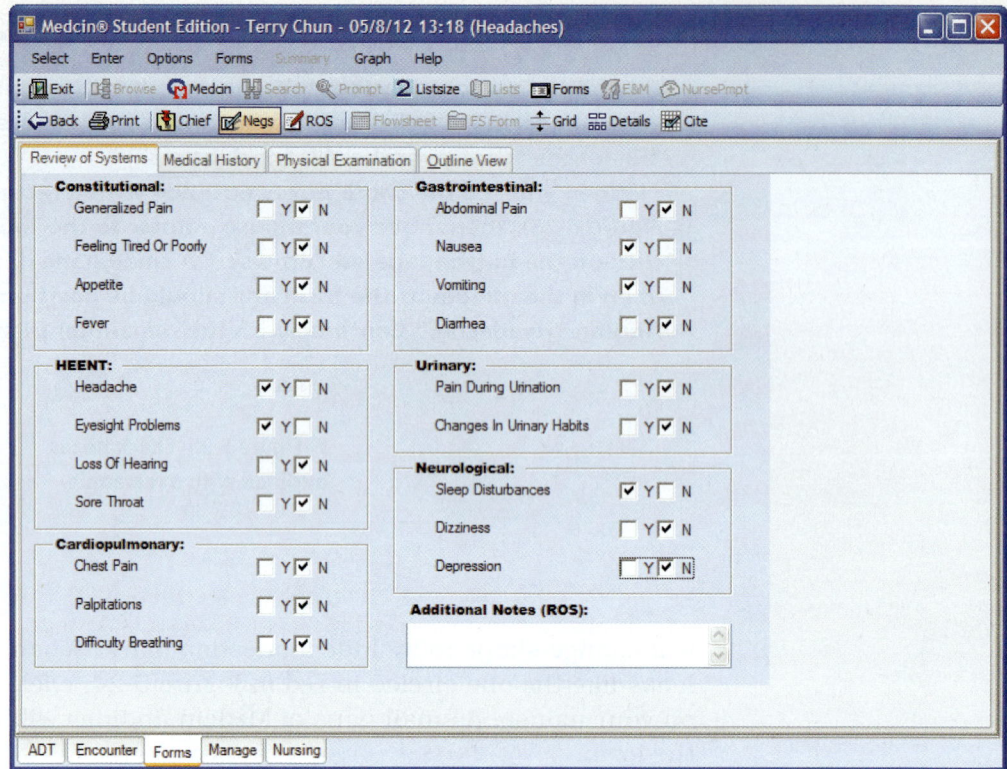

Locate the "Negs" button in the Toolbar at the top of your form. Click your mouse on the Negs button (highlighted in Figure 5-26).

Compare your screen to Figure 5-26. Note what happened. Note that Auto Negative does not alter findings that are already recorded, such as "Headache," "Eyesight Problems," and "Sleep Disturbances."

Step 10

Forms also can allow entry of free-text notes right on the form. This saves the clinician the time it takes to add notes to Entry Details, or open free-text findings. In this step, add a clinical impression to the ROS findings.

In the box at the bottom of your screen labeled "Additional Notes ROS," type the following text: **Pt. denies depression but seems very sad**.

Compare your screen to Figure 5-27 before proceeding.

Step 11

During the course of this exercise, you have been recording findings in the encounter note with every click of your mouse on the form, but you cannot see them as you can on the Encounter tab.

In Forms, the Outline View tab allows you to take a quick look at the findings you have selected for the encounter note. Before entering data in the rest of the form, take a moment to look at what has been entered so far.

Locate and click on the tab labeled "Outline View" at the top of your form (circled in red in Figure 5-28).

178 Chapter 5 | Data Entry at the Point of Care

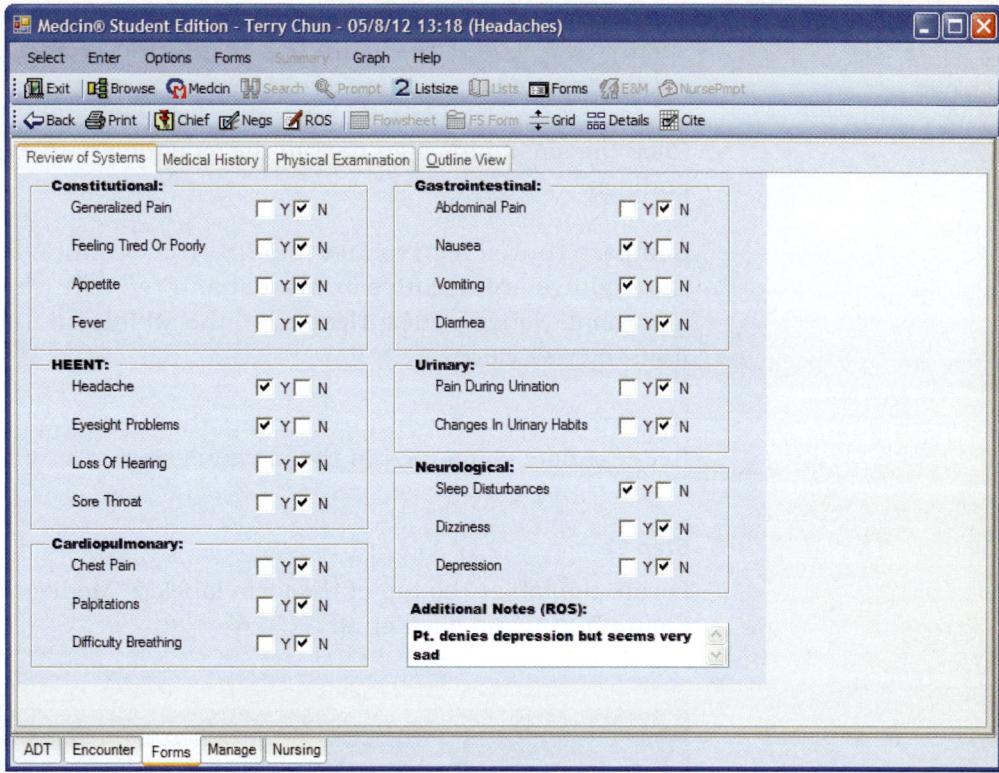

▶ Figure 5-27 Free-text clinical impressions in a form.

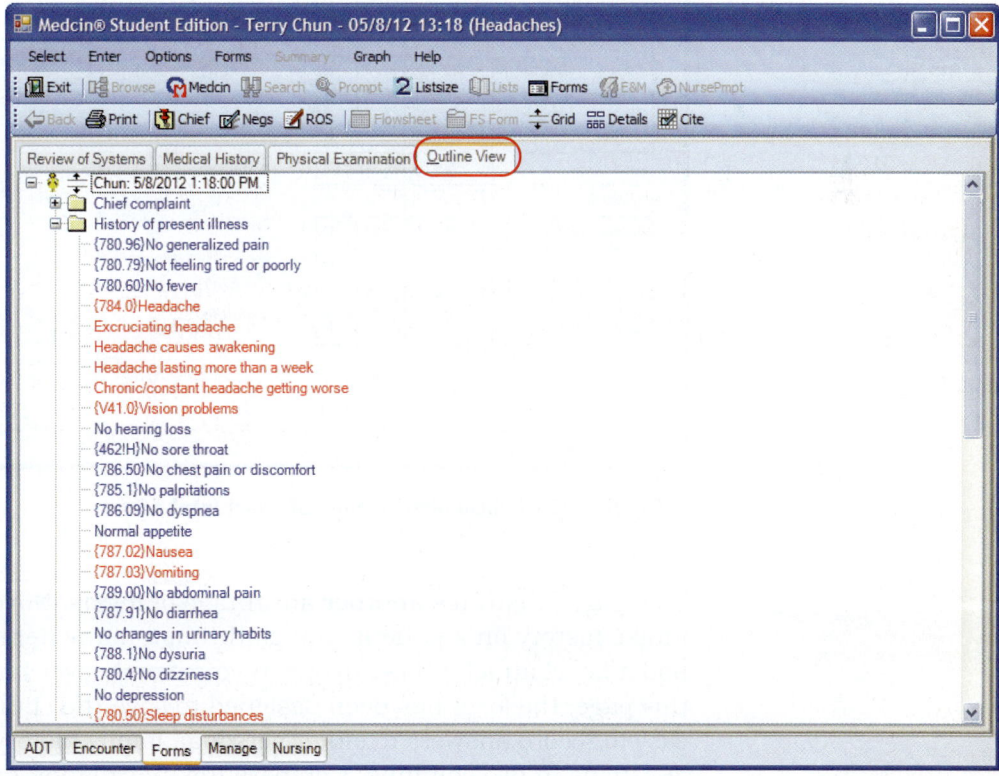

▶ Figure 5-28 Outline View.

Chapter 5 | Data Entry at the Point of Care 179

The outline view shows small folders for each section of the encounter. The small folder icons are the finding group titles you normally see in the encounter note.

Click the small plus sign next to the icon folders to expand them to show the findings.

Compare your screen to Figure 5-28. The Outline View uses blue text when the findings are negative or normal and red text when they are positive or abnormal. Notice under "Headache" the additional findings that you entered from the tree view.

Scroll the outline downward to locate the "Review of Systems" folder. Notice the free-text note you added in the previous step.

Step 12

Locate the tab at the top of the form labeled "Medical History" (circled in red in Figure 5-29), and click on it.

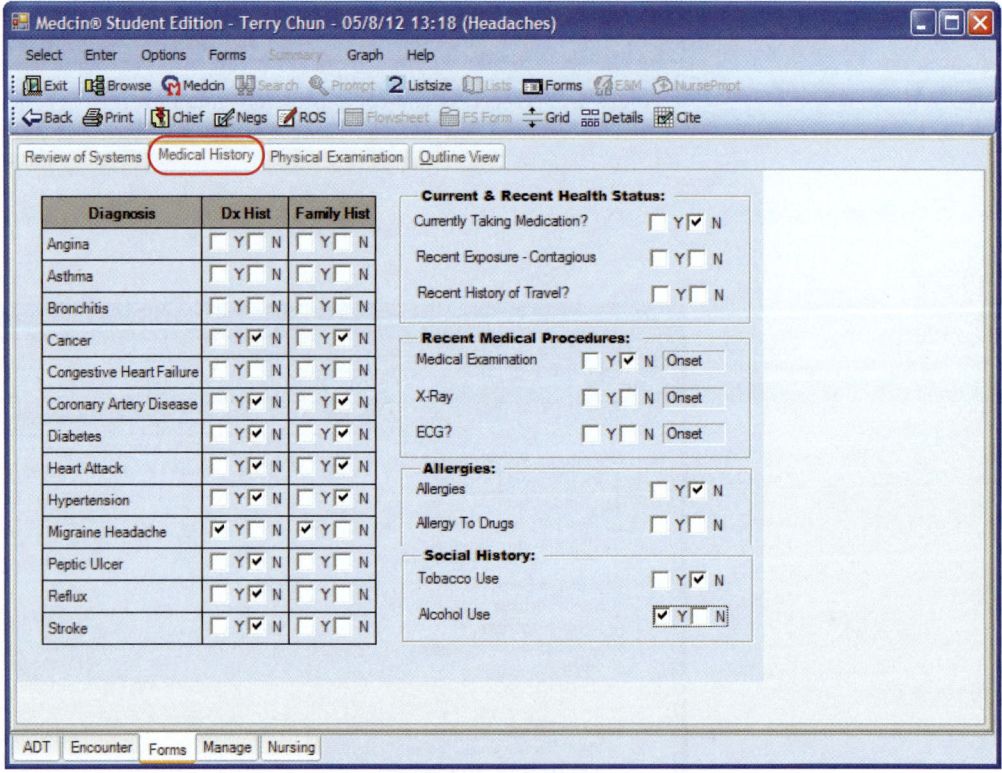

▶ Figure 5-29 Medical History page of Short Intake Form.

This page illustrates another advantage of forms. Normally, when you do an intake history on a patient, you go through many items twice: "Have you ever had a heart attack? Has anyone in your family ever had a heart attack?" On this page, the form has been designed to save the clinician time, by making it easy to record answers to either personal, family history, or both types of history questions in two columns. Compare the information on this tab of the EHR form with the paper form in Figure 5-17.

Step 13

Sometimes patients do not know the medical history of other family members; therefore, you will only record findings the patient is sure about. As the medical assistant asks Ms. Chun the history questions, the patient will only know the answer to some of them.

Enter the Dx History and Family History only for the following items:

Diagnosis	Dx HIST	Family History
Cancer	✓ N	✓ N
Coronary Artery Disease	✓ N	✓ N
Diabetes	✓ N	✓ N
Heart Attack	✓ N	✓ N
Hypertension	✓ N	✓ N
Migraine	✓ Y	✓ Y
Peptic Ulcer	✓ N	
Reflux	✓ N	
Stroke	✓ N	

Complete the rest of her medical history in the right side of the form by locating and clicking on the check boxes as follows:

Currently Taking Medication	✓ N
Recent Medical Examination	✓ N
Allergies	✓ N
Tobacco	✓ N
Alcohol	✓ Y

Carefully compare your screen to Figure 5-29 before proceeding.

Step 14

Locate the tab at the top of the form labeled "Physical Examination" (circled in red in Figure 5-30), and click on it.

The first thing you will notice about this page is that it includes the Vital Signs (in the upper left corner of the page). Recording vital signs as part of the intake physical saves the time it would take to load the vitals form separately. This page illustrates how forms can combine many different elements to make data entry more convenient.

Enter the following vital signs for Terry Chun:

Temperature:	**98**
Respiration:	**14**
Pulse:	**78**
BP:	**130/86**
Weight:	**133**

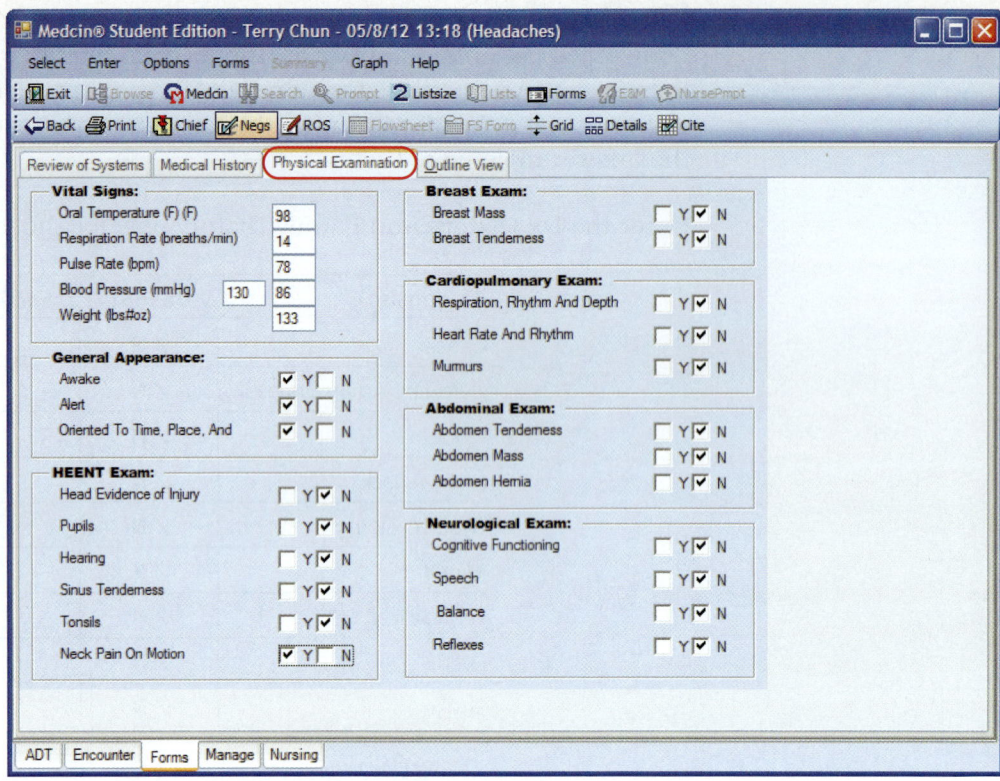

▶ Figure 5-30 Physical Exam page of Short Intake Form.

Step 15

During the physical, the nurse observes the patient has neck pain elicited by motion. Locate the finding **Neck pain on motion** and click the check box for **Y**.

Everything else is normal. Click on the button labeled "Negs" on the Toolbar at the top of your screen (highlighted in Figure 5-30).

Remember you can use the button to quickly document "normals" on Symptoms and Physical Exam findings.

Compare your screen to Figure 5-30.

Did you see that the findings in the General Appearance group were checked Y instead of N by the Auto Negative feature? That is because for some findings such as these, the normal state is to be awake, alert, and oriented. If these were checked No, the condition would be abnormal. The Auto Negative feature is really an Auto Normal feature.

Step 16

Click on the Encounter tab at the bottom of your screen, to view the full text of the encounter note that was completed from within the form.

Click on the Dx tab in the left pane and enter an admitting diagnosis.

Locate and expand the tree for "Neurologic Disorders," and "Headache Syndromes."

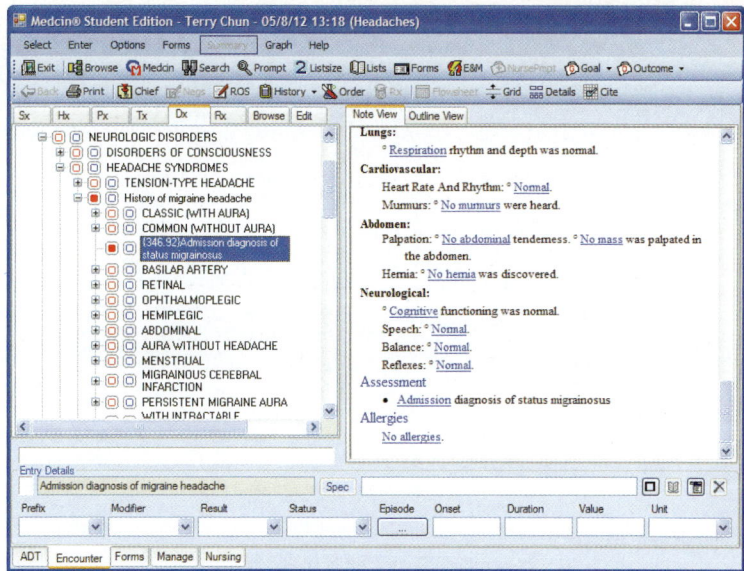

▶ Figure 5-31 Encounter note entered using a form.

Locate and highlight the finding status migrainosus.

Locate and click on the down arrow button in the Entry Details Prefix field and select "Admission diagnosis of"; the description should change to "Admission diagnosis of status migrainosus."

Compare your screen to Figure 5-31. Scroll the right pane so that you can view the entire contents of the note.

This exercise was intended to demonstrate how forms can be used to speed through pages of routine questions, and provide the convenience of free-text or Entry Details fields as part of the form. Although the exercise does not create a medically complete intake history and a physical, you have successfully completed the goals of this exercise.

 **Alert** Do not close or exit the encounter until you have a printed copy in your hand. *You will lose your work if you exit before printing.*

Step 17

Click on the Print button on the Toolbar at the top of your screen to invoke the Print Data window.

Be certain there is a check mark in the box next to "Current Encounter" and then click on the appropriate button to either print or export a file, as directed by your instructor.

```
Terry Chun                                                       Page 1 of 2

   Student: your name or id here
   Patient: Terry Chun: F: 6/10/1980: 5/08/2012 01:18PM
Chief complaint
The Chief Complaint is: Severe headaches.
History of present illness
      Terry Chun is a 31 year old female.
      She reported: Headache is excruciating - 'worst I ever had', causing awakening,
      lasting for more than a week, and chronic/unremitting getting progressively worse.
      Vision Problems.
      Normal appetite. Nausea and vomiting. ° No abdominal pain and no diarrhea.
      No depression. ° Sleep disturbances.
      No generalized pain, not feeling tired or poorly, and no fever. ° No hearing loss
      and no sore throat. ° No chest pain or discomfort and no palpitations. ° No dyspnea.
      No changes in urinary habits and no dysuria. No dizziness.
Past medical/surgical history
   Reported History:
      Medical: No recent medical examination.
      Medications: Not taking medication.
   Diagnosis History:
      No coronary artery disease
      No acute myocardial infarction.
      No hypertension.
      No esophageal reflux
      No peptic ulcer.
      No diabetes mellitus.
      Migraine headache.
      No stroke syndrome.
      No cancer
Personal history
      Behavioral: No tobacco use.
      Alcohol: Alcohol use.
Family history
      No coronary artery disease
      No acute myocardial infarction
      No hypertension
      No diabetes mellitus
      Migraine headache
      No cancer.
Review of systems
Pt. denies depression but seems very sad.

Continued on the following page...
```

▶ **Figure 5-32a** Printout of encounter note for Terry Chun created using a form (page 1 of 2).

Compare your printout or file output to Figure 5-32. (Note your computer will print out two pages; the page breaks vary by printer and may not be in the same place as the figure in the book. However, the contents should be the same except for the encounter date and patient's age.) If your work is correct, hand it in to your instructor. If there are any differences, review the previous steps in the exercise and find your error.

Customized Forms

Forms are not limited to the pages used in this exercise. Forms also allow you to organize questions in the order you would ask them, regardless of where the findings may be grouped in the Medcin Nomenclature hierarchy.

Terry Chun   Page 2 of 2

Physical findings
Vital signs:

Vital Signs/Measurements	Value	Normal Range
Oral temperature	98 F	97.6 - 99.6
RR	14 breaths/min	18 - 26
PR	78 bpm	50 - 100
Blood pressure	130/86 mmHg	100-120/56-80
Weight	133 lbs	98 - 183

General Appearance:
  °~Awake. °~Alert. °~Oriented to time, place, and person.
Head:
  Injuries: °~No evidence of a head injury.
Neck:
  Maneuvers: •~Neck pain was elicited by motion.
Eyes:
  General/bilateral:
  Pupils: °~Normal.
Ears:
  General/bilateral:
  Hearing: °~No hearing abnormalities.
Nose:
  General/bilateral:
  Sinus Tenderness: °~No sinus tenderness.
Pharynx:
  Oropharynx: °~Tonsils showed no abnormalities.
Breasts:
General/bilateral:
  °~No breast mass was found. °~No tenderness of the breast.
Lungs:
  °~Respiration rhythm and depth was normal.
Cardiovascular:
  Heart Rate And Rhythm: °~Normal.
  Murmurs: °~No murmurs were heard.
Abdomen:
  Palpation: °~No abdominal tenderness. °~No mass was palpated in the abdomen.
  Hernia: °~No hernia was discovered.
Neurological:
  °~Cognitive functioning was normal.
  Speech: °~Normal.
  Balance: °~Normal.
  Reflexes: °~Normal.
Assessment
  •~Admission diagnosis of status migrainosus
Allergies
  No allergies.

▶ **Figure 5-32b** Printout of encounter note for Terry Chun created using a form (page 2 of 2).

Forms can be designed to include pages for any of the findings expected to be needed for a particular type of visit. For example, a therapy page is an excellent means of having quick access to standard treatments for specific conditions.

Medical facilities that have a large number of forms customized for their providers succeed very well in implementing an EHR. Form Design tools are a part of almost every EHR system on the market. Forms take longer for the designer to create than Lists, but, if well constructed, make it significantly easier to record patient exams as they happen. Figure 5-33 shows an actual form created and used daily by Dr. Michael Lukowski, M.D., a specialist in obstetrics and gynecology. (See the Real-Life Story by Dr. Lukowski in this chapter.)

Real-Life Story

How I Learned to Stop Worrying and Love Forms

By Michael Lukowski, M.D.

Michael Lukowski is a specialist in obstetrics and gynecology. He has been practicing more than 20 years. He uses an EHR in his practice, enters his own data, and has designed his own EHR forms.

I started using forms right away. When the trainer told me about forms, I thought, "This is the way to go." It slows you down if you have to search a lot. Forms gave me a discrete window into the database so that I could pick out things that I use day in and day out.

I try to put as much of my exam in as data points (findings) rather than just free text. I use free text only as a comment to a finding. To me the whole idea of this is to have retrievable information that I can analyze over time. So I always try to use the (nomenclature) database as my main way to construct a note and then add free text to that if I have to. I find that I use less and less free text because I can pick out findings that say pretty much what I need to say.

Workflow

Using forms, I do what I have always done. My nurse puts in the vital signs; we do some simple lab tests like a hematocrit. The patient is sitting in the exam room when I go in. I sit down and talk with her. As we are talking, I am filling in her history using a tablet computer, just like I used to do with a paper chart. When I am done with that part of the exam, I call my nurse in and do the physical exam.

When the physical exam is finished, I leave and come back to my office. While the patient gets dressed, I finish filling out the rest of the encounter. The patient comes to my office once she is dressed and we talk a little bit more; I finalize her note and write any prescription. If the patient has a pharmacy that receives electronic prescriptions, I transmit them directly to the pharmacy. If the pharmacy does not, I print it on paper and the staff brings it to me to sign.

Forms

I use four forms: Gyn, Post-partum, Pre-op, and then one that contains all the procedures I do, which is still a work in progress, but it covers a lot.

I have a number of tabs within each form. For instance, the Gyn form starts with the intake page. My assistant fills in the menstrual history, pap smear, mammograms, methods of birth control, and so on.

I move through the rest of the tabs, except at the right end of the form; I use three different tabs for assessment so that I can have all the diagnoses I normally use available without searching.

Figure 5-33 shows one of the forms I use every day. The Tabs are: Intake info, VS and Off Labs, Pain Hx, V & V, GI and UTI Sx, Meno & PMS, Fertility Eval, BC Counseling, Soc Hx, Med Hx, and three tabs for assessment.

The tabs are not necessarily in the order I use them but, rather, the order I made the form in—but I know where everything is. If I do want to browse, I have a search box right at the top of my form. I can type in a term I want and hit my search button.

This system—I'm in love with it. It takes either the same time or less time than it used to on paper and I get a note that is 10 times better.

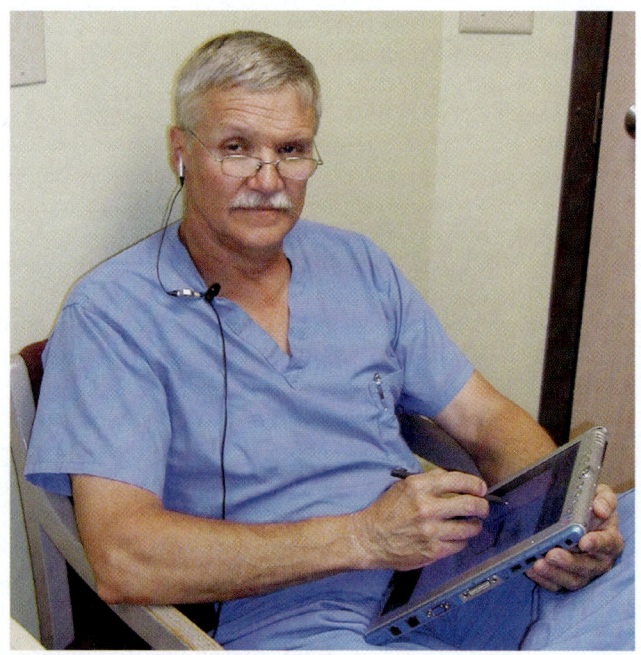

Photo by Richard Gartee

Dr. Lukowski enters data in the exam room on a Tablet PC using an EHR form he designed.

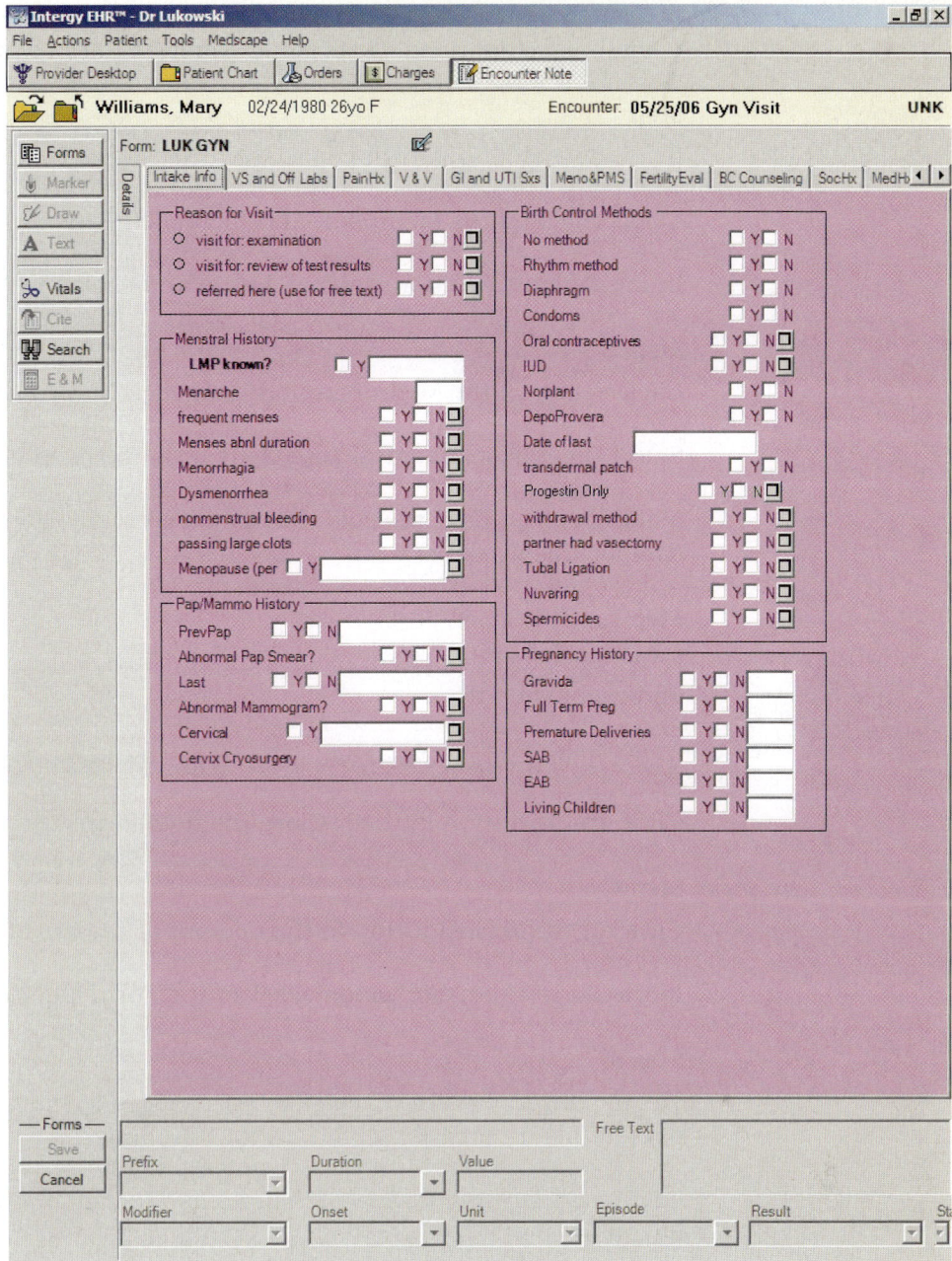

▶ Figure 5-33 Intake tab of gynecology form designed and used by Dr. Lukowski.

Critical Thinking Exercise 35: Using a Form and a List

In this exercise you will use both the form and the list from the previous exercises. Using what you have learned so far, document Mr. Green's hospital admission.

Case Study

Charles Green is a 33-year-old male with a complaint of a new onset frequent cough that is progressively worse especially at night. His chest hurts when he coughs and sometimes vomits because of the coughing. The patient was previously seen at his doctor's office and diagnosed with acute sinusitis. His condition has deteriorated. He is being admitted to the hospital for acute bronchitis.

Step 1

If you have not already done so, start the Student Edition software.

Click Select on the Menu bar, and then click Patient.

In the Patient Selection window, locate and click on Charles Green.

Step 2

Click Select on the Menu bar, and then click New Encounter.

Select the reason **Hospital Inpatient** from the drop-down list.

Make sure you have selected the reason correctly. You may use the current date for this exercise.

Step 3

Enter the Chief complaint by locating the button in the Toolbar labeled "Chief" and clicking on it.

In the dialog window that will open, type "**Recurrent cough and dyspnea**."

Click on the button labeled "Close the note form."

Step 4

Click on the Forms button in the Toolbar at the top of the screen.

In the Forms Manager window, select the Form labeled "Short Intake."

Step 5

The patient reports that he is feeling poorly, and has a fever, headaches, chest pain, difficulty breathing, and trouble sleeping.

On the tab labeled "Review of Symptoms," locate and click in the check box next to the letter **Y** for the following findings:

- ✓ **Y** Feeling Tired or Poorly
- ✓ **Y** Fever
- ✓ **Y** Headache
- ✓ **Y** Chest Pain
- ✓ **Y** Difficulty Breathing
- ✓ **Y** Vomiting
- ✓ **Y** Sleep Disturbance

Step 6

Locate and click on the "Negs" button in the Toolbar at the top of your form.

All items on the Review of Symptoms tab should now have a check in either the Y or N boxes.

Step 7

Locate the tab at the top of the form labeled "Medical History."

Locate the finding "**Currently Taking Medication**" and click in the check box next to the letter **Y**.

Position the mouse pointer over the finding "Currently Taking Medication" (not over the Y/N check boxes) and click the **right-click button** on your mouse.

Scroll the list of Medcin findings that opened on the left of the form, to locate and click on the plus sign next to "over-the-counter medications." Click on the following finding:

- ● (red button) for colds

Click on the button labeled "Close Trees" at the top of the pane.

Step 8

Locate the finding Allergies and click in the check box next to the letter **N**.

Locate the finding Tobacco use and click in the check box next to the letter **Y**.

Step 9

Enter the Dx History and Family History only for the following items:

Diagnosis	Dx Hist	Family Hist
Cancer	✓ N	✓ N
Coronary Artery Disease	✓ N	✓ N
Diabetes	✓ N	✓ N
Heart Attack	✓ N	✓ N
Hypertension	✓ N	
Migraine	✓ N	
Peptic Ulcer	✓ N	
Reflux	✓ N	
Stroke	✓ N	

Step 10

Locate the tab at the top of the form labeled "Physical Examination."

Enter Mr. Green's vital signs in the corresponding fields as follows:

Temperature: 101

Respiration: 26

Pulse: 88

BP: 130/86

Weight: 170

Chapter 5 | Data Entry at the Point of Care

Step 11

On the Physical Examination tab, locate and click in the check box next to the letter **Y** for the following findings:

✓ **Y** Sinus Tenderness

✓ **Y** Neck Pain On Motion

✓ **Y** Respiration Rhythm And Depth

Locate and click on the "Negs" button in the Toolbar at the top of your form.

All items on the Physical Examination tab should now have data.

Step 12

Locate and click on the Encounter tab at the bottom of your screen to return to the encounter view.

Locate and click on the Lists button in the Toolbar at the top of your screen. The List Manager window will be invoked.

Locate and highlight the list named Adult URI. Click your mouse on the button labeled "Load List."

Step 13

Verify that the first line of the Medcin Nomenclature in the left pane reads: "Templates (Symptoms)."

Locate and click on the following symptom findings:

- (red button) sinus pain
- (red button) cough
- (red button) coughing up sputum

Locate and click the small plus sign next to "Cough."

Locate and click the findings:

- (red button) worse at night
- (red button) causing awakening from sleep

Step 14

Locate and click on the ROS button in the Toolbar at the top of your form. Verify that the ROS button is orange.

Locate and click on the Negs button in the Toolbar at the top of your form.

Step 15

Click on the Hx tab. Locate and click on the following History findings:

- (red button) Recent upper respiratory infection (URI)
- (red button) current smoker

In the Value field at the bottom of your screen type the number **20**.

Step 16

Click on the Dx tab to document a history of bronchitis.

Locate and highlight **Sinusitis Acute**.

Locate and click on the down arrow button in the Prefix field. Select "**Recurrent history of**" from the drop-down list.

Step 17

Click on the Px tab to document the physical exam.

Locate and click on the following Physical Exam findings:

- (red button) Wheezing
- (red button) Ronchi

Locate and click on the small plus sign next to "Respiratory movements" to expand the tree.

Locate and click on the following Physical Exam finding:

- (red button) Exaggerated Use Of Accessory Muscles For Inspiration

Locate and click on the Negs button in the Toolbar at the top of your form.

Step 18

Click on the Dx tab and then locate and highlight the finding:

Acute bronchitis.

Locate and click on the down arrow button in the Entry Details Prefix field and select "Admission diagnosis of" as you have in previous exercises.

 **Alert** Do not close or exit the encounter until you have a printed copy in your hand. *You will lose your work if you exit before printing*.

Step 19

Click on the Print button on the Toolbar at the top of your screen to invoke the Print Data window.

Be certain there is a check mark in the box next to "Current Encounter" and then click on the appropriate button to either print or export a file, as directed by your instructor.

```
Charles Green                                              Page 1 of 2

Student: your name or ID here
Patient: Charles Green: M: 5/06/1979: 5/08/2012 01:45PM
```
Chief complaint
```
The Chief Complaint is: Recurrent cough and dyspnea.
```
History of present illness
```
    Charles Green is a 33 year old male.
      He reported: No generalized pain and not feeling tired or poorly.
      Fever, Headache and sinus pain.
      Chest pain or discomfort.No palpitations.
      Dyspnea,cough worse at night,causing awakening from sleep,and coughing up sputum.
      Normal appetite and no nausea.Vomiting.No abdominal pain and no diarrhea.
      No depression.Sleep disturbances.
      No vision problems.No hearingloss and no sore throat.No changes in urinary habits
      and no dysuria.No dizziness.
```
Past medical/surgical history

Reported History:
```
    Medical: A recent URI.
    Medications: Taking over-the-counter cold medication.
```
Diagnosis History:
```
    Recurrent history of acute sinusitis.
    No coronary artery disease
    No acute myocardial infarction.
    No hypertension
    No esophageal reflux
    No peptic ulcer.
    No diabetes mellitus.
    No Migraine headache
    No stroke syndrome.
    No cancer
```
Personal history
```
Behavioral: Current smoker was 20 years
```
Family history
```
    No coronary artery disease
    No acute myocardial infarction
    No diabetes mellitus
    No cancer
```
Review of systems
Systemic: No chills.
Neck: No swollen glands in the neck.
Otoplaryngeal: No earache,no discharge from the ears, no nasal discharge, and no nasal passage blockage.
Pulmonary: No hemoptysis.
Musculoskeletal: No muscle aches.

Continued on the following page…

▶ **Figure 5-34a** Printed encounter note for Charles Green's hospital intake (page 1 of 2).

Compare your printout or file output to Figure 5-34. (Note your computer will print out two pages; the page breaks vary by printer and may not be in the same place as the figure in the book. However, the contents should be the same except for the encounter date and patient's age.) If your work is correct, hand it in to your instructor. If there are any differences, review the previous steps in the exercise and find your error.

Charles Green   Page 2 of 2

Physical findings

Vital signs:

Vital Signs/Measurements	Value	Normal Range
Oral temperature	101 F	97.6 - 99.6
RR	26 breaths/min	18 - 26
PR	88 bpm	50 - 100
Blood pressure	130/86 mmHg	100-120/60-80
Weight	170 lbs	125 - 225

General appearance:
    ° Awake. ° Alert. ° Oriented to time, place, and person.

Head:
    Injuries:° No evidence of a head injury.

Neck:
    Maneuvers: • Neck was elicited by motion.

Eyes:
    General/bilateral:
    Pupils: ° Normal.

Ears:
    General/bilateral:
    Hearing: ° No hearing abnormalities.

Nose:
    General/bilateral:
    Discharge: ° No nasal discharge seen.
    Cavity: ° Nasal septum normal. ° Nasal turbinate not swollen.
    Sinus Tenderness: • Tenderness of sinuses.

Pharynx:
    Oropharynx: ° Tonsils showed no abnormalities.
    Mucosal: ° Pharynx was not inflamed.

Lymph Nodes:
    ° Normal.

Breasts:
    General/bilateral:
    ° No breast mass was found. ° No tenderness of the breast.

Lungs:
    • Respiration rhythm and depth was abnormal.• Exaggerated use of accessory muscles for inspiration was observed.• Wheezing was heard.• Rhonchi were heard. ° Chest was normal to percussion. ° No rales/crackles were heard.

Cardiovascular:
    Heart Rate And Rhythm: ° Normal.
    Murmurs: ° No murmurs were heard.

Abdomen:
    Palpation: ° No abdominal tenderness. ° No mass was palpated in the abdomen.
    Hernia: ° No hernia was discovered.

Neurological:
    ° Cognitive functioning was normal.
    Speech: ° Normal.
    Balance: ° Normal.
    Reflexes: ° Normal.

Assessment
    • Admission diagnosis of acute bronchitis

Allergies
    No allergies.

▶ **Figure 5-34b** Printed encounter note for Charles Green's hospital intake (page 2 of 2).

Chapter Five Summary

In this chapter you learned to use Lists and Forms. Lists are selected from the List Manager window. Forms are selected from the Form Manager window. Both windows are invoked by clicking buttons on the Toolbar.

Forms Invokes the Forms Manager window from which you may select and load a Form as you have in previous chapters.

List Invokes the List Manager window from which you may select and load a List.

List Size Increases or decreases the number of findings in the displayed list. List Sizes are 1-3.

Lists allow the clinician or medical practice to create a subset of the nomenclature typically used for a particular condition or type of exam. A List usually contains findings in every tab.

Because shorter lists mean less scrolling, Lists are a sure way to speed up data entry of routine exams and increase adoption of the EHR by clinicians in the practice. Over time, medical practices should build up a library of Lists covering the medical conditions that are frequently seen at their practice.

A List is accessed by clicking on the button labeled Lists in the Toolbar at the top of the screen and then selecting it from the List Manager window.

Forms display a desired group of findings in a presentation that allows for quick entry of not only positive and negative findings but of any Entry Details fields such as value or results as well. Forms also provide other features that lists cannot, for example:

1. Forms are static; findings have a fixed position on Forms, and will consistently remain in that position, every time the form is used.
2. Findings from multiple sections of the nomenclature can be mixed on the same page of the form in any way that will enable the quickest data entry.
3. Forms may include check boxes, drop-down lists, the fields in the Entry Details section, the onset date, and free-text boxes to record comments.
4. Forms can control which findings are required and which are optional; every question on a Form does not have to be answered for every visit.

The Outline View allows you to see the findings that have been selected without leaving the Forms tab.

A form is accessed by clicking on the Forms tab at the bottom of the screen, then selecting it from the Forms Manager window.

In addition to the List and Forms buttons, you learned to use the following new buttons:

Neg Auto Negative button will automatically click set all the findings (that are not already set) to "normal" when you are on the Sx or Px tab.

ROS On/Off button: when On (orange) history findings are recorded in the Review of Systems section; when Off (blue) history findings are recorded in the History of Present Illness section.

Browse   Displays the current finding's position in the Medcin nomenclature hierarchy. This button was used in this chapter only if you did not have a right-click button on your mouse.

After completing this chapter, you should be comfortable with the general process of locating findings and expanding the tree to view additional findings, using Lists, Forms Search, and Prompt features to create Patient Encounter notes. If you are having difficulty with any area, it is suggested that you repeat Exercises 32 and 34 before proceeding further in the book.

Task	Exercise	Page #
Load and use a list	32	155
How the ROS button works	32	159
HPI/ROS button on individual findings	32	162
Auto Negs Button	32	160
Load and use Forms	34	173
How to access the nomenclature while in a Form	34	176

Testing Your Knowledge of Chapter 5

You may run the Medcin Student Edition software and use your mouse on the screen to answer the following questions:

1. How do you select a List?
2. How do you select Forms?
3. List three features Forms have that Lists do not.
4. Describe what the ROS button on the Toolbar does.

Write the meaning of each of the following medical abbreviations (as they were used in this chapter):

5. ROS   _____
6. HPI   _____
7. HEENT   _____
8. URI   _____
9. Sig   _____

10. Which section of the encounter note is allergy information written into?
11. Auto Negative (the Negs button) functions on what two tabs?
12. An extra icon appears next to Sx findings while using a List. Describe the function of this special button.
13. What Entry Details field is used with a finding to indicate the patient's fever was "mild"?
14. How do you change the numbers on the List Size button and what do the numbers do?
15. You should have produced four narrative documents of patient encounters, which you printed. If you have not already done so, hand these in to your instructor with this test. The printed encounter notes will count as a portion of your grade.

Chapter Six

Understanding Electronic Orders

Learning Outcomes

After completing this chapter, you should be able to:

- Discuss the importance of electronic orders and results
- Compare paper and electronic workflow of orders and results
- Search for a finding using the Search button
- Understand and use the Prompt feature
- Record orders for tests
- Describe the workflow of radiology orders and reports
- Use a CPOE to write a prescription
- Discuss Closed Loop Safe Medication Administration
- Name the five rights of medication administration
- Order medications using a quick-pick list
- Compare ICD-9-CM codes and ICD-10 codes
- Use a diagnosis to find protocols
- Order tests to confirm or rule out a diagnosis

The Importance of Electronic Orders and Results

As you learned in Chapter 1, computerized provider order entry, or CPOE, is viewed by IOM, Leapfrog, and others as one of the key features of an EHR that can improve quality of care, patient safety, and clinician efficiency.

According to the IOM report[1] CPOE systems can improve workflow processes by:

- Preventing lost orders
- Eliminating ambiguities caused by illegible handwriting
- Reduce the medication errors of dose and frequency, drug–allergy, and drug–drug interactions
- Monitoring for duplicate orders
- Reducing the time to fill orders
- Automatically generating related orders
- Improve clinician productivity

Computerized results improve workflow processes because:

- They can be accessed more easily than paper reports by the provider at the time and place they are needed.
- They reduce lag time allowing for quicker recognition and treatment of medical problems.
- Automated display of previous test results makes it possible to reduce redundant and additional testing.
- They allow for better interpretation and for easier detection of abnormalities, thereby ensuring appropriate follow-up.
- Access to electronic consults and patient consents can establish critical linkages and improve care coordination among multiple providers, as well as between provider and patient.

All types of treatments and care events are the result of provider orders. Examples include labs, x-rays, other diagnostic tests, medications, oxygen, diet, therapy, and even home medical devices such as a walker or wheelchair. As the IOM report suggests, when care is ordered electronically, the care is expedited and the workflow process is improved to the benefit of the patient.

CPOE is used by many types of healthcare providers. Some examples include licensed nurse practitioners, physician assistants, registered nurses, and other types of doctors such as osteopaths, dentists, and chiropractors.

Recording Orders in the Student Edition

In this chapter, we will discuss several types of orders, the effect of an EHR on the process, and the workflow. In subsequent exercises you will have the opportunity to record orders and view test results. Although you may not be a provider who writes orders, there are a number of reasons we include orders in this course:

1. Orders are an essential component of any patient chart and a key objective for the IOM, Leapfrog, HITECH Act, and the CMS "meaningful use" criteria.

---

[1] R. S. Dick and E. B. Steen, *The Computer-based Patient Record: An Essential Technology for Health Care* (Washington, DC: Institute of Medicine, National Academy Press, 1991, revised 1997, 2000).

2. Charts that include electronic orders and results offer the student a more realistic view of the complete EHR workflow.

3. Nurses, medical assistants, ward clerks, and other allied health professionals often enter verbal orders into an EHR on behalf of the ordering clinician.

4. Nurses or other allied health professionals may enter their own patient orders directly in the EHR within their particular scope of practice.

5. Nurse practitioners and physician assistants in nearly all states are licensed to write prescriptions and thus will use an electronic prescription writer. Nurse practitioners order laboratory, radiology and other diagnostic tests with the same authority as their physician counterparts.

6. In some critical care units a nurse will act as a scribe for the *code* team, documenting the emergency care as it is being delivered, including the ordering of stat tests and meds.

You will learn to record orders for lab tests in the EHR and later exercises will simulate the process of ordering and tracking lab results on a computer. However, the Student Edition does not contain a working electronic lab order system. You cannot use the Student Edition software to write or send actual orders to a lab, as this ability would be inappropriate in a student edition.

Similarly, exercises later in the chapter include a simulation of writing prescriptions electronically. Again, the Student Edition does not contain a real electronic prescription system. You cannot use it to write or send actual prescriptions to a pharmacy; this also would be inappropriate in a student edition.

Lab Orders and Reports

Laboratory and other diagnostic tests are ordered to determine the health status of the patient, to confirm, or to rule out a suspected diagnosis. The order is assigned a unique ID called a *requisition or accession* number.

Laboratory services consist of nine sciences:

- Hematology
- Chemistry
- Immunology
- Blood bank (donor and transfusion)
- Pathology
- Surgical pathology
- Cytology
- Microbiology
- Flow cytometry

Many laboratory tests use automated instruments to analyze blood and other samples. These instruments typically have an electronic interface to the

Laboratory Information System (LIS). This enables automated test equipment to transfer test results directly to the LIS database. Test results are first stored in the LIS and then transferred to the EHR or printed on a paper lab result report.

Some lab work cannot be performed by automated equipment. For example, some pathology tests are performed by growing cultures and examining them, or examining tissue samples through a microscope. There are three areas of pathology:

- Clinical pathology uses chemistry, microbiology, hematology, and molecular pathology to analyze blood, urine, and other body fluids.
- Anatomic pathology performs gross, microscopic, and molecular examination of organs and tissues and autopsies of whole bodies.
- Surgical pathology performs gross and microscopic examination of tissue removed from a patient by surgery or biopsy.

Hospitals and some medical offices have labs within the medical facility. There are also outside testing facilities called *reference laboratories*. These labs process tests for offices that do not have their own labs and perform esoteric tests that are beyond the capability of the hospital laboratory.

There are also medical tests that do not have to be performed in a laboratory. Certain tests may be performed by handheld instruments at the patient's bedside or even the patient's home. This is called *point-of-care testing*. One example of such an instrument is a *glucose monitor*. The glucose monitor measures the amount of a type of sugar in a patient's blood. The results of this test can be electronically transferred from the glucose monitor device to the EHR. In a hospital, the data is usually transferred via the LIS.

The fluid or tissue to be examined is called the *specimen*. The specimen may be collected from the patient at the medical facility and then transported to the laboratory or the patient may be sent to the laboratory to have his or her blood drawn there.

Here are various ways a sample for a blood test might be obtained:

- A nurse in the emergency department may draw blood from a patient, but a different person may carry the sample to the hospital laboratory.
- A laboratory at an inpatient hospital may send a phlebotomist to patient's room to draw the blood required for ordered tests.
- A surgery patient may be directed to the hospital laboratory during preadmission, where a phlebotomist or laboratory technician may draw the sample before the patient is admitted.
- A physician's office may have a small laboratory where certain tests can be performed in the office.
- A physician's office may draw the blood but send the specimen to an outside reference lab. In this case a courier will collect the specimens from the medical office and transport them to the lab.
- A physician's office may give a written lab requisition to the patient and send them to the outside reference lab. When the patient arrives at the lab, a phlebotomist employed by the lab company will draw the blood.

Whether blood is drawn at a medical office, laboratory, or in a hospital at the patient's bedside, a phlebotomist or nurse will collect a specified amount of blood from the patient in one or more vials.

A provider usually only collects the specimen when it is part of the exam or procedure—for example, taking a swab for a throat culture, or removing a mole that is to be sent to pathology.

If a test requires a urine sample or stool specimen, this might be obtained from the patient at the medical facility or might be brought by an outpatient to his or her appointment.

Certain tests may not be covered by the patient's insurance and the patient must sign an acknowledgment that he or she has been advised that the test will not be paid by insurance. This is called an Advance Beneficiary Notice, or ABN. A sample ABN is shown in Chapter 2, Figure 2-23.

If the clinician's diagnosis or plan of treatment is dependent on the outcome of the test, then timeliness is important. In such a case, the patient cannot be treated until the provider receives and reviews the results. Although many of the steps are the same, electronic lab orders enable the provider to begin treatment sooner because the provider is aware of the results sooner.

Similarly, tissue samples need to be examined for certain surgical pathologies and the results made available to the surgeon during the surgery.

The results of tests that are performed by automated equipment are communicated to the LIS, which assigns codes and records values for each component of the test. The lab system computer then compiles the results into a report that includes the information from the original requisition, test codes, codes for each component of the test, as well as standard reference ranges for each associated with the actual value measured with the component. Additional notes, such as whether the value is considered outside the reference range (high or low) and whether the results were verified by repeat testing, also are merged into the report data.

When the report is complete, it is sent to the ordering clinician. The clinician will review the results of the test and take appropriate action.

From the beginning of the order to completion of the review by the clinician, the status of the order is important. If too much time lapses between when the patient needs the test and a treatment is given based on that test's results, the patient's condition could deteriorate.

To determine how much time has elapsed, the medical office must know which patients have tests pending results and when they were ordered. The office is then in a position to follow up on the test by calling the lab or the patient.

Orders are tracked in an EHR from the moment they are entered in the system. If a patient fails to show up for a test, the lab can inform the medical office because the lab received the requisition electronically and is expecting the patient.

In the EHR system, all orders have a status. Lab orders that have been sent but have no results are "pending." A report of pending orders is always available.

Labs may sometimes send "preliminary" results to give the clinician an early indication of the test and then send "final" results once the test has been repeated for verification. For example, a bacterial culture's preliminary results may appear after 24 hours, but the culture may be monitored for 72 hours before the final results.

EHR systems may connect to the lab system frequently as new orders are written or at predefined intervals throughout the day. Whenever a connection is established between the two systems, all available results for all of the clinic's patients are downloaded to the EHR. When lab results are received, most systems merge the data instantly into the patient's chart. Software matches each result to the original requisition order.

The status will then be preliminary, final, or corrected, as designated by the lab.

With an electronic order system, the patient's results are usually available the same day or the next morning. The clinician is notified as soon as results are ready. The clinician may order follow-up tests, a follow-up visit, send a "task" to have the patient called, add comments or annotations to the test, and compare the results to previous similar test results. The EHR system also keeps track of which results have not yet been reviewed by the clinician.

An important tool clinicians use to care for their patients is "trending," which is comparing the change of certain test components or vital signs over a period of time.

In a paper chart, the trend is observed by paging through past tests, locating the desired component on each report, and making a mental comparison. However, when the lab results are stored as data in the EHR, the computer can instantly find all instances of any component the clinician wishes to consider. Additionally, with computerized data, graphs and charts can be easily created for any finding that has numerical results. Examples of trending lab data are shown in Chapter 2, Figure 2-19 and Figure 2-20.

The benefit of electronic lab results is that the codified data is merged into the EHR. Most practices cannot afford the personnel to have paper lab results keyed into the computer. Without an electronic laboratory interface, the provider and the patient both miss the advantages that codified lab data provides.

Electronic lab orders and results benefit both the patient and the practice. Waiting for the results of an important test is stressful to patients. Electronic laboratory interfaces help expedite the process, ensuring the provider knows about the results as soon as they are ready at the lab. Whether the patient is subsequently contacted by the phone or has access to lab results via the web, the waiting time (and accompanying anxiety) is reduced.

Comparison of Orders and Results Workflows

In Chapter 1 we compared the workflow of an office using paper charts with an office that fully uses an EHR. Let us now compare the workflow of a facility that writes orders on paper with one that uses electronic orders and results. As we previously used the example of laboratory tests to compare forms of data, let us use the workflow surrounding lab tests in this comparison as well.

In this scenario the clinician wants additional information about the patient's health that can be obtained by analyzing the patient's blood. The provider "orders" a blood test. Implied within the order is a request for a nurse, phlebotomist, or other medical personnel to draw a sample of the patient's blood.

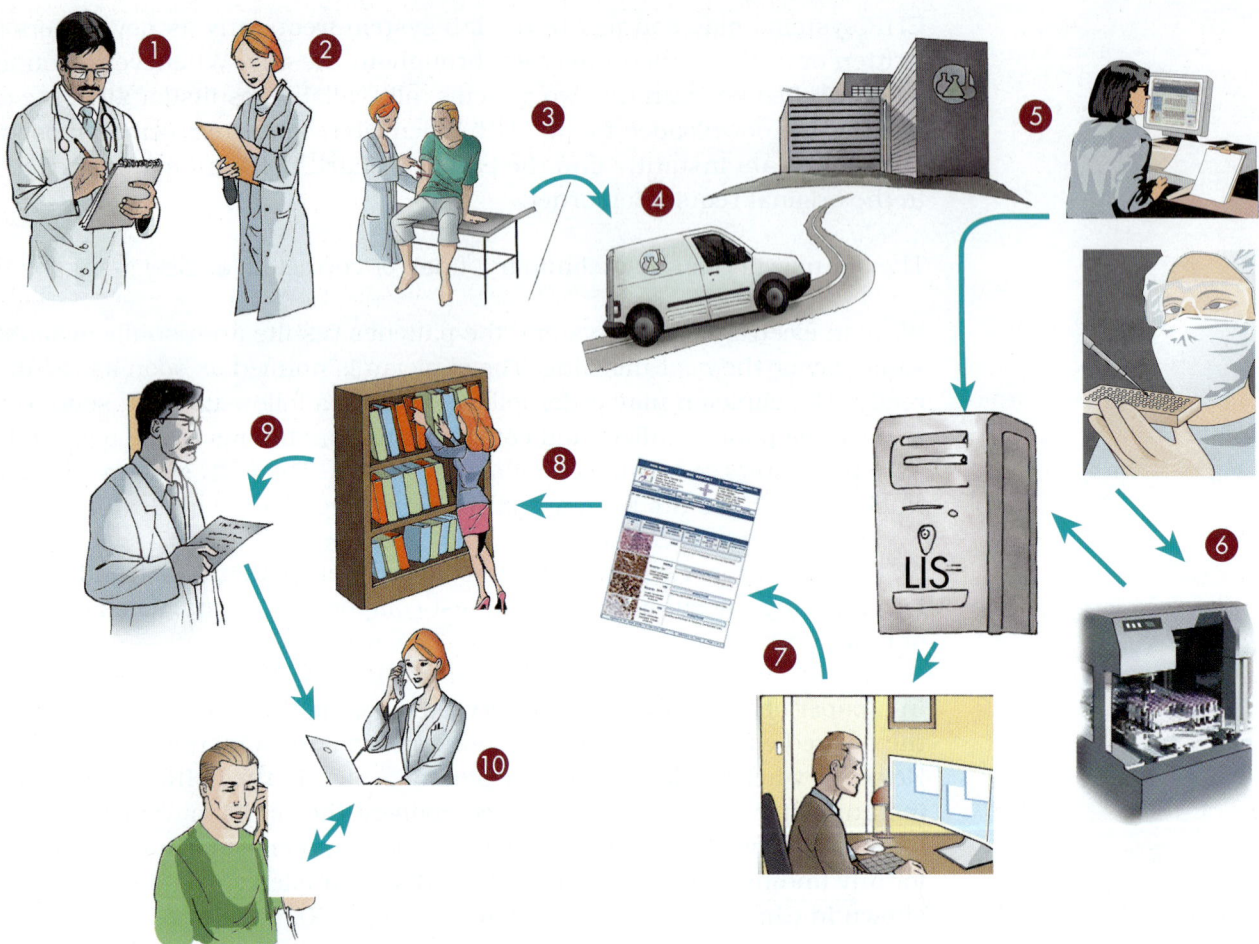

▶ Figure 6-1 Workflow of paper-based lab orders and results.

Workflow of Paper Lab Orders and Results

Figure 6-1 illustrates the workflow of paper-based lab orders and results. Follow the workflow as you read the following:

❶ The workflow begins when the clinician decides a lab test will be useful and writes an order. In a facility that uses paper orders, this may be a verbal order to the nurse or medical assistant who will obtain and complete the paper requisition form. The test order may be noted in the handwritten paper chart or mentioned in the clinician's dictation.

❷ A paper requisition form supplied by the reference laboratory is filled out. The patient's demographic and insurance information is copied by hand, onto the form, with inherent risks of a mistake while copying by hand.

Certain tests may not be covered by the patient's insurance and the patient must sign an ABN. Whether an ABN will be required for a particular test relies on either a call to the lab, a call to the insurance plan, or the nurse's memory.

③ The specimen of the patient's blood is drawn.

The paper form is accompanied by uniquely numbered labels. The nurse will write the patient name and ID on the labels and attach them to the specimen vial or container.

④ If the blood is drawn in the clinic, the sample is picked up by a courier and transported to the lab.

If the specimen is delivered to the lab by courier, the paper requisition will accompany the specimen. If the patient is going to have the blood drawn at the lab, the patient will bring the requisition form.

⑤ The paper requisition is keyed into the lab system computer by a lab employee. There is an inherent risk of a typing error.

⑥ The laboratory performs the tests, assigns codes and values for each component of the test, and then compiles the results into a report.

⑦ A pathologist reviews the results and a printed copy of the results will be faxed, mailed, or sent by courier to the ordering clinic or facility.

⑧ A staff person at the medical facility will file the paper copy in the patient's chart and make the clinician aware that the report has arrived.

⑨ The clinician will review the results in the paper chart. To compare results with any previous tests, the clinician will thumb through the pages of the chart.

⑩ The doctor will handwrite notes, or leave voice mail for his staff, who will call the patient with the results.

Although a copy of the order is in the paper chart, unless a separate list is maintained of what tests are ordered and when results are received, the clinician never knows if a test is lost.

If the patient was sent to an outside lab with a paper requisition in hand and fails to show up, neither the lab nor the medical office knows that the test is pending.

Workflow of Electronic Lab Orders and Results

EHR systems allow the clinician to order a test while the clinician is creating the encounter note. The order is automatically documented as part of the encounter note (in the Plan section). You will see this in Guided Exercise 37.

Figure 6-2 illustrates the workflow of electronic lab orders and results. Follow the workflow as you read the following:

① The workflow begins when the provider orders a lab test. Using an EHR at the point of care, the provider can create the order from within the EHR.

The electronic order system compares the test codes on the order to coverage rules for the patient's insurance and automatically alerts the user if a signed ABN is required.

CPOE systems also display a list of recent and pending orders for the patient. This serves two purposes. First it prevents unintentional duplicate orders as the clinician is aware if another provider has already ordered the same or similar test. Second, the clinician is made aware of regular preventative or health maintenance tests for which the patient is due.

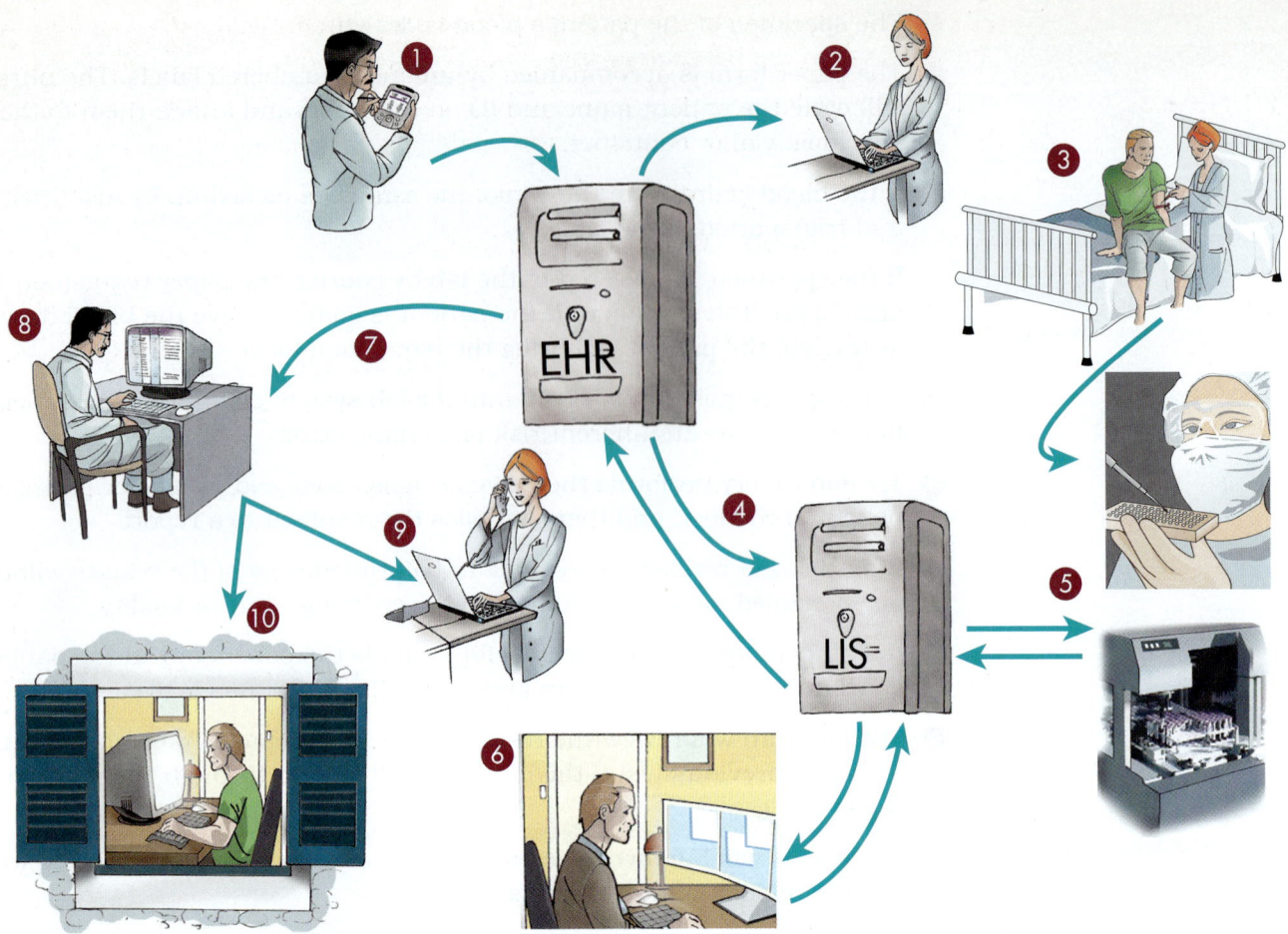

▶ Figure 6-2 Workflow of electronic lab orders and results.

❷ In CPOE systems the provider does not complete the actual requisition form. The lab order initiates a "task" for a nurse, medical assistant, or phlebotomist to act on. The task involves at least two actions: completing the requisition and obtaining a specimen.

A nurse, phlebotomist, or other staff person will complete the electronic requisition in a computer. The patient's demographic and insurance information is populated automatically, eliminating mistakes caused by retyping.

Uniquely numbered labels are automatically printed as part of the electronic requisition process.

❸ The specimen of the patient's blood is drawn. The labels are attached to the specimen vial or container.

❹ The requisition is transmitted electronically to the lab system computer and contains the information required to process the test. Electronic orders are transmitted to the lab either in real time as each requisition is completed or in batches throughout the day.

Specimens obtained at the medical office for tests performed at an outside lab are picked up by a courier and transported to the lab one or more times a day.

If the patient is sent to an outside lab for the blood to be drawn, the requisition is already waiting in the lab system when the patient arrives because it was sent electronically.

❺ The lab performs the requested tests and communicates the results through the Laboratory Information System (LIS).

❻ As soon as any results are ready at the lab, they are reviewed by the pathologist and made available to the medical facility's EHR.

❼ The results are returned electronically and merged into the patient's EHR.

The EHR will alert the clinician that the results are ready.

❽ The clinician will review the results on screen. Access to other components of the EHR allows easy comparison of current results with previous tests and allows the clinician to graph trends. The clinician can then order the treatments and follow-up tests, send messages to the staff or the patient, and do it all from the EHR.

❾ In an outpatient setting, a nurse or other staff member receives an electronic "task" to call the patient.

❿ Alternatively, some facilities allow the patient to view the test results online via a secure web site.

Electronic lab orders are assigned a status the moment they are created. This means it is easy for a clinician to see that a test has already been ordered by another provider. It also means that the order is not buried in some paper chart, but electronically tracked so the clinic is alert to missing or overdue results.

Learning to Use the Search and Prompt Features

As you learned in Chapter 2, medical nomenclatures such as SNOMED-CT and Medcin have hundreds of thousands of findings. The challenges with large clinical vocabularies include:

- How can you locate a finding among hundreds of thousands?
- Does the nomenclature use the same term for the finding as you do?
- Where are other related findings?

The Search feature provides a quick way for the provider to locate a desired finding in the nomenclature. Search produces a list of the findings almost instantly. Medcin addresses semantic differences in medical terms in several ways:

1. Search performs automatic word completion so if you search for "knee" but the finding is for "knees" it will still find it.

2. Medcin includes an extensive list of synonyms that are used in an alternate word search. For example, if you search for knee injury, the search results will also include findings for knee burns, knee trauma, and fractured patella, among others.

3. Search identifies related findings in other tabs so that when you search for a word or phrase in a particular tab, related findings are automatically available in the other tabs. This means that when you are using search while documenting a patient exam, as you proceed through the exam, the other tabs may already have related findings that you will use.

How Search Works

Search is not designed to find every instance that contains the words being searched because the search results would often have too many findings. Instead, search uses the Medcin hierarchy (the tree view you have expanded in previous exercises). It finds and shows the highest level match and does not list all the expanded findings below it.

For example, in Chapter 3 you did an exercise with Headache during which you expanded the tree to show many types of headache. If you searched for Headache, the search results would display the finding "Headache" with a small plus sign next to it. If you wanted to peruse the various types of headaches, you would click on the plus sign to expand the next level of the tree. If, however, you were searching for "migraine headache," the search results would have expanded the tree for Headache to show migraine, which is at a lower level.

Search always begins in the tab you are currently in when you start the search. If there are search results in another tab but none in the current tab, the software will automatically change tabs to the first one with results. The order of the tabs you see on the screen is the same order in which it will display the search results. For example, if you are on the Tx tab when you search and there are no results but there are results for the other tabs, it will automatically change the left pane to the Dx tab to display those results because that is the next tab in order.

Guided Exercise 36: Using Search and Prompt

When patients are referred for diagnosis or follow-up care, a battery of diagnostic test may be ordered to be done before the patient's scheduled appointment so the results can be available when the clinician sees the patient. This is especially true of tests that require more time to result or require the capabilities of an outside lab or radiology center.

Having the results ready when the clinician sees the patient allows the results to be considered during the exam, used in the current assessment, and used to educate and counsel the patient.

Case Study

The patient, Gary Yamamoto, has been referred to the cardiology clinic with suspected angina. The patient did not seem in any immediate danger when he was seen by his family physician at the time of the referral and has been given an appointment at the clinic later this week. In the meantime, we are going to enter orders for some tests to be done prior to the scheduled appointment so the results will be available at the scheduled clinic visit.

In this exercise, you will learn to use the Search and Prompt features as well as several new buttons on the Toolbar. The exercise will not produce a very thorough exam note, but it will give you experience using the features.

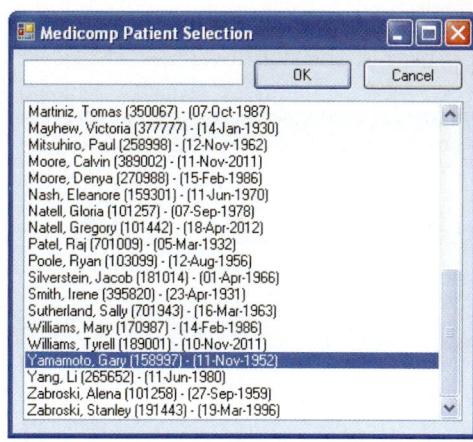

▶ Figure 6-3 Selecting Gary Yamamoto from the Patient Selection menu.

Rather than navigate the entire Medcin nomenclature, you can start with a known symptom or disease and work forward. To quickly locate the desired findings, we will use the Search function.

Step 1

If you have not already done so, start the Student Edition software.

Click Select on the Menu bar, and then click Patient.

In the Patient Selection window, locate and click on **Gary Yamamoto**, as shown in Figure 6-3.

Step 2

Click Select on the Menu bar again, and then click New Encounter.

You may use the current date and time for this exercise.

Select the reason **Pre-visit Workup** from the drop-down list. Click on the OK button.

In the next two steps, the medical assistant enters the Chief complaint and Vital Signs.

Step 3

Enter the Chief complaint by locating the button in the Toolbar labeled "Chief" and clicking on it.

In the dialog window that will open, type "**Pt. referred with suspected Angina.**"

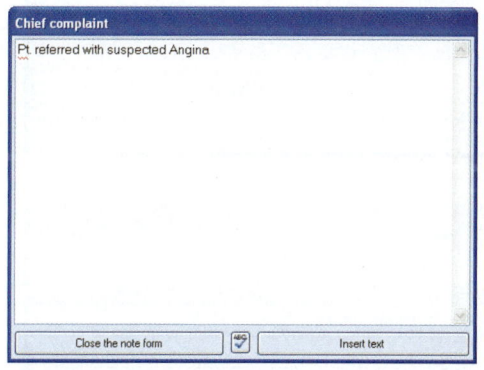

▶ Figure 6-4 Chief complaint dialog referral for suspected angina.

Compare your screen to Figure 6-4 before clicking on the button labeled "Close the note form."

Step 4

Enter Mr. Yamamoto's vital signs using the Vitals Form.

Locate and click on the button labeled "Forms" in the Toolbar at the top of your screen.

Select the form labeled "Vitals" from the list in the Form Manager window.

Enter Gary Yamamoto's vital signs in the corresponding fields as follows:

Temperature:	**98.6**
Respiration:	**20**
Pulse:	**70**
BP:	**130/86**
Height:	**65**
Weight:	**138**

Chapter 6 | Understanding Electronic Orders

When you have finished, compare your screen to Figure 6-5. If it is correct, click on the tab labeled "Encounter" at the bottom of the window.

▶ Figure 6-5 Vital Signs form for Gary Yamamoto.

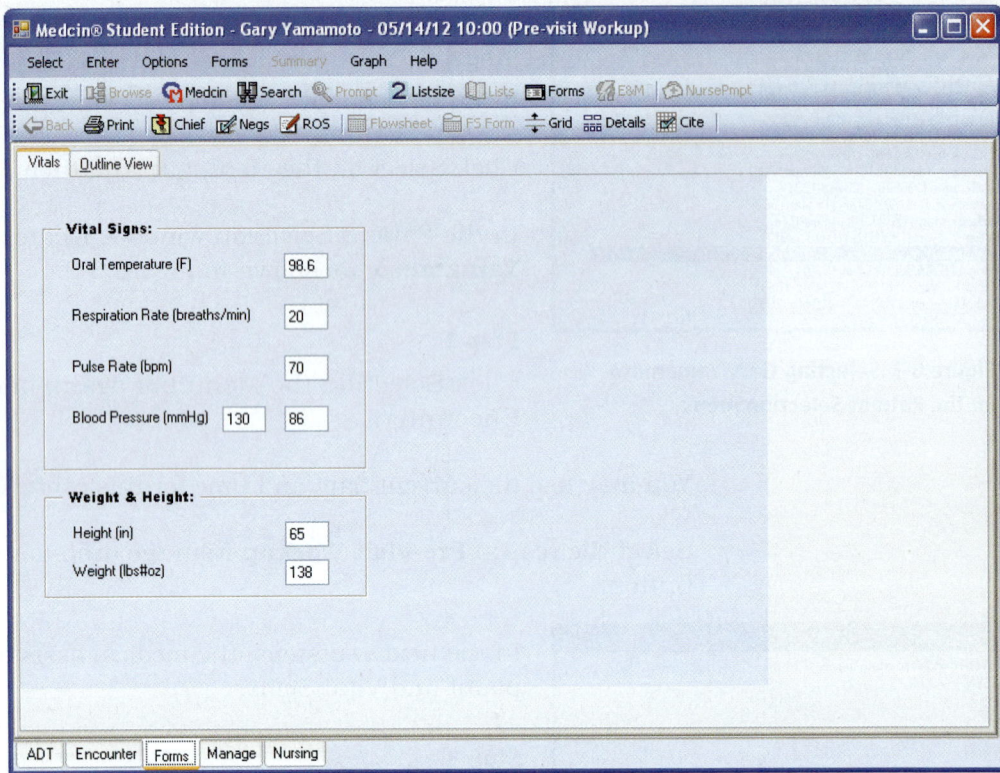

▶ Figure 6-6 Search button (highlighted) invokes Search Dialog window.

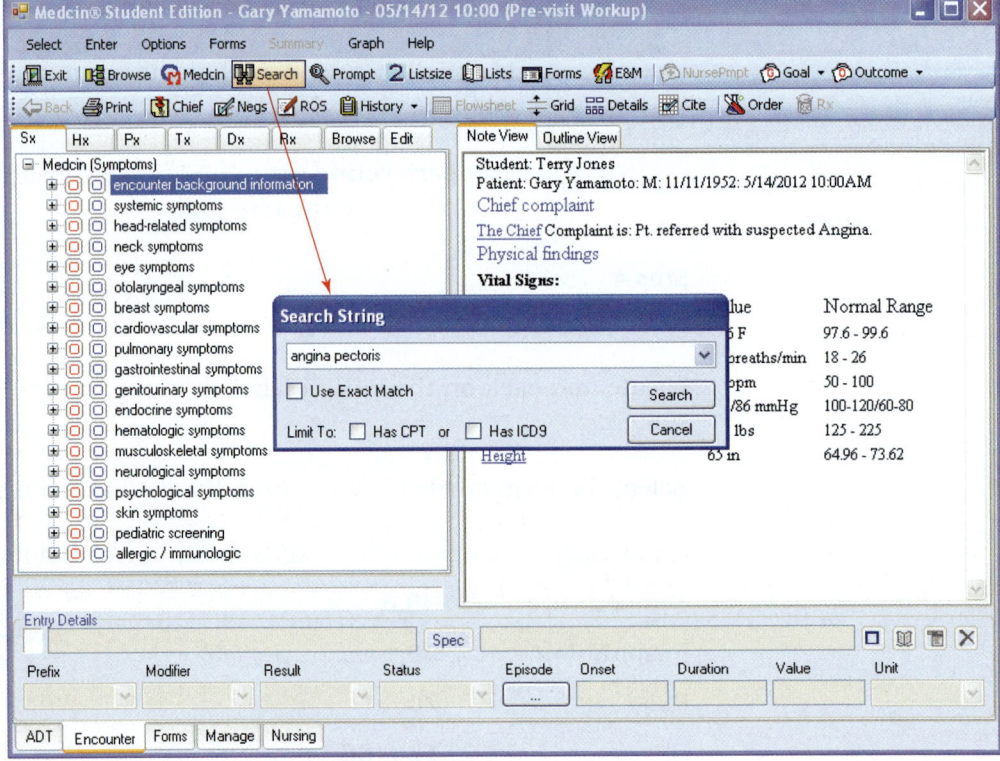

Step 5

Locate the Search button on the Toolbar near the top of the screen. The search icon resembles a small pair of binoculars. It is highlighted in Figure 6-6.

Click your mouse on it to invoke the "Search String" window. Position your mouse in the Search String field and enter the medical term "**angina pectoris**." Verify that you have spelled this correctly, then click the button in the box that says "Search."

▶ Figure 6-7 Search results (List Size button circled in red).

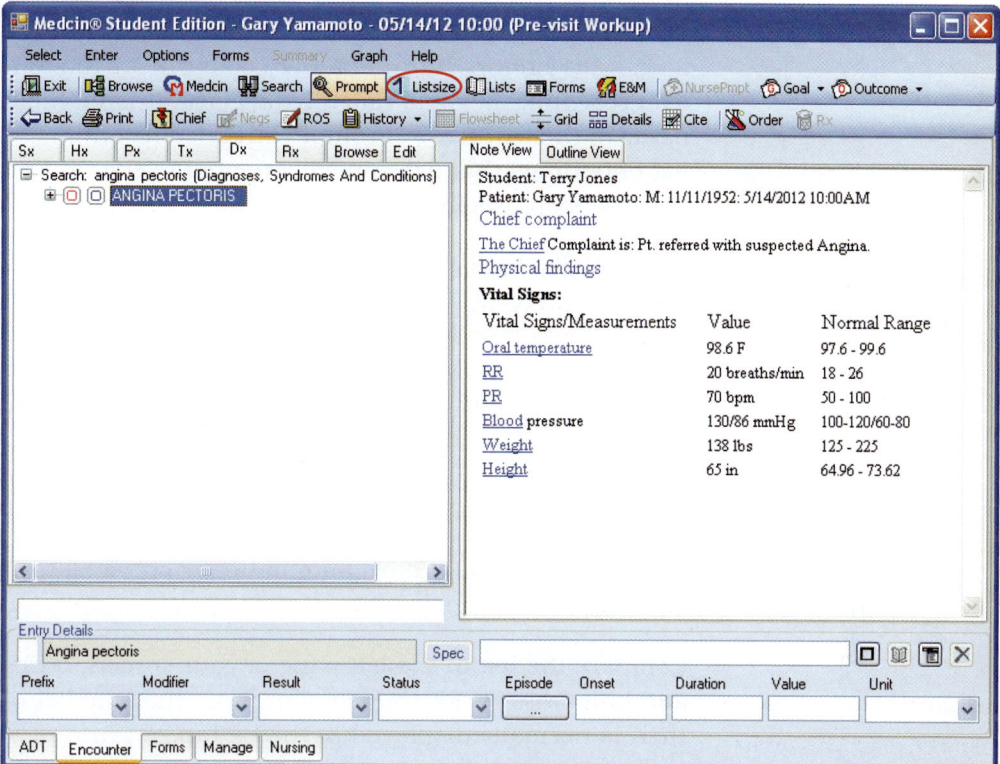

Step 6

Compare your screen to Figure 6-7, which shows the search has succeeded. Notice that you started the search on the Sx tab but the screen is now on the Dx tab. This is because the search was for a very specific pair of words that did not exist in the other tabs.

As discussed earlier in this section, the Search result displays in the current tab if there are any findings that match the search string; otherwise, it displays in the first tab with findings that match. Had the search simply been for angina, History of Angina would have been found and the Hx tab would have been displayed.

Note

No Results?

If your screen does not match Figure 6-7, or you received the message "nothing found to match search," repeat step 5 and verify that you have spelled the medical terms correctly. In this exercise you are searching for a very specific match, and a spelling error will alter the search results.

Step 7

Locate the button labeled "List Size" on the Toolbar near the top of the screen. The List Size button is circled in red in Figure 6-7, and you have used the button in previous chapters. As the name implies, the List Size controls the number of findings that will be displayed in a "prompt list."

For this step, set the List Size to **1**. If the List Size is currently greater than 1, click your mouse on the List Size button repeatedly until it displays a **1**.

Step 8

Locate the Prompt button on the Toolbar near the top of the screen. The Prompt icon resembles a small magnifying glass. It is highlighted in Figure 6-7. The full name of the feature is "Prompt with current finding." This feature generates a list of findings that are clinically related to the finding currently highlighted. For this step, Angina Pectoris should be highlighted in blue on your screen.

Once the list is displayed, you can use it just like you have been using Lists in previous exercises. That is, you can record findings by clicking on the red or blue buttons next to the findings. You also can change tabs; however, the findings displayed in the other tabs will be limited to those that are clinically related to the finding that was highlighted when you clicked the Prompt button.

Click your mouse on the Prompt button at this time.

Step 9

The left pane should have automatically changed to the Sx tab; if it did not, click on the tab labeled "Sx."

Compare the list in the left pane of your screen to Figure 6-8, ignoring the red and blue buttons for the moment. Note that the list of findings is much shorter than is normally displayed in the Sx tab.

The first line in the left pane usually includes the name or source of the list. Heretofore, this was just the name of the tab, for example, Medcin (Symptoms);

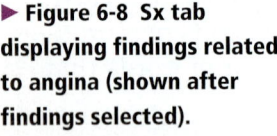

▶ **Figure 6-8** Sx tab displaying findings related to angina (shown after findings selected).

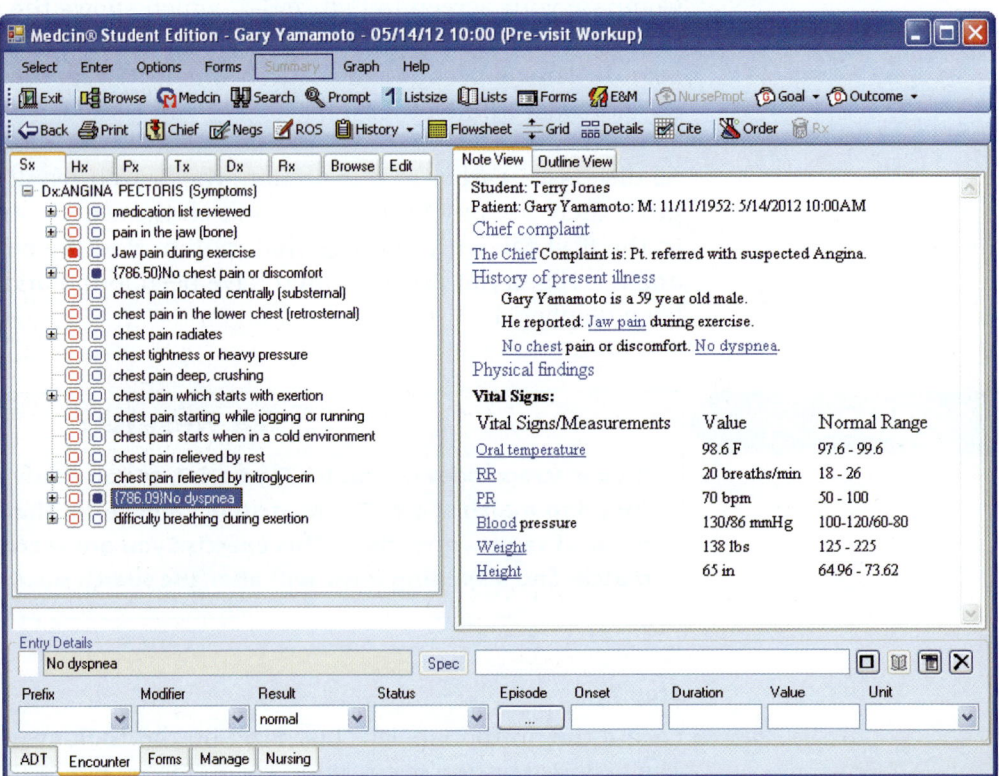

now, however, the first line reads "Dx: ANGINA PECTORIS (Symptoms)." This indicates that the list is limited to findings that are clinically related to the diagnosis of angina pectoris.

Proceed with the exercise by locating and clicking on the following symptoms reported by the patient:

- ● (red button) jaw pain during exercise (myocardial)
- ● (blue button) chest pain or discomfort
- ● (blue button) difficulty breathing (dyspnea)

Compare your screen to the selected red and blue buttons in Figure 6-8 before proceeding.

Step 10

The patient does not smoke, and denies any history of high blood pressure or diabetes. Click on the Hx tab and enter the patient's history information by locating and clicking on the following history findings:

- ● (blue button) current smoker
- ● (blue button) history of HYPERTENSION (Systemic)
- ● (blue button) history of DIABETES MELLITUS

▶ Figure 6-9 Hx tab displaying findings related to angina.

Compare your screen to Figure 6-9.

Step 11

The first test to be ordered is an electrocardiogram (ECG). Although some tests, such as electrocardiograms, are performed in the clinic, most lab tests and many radiology procedures are "ordered" at the clinic, but the test is performed elsewhere.

▶ Figure 6-10 Recording the finding "An ECG Was Performed."

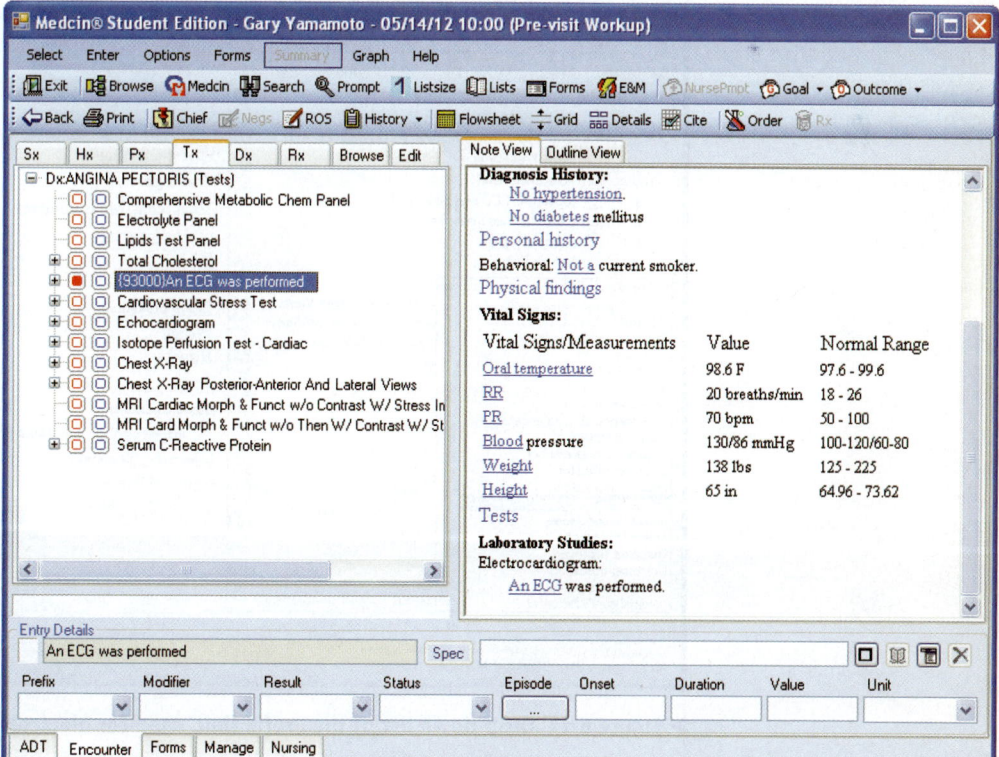

Chapter 6 | Understanding Electronic Orders 211

The ECG was performed today at the clinic.

Verify the List Size displays the numeral **1**.

Click on the Tx tab, which will display a list of tests that might be ordered for angina pectoris.

You can indicate that your office performed a test by clicking on the red button next to its name. Locate and click on the following finding:

- (red button) Electrocardiogram

The encounter note should now read, "An ECG was performed," as shown in Figure 6-10.

Do not exit the program until you have completed the following exercise.

Guided Exercise 37: Ordering Diagnostic Tests

Continuing with Mr. Yamamoto's visit, this exercise will explore several methods of recording tests and orders.

In this exercise, you will order several lab tests. There are two ways to do this: by using the Entry Details Prefix field or by using the Orders button on the Toolbar. In this step, you are going to use a prefix.

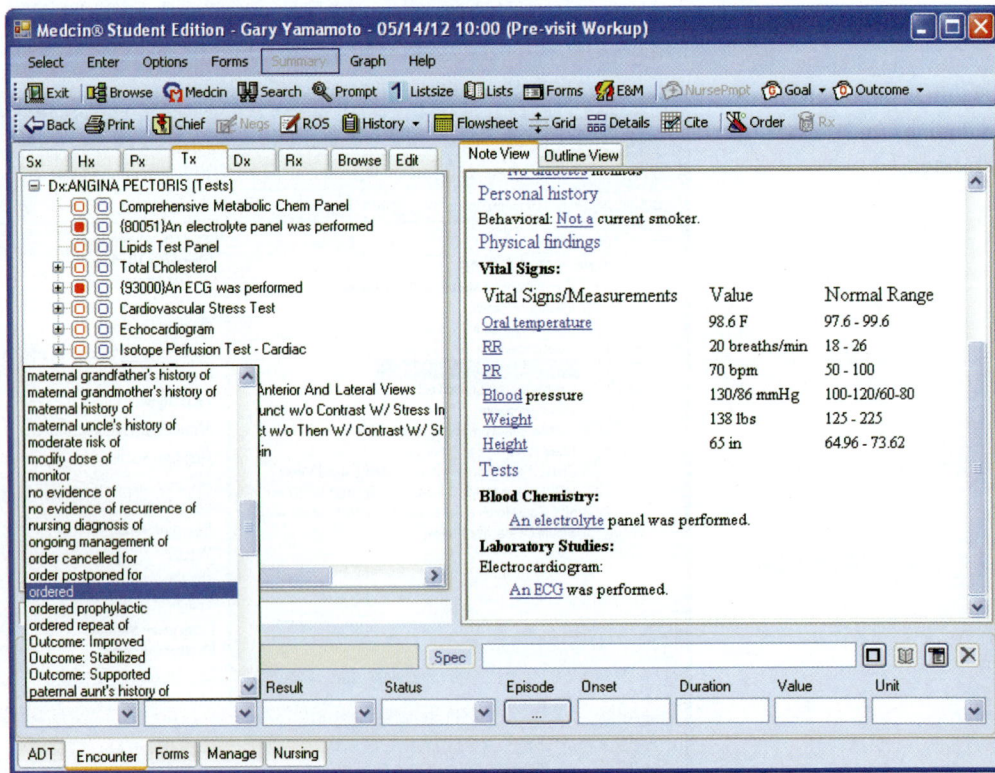

▶ Figure 6-11 Drop-down list of the Prefix field used for electrolyte panel.

212　Chapter 6 | Understanding Electronic Orders

Step 12

Locate and click on the following test:

- (red button) Electrolyte panel

Note that the electrolyte panel appears in the encounter note under Tests: "An electrolyte panel was performed." However, your clinic did not really perform the electrolyte panel test; the clinician just wanted to order it.

With the finding of "An electrolyte panel was performed" still highlighted, click on the Prefix field in the bottom of the screen. A drop-down list will appear as shown in Figure 6-11. Locate and click on the word "Ordered" in the list of prefixes.

▶ Figure 6-12 Electrolyte panel "ordered."

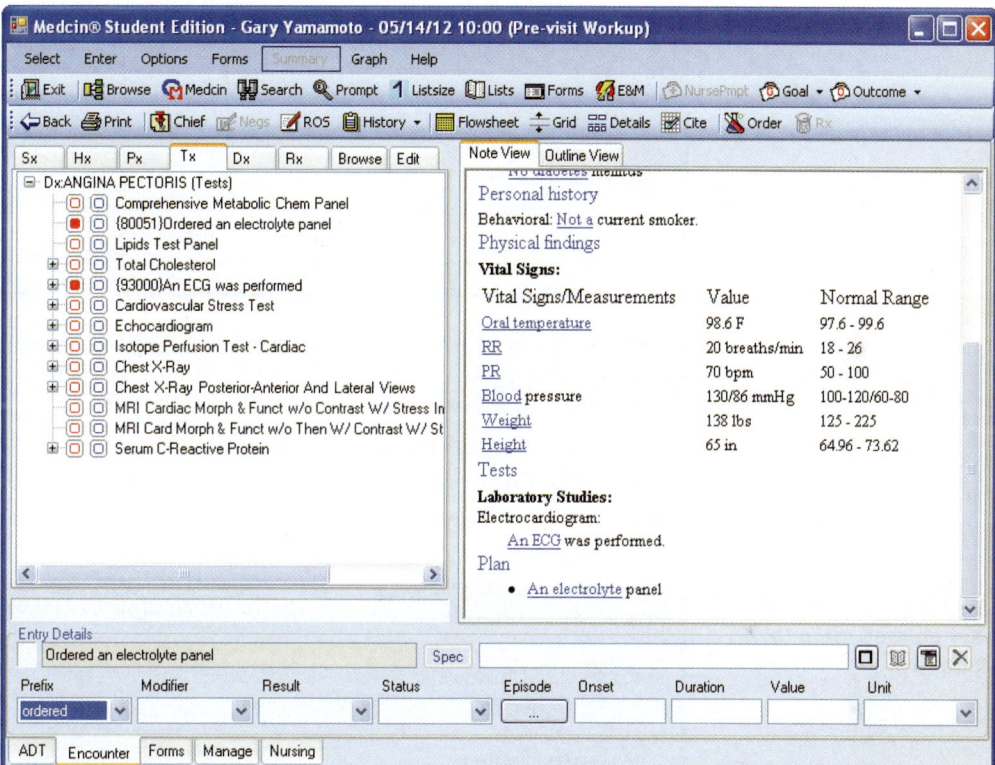

Step 13

Compare your screen to Figure 6-12. Notice that when you added the prefix "Ordered" to the finding of Electrolyte Panel, it not only changed the meaning in the encounter note but also moved the test to a different category in the encounter notes. Medcin assigns a test that was performed or has a result status to the category of test procedures but assigns a test that is ordered to the category "Plan."

Step 14

Now that you are familiar with one method of ordering, you can see that it requires two steps, clicking the finding and then setting the prefix. However, both of these actions can be accomplished in a single step by using the "Order" button on the Toolbar. To order a test using the order button, you only need to highlight the finding and click the "Order" button. You do not have to click either the red or blue button for the finding.

Chapter 6 | Understanding Electronic Orders   213

▶ Figure 6-13 Lipids test panel is highlighted and Order button is orange.

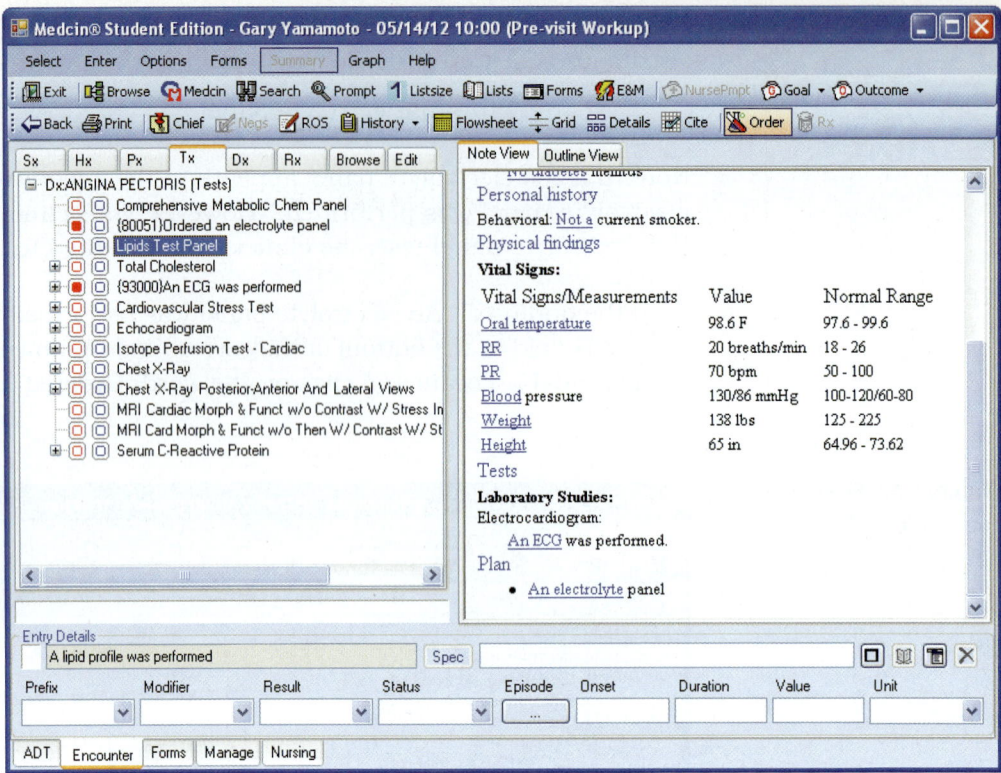

Locate and click on the description "Lipids Test Panel" to highlight it (as shown in Figure 6-13).

Locate and click on the button labeled "Order" in the Toolbar at the top of your screen. The Order icon resembles a lab beaker and test tube. It is highlighted orange in Figure 6-13.

▶ Figure 6-14 Tests and x-rays ordered using the Order button.

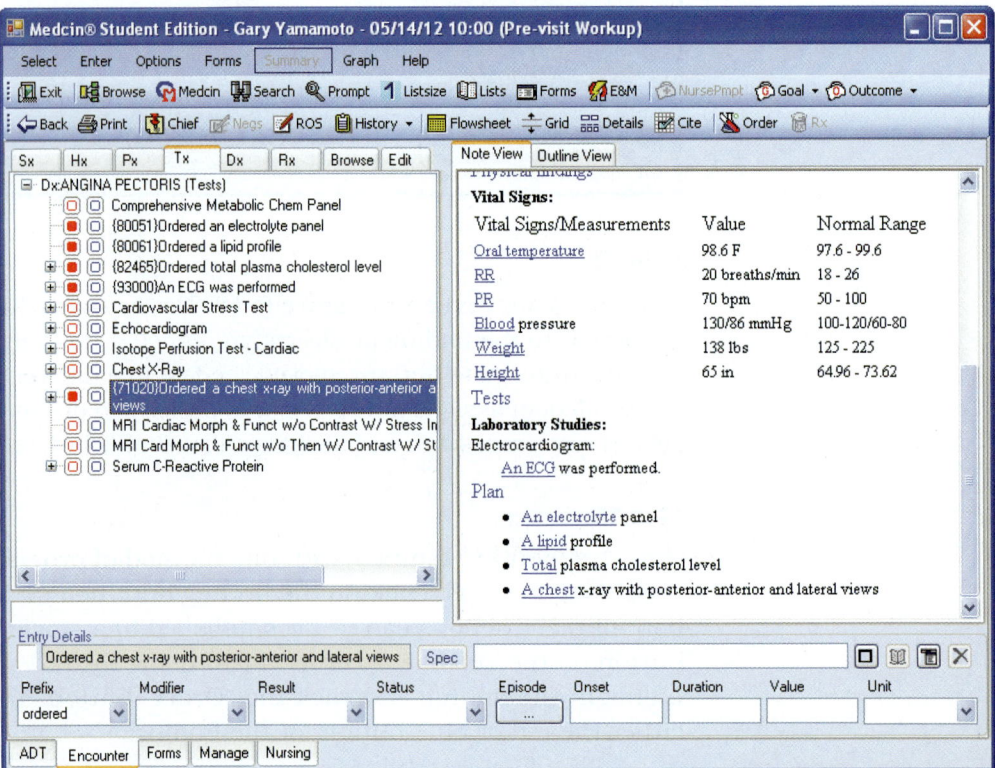

214   **Chapter 6** | Understanding Electronic Orders

Step 15

Using what your have learned in the previous step, order an additional test and an x-ray. Highlight each of the following findings and then click on the Order button. Do not click on the red or blue buttons beside these findings. The Order button will set them once they are ordered.

- 🧪 Total Cholesterol
- 🧪 Chest X-Ray Posterior-Anterior and Lateral Views

Compare your screen to Figure 6-14. From this example, you can see the advantage of using Toolbar buttons for orders. Similar buttons also are useful for History items and prescriptions, as you will learn in subsequent exercises.

> **Note**
>
> **Electronic Lab Orders**
>
> Most commercial EHR systems offer sophisticated laboratory interface systems that electronically send orders, receive results, and automatically populate the EHR with lab data. In an EHR, a button similar to the lab orders button shown here typically will invoke a window in which you create the actual electronic lab order and send it to the lab.

▶ Figure 6-15 Dx tab with drop-down list for Prefix—referral diagnosis Angina Pectoris.

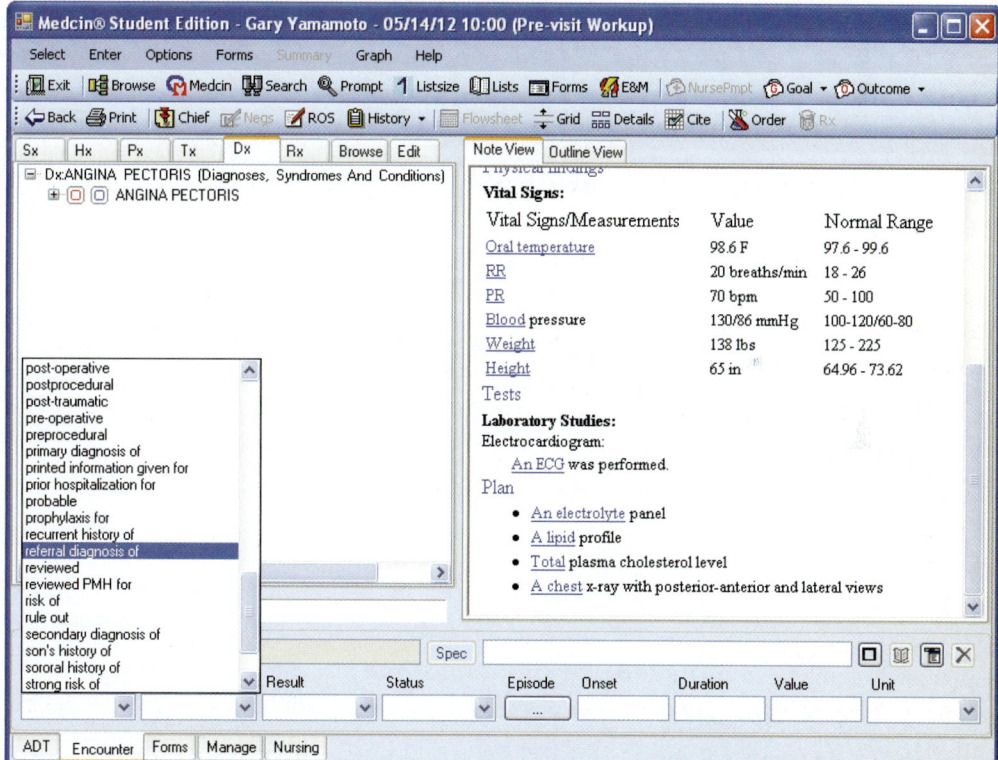

Step 16

The clinician will determine the final assessment after the complete workup later this week. Therefore, the diagnosis at this time will be the referral diagnosis angina pectoris.

Click on the Dx tab and record the assessment.

Locate and highlight Angina Pectoris.

Chapter 6 | Understanding Electronic Orders

Alert

Do not close or exit the encounter until you have a printed copy in your hand. *You will lose your work if you exit before printing.*

Locate the Prefix field in the Entry Details section. Click the mouse on the button with the down arrow in the Prefix field.

Scroll the drop-down list to locate and click on the words **Referral diagnosis**, as shown in Figure 6-15.

Step 17

This completes Mr. Yamamoto's pre-visit workup. Print your completed encounter note. Click on the Print button on the Toolbar at the top of your screen to invoke the Print Data window.

Be certain there is a check mark in the box next to "Current Encounter" and then click on the appropriate button to either print or export a file, as directed by your instructor.

Compare your printout or file output to Figure 6-16. If it is correct, hand it in to your instructor. If there are any differences (other than date or the patient's age), review the previous steps in the exercise and find your error.

```
Gary Yamamoto                                                         Page 1 of 1

Student: your name or id here
Patient: Gary Yamamoto: M: 11/11/1952: 5/14/2012 10:00AM
Chief complaint
The Chief Complaint is: Pt. referred with suspected Angina.
Referred here
Referral diagnosis of angina pectoris.
History of present illness
      Gary Yamamoto is a 59 year old male.
      He reported: Jaw pain during exercise.
      No chest pain or discomfort. No dyspnea.
Past medical/surgical history
   Diagnosis History:
      No hypertension.
      No diabetes mellitus
Personal history
Behavioral: Not a current smoker.
Physical findings
Vital signs:
Vital Signs/Measurements            Value                       Normal Range
Oral temperature                    98.6 F                      97.6 - 99.6
RR                                  20 breaths/min              18 - 26
PR                                  70 bpm                      50 - 100
Blood pressure                      130/86 mmHg                 100-120/60-80
Weight                              138 lbs                     125 - 225
Height                              65 in                       64.96 - 73.62
Tests
   Laboratory Studies:
      Electrocardiogram:
      An ECG was performed.
Plan
      • An electrolyte panel
      • A lipid profile
      • Total plasma cholesterol level
      • A chest x-ray with posterior-anterior and lateral views
```

▶ **Figure 6-16** Printed encounter note with angina orders for Gary Yamamoto.

Radiology Orders and Reports

Most acute care hospitals have radiology departments. Radiology departments typically have a radiology information system (RIS), a picture archiving and communication system (PACS) for storing diagnostic images, and a dictation/transcription or voice recognition system for reports.

When diagnostic information is needed, the provider may order an x-ray or other radiology study. CPOE systems in hospitals may send orders to the radiology department RIS system electronically. Radiology orders may also be handwritten or verbal orders. Most medical offices do not yet send electronic radiology orders unless the x-ray or other device is located in the same facility as the ordering provider. Whatever the original form of the order, virtually all radiology department orders are entered into the RIS, where they become electronic orders for the remainder of the process.

Many of the diagnostic imaging devices used in the radiology department are capable of receiving order and patient data electronically from the RIS system. Patient data is then incorporated in the image data. Once the image is captured, it will transfer electronically into the PACS.

Traditional x-rays used to be taken on photographic film. To be stored in a PAC system, the film then had to be digitized using a scanner. Today, x-ray systems can record the image on a special plate that captures the image digitally, eliminating the steps of developing the film and then scanning it. In addition to x-rays, other types of diagnostic images studied by radiologists include:

- Computerized axial tomography (CAT) systems use x-rays to see into the patient's body and capture thousands of digital images. Using computer software, it then constructs a view of cross sections of the body from the digital images. In some facilities this is also referred to as CT or computed tomography.

- Magnetic resonance imaging (MRI) uses magnetic fields and pulses of energy to create images of organs and structures inside the body that cannot be seen by x-ray or CAT scan.

- Positron emission tomography (PET) combines CT and nuclear scanning using a radioactive substance called a *tracer*, which is injected into a patient's vein. A computer records the tracer as it collects in certain organs, then converts the data into three-dimensional (3-D) images of the organ. PET can be used to detect or evaluate cancer.

A set of related images interpreted by the radiologist is called a *study*; a *hanging protocol* refers to the number of images that simultaneously display on the radiologist's monitor.

Once the x-ray, CAT scan, or other study images have been captured, a radiologist interprets the results. Increasingly, these images are stored and read in a digital format. The radiologist uses a computer monitor with much higher resolution than standard computer screens to view the images. Special software not only displays the image but also allows the radiologist to manipulate it, zooming in and out, changing the contrast, reversing the image colors, and offering many other capabilities that help the radiologist.

While looking at the image, radiologists dictate a report; describe what they see, its size, location, and any other comments. Because the radiologists are using the computer controls to manipulate and control the image, their observations are seldom keyed into an EHR program. It is standard practice for a radiologist's report to be dictated, and then typed by a medical transcriber. However, some radiology practices use speech recognition software, which converts the human voice into typed reports. This was discussed in Chapter 1.

When the report is complete and reviewed by the radiologist, it is sent to the ordering provider. Radiology reports are almost always originated in an electronic text format at the radiologist's office, and are usually sent on paper as a letter or fax.

Radiology reports are seldom available as a codified EHR record, but some medical offices may scan the paper reports as document images in the patient's EHR. Radiological observations that are codified are those related to the size and stage of tumors.

Additionally, within most hospital systems and between some medical offices, electronic text files of the reports may be available. Copies of the images studied by the radiologist also are sometimes sent to the ordering provider. These images are usually in an electronic format, although x-rays may be sent as film. Electronic transmission of images uses a national standard called DICOM which stands for Digital Imaging and Communications in Medicine. Electronic orders, results, and other data may be communicated between the hospital systems using another standard, called HL-7. Both DICOM and HL7 were discussed in Chapter 2.

Critical Thinking Exercise 38: Ordering an X-Ray

Patient Juan Garcia has injured his knee and is examined by a nurse practitioner, who will order an x-ray. Using what you have learned in this chapter, document his visit and the nurse practitioner's orders.

Step 1

Click Select on the Menu bar, and then click Patient.

In the Patient Selection window, locate and click on **Juan Garcia**.

Step 2

Click Select on the Menu bar, and then click New Encounter.

You may use the current date and time for this exercise.

Select the reason **Office Visit** from the drop-down list. Click on the OK button.

Step 3

Enter the Chief complaint by locating the button in the Toolbar labeled "Chief" and clicking on it.

In the dialog window that will open, type "**Twisted his knee**."

Click on the button labeled "Close the note form."

Step 4

Locate and click on the Search button on the Toolbar near the top of the screen. (The Search button was highlighted in Figure 6-6.)

Click your mouse in the Search String field and enter the medical term "**knee sprain**." Verify that you have spelled this correctly, and then click the button in the box labeled "Search."

If you see the message "nothing found to match search," repeat step 4 and verify that you have spelled the medical term correctly.

Step 5

Locate and click on the Prompt button on the Toolbar near the top of the screen. (The Prompt button was highlighted in Figure 6-7.)

Step 6

If the left pane is not automatically on the Symptoms tab, click the Sx tab. List Size should be 1.

Locate and click on the following findings:

- (red button) joint pain localized in the knee
- (red button) joint swelling of the lateral left knee

Step 7

Click the Hx tab.

Click on the small plus sign next to "Reported trauma to the knee"

Locate and click on the following finding:

- (red button) due to twisting

Step 8

Click the Px tab.

Click on the small plus sign next to "Knee swelling."

Locate and click on the following findings:

- (red button) Left

Scroll the list and then click on the small plus sign next to "Knee tenderness on palpitation."

Locate and click on the following findings:

- (red button) On the left

Step 9

Click the Dx tab.

Locate and click on the following finding:

- (red button) Knee sprain

Chapter 6 | Understanding Electronic Orders

Step 10

Click the Tx tab.

Locate and highlight the following finding. When the finding is highlighted, locate and click the order button on the Toolbar:

 (order button) X-Ray Knee Views W/oblique(s), 3 or more views

Step 11

Click the Rx tab.

Locate the List Size button on the Toolbar and click on it. It should change to size **2**.

Locate and click on the following findings:

- (red button) ordered knee brace
- (red button) ordered pain management by immobilization

Alert Do not close or exit the encounter until you have a printed copy in your hand. *You will lose your work if you exit before printing.*

Step 12

Click on the Print button on the Toolbar at the top of your screen to invoke the Print Data window.

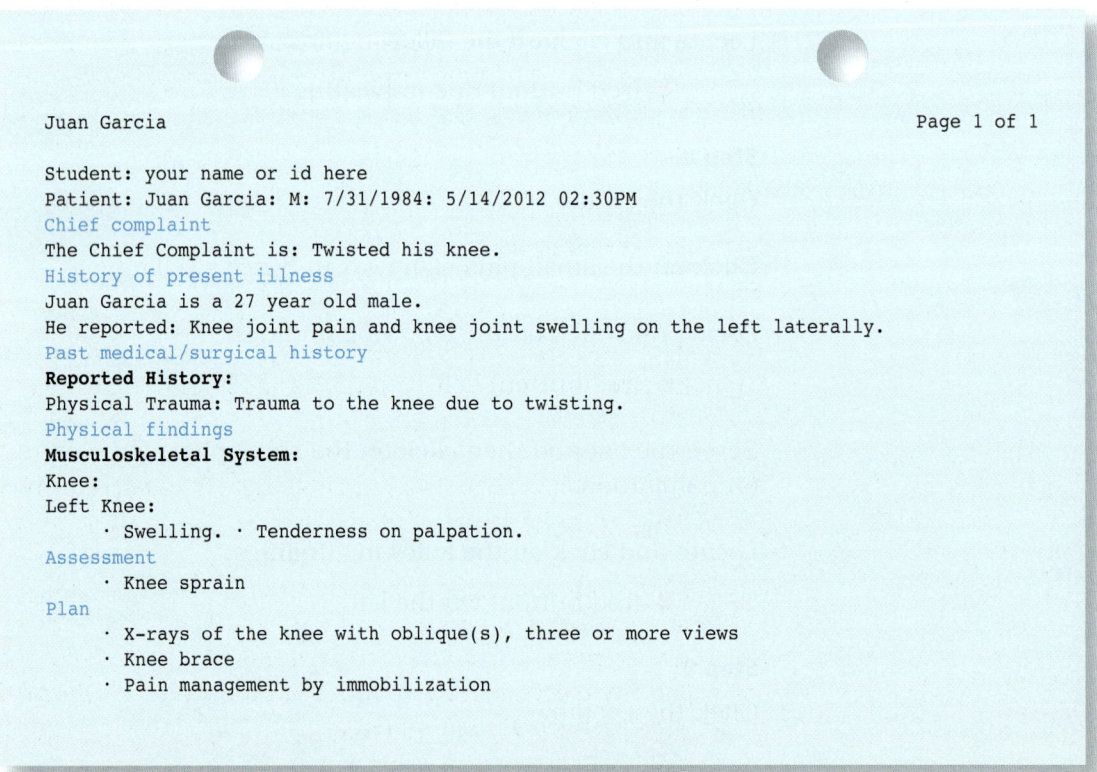

▶ Figure 6-17 Printed encounter note with radiology orders for Juan Garcia.

Be certain there is a check mark in the box next to "Current Encounter" and then click on the appropriate button to either print or export a file, as directed by your instructor.

Compare your printout or file output to Figure 6-17. If it is correct, hand it in to your instructor. If there are any differences, review the previous steps in the exercise and find your error.

Medication Orders

The most common type of order is for medication. Ever since the IOM report revealed that high numbers of deaths have occurred because of preventable medical errors, hospitals have increased their focus on patient safety. Hospital's efforts have included CPOE, computerizing the pharmacy, and using positive identification systems to correctly match the medication with the patient, thus ensuring the right patient receives the right medication. In ambulatory settings, electronic prescription writers have been incorporated into EHR software and include drug utilization review and formulary checking functions (described in Chapter 2 and below).

Written Prescriptions

At an inpatient facility using paper charts, the order is written on a Doctor Order sheet and a copy is sent to the hospital pharmacy. The clerk or nurse transcribes the medication order onto an administration record form in the patient's chart.

In an outpatient facility using a paper system, drug prescriptions are written by hand on a prescription pad and given to the patient to have filled at a pharmacy. Information about the medication is recorded in the chart by hand or the prescription is copied and filed in the paper chart. Alternatively, a member of the clinic staff may phone the prescription to the pharmacy or the clinician may give the patient samples of drugs provided by pharmaceutical companies.

When the patient goes to the pharmacy to have the prescription filled, the pharmacist will enter the information in the pharmacy computer system. The patient's insurance may require that a generic or less costly drug be substituted for a brand-name drug on the prescription. Unless the provider has indicated DAW or "Dispense As Written" on the prescription, it is very likely that the pharmacist will substitute a medically equivalent drug for the one prescribed by the provider.

The pharmacy computer system is also likely to perform two other functions: "formulary compliance checking" and "drug utilization review," or "DUR."

Formulary compliance was discussed earlier in Chapter 2 as an example of decision support. Formulary lists are usually per insurance plan, and because there are so many different plans, the pharmacy system usually checks the formulary by electronically communicating with an intermediary company called a *pharmacy benefit manager*.

DUR is also performed by the pharmacy computer system. The computer compares the prescription about to be filled with other prescriptions the patient is currently taking to determine if harmful interactions could occur when two or more medicines are combined. DUR is also capable of checking for potential errors where the dose in the prescription is too large or too small. If allergy information about the patient is available to the DUR system, warnings also can be given where allergic reactions might occur.

If either the formulary checking or the DUR indicates any problem with the handwritten prescription, the pharmacist must contact the prescribing provider. Often the call from the pharmacist comes when the provider is with another patient, so a message is left and the call is returned at a later time. This creates a delay for the patient and pharmacist and consumes extra time for the provider, who has to return the phone calls.

Electronic Prescriptions

Writing prescriptions electronically has several advantages over the paper chart method. First, the provider issues the prescription and records it in the chart in one step. Second, the prescription can be transmitted electronically from the provider's computer system to the pharmacy, saving time for the patient, eliminating the need for the provider's staff to call in the prescription, and reducing errors caused by handwritten prescriptions. Finally, the DUR and formulary compliance checking can be performed by the clinician's computer at the time the prescription is written. This allows any problems with the prescription to be corrected prior to sending it to the pharmacy. This drastically reduces phone calls back to the prescribing provider from the pharmacy, saving everyone time. Figures 2-21 and Figure 2-22 in Chapter 2 show examples of DUR and formulary compliance screens in an electronic prescription system.

DUR is a very important feature that reduces the patient's risk of adverse drug reactions. DUR works best when all of the known drugs and allergy information is available and current. Therefore, an EHR should record not only prescriptions issued by the provider's system but also medications prescribed elsewhere. These are usually reported by the patient during the nurse's interview or during the exam. The current medications list should be updated each visit before the provider issues any prescriptions.

The electronic prescription component of an EHR can provide additional benefits to both the clinician and the patient. Because each medication is automatically recorded in the medications list as the prescription is created, a current and recent medications list is available to the clinician when writing the prescription. This reduces prescribing errors.

EHR systems also shorten the time it takes to write a prescription by maintaining a list of prescriptions the clinician writes frequently. This speeds up the writing of prescriptions for common ailments seen at the practice. Physicians of patients with chronic diseases frequently write renewals for existing prescriptions; with EHR systems, they perform this task with a few clicks of the mouse. Additional time is saved because all FDA-approved drugs are listed in the computer, eliminating the need to use a drug reference book to find less frequently prescribed drugs. An example of an EHR prescription writer will be used in Exercise 39.

Closing the Loop on Safe Medication Administration

Hospital EHR systems help protect patients by closing the loop on medication administration. This safety initiative starts with electronic medication prescription from CPOE to the pharmacy computer system, where the order is checked and approved by the pharmacist for dispensing to the nurse. The nurse can then use an electronically document process to ensure the five patient rights of medication administration safety. Before administering the medication, a handheld scanner device is used to read a barcode on the patient's armband to ensure the medication is being given to the right patient. Next the nurse scans the barcodes on each medication or intravenous solution and the computer program checks the electronic order and warns the nurse of any discrepancies. If the medication dose, route, and time match the order for the patient, the nurse can then administer the medication to the patient. In some electronic systems a repeat scan of the patient armband or the scan of the nurse's identification badge completes the documentation, confirming that the medication has been administered.

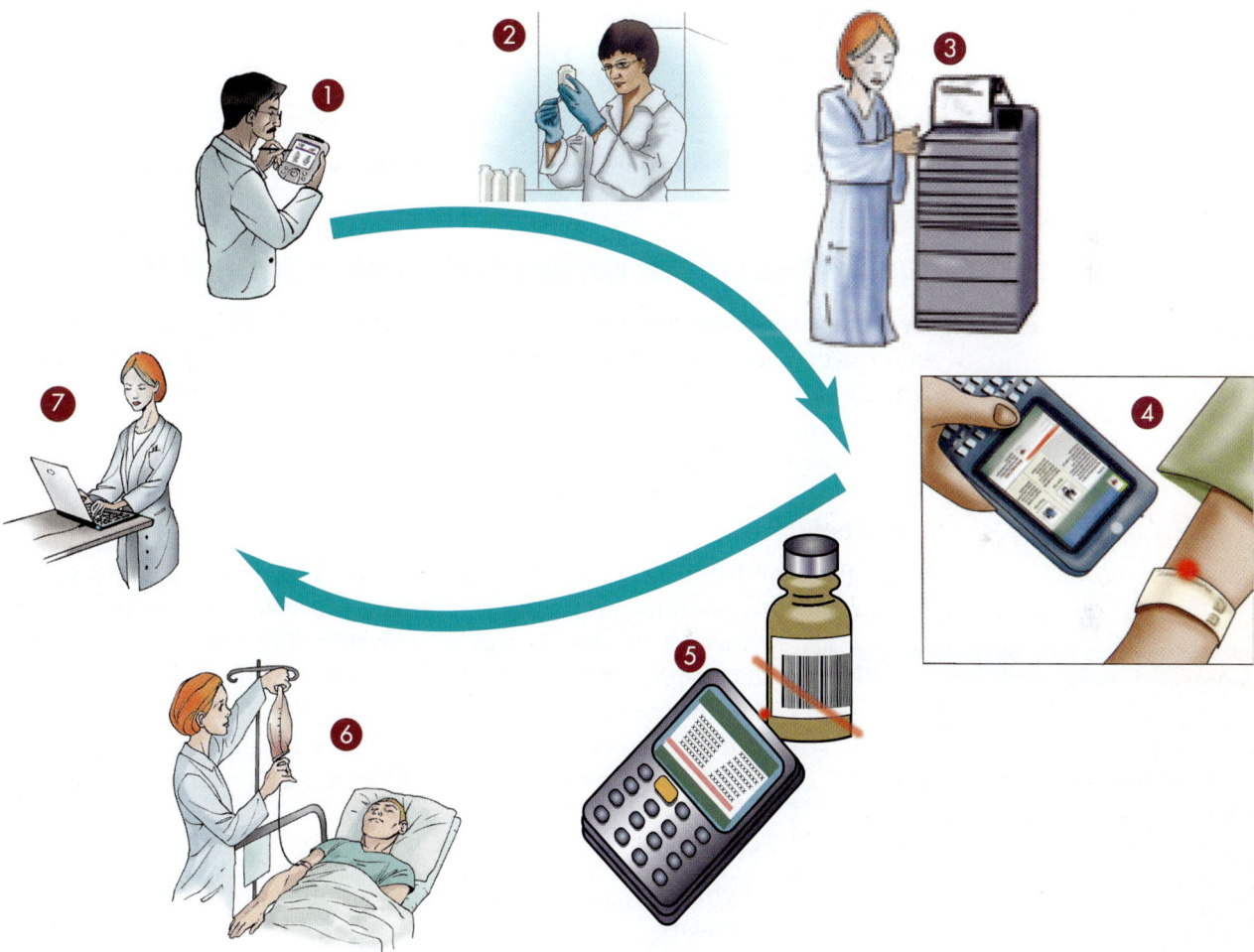

▶ Figure 6-18 Medication safety—the closed loop process.

Follow the numbers in Figure 6-18 as you read the following:

❶ Clinician writes prescription using CPOE.

❷ Prescription is checked and approved by the pharmacist.

❸ Nurse receives order electronically and removes vial from medication-dispensing system.

Chapter 6 | Understanding Electronic Orders

④ A handheld scanner device is used to read a barcode on the patient's armband to ensure the medication is being given to the right patient.

⑤ Nurse scans the barcodes on each medication or intravenous solution and the computer program checks the electronic order and warns the nurse of any discrepancies.

⑥ Nurse administers the medication to the patient.

⑦ Nurse documents the patient's chart. (In some EHR systems a repeat scan of the patient's armband or the scan of the nurse's identification badge completes the chart documentation, without manual entry.)

Medication Administration—The Five Rights

1. Right patient
2. Right time and frequency
3. Right medication
4. Right dose
5. Right route of administration

Guided Exercise 39: Writing Prescriptions in an EHR

In this exercise you will learn to use the Student Edition prescription writer to enter orders a nurse has received by phone from the doctor. It is necessary for the nurse to enter the prescription, because the patient needs to start taking the antibiotic immediately and the doctor does not have remote access to his EHR to write the prescription himself.

Case Study

You will recall from the previous chapter that Kerry Baker is a 36-year-old female recently seen for an upper respiratory infection. It has been 10 days since she was seen and her condition has not improved. She would like a prescription for an antibiotic, but the physician has already left for the day. The nurse contacts the physician, who verbally orders amoxicillin. The nurse will write the prescription and the doctor will cosign the order later, usually within 24 hours.

Step 1

If you have not already done so, start the Student Edition software.

Click Select on the Menu bar, and then click Patient.

In the Patient Selection window, locate and click on **Kerry Baker**, as shown in Figure 6-19.

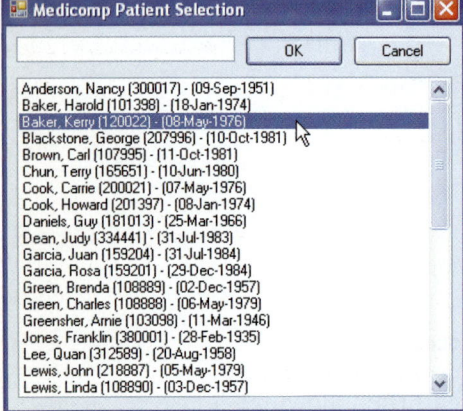

▶ Figure 6-19 Select Patient Kerry Baker.

Step 2

Enter the Chief complaint by locating the button in the Toolbar labeled "Chief" and clicking on it.

224 Chapter 6 | Understanding Electronic Orders

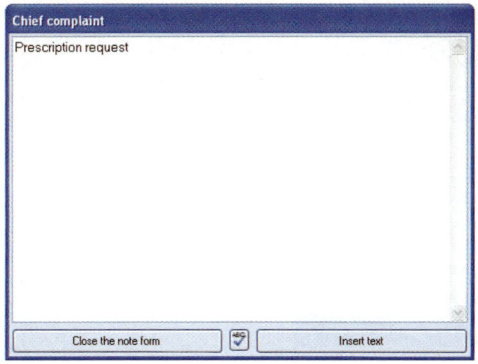

▶ Figure 6-20 Chief complaint prescription request.

In the dialog window that will open, type "**Prescription request**."

Compare your screen to Figure 6-20 before clicking on the button labeled "Close the note form."

Step 3

Click on the Dx tab.

Locate and click on the small plus signs next to "ENT Disorders," "Nose," and "Sinusitis."

Locate and click on the following finding:

● (red button) Acute

▶ Figure 6-21 Diagnosis acute sinusitis.

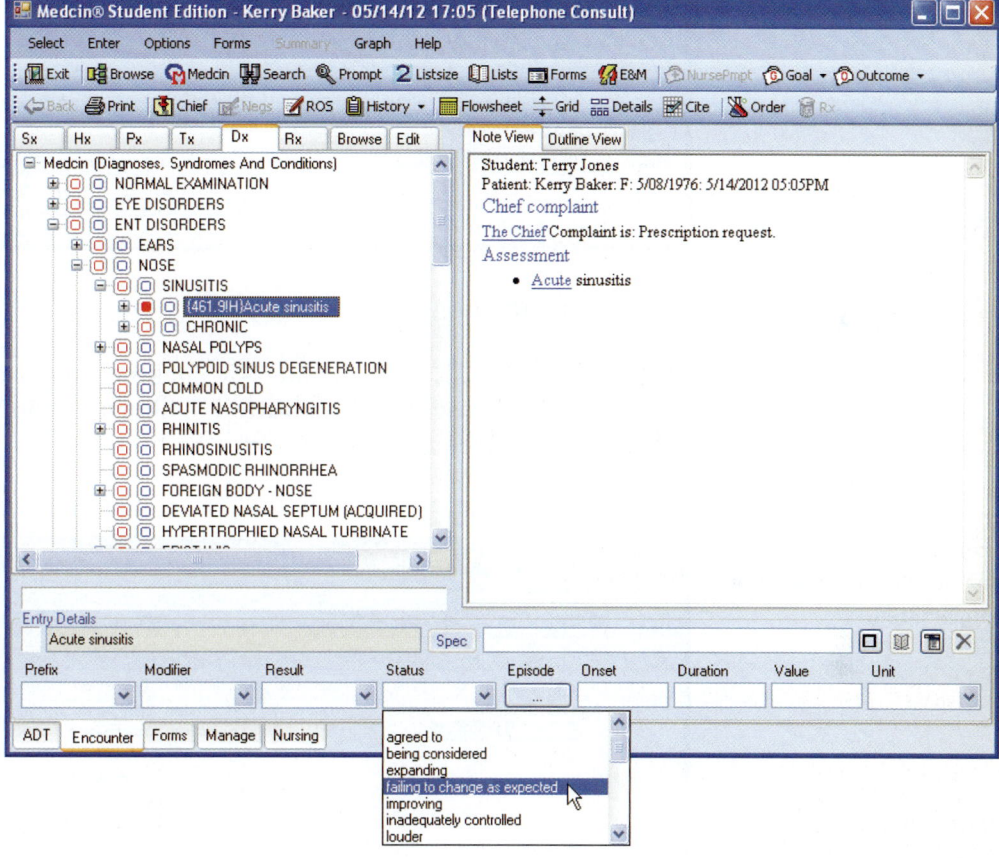

Compare your screen to Figure 6-21.

Locate the Entry Details "Status" field and click the down arrow to display a drop-down list (also shown in Figure 6-21).

Locate and click on the status "**Failing to change as expected**."

Step 4

You will now enter the medication order using the prescription writer. Although clinicians usually have personal order sets that allow them to quickly pick from a list of frequently prescribed drugs, you do not have access to this doctor's list. Therefore you will use search to locate the ordered drug.

Chapter 6 | Understanding Electronic Orders

▶ Figure 6-22 Search for amoxicillin (Rx button circled in red).

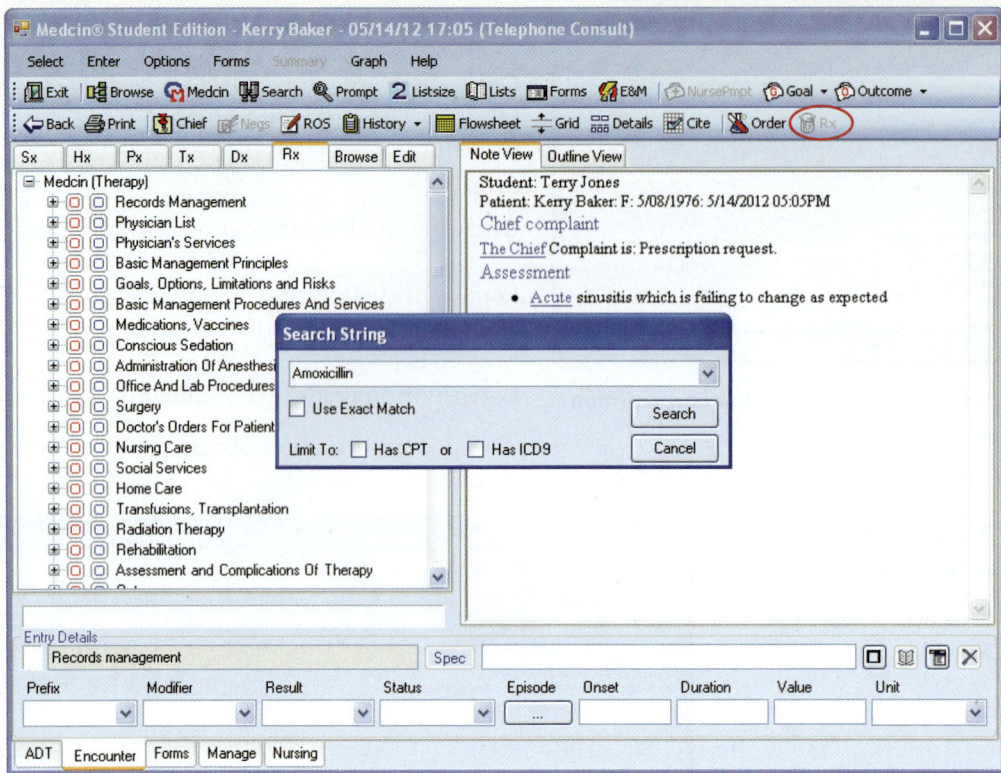

Click on the Rx tab.

The prescription writer is invoked by clicking the Rx button in the Toolbar at the top of your screen. The button is shown circled in red in Figure 6-22. The icon resembles a small prescription bottle, but notice that the button is grayed out.

▶ Figure 6-23 Rx button enabled when amoxicillin is highlighted.

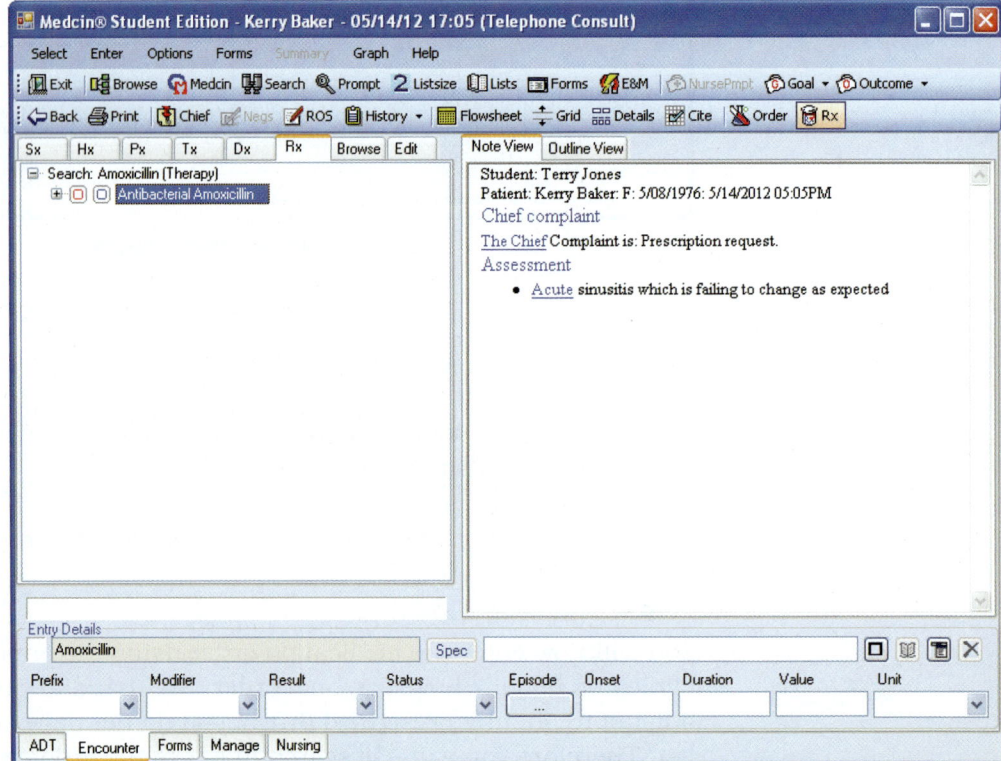

226   Chapter 6 | Understanding Electronic Orders

Step 5

Locate and click on the Search button on the Toolbar to invoke the Search String window.

Type "**Amoxicillin**" in the search dialog window and click on the button labeled "Search." Note that amoxicillin is a generic drug, but even when you type in a brand name, the search will automatically find the generic version of the drug for you.

Step 6

The finding "Antibacterial Amoxicillin" should be highlighted.

The Rx button on the Toolbar is now active. If you position the mouse pointer over it, it will change color (as shown in Figure 6-23.) The prescription (Rx) button is enabled only when you are on the Rx tab and only if the highlighted finding is a medication.

With the finding "Antibacterial Amoxicillin" highlighted, click on the Prescription button in the Toolbar. A simple Prescription writer window will be invoked, as shown in Figure 6-24.

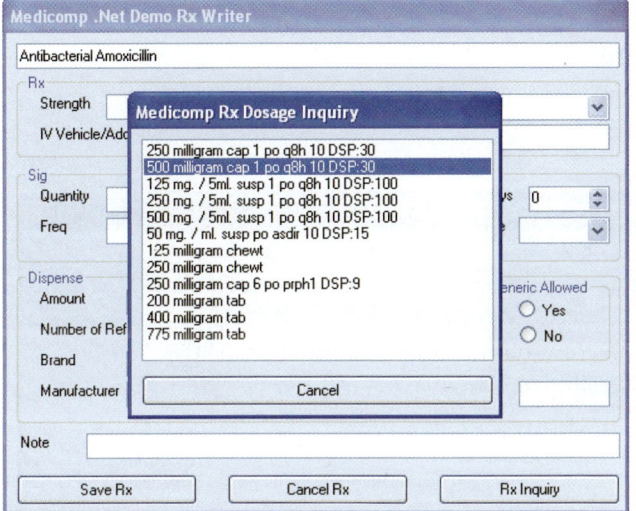

▶ **Figure 6-24** Prescription writer with Dosage Window.

Step 7

When you clicked on the prescription (Rx) button and invoked the prescription writing window, the drug was automatically selected from the finding. A list of available dosages is automatically displayed. This is the "Sig"[2] information that the pharmacist will include on the label. It consists of the quantity prescribed, the number of times per day, capsules to take each time, number of days to take the drug, the total quantity prescribed, the number of refills allowed, and any free-text instructions to the patient. The list of available Sig choices makes writing the prescription very fast. It is found in virtually all commercial EHR prescription systems.

Locate and click your mouse on the Sig: "**500 milligram cap 1 po q8h 10 DSP:30**," shown highlighted in Figure 6-24.

The next window displaying available brands (as shown in Figure 6-25) will be displayed automatically.

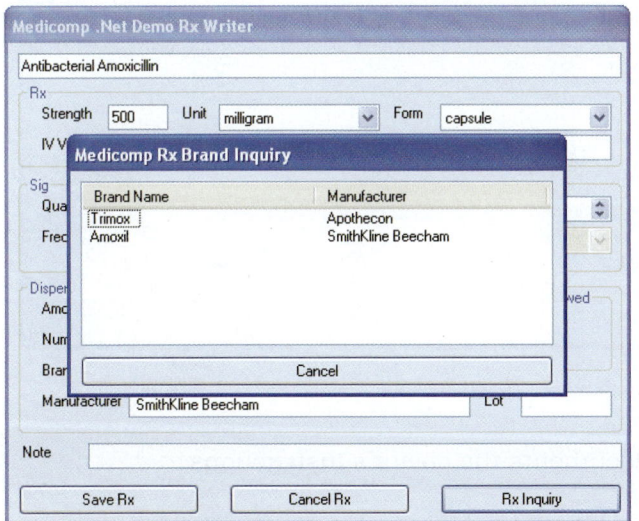

▶ **Figure 6-25** Prescription brand selection.

Step 8

Locate and click on "**Amoxil SmithKline Beecham**," as shown in Figure 6-25.

---

[2]Sig, from the Latin *signa*, are instructions for labeling a prescription.

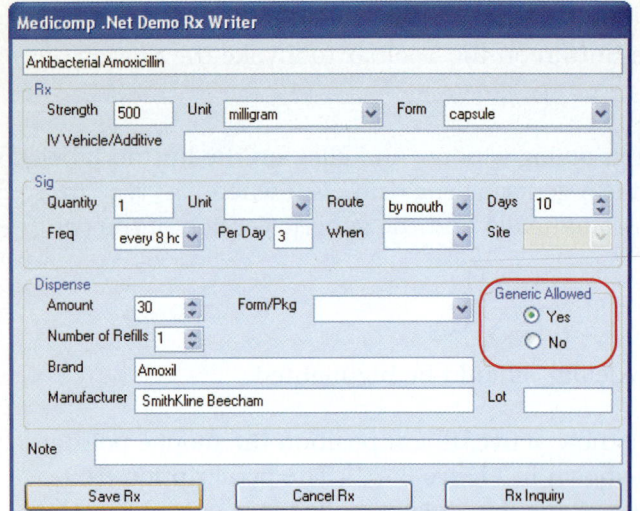

▶ **Figure 6-26** Prescription for amoxicillin (generic circled in red).

Step 9

Compare your screen to Figure 6-26. Locate the "Generic Allowed" fields. The "Yes" and "No" indicate if the pharmacist is allowed to substitute a generic drug for a prescribed brand. Click in the small circle next to **Yes**. The small circle is then filled in.

If you need to make any changes or corrections in the prescription, click on the button labeled "Rx Inquiry" to invoke the Dosage and Brand windows again.

When everything in your prescription screen matches Figure 6-26, click on the Save Rx button.

Step 10

The prescription information will be written into your patient encounter note as shown in Figure 6-27.

▶ **Figure 6-27** Encounter note shows prescription.

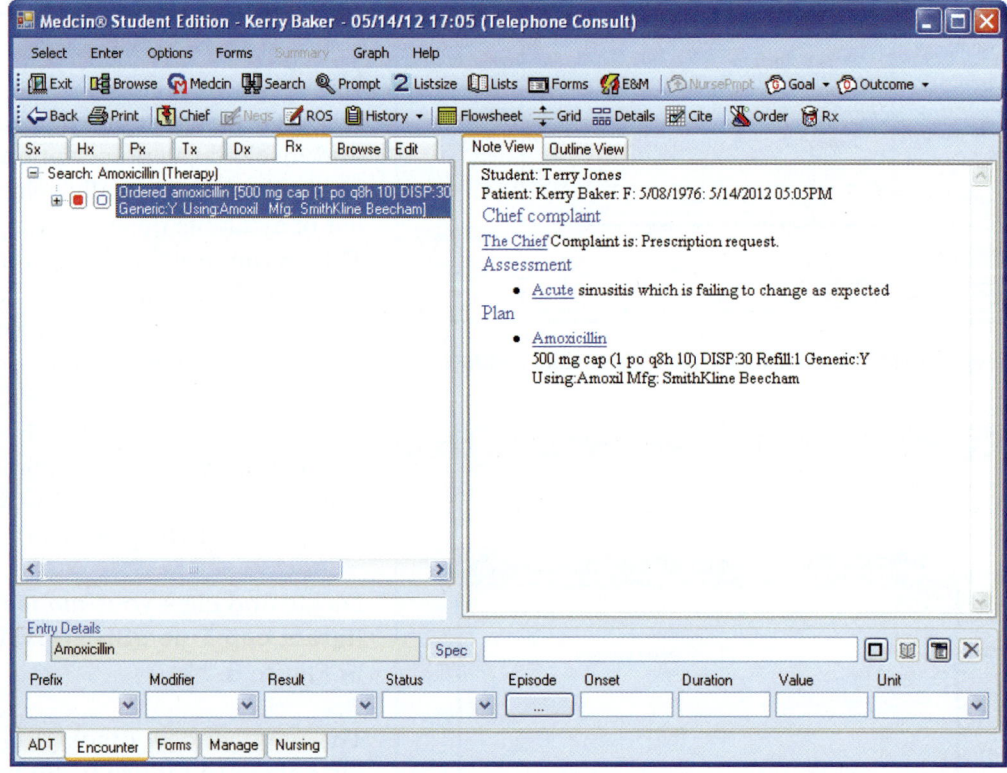

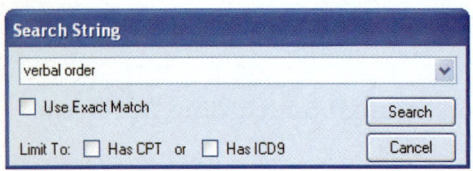

▶ **Figure 6-28** Search dialog for verbal orders.

Step 11

The nurse now documents the doctor's instructions.

Locate and click on the Search button on the Toolbar to invoke the Search String window.

Type "**verbal orders**" in the search dialog window (shown in Figure 6-28) and click on the button labeled "Search."

228 Chapter 6 | Understanding Electronic Orders

▶ Figure 6-29 Record of verbal order from Dr. Thomas.

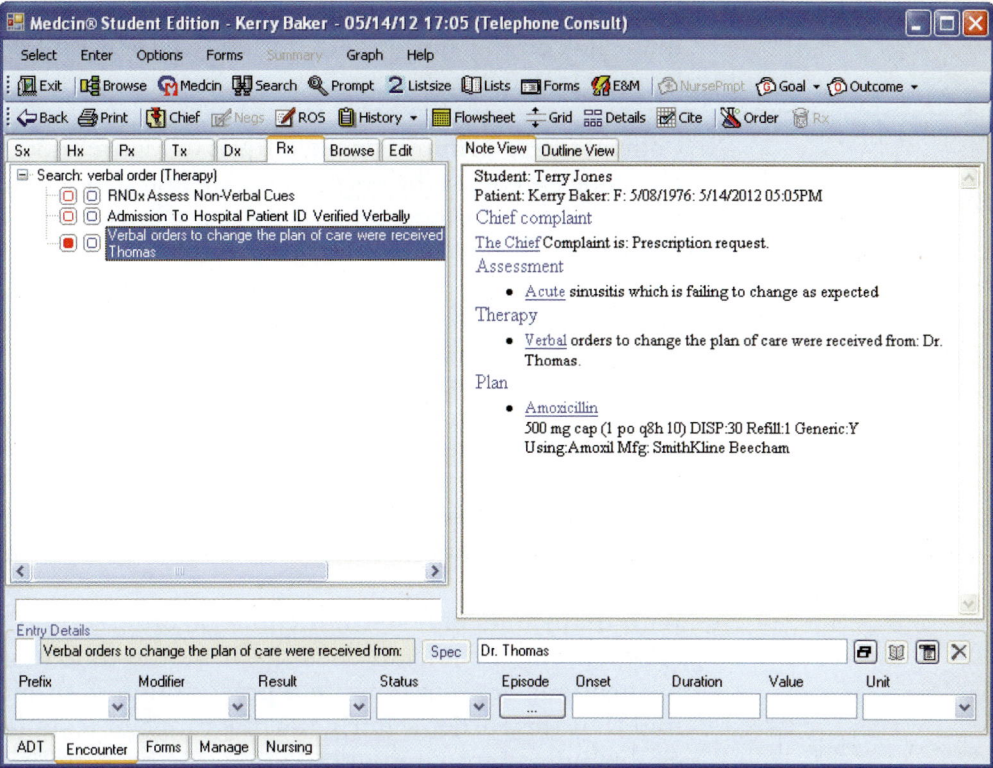

Alert

Do not close or exit the encounter until you have a printed copy in your hand. *You will lose your work if you exit before printing.*

Step 12

Locate and click on the following finding:

● (red button) Verbal orders to change plan of care

Locate the free-text field just below the right pane. Type "**Dr. Thomas**" and press the Enter key.

Compare your screen to Figure 6-29.

Step 13

Click on the Print button on the Toolbar at the top of your screen to invoke the Print Data window.

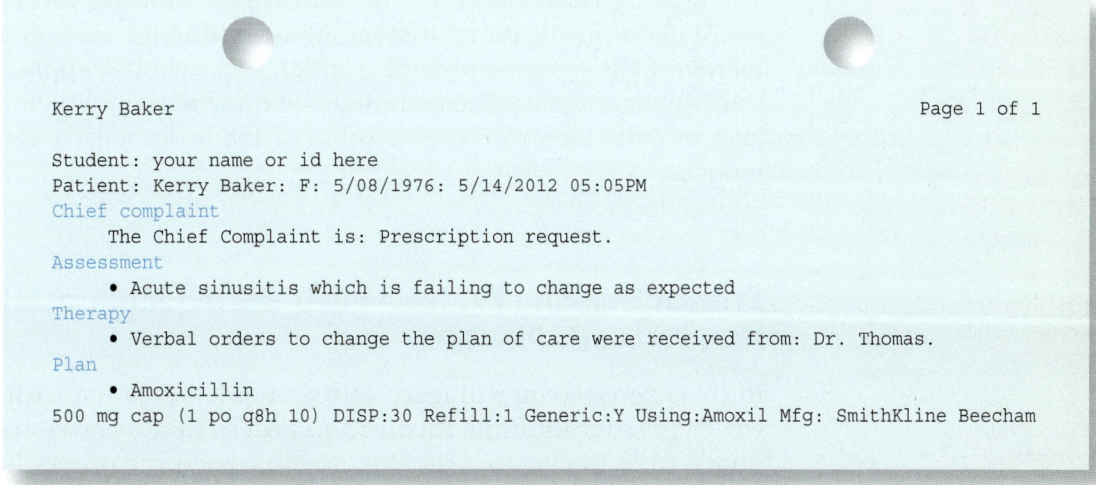

▶ Figure 6-30 Printed encounter note with Rx order for Kerry Baker.

Chapter 6 | Understanding Electronic Orders   229

Be certain there is a check mark in the box next to "Current Encounter" and then click on the appropriate button to either print or export a file, as directed by your instructor.

Compare your printout or file output to Figure 6-30. (The contents should be the same except for the encounter date and patient's age.) If your work is correct, hand it in to your instructor. If there are any differences, review the previous steps in the exercise and find your error.

Quick Access to Frequent Orders

In the previous exercise we mentioned a time-saving feature that is typical in all CPOE systems is a quick-pick list of a clinician's frequently used orders. These may take the form of diagnosis-based order sets, or a more generalized list of the prescriptions the clinician writes most frequently.

With thousands of tests that could be ordered and thousands of drugs to choose from, a clinician does not have the time to go through a search of medications or tests to write a prescription or order a lab. Many clinicians find that they order a fairly narrow range of tests (appropriate to their specialty and patient population) and write prescriptions for only a small group of medications.

It makes sense for clinicians to keep a list of the items they most frequently use from which they can select when writing the order. Commercial EHR systems handle this in different ways; some automatically create the list by memorizing what the clinician has been ordering, whereas other systems allow the clinicians to build their own lists. Most EHR systems offer a combination of both.

The EHR system you will use in a medical facility will most certainly have this type of feature. Making use of the feature is definitely a good way to speed up data entry at the point of care. Creating or customizing Rx and orders lists will certainly save time when the clinician is with the patient.

The next exercise emulates this feature by allowing you to select from a small list of medications instead of searching for each drug. However, commercial EHR systems provide a much more robust application that allows the clinician to save the complete sig information, which enables the clinician to write an entire prescription or lab order with a single click of the mouse.

Critical Thinking Exercise 40: Ordering Medications Using a Quick-Pick List

In this exercise you will learn to use a quick-pick list with the prescription writer to enter multiple medication orders that a nurse has received by phone from the doctor. The doctor will cosign the orders later, usually within 24 hours.

Case Study

Nancy Anderson is a 61-year-old female who was admitted to the hospital for congestive heart failure. She is to be discharged today and is anxious to leave. Her doctor has called you with orders for her discharge medications. As you have in the previous exercise, you will enter medication orders on the doctor's behalf. The doctor has ordered Lasix 40 mg BID, Lanoxin 0.125 mg daily, Potassium chloride 20 mg BID, and Nitroglycerine sl PRN.

Step 1

If you have not already done so, start the Student Edition software.

Click Select on the Menu bar, and then click Patient.

In the Patient Selection window, locate and click on **Nancy Anderson**.

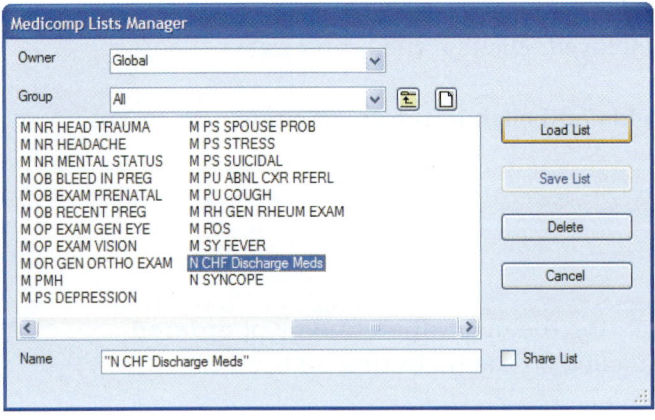

▶ Figure 6-31 Load the list "N CHF Discharge Meds."

Step 2

Locate and click on the "List" button on the Toolbar.

Scroll the List Manager window to the right until you see the list named "N CHF Discharge Meds." Highlight it (as shown in Figure 6-31) and then click the button labeled "Load List."

Step 3

You should automatically be on the Rx tab.

The CHF Discharge Meds list displays medications typically prescribed to CHF patients when they are discharged.

Locate and highlight the medication finding of **ordered Anginal Preparations Nitroglycerine**, and then click on the Rx button on the Toolbar. This will invoke the prescription writer.

Step 4

The dosage selection will automatically be displayed. Select the first dosage **0.15 mg**.

When the brand window is displayed click on the brand **Nitrostat**.

When the prescription is displayed, locate the "Generic Allowed" fields and click in the small circle next to **Yes**.

Click on the Save Rx button.

Step 5

Enter the next order by highlighting the medication finding of **ordered Cardiac Glycosides Digoxin** and then click on the Rx button on the Toolbar.

When the dosage selection is displayed, select the first dosage on the list **0.125 mg tab**.

When the brand window is displayed click on the brand **Lanoxin**.

Locate the Generic Allowed fields and click in the small circle next to **Yes**.

Click on the Save Rx button.

Step 6

Enter the next order by highlighting the medication finding of **ordered Diuretic Loop Acting Furosemide** and then click on the Rx button on the Toolbar.

When the dosage selection is displayed, select the second dosage on the list **40 milligram tab 1 po BID**.

When the brand window is displayed, click on the brand **Lasix**.

Locate the Generic Allowed fields and click in the small circle next to **Yes**.

Click on the Save Rx button.

Step 7

Enter the last order by highlighting the medication finding of **ordered Potassium Chloride** and then click on the Rx button on the Toolbar.

When the dosage selection is displayed, select the last dosage on the list: **20 mEq tab**.

The brand will not be selected; click the button labeled Cancel in the brand window.

When the prescription is displayed, locate and click your mouse in the "Quantity" field, and then type **1**.

Locate the frequency field (labeled "Freq") and click on the down arrow in the field to display the drop-down list. Select **twice daily**, from the list.

Locate the field labeled "Per Day" and type the numeral **2**.

Locate the field labeled "Route" and click on the down arrow in the field to display the drop-down list. Select **by mouth**, from the list.

Locate the field labeled "Days" and type the numeral **30**.

In the Dispense section, locate the field labeled "Amount" and type the numeral **60**.

Locate the field labeled "Number of Refills" and type the numeral **3**.

Locate the Generic Allowed fields and click in the small circle next to **Yes**.

Click on the Save Rx button.

 **Alert** | *Do not close or exit the encounter until you have a printed copy in your hand. You will lose your work if you exit before printing.*

```
Nancy Anderson                                                    Page 1 of 1

Student: your name or id here
Patient: Nancy Anderson: F: 9/09/1951: 5/15/2012 11:15PM
Plan
      • Nitroglycerin
0.15 mg tab (1 sl prn) DISP:100 Refill:5 Generic:Y Using:Nitrostat Mfg: Parke Davis
      • Digoxin
0.125 mg tab (1 po qd) DISP:100 Refill:5 Generic:Y Using:Lanoxin Tablets Mfg:
      Burroughs Wellcome
      • Furosemide
40 mg tab (1 po bid) DISP:100 Refill:3 Generic:Y Using:Lasix Mfg: Hoechst
      • Potassium chloride
20 mEq tab (1 po bid) DISP:60 Refill:3 Generic:Y
```

▶ **Figure 6-32** Printout of Nancy Anderson's medication orders.

Step 8

Click on the Print button on the Toolbar at the top of your screen to invoke the Print Data window.

Be certain there is a check mark in the box next to Current Encounter and then click on the appropriate button to either print or export a file, as directed by your instructor.

Compare your printout or file output to Figure 6-32. (The contents should be the same except for the encounter date and patient's age.) If your work is correct, hand it in to your instructor. If there are any differences, review the previous steps in the exercise and find your error.

Real-Life Story

When Orders and Results Are Critical

By Marney Thompson, RN

Marney Thompson is a registered nurse working in the critical care unit of a large hospital.

When I was in nursing school I did a 16-week rotation in a critical care setting and I loved it. Since then I have always worked in medical intensive care, or critical care units. I like the challenges of that type of nursing where you have an intensive patient with multiple needs and you are managing all the complications that come along with the acute phase—so you can get that patient to the next phase, which is recovery. I feel a strong sense of purpose being part of the team who responds when there is a patient who is coding.

I have been fortunate that all the hospitals I have worked in used electronic records. The patient's vital signs, CVP (cerebral vascular pressure) monitoring, heart rate, oxygenation, blood pressure—all transfer directly into our charts electronically. Our hospital EHR also has CPOE, so all lab and medication orders are electronic. The lab results are also electronic, which means the intensivist and I can both be looking at a patient's most recent results at the same time, even though the doctor might be in a different part of the hospital.

In addition, our hospital pharmacy is computerized, which means that when a situation is critical I can order meds on behalf of the doctor; the pharmacist can then review them and communicate with the Pyxsis Medstation in the nursing unit to dispense them. Here is a situation that happened recently.

This patient was on BIPAP (bilevel positive airway pressure) and his respirations were agonal looking. He was not responsive—had not been responsive since coming to the unit—but he started to look like he was going downhill. I contacted the doctor (our intensivist), who ordered some stat lab tests: a BMP (basic metabolic panel), a CBC (complete blood count), and a magnesium level–pretty standard stuff for any patient who is crashing. We drew the specimens and sent them to the lab stat. The BMP takes about 45 minutes to be processed. In the meantime, I noticed that his QRS intervals started to widen. I suspected that it was related to possible electrolyte imbalances because his urine output had significantly decreased despite fluid boluses. I got an EKG, which confirmed it. I, another nurse, and an RT (respiratory therapist) were in the room trying to get an ABG (arterial blood gas) from the femoral artery, when suddenly none of us could feel a pulse. Basically, he was in PEA (pulseless electrical activity). Of course at that point we called the code.

The code team arrived. We had started CPR (cardio-pulmonary resuscitation) and shortly after starting CPR we got a pulse back. We still had to intubate the patient because of his respiratory status. While the CRNA (Certified Registered Nurse Anesthesiologist) was intubating, I was able to bring up his lab results so we could get a bigger picture. At that time his potassium was extremely high. The doctor was at the bedside assessing the patient, assisting with intubation and calling out orders. I was at the computer looking at the labs and entering orders.

The doctor said, "Let's go ahead and push an amp of D-50 (dextrose) and ten units of insulin. Then we'll push an amp of calcium chloride after that. His bi-carb is low—push 2 amps of bi-carb and put an order in for another ABG right away."

The doctor was ordering this in rapid succession, while I entered the orders and transmitted them to the pharmacist, who cleared them very quickly; my co-worker went to pull the meds from the Pyxis machine. Literally in a matter of minutes, people were handing the drugs through the door, scanning and administering them. It was over and done, just that quick.

Our hospital policy supports the closed loop medication administration safety initiative which you will read about elsewhere in this chapter. Let me describe how that works. When the doctor was giving me verbal orders, I was entering them in the CPOE. The medication orders were automatically sent to the pharmacy. The pharmacist interacted with that order on the pharmacy system, validated that the orders were safe and ready to dispense, and sent an order to the dispensing system. When the nurse went to the drawer to pull it out of the machine, the order was in there and allowed her to get it. Then she gave it to the nurse in the room, who scanned the patient's arm band, scanned the medication, and then administered it. The system also documented it. So there is no transcription error, no misinterpretation of the orders errors—it is all electronically one order moving through the systems. I love it. I feel like I am getting double-checked five times. The pharmacist is also getting double-checked because when the order goes to the Pyxis machine it also comes up on my order list screen, highlighted in yellow for the nurse to confirm this is in fact the correct order for the correct patient. I know instantly what the pharmacist is dispensing. If there is any miscommunication, the nurse will have the ability to catch any error from the pharmacy.

When the crisis is over and the doctor has time to get into his own CPOE system, there is a button there labeled "cosign." He can click the cosign button and it will show him all the verbal orders that he has given—that someone else has entered for him. He can select them and cosign them at that time. Also, each doctor has a work folder in the EHR, so if he does not cosign them at that time they will show up in his work folder as items he needs to attend to. Most of the intensivists on our unit cosign their orders before the end of their shift.

Even when we are not in a code situation, there are times throughout the night when nurses are entering orders. For example, last night I had a patient come in who was already on a dopamine drip at 20 micrograms. The patient was tachycardic; blood pressure was 70 and 80 systolic. The doctor was at the bedside speaking with the surgeon when the anesthesiologist came to intubate. I said to the doctor, "Can I have Levophed?" and entered the order. I got the Levophed hanging, but the patient's pressure was still dumping. Because the physicians were evaluating the patient for septic versus cardiogenic shock, I asked, "How about some dobutamine?" The doctor told me to go ahead with the order.

Even with all three of those hanging, the patient still was not improving, and the anesthesiologist was requesting a better BP before sedation for intubation. I asked, "What else do we want to hang to get some blood pressure—can I have some vasopressin?" The doctors preferred to have me enter the orders in the computer while they continued to confer about the patient. By me entering the orders at the bedside, pharmacy was able to get the drugs to me more quickly as well.

I enjoy working in the CCU. You are responsible for almost every aspect of your patient's care. You have to be an advocate for your patient, someone who can handle herself in stressful situations, and think quickly in crisis.

Protocols Based on Diagnosis Codes

Disease-based protocols can help the clinician write the orders and document the exam more quickly. Instead of searching through a list of a thousand prescription drugs, the clinician can access a short list of drugs that are regularly prescribed for a particular type of infection. These lists can be created for individual prescribing clinicians, for the practice as a whole, or by some recognized authority such as a medical association.

Similarly, the clinician can create a specific group of orders used to test for certain conditions. When a diagnosis is suspected, the list can be quickly located and the clinician can order tests, consults, or radiological studies all at once.

Introducing Diagnosis Codes

Each of the encounters you have documented in the previous exercises included an Assessment finding that was selected on the Dx tab of the software. As you are already aware, Dx is an acronym for "Diagnosis." Diagnoses are assigned codes using the ICD-9-CM code set (or ICD-10 after 2013).

People sometimes erroneously think of ICD-9-CM codes as "billing" codes, because reimbursement is tied to the diagnoses codes and they are required on health insurance claims. However, ICD-9-CM codes are important for reasons other than billing, including statistical studies of causes of death, disease, and injury. ICD-9-CM provides an internationally recognized system of codifying the patient's condition.

Because ICD-9-CM are standardized codes for diseases, those codes can be used for problem lists and associated with protocols and treatment plans. Many professional journals, associations, and practices create protocols for treating certain diseases. These may consist of specific regimens such as an oncologist might use to treat a particular form of cancer, or they might consist of a list of all possible antibiotics known to be effective for a certain type of infection. In either case, the protocol or plan of treatment can be easily communicated to other clinicians by linking it to the diagnoses for which it is effective.

Even without creating specific protocols, the diagnosis can be used to help locate orders and treatment plans. Guided Exercise 37, earlier in this chapter, demonstrated this with Gary Yamamoto's encounter. Once you found the diagnosis "413.9 Angina Pectoris," the Prompt feature was able to find a list of appropriate test orders related to the condition. Now we will further study how the diagnosis aids the clinician in locating appropriate orders.

History of ICD-9-CM

ICD stands for International Classification of Diseases, which is a system of standardized codes developed collaboratively between the World Health Organization (WHO) and 10 international centers. The number "9" represents the ninth revision of the coding system, which was revised about every 10 years from 1900 to 1979.

Today's coding system evolved from the International List of Causes of Death, which was used by physicians, medical examiners, and coroners to facilitate standardized mortality studies. In 1948, WHO expanded and renamed the system to make it useful for coding patient medical conditions as well.

By the time the ninth revision was published, the U.S. National Center for Health Statistics began to modify the statistical study with clinical information. The letters "CM" stand for Clinical Modification. Clinical modifications provided a way to code the clinical information about the health of a patient beyond that needed for statistical reports. With the addition of clinical modifications, the codes became useful for indexing medical records and medical case reviews, and communicating a patient's condition more precisely.

ICD-9-CM is currently published in three volumes. The first two volumes provide a listing and an index of diagnosis codes; the third volume lists codes for hospital inpatient procedures. Figure 6-33 shows a sample list of codes from volumes 1 and 2.

The diagnosis codes are three characters, followed by a decimal point and up to two numerals. The first three characters of an ICD-9-CM code identify the primary diagnosis; the two digits to the right of the decimal point further refine the diagnosis specificity.

Insurance billing allows for the use of multiple ICD-9-CM codes for a single procedure, indicating one code as the primary diagnosis and additional codes as secondary conditions for which the treatment was done.

The historical intent of the ICD was to classify similar causes of mortality and disease conditions into statistical reportable data. When in 1989 ICD-9-CM codes became required by insurance carriers to process claims, the code set had to be further modified. The problem was that if an ICD-9-CM code was required for an insurance claim, but the patient was perfectly healthy, what code should be used? To solve this problem, ICD-9-CM added a section of codes that start with the letter "V"; these V codes indicate nonillness conditions that can be used for billing. For example, children have regular pediatric checkups, these are coded as "V20.2 Well-Child Checkup."

▶ **Figure 6-33** Small sample of ICD-9-CM codes.

ICD-9-CM Codes (Diagnosis)	
Code	**Description**
Diseases of Other Endocrine Glands	
250	Diabetes mellitus
250.0	Diabetes mellitus without mention of complication (NOS)
250.00	Diabetes mellitus type II, not stated as uncontrolled
250.01	Diabetes mellitus type I (juvenile) not stated as uncontrolled
250.02	Diabetes mellitus type II, uncontrolled
250.03	Diabetes mellitus type I, (juvenile) uncontrolled
250.1	Diabetes with ketoacidosis
250.2	Diabetes with hyperosomolarity
250.3	Diabetes with other coma
V Codes (Circumstances other than disease or injury)	
V22.0	Supervision of normal first pregnancy
V22.1	Supervision of other normal pregnancy
V70.0	Routine general medical examination (health check up)
V72.1	Examination of ears and hearing
V72.1	Encounter for hearing following a failed hearing screening
E Codes (Classification of external causes of injury or poisoning)	
E813.0	Driver in a motor vehicle accident involving collision with other vehicle
E813.1	Passenger in a motor vehicle accident involving collision with other vehicle
E813.3	Motorcyclist in a motor vehicle accident involving collision with other vehicle

Volume 1 also includes "E" codes (listed at the bottom of Figure 6-33). These are not used for diagnosis, but to classify the cause of an injury or poisoning. For example, the billing diagnosis 823.0 indicates the patient had a closed fracture of the tibia. The code E813.1 provides further detail that the broken leg is the result of a motor vehicle crash in which the patient was a passenger.

Future Developments: ICD-10

ICD-10 is the latest revision to the International Classification of Diseases. It was released by WHO in 1992 and is used broadly in Europe and Canada. ICD-10 contains about twice as many categories as ICD-9 and uses more alphanumeric codes. Effective January 1, 1999, ICD-10 was officially implemented in the United States for reporting the cause of death on death certificates. It has not been implemented for billing, and should not be used in place of ICD-9-CM for reporting diagnoses on insurance claims. The U.S. Department of Health and Human Services (HHS) has proposed that the ICD-10 code sets be used for billing effective October 1, 2013.

▶ Figure 6-34 A comparison of ICD-10 codes and ICD-9-CM codes.

| Comparison of ICD-10 and ICD-9-CM Codes ||||
ICD-10	Description	ICD-9-CM	Description
R31.0	Gross hematuria	599.7	Hematuria
R31.1	Benign essential microscopic hematuria	599.7	Hematuria
R31.2	Other microscopic hematuria	599.7	Hematuria
R31.9	Hematuria, unspecified	599.7	Hematuria
N36.41	Hypermobility of urethra	599.81	Urethral hypermobility
N36.42	Intrinsic sphincter deficiency	599.82	Intrinsic sphincter deficiency
N36.43	Combined hypermobility of urethra and intrinsic sphincter deficiency		
N364.4	Muscular disorders of urethra		
N36.8	Other specified disorders of urethra	599.83	Urethral instability
N36.8	Other specified disorders of urethra	599.84	Other specified disorders of urethra

Use Figure 6-34 to compare several ICD-9-CM and ICD-10 codes.

ICD-9-CM and EHR Nomenclatures

The ICD-9-CM is not an EHR nomenclature. However, most EHR systems contain a "cross-walk" or internal reference table that can produce ICD-9-CM codes automatically. The advantage of using an EHR with a codified nomenclature is that the ICD-9-CM codes will always be in sync with the encounter documentation that is produced. Another advantage is that the EHR allows the clinician to record nuances that are beyond the scope of ICD-9-CM such as "mild" or "improving." The EHR software will automatically translate the assessment to the correct diagnosis code.

Primary and Secondary Diagnoses

The concept of the primary diagnosis is also important. The primary diagnosis is the reason why the patient came to the office or hospital. Other conditions that are addressed during the visit are listed as secondary diagnoses (also called *comorbidity*). In a hospital, secondary diagnoses are classified as POA, present on admission, or HAC, hospital acquired condition.

Any conditions that exist concurrently with the primary diagnosis should be reviewed, examined, or treated and documented in the exam note. Often this is facilitated by a "problem list," which is a summary of ongoing or previous conditions. The problem list helps the clinician keep track of the patient's needs beyond the scope of the chief complaint for today's visit. You will see an example of a problem list in Chapter 7.

Multiple Diagnoses

Multiple diagnoses occur mainly in patients with ongoing or chronic conditions requiring regular visits. It is correct and appropriate to continue to use diagnosis codes from past visits for as long as the patient continues to have the illness or condition and that condition is clearly documented in the record. For example, a patient with diabetes mellitus—poorly controlled might be seen regularly. With this disease, on some visits the patient will likely have other problems as well. Therefore, the diagnosis 250.2, "Diabetes Mellitus," should be included in every visit note and on insurance claims for those visits.

The Rule-Out Diagnosis

The ICD-9-CM code set has neither specific codes nor modifiers to use with diagnosis codes to communicate the concept of "ruling out" a disease or condition. One inconsistency in the ICD-9-CM guidelines is that services performed during inpatient settings support the concept of "rule-out," but guidelines for the outpatient setting does not.

The diagnosis for a patient may take more than one visit to be determined or confirmed, but the outpatient visit guidelines do not allow for "possible," "probable," "suspected," "rule-out," or similar diagnoses. Although the prefix "possible" may be appropriate and necessary in the exam note, the insurance claim for an outpatient visit should not be coded with a diagnosis for the suspected disease.

This creates a dilemma when ordering diagnostic tests from outside facilities. Reference laboratories cannot bill for the test unless they have a diagnosis. Only the clinician ordering the test is allowed to assign the diagnosis; the reference lab cannot. Therefore, the labs require an order for a test to include a diagnosis code, even though the purpose of the test is only to determine if the patient in fact has the disease. Again, Guided Exercise 36 was an example of this in that you practiced ordering tests for Gary Yamamoto, a patient with *possible* angina pectoris.

Using Diagnosis to Find Orders and Treatments

In the next two exercises, you will learn to use multiple diagnoses and to create different sets of orders based on established plans associated with each diagnosis. You must complete both Exercise 41 and Exercise 42 in one session. **Do not begin this exercise unless there is enough class time remaining to complete both exercises.**

Guided Exercise 41: Orders Based on Diagnosis

Case Study

Alena Zabroski is a 53-year-old female who complains of jaw pain. She has been to her dentist, who has found nothing wrong. The clinician initially suspects angina and orders tests to confirm or rule out the diagnosis. However, Alena mentions that she has moved back to her childhood home and has been restoring it. Knowing that the patient was born in 1959 and therefore her home is an old house, the clinician realizes there is a possibility that she is being exposed to lead-based paints. This fact alters the direction of inquiry and of the tests ordered.

Step 1

If you have not already done so, start the Student Edition software.

Click Select on the Menu bar, and then click Patient.

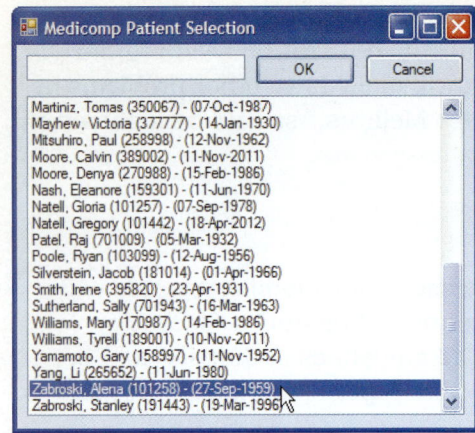

▶ Figure 6-35 Select Patient Alena Zabroski.

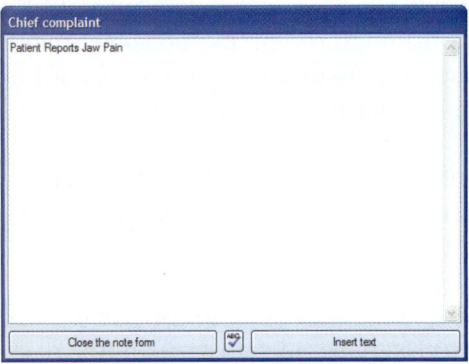

▶ Figure 6-36 Chief complaint dialog for "Patient Reports Jaw Pain."

In the Patient Selection window, locate and click on **Alena Zabroski** as shown in Figure 6-35.

Step 2

Click Select on the Menu bar, and then click New Encounter.

Use the current date and time. Select the reason **Office Visit** from the drop-down list and click on the OK button.

Step 3

Enter the Chief complaint by locating the button in the Toolbar labeled "Chief" and clicking on it.

In the dialog window which will open, type: "**Patient reports jaw pain**."

Compare your screen to Figure 6-36 before clicking on the button labeled "Close the Note form."

Step 4

In this exercise, the medical assistant will begin the visit by taking Alena's vital signs.

Use the form labeled "Vitals," which you will select from the Forms Manager, invoked on the Active Forms tab (as you have done in previous exercises).

▶ Figure 6-37 Vital Signs form for Alena Zabroski.

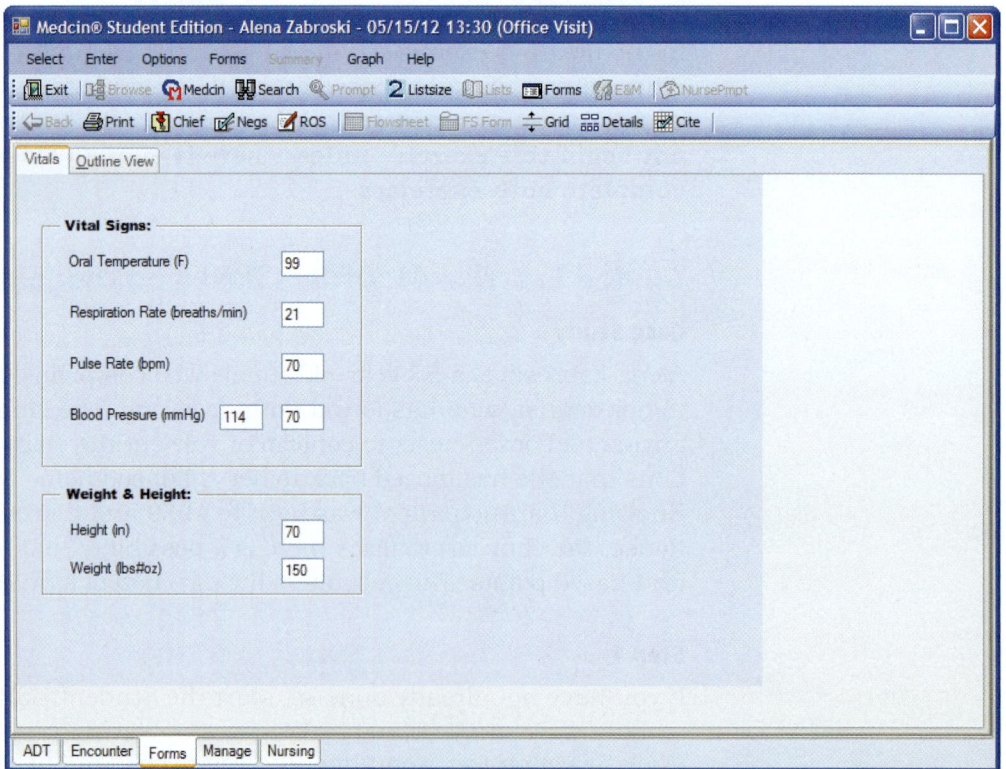

Enter Alena's vital signs in the corresponding fields on the Form as follows:

Temperature: **99**

Respiration: **21**

Pulse: **70**

BP: **114/70**

Height: **70**

Weight: **150**

When you have finished, compare your screen to Figure 6-37 and, when it is correct, click on the Encounter tab at the bottom of the screen.

Step 5

Locate and click on the Lists button in the Toolbar at the top of your screen. The List Manager window will be invoked.

As you learned in the previous chapter, the List Manager displays the various Lists available to providers in the practice. Two fields at the top of the screen organize the display of List names, filtering them by Owner and Group.

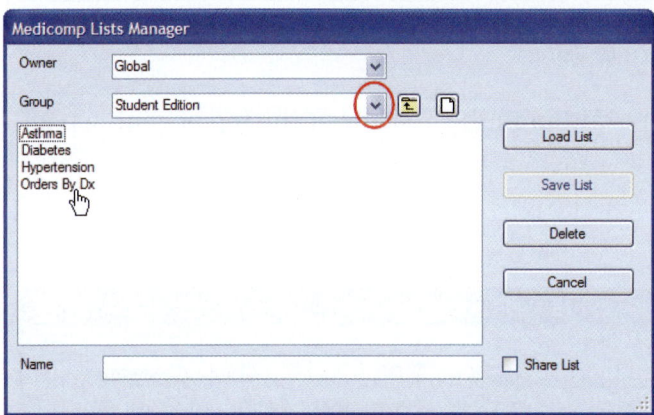

The Group field allows a user to quickly find a list by limiting the display to a desired group. The Student Edition has two groups: "All" and "Student Edition." In this step, you are going to change the lists displayed from All to Student Edition.

Locate and click on the button with a down arrow in the Group field; a drop-down list will be displayed. Select Student Edition. Compare your List Manager window to Figure 6-38.

▶ **Figure 6-38 Load Orders by Dx list (down arrow for group circled in red).**

Locate and highlight the list labeled "**Orders By Dx**" and then click on the button labeled "Load List."

The Orders By Dx List has been especially created for this exercise. It demonstrates the use of protocols of orders and treatments by associating them with particular diseases. In this exercise there is one list for several diseases. In an actual medical office, there would likely be many separate lists.

Step 6

The list will load and automatically change to the Dx tab. If the left pane is not on the Dx tab, click on the tab labeled "Dx."

Locate the list size button in the Toolbar at the top of your screen and click it until it is set to **2**.

Locate and click on the finding:

- (red button) ANGINA PECTORIS

▶ Figure 6-39 Dx: Angina Pectoris with List Size 2.

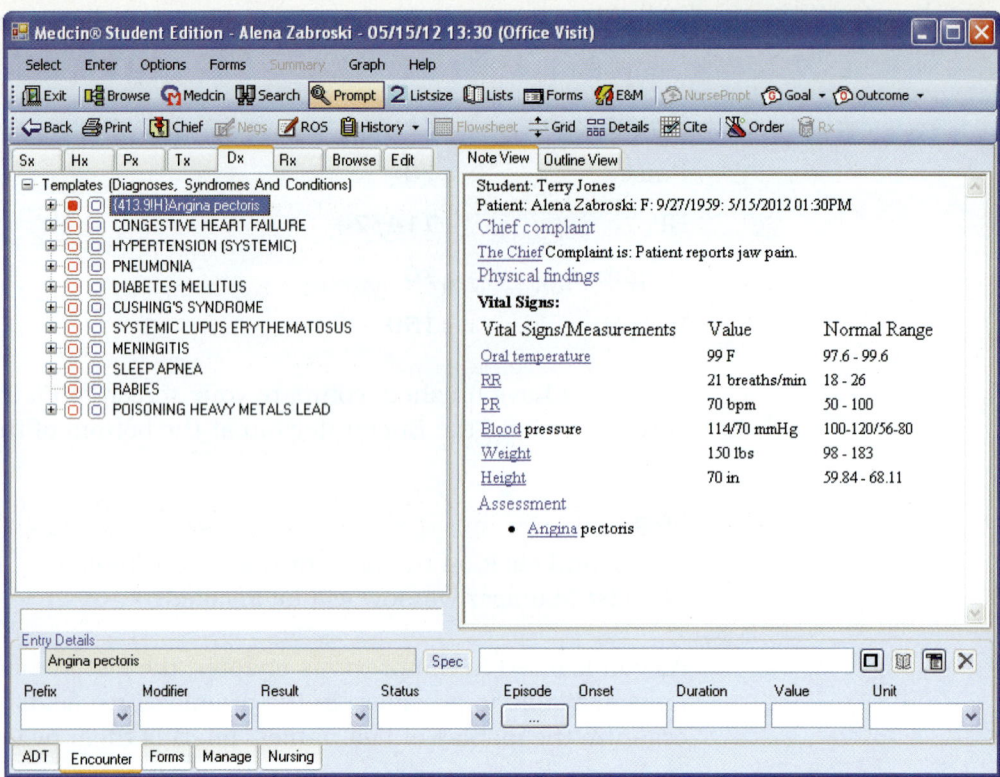

Compare your screen to Figure 6-39.

Locate and click on the Prompt button in the Toolbar at the top of your screen.

Step 7

Click on the Sx tab.

▶ Figure 6-40 Sx tab with Dx: Angina Pectoris List Size 2 and ROS On.

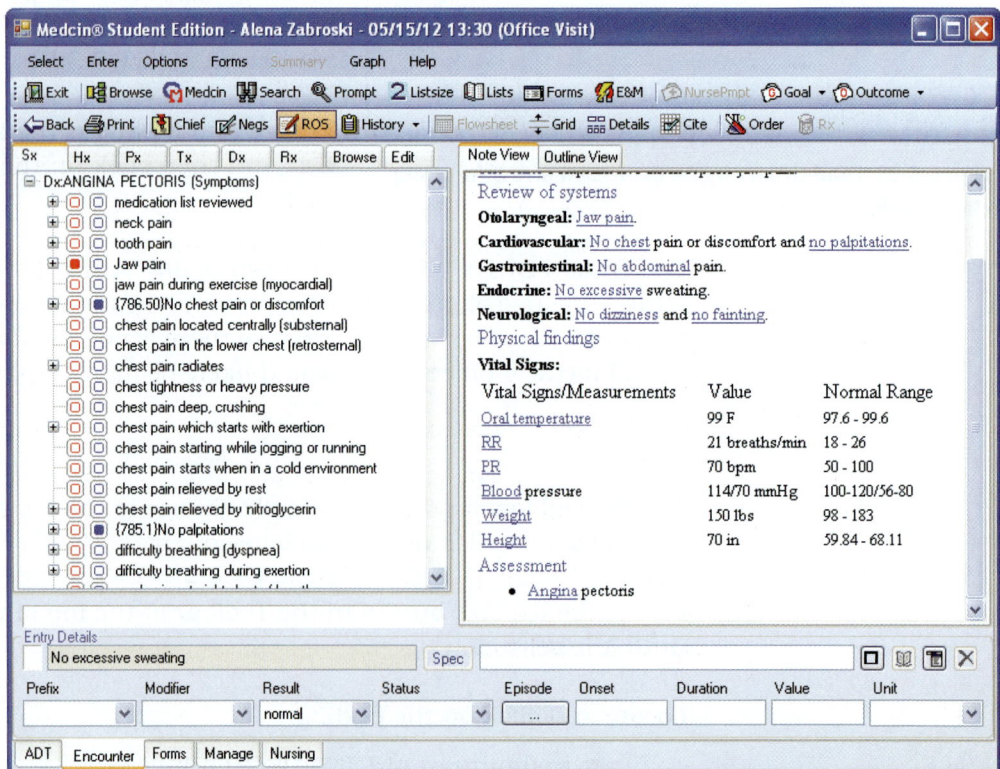

242   Chapter 6 | Understanding Electronic Orders

Locate the ROS button in the Toolbar at the top of your screen and click it. It should change color (as shown in Figure 6-40).

Locate and click on the following findings (you will need to scroll the left pane to find them all):

- (red button) jaw pain (in jaw bone)
- (blue button) chest pain or discomfort
- (blue button) palpitations
- (blue button) abdominal pain
- (blue button) excessive sweating
- (blue button) dizziness
- (blue button) fainting (syncope)

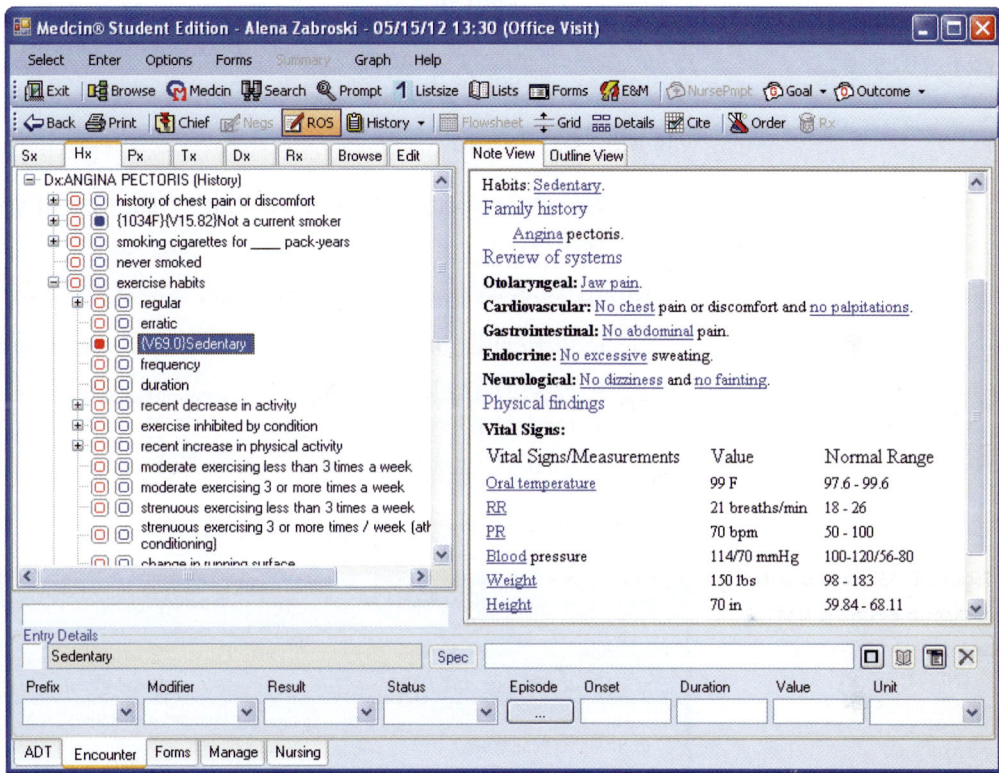

▶ Figure 6-41 Hx tab with Dx: Angina Pectoris List Size 2.

Step 8

Click on the Hx tab.

Locate and click on the following findings:

- (blue button) current smoker
- (red button) Family history of Angina Pectoris

Locate and expand the tree for "exercise habits."

Locate and click on the following finding:

- (red button) Sedentary

Compare your screen to Figure 6-41.

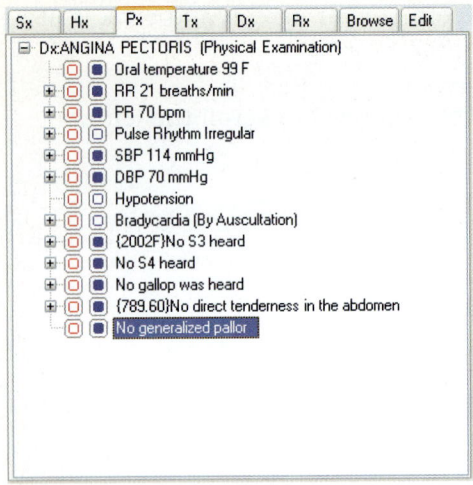

▶ Figure 6-42 Px tab with Dx: Angina Pectoris List Size 2.

Step 9

Click on the Px tab. Notice that the physical findings from Vitals are already recorded.

Locate and click on the following findings:

- (blue button) Heart Sounds S3
- (blue button) Heart Sounds S4
- (blue button) Heart Sounds Gallop
- (blue button) Abdomen Tenderness Direct
- (blue button) Pallor, Generalized

Compare your screen to Figure 6-42.

Step 10

Locate the List Size button in the Toolbar and click it until it is set to **1**.

Click on the Tx tab.

Locate the Order button in the Toolbar at the top of your screen (highlighted in Figure 6-43).

Highlight each of the following findings and then click on the Order button.

- (order) Comprehensive Metabolic Chem Panel
- (order) Lipids Test Panel
- (order) Electrocardiogram
- (order) Cardiovascular Stress Test

Compare your screen to Figure 6-43.

▶ Figure 6-43 Tx tab with Dx: Angina Pectoris List Size 1.

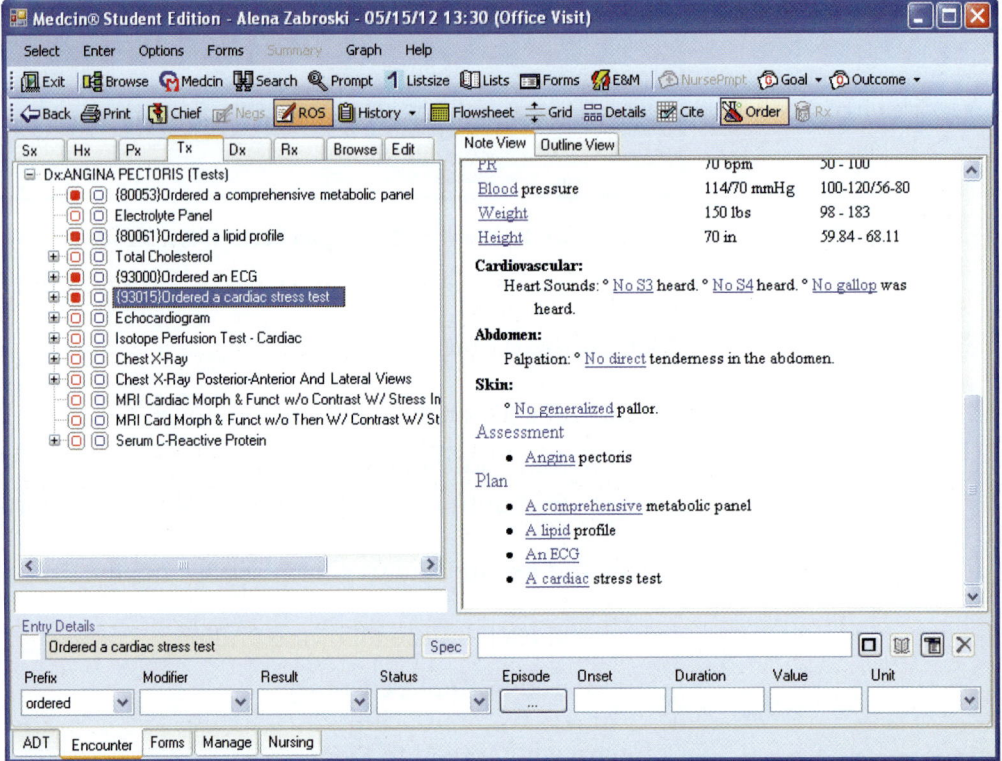

244 Chapter 6 | Understanding Electronic Orders

▶ Figure 6-44 Rx tab with Dx: Angina Pectoris List Size 1.

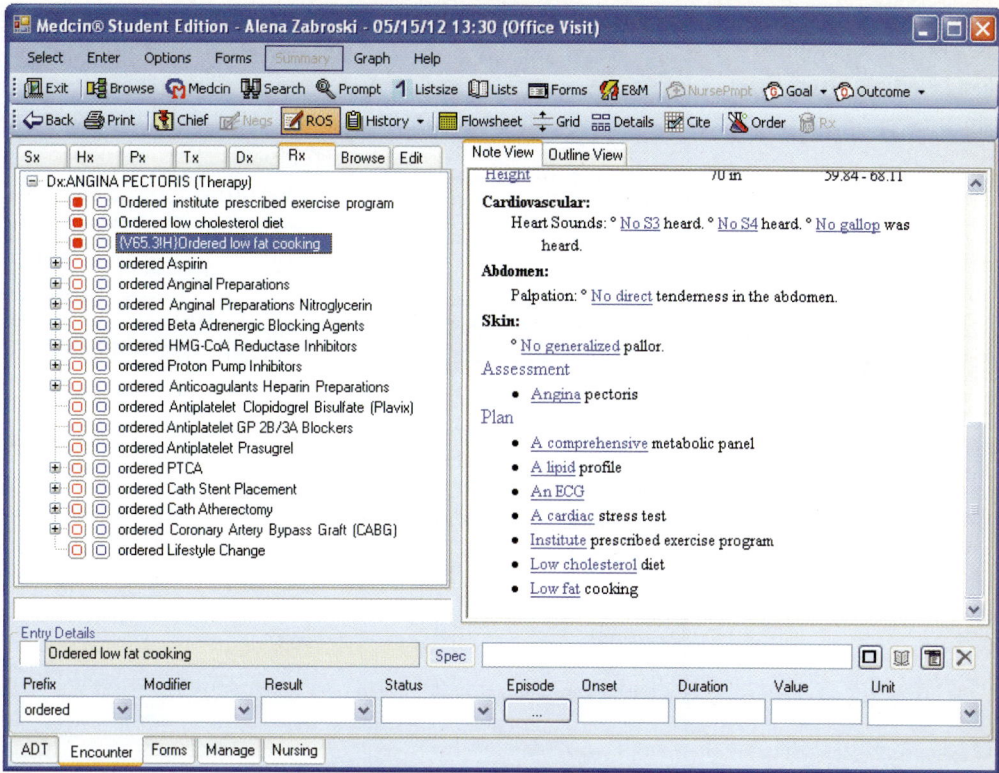

Step 11

Click on the Rx tab.

Locate and click on the following findings (you do not need to use the order button):

- (red button) ordered Institute Prescribed Exercise Program
- (red button) ordered Low Cholesterol Diet
- (red button) ordered Patient Education Dietary Low Fat Cooking

Compare your screen to Figure 6-44.

Continue with Guided Exercise 42. Do not exit the Student Edition software or you will lose your work.

Guided Exercise 42: Multiple Diagnoses

It is not unusual during the course of an office visit for a patient to bring up additional problems or provide a piece of information to the clinician that suddenly brings focus on another area of the patient's health.

When Alena Zabroski mentions that she has been scraping a lot of old layers of paint off the walls of her childhood home, the clinician realizes that the patient was born in 1959 and there is a possibility that she is being exposed to lead-based paints.

Step 12

Locate the List button in the Toolbar at the top of your screen and click it to invoke the List Manager window.

Reload the List "Orders By Dx" by selecting it and clicking the button labeled "Load List." If you have difficulty, see Figure 6-38 and review step 5 above.

▶ Figure 6-45 Dx tab with Heavy Metals highlighted—select "Possible" from list.

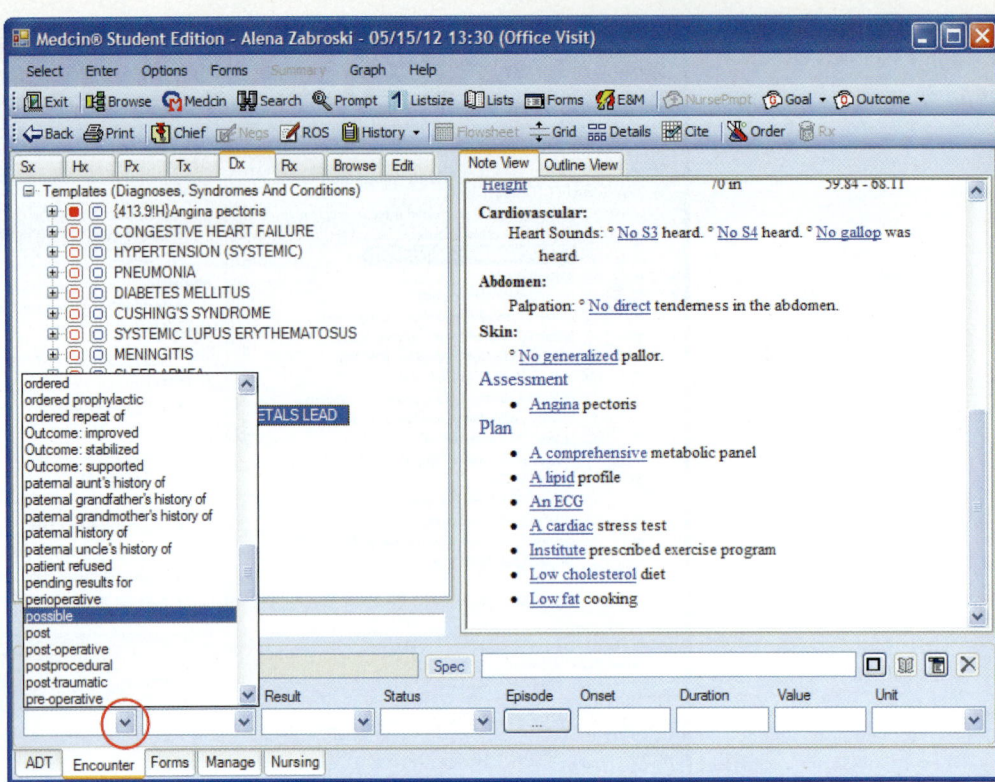

Step 13

The list will be reloaded and the Dx tab will be displayed.

Verify the List Size is 1. If it is not, then locate and click on the button labeled "List Size" in the Toolbar until it is set to 1.

Locate and highlight the finding "Poisoning Heavy Metals Lead."

▶ Figure 6-46 Hx tab with List from Dx: Poisoning Heavy Metals Lead.

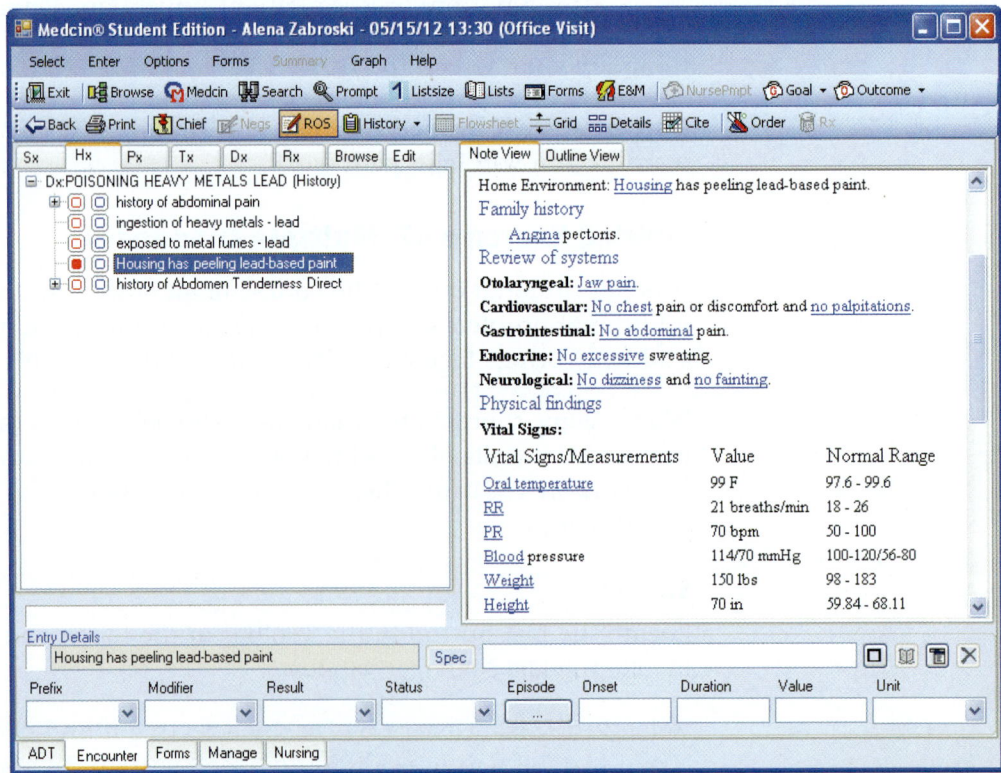

246   Chapter 6 | Understanding Electronic Orders

Locate the field labeled "Prefix" in the Entry Details section of your screen. Click the button with the down arrow in the Prefix field (circled in red in Figure 6-45). A drop-down list of Prefix terms will be displayed.

Scroll the list of prefixes. Locate and click on the term "Possible."

The finding will automatically be recorded and the text of the finding will change to "Possible poisoning by lead."

Locate the list size button in the toolbar at the top of your screen; if it is not currently set to 1, click it until it is set to 1.

With the finding "Possible Poisoning by Lead" still highlighted, locate and click on the Prompt button in the Toolbar at the top of your screen.

Step 14

The clinician is going to first record this new piece of information. Click on the Hx tab. Locate and click on the following finding:

- (red button) house has peeling paint which is lead based

Compare your screen to Figure 6-46.

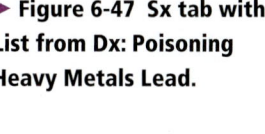

▶ Figure 6-47 Sx tab with List from Dx: Poisoning Heavy Metals Lead.

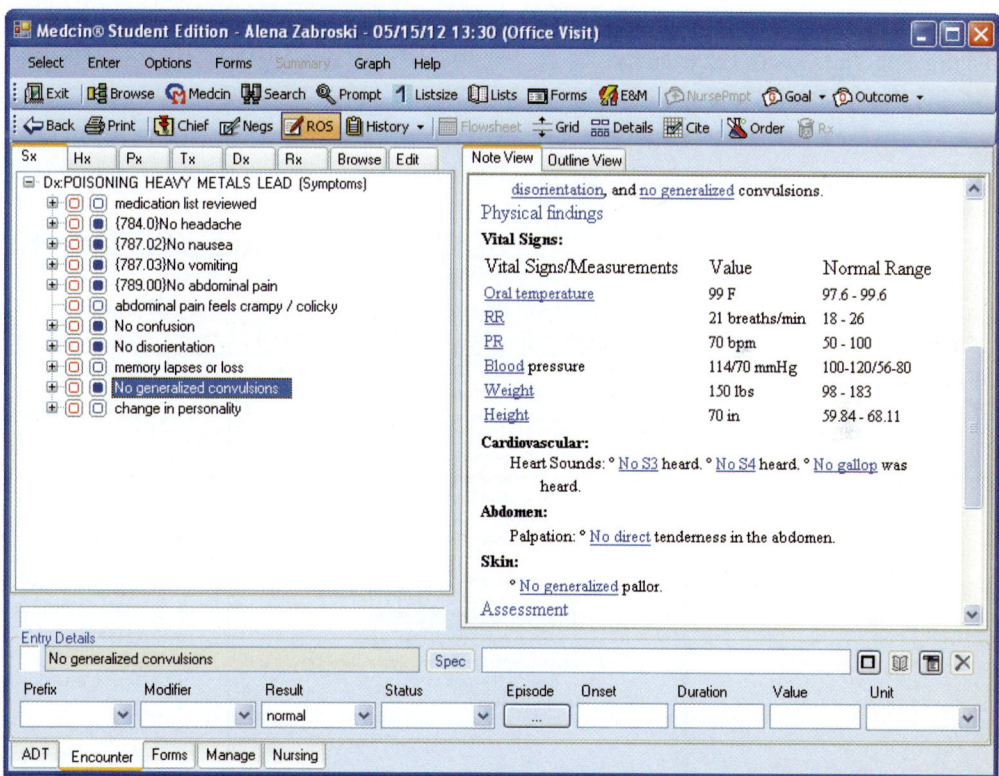

Step 15

Click on the Sx tab. Verify the ROS button in the Toolbar at the top of your screen is still depressed. If it is not, then click it.

Locate and click on the following findings:

- (blue button) headache
- (blue button) nausea

- (blue button) vomiting
- (blue button) confusion
- (blue button) disorientation
- (blue button) convulsions, generalized

Compare your screen to Figure 6-47.

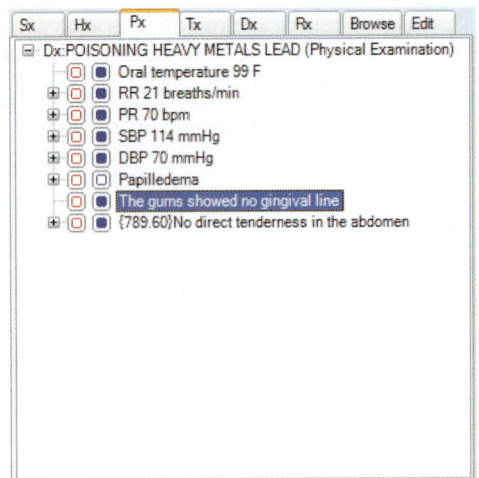

▶ Figure 6-48 Px tab with List from Dx: Poisoning Heavy Metals Lead.

Step 16

Click on the Px tab. Note some findings are already selected (from the previous exercise).

Locate and click on the following finding:

- (blue button) Gums Gingival Line

Compare your screen to Figure 6-48.

Step 17

Click on the Tx tab.

Locate the Order button in the Toolbar at the top of your screen.

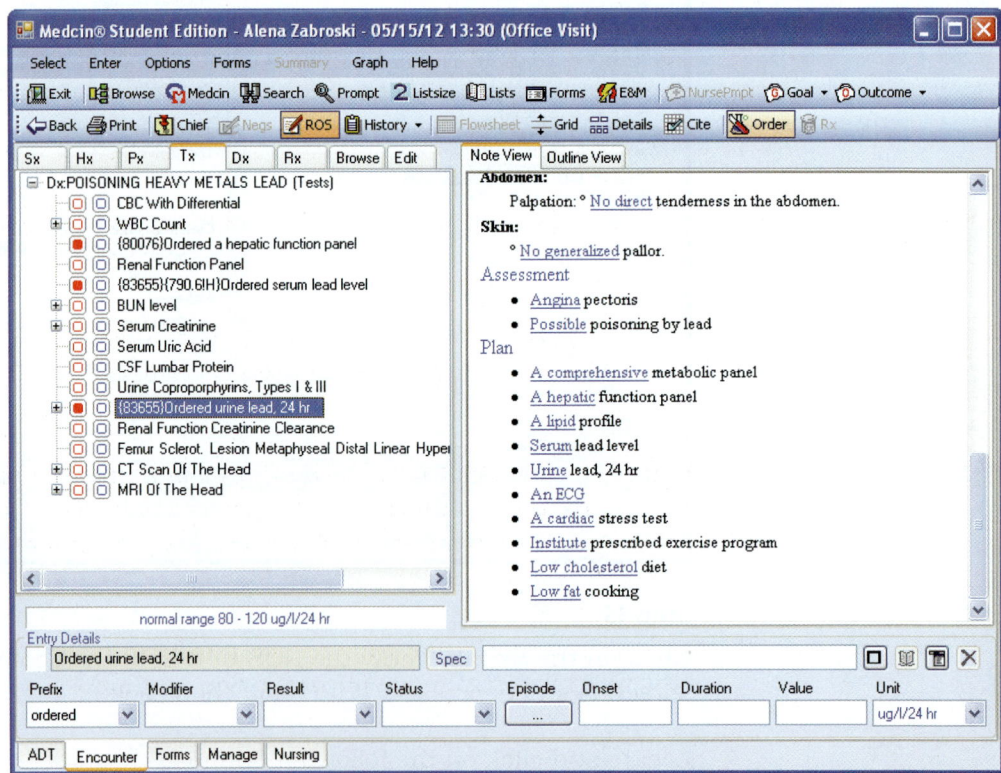

▶ Figure 6-49 Tx tab with list from Dx: Poisoning Heavy Metals Lead.

248   Chapter 6 | Understanding Electronic Orders

Locate and highlight each of the following findings and then click on the Order button. Do not click on the red or blue buttons next to these findings.

- (order) Hepatic Function Panel
- (order) Serum Lead Level
- (order) Urine Lead, 24 hr

Compare your screen to Figure 6-49.

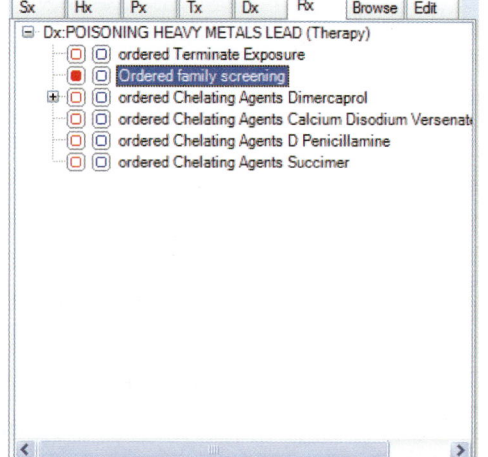

▶ Figure 6-50 Rx tab with Dx: Poisoning Heavy Metals (List Size 1).

Step 18

The clinician is also concerned about others who might be in the home and will need to be screened for lead poisoning as well.

Click on the Rx tab.

Locate and click on the following findings (you do not need to use the Order button):

- (red button) Screen Family

Compare your screen to Figure 6-50.

 **Alert** | **Do not close or exit the encounter until you have a printed copy in your hand. You will lose your work if you exit before printing.**

Step 19

Click on the Print button on the Toolbar at the top of your screen to invoke the Print Data window.

Be certain there is a check mark in the box next to "Current Encounter" and then click on the appropriate button to either print or export a file, as directed by your instructor.

Compare your printout or file output to Figure 6-51. If your work is correct, hand it in to your instructor. If there are any differences (other than encounter date or patient's age), review the previous steps in the exercise and find your error.

This exercise has shown how a diagnosis can be used to find and display lists of orders and treatments for particular conditions.

Chapter 6 | Understanding Electronic Orders   249

Alena Zabroski   Page 1 of 1

Student: your name or id here
Patient: Alena Zabroski: F: 9/27/1959: 5/15/2012 01:30PM

Chief complaint
The Chief Complaint is: Patient reports jaw pain.

Personal history
    Behavioral: Not a current smoker.
    Habits: Sedentary.
    Home Environment: Housing has peeling lead-based paint.

Family history
Angina pectoris.

Review of systems
    Head: No headache.
    Otolaryngeal: Jaw pain.
    Cardiovascular: No chest pain or discomfort and no palpitations.
    Gastrointestinal: No nausea, no vomiting, and no abdominal pain.
    Endocrine: No excessive sweating.
    Neurological: No dizziness, no fainting, no confusion, no disorientation, and no generalized convulsions.

Physical findings
Vital Signs:

Vital Signs/Measurements	Value	Normal Range
Oral temperature	99 F	97.6 - 99.6
RR	21 breaths/min	18 - 26
PR	70 bpm	50 - 100
Blood pressure	114/70 mmHg	100-120/56-80
Weight	150 lbs	98 - 183
Height	70 in	59.84 - 68.11

Oral Cavity:
Gums: ° Showed no gingival line.
Cardiovascular:
Heart Sounds: ° No S3 heard. ° No S4 heard. ° No gallop was heard.
Abdomen:
Palpation: ° No direct tenderness in the abdomen.
Skin:
° No generalized pallor.

Assessment
- Angina pectoris
- Possible poisoning by lead

Plan
- A comprehensive metabolic panel
- A hepatic function panel
- A lipid profile
- Serum lead level
- Urine lead, 24 hr
- An ECG
- A cardiac stress test
- Institute prescribed exercise program
- Low cholesterol diet
- Low fat cooking
- Family screening

▶ Figure 6-51 Printed encounter note for Alena Zabroski.

Chapter Six Summary

This chapter introduced several new buttons on the Medcin Toolbar. In this chapter you learned to use the Search and Prompt features and one way of recording a clinician's order. You also learned to use more icons on the Medcin Toolbar.

Search provides a quick way to locate a desired finding in the nomenclature. Medcin addresses semantic differences in medical terms in three ways:

1. Search performs automatic word completion, so if you search for knee but the finding is for knees, it will still find it.

2. Medcin includes an extensive list of synonyms that are used in an alternate word search. For example, if you search for knee injury, the search results will also include findings for knee burns, knee trauma, and fractured patella, among others.

3. Search identifies related findings in other tabs so that when you search for a word or phrase in a particular tab, related findings are automatically available in the other tabs. This means that when you are using search while documenting a patient exam, as you continue through the exam, the other tabs may already have findings that you will use.

Search is not designed to find every instance that contains the words being searched because the search results will often have too many findings. Instead, Search finds and displays the highest level match but does not list all the expanded findings below it.

Prompt is short for "prompt with current finding." Prompt generates a list of findings that are clinically related to the finding currently highlighted.

The prompt list that is displayed is shorter than the full nomenclature, containing only relevant findings, making it easier to read and navigate. The list generated by the prompt feature populates all the tabs, creating shorter lists of any relevant findings in each tab (Sx, Hx, Px, Tx, Dx, and Rx).

The **Order** button orders a test. Clicking on the red button for a test records the test as performed. Highlighting the name of the test and clicking the order button records the test as ordered.

The **Rx** button on the Toolbar is available only on the Rx tab and only when the highlighted finding is a drug or medication. Clicking the Rx button invokes the prescription writer.

ICD-9-CM codes are an international standard for coding diseases and death. A supplemental section of ICD-9-CM also provides codes for reasons that patients come to the doctor other than illness or injury. These codes are called "V Codes" and start with the letter "V." They are used for checkups, physicals, vaccinations, maternity care, screening for diabetes, and so on.

Another supplemental section of the ICD-9-CM codes is titled "External Causes of Injury and Poisoning." These codes begin with the letter "E." E codes cover injuries ranging from bee stings to war; other examples include falling and vehicle crash injuries. E codes are used in addition to the numeric ICD-9-CM codes, never alone. E codes are used to codify the cause of an injury or adverse event.

The ICD-9-CM codes are from three to five digits long. The fourth and fifth digits add specificity. Insurance billing rules require that clinicians code to the most specific level. EHR systems automatically reference ICD-9-CM codes at the fourth or fifth digit specificity. EHR systems based on Medcin can automatically resolve the assessment to the most specific level of diagnosis code.

ICD-9-CM codes also are used as a key to problems and protocols in healthcare. Examples of protocols might be a specific set of tests used to monitor a particular disease or a list of antibiotics known to be effective for a certain type of infection. Creating protocols and finding them based on the assessment can help the clinician write orders and document the exam quickly.

Multiple diagnoses codes can be assigned to a single encounter. This occurs mainly because patients with ongoing or chronic conditions require regular visits. It is correct and appropriate to continue to use diagnosis codes from past visits for as long as the patient continues to have that illness or condition.

ICD-10 is the latest revision to the International Classification of Diseases. HHS has proposed that ICD-10 codes should begin being used in the United States effective October, 2013.

As you continue through the course, you can refer to the Guided Exercises in this chapter when you need to remember how to perform a particular task.

Task	Exercise	Page #
Search for a finding in the nomenclature	36	208
Prompt (locate findings related to highlighted finding)	36	210
Record orders (or change order status) using the drop-down list	37	213
Use the prescription writer	39	226
Use a quick-pick list to write prescriptions	40	230
Order tests based on diagnosis	41 and 42	239

Testing Your Knowledge of Chapter 6

You may run the Medcin Student Edition software and use your mouse on the screen to answer the following questions:

1. Describe how to record a test that was ordered and describe how to record a test that was performed.
2. How do you indicate a "possible" diagnosis?

Describe the function of each of the following buttons on the Toolbar:

3. Exit
4. Browse
5. Chief
6. Search
7. Order
8. Print
9. Prompt
10. When you click the Prompt button, what List will be generated?
11. How do you change the numbers on the List Size button and what do the numbers do?

Circle True or False for the following statements:

12. Orders are an essential component of any patient chart.

    True   False

13. Nurses and medical assistants sometimes enter verbal orders into an EHR on behalf of the ordering clinician.

    True   False

14. The use of CPOE, in conjunction with an EHR, also improves clinician productivity.

    True   False

15. You should have produced five narrative documents of patient encounters, which you printed. If you have not already done so, hand these in to your instructor with this test. The printed encounter notes will count as a portion of your grade.

Comprehensive Evaluation of Chapters 1–6

This comprehensive evaluation will enable you and your instructor to determine your understanding of the material covered so far. Complete both the written test and the two exercises provided below. Depending on the time provided, it may be necessary to do this in two separate sessions. Your instructor will advise you. Do not begin the critical thinking exercise if there will not be enough class time to complete it.

Part I—Written Exam

You may run the Student Edition software and use your mouse on the screen to answer the following questions. You will also need access to the Internet to answer some of the questions.

Give a brief description of the purpose of each of the following coding systems:

1. Medcin _____
2. ICD-9-CM _____
3. Explain the difference between an EHR nomenclature and a billing code set.
4. Which screen do you use to set the reason for the visit?
5. How do you enter vital signs?
6. How do you load a list?

Write the meaning of each of the following medical abbreviations:

7. ROS _____
8. Hx _____
9. HPI _____
10. Dx _____
11. HEENT _____
12. URI _____
13. Describe how to record a test that was performed.
14. What Entry Details field is used with a finding to indicate a "possible" diagnosis?
15. What month and year is the United States scheduled to begin using ICD-10?
16. Describe the closed loop of medication administration.
17. Compare the advantages of codified EHR data over scanned document data.
18. Name at least three things that are checked by a DUR alert system.

Describe the purpose of the following buttons on the Medcin Toolbar:

19. List Size   _____
20. Rx   _____
21. Search   _____
22. Negs   _____
23. ROS   _____
24. Prompt   _____
25. Order   _____

Part II—MyHealthProfessionsKit Questions

Use the document image simulation program on the MyHealthProfessionskit.com web site to answer the next five questions.

Case Study

Raj Patel is an 80-year-old male who arrives in the emergency department accompanied by his daughter. His daughter informs the triage nurse that Mr. Patel was previously an inpatient at this hospital.

Using what you have learned in Guided Exercise 5, find the information the triage nurse needs about Mr. Patel's previous stay.

Step 1

Start your web browser, go to the MyHealthprofessionskit.com web site and log in as you did in Guided Exercise 5.

Locate and click the link "Document/Image System program."

Step 2

Select patient **Raj Patel**.

Step 3

Locate and click on the catalog entry for his Admission Face Sheet.

26. What was the date of admission?
27. What was the date of discharge?
28. What was the principle diagnosis?
29. What was the name of the attending physician?

Step 4

Locate and click on the catalog entry for his Discharge report.

30. Where was the patient discharged to?

Part III—Hands-on Exercise

The following exercise will use features of the software with which you have become familiar. Complete each step in sequential order using the instructions and other information provided.

When you have finished the complete exercise, print out the exam note and hand it to your instructor. Do not begin the hands-on exercise if there will not be enough class time to complete it.

Critical Thinking Exercise 43: Examination of a Patient with Asthma

In this exercise, you use the skills you have acquired to document this exam.

Case Study

Carl Brown is a 30-year-old established patient with possible mild asthma who comes to the office complaining of awakening in the night short of breath. Carl does not smoke, but he is exposed to second-hand smoke and has pets in the house.

Step 1

If you have not already done so, start the Student Edition software.

Click Select on the Menu bar, and then click Patient.

In the Patient Selection window, locate and click on **Carl Brown**.

Step 2

Click Select on the Menu bar, and then click New Encounter.

Select the date **May 16, 2012**, the time **4:30 PM**, and the reason **10 Minute Visit**.

Make certain that you set the date and reason correctly. Compare your screen to the date, time, and reason printed in bold type before clicking on the OK button.

Step 3

Enter the Chief Complaint by locating the button in the toolbar labeled "Chief" and clicking on it.

In the dialog window that will open, type "**Patient reports waking at night short of breath**."

When you have finished typing, click on the button labeled "Close the note form."

Step 4

Begin the visit by recording Carl's vital signs and medical history.

Use the form labeled "Vitals," which you will select from the Forms Manager.

Enter Carl's vital signs in the corresponding fields on the form as follows:

Temperature:	**98.6**
Respiration:	**18**
Pulse:	**68**
BP:	**120/80**
Height:	**71**
Weight:	**175**

When you have finished, check your work. If it is correct, proceed to step 5.

Step 5

Remain on the Forms tab. Take the patient's medical history by using the Short Intake form, which you will load by invoking the Forms Manager window again.

When the Short Intake form is displayed, locate and click on the tab labeled "Medical History."

Step 6

Enter the Dx History and Family History by clicking on the Y (yes) check box or the N (no) check box for the following items:

Diagnosis	Dx Hist	Family Hist
Angina	✓ N	✓ N
Asthma	✓ Y	✓ N
Bronchitis	✓ Y	✓ N
Cancer	✓ N	✓ N
Congestive Heart Failure	✓ N	✓ N
Coronary Artery Disease	✓ N	✓ N
Diabetes	✓ N	✓ N
Heart Attack	✓ N	✓ N
Hypertension	✓ N	✓ N
Migraine Headache	✓ N	✓ N
Peptic Ulcer	✓ N	✓ N
Reflux	✓ N	✓ N
Stroke	✓ N	✓ N

Complete the rest of his medical history on the right side of the form by locating and clicking on the check boxes as follows:

Currently Taking Medication	✓ N
Recent Exposure (Contagious Disease)	✓ N
Recent History of Travel	✓ N
Recent Medical Examination	✓ Y
Recent X-Ray	✓ N
Recent ECG	✓ N
Allergies	✓ Y
Allergy to Drugs	✓ N
Tobacco	✓ N
Alcohol	✓ Y

When you have finished, check your work. If it is correct, click on the Encounter tab at the bottom of the screen.

Step 7

Locate and click on the Lists button in the Toolbar at the top of your screen. The List Manager window will be invoked.

Two fields at the top of the List Manager window organize the display of List names, filtering them by Owner and Group.

Click on the down arrow in the Group field and select the Group "Student Edition," as you have done in Chapter 6.

Locate and highlight the list named **Asthma**. Click your mouse on the button labeled "Load List."

Step 8

The left pane should be on the Sx tab and the title of first line should be "Templates (Symptoms)."

Locate and click on the following symptom findings:

- ● (red button) awaking in night short of breath

The text will change to Paroxysmal Nocturnal Dyspnea.

Step 9

Locate and click on the ROS button in the Toolbar at the top of your screen.

Verify that the ROS button is orange.

Locate and click on the button labeled "Negs" in the Toolbar at the top of your screen.

All unselected symptoms findings will be set by Auto Negative.

Step 10

Next, click on the Hx tab to enter the patient's history. Note that "No family history of Asthma" was already set via the Short Intake form.

Locate and click on the following findings:

- (blue button) previous hospitalization for pulmonary problem
- (red button) exposure to secondhand cigarette smoke
- (red button) exposure to dust mites
- (red button) exposure to animal dander
- (blue button) current smoker

Step 11

Click on the Px tab to document the physical exam. Notice that the findings from the vitals form are already displayed.

Locate and highlight the finding: **IntranasalMass Polyp** (note the finding may currently display either cm or mm; you will set this unit field after the finding is selected.)

In the Entry Details section of your screen, locate the field labeled "Value," and enter the numeric value **0.2** (two tenths).

Locate the unit field and verify it is set to **cm**. If it is not, click on the down arrow in the unit field and select cm.

The finding text should change to read "0.2 cm intranasal polyp."

Step 12

Locate the button labeled "Negs" in the Toolbar and click it once.

Px findings not previously set will be set by Auto Negative.

Step 13

Click on Tx tab.

Locate "Pulmonary function tests" and expand the tree of findings for Pulmonary Function Tests.

Locate, highlight the finding, and click on the order button for each of the following tests:

- (order button) CBC with Differential
- (order button) Spirometry

Verify that both tests appear in the plan before proceeding.

Step 14

Click on the Dx tab.

Locate and click on the following finding:

- (red button) Asthma mild persistent

Click the down arrow button in the prefix field. Select the prefix "possible" from the drop-down list displayed.

Step 15

Click on the Rx tab.

Expand the tree for Environmental Control Measures.

Locate and click on the following finding:

- (red button) Frequent vacuuming
- (red button) Avoid Allergens
- (red button) Patient Education – Asthma
- (red button) Follow-up Visit

Step 16

Enter a prescription.

Expand the tree for Bronchodilators.

Locate and highlight **Albuterol**.

Click on the Rx button in the Toolbar. The prescription writer window will be invoked.

Step 17

In the Rx Dosage Inquiry window, locate and click on the following Sig:

90 microgram puffs 1 inh prn DSP1

Do not close or exit the encounter until you have a printed copy in your hand. *You will lose your work if you exit before printing.*

When the Rx Brand Inquiry window is displayed, position your mouse over the brand **Proventil** and click your mouse button.

Locate the field labeled "Generic Allowed."

Click your mouse in the white circle next to Yes. It should then be filled in.

Review the completed prescription. If anything is incorrect, click on the button labeled "Rx Inquiry" to correct it.

When the prescription is correct, locate and click on the button labeled "Save Rx."

Step 18

Click on the Print button on the Toolbar at the top of your screen to invoke the Print Data window.

Be certain there is a check mark in the box next to "Current Encounter" and then click on the appropriate button to either print or export a file, as directed by your instructor. Your print out or file should consist of two pages. Hand them into your instructor.

Chapter Seven

Problem Lists, Results Management, and Trending

Learning Outcomes

After completing this chapter, you should be able to:

- Understand and use Patient Management
- Understand and use Problem Lists
- Cite information from previous visits in a new encounter
- View pending orders
- Review lab test results
- Create a graph of lab results
- Create a graph of vital signs in the chart

Important Information about the Exercises in This Chapter

The exercises thus far have permitted you to skip setting the encounter date and time. In the next few chapters, you will work with patients' complete medical history using information from several previous encounters. In certain exercises it will be necessary to match the encounter date and time exactly as instructed in step 2 of the exercise in order to maintain the correct chronology of data in the exercise. If you need to review how to set the date and time when creating a new encounter, see Chapter 3, Guided Exercise 13.

Longitudinal Patient Records to Manage Patients' Health

In this chapter we shift from inpatient to outpatient facilities. In medical offices the electronic health record is a longitudinal record encompassing numerous encounters over an extended period of time. In contrast, inpatient records typically concern a particular inpatient stay or episode of care. In addition to the traditional medical office, hospitals are increasingly operating specialty clinics focusing on problematic diagnoses—for example diabetes, asthma or hypertension.

In a medical office or outpatient clinic, patients are frequently seen by nurse practitioners instead of physicians. In this chapter we use the term *clinician* or *provider* to represent equally a nurse practitioner or doctor.

Providers in a specialty clinic or primary care practice come to know their regular patients, helping to monitor and hopefully improve the patient's health. To do so, the clinician must review the records from the patient's past visits and recheck previous problems on every new encounter.

Providers also must keep track of what medications the patient is currently taking, which tests have results, and any other orders that have been issued. A clinician will always check the medications list before writing a new prescription, as well as to renew any that were about to expire.

In a world of paper charts, this is done by flipping through the papers in the chart and reviewing the previous notes. In some offices, current medications and current problems are copied by hand to a list in the front of the paper chart. In other cases, the clinician simply remembers them while skimming the chart, keeping a mental list as he or she reads the chart.

In a codified electronic chart, the software itself can dynamically locate the necessary information and organize it for quick review. Additionally, the clinician can note the items reviewed, make updates to the problems, and then record them in the current encounter. The clinician does not have to search for findings in the system because the findings are already identified in the previous encounter notes.

The Student Edition software includes a Patient Management feature that will allow you to explore some of these concepts. Although commercial EHR vendors use national standard nomenclatures such as Medcin, they differentiate their software with unique visual styles. Software you will use in a clinic or medical office will have concepts and features for Patient Management similar to the Student Edition, but the presentation of the information is likely to have a different appearance.

Understanding Problem Lists

Clinicians of all levels are trained to work with Problem Lists and depend on the information contained in the problem lists when providing care. Furthermore, maintaining a Problem List is a requirement for accreditation by organizations such as the Joint Commission (JCAHO).

Problem Lists are used to track both acute and chronic conditions related to the care of the patient. Clinic staff should be able to easily see the active problems for a patient and view the history of problems. Although chronic diseases that are poorly controlled or malignancies take precedence in clinical decision making over mild conditions that are not life threatening, the idea of a Problem List is to make sure everyone who touches the patient knows what conditions are present.

The relationship between diagnoses and problems is very close. In most EHR software, they are synonymous. Most clinical information recorded in the chart will be related to one or more problems. However, the concept of a primary diagnosis used for billing does not apply to a Problem List.

The concept of a "problem-oriented" view is to organize entries in a patient record by problem. The Problem List provides an up-to-date list of the diagnoses and conditions that affect that particular patient's care. Typically, it links the data from all encounters, orders, and prescriptions to the respective problem. This problem-oriented view allows the clinician to quickly see the patient's problems and what has been done thus far.

Problem Lists usually have an onset date, indicate Chronic or Acute, and show whether or not the problem is active. Problems are removed from the list or set inactive once the patient is "cured" or the problem is "resolved." Some problems have a natural period of time in which they normally resolve themselves. These problems are called Acute Self-Limiting.

In some systems, Problem Lists can include findings that are not disease related but are, rather, wellness conditions. Wellness conditions are based on the age and sex of the patient and used in health maintenance and preventative screening programs to keep healthy patients healthy. Both disease conditions and wellness conditions have activities that are typically performed for patients with that condition, including:

- an annual EKG for a person with congestive heart failure
- a quarterly blood sugar test for a patient with diabetes
- a mammogram for a healthy woman over 35
- immunizations for a healthy infant

These recommendations can be driven by the data in the Problem List. An example of a health maintenance preventive screening program was discussed in Chapter 2.

In many EHR systems, a problem is added to the Problem List either manually or automatically from the assessment in the encounter note. Some clinicians prefer to add the problems manually so that diagnoses for "possible" and "rule-out" conditions do not appear on the Problem List until the diagnosis is confirmed. Manually adding a problem to the Problem List is especially useful when the problem is being treated by a specialist at another office, but the clinician wants to remain aware of the condition. It is also possible to manually add findings to the Problem List that would normally be in other sections of the narrative, such as Past Medical History or Symptoms.

Guided Exercise 44: Exploring Patient Management

The Patient Management tab in the Student Edition software is used to manage a patient's problems over time. It presents a clinical summary view of the patient's previous visits. The view presents historical data that is obtained from findings recorded in past encounters. The view can be updated from the current encounter or, conversely, the encounter note for the current visit can be created using data from Patient Management.

In this exercise you are going to start a new encounter but the system will automatically retrieve and display information from previous encounters. For the first exercise, you are just going to become familiar with the Patient Management features of the software. In the subsequent exercise you will learn to cite information from previous encounters into the current encounter note.

Case Study

Juan Garcia, an outpatient who has been treated, previously, is returning for a follow-up visit.

Step 1

If you have not already done so, start the Student Edition software.

Click Select on the Menu bar, and then click Patient.

In the Patient Selection window, locate and click on **Juan Garcia**, as shown in Figure 7-1.

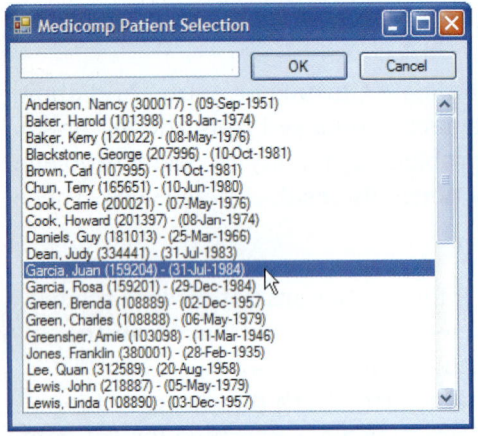

▶ **Figure 7-1** Selecting Juan Garcia from the Patient Selection window.

 **Alert** Make certain you set the date and time correctly for this exercise. If you need help, review Chapter 3, Guided Exercise 13.

Step 2

Click Select on the Menu bar, and then click New Encounter.

Select the date **May 21, 2012**, the time **9:00 AM**, and the reason **Office Visit**.

Compare your screen to Figure 7-2. Make certain the date and time match before clicking on the OK button.

Step 3

Enter the Chief complaint by locating the button in the Toolbar labeled "Chief" and clicking on it.

In the dialog window, type "**Knee injury follow-up**."

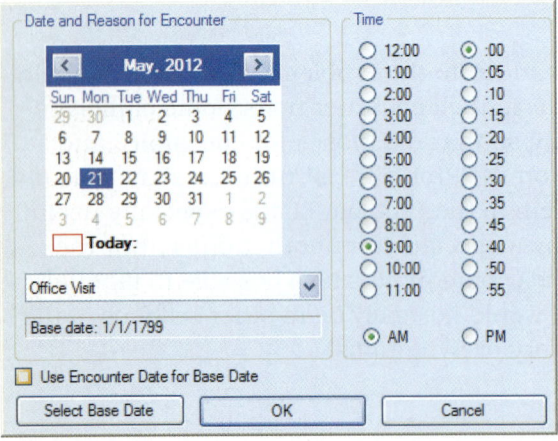

▶ **Figure 7-2** New encounter for an office visit, May 21, 2012 9:00 AM.

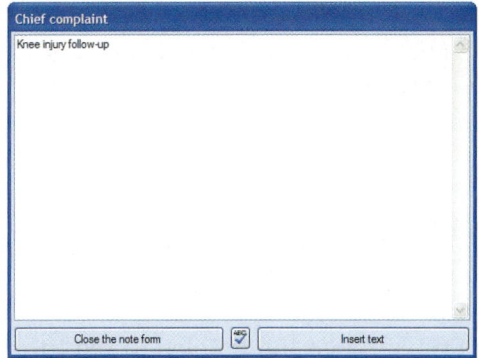

▶ **Figure 7-3** Chief complaint dialog for knee injury follow-up.

▶ **Figure 7-4** Manage tab (circled in red) and Details button (highlighted orange).

Compare your screen to Figure 7-3 before clicking on the button labeled "Close the note form."

Step 4

Locate and click on the tab labeled "Manage" at the bottom of your screen. It is circled in red in Figure 7-4.

Compare your screen to Figure 7-4. The Medcin Nomenclature normally displayed in the left pane of your screen has been replaced by an information window displaying information from previous encounters.

When you are on the Manage tab, the Toolbar (at the top of the screen) has some additional buttons.

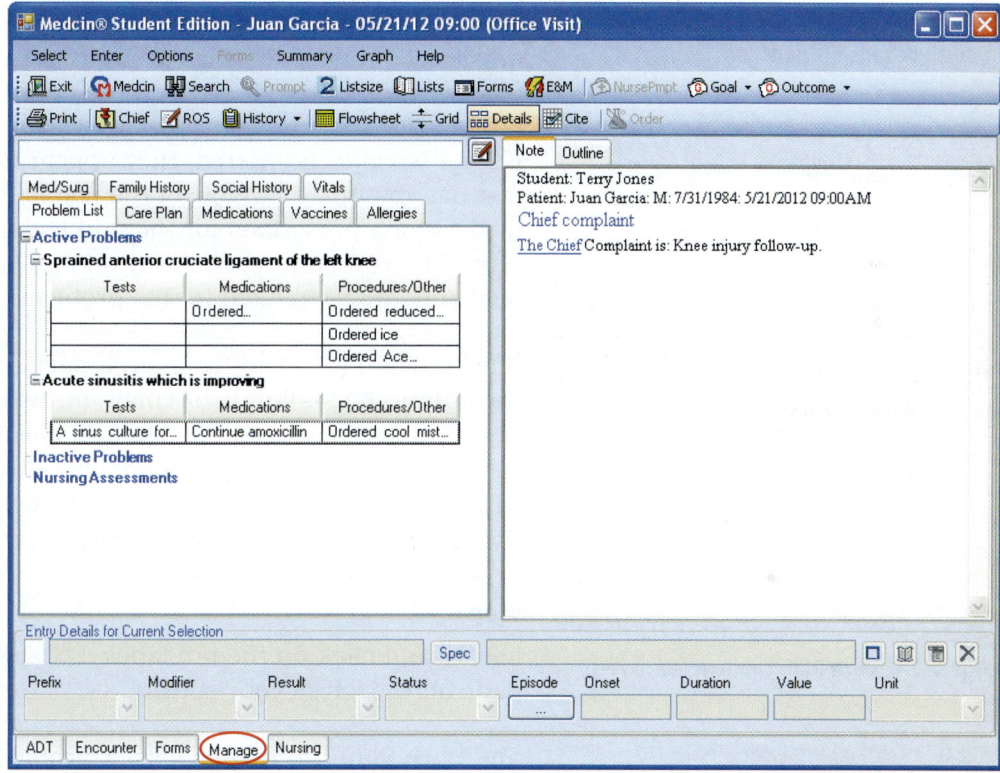

Locate and click on the button in the Toolbar labeled "Details." This action allows you to see more of Patient Management by hiding the Entry Details section at the bottom of the screen. The Entry Details section can be restored when it is hidden by clicking the Details button again.

Look at the left pane of your screen. Note that the pane contains nine tabs:

- Problems (The Patient Management feature opens on the Problem List tab.)
- Care Plan
- Medications
- Vaccines
- Allergies

Chapter 7 | Problem Lists, Results Management, and Trending   265

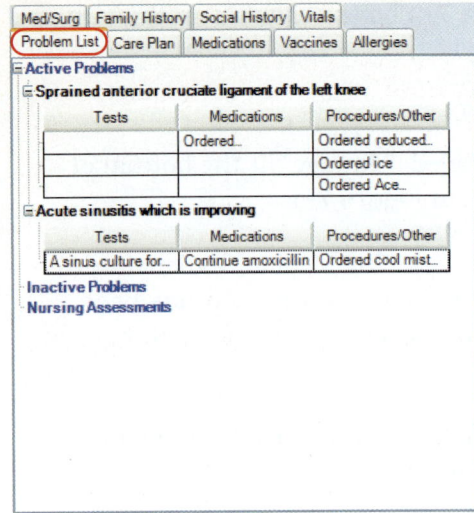

▶ Figure 7-5 Problem List tab (circled in red) with details hidden.

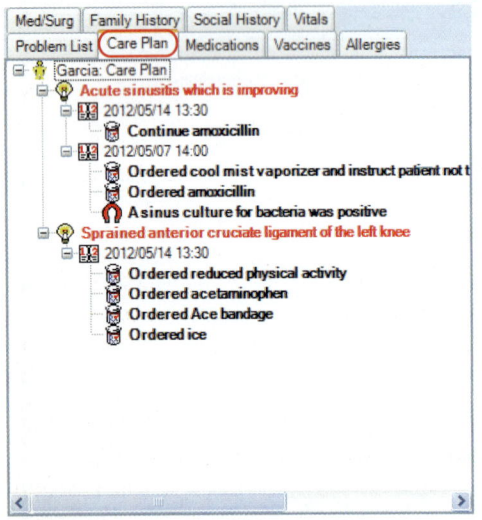

▶ Figure 7-6 Care Plan tab (circled in red)

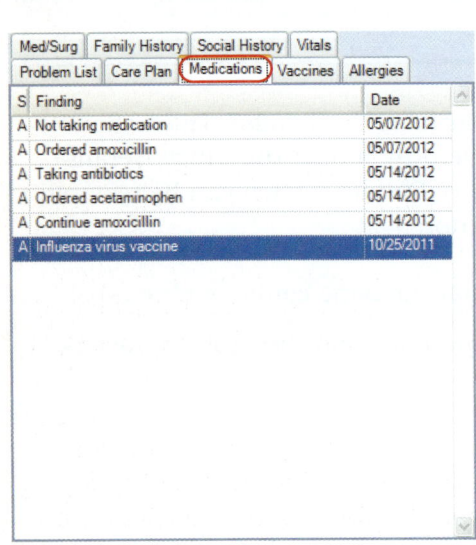

▶ Figure 7-7 Medications tab (circled in red).

◆ Past Medical/Surgical History (Med/Surg)

◆ Family History

◆ Social History

◆ Vitals

In the following steps, you will examine each tab.

Step 5

The Manage tab opens on the Problem List tab (circled in red in Figure 7-5). The Problem List includes a view of both active and inactive problems, as well as nursing assessments. This example has two active problems.

Compare your screen to Figure 7-5. Within the Problem List, there are three columns: Tests, Medications, and Procedures/Other. The most recent active findings (from the Tx and Rx sections of previous encounters) are listed in these columns for each problem.

If tests have been ordered, they appear in the first column. If a test has results, the name of the test is displayed in bold. Any medications prescribed for the problem appear in the second column. The last column lists any other orders or procedures from past encounters related to this problem.

The clinician also can focus on a particular problem by closing the others. A small plus or small minus sign next to a problem description allows you to open and close the details of the problem in the same way you expand or contract the tree structure when browsing the Nomenclature List. You will work more with the Problem List in the next exercise.

Step 6

Locate and click on the tab labeled "Care Plan" in the information pane on the left of your screen.

The Care Plan tab displays each problem, followed by the date of each encounter that the patient was seen for that problem. Small plus signs next to the encounter allow you to expand the encounter to display the Care Plan for that date.

Click on the plus sign beside each encounter date. Compare your screen with Figure 7-6.

Findings from the Plan section of the encounter note are displayed beneath the encounter date; however, findings from any group can be manually added to the Care Plan.

Step 7

Locate and click on the tab labeled "Medications" in the information pane on the left of your screen. Compare your screen to Figure 7-7.

266   Chapter 7 | Problem Lists, Results Management, and Trending

The Medications tab provides a traditional medications list. Although the two previous tabs (Problem and Care Plan) listed the medications ordered for each problem, the Medications tab displays all medications ordered by any clinician in the practice as well as those reported by the patient.

Step 8

Locate and click on the tab labeled "Vaccines" in the information pane on the left of your screen. Compare your screen to Figure 7-8.

The tab displays the patient's history of vaccines. Note that vaccines also appear in the Medications list; these are not duplicate findings. The software deliberately shows vaccines in both lists.

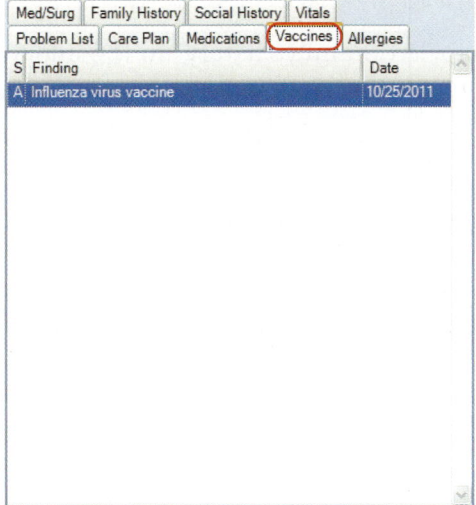

▶ Figure 7-8 Vaccines tab (circled in red).

Step 9

Locate and click on the tab labeled "Allergies" in the information pane on the left of your screen. Compare your screen to Figure 7-9.

The tab displays any allergy information from any of the patient encounters. In this case, the pertinent fact is that the patient reported "No allergies."

Before writing a prescription, a provider would check both the Medications and Allergies tabs. Most electronic prescription systems also check allergy data automatically at the time the prescription is written. Drug utilization review was discussed in Chapter 2 and Chapter 6.

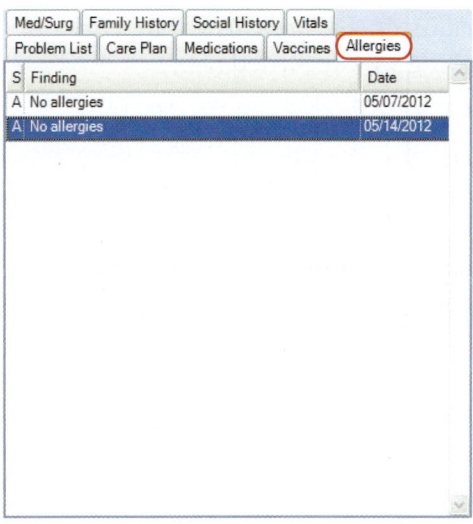

▶ Figure 7-9 Allergies tab (circled in red).

Step 10

Locate and click on the tab labeled "Med/Surg" in the information pane on the left of your screen. Compare your screen to Figure 7-10. Note that the tabs in the left pane are arranged in two rows; when you click any tab in the upper row, the entire row moves down. The tab for the data currently displayed in the left pane is always in the (bottom) row of tabs closest to the grid.

"Med/Surg" stands for Medical and Surgical History and displays all findings that have been recorded in the Past History section of previous encounters. The date column displays the date the finding was recorded.

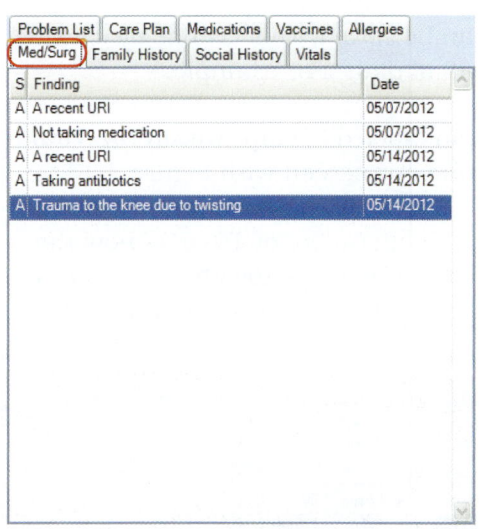

▶ Figure 7-10 Past Medical and Surgical History tab.

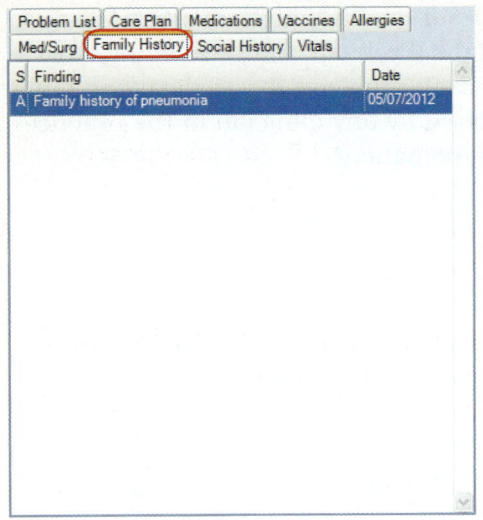

▶ **Figure 7-11** Family History tab (circled in red).

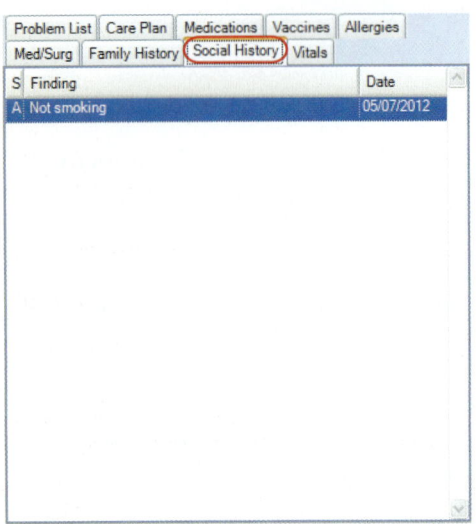

▶ **Figure 7-12** Social History tab (circled in red).

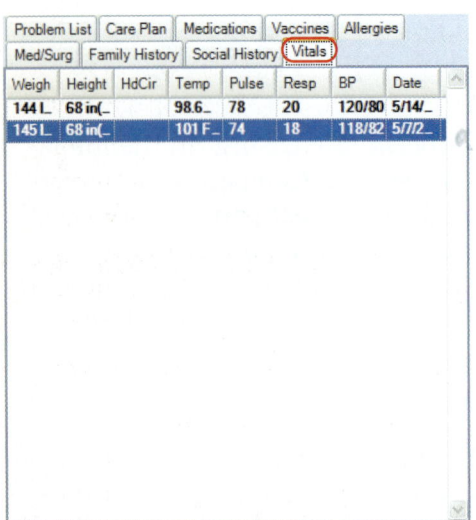

▶ **Figure 7-13** Vitals Signs tab (circled in red).

Step 11

Locate and click on the tab labeled "Family History" in the information pane on the left of your screen. Compare your screen to Figure 7-11.

The tab displays all findings that have been recorded in the Family History section of previous encounters. The date column displays the date that the finding was recorded.

Step 12

Locate and click on the tab labeled "Social History" in the information pane on the left of your screen. Compare your screen to Figure 7-12.

The tab displays all findings that have been recorded in the Social History section of previous encounters. The date column displays the date that the finding was recorded.

Step 13

Locate and click on the tab labeled "Vitals" in the information pane on the left of your screen. Compare your screen to Figure 7-13.

The tab displays the Vital Signs findings that have been recorded in multiple encounters.

Step 14

In each of the tabs the data can be sorted. This is done by clicking on the labels over the columns of data. For example:

Locate and click on the column labeled "Temp" within the Vitals tab. Compare the Vitals tab on your screen with Figure 7-14. You will notice that the rows of vital signs data changed places and the date that Juan had a temperature of 101°F is now the top row. When sorting, the entire row stays together. To restore the Vitals tab to its original order, click on the column labeled "Date."

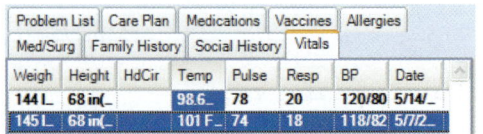

▶ **Figure 7-14** Vital signs sorted by patient temperature.

This example used the Vitals tab, but the data in any tab of Patient Management can be sorted by clicking on the column labels.

If there is not enough class time remaining to complete the next exercise, you may stop at this point. You do not need to print the encounter.

Citing Previous Visits from Problem Lists

Patient Management is an excellent tool for reviewing information from the patient's previous encounters without having to open and read each one individually. Presenting the information in a "problem-oriented" view and having the previous findings at hand enables the clinician to quickly record the reexamination of each area examined during the previous visits. Patient Management is much more than just a review tool; it also is a very efficient method of documenting a follow-up exam.

In an EHR, citing from a previous encounter note means to bring a finding into the current encounter, usually as a follow-up to a previous visit.

Guided Exercise 45: Following Up on a Problem

You will recall from a previous chapter that the mouse typically has at least two buttons, a left button and a right button. In this exercise, when instructed, you are going to be using the right button on the mouse as well as the left button.

Case Study

Juan Garcia has returned for a follow-up on his previous knee injury. Using Patient Management, you will see how easy it is to document this type of visit.

Make certain you set the date and time correctly for this exercise. If you need help, review Chapter 3, Guided Exercise 13.

Step 1

If you are continuing from the previous exercise, proceed to step 4.

Otherwise, start the Student Edition software.

From the Select Menu, click Patient, and from the Patient Selector window select **Juan Garcia** (see Figure 7-1).

Step 2

From the Select Menu, click New Encounter. Use the date **May 21, 2012, the time 9:00 AM**, and the reason **Office Visit**.

Make certain the date and time match before clicking on the OK button (see Figure 7-2).

Step 3

Enter the Chief complaint by locating the button in the Toolbar labeled "Chief" and clicking on it.

Chapter 7 | Problem Lists, Results Management, and Trending 269

In the dialog window, type "**Knee injury follow-up**."

When it is correct, click on the button labeled "Close the note form" (see Figure 7-3).

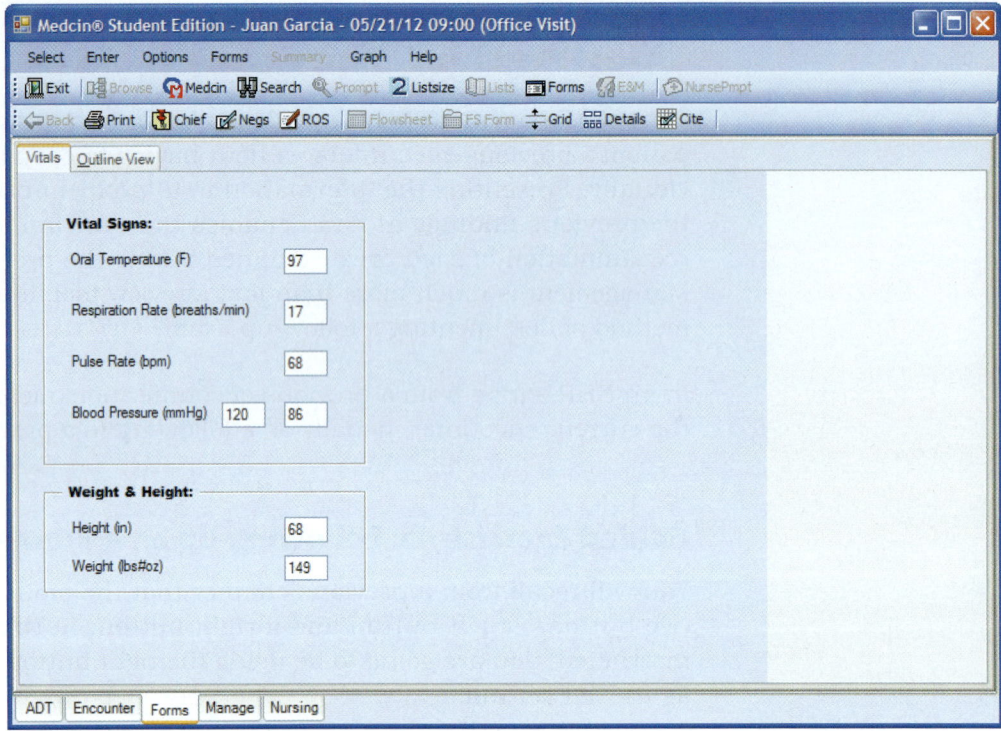

▶ Figure 7-15 Vital Signs form for Juan Garcia.

Step 4

Enter Juan Garcia's vital signs using the Vitals Form in the corresponding fields as follows:

Temperature:	**97**
Respiration:	**17**
Pulse:	**68**
BP:	**120/86**
Height:	**68**
Weight:	**149**

When you have finished, compare your screen to Figure 7-15. If it is correct, click on the tab labeled Manage at the bottom of the window. (If you have difficulty locating Manage, refer to Figure 7-4.)

Step 5

Verify that you are on the Manage tab.

If the information pane on the left of your screen is not already displaying the Problem List, click on the tab labeled "Problem List" (circled in red in Figure 7-5).

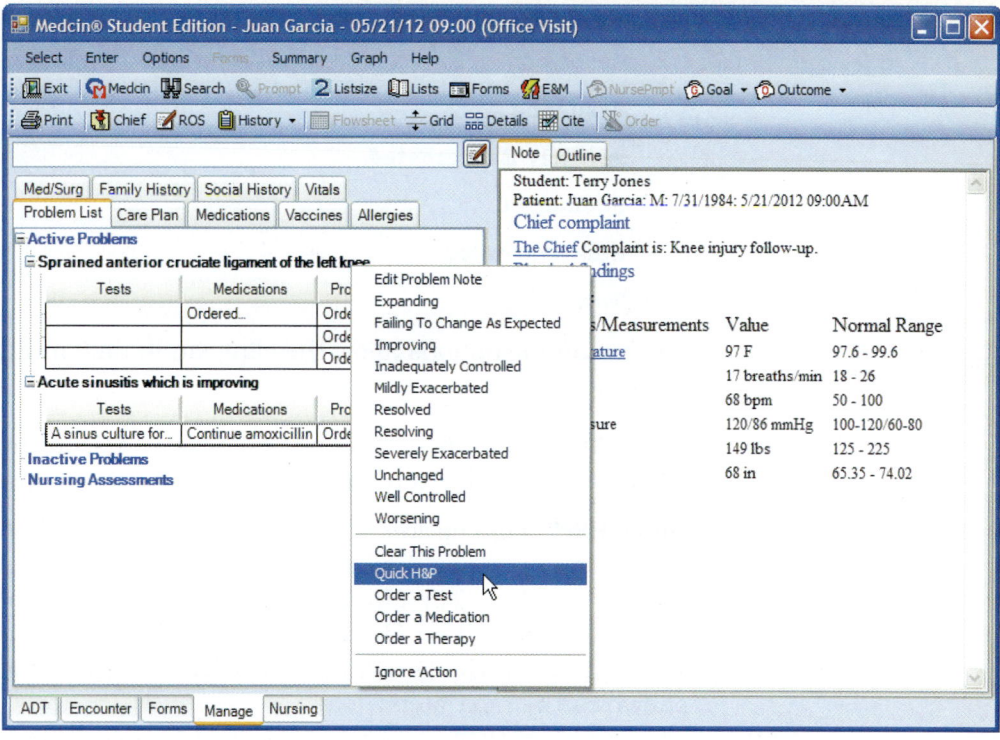

▶ **Figure 7-16** Problem List tab with drop-down list from right click of mouse.

If the Entry Details section is currently covering the bottom of your screen, locate the button labeled "Details" in the Toolbar at the top of your screen and click it until the Entry Details section is hidden.

Position the mouse pointer over the first problem, "Sprained anterior cruciate ligament of the knee," and click the **Right** button on your mouse. A drop-down list will be displayed, as shown in Figure 7-16.

If the drop-down list does not match the list shown in Figure 7-16, your mouse was not positioned correctly on the problem description. Reposition your mouse and click the **Right** mouse button again.

Without clicking on any of the options, study the options on the drop-down list. Most of these options are used to cite updated findings into the new encounter. Do not select any option until directed to do so. The following is a brief explanation of each option in the drop-down list:

Edit Problem Note: Allows you to edit a free-text note that is attached to the problem.

The next 11 options are used to record the status of the problem. Selecting any of the following items from the drop-down list will add a new finding to today's encounter. The finding will have a status set with one of the following:

Expanding

Failing to Change as Expected

Improving

Inadequately Controlled

Chapter 7 | Problem Lists, Results Management, and Trending   **271**

> **Mildly Exacerbated**
>
> **Resolved**
>
> **Resolving**
>
> **Severely Exacerbated**
>
> **Unchanged**
>
> **Well Controlled**
>
> **Worsening**

The remaining options allow the clinician to take multiple actions quickly. They are as follows:

Clear This Problem: Clears all test orders, discontinues medications related to the problem, clears therapy orders, and sets the problem as inactive.

Quick H&P: This option invokes a data entry window that lists symptoms, history, and physical findings as they appeared in the most recent encounter for this problem. The clinician can quickly review the last History and Physical (H&P) taken for this problem and update the new encounter with any findings in the Quick H&P window. The Quick H&P window will be shown in the next step.

Order a Test: This option is provided to allow the clinician to order a new test for this problem. When the option is selected, the right pane will temporarily display a list of tests you would normally see in Tx tab. When the Tx list is displayed, you can order directly from the list in the right pane.

Order a Medication: This option is provided to allow the clinician to order a new medication for this problem. When the option is selected, the right pane will temporarily display the Rx list of medications. When the Rx list is displayed, you can order directly from the list in the right pane. If the drug selected requires a prescription, the prescription writer will be invoked automatically.

Order a Therapy: This option is provided to allow the clinician to quickly order any type of therapy other than medications. As with the previous two options, a list of therapies will temporarily display in the right pane. You can order directly from the displayed list.

Ignore Action: This option cancels the drop-down list without recording anything. You also can cancel the drop-down list by clicking anywhere else on the screen.

Step 6

Locate and click on the Quick H&P option in the drop-down list (shown highlighted in Figure 7-16). The Quick History and Physical window will be invoked.

Compare your screen to Figure 7-17. The window displays findings from the previous exam for this condition.

Using the findings in the list, the clinician can be certain to update anything that was observed in the previous visit. Items that have already been entered in today's encounter appear on the Quick H&P list in gray. Examples in this exercise include Chief complaint and Vital Signs.

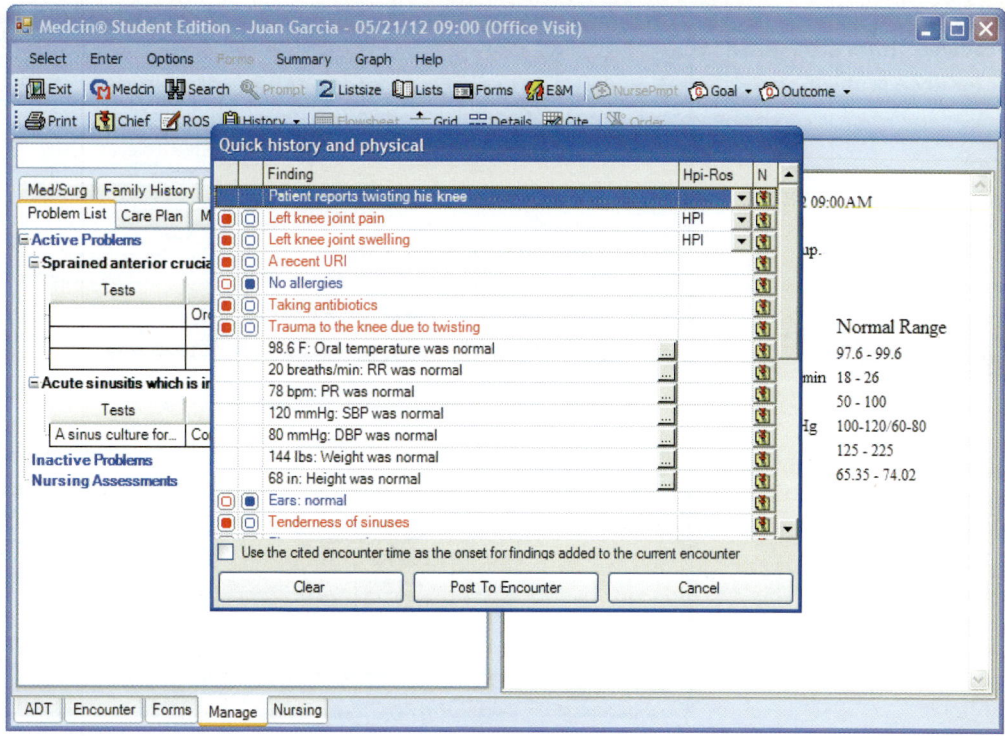

▶ Figure 7-17 Quick history and physical for knee injury.

The patient reports that his knee is better. Locate and click on the following findings (you will need to scroll the window to get them all):

- (blue button) Left knee joint pain
- (blue button) Left knee joint swelling
- (blue button) Taking antibiotics
- (blue button) Localized swelling of the left knee
- (blue button) Warmth of the left knee
- (blue button) Pain was elicited by motion of the left knee

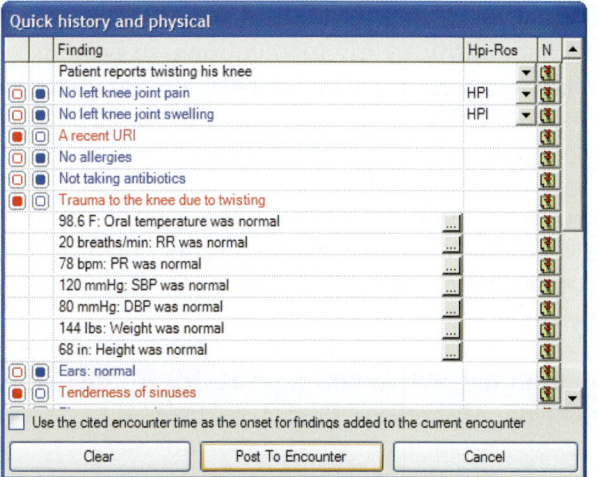

▶ Figure 7-18 Knee injury findings set to normal, ready to post to encounter.

Important—do not click every finding that is listed. Click only those indicated above.

Step 7

Compare your screen to Figure 7-18. Scroll the window and verify that you have selected only the items listed in step 6. If you find an error, click on the button labeled "Cancel," and repeat steps 5 and 6.

When all the findings have been selected correctly, click on the button labeled "Post To Encounter."

▶ Figure 7-19 Select "Resolved" from drop-down list for knee problem.

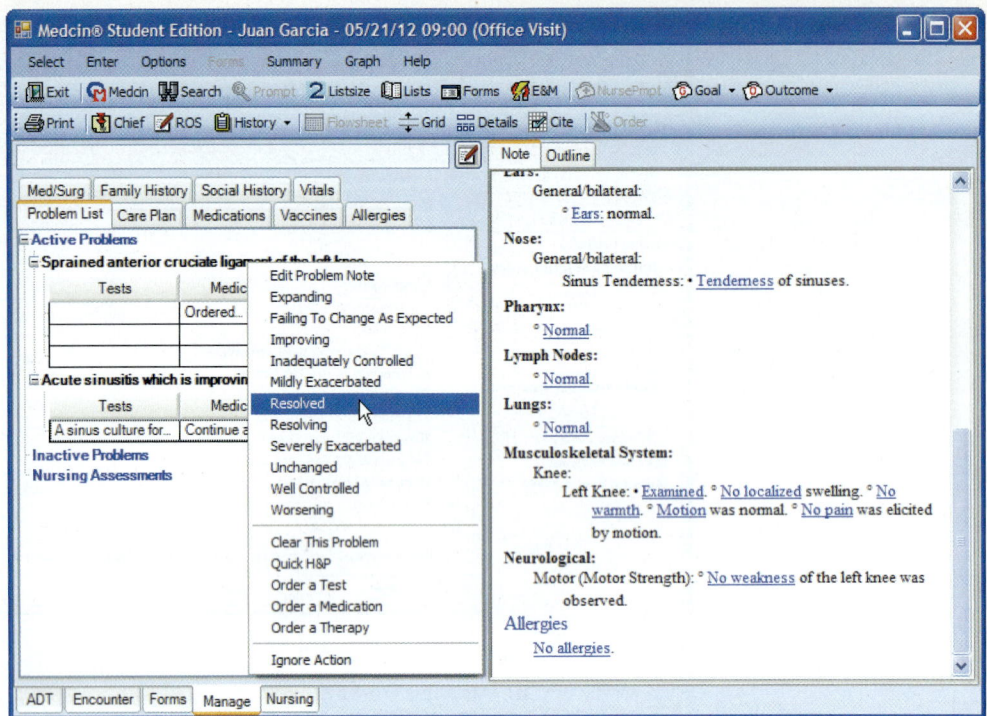

Step 8

The findings you selected in the Quick H&P window should now be displayed in the patient encounter note (as shown in the right pane of Figure 7-19).

The problem is resolved. To indicate this in today's encounter note, position the mouse over the first problem, "Sprained anterior cruciate ligament of the right knee," and click the **Right** button on your mouse. Again the drop-down list will be displayed, as shown in Figure 7-19.

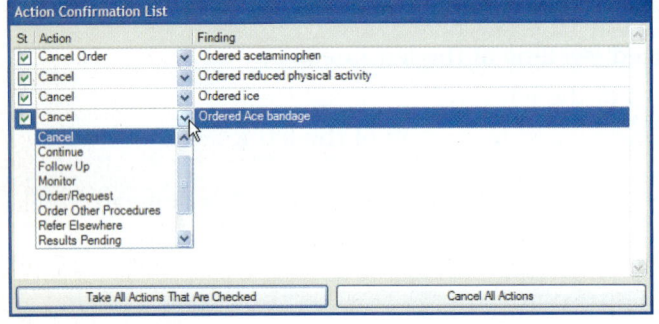

▶ Figure 7-20 Resolving a problem—Action Confirmation List.

Locate and click on the option labeled "Resolved." The window shown in Figure 7-20 will be invoked.

Step 9

When a problem is resolved, there are certain actions the clinician may want to take: canceling previous orders, discontinuing any medications, or setting the problem as inactive. The Resolved option invokes a window of all active orders related to the problem and sets appropriate default actions.

A check box next to each item indicates that you wish to take the action indicated. A drop-down list of possible actions is available for each order, as shown in Figure 7-20. You can use the list to select a different action or you can indicate that no action is to be taken by unchecking the box.

Do not make any changes to the default list. When you have reviewed the list, locate and click the button labeled "Take All Actions That Are Checked."

Step 10

The knee problem in the left pane has moved to the section labeled "Inactive Problems." If it is not currently displayed, locate and click the small plus sign next to "Inactive Problems."

▶ Figure 7-21 Inactive problem on Problem List.

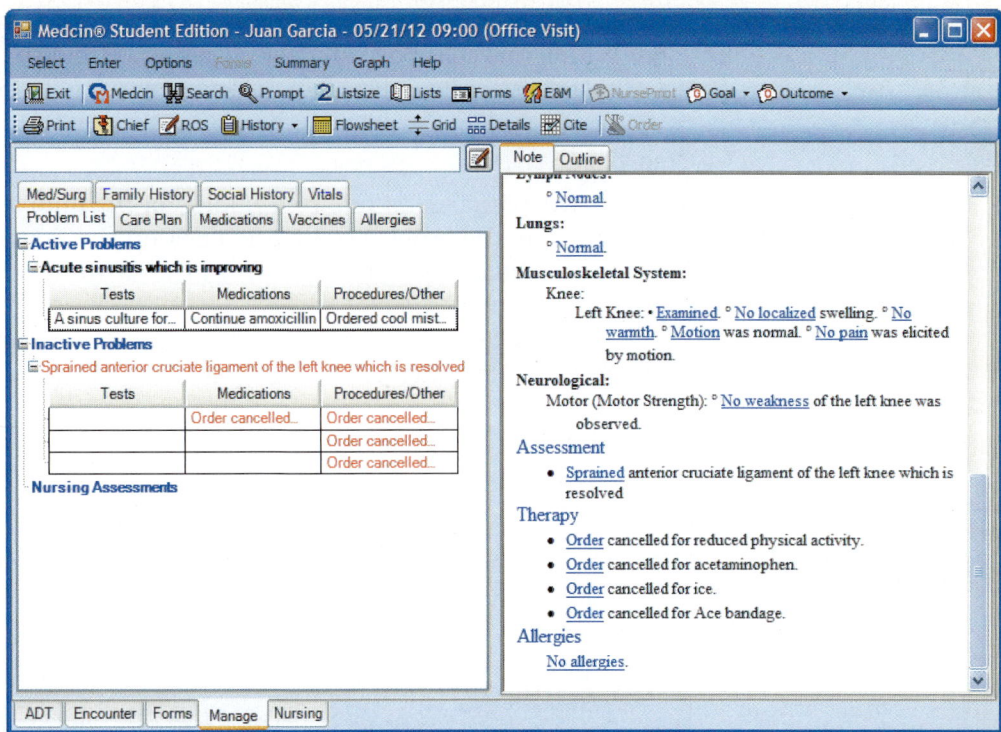

Compare your screen with Figure 7-21. Note in the right pane that the previous therapy orders have been canceled.

Step 11

The Problem List also listed a second problem, acute sinusitis, for which the patient was recently treated. The patient reports that his sinusitis has cleared up and that he has finished the prescribed course of antibiotics. Using what you have learned in the previous steps, resolve the acute sinusitis problem.

▶ Figure 7-22 Resolve acute sinusitis Action Confirmation List.

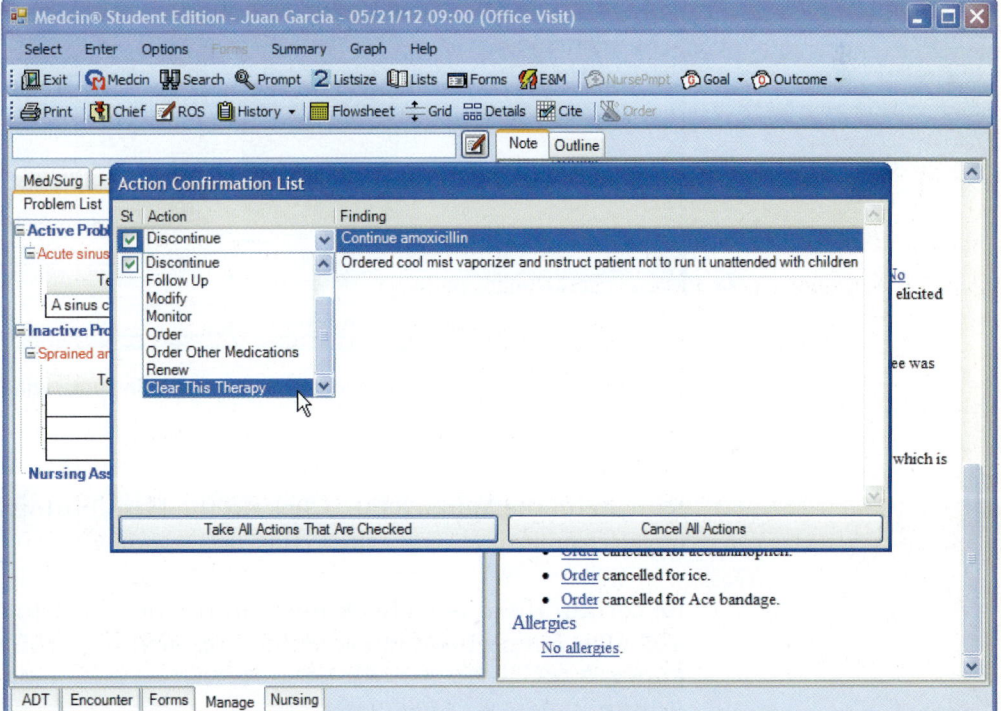

Chapter 7 | Problem Lists, Results Management, and Trending   275

Position your mouse pointer on the active problem, "Acute sinusitis." Click the Right button on the mouse and select Resolved from the options on the drop-down list. The action confirmation list window (shown in Figure 7-22) will be invoked.

Step 12

Because the patient has reported taking all the amoxicillin, there is no reason to discontinue the order. Locate and click on the down arrow next to "Cancel" and select "Clear This Therapy" from the drop-down list as shown in Figure 7-22.

Click on the button labeled "Take All Actions That Are Checked."

When you have completed this step, you will notice that both problems are now in the inactive problem list.

 **Alert** Do not close or exit the encounter until you have a printed copy in your hand. You will lose your work if you exit before printing.

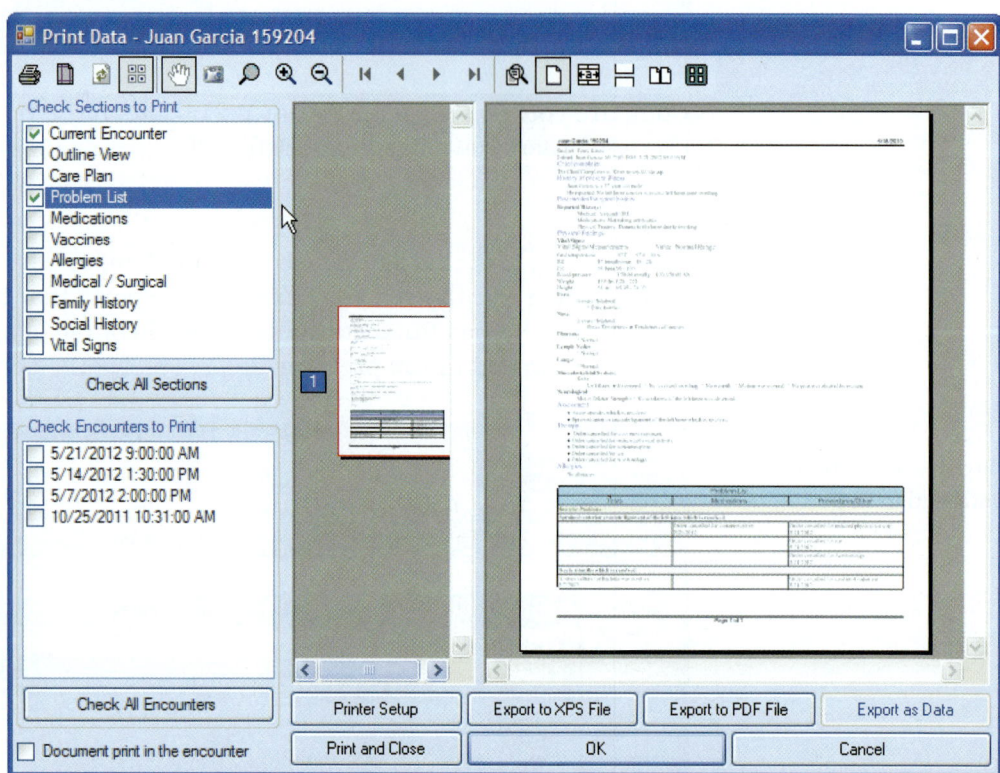

▶ **Figure 7-23 Check mark next to Problem List in Print Data window.**

Step 13

Remain on the Manage tab. Click on the Print button on the Toolbar at the top of your screen to invoke the Print Data window.

Be certain there is a check mark in the box next to "Current Encounter" and also put a check mark in the box next to "Problem List" as shown in Figure 7-23.

Click on the appropriate button to either print or export a file, as directed by your instructor.

```
Juan Garcia                                                        Page 1 of 1

Student: your name or id here
Patient: Juan Garcia: M: 7/31/1984: 5/21/2012 09:00AM
Chief complaint
The Chief Complaint is: Knee injury follow-up.
History of present illness
     Juan Garcia is a 27 year old male.
     He reported: No left knee joint pain and no left knee joint swelling.
Past medical/surgical history
     Reported History:
     Medical: A recent URI.
     Medications: Not taking antibiotics.
     Physical Trauma: Trauma to the knee due to twisting.
Physical findings
Vital Signs:
Vital Signs/Measurements        Value                  Normal Range
Oral temperature                97 F                   97.6 - 99.6
RR                              17 breaths/min         18 - 26
PR                              68 bpm                 50 - 100
Blood pressure                  120/86 mmHg            100-120/60-80
Weight                          149 lbs                125 - 225
Height                          68 in                  65.35 - 74.02
Ears:
General/bilateral:
° Ears: normal.
Nose:
General/bilateral:
Sinus Tenderness:
     • Tenderness of sinuses.
Pharynx:
° Normal.
Lymph Nodes:
° Normal.
Lungs:
° Normal.
Musculoskeletal System:
Knee:
Left Knee:
     • Examined. ° No localized swelling. ° No warmth. ° Motion was normal.
° No pain was elicited by motion.
Neurological:
Motor (Motor Strength): ° No weakness of the left knee was observed.
Assessment
     • Acute sinusitis which is resolved
     • Sprained anterior cruciate ligament of the left knee which is resolved
Therapy
     • Order cancelled for cool mist vaporizer.
     • Order cancelled for reduced physical activity.
     • Order cancelled for acetaminophen.
     • Order cancelled for ice.
     • Order cancelled for Ace bandage.
Allergies
No allergies.
```

▶ Figure 7-24a Printed encounter note for Juan Garcia (page 1 of 2).

Problem List		
Tests	Medications	Procedures/Other
Inactive Problems		
Sprained anterior cruciate ligament of the left knee which is resolved		
	Order cancelled for acetaminophen 5/21/2012	Order cancelled for reduced physical activity 5/21/2012
		Order cancelled for ice 5/21/2012
		Order cancelled for Ace bandage 5/21/2012
Acute sinusitis which is resolved		
A sinus culture for bacteria was positive 5/7/2012		Order cancelled for cool mist vaporizer 5/21/2012

▶ Figure 7-24b Printed encounter note for Juan Garcia (page 2 of 2).

Compare your printout or file output to Figures 7-24a and 7-24b. If it is correct, hand it in to your instructor. If there are any differences, review the previous steps in the exercise and find your error.

Orders and Results Management

You will recall from Chapter 1 that Results Management was one of the eight criteria for an EHR in the IOM report. Orders are tracked in an EHR from the moment they are entered in the system. In Chapter 6 we discussed one of the benefits of CPOE systems is that they keep track of what has been ordered for each patient. Benefits of CPOE order tracking include:

◆ Preventing lost orders.

◆ Preventing duplicate orders.

◆ Detecting when a patient sent to an outside lab has failed to show up.

Benefits of results tracking include:

◆ Notifying the provider as soon as "preliminary" results are available.

◆ Notifying the provider anytime results status are updated to "final" or "corrected."

◆ Keeping track of which results need to be reviewed by the clinician.

As you will see in subsequent exercises, the benefits of having test results available to the provider during the patient encounter include the ability to graph or "trend" the results. Another benefit is the ability to review results online and to quickly order subsequent or additional tests when it is warranted.

The Student Edition software does not contain an electronic laboratory order and result system. It would be inappropriate to order tests from a classroom.

Because the Student Edition does not contain the electronic lab interface, the following two exercises have been created solely to demonstrate how useful it is to have lab data at hand while seeing the patient. The features you will find in commercial EHR software automate the lab order/result workflow differently and more elegantly than these simple exercises.

Guided Exercise 46: Viewing Pending Orders and Lab Results

Case Study

In Guided Exercise 42 this patient's mother reported the possible exposure to lead-based paints while remodeling their older home. You will recall her treatment plan recommended screening other family members. The clinician has since ordered tests for her son Stanley and he has already visited the lab before his appointment. Today is his office visit for examination and to review the test results.

Step 1

If you have not already done so, start the Student Edition software.

Click Select on the Menu bar, and then click Patient.

Figure 7-25 Selecting Stanley Zabroski from the Patient Selection Window.

In the Patient Selection window, locate and click on **Stanley Zabroski** as shown in Figure 7-25.

Alert — Make certain you set the date and time correctly for this exercise. If you need help, review Chapter 3, Guided Exercise 13.

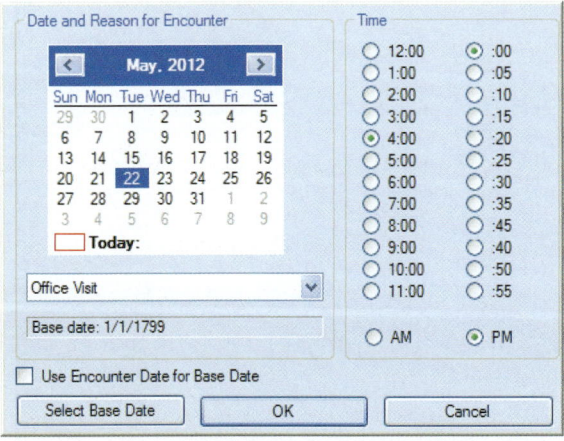

Figure 7-26 New encounter for an office visit, May 22, 2012 4:00 PM.

Step 2

Click Select on the Menu bar, and then click New Encounter.

Select the date **May 22, 2012**, the time **4:00 PM**, and the reason **Office Visit**.

Compare your screen to Figure 7-26. Make certain the date and time match before clicking on the OK button.

In the next two steps, the medical assistant enters the Chief complaint and Vital Signs.

Chapter 7 | Problem Lists, Results Management, and Trending   279

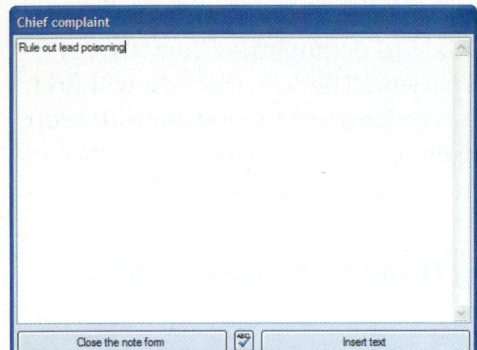

Step 3

Enter the Chief complaint by locating the button in the toolbar labeled "Chief" and clicking on it.

In the dialog window that will open, type "Rule out lead poisoning."

Compare your screen to Figure 7-27 before clicking on the button labeled "Close the note form."

▶ Figure 7-27 Chief complaint dialog for "Rule out lead poisoning."

Step 4

Enter the patient's Vital Signs using the Vitals Form. Vital Signs for Stanley Zabroski are as follows:

Temperature:	**98.6**
Respiration:	**20**
Pulse:	**76**
BP:	**120/80**
Height:	**73**
Weight:	**155**

When you have finished, compare your screen to Figure 7-28. If it is correct, click on the tab labeled Encounter at the bottom of the window.

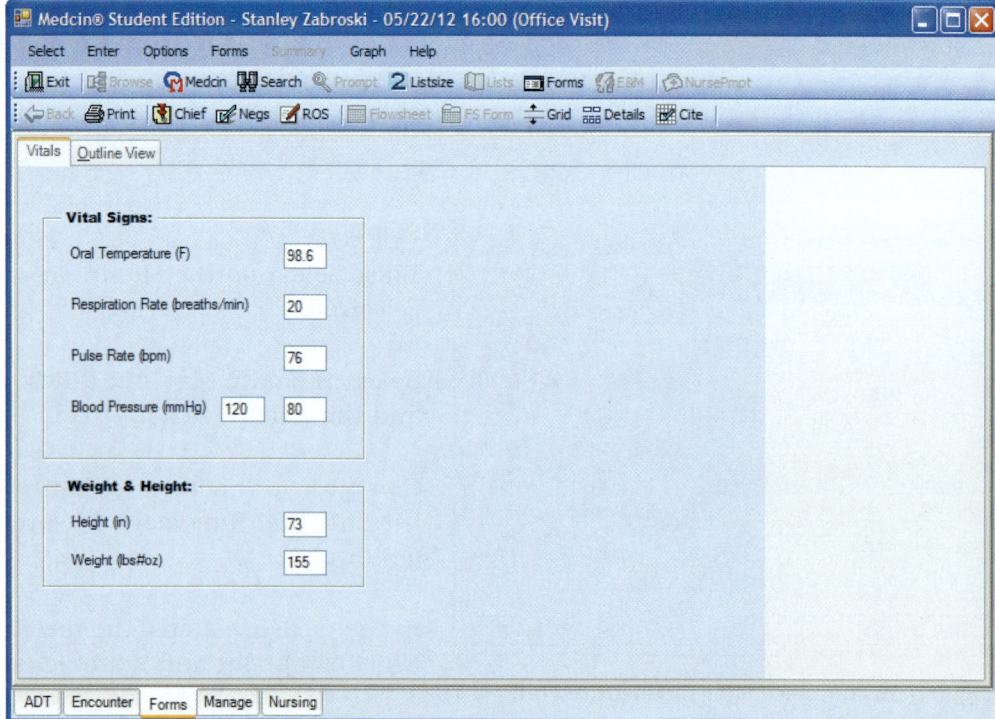

▶ Figure 7-28 Vital Signs form for Stanley Zabroski.

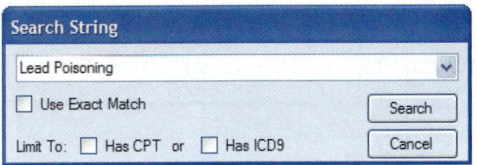

▶ **Figure 7-29** Search for Lead Poisoning.

Step 5

Click on the Dx Tab.

Click on the button labeled "Search" on the Toolbar near the top of the screen. (The Search button icon resembles a small pair of binoculars.) The Search String window will be invoked.

Enter the search string "Lead poisoning" and click on the button labeled "Search" in the window, as shown in Figure 7-29.

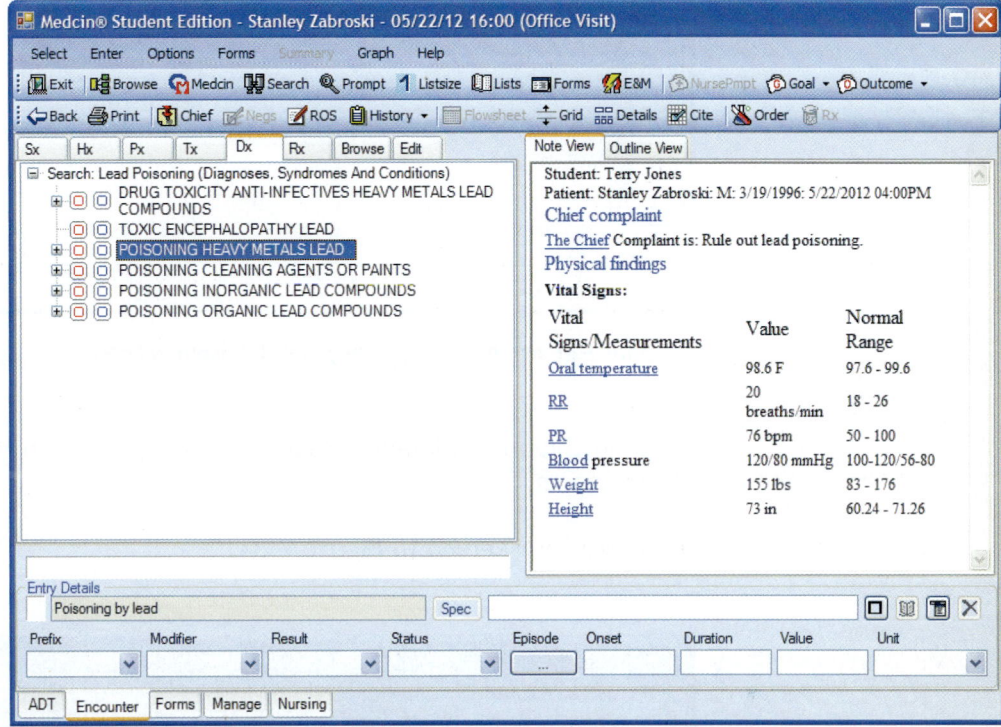

▶ **Figure 7-30** Search results with Poisoning Heavy Metals Lead highlighted.

Step 6

Click on the Dx tab.

Locate and highlight the finding "POISONING HEAVY METALS LEAD."

Click on the List Size button until the list size is **1**.

Compare your screen to Figure 7-30, and then click on the button labeled "Prompt" on the Toolbar near the top of the screen.

Step 7

Click on the Sx tab.

Verify that List Size is set to **1**.

Click on the button labeled "ROS" on the Toolbar near the top of the screen.

Chapter 7 | Problem Lists, Results Management, and Trending

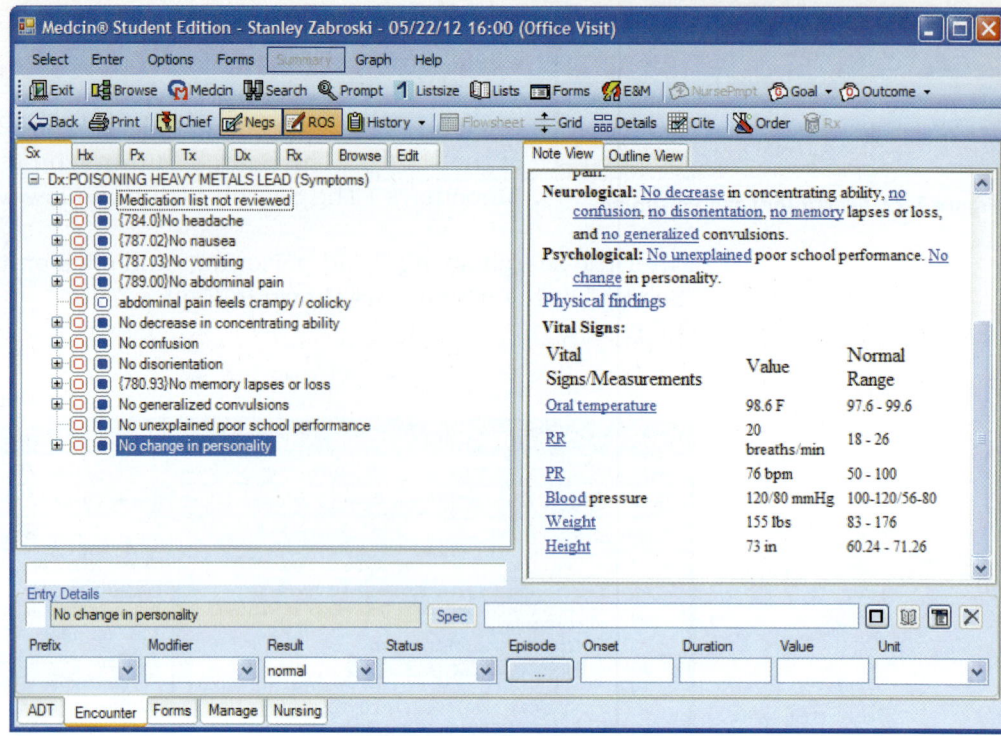

▶ Figure 7-31 Symptoms for Heavy Metal Poisoning Lead.

Click on the button labeled "Negs" (Auto Negative) on the Toolbar near the top of the screen.

Compare your screen to Figure 7-31.

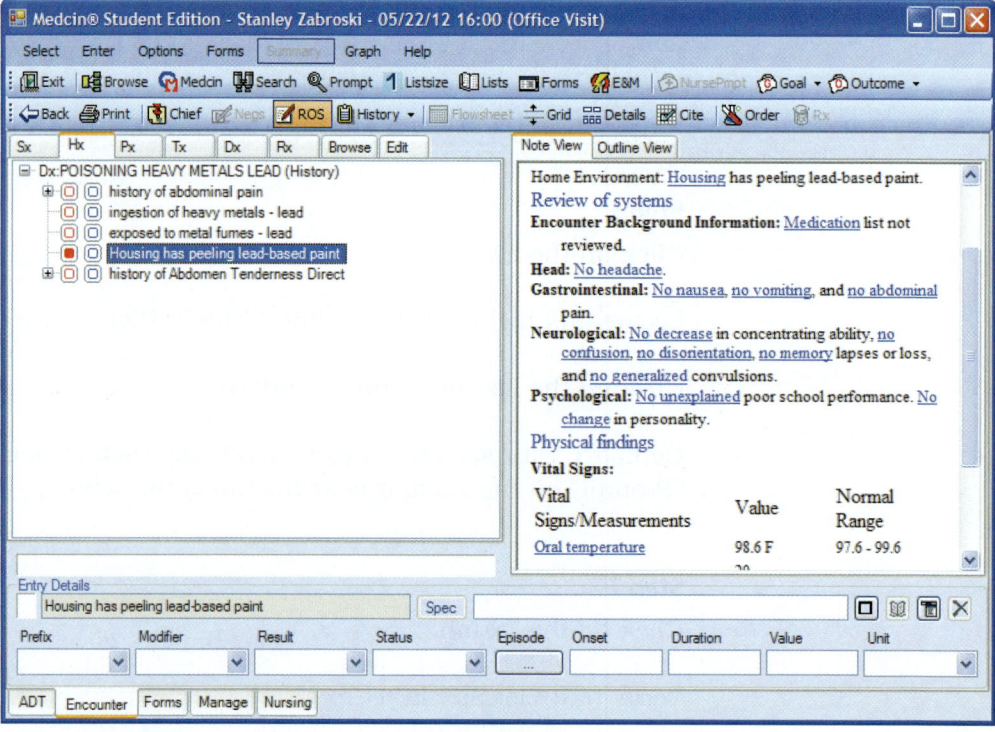

▶ Figure 7-32 History for Heavy Metal Poisoning Lead.

Step 8

Click on the Hx tab. Locate and click on the following finding:

- (red button) house has peeling paint which is lead based

Compare your screen to Figure 7-32.

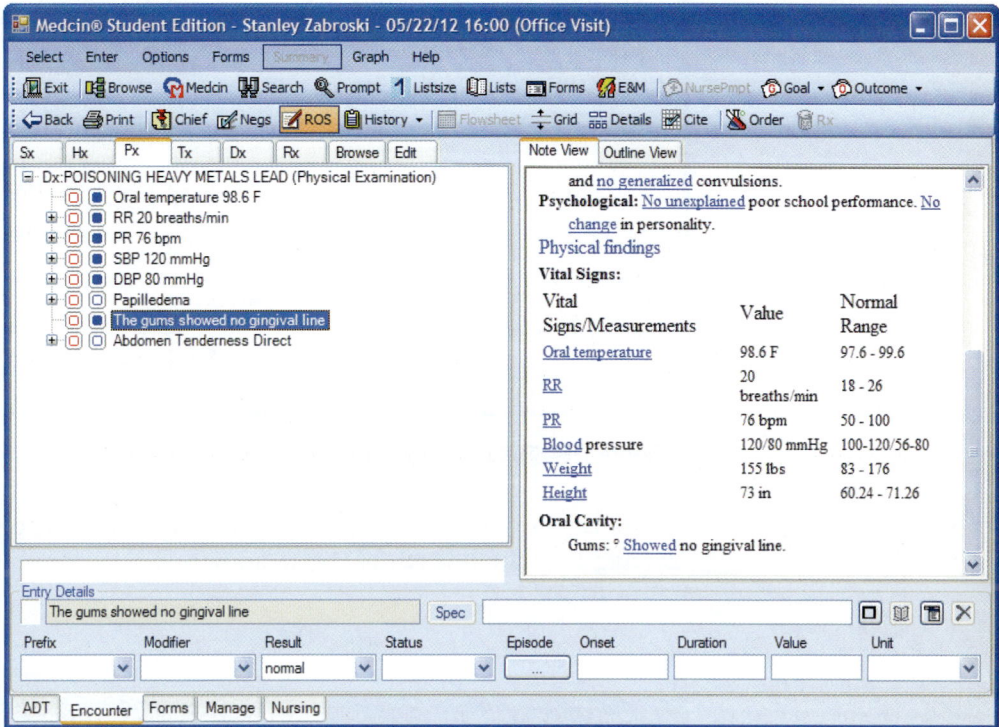

▶ Figure 7-33 Physical Exam for Heavy Metal Poisoning Lead.

Step 9

Click on the Px tab. Locate and click on the following finding:

- (blue button) Gums gingival line

Compare your screen to Figure 7-33.

Step 10

As discussed at the beginning of the exercise, the patient has had several lab tests performed before the office visit. The results were within normal limits. The clinician will review results of the tests and document them in the encounter note.

Click on the Tx tab. Locate and click on the following finding:

- (blue button) CBC with differential
- (blue button) Serum Lead Level
- (blue button) Urine Lead, 24 hr

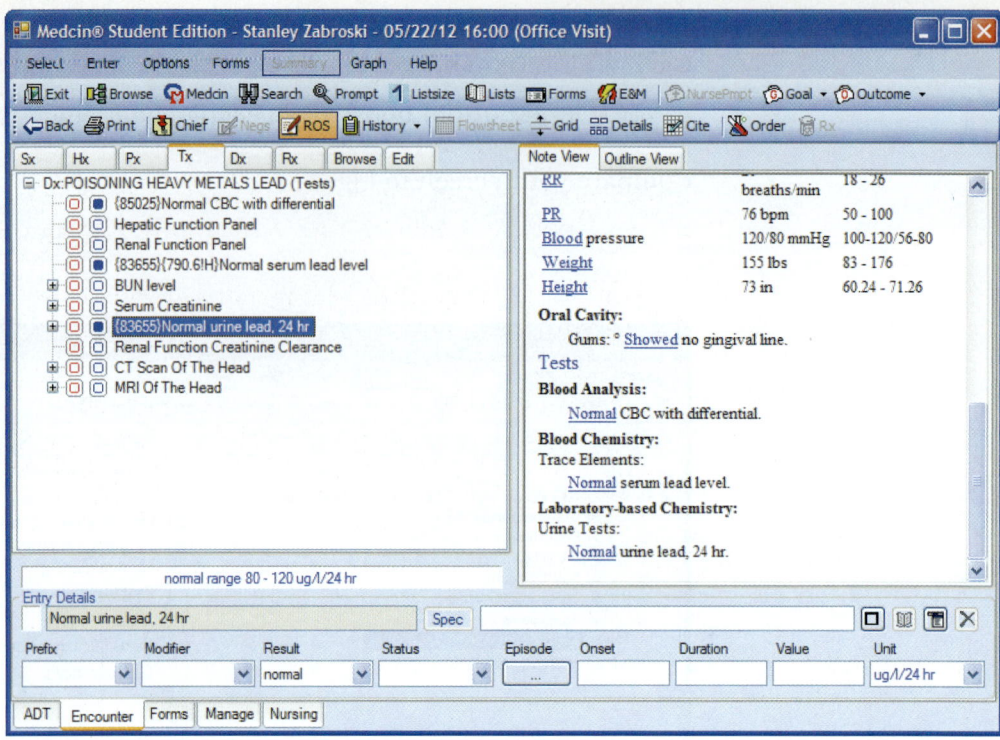

▶ Figure 7-34 Tx tab showing test results with normal results.

Compare your screen to Figure 7-34. If it is correct, click on the tab labeled "**Manage**" at the bottom of the window.

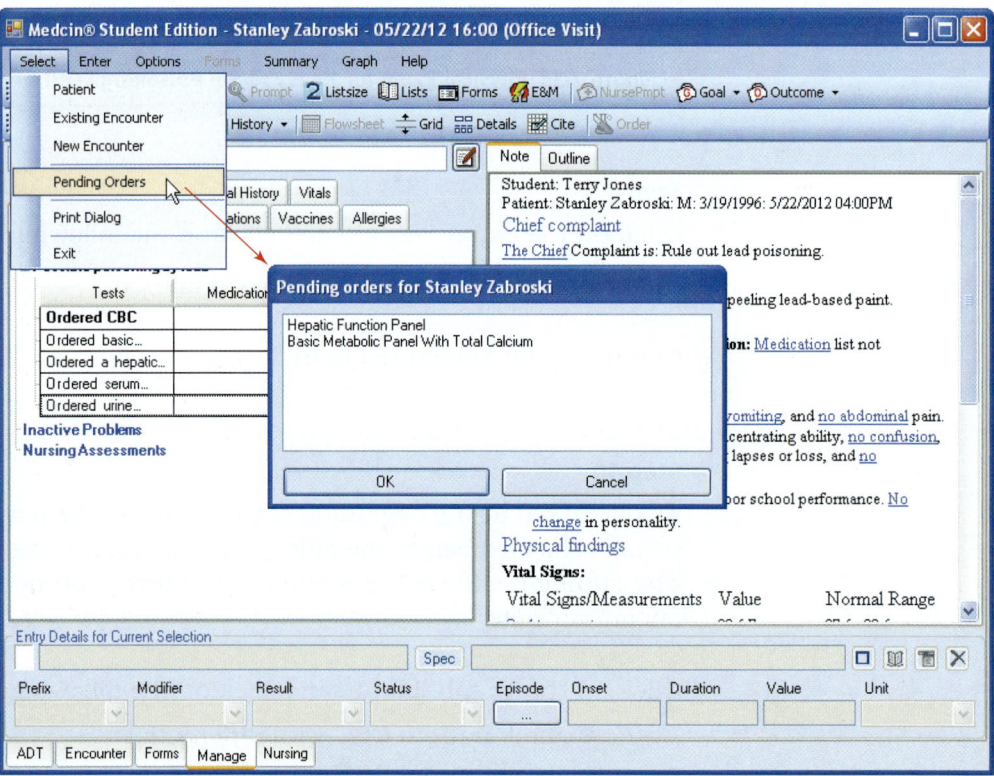

▶ Figure 7-35 Patient Management—Pending Orders window.

284 **Chapter 7** | Problem Lists, Results Management, and Trending

Step 11

Your screen should display the Problem List. If the information pane on the left of your screen is not already displaying the Problem List, click on the tab labeled "Problem List."

If the Entry Details pane is covering part of your list, locate and click on the button labeled "Details" in the Toolbar at the top of your screen.

Knowing which orders are still pending results is especially useful in offices in which multiple clinicians share patients, because it prevents duplicate orders. A nurse practitioner can see what orders are outstanding on a patient, including those ordered by another provider.

Click Select on the Menu bar, and then click **Pending Orders**. A window of pending orders will be displayed.

Compare the window in your screen labeled "Pending Orders for Stanley Zabroski" to Figure 7-35. This window contains a list of tests that have been ordered but for which results have not yet been entered.

Close the window by clicking on the Cancel button. Note: If you click OK by mistake, you will invoke a results entry window. Simply click the Cancel button in that window, and proceed to the next step.

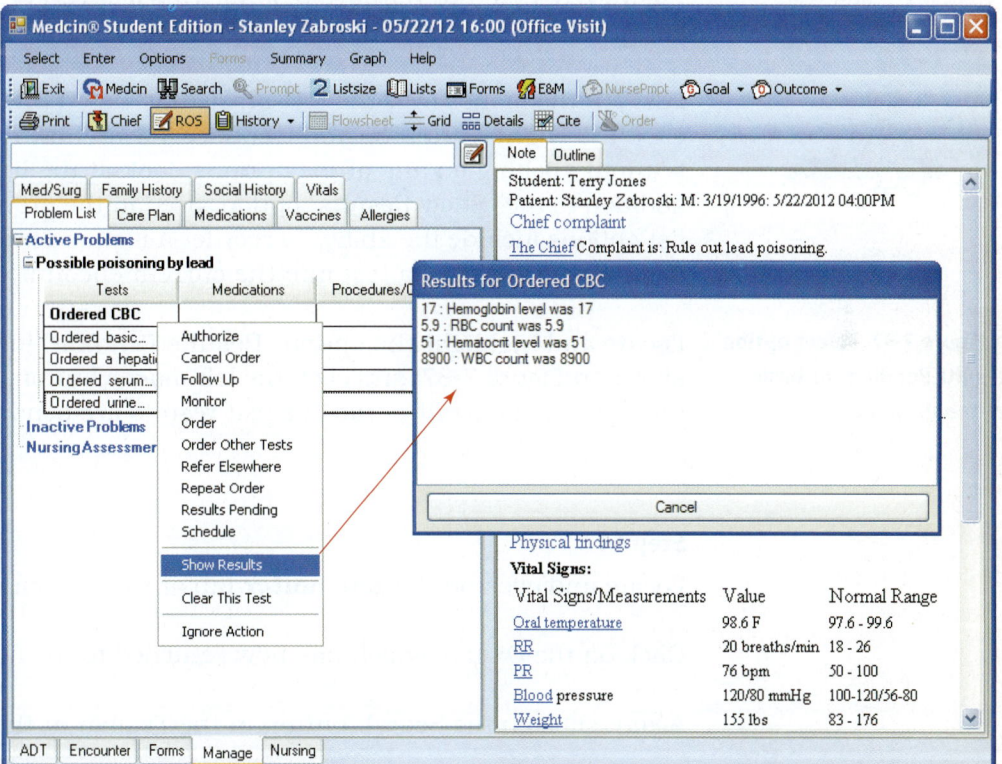

▶ Figure 7-36 Right-click menu: "Shows Results" invokes window of ordered CBC results.

Step 12

From the Manage tab, you also can see the results of any tests that have been entered. As we discussed earlier, EHR systems can receive results from the lab electronically and merge them directly into the patient's chart. Typically, the ordering provider is notified that results are ready for review.

Look at the Problem List in the left pane of your screen, under the test column.

Test names that are in bold type in the list indicate those that have results in the system.

Position the mouse over the test labeled "Ordered CBC" and click the **Right** button on your mouse. A drop-down list will be displayed.

If the drop-down list does not match the list shown in Figure 7-36, your mouse was not positioned correctly on the test. Reposition your mouse and click the right mouse button again.

Locate the option to Show Results and click the left mouse button. A window displaying the "Results for Ordered CBC" will be displayed, as shown in Figure 7-36.

The clinician can review the actual test results. Click the Cancel button to close the results window.

Step 13

You will recall that tests displayed in the Pending Orders window (shown in Figure 7-35) did not yet have results. This fact can be easily noted in the encounter note using Patient Management.

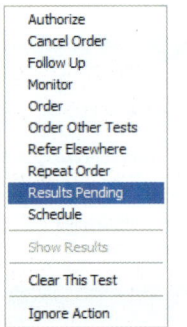

▶ **Figure 7-37** Select option Results Pending for basic metabolic panel.

Position the mouse over the test labeled "Ordered Basic Metabolic Panel" and click the **Right** button on your mouse. A drop-down list will be displayed. Without clicking on any of the options, look at the list that is displayed. In addition to the "Show Results" option, used in the previous step, the drop-down list options include the ability to reorder a test, order additional follow-up tests, or enter the status of a test into the current encounter.

Locate and highlight the option "Results Pending" in the drop-down list (as shown in Figure 7-37) and click the left mouse button. This will record a finding into the exam narrative that the test results are pending.

Step 14

Locate and click on the **Encounter** tab at the bottom of your screen.

Click on the Dx tab (which has now returned to the full list of findings).

Again, click on the Search button in the Toolbar at the top of your screen.

The Search String window will be invoked and should still contain the words "**lead poisoning**." If it does not, type them again.

Click on the button in the window labeled "Search." (If you need help, refer to Figure 7-29.)

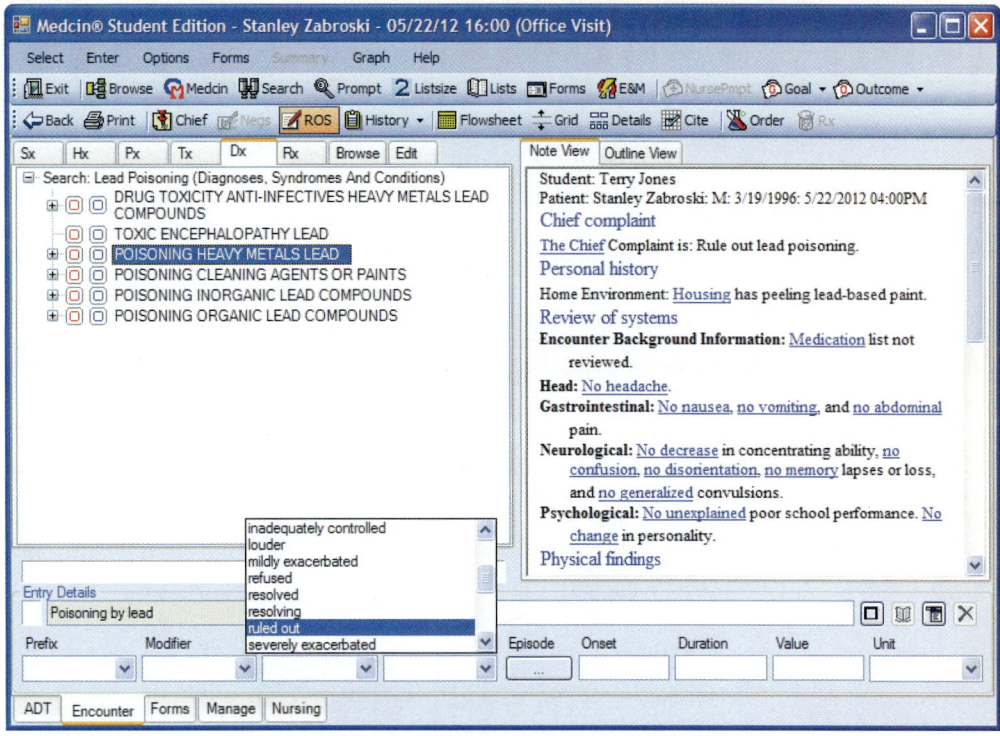

▶ Figure 7-38 Dx tab—Select the status "Ruled out" for Poisoning Heavy Metals Lead.

When the list of diagnoses is displayed, locate and highlight the finding "POISONING HEAVY METALS LEAD." (If you need help, refer to Figure 7-30.)

In the Entry Details section at the bottom of your screen, locate the Status Field and click on the down arrow button in it.

Scroll the drop-down list that is displayed to locate and click on "ruled out" as shown in Figure 7-38.

 **Alert** Do not close or exit the encounter until you have a printed copy in your hand. You will lose your work if you exit before printing.

Step 15

Click on the Print button on the Toolbar at the top of your screen to invoke the Print Data window.

Be certain there is a check mark in the box next to "Current Encounter" and then click on the appropriate button to either print or export a file, as directed by your instructor.

Stanley Zabroski   Page 1 of 1

Student: your name or id here
Patient: Stanley Zabroski: M: 3/19/1996: 5/22/2012 04:00PM
Chief complaint
The Chief Complaint is: Rule out lead poisoning.
Personal history
Home Environment: Housing has peeling lead-based paint.
Review of systems
Encounter Background Information: Medication list not reviewed.
Head: No headache.
Gastrointestinal: No nausea, no vomiting, and no abdominal pain.
Neurological: No decrease in concentrating ability, no confusion, no disorientation, no memory lapses or loss, and no generalized convulsions.
Psychological: No unexplained poor school performance. No change in personality.
Physical findings
Vital Signs:

Vital Signs/Measurements	Value	Normal Range
Oral temperature	98.6 F	97.6 - 99.6
RR	20 breaths/min	18 - 26
PR	76 bpm	50 - 100
Blood pressure	120/80 mmHg	100-120/56-80
Weight	155 lbs	83 - 176
Height	73 in	60.24 - 71.26

Oral Cavity:
Gums: ° Showed no gingival line.
Tests
Blood Analysis:
Normal CBC with differential.
Blood Chemistry:
Pending results for basic metabolic panel with total calcium.
Trace Elements:
Normal serum lead level.
Laboratory-based Chemistry:
Urine Tests:
Normal urine lead, 24 hr.
Assessment
- Poisoning by lead which is ruled out

▶ **Figure 7-39** Printed encounter note for Stanley Zabroski.

Compare your printout or file output to Figure 7-39. If it is correct, hand it in to your instructor. If there are any differences, review the previous steps in the exercise and find your error.

Real-Life Story

Experiencing the Functional Benefits of an EHR

By Henry Palmer, M.D.

Henry Palmer, M.D., specializes in internal medicine and is affiliated with Rush University Medical Center.

I am a physician practicing at two locations, neither of which is where my EHR computer is located. I have computers in the exam rooms and I am documenting with the patients, but the data is going over the Internet into the servers in real time.

Rush University Medical Center, like other large institutions, had many different computer systems in its departments. Trying to unite all these legacy systems was very difficult, but the center wanted to be able to access all the information relatively easily from one system. Rush has a CDR, or clinical data repository, which stores the data from various legacy systems. For example, the clinical notes section includes all of the radiology, ultrasound, stress testing, cardiology, and operative reports; these are transcribed reports, all text based.

Lab results, however, come in as data. The results are imported automatically. You can set how far back in time you want to default your view of them. This is very handy because you are able to see the trends. You can also graph it. You can rearrange the view to see your results horizontally or vertically.

The CDR has demographic information for the patient, of course, and helpful information about admission and discharge. Let us say I want to look at the admission from two months ago. I can highlight it and find out who the providers were for that admission, the insurance information for that admission, as well as the diagnosis.

Rush also has an order entry system. When I sign in, it automatically shows if I have a patient who is in the hospital. This is handy, particularly in the case of primary care physicians, because sometimes your patients get admitted without your knowledge. A patient may get admitted into the surgical service and you might never be called.

The order entry screen first shows if there are any orders approaching expiration. It also asks me to authenticate any verbal orders I had given over the phone, but had not yet countersigned.

I can pull up a patient and view results through the order system. I can look at results in different ways—results for the last five days, all the results since admission, or just the ones that were critical. I can see details about particular results, the normal ranges, and some additional information about how to interpret those results.

When I write a medication order, it goes electronically to the pharmacy. The order system will also provide alerts to drug interactions or areas of concern the hospital has identified with the drug. When ordering potassium, for example, the system would advise me that it should only be given in a certain quantity if the patient is on certain medications that tend to increase potassium levels anyway.

It is easy to order labs by just clicking one box. I can also order a consult. CPOE works. It is not perfect, but in a large institution like this it has to work or it would not be used.

Our PAC system eliminates the need to have to go down to radiology to see x-rays. On the average workstation I can view the images of the patients' x-rays with reasonable definition. If I want really fine detail, I can go to any of the high-definition monitors that are scattered around the hospital. I can also display the radiologist's report. Reading the report will guide me toward the areas of concern.

Additionally, we use an electronic signature program for signing off on charts. Basically this brings up the document, allowing me to edit it and finalize my signature. I can also indicate which doctors I want to receive copies of my document. The system will then automatically fax them to the doctors involved with the patient care.

Dr. Palmer reviews a CAT scan.

Decision support includes access to the Rush medical library from inside our system. I enter my search term and it will retrieve an index of the article. I can go directly to what I want to read, for example, the treatment or the diagnostic approach to the disease.

One of the challenges as a primary care physician is that my patients search the Internet. They will often come in with research in hand and ask some very cogent questions. I think the downside can be that people assume because they have read it on the Internet that it applies to them or that they know what to do with the information—and that is not always the case.

The biggest problem I see in health information technology today is the segregation of records, particularly between inpatient and outpatient systems. When patients are admitted, their outpatient records are not there. Synchronizing those, I think, would be a big step forward and also eliminate redundancy in testing.

Trending

One important service that clinicians want to perform for their patients is "trending," which is comparing the change of certain test components or measurements over a period of time. In Chapter 1 the IOM identified this as one of the functional benefits derived from an EHR.

In a paper chart, the trend is observed by paging through past tests, locating the desired component on each report, and making a mental comparison. However, when the lab results or other measurements are stored as data in the EHR, the computer can instantly find all instances of any component the clinician wishes to compare.

Additionally, with computerized data, graphs and charts can be easily created for any finding that has numerical results. This provides the clinician with a quick picture of the changes over time. Not only are graphs useful to the clinician, but they also provide an excellent means of clarification when counseling patients or for patient education.

Using Graphs to View Trends of Lab Results

Chapter 2 discussed the advantages of EHR records with codified results as opposed to EHR records that are scanned images of printed reports. Nowhere is that more evident than with lab result reports.

An EHR system can graph any component of a lab test that has numerical values. However, to create a meaningful graph, the test must have been performed multiple times.

Guided Exercise 47: Graphing Lab Results

In the next exercise you will learn to graph a specific lab test by locating it using the search tool. You will also learn to retrieve an existing encounter.

Case Study

Guy Daniels has been seen at the clinic for several years. He has hypertension, Type II diabetes, and a weight problem. He is scheduled for a clinic visit tomorrow and his pre-visit lab work has been received from the lab. You have been asked to generate two graphs to be used for patient education.

Step 1

If you have not already done so, start the Student Edition software.

Click Select on the Menu bar, and then click Patient.

In the Patient Selection window, locate and click on **Guy Daniels**, as shown in Figure 7-40.

Step 2

In this exercise you will use a new feature you have not used before; you are going to retrieve and work with an encounter already in progress.

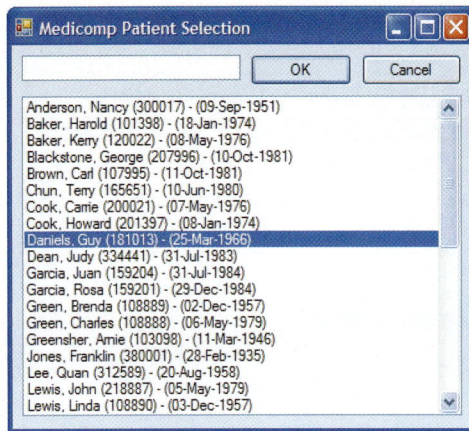

▶ Figure 7-40 Selecting Guy Daniels from the Patient Selection window.

Click Select on the Menu bar, and then click **Existing Encounter**.

A small window of previous encounters will be displayed. Compare your screen to the window in the center of Figure 7-41.

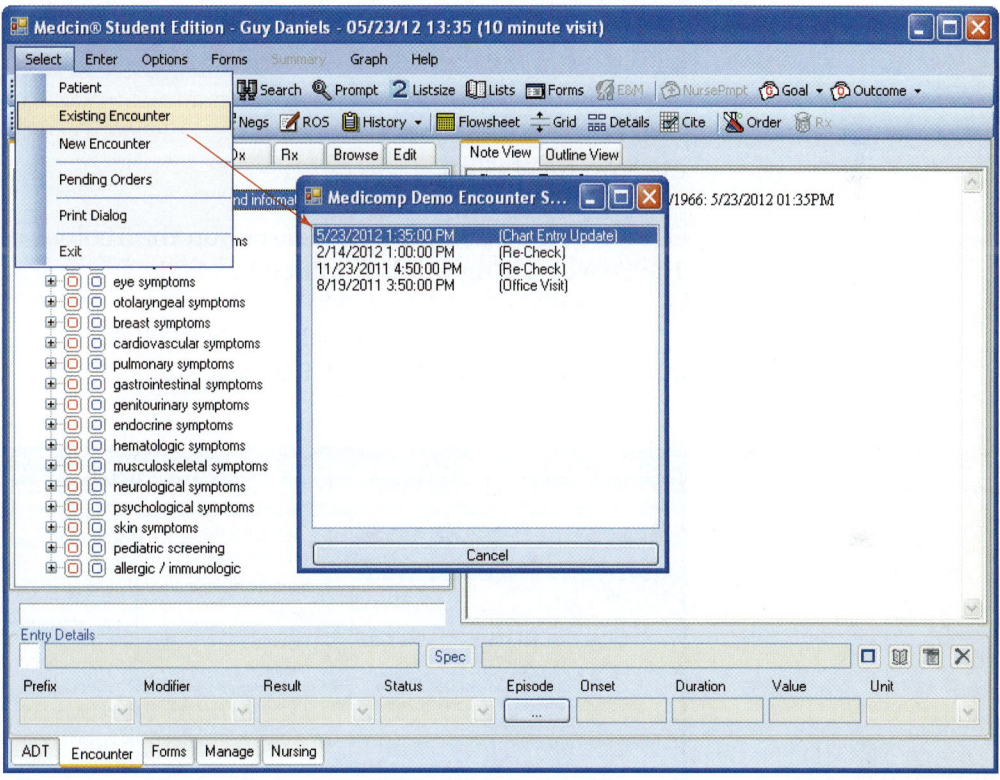

▶ Figure 7-41 Select Existing Encounter for May 23, 2012 10:00 AM.

Position your mouse pointer on the first encounter in the list, dated **5/23/2012 1:35 PM** (as shown in Figure 7-41) and click on it.

Because this is the first time that you have retrieved an existing encounter, take a moment to look at the encounter note in the right pane of your screen. This encounter is simply the result record of a number of tests that were ordered before Mr. Daniel's scheduled visit. It is not uncommon for patients to have lab work done ahead of their clinic visit so that the results will be ready when the doctor or nurse practitioner sees them. While having his blood drawn, Mr. Daniels felt faint, so the nurse took his blood pressure and recorded it in the chart.

Chapter 7 | Problem Lists, Results Management, and Trending

▶ Figure 7-42 Search for Creatinine.

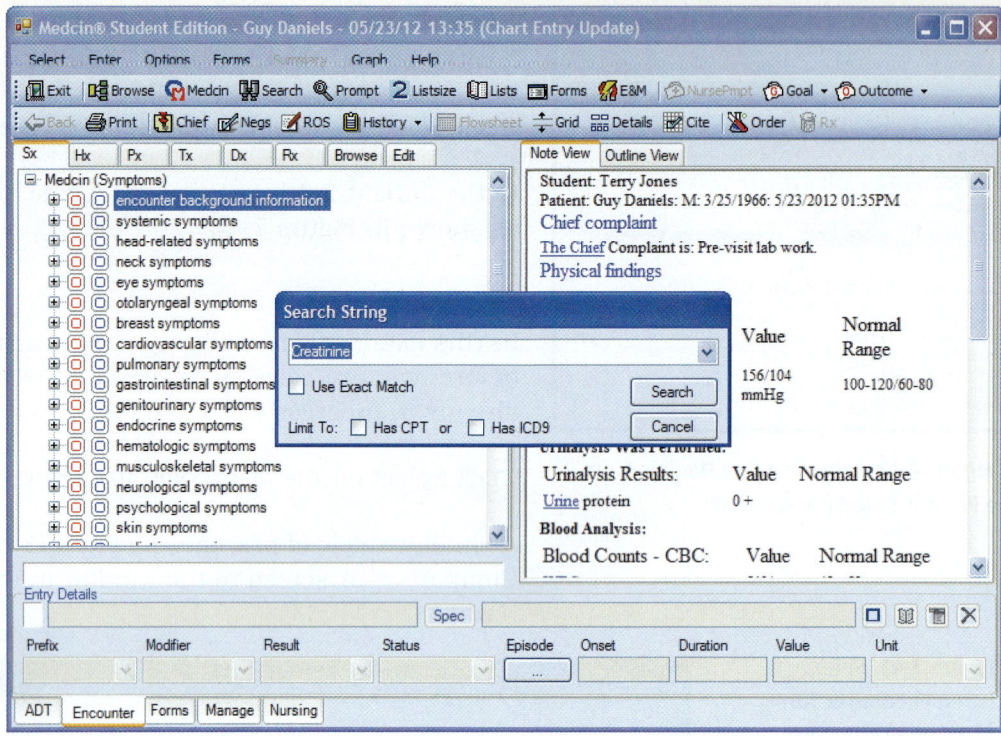

Step 3

Click on the Tx Tab.

Click on the button labeled "Search" on the Toolbar near the top of the screen. The Search String window will be invoked.

Type the search string "**Creatinine**" and click on the button in the window labeled "Search" as shown in Figure 7-42.

▶ Figure 7-43 Select Graph Current Finding from the menu.

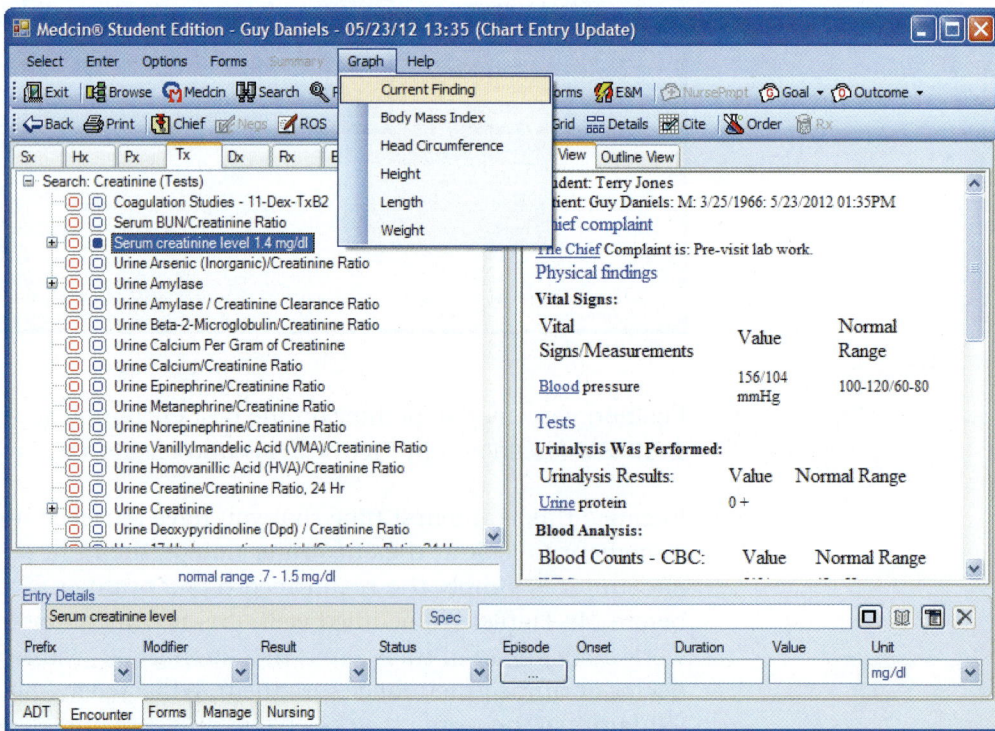

292   Chapter 7 | Problem Lists, Results Management, and Trending

Step 4

Your left pane should automatically be on the Tx tab.

Locate and highlight the finding of Serum Creatinine (as shown in Figure 7-43).

Click Graph on the Menu bar, and then click "Current Finding" from the drop-down list

The Medcin Graph window will be invoked.

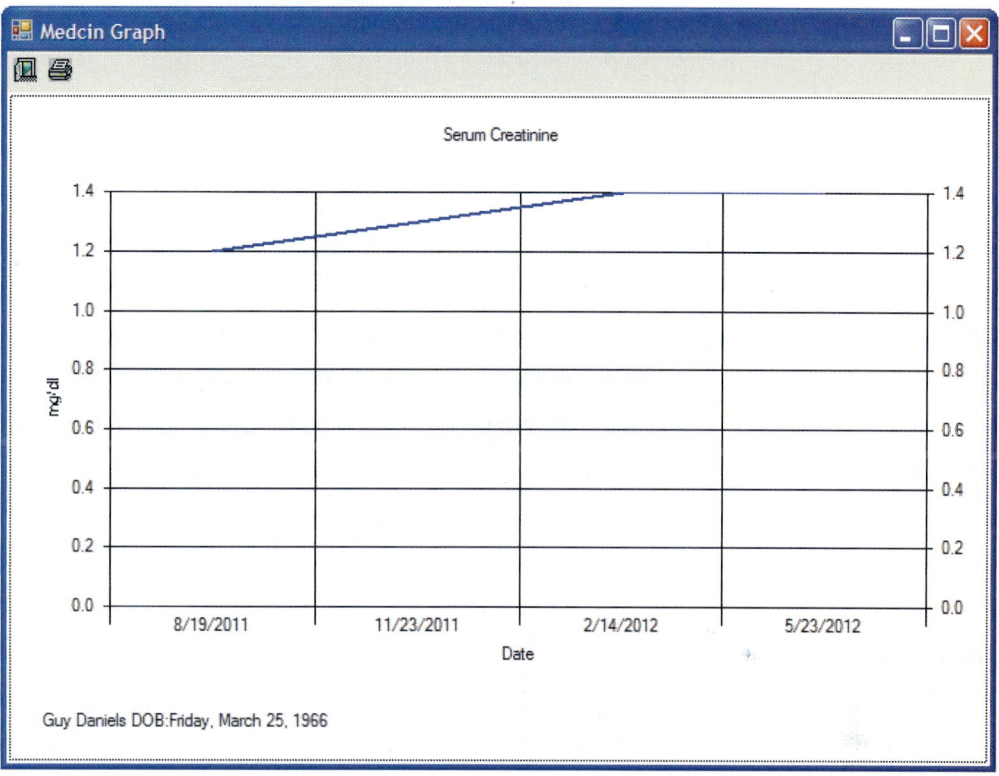

▶ **Figure 7-44** Graph of Guy Daniel's serum creatinine.

Step 5

The software will find and graph Mr. Daniel's creatinine over the last four tests. Compare your screen to Figure 7-44.

This example shows the increase in creatinine level. Similar graphs could have been created for any of the lab results that have numeric values for their results.

Step 6

The Graph window has two buttons in the upper left corner that are identical in appearance and purpose to the corresponding buttons on the Student Edition Toolbar. The first button is Exit, which closes the graph window. The second button is the Print button, which prints your graph.

Chapter 7 | Problem Lists, Results Management, and Trending

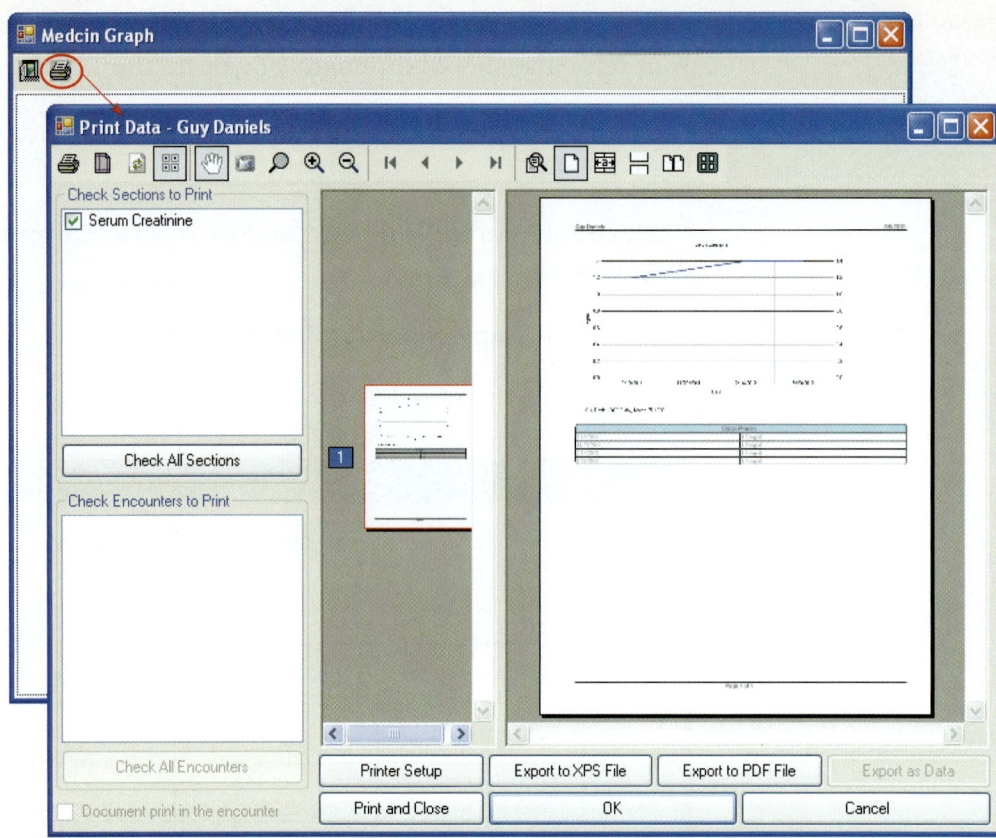

▶ Figure 7-45 Print Data window for Graphs is invoked from Graph window Print icon.

Locate and click on the Print button (circled in Figure 7-45) in the upper left corner of the graph window to invoke the Print Data window.

In the left column of the Print Data window where you normally see a check box for Current Encounter, you will see a check box with the name of the graph. Click your mouse in the check box next to Serum Creatinine and then click on the appropriate button to either print or export a file, as directed by your instructor.

When your graph has printed successfully, click on the Exit button in the window displaying the Serum Creatinine graph.

Do not close or exit the Student Edition software until you have completed the next exercise.

Guided Exercise 48: Graphing Vital Signs in the Chart

As previously stated, any finding with a numeric value can be graphed. For example, vital signs are recorded at every encounter. A chart of the patient's blood pressure and weight measurements could be used for patient education and might stimulate the patient to keep his own chart at home.

Step 7

In the right pane, the encounter note, locate and click on the vital sign **Blood Pressure** as shown in Figure 7-46.

▶ **Figure 7-46** Selecting Guy Daniels blood pressure from the encounter.

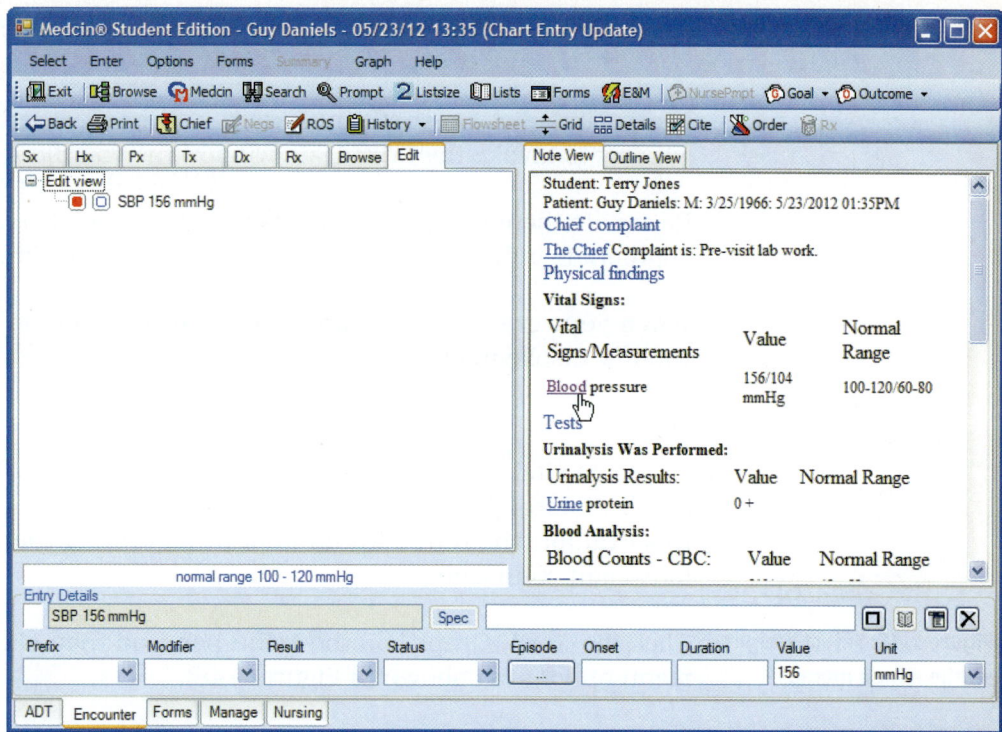

Step 8

Click the word "Graph" on the Menu bar, and then click "Current Finding" on the list of menu options, as you did in the previous exercise.

Step 9

The software will find and graph Guy's blood pressure over the last four visits. Compare your screen to Figure 7-47. The blue line is his systolic blood pressure

▶ **Figure 7-47** Blood pressure graph for Guy Daniels.

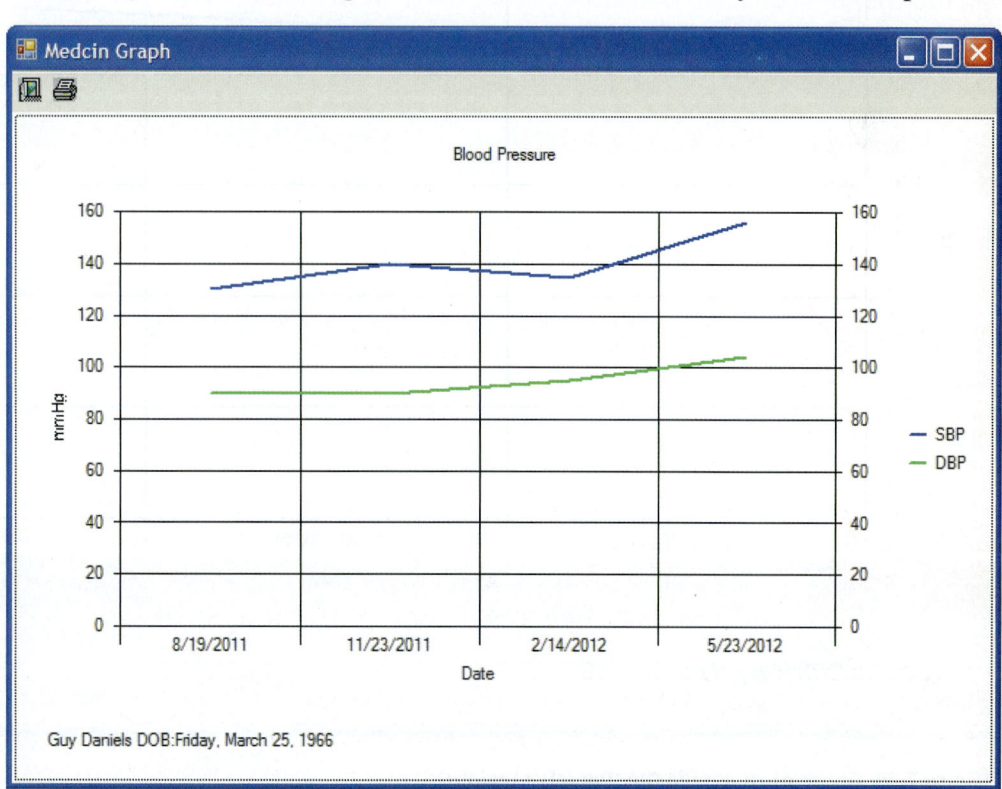

Chapter 7 | Problem Lists, Results Management, and Trending

readings and the green line is his diastolic readings, as noted in the graph legend, SBP and DPB, respectively.

Locate and click on the Print button in the upper left corner of the graph window to invoke the Print Data window, as you did in the previous exercise.

Be certain there is a check in the box next to Blood Pressure and then click on the appropriate button to either print or export a file, as directed by your instructor.

When your graph has printed successfully, click on the exit button in the window displaying the graph.

Step 10

For some vital signs it is not necessary to locate the finding to generate a graph. Several popular measurements are always available for graphing. In this example the nurse wants to print a graph of the patient's weight to use for weight counseling.

▶ **Figure 7-48** Select Weight from the Graph menu.

Click the word "Graph" on the Menu bar, and then click "Weight" on the list of menu options (as shown in Figure 7-48).

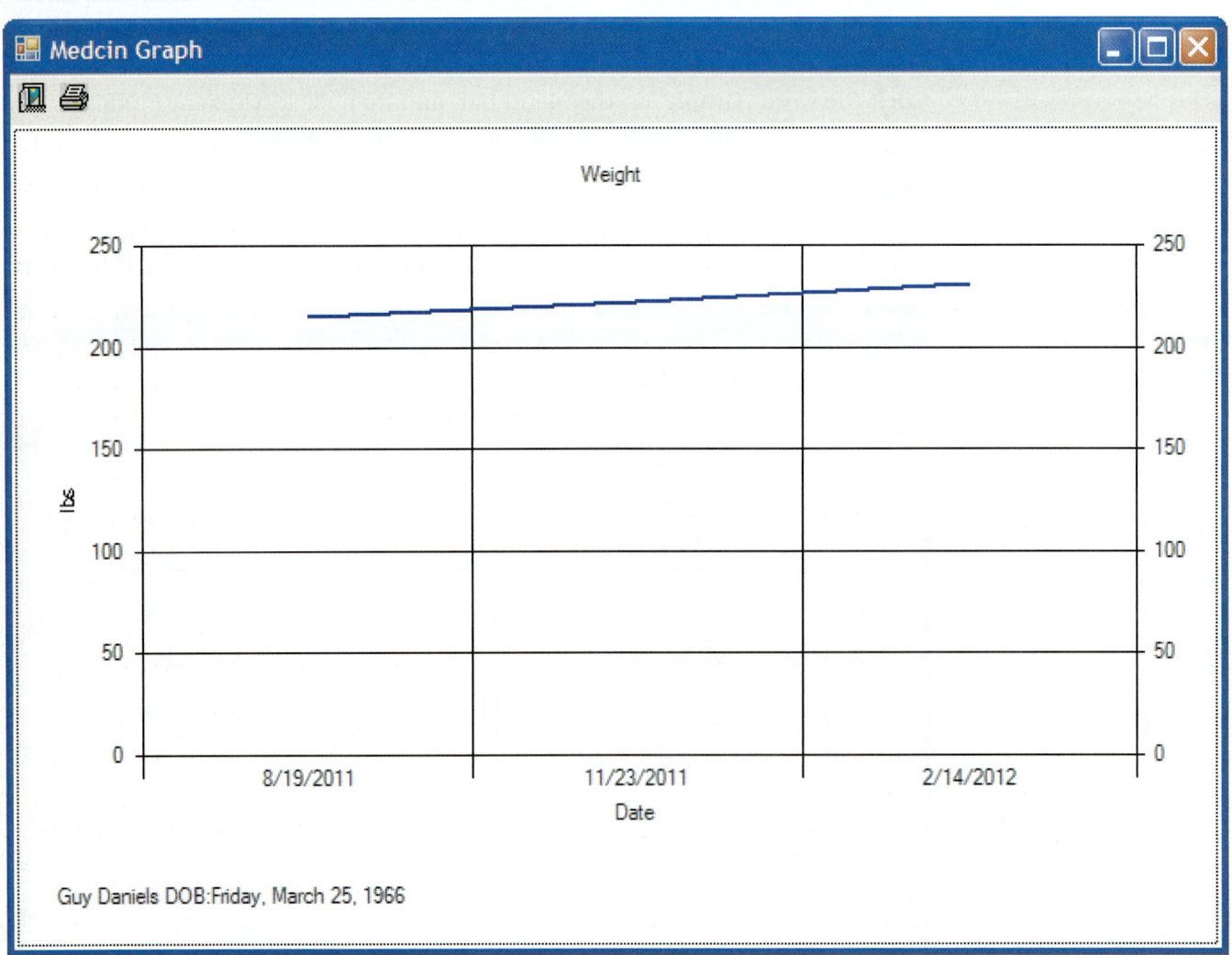

▶ **Figure 7-49 Graph of change in Guy Daniels's weight.**

Step 11

Compare your screen to Figure 7-49.

A graph of the patient's weight measurements from previous visits is instantly displayed. You do not have to select a finding or even load an existing encounter. The graph menu allows the clinician to instantly create graphs of several key measurements without having to locate a specific finding.

Step 12

Locate and click on the Print button in the upper left corner of the graph window to invoke the Print Data window.

Locate the check box for Weight, in the left column and click on it.

Locate and click on the appropriate button to either print or export a file, as directed by your instructor. When your graph has printed successfully, click on the exit button in the window displaying the Weight graph.

Hand your graphs in to your instructor.

Visual Aides to Engage Patients in Their Own Healthcare

Patients must become involved in their own healthcare to effectively manage and prevent diseases. A chart of the patient's weight measurements and graphs of key indicators such as cholesterol and blood glucose levels can be effective visual aides for patient education and may help to stimulate compliance with health regimens.

Critical Thinking Exercise 49: Graphing Total Cholesterol and Weight

Case Study

The clinic has been helping Sally Sutherland monitor her cholesterol by testing her at each annual exam. In this exercise, you are going to create a graph of Sally's total cholesterol and her weight. You will not enter any new data.

Step 1

If you are continuing from the previous exercise, proceed to select the patient, otherwise start the Student Edition software.

Click Select on the Menu bar, and then click Patient.

In the Patient Selection window, locate and click on **Sally Sutherland**.

You do not have to set the date or time.

Step 2

Click the word "Graph" on the Menu bar, and then click "Weight" on the list of menu options.

Step 3

Locate and click on the Print button in the upper left corner of the graph window to invoke the Print Data window.

Locate the check box for Weight in the left column and click on it.

Locate and click on the appropriate button to either print or export a file, as directed by your instructor. When your graph has printed successfully, click on the exit button in the window displaying the Weight graph.

Click on the Exit button in the window displaying the weight graph.

Step 4

Locate and click the button labeled "Search" on the Toolbar to invoke the Search String window. Type the words "**Total Cholesterol**" in the Search String window and click on the Search button.

Step 5

Verify you are on the Tx tab.

Locate and highlight the finding of Total Cholesterol.

Click Graph on the Menu bar, and then click "Current Finding" from the drop-down list

The Graph window will be invoked, displaying a graph of Sally's Total Cholesterol test results over the last four years.

Step 6

Locate and click on the Print button in the upper left corner of the graph window to invoke the Print Data window.

Locate the check box for Total Cholesterol in the left column and click on it.

Locate and click on the appropriate button to either print or export a file, as directed by your instructor. When your graph has printed successfully, click on the Exit button in the window displaying the Total Cholesterol graph.

Hand your graphs in to your instructor.

Chapter Seven Summary

This chapter explored the Patient Management feature to demonstrate the way an EHR can organize information from past encounters. Patient Management has the following tabs:

Problems—Problem lists and problem-oriented views of the chart organize the data by problem and encounter date.

Problem lists provide an up-to-date list of the diagnoses and conditions that affect that particular patient's care. Problem lists track both acute and chronic conditions. Problems are removed from the list or set inactive once the patient is "cured" or the problem is "resolved." Problems that normally resolve themselves over a short period of time are called "Acute Self-Limiting." The status of the problem is updated at each visit.

The following are typical of the types of status assigned to active problems:

Resolved

Resolving

Improving

Well controlled

Unchanged

Inadequately controlled

Mildly exacerbated

Failing to change as expected

Expanding

Worsening

Severely exacerbated

Care Plan—Provides a quick review of the plan from each previous encounter. It is organized by problem and encounter date for which the patient was seen for that problem. Clicking on the encounter reveals the findings recorded in the plan for that visit.

Medications—Keeps track of what medications the patient is currently taking. The Medications list is always reviewed before writing new prescriptions.

Vaccines—Lists the patient's immunizations that have been administered at the clinic.

Allergies—Lists food, drug, and other allergies the patient may have. This information is reviewed before writing a prescription.

Past Medical/Surgical History—Lists past history items recorded in the EHR during all previous encounters.

Family History—Lists family history items recorded in the EHR during all previous encounters.

Social History—Lists social and behavioral history items recorded in the EHR during all previous encounters.

Vitals—Displays key vital signs taken on previous visits in a column format.

Clicking the mouse on the label of a column within any tab of Patient Management will sort the rows in the tab by the values in the column that was clicked.

The Patient Management feature allows information from previous encounters to be updated and cited in the current encounter.

Citing means to bring a finding from a previous encounter note into the current encounter. Tests can be ordered, reordered, or the results can be viewed. Prescriptions can be renewed or discontinued as well. In this chapter you also learned how to view pending orders and lab results.

You also learned to view pending lab orders. All lab orders have a status; these include:

Pending—Sent but have no results.

Preliminary—Results provide an early indication of the test but awaiting verification.

Chapter 7 | Problem Lists, Results Management, and Trending

Final—Results have been verified and are ready for review.

Corrected—A change occurred as a result of repeat verification.

The ability for the clinician to see what tests are pending helps prevent duplicate orders.

The ability to graph weight, height, and test results can provide an excellent means of clarification when counseling patients or for the clinician to observe trends in the patient's condition.

Any finding with a numerical value can be graphed. Several standard graphs—for example, height and weight—can be generated without locating the specific finding, simply by selecting them from the Graph menu.

As you continue through the course, you can refer to the Guided Exercises in this chapter when you need to remember how to perform a particular task.

Task	Exercise	Page #
How to use Patient Management	44	263
How to use problem lists and cite findings	45	269
Viewing pending orders and lab results	46	279
How to graph lab results or any current finding	47	290
How to print a graph	47	293
How to graph weight or height	48	294

Testing Your Knowledge of Chapter 7

1. What is a Problem List?
2. What is the idea of a Problem List?
3. Name at least two reasons why clinicians use a Problem List.
4. What is a reason that a "wellness" condition would appear on a Problem List?
5. Where does the data that appears in the Manage tab come from?
6. What does it mean to cite a finding?
7. Define trending of lab values.
8. Describe how to graph a patient's weight.
9. What type of lab results can be graphed?
10. What is a pending order?
11. List the steps you would take to graph a lab value.
12. What type of data is on the Care Plan tab?
13. How do you sort the data display on the Vitals Signs tab?
14. How do you set a problem as inactive?
15. You should have produced two narrative documents of patient encounters, and five graphs. If you have not already done so, hand these in to your instructor with this test. The printed encounter notes and graphs will count as a portion of your grade.

Chapter Eight

Data Entry Using Flow Sheets and Anatomical Drawings

Learning Outcomes

After completing this chapter, you should be able to:

- Describe flow sheets
- Work with a flow sheet
- Create a Form-based flow sheet
- Create a Problem-based flow sheet
- Use an EHR drawing tool to annotate drawings in an encounter

Learning to Use Flow Sheets

Flow sheets present data from multiple encounters in column form. This format allows for a side-by-side comparison of findings over a period of time. Some clinicians prefer to view a patient chart this way because it is easier to spot trends in the patient's health conditions. It is ideal for chronic disease management such as diabetes or long-term conditions such as pregnancy. OB offices use flow sheets to monitor pregnancy because it affords them a view of the previous visits when documenting the current one. Paper flow sheets have been in use long before flow sheets were developed for EHR systems. The difference is that EHR systems have the ability to create them dynamically.

Not all EHR systems implement flow sheets in the same manner, so flow sheets in the workplace may vary from these exercises. Some EHR systems limit flow sheets to lab results or vital signs. However, by using a codified nomenclature, it is possible to create clinical flow sheets that present findings from entire encounters in columns by encounter date. Additionally, there are several different ways for an EHR to create a flow sheet based on a list, a problem, or a form.

Patients with chronic diseases such as diabetes often develop additional chronic diseases, for example, hypertension, cardiovascular disease, macular degeneration, and a number of other diseases. Rather than try to develop complicated forms that cover different combinations of diseases, a clinic can simply develop one form for each. As you will see in this exercise, you can switch forms throughout the exam without reentering findings. Because the forms share the same nomenclature, a finding that is used on both forms automatically displays the entered data when either form is loaded.

Guided Exercise 50: Working with a Flow Sheet

In previous exercises, you worked with multiple diagnoses for a single patient. You also have learned that creating and using forms for specific diseases, conditions, or types of visits can speed up data entry because the form presents all of the findings likely to be needed by the clinician for a particular type of exam. This exercise will combine those two concepts and add a third concept, the flow sheet. In this exercise you will learn to use a flow sheet to document a patient encounter.

Case Study

Guy Daniels is a patient with hypertension and borderline diabetes who has been seen quarterly at the outpatient clinic to better manage his health. Mr. Daniels returns for a three month checkup. Lab tests have been ordered and performed before his visit. The results were reviewed by the clinician when they arrived electronically earlier today.

Step 1

If you have not already done so, start the Student Edition software.

Click Select on the Menu bar, and then click Patient.

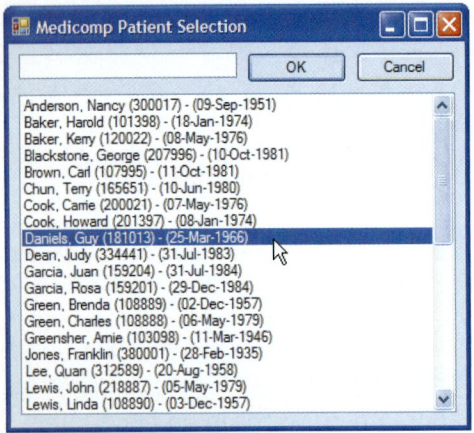

▶ Figure 8-1 Selecting Guy Daniels from the Patient Selection window.

In the Patient Selection window, locate and click on **Guy Daniels**, as shown in Figure 8-1.

 **Alert** | Make certain you set the date and time correctly for this exercise. If you need help, review Chapter 3, Guided Exercise 13.

Step 2

Click Select on the Menu bar, and then click New Encounter.

Select the date **May 24, 2012**, the time **4:15 PM**, and the reason **Office Visit**.

Compare your screen to Figure 8-2. Make certain that the date and time match before clicking on the OK button.

Step 3

Enter the Chief complaint by locating the button in the Toolbar labeled "Chief" and clicking on it.

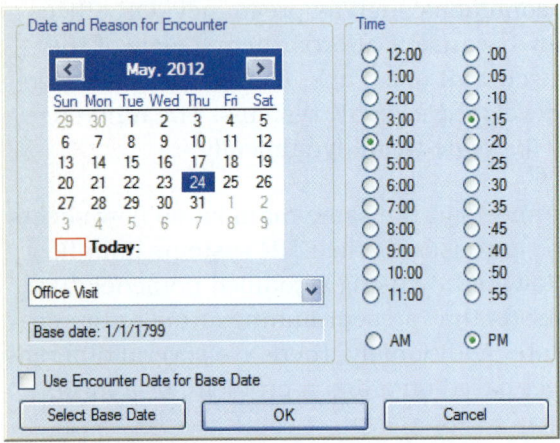

▶ Figure 8-2 New encounter for an office visit, May 24, 2012 4:15 PM.

In the dialog window that will open, type "**3 month check up**."

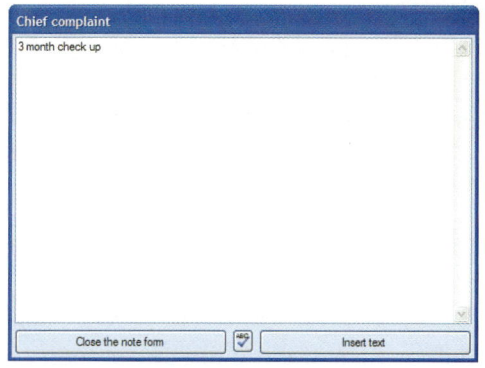

▶ **Figure 8-3** Chief complaint dialog for three-month check-up.

▶ **Figure 8-4** Select Hypertension Form.

▶ **Figure 8-5** Hypertension Form.

Compare your screen to Figure 8-3 and then click on the button labeled "Close the note form."

Step 4

Locate and click on the Forms button in the Toolbar at the top of your screen, as you have done in previous exercises.

Select the form labeled "Hypertension," as shown in Figure 8-4.

Step 5

Locate the Diagnosis Hypertension at the top of the form.

Click the **Y** check box for Hypertension. A circle next to the finding will turn red.

To save time at the practice, the form designer has incorporated the vital signs fields into the first page of the form. Enter the following vital signs for Guy Daniels:

Temperature:	**98.2**
Respiration:	**20**
Pulse:	**68**
BP:	**125/85**
Weight:	**229**

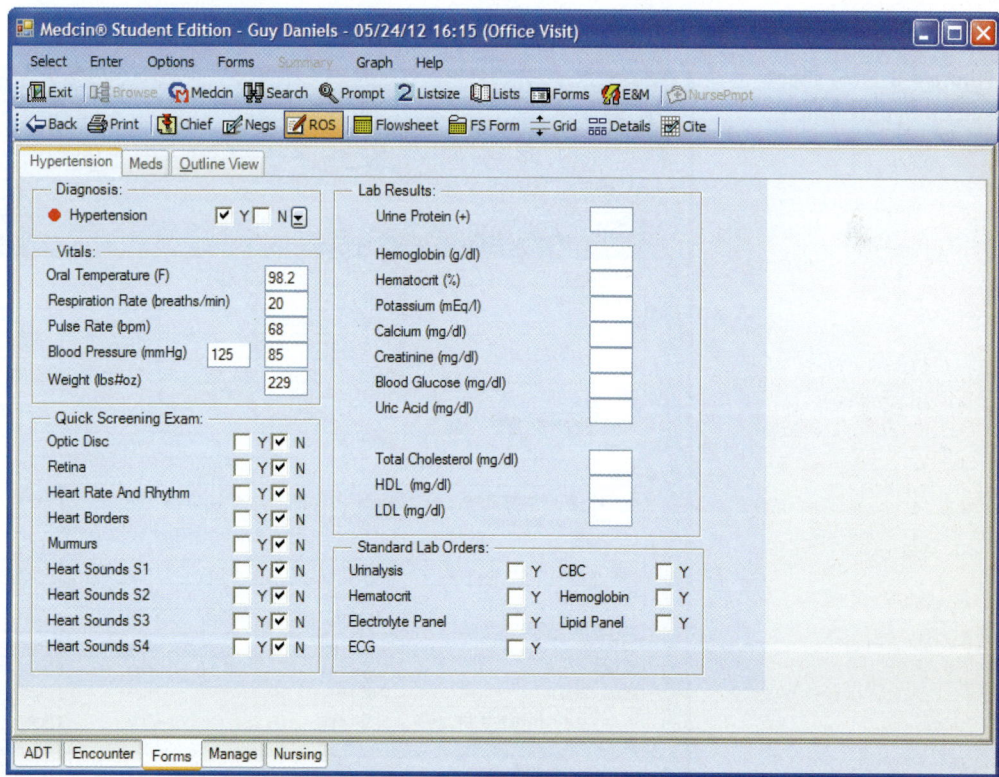

Step 6

The clinician performs the Quick Screening exam.

Chapter 8 | Data Entry Using Flow Sheets and Anatomical Drawings

Locate and click on ROS button in the Toolbar near the top of your screen. The button should appear orange.

Locate and click the Negs (auto negative) button to quickly document the clinician's physical findings.

Compare your screen to Figure 8-5.

Step 7

You may have noticed previously that the Toolbar near the top of your screen has additional buttons when you are on the Forms tab. Two of the buttons are used for invoking the Flow Sheet view. One button creates a flow sheet based on a form and the other creates a flow sheet based on a problem or list. In this exercise, you will learn to create a flow sheet based on the form.

To invoke the Flow Sheet view of Guy Daniels's chart, follow these steps:

Click on the button labeled List Size until the list size is set to 1.

Locate and click on the button labeled "FS Form" in the Toolbar near the top of your screen. (The icon resembles a file folder with a grid pattern.)

The screen will change to the Flow Sheet view. The button should now be orange.

The FS Form button is used to view a flow sheet when you are in the Forms tab.

▶ Figure 8-6 Flow sheet based on Hypertension Form.

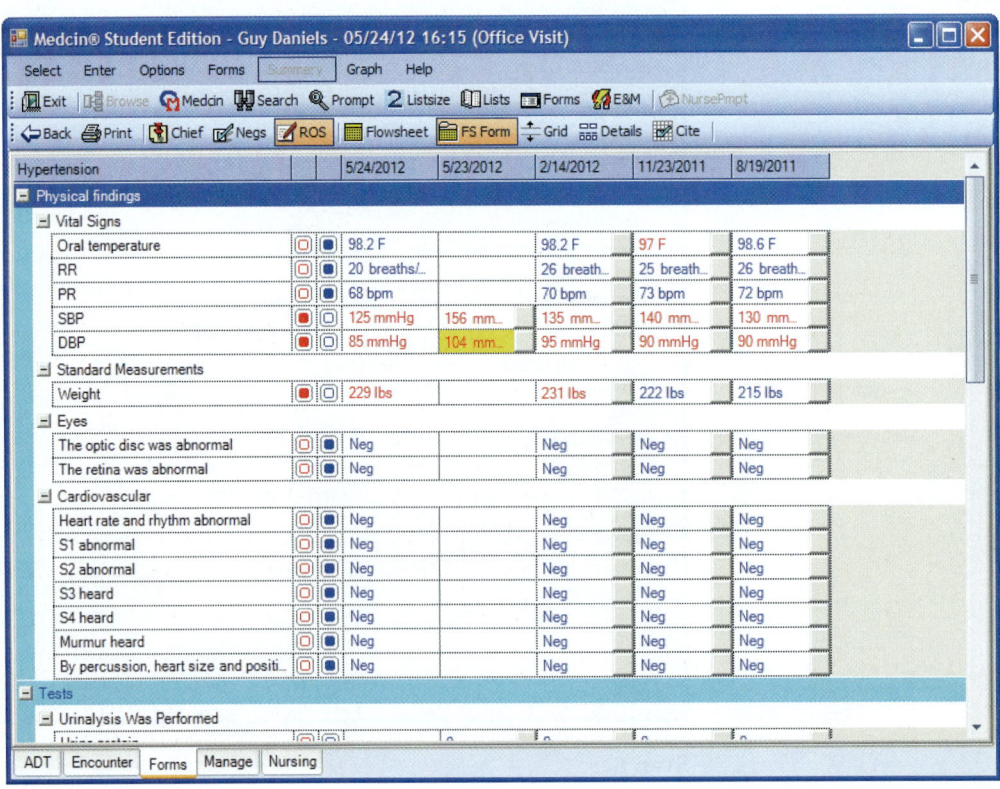

Compare your screen to Figure 8-6 as you read the following information.

About the Flow Sheet View The Flow Sheet view resembles a spreadsheet similar to Microsoft Excel® or Lotus 1-2-3®; that is, it is made up of rows and columns of "cells." The first column displays descriptions as well as red and blue buttons for findings on the current form. The date of the current encounter is at the top of the column. The remaining columns to the right display encounter data from previous visits.

The flow sheet rows are grouped vertically into logical sections that match the sections you are accustomed to seeing in the encounter note. The title of each section is printed in blue on a teal background. For example, sections in Guy Daniels's flow sheet are titled "Physical Findings" and "Tests," "Assessment," and "Plan." A small plus or minus sign next to the section title allows you to collapse or expand the findings below it. Functionally, this is comparable to the ability to expand or collapse trees in the Nomenclature Pane or to expand folders in the Outline view.

The list of findings in the first column and how they are displayed is determined by the way the flow sheet is invoked as follows:

FS Form—When a flow sheet is invoked from a form, the software uses the data elements on the form to populate the first column.

Problem—If the flow sheet were invoked instead from the Problem List on the Manage tab, the first column would be populated with findings pertinent to the selected problem in the Problem List.

List—A third type of Flow Sheet view can be created from a list. When a list is used, the first column of the flow sheet is populated with findings in the list, findings that are within the tree view of the list, and findings of similar body systems.

Step 8

The columns on the right display the dates of previous visits. The cells within the column display the words POS (in red) or NEG (in blue), or a numerical value for the finding. A blank cell indicates no finding was recorded on that encounter date.

Each cell that has a finding recorded can display only one field of data. Where there is more than one type of data (for example, if entry detail fields have been used for a finding), the cell will contain a button with an ellipsis (three dots). Clicking on the ellipsis button will invoke a small window allowing you to view the additional details.

Try this yourself. Locate the row under vital signs labeled RR (respiration rate); next, locate the column dated 02/14/2012; now position your mouse on the gray ellipsis button in the cell containing the value "26 breaths." Click on the ellipsis button.

▶ **Figure 8-7** Data Details window invoked from Ellipsis button for 02/14/2012 Respiration Rate.

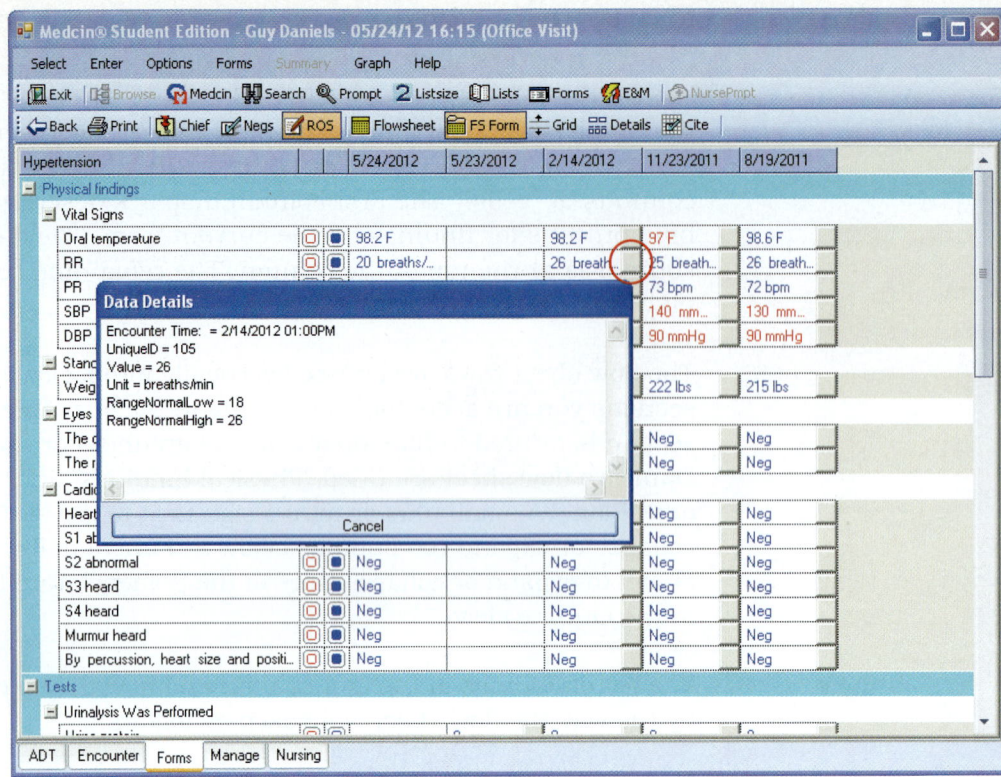

A Data Details window will be invoked, as shown in Figure 8-7.

When you have finished looking at the data details, click on the button labeled "Cancel" to close the data details window.

▶ **Figure 8-8** Narrative window of previous encounter (02/14/2012).

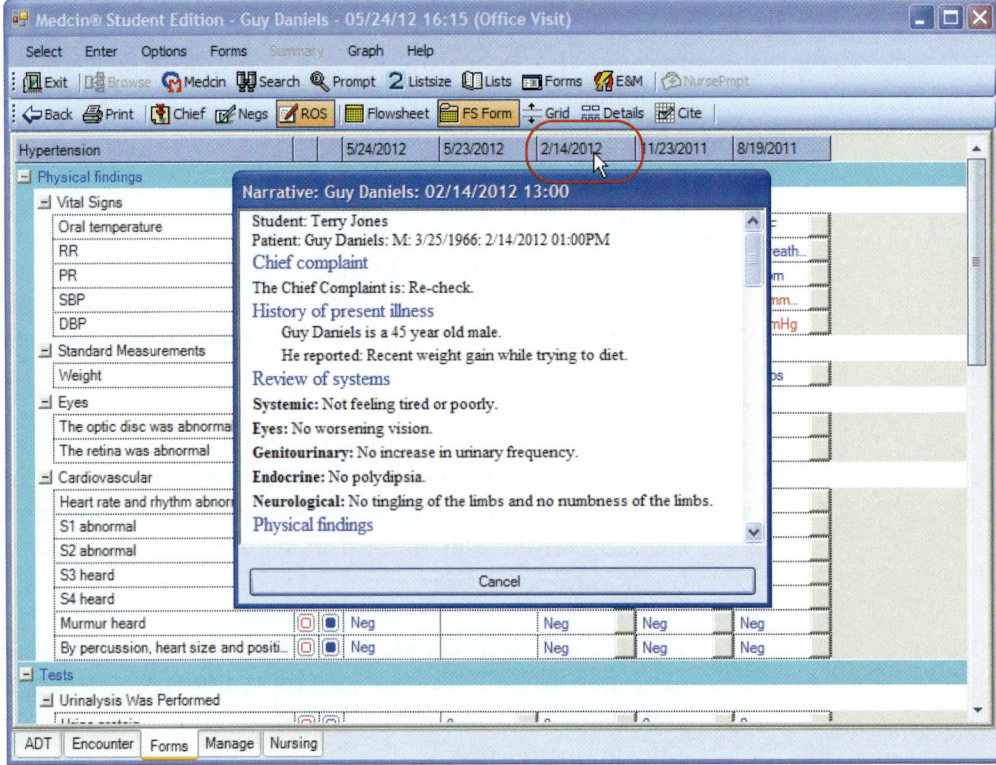

Step 9

The full encounter note for any previous encounter can be viewed by positioning the mouse over the date at the top of any of the columns on the right and clicking the mouse on the date.

Locate and click on the column header date **02/14/2012**.

(Note that you must click on the date itself, not on the row or spaces adjoining it.)

A window displaying the full encounter note will be invoked. Compare your screen to Figure 8-8.

Click on the Cancel button to close the Narrative window for 2/14/2012.

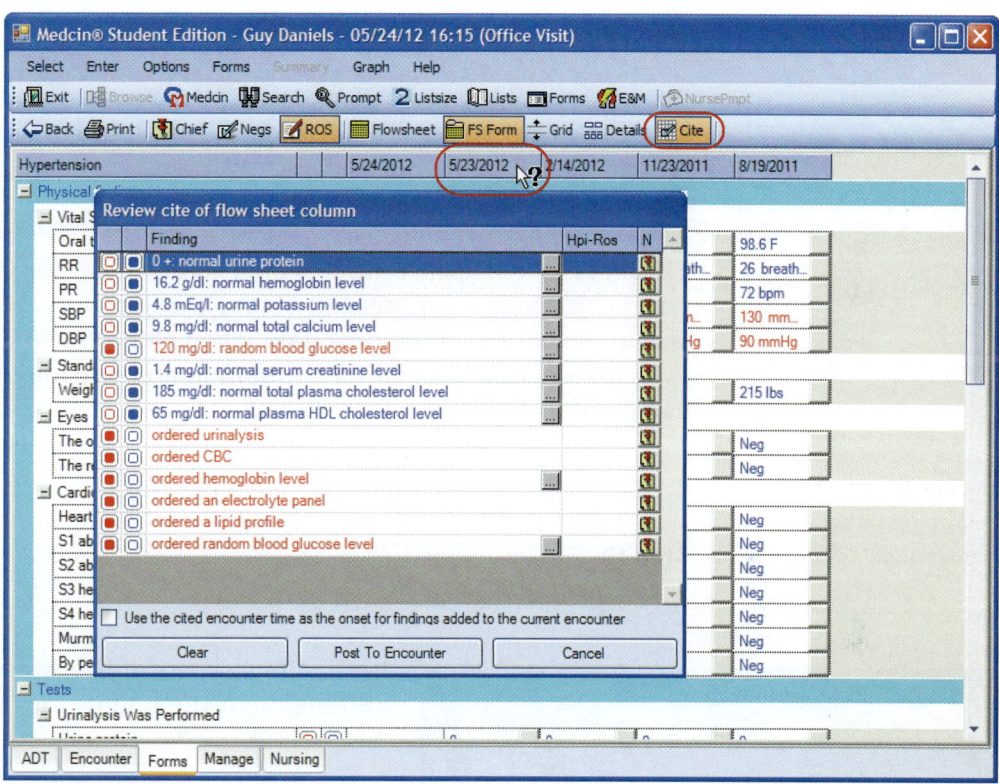

▶ Figure 8-9 Window used to cite items from previous encounter into current encounter.

Step 10

Locate and click on the button labeled "Cite" in the Toolbar at the top of your screen. The button icon resembles a teal check mark over a grid. Whenever Cite mode is enabled, the Cite button will be orange. (The Cite button is circled in red in Figure 8-9.)

Cite is used to bring information forward from previous encounters into the current one. The information can be updated as it is brought forward. The findings also could be edited after they are in the current encounter, but the Cite feature allows you to bring the finding into the current note and edit it in one step.

Chapter 8 | Data Entry Using Flow Sheets and Anatomical Drawings   307

Step 11

When the Cite button is on (orange), clicking on the date of a column header will invoke a different window. The "Review cite" window will list findings from that encounter instead of the encounter narrative. The Cite button changes which window is invoked. When the Cite button is on, a window of findings is invoked; when it is off, the Narrative window is invoked.

When the Cite button is on, the mouse pointer will change to resemble a large question mark whenever you move over the cells of the flow sheet. With the cite button **on**, position the mouse pointer on the column header date **05/23/2012**, as shown in Figure 8-9, and click the mouse.

(Note that you must click on the date itself, not on the row or spaces adjoining it.)

A window of findings from the May 23 2012, encounter will be invoked. Compare your screen to Figure 8-9.

The red and blue buttons for each finding are used to select the finding just as they are elsewhere in the software. The description of the finding will include any numerical values entered in the previous encounter. Two additional buttons appear on the right of each finding.

The first is the Ellipsis button, which you used in step 7 to view results. However, when Cite mode is on, instead of displaying results, the Ellipsis button allows you to modify any numerical data when citing the finding. The second button (whose icon resembles a red pushpin in a note pad) is used to add a free-text comment to a finding when citing it.

Step 12

A new glucose test has been performed.

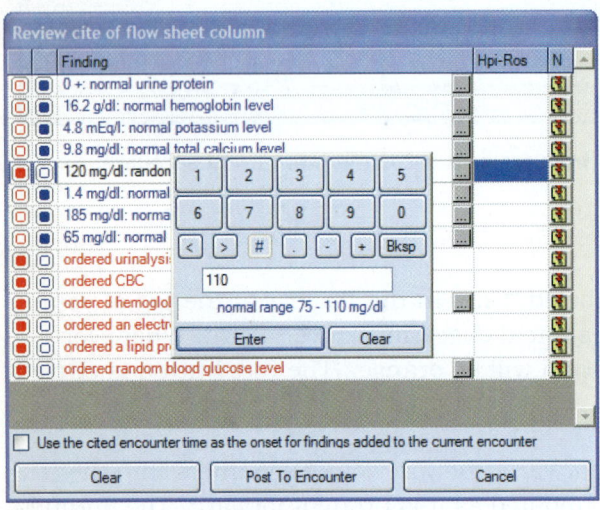

▶ Figure 8-10 Modify numeric values of finding in Cite window with Ellipsis button.

In the "Review cite of flow sheet column" window, locate and highlight the finding for the "random blood glucose test" result.

Click on the ellipsis button for that finding. A small window resembling a calculator will appear.

Use your mouse to point to the numeric buttons and click on each number to change the previous test result from 120 to the current test result 110.

(You can also type the numbers on a keyboard.)

Click the number buttons **1 1** and **0**. Compare your screen to Figure 8-10, and then click on the button labeled "**Enter**." This will record your modification and close the number pad.

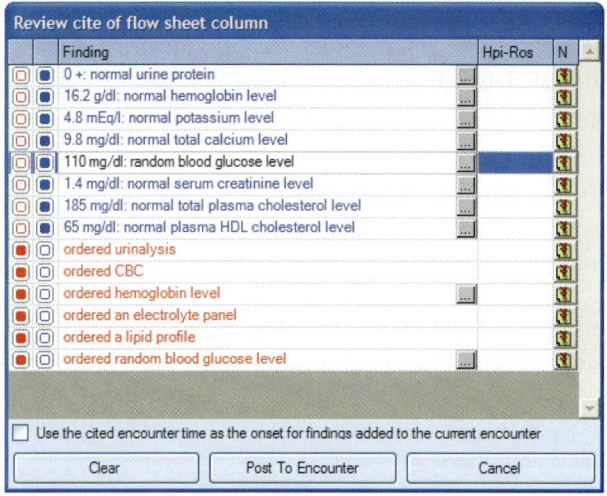

▶ Figure 8-11 Random blood glucose level after modification.

Step 13

From the Cite window you can also select or deselect the red or blue buttons for any of the findings listed. Although it may appear that you are editing a past encounter, you are not. You are simply selecting and editing the findings that will copy to the current encounter. Do not be concerned that this will change any of the findings in a previous encounter.

Compare your screen to Figure 8-11.

Click on the button labeled "Post To Encounter" to cite the findings.

Step 14

Individual findings can be cited without invoking the cite review window. When the Cite button is on, instead of positioning the mouse pointer on the date in the column header to invoke a window, you can position the mouse pointer on an individual cell of the flow sheet and click the mouse button. The data from that specific cell will be copied into the current encounter.

Scroll the flow sheet downward until you can see all the rows of the section labeled "Tests."

Locate the finding "Plasma LDL cholesterol" in the last row of that section.

Position your mouse pointer in that row, under the column dated 02/14/2012; click the mouse on the cell that reads "120 mg/dl," as shown in Figure 8-12.

▶ Figure 8-12 Cite the individual finding plasma LDL from the 02/14/2012 column.

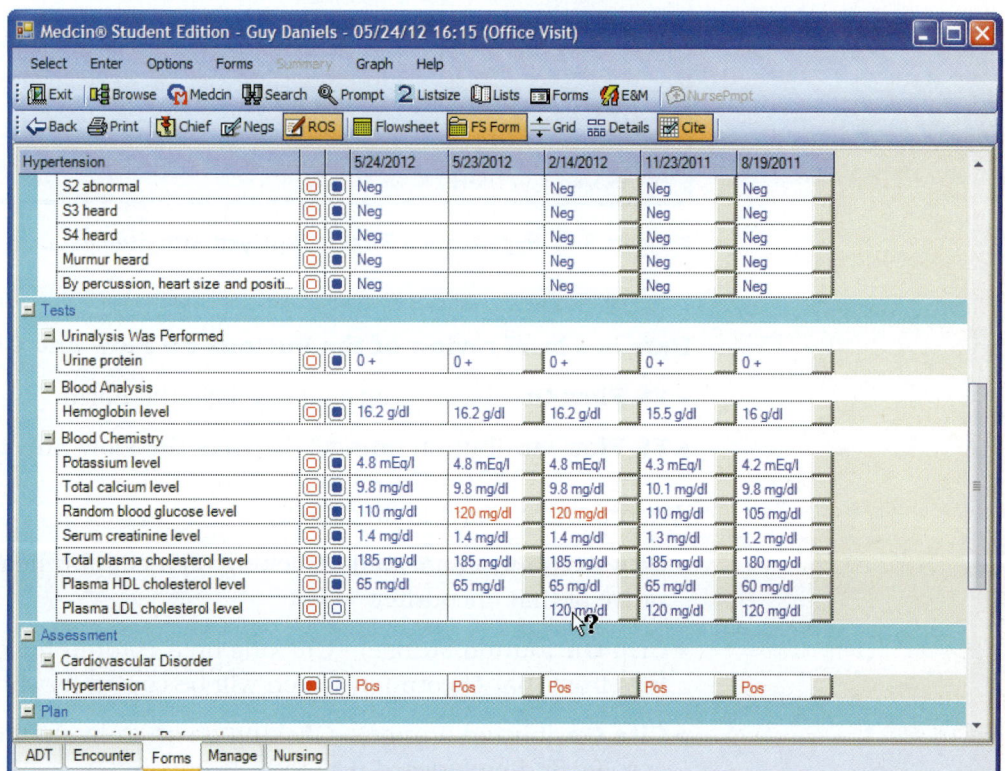

Chapter 8 | Data Entry Using Flow Sheets and Anatomical Drawings   309

This will cite a normal Plasma LDL in the column for the current encounter.

Locate and click on the button labeled "Cite" in the Toolbar at the top of your screen. This will turn Cite off.

Step 15

As you learned earlier in this exercise, this FS form button acts like a toggle, shifting the screen between the flow sheet view and the form view.

Locate and click on the button labeled "FS Form" in the Toolbar at the top of your screen. The form will redisplay. Compare your screen to Figure 8-13; notice the lab results in the center of the screen now have values that have been filled by using Cite.

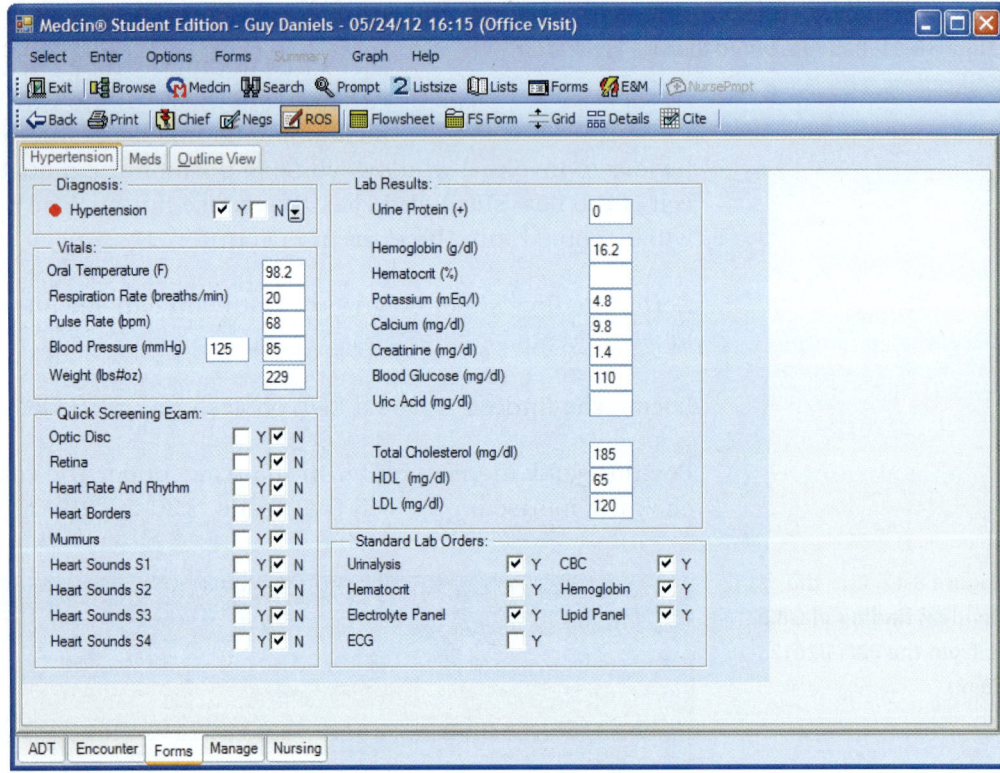

▶ Figure 8-13 Hypertension Form redisplayed with cited data.

Here is a brief review of the buttons FS Flow and Cite:

◆ **FS Flow Off** (button normal) displays the Form.

◆ **FS Flow On** (button orange) displays the Flow Sheet view.

When the flow sheet is displayed:

◆ **Cite Off** (button normal)—Clicking on a column header date invokes the narrative of that encounter.

◆ **Cite On** (button orange)—Clicking on a column header date invokes the findings from that encounter, which will be copied forward into today's encounter.

◆ **Cite On** (button orange)—Clicking on an individual cell will copy only the specific finding forward into today's encounter.

310   Chapter 8 | Data Entry Using Flow Sheets and Anatomical Drawings

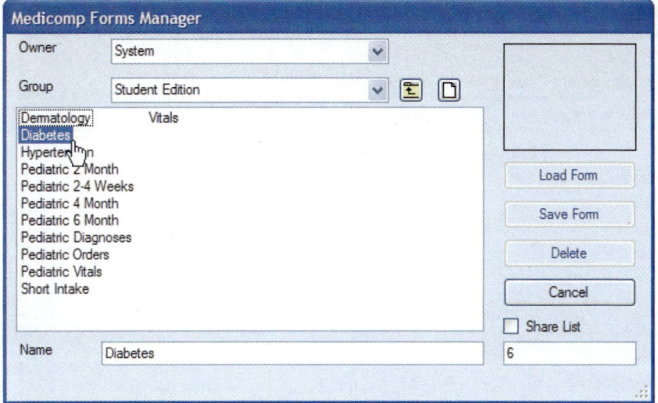

▶ Figure 8-14 Selecting the Diabetes Form from the Form Manager window.

▶ Figure 8-15 Diabetes Form shows data entered on Hypertension Form.

Step 16

To document the patient's second problem, locate and click on the Forms button in the Toolbar at the top of your screen.

Select and load the form for diabetes (as shown in Figure 8-14).

Step 17

Compare your screen to Figure 8-15. Notice that vital signs and several of the fields on the diabetes form already contain data, because these findings were entered on the hypertension form. As mentioned earlier, any findings already in the current encounter will appear automatically as you change forms.

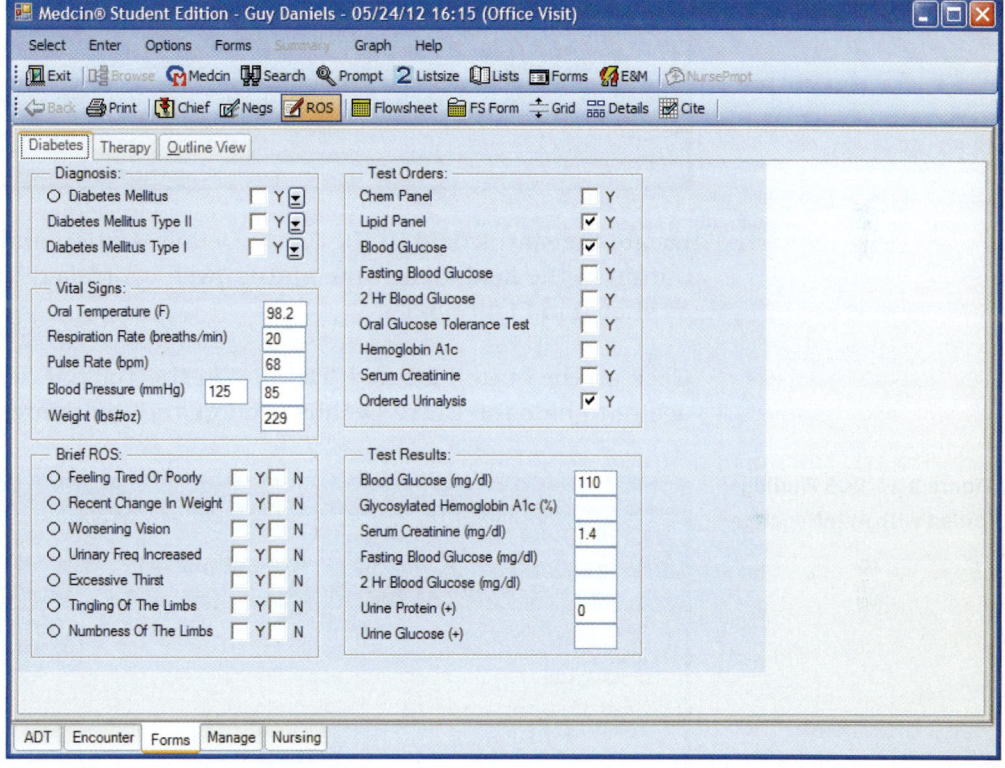

Step 18

Record the second diagnosis.

Locate the diagnosis Diabetes Mellitus Type II at the top of the form. Click on the check box next to the **Y**. A circle next to the finding will turn red.

Locate and click on the button labeled "Details" in the Toolbar at the top of your screen. This will open the Entry Details section over the bottom of the form.

In previous exercises, you have used the Details button to hide the details entry fields. In this step, we will display the fields so the status of the disease can be updated.

▶ Figure 8-16 Setting the diagnosis diabetes mellitus well controlled.

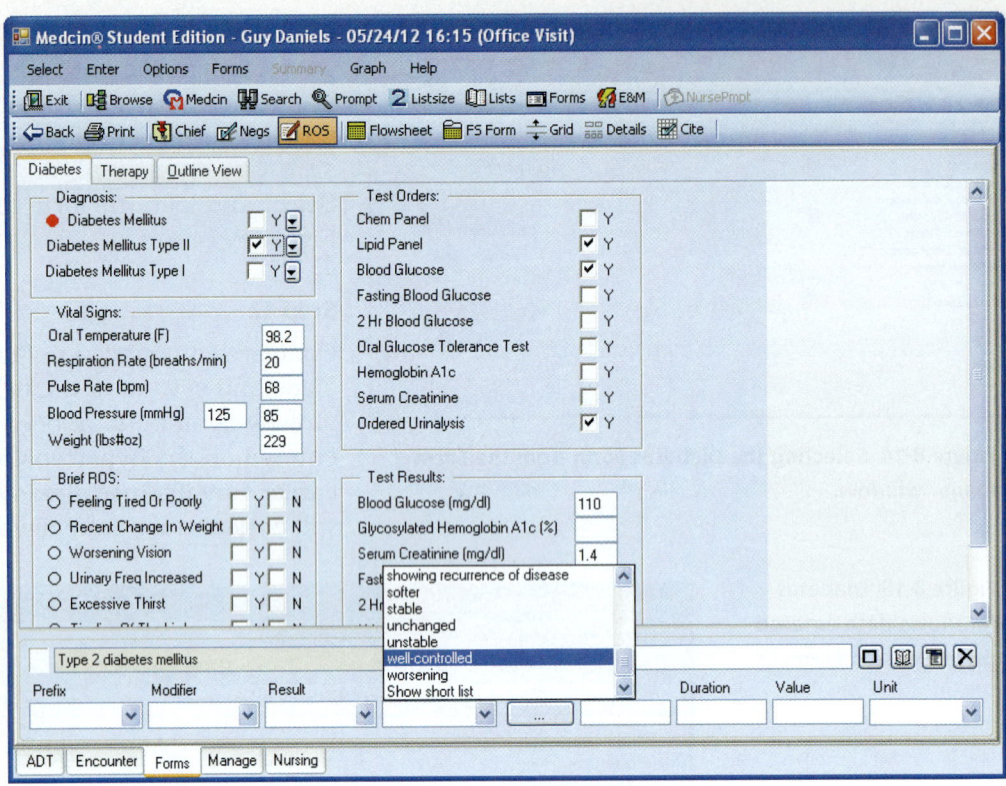

Locate the status field in the Entry Details section and click on the down arrow button in the field. Select the status "well controlled" from the drop-down list, as shown in Figure 8-16.

Click on the button labeled "Details" in the Toolbar at the top of your screen again, to hide the Entry Details section and to restore the full view of the form.

▶ Figure 8-17 ROS Findings recorded with AutoNegative.

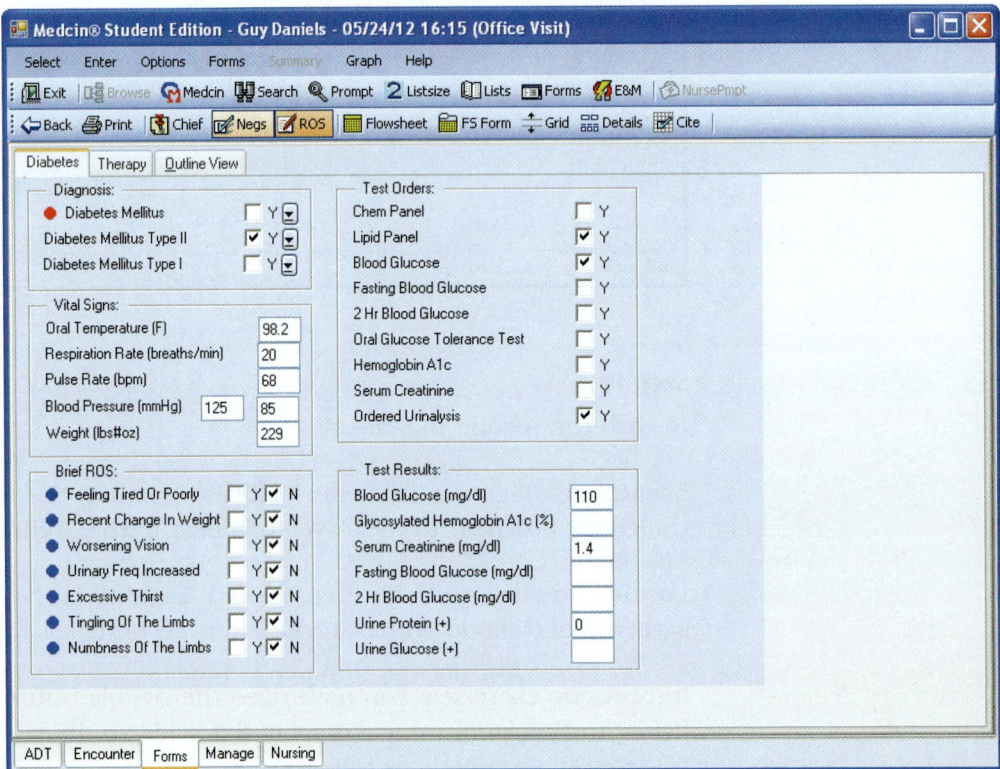

312 Chapter 8 | Data Entry Using Flow Sheets and Anatomical Drawings

Step 19

Verify that the ROS button is still on, and then click on the button labeled "Negs" (Auto Negative) in the Toolbar near the top of your screen.

Compare your screen to Figure 8-17.

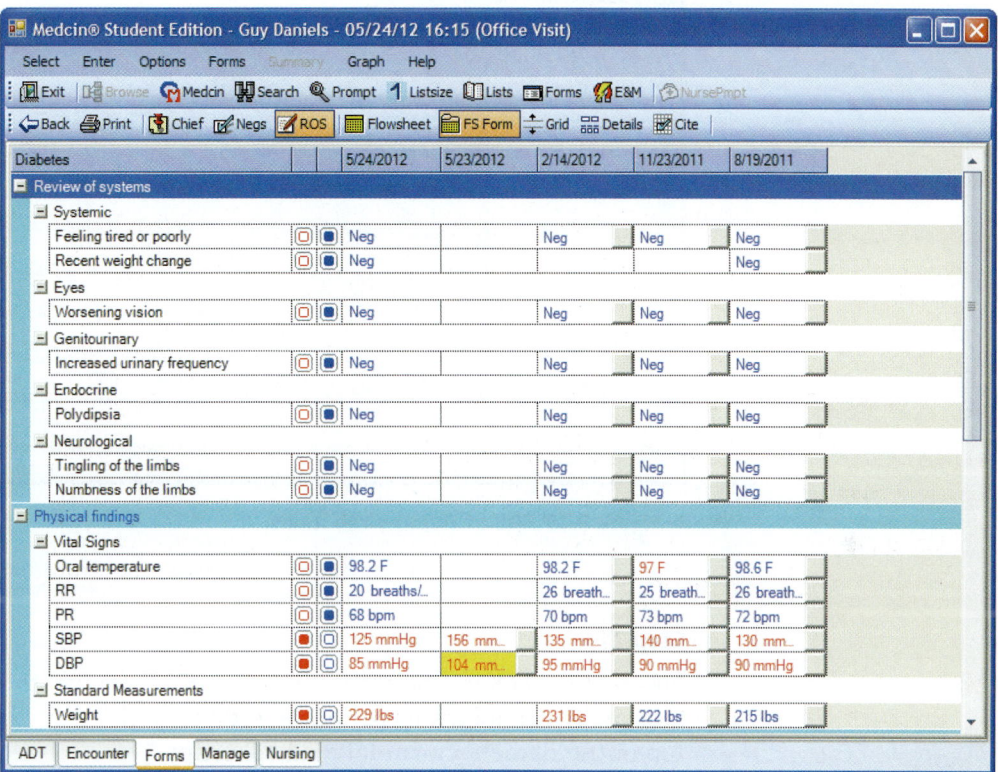

▶ **Figure 8-18** Flow Sheet view based on Diabetic Form.

Step 20

Not all findings from previous encounters are displayed in a form-based flow sheet. Only those findings that match the items in the form design are listed in the columns. Similarly, flow sheets based on a list only display findings that match the list. This step will demonstrate the difference a form design makes in a flow sheet.

Verify that the List Size is still set to **1**; if it is not, then locate and click on the List Size button until it is **1**.

Locate and click on the button labeled "FS Form" in the Toolbar at the top of your screen. The diabetes flow sheet will be displayed. Your screen should resemble Figure 8-18.

Turn back in your book and compare your screen with the earlier flow sheet shown in Figure 8-6. Notice that the diabetes flow sheet has a review of system section, which the hypertension does not. There also are differences in the tests ordered for the two diseases. From this comparison, you can easily see how the flow sheets for diabetes and hypertension differ.

Chapter 8 | Data Entry Using Flow Sheets and Anatomical Drawings   313

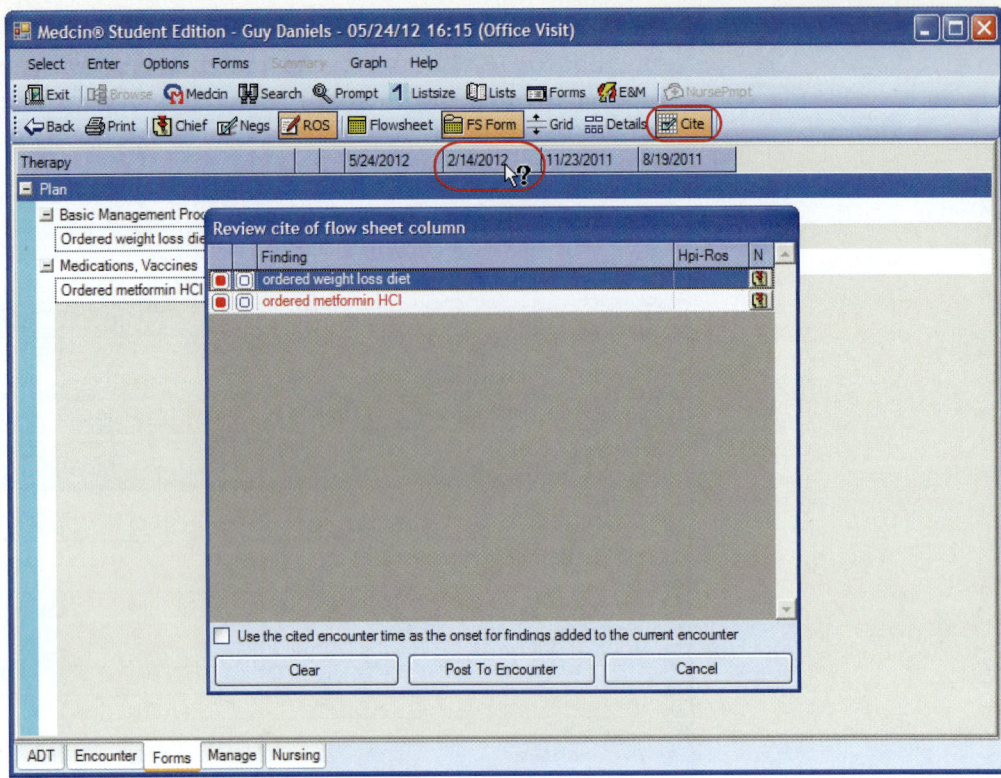

▶ Figure 8-19 Cite of Therapy tab items.

Step 21

Locate and click on the button labeled "FS Form" in the Toolbar at the top of your screen. The diabetes form will be redisplayed. Locate and click on the tab at the top of the diabetes form labeled "Therapy."

Locate and click on the button labeled "FS Form" in the Toolbar at the top of your screen. The flow sheet of the diabetes plan will be displayed.

Locate and click the Cite button on as you did early in this chapter (the button will appear orange).

Locate and click on the column header date **02/14/2012**.

A small window of findings from that encounter will appear. Compare your screen to the review cite findings window in Figure 8-19. Notice that because these findings do not have numerical values, the gray ellipsis button is not present.

There also are fewer findings to cite. This is partly because of the items on the form, but also because the Cite feature is intelligent. It omits findings already recorded in the current encounter during previous steps of the exercise.

After you have looked at the findings that are displayed, click the button labeled "Post To Encounter" to cite the findings.

Because one of the items in the list is a prescription, the prescription writer window will be invoked automatically.

Step 22

The prescription is for metformin HCL. The prescription writer will display the Rx dosage inquiry window, as shown in Figure 8-20.

Locate and click on the Rx dosage **500 mg tab**; the window will next display a list of manufacturers.

Click on the default manufacturer when that window is displayed.

Step 23

Using what you have learned in Chapter 6, enter the following prescription information in the appropriate fields.

Sig

    Quantity: **1**

    Freq: **Twice daily**

    Per Day: **2**

    Days: **30**

Dispense

    Amount: **60**

    Refill: **3**

Generic

    Locate and click on the circle next to **Yes**.

Compare your screen to Figure 8-21. When everything is correct, click on the button labeled "Save Rx."

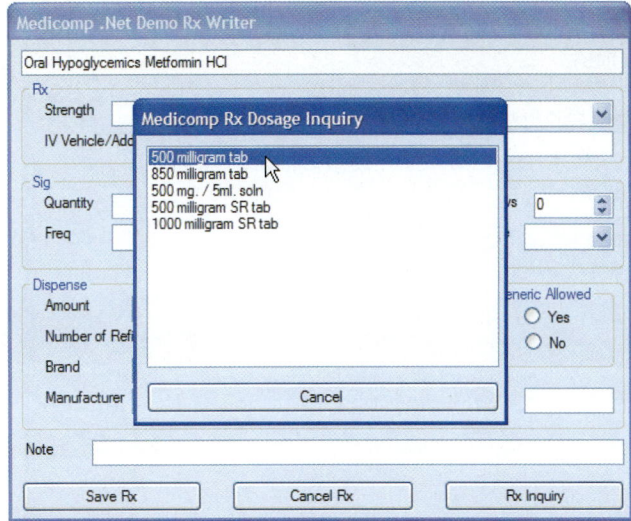

▶ **Figure 8-20** Select 500 mg metformin HCL.

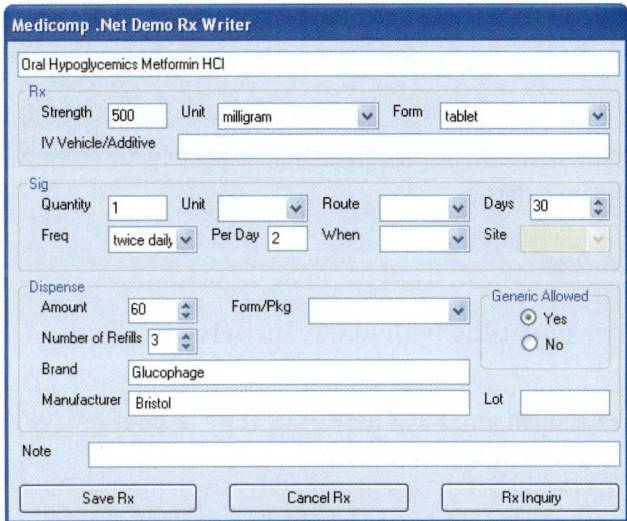

▶ **Figure 8-21** Writing Guy Daniels's prescription for Metformin HCL.

Step 24

Locate and click on the button labeled "Cite" in the Toolbar at the top of your screen to turn Cite off.

Locate and click on the button labeled "FS Form" in the Toolbar at the top of your screen to return to the view of the form. If the form is not on the Therapy tab, locate and click on the tab labeled "Therapy" (at the top of the form).

Locate the section labeled "Dietary Orders" in the upper right corner of the form. Note that Weight Loss should already have a check next to the Y. This box was checked by citing the findings in step 21.

Click the check box next to **Y** for the following findings:

✓ **Y** Diabetic (diet)

✓ **Y** Controlled Carbohydrate

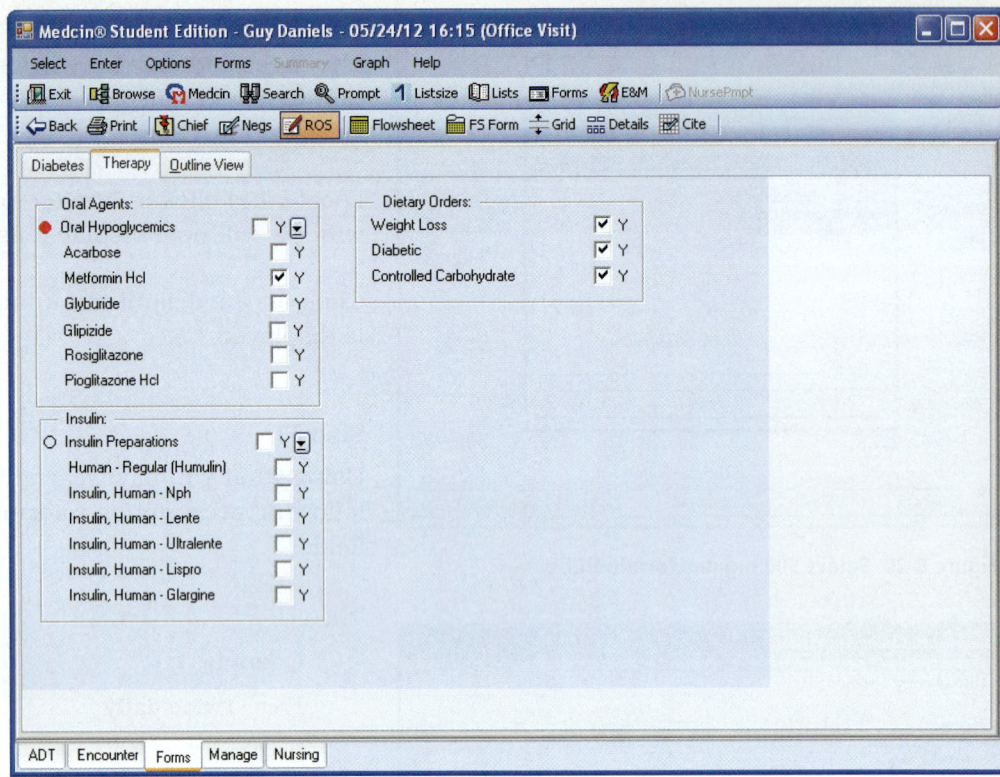

▶ Figure 8-22 Diabetic Form—enter dietary orders.

Compare your screen to Figure 8-22.

Locate and click on the Encounter tab at the bottom of your screen.

 **Alert** — Do not close or exit the encounter until you have a printed copy in your hand. You will lose your work if you exit before printing.

Step 25

Click on the Print button on the Toolbar at the top of your screen to invoke the Print Data window.

Be certain there is a check mark in the box next to "Current Encounter" and then click on the appropriate button to either print or export a file, as directed by your instructor.

Compare your printout or file output to Figure 8-23. If it is correct, hand it in to your instructor. If there are any differences, review the previous steps in the exercise and find your error.

> **You may stop at this point or, if time permits, you may continue with the next exercise without exiting.**

Guided Exercise 51: Creating a Problem-Oriented Flow Sheet

In this exercise, you are going to view a flow sheet that is focused on a particular problem, rather than a form.

316 Chapter 8 | Data Entry Using Flow Sheets and Anatomical Drawings

Guy Daniels   Page 1 of 1

Student: your name or ID here
Patient: Guy Daniels: M: 3/25/1966: 5/24/2012 04:15PM

Chief complaint
The Chief Complaint is: 3 month check up.

Review of systems
Systemic: Not feeling tired or poorly and no recent weight change.
Eyes: No worsening vision.
Genitourinary: No increase in urinary frequency.
Endocrine: No polydipsia.
Neurological: No tingling of the limbs and no numbness of the limbs.

Physical findings
Vital Signs:

Vital Signs/Measurements	Value	Normal Range
Oral temperature	98.2 F	97.6 - 99.6
RR	20 breaths/min	18 - 26
PR	68 bpm	50 - 100
Blood pressure	125/85 mmHg	100-120/60-80
Weight	229 lbs	125 - 225

Eyes:
    General/bilateral:
    Optic Disc: ° Normal.
    Retina: ° Normal.

Cardiovascular:
    Heart Rate And Rhythm: ° Normal.
    Heart Sounds: ° S1 normal. ° S2 normal. ° No S3 heard. ° No S4 heard.
    Murmurs: ° No murmurs were heard.
    Heart Borders: ° By percussion, heart size and position were normal.

Tests
Urinalysis Was Performed:

Urinalysis Results:	Value	Normal Range
Urine protein	0 +	

Blood Analysis:

Blood Counts - CBC:	Value	Normal Range
Hemoglobin level	16.2 g/dl	14 - 18

Blood Chemistry:

Electrolytes:	Value	Normal Range
Potassium level	4.8 mEq/l	3.5 - 5.5
Total calcium level	9.8 mg/dl	8.5 - 10.5
Endocrine Laboratory Tests:	Value	Normal Range
Random blood glucose level	110 mg/dl	75 - 110
Metabolic Tests:	Value	Normal Range
Serum creatinine level	1.4 mg/dl	0.7 - 1.5
Total plasma cholesterol level	185 mg/dl	140 - 200
Plasma HDL cholesterol level	65 mg/dl	30 - 70
Plasma LDL cholesterol level	120 mg/dl	80 - 130

Assessment
- Hypertension
- Type 2 diabetes mellitus which is well-controlled

Plan
- Urinalysis
- CBC
- Hemoglobin level
- An electrolyte panel
- A lipid profile
- Random blood glucose level
- Weight loss diet
- Diabetic diet
- Controlled carbohydrate diet
- Metformin HCl

500 mg tab (1 bid 30) DISP:60 Refill:3 Generic:Y Using:Glucophage Mfg: Bristol

▶ **Figure 8-23** Printed encounter note for Guy Daniels.

Alert

Make certain you set the date and time correctly for this exercise. If you need help, review Chapter 3, Guided Exercise 13.

Step 1

If you are continuing from the previous exercise, proceed to step 3.

Otherwise, start the Student Edition software.

Click Select on the Menu bar, and then click Patient.

In the Patient Selection window, locate and click on **Guy Daniels**.

Step 2

Click Select on the Menu bar, and then click New Encounter.

Select the date **May 24, 2012**, the time **4:15 PM**, and the reason **Office Visit**.

Make certain you set the date, time, and reason correctly. If necessary, refer to Figure 8-2.

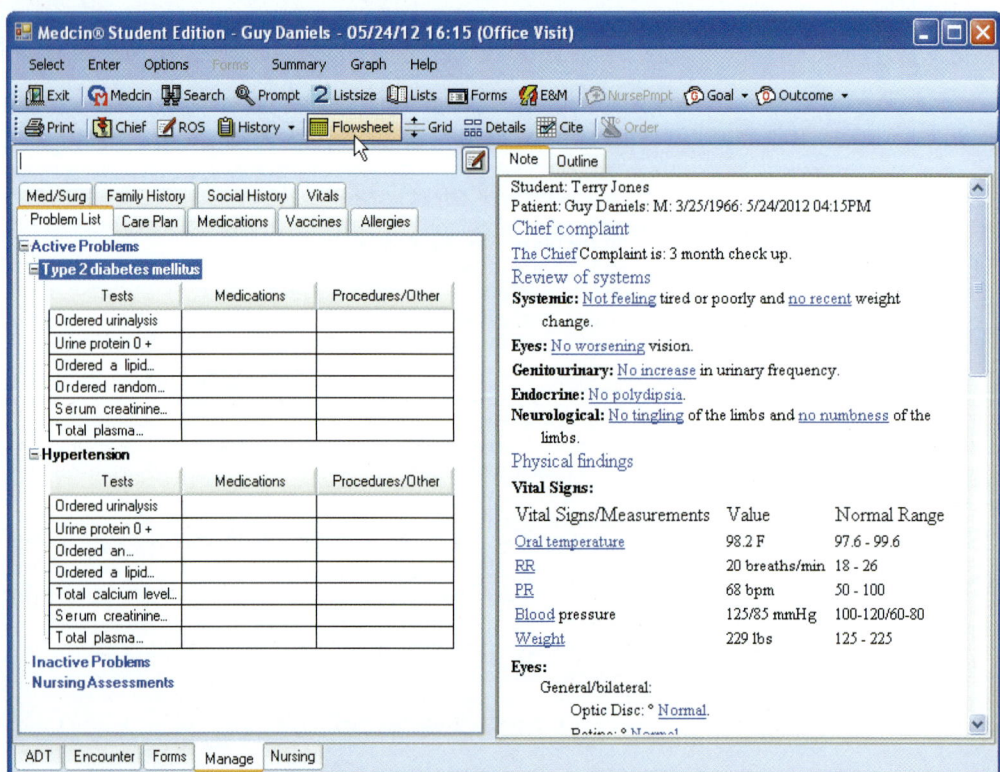

▶ Figure 8-24 Problem List for Guy Daniels.

Step 3

Locate and click on the Manage tab at the bottom of your screen.

If the left pane of your screen is not currently displaying the Problem List, click on the tab labeled "Problem List."

(Note that the right pane of Figure 8-24 is showing the encounter note as if you were continuing from the previous exercise. If you are not, the right pane will contain less information; that is acceptable for this exercise.)

318 Chapter 8 | Data Entry Using Flow Sheets and Anatomical Drawings

Step 4

Verify that the button labeled "List Size" in the Toolbar at the top of your screen is **1**. If it is not, click on it until the list size is 1.

Locate and click the Details button on the Toolbar to hide the Details section.

Locate and click on the diagnosis **Type 2 diabetes mellitus** in the problem list (left pane). This will highlight the diagnosis as shown in Figure 8-24.

Locate and click on the button labeled "Flowsheet" in the Toolbar at the top of your screen. (Note that this is not the FS Form button that you used in the previous exercise.)

A flow sheet similar to that in Figure 8-25 will be displayed.

▶ Figure 8-25 Flow sheet from Problem List for Guy Daniels.

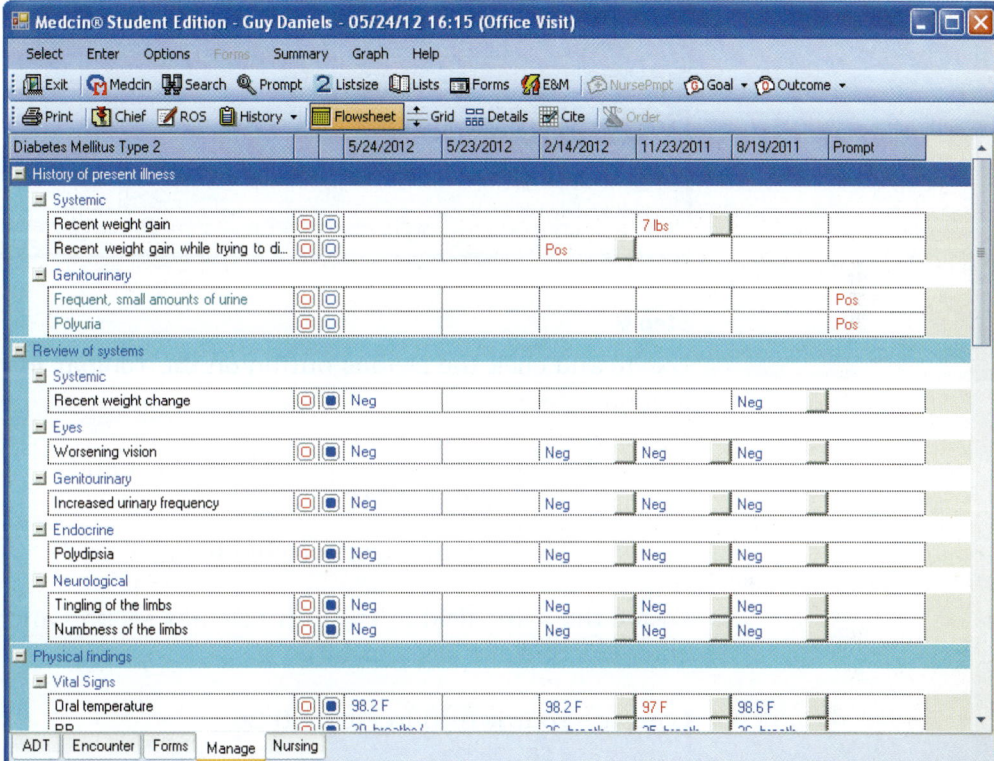

Step 5

Turn back to Figure 8-16. Compare your screen to the flow sheet in that figure.

The purpose of a problem-oriented flow sheet is to provide a historical view of the patient's data pertinent to the current problem. The difference in this type of flow sheet is that it is not constrained by the design of the form. Any finding related to the selected problem will be listed in the flow sheet.

The function of the Cite button is the same in either flow sheet. That is, Cite can be used to copy relevant findings into the current encounter.

As you learned in the previous chapter, most clinicians use a Problem List at some point during the examination. The ability to quickly view and cite from a flow sheet specific to the problem not only can speed up the documentation process but also can ensure that the clinician recalls significant findings from previous visits.

▶ Figure 8-26 Weight Change -2 lbs.

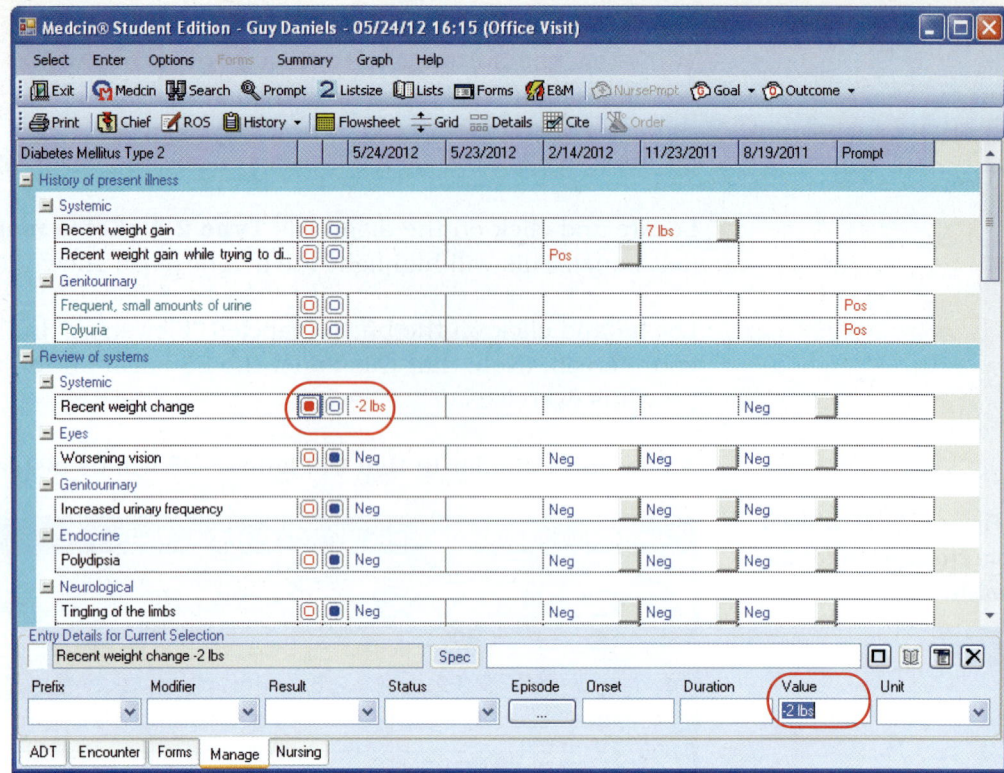

Step 6

Locate and click the Details button on the Toolbar to restore the Details Entry section.

Locate the following finding in the flow sheet and click on the red button in the column dated **05/24/2012**.

- (red button) recent weight change

Locate the Value field in the Entry Details section and type **-2 lbs**. Press the enter key on your keyboard.

Compare your screen to Figure 8-26.

Step 7

Ask your instructor if you should print another copy of Guy Daniel's encounter note. If so instructed, follow the directions in step 25 of the previous exercise. Note that if you did not continue from the previous exercise, your print out will contain less data. This is acceptable for the purposes of this exercise.

Use of Anatomical Drawings in the EHR

Another method of entering data about the patient into the EHR involves the use of anatomical drawings of the body and body systems. These drawings are used in two different ways, as an alternative method of navigating the Nomenclature or by actually annotating a drawing and including it in the patient record. In this chapter we will discuss both. Anatomical drawings are particularly easy to navigate or annotate on a Tablet PC, but the same or similar result can be achieved on a laptop or workstation computer using a mouse.

Navigation by Body System

Some EHR systems have navigation pages that allow the clinician to quickly locate findings by pointing to a particular body part in a drawing that opens a list of findings relevant to that body system. The clinician then selects the findings appropriate to the visit. In this case, the pictures do not become part of the patient note; they are just a visual tool for navigation (see Figure 8-27 for an example). Think of this as searching with pictures rather than words.

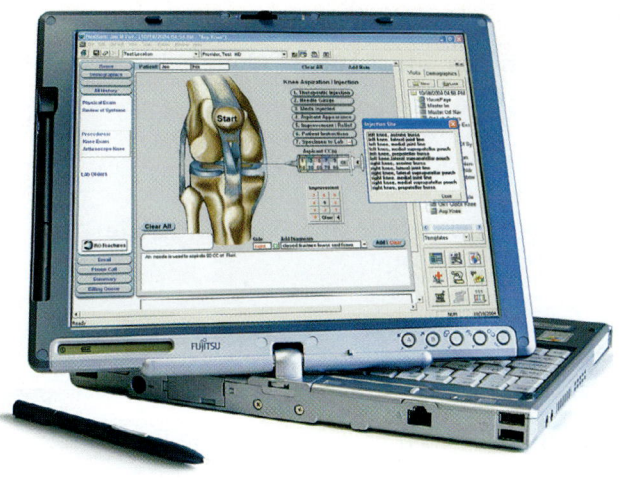

Courtesy of NextGen.

▶ **Figure 8-27 Entering findings using an image on a Tablet PC.**

Annotated Drawings as EHR Data

Another type of EHR data is the visual representation of the finding. Certain specialties routinely record information about the physical exam in the form of drawings or sketches. Two examples are dermatologists, who sometimes note the location of nevi (moles) on an outline of the body, and ophthalmologists, who frequently document observations on a drawing of the eye. These annotated drawings have long been a part of the patient's paper chart and most EHR systems today support a tool to annotate drawings in the computer. The images created using the tools in the EHR become part of the electronic encounter. Annotated drawings are also useful for patient education, as we shall see in a later exercise.

Annotated images in an EHR are often attached to the note using special findings. These images might be annotated with the size and location of nevi, but handwritten notes within the images are not codified data. This means that for the purpose of subsequent analysis of the EHR records, the system will be able to locate patient records with a finding that denotes an attached image, but it would not be able to find patients with "> 20 nevi" unless the clinician had entered them as findings in the narrative as well.

Guided Exercise 52: Annotated Dermatology Exam

This exercise will give you an opportunity to practice the annotation of a drawing using a simplified tool in the Student Edition software. As with previous exercises, the purpose here is to let you experience a function that is often available in commercial EHR systems. The drawing tools you will use here will be similar in principle but not identical to those you might use in your medical office. The method of invoking the annotation tool and the manner in which a drawing is subsequently merged into the patient note will vary by EHR vendor.

Case Study

Arnie Greensher is a 66-year-old male who has a large number of moles on his back, the result of years of working in the sun without a shirt. His doctor has been monitoring them through regular follow-up visits. In addition to the encounter notes created at those visits, the clinician finds it useful to save annotated drawings, which show the placement of the moles. In subsequent visits, the doctor will compare the drawings from past encounters to the current state of the patient's skin to quickly identify new moles or changes from a previous visit.

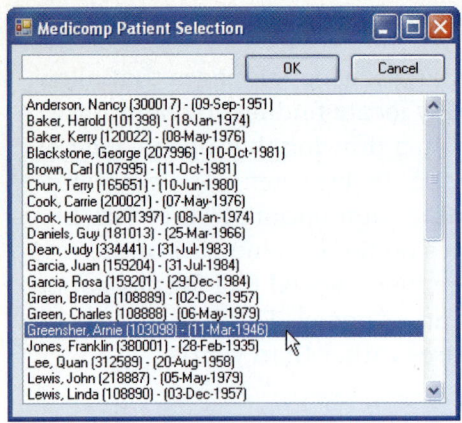

▶ **Figure 8-28** Select Patient Arnie Greensher.

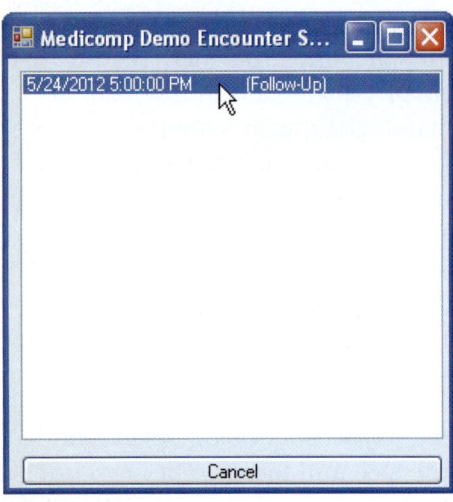

▶ **Figure 8-29** Select existing encounter for May 24, 2012.

▶ **Figure 8-30** Patient encounter note for May 24, 2012 encounter.

Step 1

If you have not already done so, start the Student Edition software.

Click Select on the Menu bar, and then click Patient.

In the Patient Selection window, locate and click on **Arnie Greensher**, as shown in Figure 8-28.

Step 2

Click Select on the Menu bar, and then click Existing Encounter.

A small window of previous encounters will be displayed. Compare your screen to the window shown in Figure 8-29.

Select the encounter dated **5/24/2012 5:00 PM** (Follow-Up).

The encounter note from that date will be displayed as shown in Figure 8-30.

Step 3

In the right pane of your screen, locate and click on the underlined portion of the finding labeled "Lesions on the back" (circled in red). The left pane should change to Edit view, as shown in Figure 8-30.

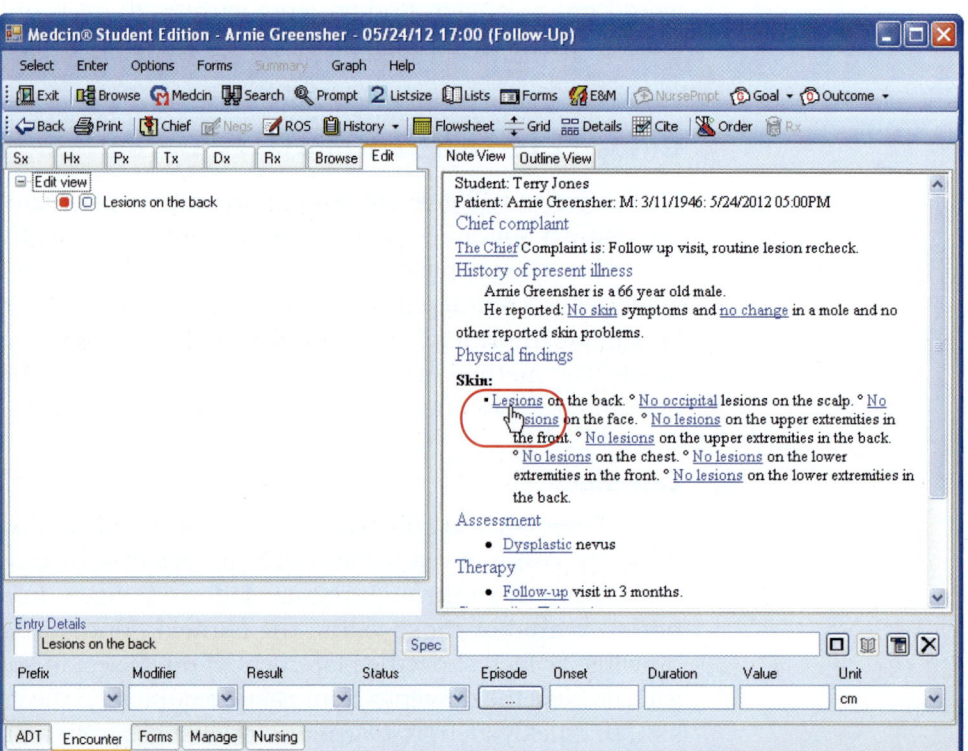

322 **Chapter 8** | Data Entry Using Flow Sheets and Anatomical Drawings

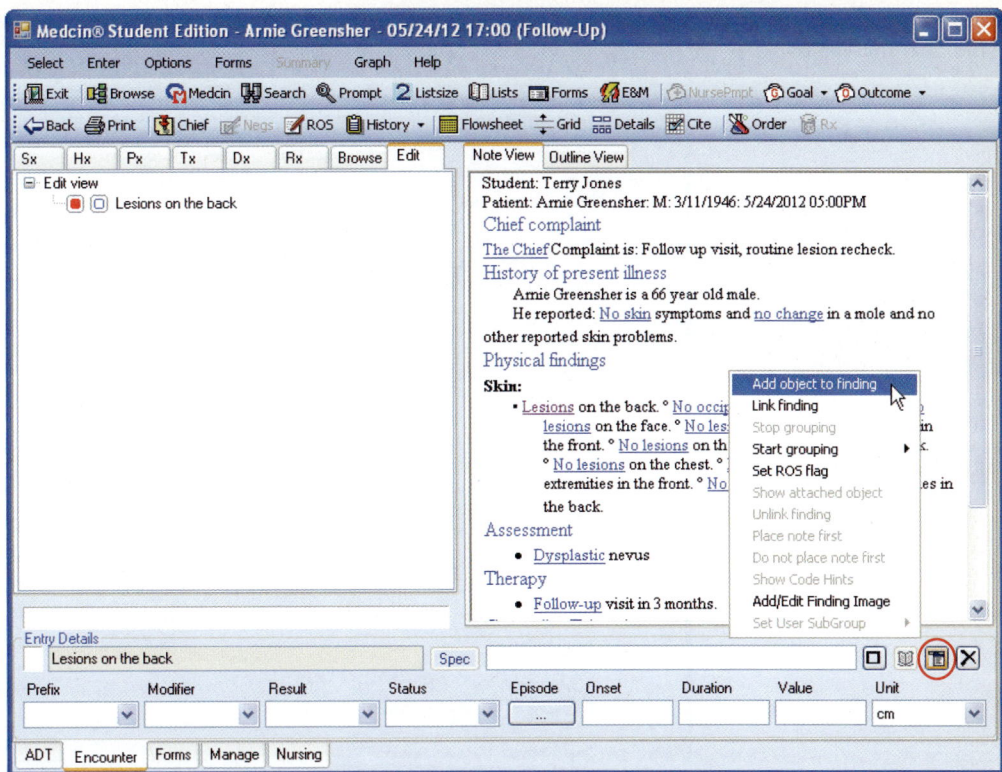

▶ Figure 8-31 Click the Context button (circled in red) and select "Add Object to Finding."

Step 4

Locate the four buttons in the lower right corner of the window. The Context button is the second button from the right (circled in red in Figure 8-31).

Click on the Context button to display a list of advanced actions that can be used with a finding.

Click the first option in the list labeled "Add object to finding." This will invoke the annotation tools in the right pane of the window (shown in Figure 8-32).

The software contains various anatomical illustrations, which may be selected for annotation. The right pane displays one of the images.

Above the image is a navigational bar consisting of three fields with drop-down lists. These are used to select images of other body systems and views.

◆ The first field can be used to select the body system to be presented (skin, circulatory, skeletal, and so on).

◆ The center field is used to select the image region within that system (full body, head and neck, lower extremities, and so on).

◆ The third field is used to select the view of the image (front, back, left, and so on).

◆ The gender of the image as well as the age range of the image is automatically determined by the demographics of the current patient. The default body system for the image is automatically determined by the selected finding.

▶ **Figure 8-32** Template image of trunk and back.

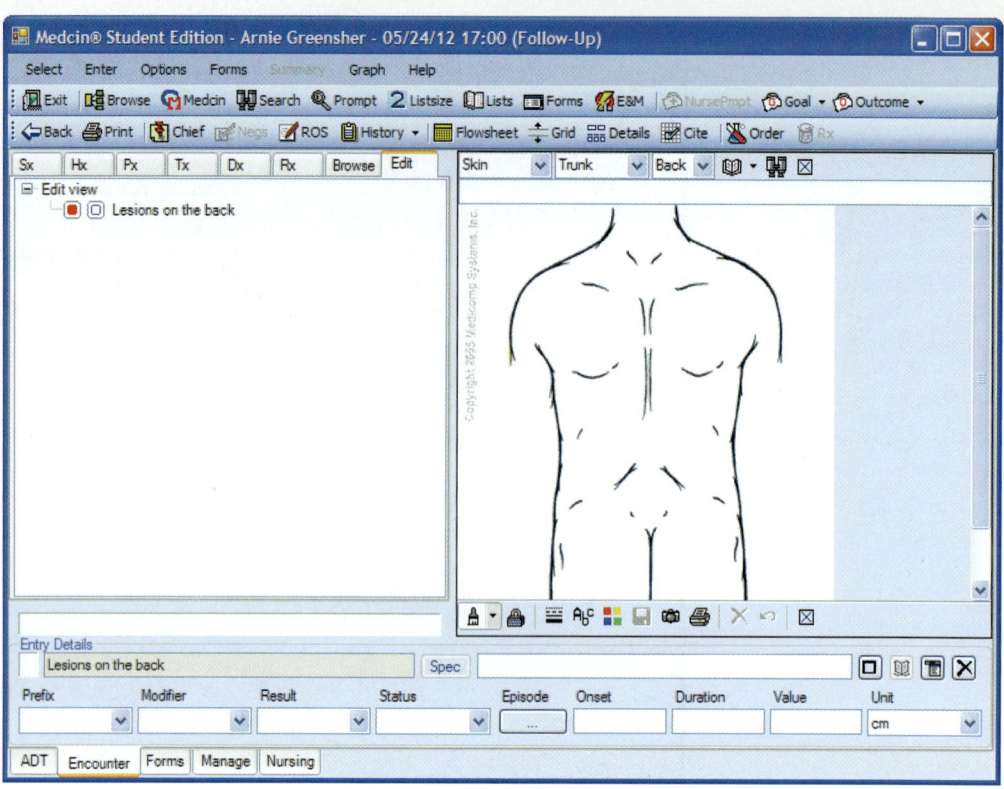

Compare your screen to Figure 8-32; if the image is not of the back of a man's trunk, click the down arrow of the center or right field to change the view. Select Trunk and Back from the respective drop-down lists.

▶ **Figure 8-33** Draw toolbar (enlarged to show detail).

At the bottom of the image is the drawing toolbar, which is shown enlarged in Figure 8-33. We will discuss each of the buttons on the drawing toolbar, from left to right.

Select Tool The first icon on the Toolbar shows the currently selected drawing shape or tool. The icon of the button will change according to the current selection. The down arrow next to the button displays a list of choices.

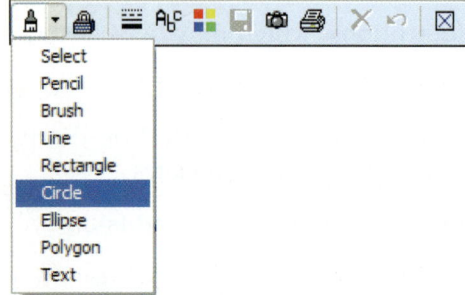

▶ **Figure 8-34** Select the shape "Circle" from the drop-down list.

Step 5

Click the down arrow next to the Select button to display the list of tools.

Figure 8-34 shows the drop-down list of shapes of the drawing tool. Most are self-explanatory, except the first one, Select. The Select option is used to select items that have been added to the drawing so they can be deleted or modified.

Locate and click on the word "Circle." The drawing tool button will display a circle in place of the pointer.

Step 6

Lock Button The icon resembles a padlock. This is used to "lock" the selected shape. When it is "locked," the button background will be white and the selections you have made for shape or the other drawing tool buttons (discussed later) stay set. When it is

324 Chapter 8 | Data Entry Using Flow Sheets and Anatomical Drawings

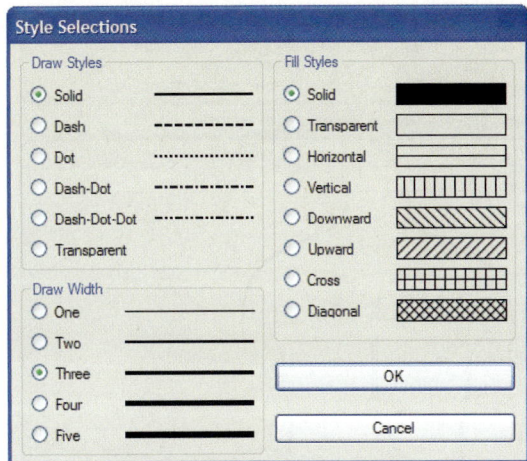

▶ Figure 8-35 Style Selections window.

not "locked" (the button background is blue), the drawing toolbar buttons return to their default state after each use.

Locate and click on the "lock" button in the drawing toolbar.

Step 7

Style This button icon consists of different horizontal lines. This button invokes the Style Selection window, which sets the pattern and thickness of the tools you will use to annotate the drawings. The style sets not only the line but also the solidity and thickness of other shapes.

Locate and click on the Style button in the drawing toolbar. A window similar to Figure 8-35 will be invoked.

Locate and click on the following:

Draw Style: **Solid**

Draw Width: **Three**

Fill Style: **Solid**

Compare your screen with Figure 8-35. Click on the OK button to close the window.

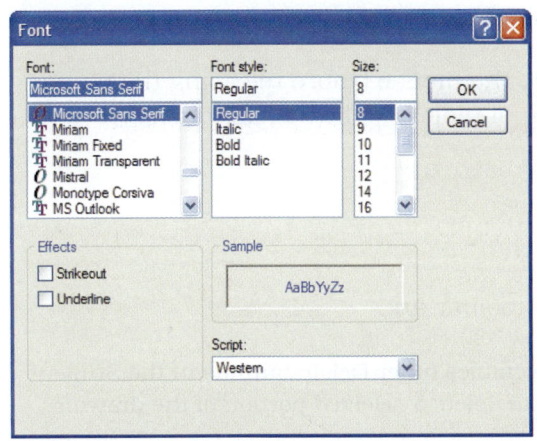

▶ Figure 8-36 The Font window is used to change the font for the Text tool.

Font This button has an icon consisting of the letters a-b-c. It is used to set the font and size of type for the text tool.

You may, optionally, click on the button to view the window, but do not change any of the settings; alternatively, you may study Figure 8-36 without invoking the window.

Step 8

Color The Color button selects the color for the annotations. The button icon consists of four colored squares.

Locate and click on the Color button and select orange by clicking on the orange square, as shown in Figure 8-37. Click the OK button to close the Color selection window.

The next two buttons on the drawing toolbar are:

Save The icon for this button represents a computer disk. This button is not used in the Student Edition software.

User Images A camera button, this is used to import external images. This button is not used in the Student Edition software.

Print This is used at the end of this exercise to print a copy of your drawing. The icon resembles a printer. Do not click it until instructed.

Step 9

In this step, you will learn how to draw on the displayed image.

Position the mouse over the patient's left shoulder in the drawing. The cursor should be shaped like a large plus sign. If it is, then hold down the left mouse key while making a slight movement. A circle should appear. The size of the

▶ Figure 8-37 Select orange in the Color pallet window.

Chapter 8 | Data Entry Using Flow Sheets and Anatomical Drawings   **325**

▶ **Figure 8-38** Draw a circle on the left shoulder to represent the position of a mole.

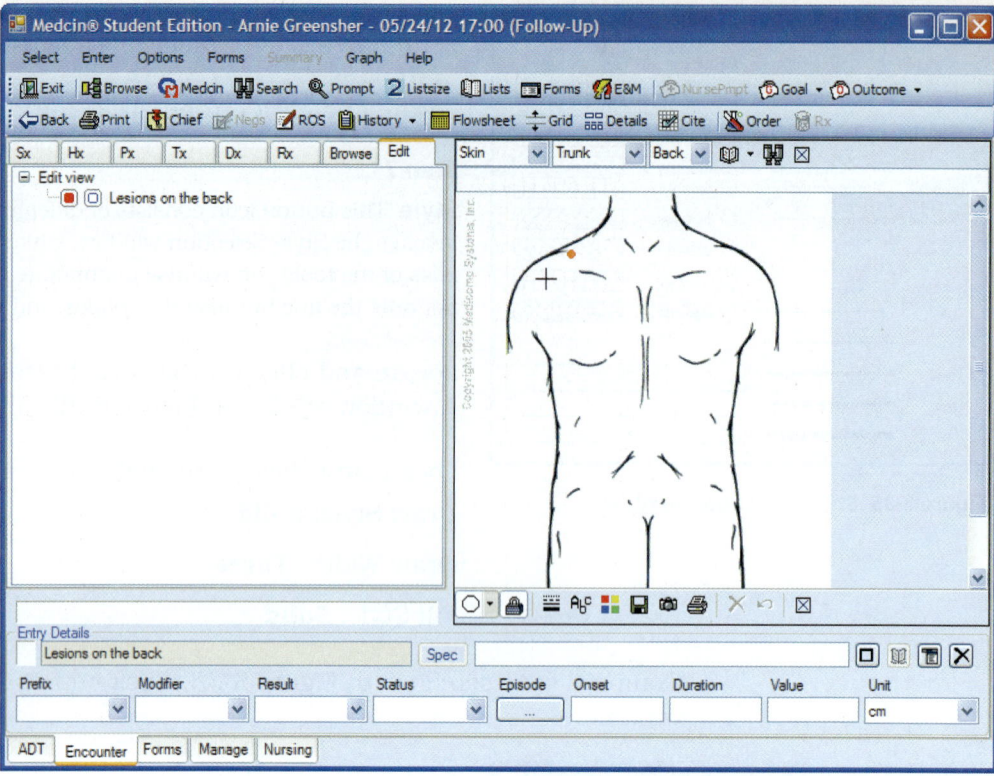

> **Note**
>
> **Note that if your cursor is not a plus sign but instead a typical mouse pointer you probably do not have the Circle tool selected; repeat step 5.**

circle is controlled by how far you move the mouse before releasing the mouse button. You are annotating the location of moles. Make a small circle.

Compare your screen to Figure 8-38.

Step 10

The remaining buttons on the drawing toolbar are:

Delete (icon is an X and resembles other Delete buttons in the Student Edition software). It is used to delete a selected portion of the drawing.

Undelete (icon is an arrow curved to the left). Used to restore the last item deleted from the drawing.

Exit (icon resembles an X in a square box). Closes the drawing and restores the encounter note narrative view. Do not click it until instructed to do so.

In this step, you will learn how to delete an item you have added and how to use the Undelete button.

Restore the drawing tool to the Select pointer by clicking on the down arrow in the drawing toolbar and clicking the first option, "Select."

Locate and click on the padlock to unlock the toolbar.

Position the mouse pointer over the mole created in step 9; the pointer should change to look like a small hand (as shown in Figure 8-39).

▶ **Figure 8-39** Selecting an object to delete (Delete button circled in red).

326 Chapter 8 | Data Entry Using Flow Sheets and Anatomical Drawings

Click on the mole. It will change to an outline of dotted lines when selected.

Locate and click on the Delete button in the drawing toolbar (circled in red in Figure 8-39). The mole will be removed from your drawing.

The Undelete button may be used to restore the last deleted item on the drawing. In this case, you deleted a mole.

Locate and click on the Undelete button (the icon resembles a curved arrow). The mole should reappear. Your drawing should once again look like Figure 8-38.

▶ **Figure 8-40** Draw 15 small moles on the back.

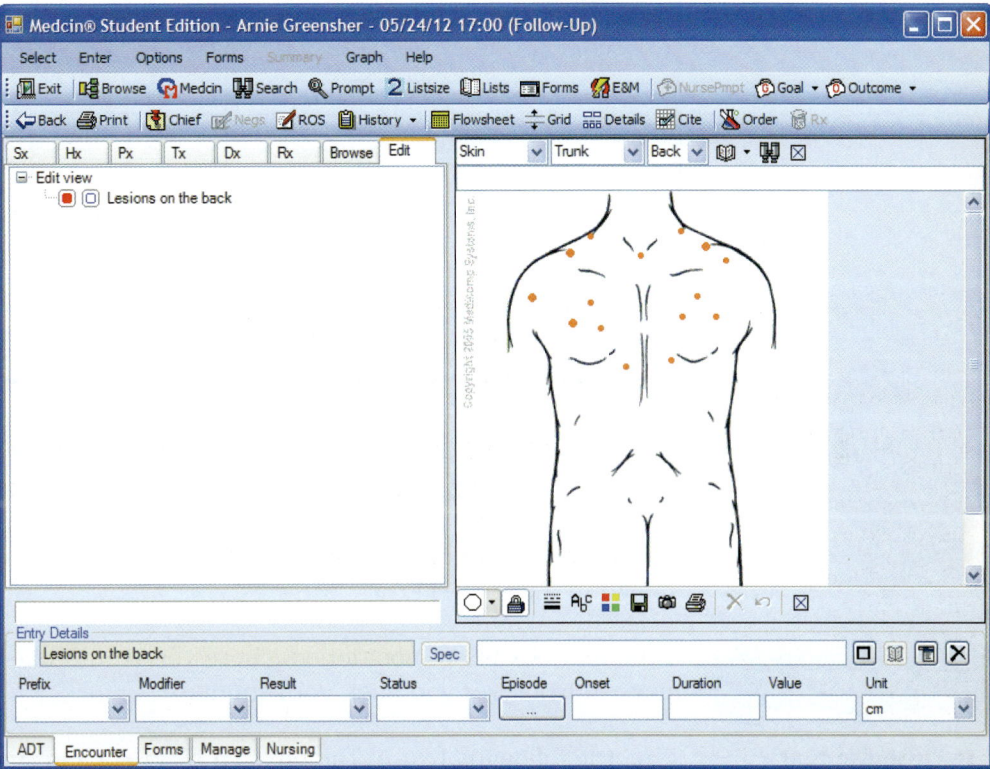

> **Note**
>
> If at any time during this step your shape tool reverts to the mouse pointer, just unlock the padlock, reselect the Circle shape, and click on the padlock to relock the shape.

Step 11

Using what you have learned in step 9, you will now illustrate the location of moles on Mr. Greensher's back using the Circle tool.

Click on the down arrow in the toolbar and reselect the circle from the drop-down list as you did in step 5. Locate and click on the padlock to lock the circle shape.

Draw **15** small moles on the patient's back, as shown in Figure 8-40. You do not have to place them exactly as they are in the figure; just get reasonably close.

Step 12

Clinicians also can annotate the images by adding text directly on the drawing canvas with the Text tool. The clinician also can select a different color for the text. It is wise to do so, as it will help the text stand out from the color and the background of the drawing.

Locate and click on the down arrow next to the Select button. Choose Text from the drop-down list.

▶ Figure 8-41 Type "15 Nevi < 1 cm. Unchanged" in text box.

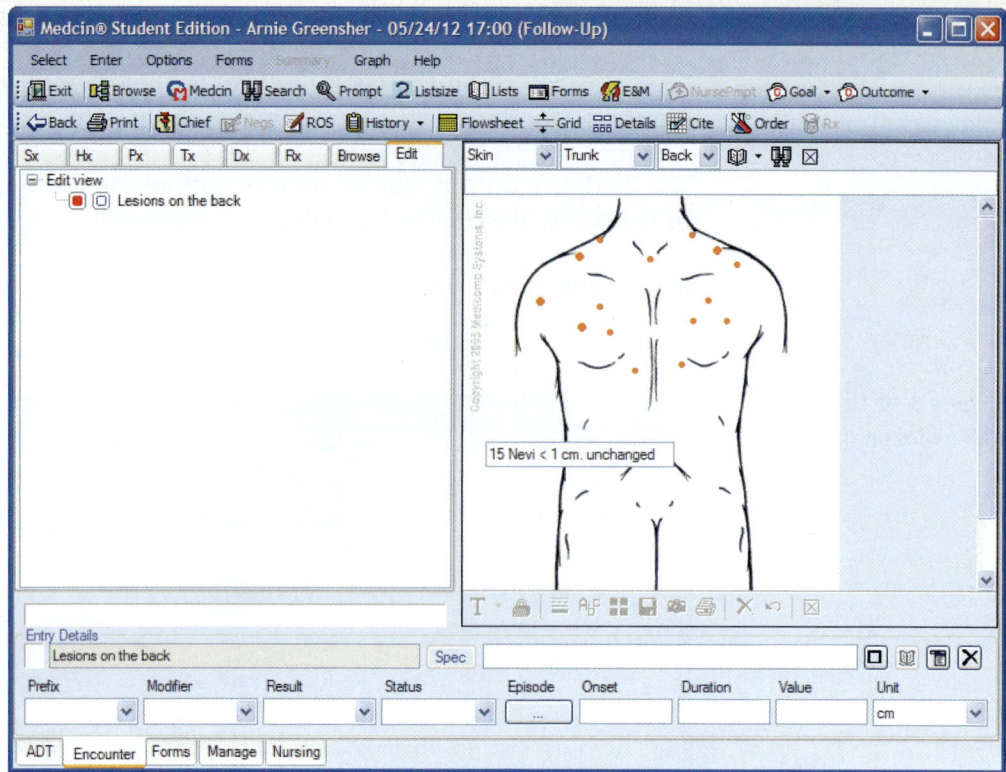

Locate and click on the Color button in the drawing toolbar. When the Color pallet window is displayed, select blue, and then click OK.

Now click over an empty portion of the drawing and a text box will appear, as shown in Figure 8-41.

If the text box is not positioned where you would like it, click elsewhere. It will move to wherever you click your mouse.

> **Note**
>
> To close the text box without saving the text, click the option "Abort Text Mode."

Type the following text in the box: **15 Nevi < 1 cm. unchanged**

Step 13

When you have finished typing, merge the text into the drawing by clicking the right mouse button anywhere on the drawing except in the text box. A drop-down menu will appear, as shown in Figure 8-42.

Locate and click on the option "Complete Text Entry."

> **Alert**
>
> Do not close or exit the drawing tool or change tabs until you have a printed copy in your hand. You could lose your work if you exit the drawing before printing has completed.

Step 14

Another useful drawing tool is the Line, which can be used to connect text to the drawing points.

Click on the down arrow in the toolbar and select Line from the drop-down list.

Position your mouse on the canvas just above the text. Hold down the left mouse button as you drag the mouse upward toward the moles on the back. When you release it, the line will end.

Compare your screen to Figure 8-43.

Chapter 8 | Data Entry Using Flow Sheets and Anatomical Drawings

▶ **Figure 8-42** Right click elsewhere in drawing and select "Complete Text Entry."

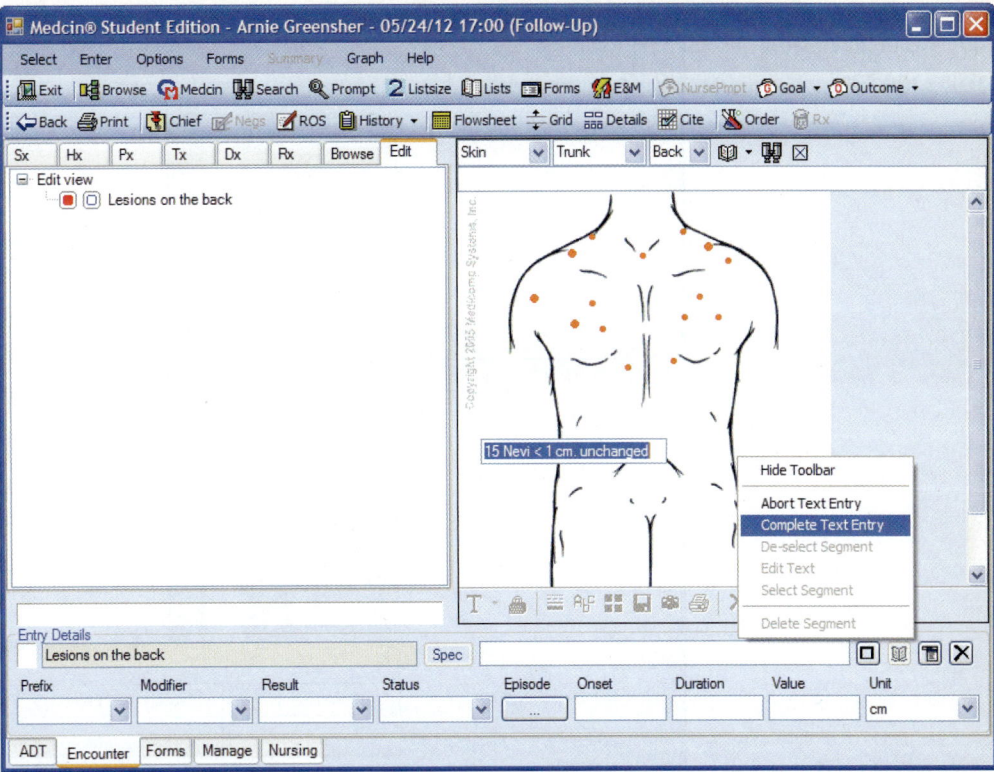

▶ **Figure 8-43** Draw a blue line from text to region of the moles.

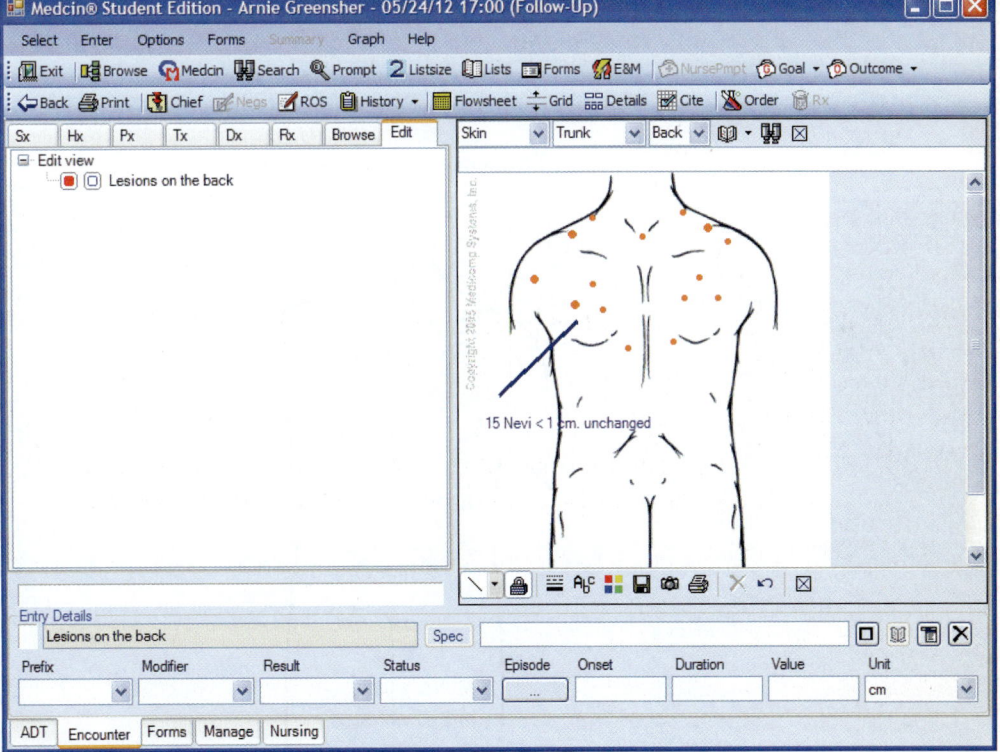

Step 15

In commercial EHR systems, you can merge your finished drawing into the narrative encounter notes for the patient visit. In the Student Edition you will only print your drawing, not merge it, because students from other classes share the data.

Chapter 8 | Data Entry Using Flow Sheets and Anatomical Drawings

▶ **Figure 8-44** Print Data window is invoked from drawing toolbar.

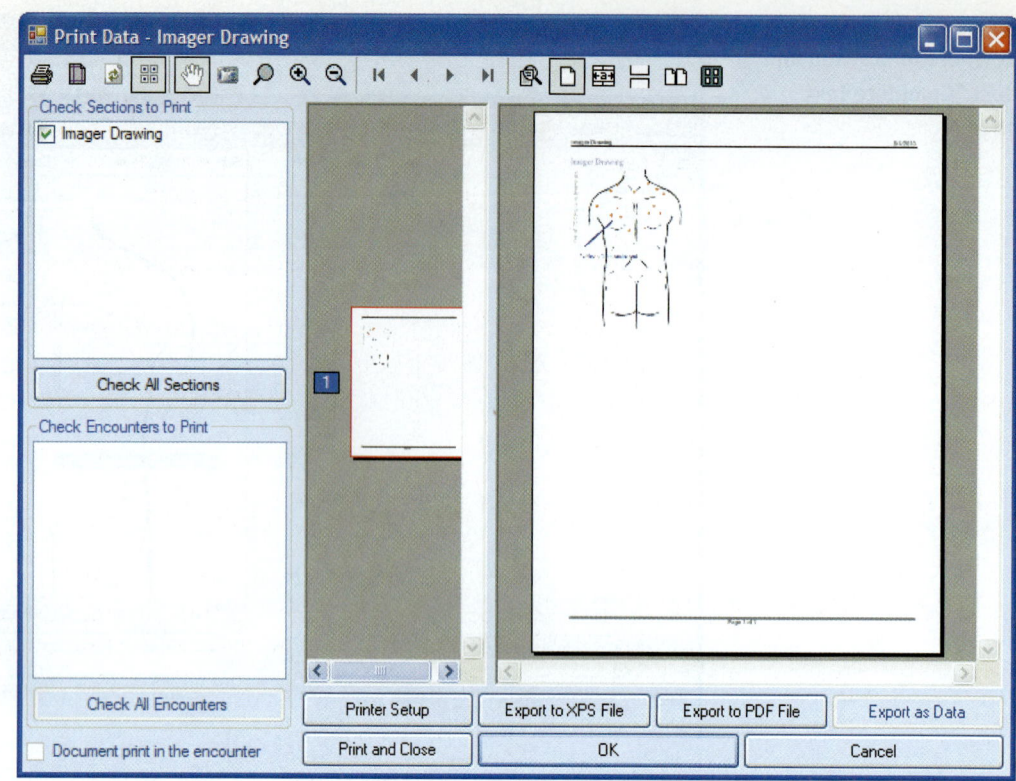

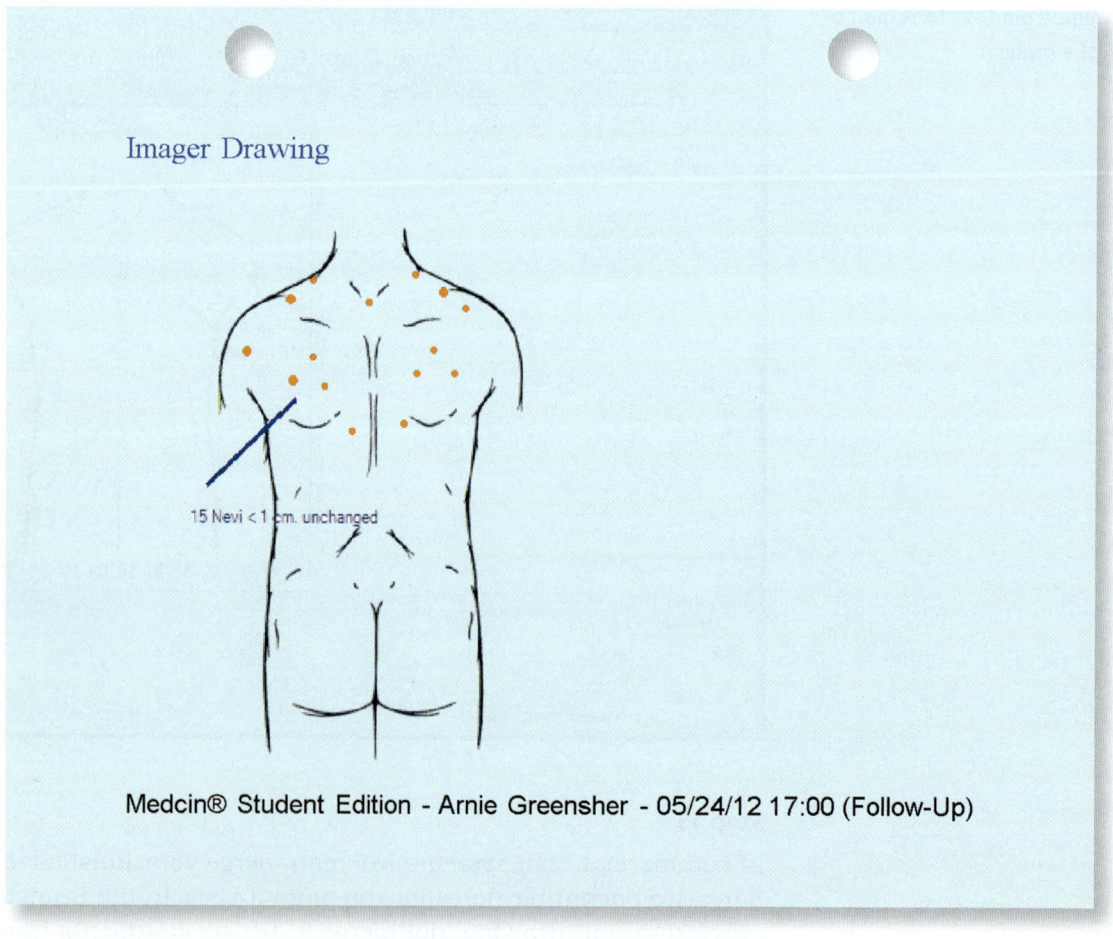

▶ **Figure 8-45** Printout of annotated drawing for Arnie Greensher.

330   Chapter 8 | Data Entry Using Flow Sheets and Anatomical Drawings

Click the Print button on the *drawing toolbar*, **not** the Print button on the main toolbar. The familiar Print Data window will be invoked.

Be certain there is a check mark in the box next to "Imager Drawing" (as shown in Figure 8-44) and then click on the appropriate button to either print or export a file, as directed by your instructor.

Compare your printout or file output to Figure 8-45.

When you have a printout of your annotated drawing in hand, close the Print Data window. Save the printed copy to give to your instructor along with the encounter note you will print in step 18.

Step 16

Return to the encounter note view by exiting the drawing tool.

▶ Figure 8-46 Exit drawing tool using X button circled in red.

Locate and click on the Exit button in the drawing toolbar (circled in red in Figure 8-46). Use only this button in this step, not any other Exit button in the window.

▶ Figure 8-47 Recording free text and value in the encounter.

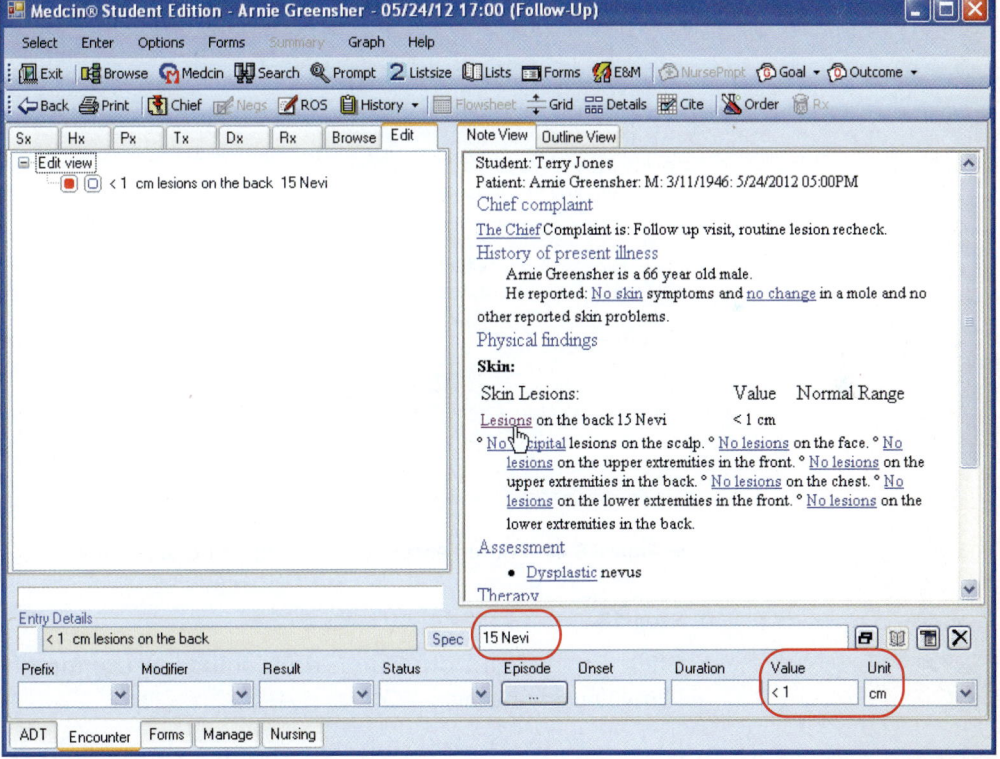

Step 17

Annotated drawings provide an excellent means of recording the location and size of certain observed findings in a physical exam. However, as we have discussed several times, the contents of the image are not codified, searchable records. In this example, the text added to the drawing became part of the image and as such can only be read by a person, not the computer.

Chapter 8 | Data Entry Using Flow Sheets and Anatomical Drawings

Alert

Do not close or exit the encounter until you have a printed copy in your hand. You will lose your work if you exit before printing.

Therefore, the clinician also will record the text of the findings in the encounter note. This will result in the best of both worlds—codified data for the computer and a visual record of the location of moles for use in future exams.

With the finding "Lesions on the back" still selected for edit, you will add data to the finding.

Locate the Entry Details free-text field just below the right pane and type: **15 Nevi**.

Locate the Value field in the Entry Details section at the bottom of the screen and type: **< 1**.

Press the enter key. Compare your screen to Figure 8-47.

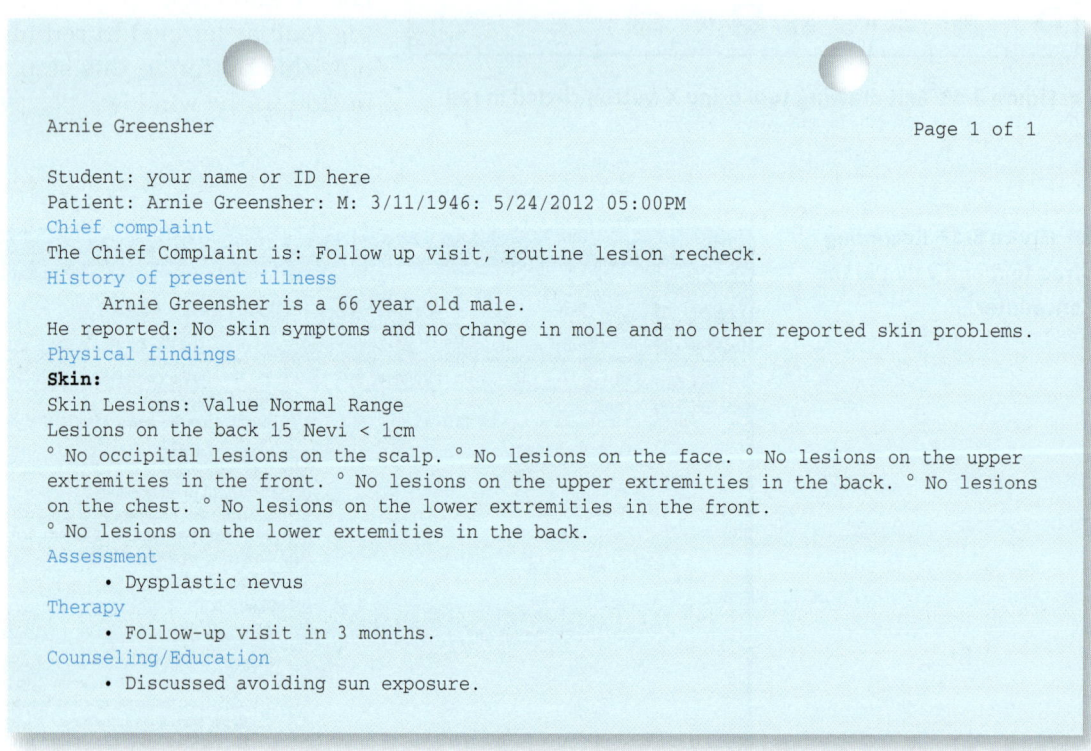

▶ Figure 8-48 Printed encounter note for Arnie Greensher.

Step 18

Click on the Print button on the Toolbar at the top of your screen to invoke the Print Data window.

Be certain there is a check mark in the box next to "Current Encounter" and then click on the appropriate button to either print or export a file, as directed by your instructor.

Compare your printout or file output to Figure 8-48. If it is correct, hand it in to your instructor. If there are any differences, review the previous steps in the exercise and find your error.

Real-Life Story

First Patient Whose Life Was Saved By Expert System Software He Operated Himself

Courtesy of Primetime Medical Software and Instant Medical History, used by permission.

Jack Gould of Columbia, South Carolina, became the first person in medical history to save his own life with software he operated himself.

One day Mr. Gould came to his physician's office to pickup a prescription renewal for his wife, who was also a patient there. In the waiting room was a computer kiosk running Instant Medical History, a patient-operated medical expert system. A sign posted near the system read, "Stay Healthy: Take our Prevention Questionnaire." While waiting for the prescription refill to be authorized, he decided to try it out.

In addition to eating and exercise recommendations, the software suggested that he needed the standard procedure to check for colon cancer because he could not recall having been checked within the timeframe suggested by standard guidelines. Normally, after the patient completes the questionnaire, the physician reviews the information with the patient. Because in this case he was not there to see the physician, he spoke with the triage nurse, who confirmed it was a wise preventive action to take and scheduled an appointment.

A few weeks later, the patient returned for his appointment. The doctor was surprised that the patient was there for such a specific preventative procedure months before his annual physical examination. The doctor asked who scheduled the procedure. In a tone reflecting his expectation that it was common for patients to schedule proctosigmoidoscopies on their own volition, he replied, "Well, your computer did."

No physician can be expected to remember the thousands of recommended interventions for each patient. The preventive health screening software queried the patient for the appropriate items based on his sex, age, and risk factors and compared them to the preventive guidelines of the U.S. Preventive Services Task Force. In the case of Mr. Gould, a flexible sigmoidoscopy was scheduled and a resectable severely dysplasic polyp was removed easily from his colon.

The large precancerous polyp that was discovered might have gone completely undetected without the intelligent prompting of the Instant Medical History program. Mr. Gould knew the importance of his decision to take the interview after his physician explained that he would not have thought to do this test until his routine annual complete medical examination. The polyps were removed without complication, before they could develop into colon cancer.

He was totally unaware of his risk for other conditions until he took the preventive interview. Now he strongly believes that Instant Medical History saved his life.

Critical Thinking Exercise 53: Examination of a Patient with Pressure Sores

In this exercise, you will use the skills you have acquired in the previous exercise to document a patient with pressure sores.

Case Study

Raj Patel is an 80-year-old male who presents complaining of sores on his back and buttocks. Two months ago he had surgery to repair cervical and thoracic spinal fractures that were the result of a motor vehicle crash. He was initially discharged to rehab, but has become sedentary post-therapy and is developing pressure sores on his shoulder blades and buttocks. Because he cannot see his sores, he mistakenly believes his pain is at the sites of his spinal and iliac incisions.

Alert

Make certain you set the date and time correctly for this exercise.

Step 1

If you have not already done so, start the Student Edition software.

Click Select on the Menu bar, and then click Patient.

In the Patient Selection window, locate and click on **Raj Patel**.

Step 2

Click Select on the Menu bar, and then click New Encounter.

Select the date **May 24, 2012**, the time **5:15 PM**, and the reason **Office Visit**.

Compare your screen to the date, time, and reason printed in bold type before clicking on the OK button.

Step 3

Enter the Chief complaint: "**Post-surgical sores on back and buttocks**."

When you have finished typing, click on the button labeled "Close the Note Dialog."

Step 4

Begin the visit by taking Mr. Patel's vital signs and history.

Locate the Forms button on the Toolbar and select the form labeled "**Vitals**." Enter Mr. Patel's vital signs in the corresponding fields on the form as follows:

Temperature:	**98.6**
Respiration:	**28**
Pulse:	**78**
BP:	**150/90**
Height:	**67**
Weight:	**210**

When you have finished, check your work; if it is correct, click on the Encounter tab at the bottom of your screen.

Step 5

Click on the Hx tab.

Expand the past medical history tree by clicking the small plus signs next to "past medical history" and "surgical/procedural."

Locate and click on following finding

- (red button) prior surgery

Locate and click in the Entry Details field "Onset" and type: **60 days**.

Press the Enter key and the software will automatically calculate the date 3/25/2012 and add it to the finding.

Step 6

Scroll the left pane downward to locate "social history." Expand the tree by clicking the small plus signs next to "social history," "habits," and "exercise habits."

Locate and click on following finding:

- (red button) sedentary

Step 7

Click on the Dx tab.

Locate and click on the small plus signs next to "Orthopedic Disorders" and "Fracture."

Click on the description "Vertebral Column" to highlight it. Locate and click the History button on the Toolbar at the top of your screen.

In the free text below the right pane type "C7, T1, T2, T3" and press the Enter key.

Click on the description "Ribs" to highlight it. Locate and click the History button on the Toolbar at the top of your screen.

Step 8

Locate and click on the Search button on the Toolbar at the top of your screen. The Search String window will be invoked.

Type the search string "**pressure sores**" and click on the Search button in the window.

Step 9

Click on the Sx tab.

Locate and click on following finding:

- (red button) red sore blanches with pressure

Step 10

Click on the Hx tab.

Locate and click on following findings:

- (red button) difficulty inspecting body for pressure sores

Step 11

Click on the Px tab.

Locate and click on following finding:

- (red button) Lesions tender to direct pressure

Locate and click on the button labeled "Medcin" on the Toolbar at the top of your screen to restore the full nomenclature.

Scroll the left pane downward to locate and click on the small plus signs next to "Skin" and "Ulcer __ cm."

Locate and click on following findings:

- (red button) On Shoulders
- (red button) Buttocks

Step 12

Click on the Dx tab.

Click again on the Search button on the Toolbar at the top of your screen. The Search String window will be invoked and should still display the search string "**pressure sores**." Click on the Search button in the window.

Locate and click on the small plus signs next to "Chronic Cutaneous Ulcer Decubitus" and "Lower Back."

Locate and click on following findings:

- (red button) Upper Back
- (red button) Coccyx

Step 13

Click on the Rx tab.

Locate and click on following finding:

- (red button) ADL Inspect body for pressure sores Short-Term

Locate and click on the button labeled "Medcin" on the Toolbar at the top of your screen to restore the full nomenclature.

Locate and click on the small plus sign next to "Basic Management Procedures and services."

Scroll the left pane downward and click on the small plus sign next to "Orthopedic services."

Locate and click on following finding:

- (red button) Regular exercise

Scroll the left pane further downward to locate and click on the small plus signs next to "Home care," "Visit," and "For Clinical Assessment."

Locate and click on the finding description "Skin" to highlight it.

Locate and click on the Order button in the Toolbar at the top of your screen.

🔔 (order button) Skin

Step 14

Create an annotated drawing to illustrate the position of his incision scars and pressure sores for the patient.

Scroll the encounter note in the right pane to locate and click on the underlined finding "Lesions." The left pane should change to the Edit tab.

Locate the context button (the second button from the right in the lower right corner of your window) and click on it. From the drop-down list displayed, choose "Add Object to Finding."

The drawing window will be invoked in the right pane.

If the drawing of the trunk is not displayed, use the fields at the top of the drawing to select the Skin, Trunk, and Back view from the drop-down lists.

Step 15

Once the correct illustration template is displayed, use the toolbar in the drawing tool to set up the tool.

Locate and click on the down arrow next to the first button; then select "Ellipse" from the drop-down list.

Locate and click on the Lock button (with the padlock). It should have a white background.

Locate and click on the Style button in the drawing toolbar. A window similar to Figure 8-35 will be invoked.

Locate and click on the following:

    Draw Style: **Solid**

    Draw Width: **Three**

    Fill Style: **Solid**

Click on the OK button to close the Style window.

Locate and click on the Color pallet button. When the window is displayed, select red. Click OK to close the Color pallet window.

Step 16

As closely as possible, replicate the drawing in Figure 8-49.

Draw a large red circle over the right shoulder blade, a red circle over the coccyx, and a vertical oval over the left shoulder blade (as shown in Figure 8-49).

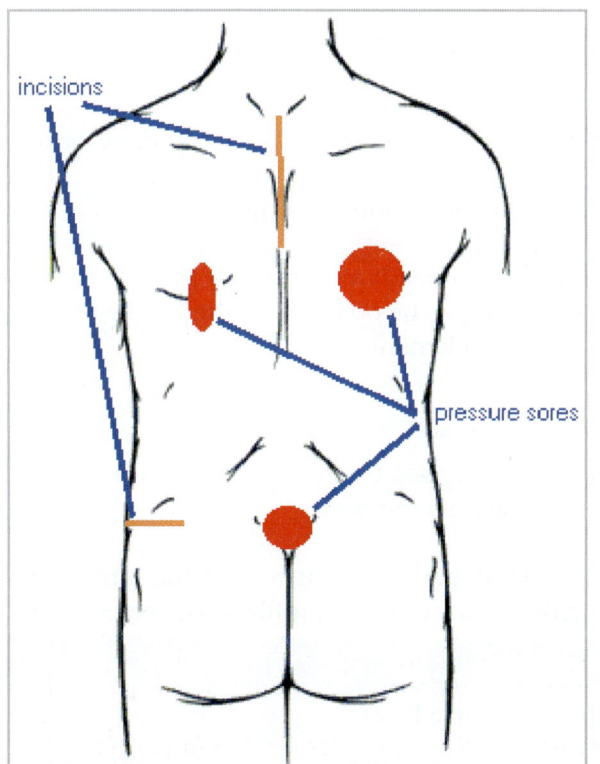

Anatomical Figure © MediComp Systems, Inc.

▶ **Figure 8-49 Drawing of incisions and pressure sores.**

Change the drawing tool.

Locate and click on the down arrow next to the first button, then select "Line" from the drop-down list.

Locate and click on the Color pallet button. When the window is displayed, select orange. Click OK to close the Color pallet window.

Draw a short horizontal line from the edge of the left hip toward the coccyx as shown in Figure 8-49.

Draw a long vertical line from the base of the neck to the center of the shoulder blades as shown in Figure 8-49.

Change the drawing tool to annotate the drawing.

Locate and click on the down arrow next to the first button, then select "Text" from the drop-down list. Next, change the color to blue by selecting the Color pallet button.

Click in the upper left of the drawing and type "incisions" in the text box.

Right click anywhere on the drawing except in the text box to display a list of options; click on "Complete Text" from the list displayed.

Click on the right side of the drawing and type "pressure sores" in the text box.

Right click anywhere on the drawing except in the text box to display a list of options.

Alert

Do not exit the drawing or change tabs until you have a printed copy in your hand. You will lose your work if you exit the drawing tool before printing is complete.

Change the drawing tool.

Locate and click on the down arrow next to the first button, then select "line" from the drop-down list.

Draw two blue lines from the word "incisions" to the orange lines you drew earlier.

Draw three blue lines from the phrase "pressure sores" to the red circles.

Compare your drawing to Figure 8-49. If you need to correct the line or circle, change the tool button to "Select" and click on the object. Use the Delete button in the Toolbar and then redraw the correct element.

Step 17

Click the Print button on the *drawing toolbar*, **not** the Print button on the main toolbar. The familiar Print Data window will be invoked.

Be certain there is a check mark in the box next to "Imager Drawing" and then click on the appropriate button to either print or export a file, as directed by your instructor.

Compare your printout or file output to Figure 8-49.

When you have a printout of your annotated drawing in hand, close the Print Data window. Save the printed copy to give to your instructor along with the encounter note you will print in step 18.

Step 18

Locate and click on the Exit button in the *drawing toolbar* to close the drawing tool and redisplay the encounter note.

Click on the Print button on the Toolbar at the top of your screen to invoke the Print Data window.

Be certain there is a check mark in the box next to "Current Encounter" and then click on the appropriate button to either print or export a file, as directed by your instructor.

Compare your printout to Figure 8-50. If anything is missing, review steps 1–13 and correct your mistake.

Hand in the printed encounter note or file output of Raj Patel's encounter and the annotated drawing of his pressure sores to your instructor.

```
Raj Patel                                                          Page 1 of 1

Student: your name or ID here
Patient: Raj Patel: M: 03/05/1932: 5/24/2012 05:15PM
Chief complaint
The Chief Complaint is: Post-surgical sores on back and buttocks.
History of present illness
     Raj Patel is an 80 year old male.
     He reported: A red sore which blanches with pressure.
Past medical/Surgical history
Reported History:
     Surgical/Procedural: Prior surgery 3/25/2012.
Diagnosis History:
     Fracture of the vertebral column C7, T1, T2, T3
     Rib fracture
Personal history
Habits: Sedentary.
Functional: Inspecting body for pressure sores with difficulty.
Physical findings
Vital signs:
Vital Signs/Measurements              Value                Normal Range
Oral temperature                      96.8 F               97.6 - 99.6
RR                                    28 breaths/min       18 - 26
PR                                    78 bpm               50 - 100
Blood pressure                        150/90 mmHg          100-120/60-80
Weight                                210 lbs              121 - 205
Height                                67 in                64.57 - 73.23
Skin:
   • Lesion was tender to direct pressure.
   • An ulcer was seen on the shoulders.
   • An ulcer was seen on the buttocks.
Assessment
   • Decubitus ulcer of the upper back
   • Decubitus ulcer of the Coccyx
Therapy
   • Regular exercise.
   • Short-term goals for inspecting the body for pressure sores.
Plan
   • Home care visit for skin assessment
```

▶ **Figure 8-50** Printed encounter note for Raj Patel.

Chapter Eight Summary

This chapter showed how codified data in the EHR could be displayed in a format called a flow sheet.

Flow sheets present data from multiple encounters in column form. This format allows for a side-by-side comparison of findings over a period of time.

The flow sheet view resembles a spreadsheet made up of rows and columns of "cells." The first column displays descriptions as well as red and blue buttons for findings on the current encounter. The date of the current encounter is at the top of the column. The remaining columns to the right display encounter data from previous visits.

The flow sheet rows are grouped vertically into logical sections that match the sections you are accustomed to seeing in the encounter note. The title of each section is printed in blue on a teal background.

The Student edition software allows you to create flow sheets three different ways based on:

- List
- Problem
- Form

You also used multiple forms during a single exam to document a patient with multiple chronic conditions. From this you have learned that you can change forms as often as you like during an examination without losing any of the data.

Citing means to bring a finding from a previous encounter note into the current encounter.

In this chapter you learned that some EHR systems have navigation pages that allow the clinician to quickly locate findings by pointing to a particular body part in a drawing, which opens a list of findings relevant to that body system. This was described as searching with pictures rather than words.

You also learned another method of entering data about the patient into the EHR with the use of anatomical drawings of the body and body systems. Annotated drawings often are included in the EHR at ophthalmology and dermatology practices. Annotated images created in the EHR become part of the electronic encounter, and are useful for patient education as well as documentation.

The Student Edition software includes a set of simple drawing tools for creating annotated drawings and associating them with findings in the encounter notes. The tools are invoked by clicking on a finding in the Edit view, then clicking on the Context button and then selecting Add Object to Finding from the drop-down list.

The software contains various anatomical illustrations, which may be selected for annotation. A special toolbar allows you to select the shape, line, thickness, and color of the drawing tool. You can also add text annotations to the drawing.

A Print button on the drawing toolbar (not the Print button on the main toolbar) is used to print your finished drawing.

Task	Exercise	Page #
How to use a flow sheet	50	302
How to cite findings in a flow sheet	50	307
How to create a flow sheet from a problem list	51	316
How to create annotated drawings	52	321
How to print annotated drawings	52	330

Testing Your Knowledge of Chapter 8

1. What were the two chronic diseases for which Mr. Daniels was being monitored?
2. Why did the practice use separate forms for each disease?
3. Why were some items already filled in when you loaded the second form?
4. What form did you use to record dietary orders?
5. What is a flow sheet?
6. What does it mean to cite a finding?
7. Describe how to create a flow sheet from a form.
8. Describe how to create a problem-oriented flow sheet.
9. Describe how to cite a finding from a flow sheet.
10. What types of specialties typically incorporate annotated drawings in an encounter note?
11. Why did the two forms create different flow sheets?
12. If you click the date of a flow sheet column when the Cite button is *off*, what data is displayed?
13. If you click the date of a flow sheet column when the Cite button is *on*, what data is displayed?
14. How do you print an annotated drawing?
15. You should have produced three narrative documents of patient encounters and two annotated drawings. If you have not already done so, hand these in to your instructor with this test. These will count as a portion of your grade.

Chapter Nine

Using the EHR to Improve Patient Health

Learning Outcomes

After completing this chapter, you should be able to:

- Document a well-baby checkup using a wellness form
- Explain the relationship between vitals signs and growth charts
- Create a pediatric growth chart
- Understand Body Mass Index
- Calculate Body Mass Index
- Understand immunization schedules
- Order immunizations for a child
- Describe how patients can be involved in their own health
- Discuss preventive care guidelines
- Understand how EHR preventive care systems work

Prevention and Early Detection

The value of an EHR increases as a practice uses it. As more of the patient's health record is stored in a codified EHR, more can be done with it. As we have seen in previous chapters, data from past encounters can be used to improve patient care through disease management, trending, and creating graphs for patient education and counseling.

Still, it is always better to prevent a disease than to treat it. Thus far, you have learned how to use an EHR to document patient visits. In this chapter, we will discuss various ways in which preventive care, immunization, preventive screening, patients' participation in their healthcare, education, and counseling can help people live longer, healthier lives.

Pediatric Wellness Visits

Whereas those of us who are adults may someday have an electronic health record, we may never have a completely codified personal health record, because too much of our medical history is isolated in paper records at medical offices that we no longer visit. Those who are just being born, however, have an excellent chance that their medical records are being created and stored electronically even today.

The care we receive in the early years is fundamental to lifelong health. Early screening, detection, education, and immunizations have all contributed to increased life spans of the population as a whole. Nowhere does this have more support than in the pediatric practice, where regular examinations are recommended for wellness visits, not just when the child is ill.

In the next exercises, you will use the Student Edition software to record a pediatric visit, create a different kind of graph called a *growth chart*, and learn about childhood immunizations. This is a lot of material to cover, and for that reason the pediatric visit will span several exercises.

Guided Exercise 54: A Well-Baby CheckUp

Case Study

Tyrell Williams is a six-month-old male who is brought by his mother to the pediatric clinic where he has always been seen. As a result, the clinic has a lifelong history of his care and growth.

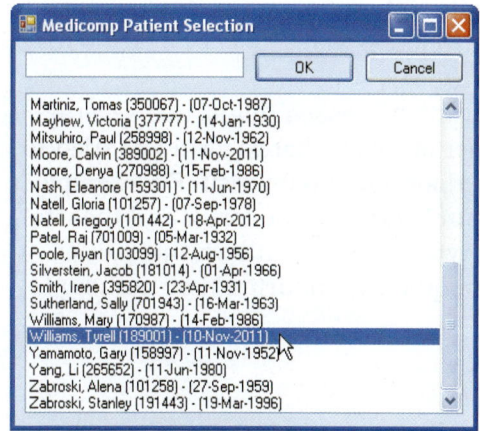

▶ **Figure 9-1** Selecting Tyrell Williams from the Patient Selection window.

Step 1

If you have not already done so, start the Student Edition software.

Click Select on the Menu bar, and then click Patient.

In the Patient Selection window, locate and click on **Tyrell Williams**, as shown in Figure 9-1.

Step 2

Click Select on the Menu bar, and then click New Encounter.

Use the date **May 25, 2012**, the time **11:00 AM**, and the reason **Well-Baby Check**.

(You will need to scroll the drop-down list of reasons to find Well-Baby Check.)

 **Alert** — Make certain the date and time are set correctly for this exercise.

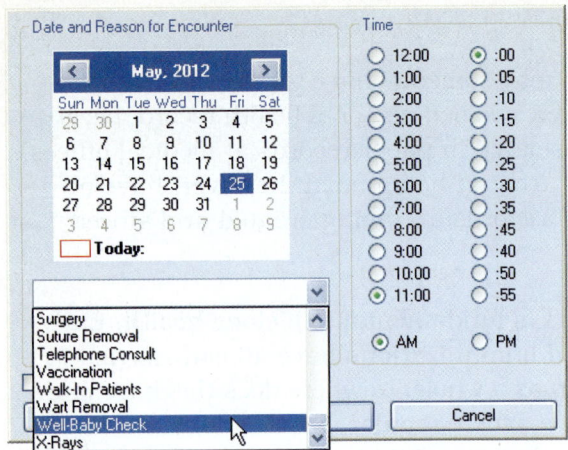

▶ Figure 9-2 New encounter for a well-baby check, May 25, 2012 11:00 AM.

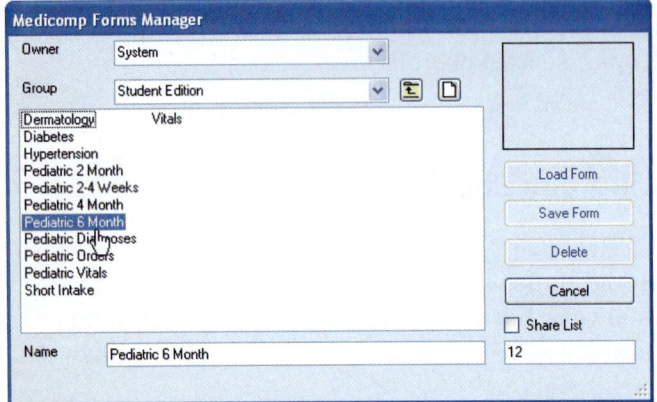

▶ Figure 9-3 Selecting the pediatric 6-month from the Form Manager window.

Compare your screen to Figure 9-2 when it is correct click on the OK button.

Step 3

Locate and click on the Forms button on the Toolbar.

Notice that there are several pediatric forms. Because there are different developmental milestones and therefore different questions appropriate to different ages, pediatric clinics typically have a form for each age-appropriate visit. In an actual pediatric practice, there would be more forms than are shown in the Student Edition.

Locate and click on the form labeled "**Pediatric 6 Month**."

Step 4

The pediatric form will be displayed. Take a moment to orient yourself. You will notice that there are quite a few tabs on the form.

Well-baby checkups are usually quite extensive, and involve the social history of the parents as well as of the baby. This form contains the items a practice might cover during a checkup for a six-month-old baby. In the interest of time, you will not enter data for every question, although you would during an actual pediatric wellness visit.

Whereas practices seeing patients with chronic illnesses might use several different forms for a patient visit, the designer of this pediatric form has tried to combine in one form all the elements required for a well-baby visit. For example, the form has a button for the chief complaint imbedded in the form, and the vital signs also are imbedded in the form. This type of design allows the nurses and pediatricians to move through the exam quickly, ensuring that nothing is forgotten or overlooked.

Step 5

Locate the finding in the form labeled "The Chief Complaint is:"

Click on the note button to the right of the finding (circled in red in Figure 9-4). The chief complaint dialog window will be invoked.

In the dialog window, type "**6 month check up**."

Compare your screen to Figure 9-4, then click on the button labeled "Close the note form."

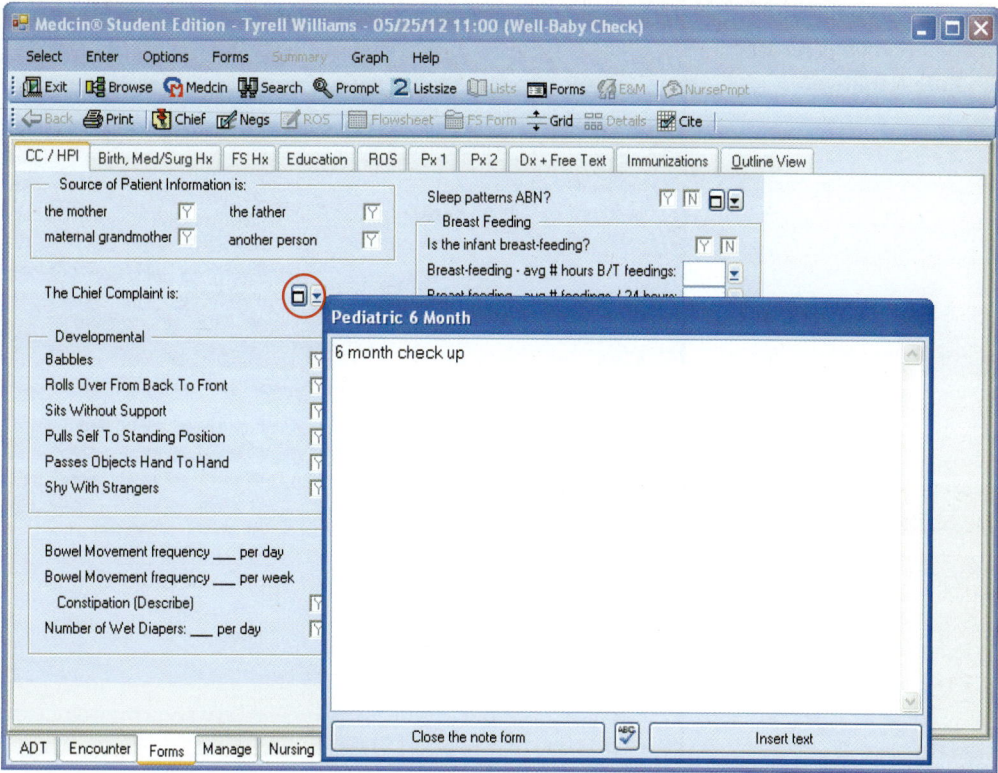

▶ Figure 9-4 Pediatric form—CC/HPI tab with Chief Complaint dialogue invoked.

Step 6

This form uses check boxes to record the findings. Notice that the letters "Y" and "N" are gray. When you click on a "Y" check box, the letter will turn red; clicking on a "N" check box will turn the letter blue.

The first thing the form asks is the source of information. Tyrell is accompanied by his mother. Click your mouse in the check box:

✓ **Y** "the mother"

Locate sleep patterns on the top right of the form and click on the check box:

✓ **N** Sleep patterns ABN

Locate and click the button labeled "Negs" (Auto Negative) in the Toolbar at the top of your screen.

Step 7

Complete the HPI by locating and clicking the check boxes indicated for the following findings about the patient's feeding:

✓ **Y** Is the infant breast-feeding?

✓ **N** Any difficulties w/ breast-feeding?

✓ **Y** Is rice cereal introduced?

▶ Figure 9-5 Pediatric form—HPI findings recorded with Auto Negative.

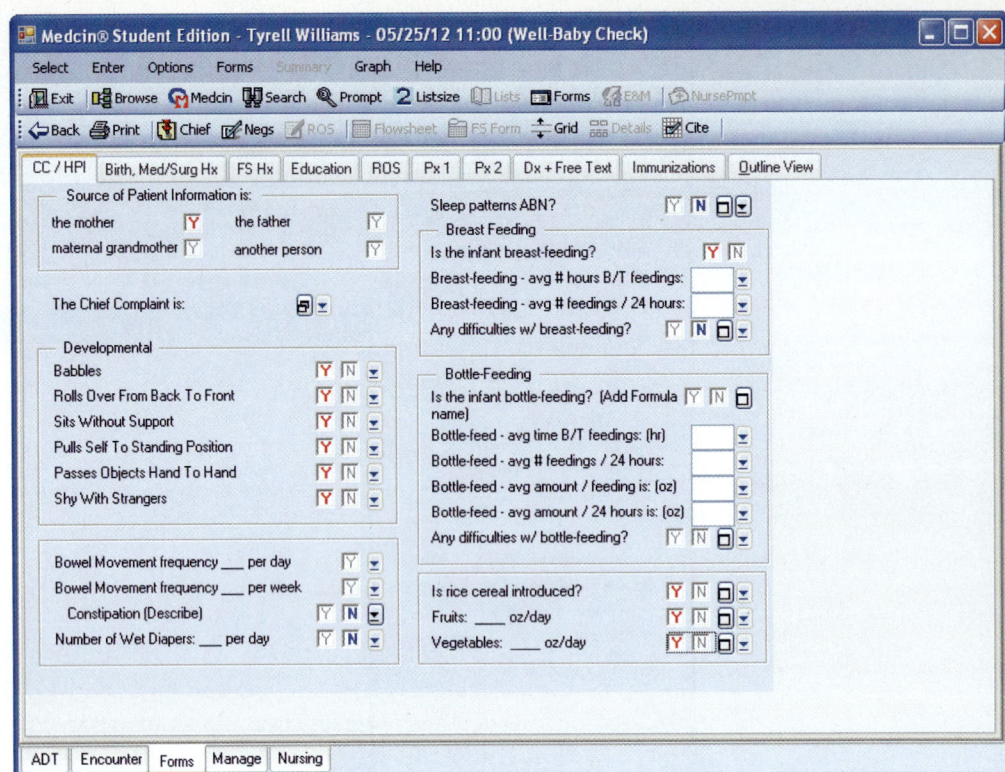

✓ **Y** Fruits: _____ oz/day

✓ **Y** Vegetables: _____ oz/day

Compare your screen to Figure 9-5.

▶ Figure 9-6 Pediatric form—Birth, Med/Surg Hx.

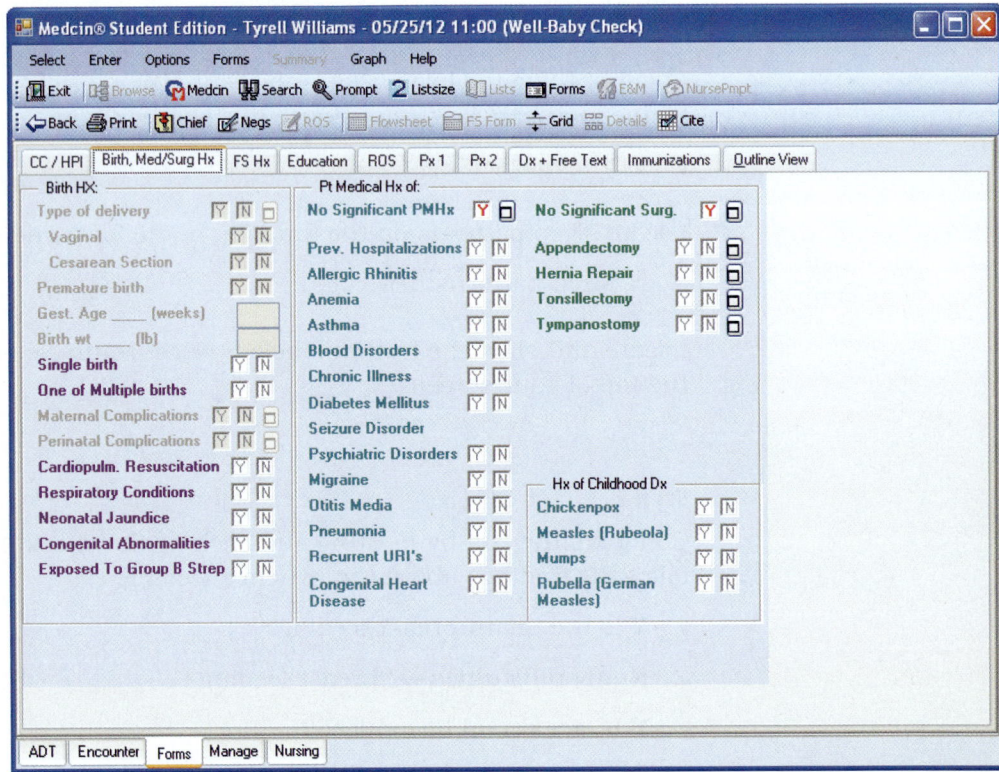

346　Chapter 9 | Using the EHR to Improve Patient Health

Step 8

Locate and click on the tab labeled "Birth, Med/Surg Hx" at the top of the form.

Tyrell has no previous medical or surgical history. This is indicated by findings at the top of the middle and right columns, as shown in Figure 9-6. Locate and click on the following check boxes:

✓ **Y** No Significant PM Hx

✓ **Y** No Significant Surg Hx

Compare your screen to Figure 9-6.

Step 9

Locate and click on the tab labeled "FS Hx" at the top of the form.

FS Hx stands for Family and Social History. In pediatric visits, the parent's social habits and environment are seen as health factors that can affect the child. This page of the form is used to record findings about the family history, the child's environment, and the parents' behavioral habits. The Family Social History section is not asking if the baby uses tobacco, alcohol, or drugs, but if the parents do.

Locate and click on the check boxes indicated for the following findings:

Family History:

✓ **Y** No Significant Family Hx

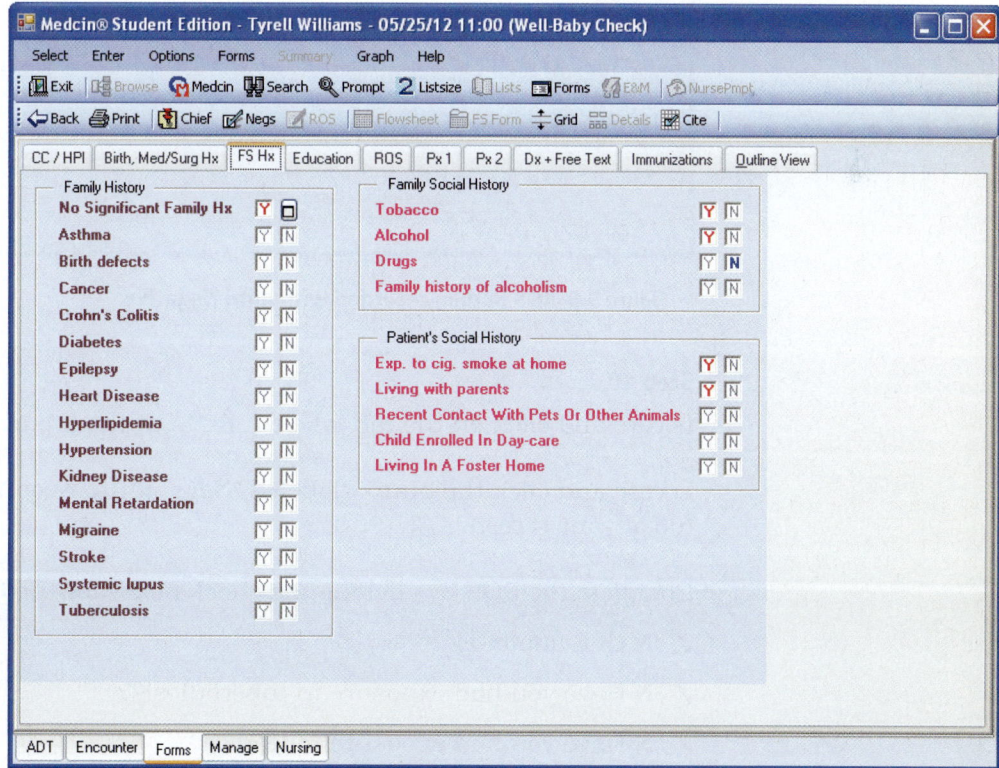

▶ Figure 9-7 Family and Social History tab.

Chapter 9 | Using the EHR to Improve Patient Health

Family Social History:

✓ **Y** Tobacco

✓ **Y** Alcohol

✓ **N** Drugs

Patient's Social History:

✓ **Y** Exposure to cig. smoke at home

✓ **Y** Living with parents

Compare your screen to Figure 9-7.

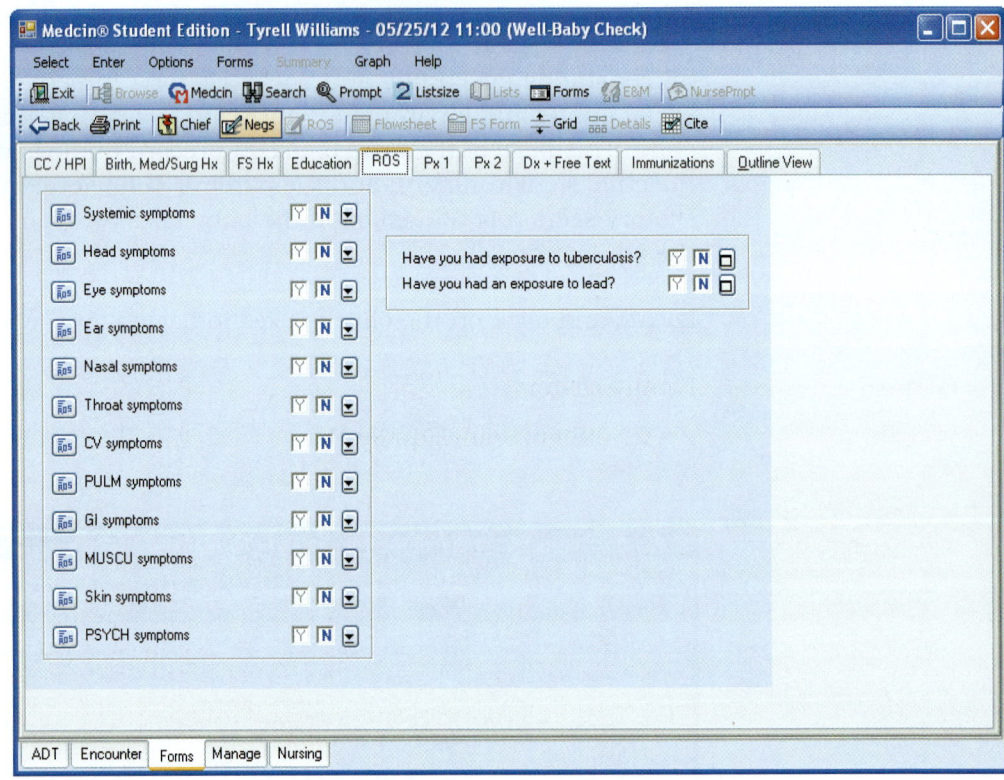

▶ **Figure 9-8** ROS finding recorded with Auto Negative.

Step 10

Locate and click on the tab labeled "ROS" at the top of the form.

Locate and click the button labeled "Negs" (Auto Negative) in the Toolbar at the top of your screen.

Complete the ROS by clicking the check boxes for the following findings:

✓ **N** GI Symptoms

✓ **N** Have you had exposure to tuberculosis?

✓ **N** Have you had exposure to lead?

Compare your screen to Figure 9-8.

▶ Figure 9-9 The first of two Px tabs includes vital signs.

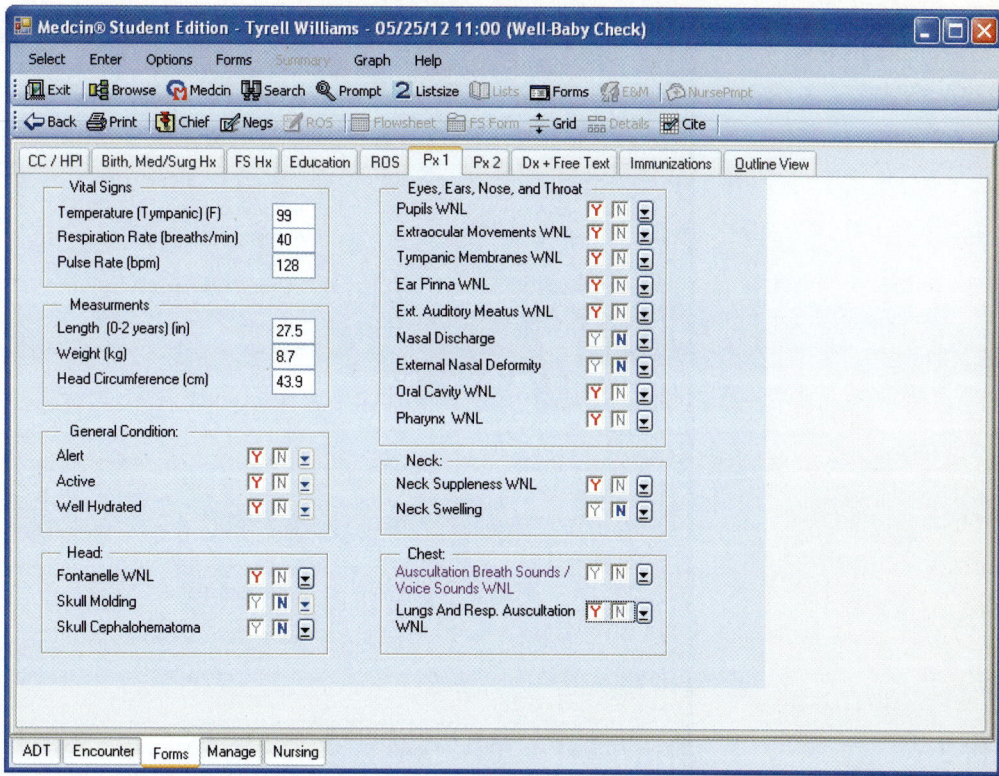

Step 11

This form uses two tabs to record the physical exam.

Locate and click on the tab labeled "Px 1" at the top of the form. The first page of the Physical Exam form will be displayed.

The Px 1 tab allows the vital signs to be entered without leaving the form. Notice that there are several differences between pediatric and adult vital signs:

◆ Infant growth is measured in length not height.

◆ The temperature is measured in the ear (tympanic).

◆ The circumference of the head is also recorded.

◆ Blood pressure readings are not typically taken in healthy children under the age of three.

Enter the following measurements for Tyrell in the corresponding Vital Signs fields:

Temperature:	**99**
Respiration Rate:	**40**
Pulse:	**128**
Length (in):	**27.5**
Weight (kg):	**8.7**
Head Circumference (cm):	**43.9**

Click the button labeled "Negs" (Auto Negative) in the Toolbar at the top of your screen to record the rest of the physical exam findings for this page.

Compare your screen with Figure 9-9.

Chapter 9 | Using the EHR to Improve Patient Health   349

▶ Figure 9-10 The second Px tab completes the physical exam.

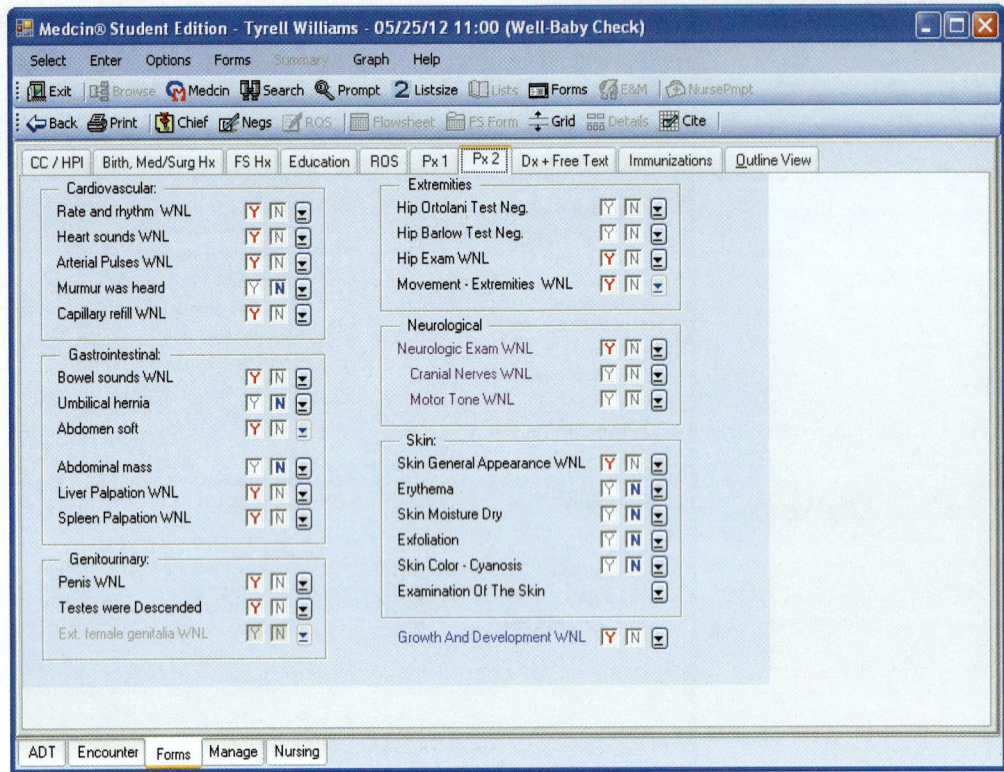

Step 12

Record the remainder of the physical exam.

Locate and click on the tab labeled "Px 2" at the top of the form. The second page of the Physical Exam form will be displayed.

Locate and click the button labeled "Negs" (Auto Negative) in the Toolbar at the top of your screen.

Locate and click the check box for the physical exam finding:

✓ **Y** Growth and Development WNL

Compare your screen with Figure 9-10.

Step 13

Locate and click on the tab labeled "Dx + Free Text" at the top of the form.

Unless the child is ill, the diagnosis for a well-baby checkup is the same for each child; therefore, the form designer has included an option to record it via the form, saving the clinician the time it would take to search the nomenclature.

Additionally, there are many possible areas of the exam in which the pediatrician may wish to record additional free text. In this form, the clinician can add notes to any area from this one tab. The type of finding and the section of the note in which it will appear have been clearly labeled for the clinician.

Locate and click on the check box for the diagnosis:

✓ **Y** Dx: Well Baby 6-month visit

Compare your screen to Figure 9-11.

350   Chapter 9 | Using the EHR to Improve Patient Health

▶ Figure 9-11 The Dx tab with free-text findings.

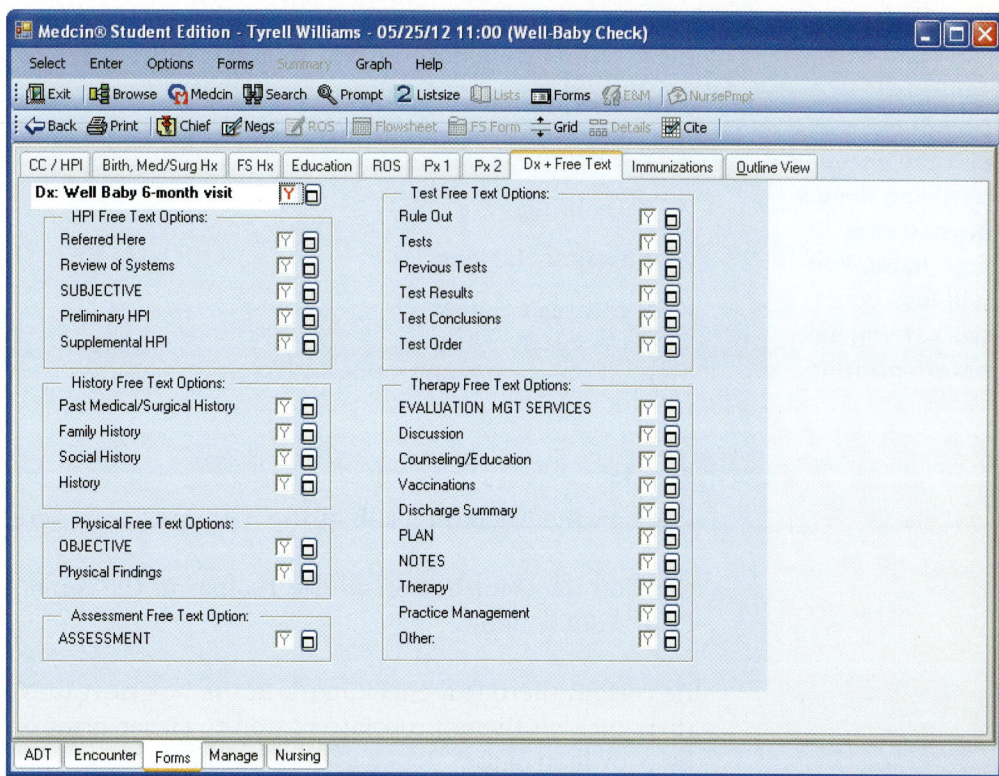

▶ Figure 9-12 Parent Education tab.

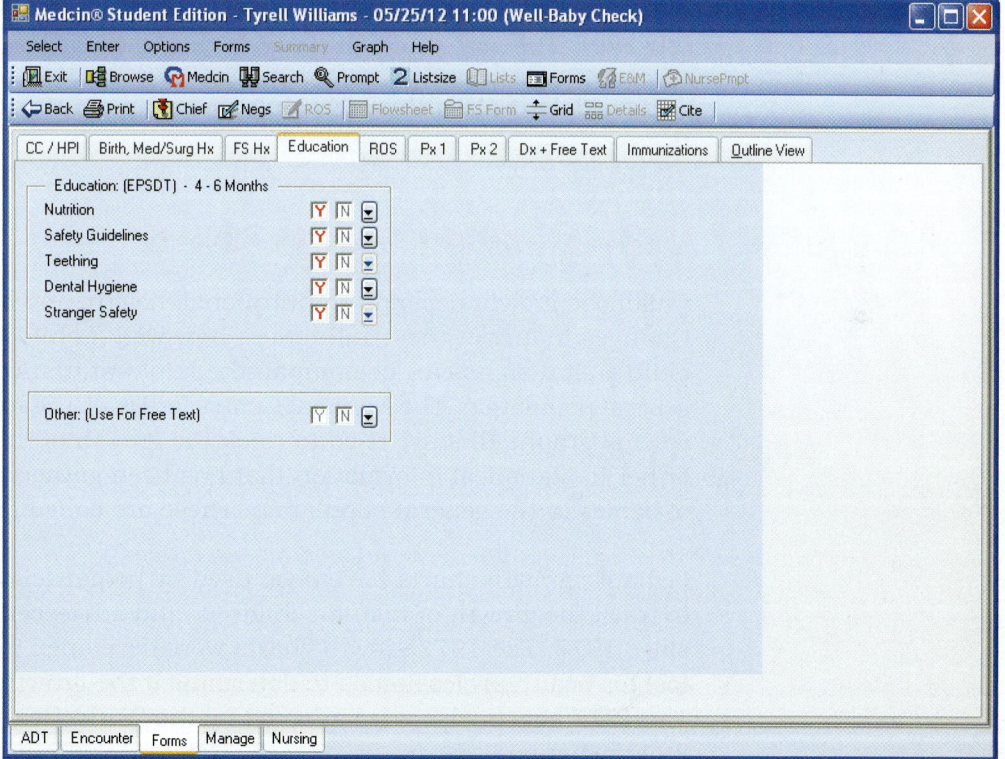

Step 14

During well-baby visits, the pediatrician provides educational information to the mother about the child's development, nutrition, immunizations, and safety.

Locate and click on the tab labeled "Education" at the top of the form.

> **! Alert**
>
> Do not close or exit the encounter until you have a printed copy in your hand. You will lose your work if you exit before printing.

Locate and click on the "Y" check box for each of the following to indicate that these points were covered during the visit:

- ✓ **Y** Nutrition
- ✓ **Y** Safety Guidelines
- ✓ **Y** Teething
- ✓ **Y** Dental Hygiene
- ✓ **Y** Stranger Safety

Compare your screen to Figure 9-12.

Step 15

Click on the Encounter tab at the bottom of your screen.

Click on the Print button on the Toolbar at the top of your screen to invoke the Print Data window.

Be certain there is a check mark in the box next to "Current Encounter" and then click on the appropriate button to either print or export a file, as directed by your instructor.

Compare your printout or file output to Figure 9-13. If there are any differences, other than page breaks, review the previous steps in the exercise and find your error.

If sufficient class time remains, you may continue with the next exercise.

Understanding Growth Charts

Childhood growth depends on nutritional, health, and environmental conditions. Changes in any of these influences how well a child grows and develops. A child's vital signs can be compared against statistical information of the general population. The National Center for Health Statistics (NCHS) has created a set of graphs that are used to track the growth of the child and compare him or her to statistical information that has been gathered about the growth rate of babies in the general population. These are called *growth charts*.

Pediatric growth charts have been used by pediatricians, nurses, and parents to track the growth of infants, children, and adolescents in the United States since 1977. The 1977 growth charts were developed by the NCHS as a clinical tool for health professionals to determine if the growth of a child is adequate. The 1977 charts also were adopted by the World Health Organization (WHO) for international use.

Today, 16 pediatric growth charts are maintained and distributed by the Centers for Disease Control and Prevention (CDC), eight for boys and eight for girls. The charts were revised in 2000, when two new charts were added. The new charts are body mass index-for-age for boys and girls ages 2 to 20 years. Body Mass Index (BMI) is explained later.

Tyrell Williams   Page 1 of 2

Student: your name or id here
Patient: Tyrell Williams: M: 11/10/2011: 5/25/2012 11:00AM

Chief complaint
The Chief Complaint is: 6 month check up.

History of present illness
    Tyrell Williams is a 6 month old male. Source of patient information was mother. No constipation. A normal number of wet diapers per day.

Past medical/surgical history
Reported History:
    Past medical history - No significant past medical history.
    Surgical / Procedural: Prior surgery - No significant surgical history.
    Exposure: No exposure to tuberculosis.
    Environmental Exposure: No exposure to lead.
    Dietary: Infant is breast-feeding.
    Pediatric: No difficulty breast-feeding, rice cereal introduced, with pureed fruit introduced, and with pureed vegetables introduced.

Personal history
Habits: A normal sleep pattern.
Home Environment: Lives with parents and the living environment has secondhand tobacco smoke.

Family history
    Family medical history - No significant family history
    Tobacco use
    Alcohol
    Not using drugs.

Review of systems
Systemic: No systemic symptoms.
Head: No head symptoms.
Eyes: No eye symptoms.
Otolaryngeal: No ear symptoms, no nasal symptoms, and no throat symptoms.
Cardiovascular: No cardiovascular symptoms.
Pulmonary: No pulmonary symptoms.
Gastrointestinal: No gastrointestinal symptoms.
Musculoskeletal: No musculoskeletal symptoms.
Psychological: No psychological symptoms.
Skin: No skin symptoms.

Physical findings
Vital Signs:

Vital Signs/Measurements	Value	Normal Range
Tympanic membrane temperature	99 F	99 - 101
RR	40 breaths/min	36 - 44
PR	128 bpm	110 - 175
Weight	8.7 kg	6.136 - 10
Body length	27.5 in	25.59 - 29.13
Head circumference	43.9 cm	42 - 47

General Appearance:
° Alert. ° Well hydrated. ° Active.
Head:
    Injuries: ° No cephalohematoma.
    Appearance: ° No skull molding was seen. ° Fontanelle was normal.
Neck:
    Appearance: ° Neck was not swollen.
    Suppleness: ° Neck demonstrated no decrease in suppleness.
Eyes:
    General/bilateral:
    Extraocular Movements: ° Normal.
    Pupils: ° Normal.
Ears:
    General/bilateral:
    Outer Ear: ° Auricle normal.
    External Auditory Canal: ° External auditory meatus normal.
    Tympanic Membrane: ° Normal.

▶ **Figure 9-13a Printed encounter note for Tyrell Williams 6-month checkup (page 1 of 2).**

Tyrell Williams

Nose:
    General/bilateral:
        Discharge: ° No nasal discharge seen.
        External Deformities: ° No external nose deformities.

Oral Cavity:
    ° Normal.

Pharynx:
    ° Normal.

Lungs:
    ° Clear to auscultation.

Cardiovascular:
    Heart Rate And Rhythm: ° Normal.
    Heart Sounds: ° Normal.
    Murmurs: ° No murmurs were heard.
    Arterial Pulses: ° Equal bilaterally and normal.
    Venous Filling Time: ° Normal.

Abdomen:
    Auscultation: ° Bowel sounds were normal.
    Palpation: ° Abdomen was soft. ° No mass was palpated in the abdomen.
    Liver: ° Normal to palpation.
    Spleen: ° Normal to palpation.
    Hernia: ° No umbilical hernia was discovered.

Genitalia:
    Penis: ° Normal.
    Testes: ° No cryptorchism was observed.

Musculoskeletal System:
    General/bilateral: ° Normal movement of all extremities.
    Hips:
        General/bilateral: ° Hips showed no abnormalities.

Neurological:
    ° System: normal.

Skin:
    ° General appearance was normal. ° Showed no erythema. ° No cyanosis. ° Not dry. ° No exfoliation was seen.

Growth And Development:
    ° Normal. ° Babbles. ° Rolls over from back to front. ° Passes objects from hand to hand. ° Sits independently. ° Pulls self to a standing position. ° Shy with strangers.

Counseling/Education
- Discussed safety practices
- Discussed stranger safety
- Discussed nutritional needs
- Discussed concerns about teething
- Discussed concerns about dental hygiene

Reason for Visit
    Visit for: 6-month visit.

▶ **Figure 9-13b** Printed encounter note for Tyrell Williams 6-month checkup (page 2 of 2).

The CDC provides the following clinical growth charts:

Infants, birth to 36 months:

◆ Length-for-age and Weight-for-age

◆ Head circumference-for-age and Weight-for-length

Children and adolescents, 2 to 20 years

◆ Stature-for-age and Weight-for-age

◆ BMI-for-age

Preschoolers, 2 to 5 years

◆ Weight-for-stature

What Is a Percentile?

Figure 9-14 shows a blank paper form of one of the CDC growth charts. This form would be used by a clinic to manually record two graphs on one page.

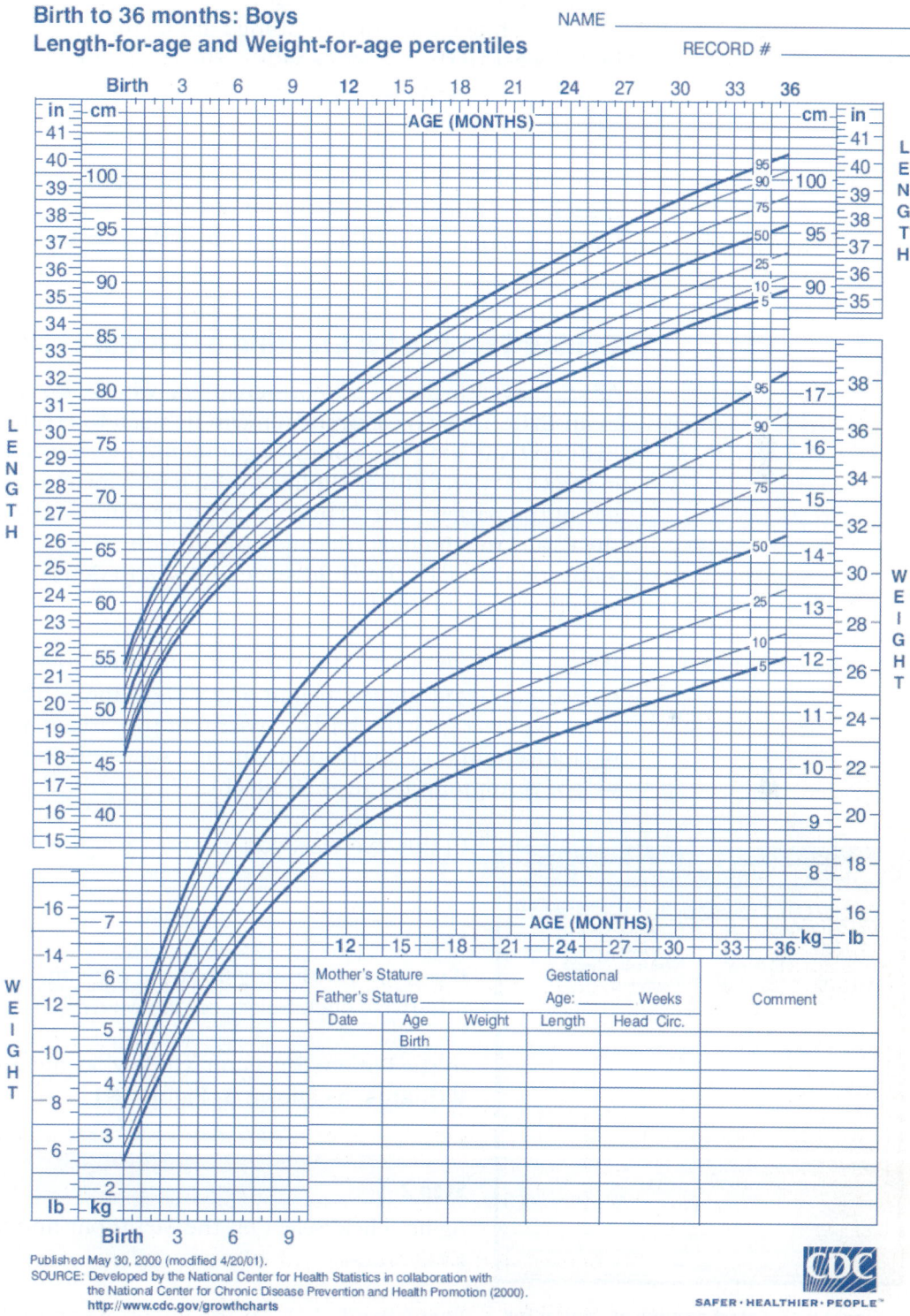

▶ **Figure 9-14** Boys birth to 36 months Length-for-age/Weight-for-age growth chart.

The age of the child is indicated horizontally across the top of the graph and the height and weight measurements are listed vertically down the sides of the graph. The curved blue lines printed across the face of the graph are called *percentiles*. The curved lines represent what percent of the reference population that the individual would equal or exceed. This graph includes the 5th through 95th percentiles; the CDC also has a version available that widens the spectrum by showing a 3rd and 97th percentile.

The patient's weight and height measurements can be marked on the chart under each age for which readings are available. By finding the percentile line closest to the patient's vitals, the clinician can assess the size and growth patterns of the individual as compared to other children in the United States.

For example, a two-year-old boy whose weight is at the 25th percentile weighs the same or more than 25 percent of the reference population of two-year-old boys but weighs less than 75 percent of the two-year-old boys.

Guided Exercise 55: Creating a Growth Chart

As you have learned in previous chapters, when vital signs are routinely entered in an EHR, those measurements can be used to create graphs. Most popular EHR systems have the ability to graph children's measurements over an image of the CDC percentiles, similar to the paper form in Figure 9-14. Using the age of the patient, the EHR software determines if the graph should include the CDC growth chart. Because the growth charts are gender specific, the software also uses the child's age and sex to determine which of the 16 growth charts to display.

Pediatric growth charts often are used for parent education during well-baby checkups. Graphing the height and weight measurements recorded in the EHR to create growth charts is useful in two areas: measuring the growth rate of children, and fighting obesity in our society by determining if a person's weight is appropriate for their height.

In this exercise, you will create a growth chart for Tyrell Williams.

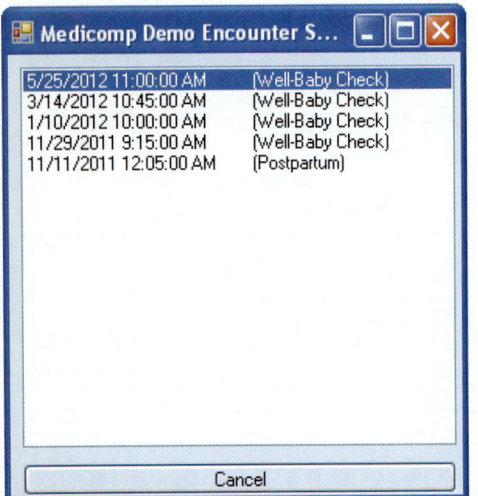

▶ Figure 9-15 Select existing encounter for May 25, 2012 11:00 AM.

Step 1

If you are continuing from the previous exercise, proceed to step 3, otherwise click Select on the Menu bar, and then click Patient.

In the Patient Selection window, locate and click on **Tyrell Williams**, as shown in Figure 9-1.

Step 2

Again, click Select on the Menu bar and then click Existing Encounter.

Locate and click on the encounter dated **May 25, 2012**, at **11:00 AM**, as shown in Figure 9-15.

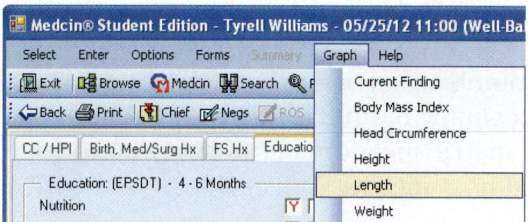

▶ Figure 9-16 Select length from graph menu to generate a Growth Chart.

▶ Figure 9-17 Growth chart for Tyrell Williams.

Step 3

Click on the word "Graph" on the Menu bar, then click "Length" as shown in Figure 9-16.

A pediatric growth chart will be displayed, as shown in Figure 9-17.

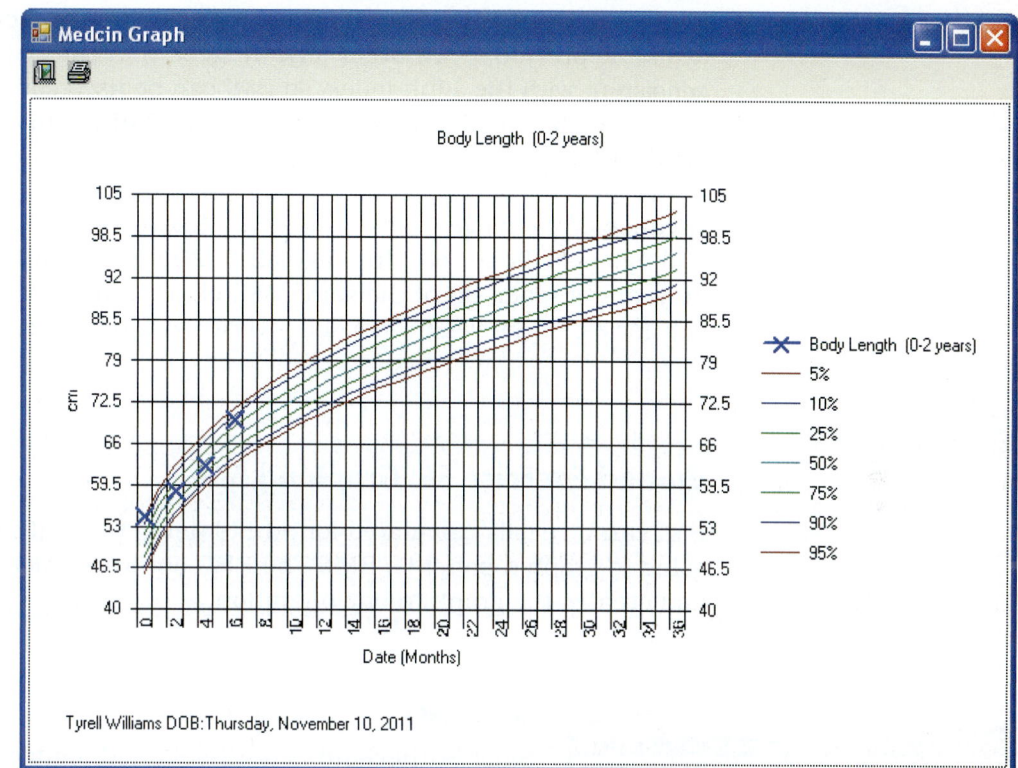

Step 4

Review the growth chart for Tyrell Williams displayed on your screen. The blue X marks the patient's length at the various months, listed across the bottom of the graph. The curved lines represent the comparable growth rate as a percentage of the general population. This is the percentile described previously. Similar growth charts also can be generated for a child's weight and head circumference.

Step 5

Print out Tyrell's growth chart. Locate and click on the Print button in the upper left corner of the graph window to invoke the Print Data window.

In the left column of the Print Data window make sure there is a check mark in the box next to "Body length (0-2 years)" and then click on the appropriate button to either print or export a file, as directed by your instructor.

When your graph has printed successfully, click on the Exit button in upper right corner of the window displaying the growth chart.

This completes Exercise 55.

Chapter 9 | Using the EHR to Improve Patient Health

Body Mass Index

BMI stands for Body Mass Index. It is a number that shows body weight adjusted for height. BMI can be calculated with a simple math formula wt/ht^2 that may be equally applied to either English or metric measurements (wt = pounds and ht = inches) or (wt = kilograms and ht = meters).

The CDC encourages pediatricians to replace use of the older weight-for-stature charts with the new BMI-for-age charts.[1] There are several advantages to using BMI-for-age as a screening tool for overweight and underweight children. BMI-for-age provides a reference for adolescents, which was not available previously. Another advantage is that the BMI-for-age measure is consistent with the adult index, so BMI can be used continuously from two years of age to adulthood. This is important, as BMI in childhood is a determinant of adult BMI.

Because BMI changes substantially as children get older, BMI is gender specific and age specific for children ages 2 to 20 years. Adults of both genders age 20 years or older share the same BMI chart. Adult BMI falls into one of four categories: underweight, normal, overweight, or obese.

Guided Exercise 56: Graphing BMI

BMI can be easily calculated for adults using the EHR. In this exercise you are going to graph a patient's BMI. The EHR software calculates the BMI for you and creates the graph in one operation.

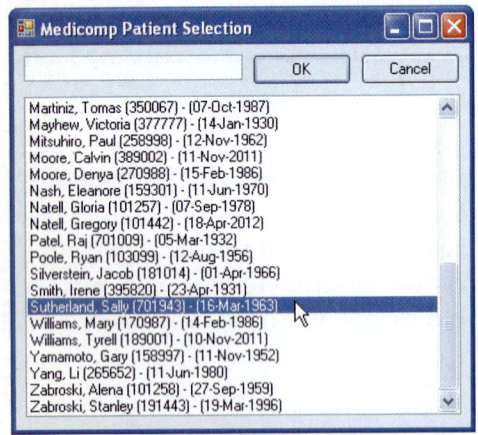

▶ Figure 9-18 Selecting Sally Sutherland from the Patient Selection window.

Case Study

Sally Sutherland is a 48-year-old female with hypertension and borderline diabetes. She has been struggling with her weight and in Chapter 7 you created a graph of her weight gain. In this exercise, you are going to create a graph of Sally's BMI.

Step 1

If you have not already done so, start the Student Edition software.

Click Select on the Menu bar, and then click Patient.

In the Patient Selection window, locate and click on **Sally Sutherland**, as shown in Figure 9-18.

---

[1]Source: U.S. Department of Health and Human Services, Center for Disease Control web site http://www.cdc.gov.

Step 2

Again, click Select on the Menu bar and then click Existing Encounter.

Locate and click on the encounter dated **5/23/2012**, at **10:00 AM**, as shown in Figure 9-19.

Step 3

Click on the word "Graph" on the Menu bar, then click "Body Mass Index" as shown in Figure 9-20.

A graph of her BMI will be displayed, as shown in Figure 9-21.

Step 4

Compare your screen to Figure 9-21 and then print out Ms. Sutherland's BMI graph.

Locate and click on the Print button in the upper left corner of the graph window to invoke the Print Data window.

In the left column of the Print Data window make sure there is a check mark in the box next to "Body Mass Index" and then click on the appropriate button to either print or export a file, as directed by your instructor.

When your graph has printed successfully, click on the Exit button in upper right corner of the window displaying the BMI graph.

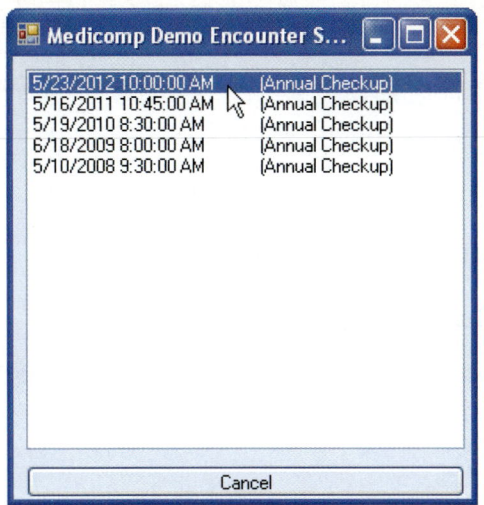

▶ Figure 9-19 Select existing encounter for May 23, 2012 10:00 AM.

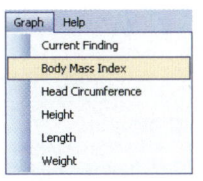

▶ Figure 9-20 Select Body Mass Index from the Graph menu.

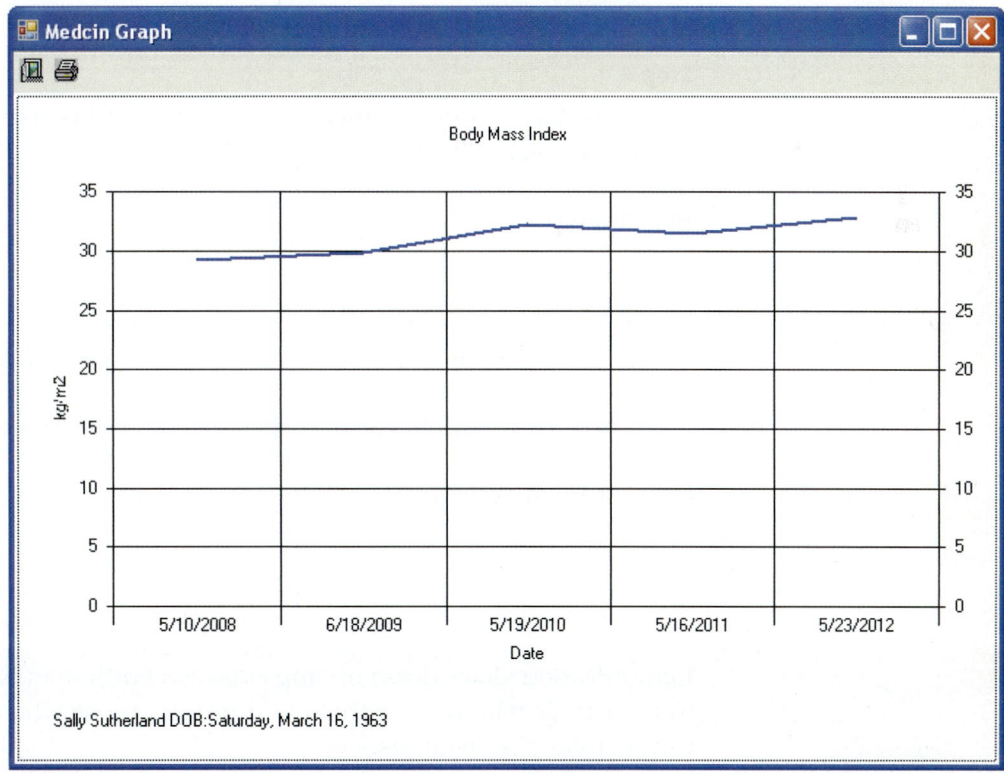

▶ Figure 9-21 Graph of Sally Sutherland's Body Mass Index.

Chapter 9 | Using the EHR to Improve Patient Health

Critical Thinking Exercise 57: Adult BMI Categories

The CDC provides a free online BMI calculator. You will need access to the Internet for this exercise.

Step 1

Start your web browser, and type the following URL in the address:

www.cdc.gov/healthyweight/assessing/bmi/index.html

Step 2

Locate and click on "Adult BMI Calculator."

Step 3

As mentioned previously, there are four categories of adult BMI. At her most recent visit, Sally Sutherland's measurements were:

Height: **5** feet **0** inches

Weight: **168** lbs.

Enter Sally's data, following the on-screen instructions.

When Sally's category is displayed, write the category on your printout of her BMI graph and give it to your instructor. If your BMI graph has been printed to a file, report Ms. Sutherland's category to your instructor separately.

Step 4

Because BMI is a useful measurement for adults as well, you may have an interest in seeing how you measure up.

Repeat step 1.

Step 5

Locate and click on "Adult BMI Calculator" if you are at least 20 years old.

If you are not yet 20, locate and click on the "Children and Teen BMI Calculator."

Follow the on-screen instructions.

The Importance of Childhood Immunizations

Immunization slows down or stops disease outbreaks. Vaccines prevent disease in the people who receive them and protect those who come into contact with unvaccinated individuals.

Although it is true that newborn babies are immune to many diseases because they have antibodies they obtained from their mothers, the duration of this immunity may last only a month to about a year. If a child is not vaccinated and is exposed to a disease germ, the child's body may not be strong enough to fight the disease. Before vaccines, many children died from diseases that vaccines now prevent.

Through childhood immunization, we are now able to control many infectious diseases that were once common in this country, including polio, measles, diphtheria, pertussis (whooping cough), rubella (German measles), mumps, tetanus, and Haemophilus influenzae type b (Hib).[2]

One of the things a pediatrician does during the first two years of well-baby checkups is to compare the child's immunization history against a recommended schedule of immunizations. At regular intervals, the well baby will receive one or more vaccines. By the age of two years, the child is then protected against a vast array of diseases that once caused the death of many children.

When the pediatrician uses an EHR system, the information from all previous immunizations is readily at hand. The clinician can then easily order the next scheduled vaccines appropriate to the patient's age and vaccine history.

Health maintenance systems, such as the one shown in Chapter 2, Figure 2-24, automatically calculate and display the next recommended immunizations. The Student Edition software does not have that feature, but the EHR system you will use in a medical office quite likely will.

Guided Exercise 58: Reviewing and Ordering Vaccines

In this exercise, you will use the Manage tab to verify what immunizations the child has had, and in a subsequent step you will order vaccines that are required.

Case Study

Before concluding Tyrell Williams's six-month checkup, the clinic will compare his immunization records with the immunization schedule recommended by the CDC and administer any vaccines for which he is due.

Step 1

If you have not already started the Student Edition software, do so at this time.

Locate and click Select on the Menu bar, and then click Patient.

In the Patient Selection window, locate and click on **Tyrell Williams** as you have previously (see Figure 9-1).

Step 2

Click Select on the Menu bar, and then click Existing Encounter.

---

[2]Ibid.

Position your mouse pointer on the first encounter in the list, dated **5/25/2012 11:00 AM** and click on it (as shown in Figure 9-15).

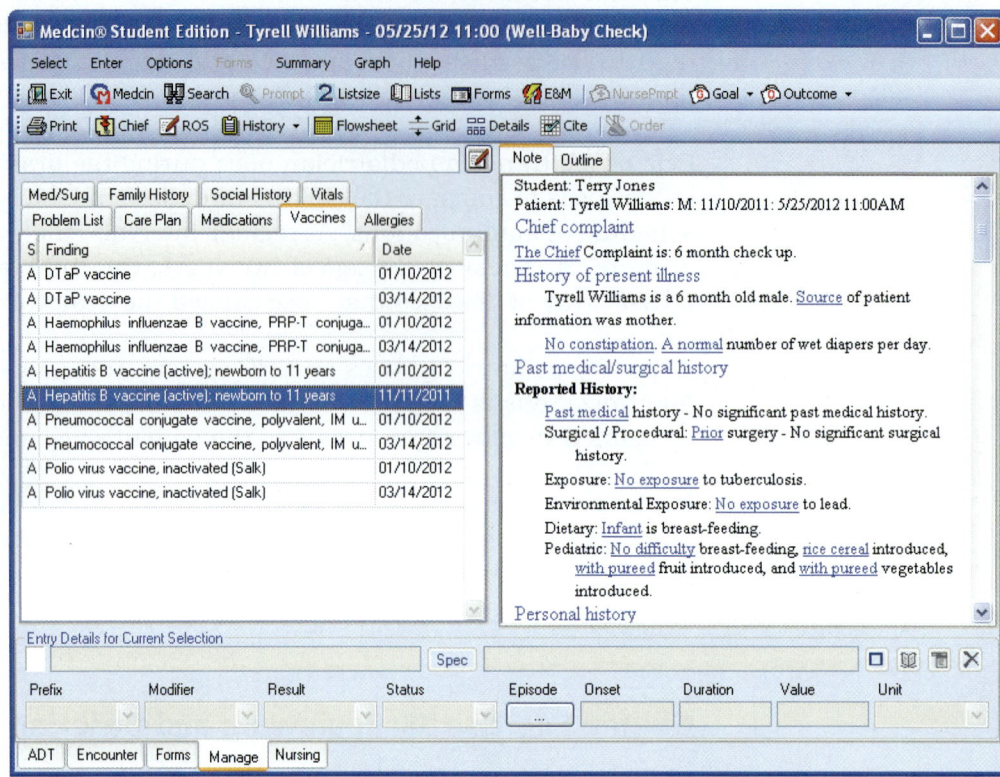

▶ Figure 9-22 Patient Management Vaccines tab history for Tyrell Williams.

Step 3

Locate and click on the tab labeled "Manage" at the bottom of your screen. Click on the tab in the left pane labeled "Vaccines."

The vaccine list can be sorted in two ways. If you click the mouse on the column header labeled "Finding," the vaccines are sorted into groups, allowing you to see easily how many doses have been given of each vaccine. If you click the mouse on the column header for date, the list will be reordered so that you can see exactly which vaccines were administered during each well-baby checkup.

Click the mouse on the column header labeled "Finding" so that the vaccines are sorted by type. Compare your screen to Figure 9-22.

Immunization Schedules from the CDC Immunizations must be acquired over time. Vaccines cannot be given all at once. Several require repeated applications over a period of time, and some such as the measles vaccine, cannot be given to children under the age of one year. Therefore, the CDC and state health departments have designed a schedule to immunize children and

Recommended Immunization Schedule for Persons Aged 0 Through 6 Years—United States • 2010

For those who fall behind or start late, see the catch-up schedule

Vaccine ▼ Age ▶	Birth	1 month	2 months	4 months	6 months	12 months	15 months	18 months	19–23 months	2–3 years	4–6 years
Hepatitis B[1]	HepB	HepB			HepB						
Rotavirus[2]			RV	RV	RV[2]						
Diphtheria, Tetanus, Pertussis[3]			DTaP	DTaP	DTaP	see footnote[3]	DTaP				DTaP
Haemophilus influenzae type b[4]			Hib	Hib	Hib[4]	Hib					
Pneumococcal[5]			PCV	PCV	PCV	PCV				PPSV	
Inactivated Poliovirus[6]			IPV	IPV	IPV						IPV
Influenza[7]					Influenza (Yearly)						
Measles, Mumps, Rubella[8]						MMR		see footnote[8]			MMR
Varicella[9]						Varicella		see footnote[9]			Varicella
Hepatitis A[10]						HepA (2 doses)			HepA Series		
Meningococcal[11]											MCV

Range of recommended ages for all children except certain high-risk groups

Range of recommended ages for certain high-risk groups

▶ **Figure 9-23** Immunization schedule from the CDC.

adolescents from birth through 18 years. The Recommended Immunization Schedules for Persons Aged 0 through 18 Years are approved by the (CDC) Advisory Committee on Immunization Practices, the American Academy of Pediatrics, and the American Academy of Family Physicians.

Figure 9-23 shows the immunization schedule recommended by the CDC for children age 0 to 6 years old. Age categories are shown across the top of the schedule. The full names of recommended vaccine combinations are shown down the left column. An abbreviation for the vaccine name is shown within the grid under the ages at which it should be administered.

Yellow bars within the grid indicate the ideal interval at which a particular series should be completed. Blue bars indicate the ages that should be given special attention if the series has not been completed. The fact that colored bars extend over multiple age categories indicates the flexibility that is built into the recommended schedule.

For example, the chart shows that the CDC recommends that infants should receive the first dose of Hepatitis B vaccine (HepB) soon after birth and ideally before hospital discharge. The second dose would be administered at least 4 weeks after the first dose. The third dose should be given at least 16 weeks after the first dose and at least 8 weeks after the second dose. The last dose in the vaccination series (third or fourth dose) should not be administered before the age of 24 weeks.

Step 4

Compare the vaccine list on your screen to the CDC schedule, as shown in Figure 9-23. Notice the following:

Tyrell was born November 10, 2011.

He had his first dose of Hepatitis B (HepB) before leaving the hospital on 11/11/2005.

He had his second dose during his 2-month checkup on 01/10/2012.

He could receive his third dose during this visit or at his 12-month visit.

Compare his DTaP (Diphtheria, Tetanus, Pertussis) vaccines to the CDC schedule.

    He had his first dose of DTaP during his 2-month checkup on 01/10/2012.

    He had his second dose during his 4-month checkup on 03/14/2012.

    He is due for his third dose during this visit.

Compare his Haemophilus influenzae type B (Hib) doses to the CDC schedule.

    He had his first dose of Hib during his 2-month checkup on 01/10/2012.

    He had his second dose during his 4-month checkup on 03/14/2012.

    He is due for his third dose during this visit.

Compare his IPV (Inactivated Polio Virus) doses to the CDC schedule.

    He had his first dose of IPV during his 2-month checkup on 01/10/2012.

    He had his second dose during his 4-month checkup on 03/14/2012.

    He is due for his third dose during this visit.

Compare his Pneumococcal Conjugate (PCV) doses to the CDC schedule.

    He had his first dose of PCV during his 2-month checkup on 01/10/2012.

    He had his second dose during his 4-month checkup on 03/14/2012.

    He is due for his third dose during this visit.

Of the vaccines remaining on the CDC schedule, he is too young for the Varicella vaccine as well as the Measles, Mumps, Rubella (MMR) vaccine, which is not administered before 12 months.

He is old enough for a flu shot, but the office visit occurs in May and annual flu shots are not available until fall.

Step 5

Now that the clinician has a clear picture of the patient's immunization needs, they can be ordered and administered.

Locate and click on the Forms button on the Toolbar.

Locate and click on the form labeled "**Pediatric 6 Month**." as you did in Exercise 54. If you need assistance, refer to Figure 9-3.

Step 6

Locate and click on the tab labeled "Immunizations" at the top of the form.

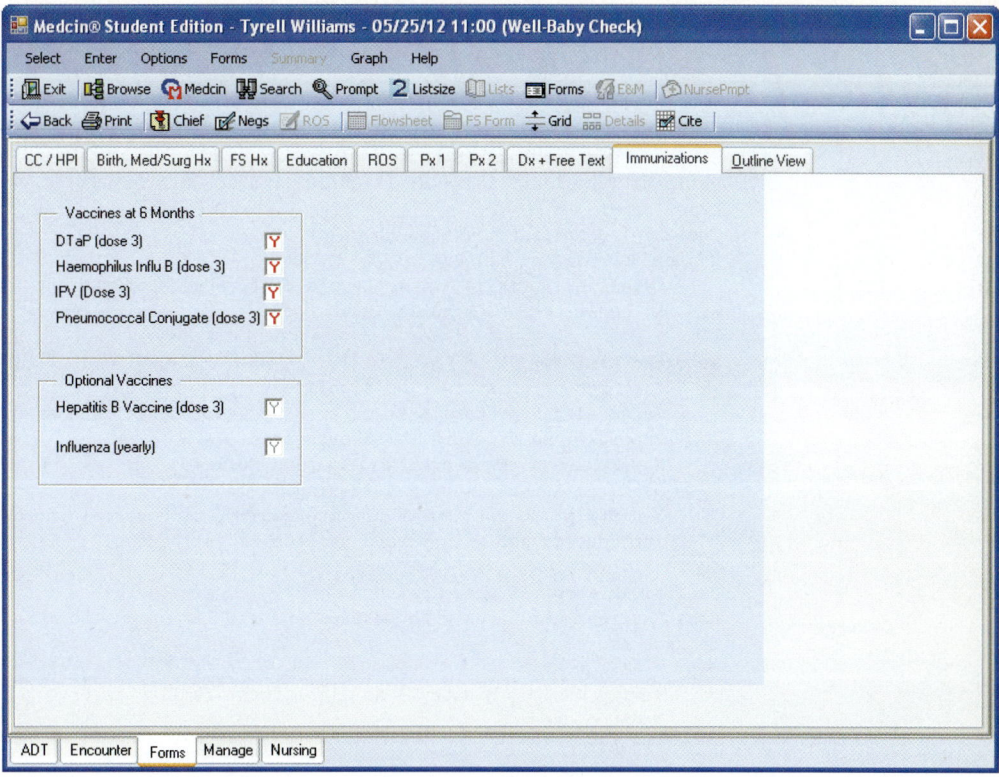

▶ Figure 9-24 Pediatric 6-month form—Immunization tab.

Locate the section labeled "Vaccines at 6 Months" and click the check box for each of the following:

✓ **Y** DTaP (dose 3)

✓ **Y** Haemophilus influ B (dose 3)

✓ **Y** IPV (dose 3)

✓ **Y** Pneumococcal Conjugate (dose 3)

Compare your screen to Figure 9-24.

Locate and click on the tab labeled "Encounter" at the bottom of your screen.

 **Alert** — Do not close or exit the encounter until you have a printed copy in your hand. You will lose your work if you exit before printing.

Step 7

Click on the Print button on the Toolbar at the top of your screen to invoke the Print Data window.

Be certain there is a check mark in the box next to "Current Encounter" and then click on the appropriate button to either print or export a file, as directed by your instructor.

Tyrell Williams   Page 1 of 2

Student: your name or id here
Patient: Tyrell Williams: M: 11/10/2011: 5/25/2012 11:00AM

Chief complaint
The Chief Complaint is: 6 month check up.

History of present illness
    Tyrell Williams is a 6 month old male. Source of patient information was mother. No constipation. A normal number of wet diapers per day.

Past medical/surgical history
Reported History:
    Past medical history - No significant past medical history.
    Surgical / Procedural: Prior surgery - No significant surgical history.
    Exposure: No exposure to tuberculosis.
    Environmental Exposure: No exposure to lead.
    Dietary: Infant is breast-feeding.
    Pediatric: No difficulty breast-feeding, rice cereal introduced, with pureed fruit introduced, and with pureed vegetables introduced.

Personal history
Habits: An abnormal sleep pattern.
Home Environment: Lives with parents and the living environment has secondhand tobacco smoke.

Family history
    Family medical history - No significant family history
    Tobacco use
    Alcohol
    Not using drugs.

Review of systems
Systemic: No systemic symptoms.
Head: No head symptoms.
Eyes: No eye symptoms.
Otolaryngeal: No ear symptoms, no nasal symptoms, and no throat symptoms.
Cardiovascular: No cardiovascular symptoms.
Pulmonary: No pulmonary symptoms.
Musculoskeletal: No musculoskeletal symptoms.
Psychological: No psychological symptoms.
Skin: No skin symptoms.

Physical findings
Vital Signs:

Vital Signs/Measurements	Value	Normal Range
Tympanic membrane temperature	99 F	99 - 101
RR	40 breaths/min	36 - 44
PR	128 bpm	110 - 175
Weight	8.7 kg	6.1 - 10
Body length	27.5 in	25.6 - 29.1
Head circumference	43.9 cm	42 - 47

General Appearance:
    ° Alert. ° Well hydrated. ° Active.
Head:
    Injuries: ° No cephalohematoma.
    Appearance: ° No skull molding was seen. ° Fontanelle was normal.
Neck:
    Appearance: ° Neck was not swollen.
    Suppleness: ° Neck demonstrated no decrease in suppleness.
Eyes:
    General/bilateral:
    Extraocular Movements: ° Normal.
    Pupils: ° Normal.
Ears:
    General/bilateral:
    Outer Ear: ° Auricle normal.
    External Auditory Canal: ° External auditory meatus normal.
    Tympanic Membrane: ° Normal.

▶ **Figure 9-25a** Printed encounter note for Tyrell Williams with immunizations (page 1 of 2).

Tyrell Williams

Nose:
    General/bilateral:
    Discharge: ° No nasal discharge seen.
    External Deformities: ° No external nose deformities.

Oral Cavity:
    ° Normal.

Pharynx:
    ° Normal.

Lungs:
    ° Clear to auscultation.

Cardiovascular:
    Heart Rate And Rhythm: ° Normal.
    Heart Sounds: ° Normal.
    Murmurs: ° No murmurs were heard.
    Arterial Pulses: ° Equal bilaterally and normal.
    Venous Filling Time: ° Normal.

Abdomen:
    Auscultation: ° Bowel sounds were normal.
    Palpation: ° Abdomen was soft. ° No mass was palpated in the abdomen.
    Liver: ° Normal to palpation.
    Spleen: ° Normal to palpation.
    Hernia: ° No umbilical hernia was discovered.

Genitalia:
    Penis: ° Normal.
    Testes: ° No cryptorchism was observed.

Musculoskeletal System:
    General/bilateral: ° Normal movement of all extremities.
    Hips:
    General/bilateral: ° Hips showed no abnormalities.

Neurological:
    ° System: normal.

Skin:
    ° General appearance was normal. ° Showed no erythema. ° No cyanosis. ° Not dry.
    ° No exfoliation was seen.

Growth And Development:
    ° Normal. ° Babbles. ° Rolls over from back to front. ° Passes objects from hand to hand. ° Sits independently. ° Pulls self to a standing position.
    ° Shy with strangers.

Assessment
- Normal routine history and physical well-baby (birth - 2 yr)

Vaccinations
- Received dose of polio virus vaccine, inactivated (Salk)
- Received dose of DTaP vaccine
- Received dose of haemophilus influenzae B vaccine, PRP-T conjugate (4 dose schedule), for intramuscular use
- Received dose of pneumococcal conjugate vaccine, polyvalent, IM use

Counseling/Education
- Discussed safety practices
- Discussed stranger safety
- Discussed nutritional needs
- Discussed concerns about teething
- Discussed concerns about dental hygiene.

▶ **Figure 9-25b** Printed encounter note for Tyrell Williams with immunizations (page 2 of 2).

Compare your printout or file output to Figure 9-25. If it is correct, hand it in to your instructor. If there are any differences, review the previous steps in the exercise and find your error.

Critical Thinking Exercise 59: Determine Your Adult Immunizations

The CDC also publishes a recommended immunization schedule for adults. Because adult immunizations are different from those you had as a child, you may have an interest in seeing what you need as an adult. You will need access to the Internet for this exercise.

Step 1

The CDC provides a free online service to determine you adult immunization needs.

Start your web browser, and type the following URL in the address:

www.cdc.gov/vaccines/recs/schedules/adult-schedule.htm

Step 2

Locate and click on the link "Adolescent & Adult Vaccine Quiz," and then on the link "Take the Quiz."

Step 3

Follow the on-screen instructions.

Step 4

Optionally, you may print out your immunization schedule. You do not have to turn it into your instructor.

Patients' Involvement in Their Own Healthcare

Patients must become involved in their own healthcare to effectively manage and prevent diseases. One such example was the immunization quiz you completed in Exercise 59. Other examples are the use of patient-specific graphs, growth charts, and BMI that are useful in patient education and counseling. Doctors Wenner and Bachman discussed in Chapter 1, the concept of giving the patient a copy of the exam note at the conclusion of the visit. One effect of that is to stimulate compliance by giving the patient written documentation of the diagnosis, therapy, and plan of care discussed during the visit. The other effect is that it improves the patient's recollection of the clinician's advice.

Patient-Entered Data Graphs

Patients can also be engaged in their own healthcare by measuring their own blood pressure at home and keeping a log that they bring to the doctor's office when they have a checkup. Although vital signs such as blood pressure readings from quarterly office visits can be graphed by the EHR software, as you have done in Chapter 7, it is also possible for patients with home computers who keep their daily blood pressure log on a computer to create a graph themselves or to bring the log as a computer file when they have their checkup and let the clinician graph it.

Dr. Allen Wenner provides a spreadsheet template to patients who have Microsoft Excel on their home computers. The template is available on his web

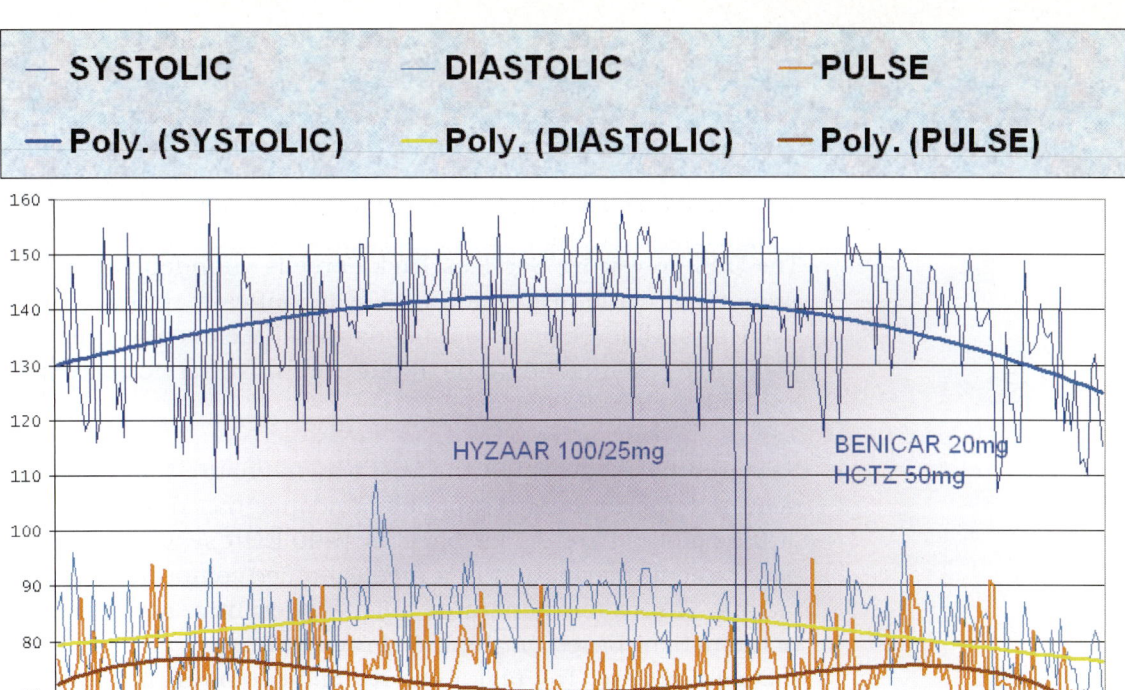

Courtesy of Primetime Medical Software and Instant Medical History.

▶ **Figure 9-26** Graph of blood pressure readings from February to May.

site or on a diskette. He encourages them to record their daily blood pressure in an Excel workbook instead of on paper, and to bring or e-mail a copy of the workbook file when they come to his office.

During the patient's office visit, the clinician and the patient discuss the graph of the daily blood pressure readings compared with the regimen of blood pressure medicine. The physician tells the patient what are the parameters of control, for example, 140/90 for most patients and 130/80 for diabetics. The patient also can view the graph at home as he builds it with his own data. Following the graph on his home computer, the patient knows whether the therapy is working.

Figure 9-26 shows a graph created in Excel by Dr. Wenner and his patient. Notice during the Hyzaar treatment that the patient's blood pressure is tending higher than 140 over 90. The graph indicates the medication needs to be changed. After the doctor shows the patient how to read the graph during the office visit, the patient understands the normal and abnormal range. The patient knows when to call the physician for advice rather than wait until the next appointment. This shared information results in shared decision making. The interaction is transformed from one of gathering information to one of managing the patient's problem. Patients can now look actively at issues of the illness, the treatment regime, and the desired outcome.

This is an example of patients using technology to improve blood pressure management. Research has shown that controlling blood pressure will reduce stroke, heart attack, and vascular disease. Nearly 200 medications are approved for use. There is a combination of drugs that will work for most patients without side effects. Currently in the United States, only about one-third of hypertensive patients have their illness under good control. A number of reasons contribute to this, but increased patient involvement can improve their health.

Preventative Care Screening[3]

The U.S. Preventive Services Task Force is an independent panel of experts in primary care and prevention that systematically reviews the evidence of effectiveness and develops recommendations for clinical preventive services. The task force recommendations about preventive services are based on age, sex, and risk factors for disease.

Research has shown that the best way to ensure that preventive services are delivered appropriately is to make evidence-based information readily available at the point of care. As far back as 1990 EHR systems were developed to compare patient information in a medical office computer with age, sex, and risk factors. The system generated a list of preventive care measures individualized to the patient based on the U.S. Preventive Services Task Force guidelines at the point of care. The task force recommendations have now been incorporated in EHR systems from several vendors.

"Evidence-based guidelines" means analyzing scientific evidence from current research and studies to determine the effectiveness of preventive services. The guidelines recommend both for and against certain measures, including screening, counseling, and preventive medications. However, the guidelines are not set in stone. They vary not only by age and sex but change at recommended intervals based on the individual patient. For example, a blood test measuring total cholesterol and high-density lipoprotein (HDL-C) is recommended every five years for a male over 35, but the interval shortens to every two years if the patient has additional risk factors such as high blood pressure, abnormal lipid levels on previous tests, or a family history of cardiovascular disease before age 50.

Using data in the EHR, the computer is able to find the appropriate guideline based on the patient's age and sex, add to it based on the patient's problem list and history findings, and then reduce the intervals based on abnormal values of previous test results. The system then generates a guideline unique to the patient and delivers it to the clinician's computer screen. Using this information, the clinician can order tests, discuss important health care options, and recommend lifestyle changes to the patient at the point of care.

Preventive care screening programs, such as the health maintenance program shown in Chapter 2, Figure 2-24, makes effective use of the EHR to present the provider with recommended tests for early detection and immunizations for prevention.

---

[3]U.S. Preventive Services Task Force, *The Guide to Clinical Preventive Services 2005*, by (Rockville, MD: Agency for Healthcare Research and Quality).

Real-Life Story

Quality Care for Pediatric and Adult Patients

By Alison Connelly, P.A.

Alison Connelly is a physician assistant in a large multispecialty group in New York City. She was instrumental in setting up the preventative screening guidelines and designing many of the forms used in the EHR at her practice. Her group has eight clinics and 350 employees.

Our practice implemented EHR and uses many of the options the system offers. These include the electronic prescription system, document imaging, a Medcin-based EHR called OmniDoc™, the referral system, and Quality Care Guidelines (the health maintenance, preventative screening component of our EHR).

The document imaging component is terrific! That was actually what got doctors who were resistant to adopting the EHR to start using the system, because they could access their results and reports instantly. Now that we are on the imaging system, any type of patient results that comes in is immediately scanned in so that doctors do not have to wait. This is especially useful in the off-site clinics. We have eight locations. Previously, a document would come in and it could float around for a couple of weeks before it got to the proper clinician, but now as soon as it arrives it is scanned and the clinicians have immediate access to the results on the report on the computer.

A little more than half our total providers use OmniDoc to enter their own exam notes, but all of the pediatric clinicians use it. We created multiple forms for pediatrics based on age and what the milestones and programs for that visit are. We have forms for well-baby visits at 2 months, 4 months, 6 months, 1 year, 15 months, 2 years, and so on. We also created one comprehensive pediatric form for all types of sick visits.

The pediatricians use the growth charts to ensure the pattern of the child's growth is appropriate and follows a trend. The vitals are automatically plotted on the growth chart after they are entered.

We use the Quality Care Guidelines module for age, sex, and disease-specific clinical reminders, primarily in the adult population. I will explain more about that later. Although the guideline system can be used for child immunization scheduling, we were not able to get rid of the manual immunization sheet in each chart.

I initially set up a system that would track immunizations from the encounters. We created multiple codes for each vaccine and every series—for example, MMR1, MMR2, HIB1, and HIB2. This allowed us to capture the right instance of the vaccine in the series. You also can set up OmniDoc to update the guidelines as vaccines are ordered, but I have not done that.

Our providers are still using the immunization sheet in the chart. There are several reasons for that. First was immunization history. We have about 150,000 visits a year and we did not have the manpower to go back and enter the old immunization records manually. With 380 employees, I also was afraid that manual entry could introduce errors. I could not come up with a method to validate the data if we did it that way, so we went forward entering only new immunizations.

The second reason was consistency. The pediatricians did not want to use the guideline system for some patients and not all of them. If a new patient started here when they were born and had all the vaccines administered here, the computer had an accurate record. However, if the patient already had an immunization record in the chart, or if the patient received some shots elsewhere, the guideline system would not be up to date. So, for vaccines it turned out that pediatric providers did not use it that frequently.

The third reason we did not use the guideline system for immunizations was because of CIR, the Citywide Immunization Registry. In New York City, we have to use CIR to report every vaccine we give to children between birth and 18 years old. So, in addition to putting it on the encounter, we have to send it into the city. If that were computerized, it would be much better; we could eliminate double entry by recording it in the EHR and then transmitting it to the city registry.

From a practical standpoint, the guideline system worked much better for adults in our practice. An adult population has more things that have to be monitored and more of the patients have chronic diseases than do children. In addition to the preventive health measures recommended by age and sex, we have special guidelines for the following conditions:

▶ Diabetes

▶ HIV

▶ Hypertension

▶ Hyperlipidemia

- Renal failure
- Ischemic heart disease
- Anemia
- Asthma

Using the guideline system, we are able to make sure, for example, that a diabetes patient has a hemoglobin A1C done every three months.

The guideline system uses patient data that is updated either manually or automatically. Many of the items on the guidelines are tests, and it is possible to have the electronic lab system update them with orders and results. However, the interface to our local lab company never worked consistently, so most of our guideline data is updated via the encounter. I created a section of the encounter that is labeled "QC Guidelines," which contains the factors that are followed. These are marked by the clinician, then our system automatically updates the guideline when the encounter is processed.

The other update process we use is related to our document image system, which updates the patient data when we scan images. For instance, we actually capture the mammogram referral and the mammogram result. When a mammogram result comes in, it is scanned and we update our system. This does three things: it stores an image of the results, it updates the patient data for the guideline, and it updates the managed care referral portion of the EMR.

We also run reports off the EHR data using the guideline system. In the case of the mammogram, this allows us to reconcile patients that are referred out with results we received back. We can then follow up with patients that just never went for their appointment.

I work in the HIV clinic and use both the guideline system and custom forms I designed for the EHR. While I write my notes in OmniDoc, I pull up the guidelines; it is a great monitor.

Because HIV has a lot of clinical guidelines to follow, clinicians can become very focused on HIV and overlook the normal orders that would be done based on age and sex, such as a mammogram or a fecal occult blood test. From that standpoint, the guideline system is very helpful, because it produces a complete list of recommendations for the patient's age and sex as well as any diseases the patient may have. I use it almost like a checklist that I go down to make sure I do not forget anything.

I also created forms in our EHR system specific for the HIV clinic that monitors certain clinical guidelines we have to follow and information such as the percentage of pills taken per week and the number of hours slept a night. I used an option in the form designer to make those fields required. The clinician cannot exit the form until those questions are answered.

The EHR system is great, but if it becomes more sophisticated we could do so much more. I like the idea that it could automatically update guidelines when results are received or automatically send vaccine data to the immunization registry. Similarly, we have to report sexually transmitted diseases within a certain time frame. If we could do that electronically when we received the lab result as well, it would be great.

Chapter Nine Summary

In this chapter you learned to create a pediatric growth chart. You also learned about pediatric forms and to document a well-baby checkup using a wellness form.

The baby's length, weight, and head circumference are measured on each visit. These measurements can be plotted on a graph called a growth chart that compares the individual's growth to statistical information from the general population. Lines on the chart called percentiles represent the percentage of the population that was the same size at the same age. A child who is at the 50th percentile weighs the same or more than 50% of the reference population at that age.

For older children, the CDC now recommends using Body Mass Index (BMI). BMI is a number (wt/ht^2) that represents body weight adjusted for height. BMI can be calculated with inches and pounds or meters and kilograms. BMI is gender specific and age specific for children, but a single BMI chart is used for adults of both genders. The CDC has replaced the older weight-for-stature charts with the new BMI charts.

Immunizations must be acquired over time. Vaccines cannot all be given at once. CDC recommended immunizations are aligned with the well-baby visit intervals. You learned how to compare a child's immunization history to the schedule recommended by the CDC (or state health department) to determine what is required each visit.

Disease prevention through periodic screening and early detection also can save lives. Preventive guidelines, also known as health maintenance guidelines, can be generated by an EHR system. Tailored by the computer, these guidelines recommend tests and preventative measures based on the patient's age and sex, but then dynamically modify the recommendations based on past history and problems unique to the individual. Using this information, the clinician can order tests, discuss important healthcare options, and recommend lifestyle changes to the patient at the point of care.

Task	Exercise	Page #
How to document a well-baby visit	54	343
How to create growth charts	55	356
How to calculate Body Mass Index	56	358

Testing Your Knowledge of Chapter 9

1. List at least three factors the EHR can use to create patient specific preventive screening or health maintenance guidelines.
2. Describe how to create a child's growth chart in the EHR.
3. Why are childhood immunizations important?
4. Describe how to change the order in which vaccines are displayed in patient management.

Give the full name for the following acronyms:

5. DTaP _____
6. HepB _____
7. BMI   _____
8. What are "evidence-based" guidelines?
9. Name the organization that developed pediatric growth charts.
10. What is a growth chart percentile?
11. Adult BMI falls into one of four categories—name them.
12. Review your graph of Sally Sutherland's BMI. Which category does she fall into?
13. At what age is the first dose of HepB recommended?
14. Name the taskforce that develops preventive screening guidelines.
15. You should have produced two narrative documents of patient encounters, one growth chart, and one BMI graph. If you have not already done so, hand these in to your instructor with this test. The printed encounter notes and graphs will count as a portion of your grade.

Chapter Ten

Privacy and Security of Health Records

Learning Outcomes

After completing this chapter, you should be able to:

- List HIPAA transactions and uniform identifiers
- Understand HIPAA privacy and security concepts
- Apply HIPAA privacy policy in a medical facility
- Discuss HIPAA security requirements and safeguards
- Follow security policy guidelines in a medical facility
- Explain electronic signatures

Understanding HIPAA

In Chapter 11 we will discuss various ways the Internet is being used for healthcare, including various implementations of EHR on the Internet, Internet-based personal health records (PHR), and remote access. In Chapter 12 we will explore the relationship of the EHR data to the determination of codes required for medical billing. Before moving to those topics it is prudent to understand HIPAA. HIPAA is an acronym for the Health Insurance Portability and Accountability Act, passed by Congress in 1996.

The HIPAA law was intended to:

- Improve portability and continuity of health insurance coverage.
- Combat waste, fraud, and abuse in health insurance and healthcare delivery.
- Promote use of medical savings accounts
- Improve access to long-term care
- Simplify administration of health insurance

> **Note**
>
> **Covered Entity**
>
> HIPAA documents refer to healthcare providers, plans, and clearinghouses as *covered entities*. In the context of this chapter, think of a covered entity as a healthcare organization and all of its employees.

HIPAA law regulates many things. However, a portion known as the Administrative Simplification Subsection[1] of HIPAA covers entities such as health plans, clearinghouses, and healthcare providers. HIPAA refers to these as *covered entities* or a *covered entity*. This means a healthcare facility or health plan and all of its employees. If you work in the healthcare field, these regulations likely govern your job and behavior. Therefore, it is not uncommon for healthcare workers to use the acronym HIPAA when they actually mean only the Administrative Simplification Subsection of HIPAA.

As someone who will work with patients' health records, it is especially important for you to understand the regulations regarding privacy and security. However, let us begin with a quick review of HIPAA, then study the privacy and security portions in more depth.

HIPAA implementation and enforcement is under the jurisdiction of several entities within the U.S. Department of Health and Human Services (HHS). This chapter will make extensive use of documents prepared by HHS.

Administrative Simplification Subsection

The Administrative Simplification Subsection has four distinct components:

1. Transactions and code sets
2. Uniform identifiers
3. Privacy
4. Security

HIPAA Transactions and Code Sets

The first section of the regulations to be implemented governed the electronic transfer of medical information for business purposes such as insurance claims, payments, and eligibility. When information is exchanged electronically, both sides of the transaction must agree to use the same format in order to make the information intelligible to the receiving system. Before HIPAA, transactions for nearly every insurance plan used a format that contained variations that made it different from another plan's format. This meant that plans could not easily exchange or forward claims to secondary payers and that most providers could only send to a few plans electronically.

Eight HIPAA Transactions

HIPAA standardized these formats by requiring specific transaction standards for eight types of EDI or Electronic Data Interchange. Two additional EDI transactions are not yet finalized. The HIPAA transactions are:

1. Claims or Equivalent Encounters and Coordination of Benefits (COB)
2. Remittance and Payment Advice
3. Claims Status
4. Eligibility and Benefit Inquiry and Response

---

[1]Health Insurance Portability and Accountability Act, Title 2, subsection f.

5. Referral Certification and Authorization
6. Premium Payments
7. Enrollment and De-enrollment in a Health Plan
8. Retail Drug Claims, Coordination of Drug Benefits and Eligibility Inquiry
9. Health Claims Attachments (Not Final)
10. First Report of Injury (Not Final)

Standard Code Sets

In an EDI transaction, certain portions of the information are sent as codes. For the receiving entity to understand the content of the transaction, both the sender and the receiver must use the same codes. In most cases, these are not the nomenclature codes discussed in Chapter 2, but rather standardized codes used to effectively communicate demographic and billing information.

For example, in an insurance claim, charges for patient visits are sent as procedure codes instead of their long descriptions. The medical reasons for the procedure are sent in the claim as diagnosis codes. HIPAA requires the use of standard sets of codes. Two of those standards are:

- Diagnoses (ICD-9-CM) codes
- Procedure (CPT-4 and HCPCS) codes

You have already been introduced to the ICD-9-CM codes. CPT-4 and HCPCS codes will be discussed in Chapter 12.

There are additional codes sets for demographic and payment information. Under HIPAA, any coded information within a transaction is also subject to standards. Just a few examples of the hundreds of other codes include codes for sex, race, type of provider, and relation of the policyholder to the patient.

HIPAA Uniform Identifiers

You can see the importance of both the sending and receiving system using the same formats and code sets to report exactly what was done for the patient. Similarly, it is necessary for multiple systems to identify the doctors, nurses, and healthcare businesses sending the claim or receiving the payment. ID numbers are used in a computer processing instead of names because, for example, there could be many providers named John Smith.

However, before HIPAA, all providers had multiple ID numbers assigned to them for use on insurance claims, prescriptions, and so on. A provider typically received a different ID from each plan and sometimes multiple numbers from the same plan. This created a problem for the billing office to get the right ID on the right claim and made electronic coordination of benefits all but impossible.

HIPAA established uniform identifier standards to be used on all claims and other data transmissions. These include:

- **National Provider Identifier** This type of identifier is assigned to doctors, nurses, and other healthcare providers.

- **Employer Identifier** This identifier is used to identify employer-sponsored health insurance. It is the same as the federal Employer Identification Number (EIN) employers are assigned for their taxes by the Internal Revenue Service.
- **National Health Plan Identifier** This identifier has not yet been implemented, but when it is it will be a unique identification number assigned to each insurance plan and to the organizations that administer insurance plans, such as payers and third-party administrators.

HIPAA Privacy Rule

The HIPAA privacy standards are designed to protect a patient's identifiable health information from unauthorized disclosure or use in any form, while permitting the practice to deliver the best healthcare possible. When the HIPAA legislation was passed, "Congress recognized that advances in electronic technology could erode the privacy of health information. Consequently, Congress incorporated into HIPAA provisions that mandated the adoption of Federal privacy protections for individually identifiable health information."[2]

> **Note**
>
> **PHI**
>
> HIPAA privacy rules frequently refer to PHI or Protected Health Information. PHI is the patient's personally identifiable health information.

Healthcare providers have a strong tradition of safeguarding private health information and have established privacy practices already in effect for their offices. For instance:

- "By speaking quietly when discussing a patient's condition with family members in a waiting room or other public area;
- By avoiding using patients' names in public hallways and elevators, and posting signs to remind employees to protect patient confidentiality;
- By isolating or locking file cabinets or records rooms; or
- By providing additional security, such as passwords, on computers maintaining personal information.

However, The Privacy Rule establishes, for the first time, a foundation of federal protections for the privacy of protected health information. The Rule does not replace federal, state, or other law that grants individuals even greater privacy protections, and covered entities are free to retain or adopt more protective policies or practices."[3]

To comply with the law, privacy activities in the average medical facility might include:

- Providing a copy of the office privacy policy informing patients about their privacy rights and how their information can be used.

---

[2]*Guidance on HIPAA Standards for Privacy of Individually Identifiable Health Information* (Washington, DC: U.S. Department of Health and Human Services Office for Civil Rights, December 3, 2002, and revised April 3, 2003).
[3]Ibid.

- ◆ Asking the patient to acknowledge receiving a copy of the policy or signing a consent form.
- ◆ Obtaining signed authorization forms and in some cases tracking the disclosures of patient health information when it is to be given to a person or organization outside the practice for purposes other than treatment, billing, or payment purposes.
- ◆ Adopting clear privacy procedures for its practice.
- ◆ Training employees so that they understand the privacy procedures.
- ◆ Designating an individual to be responsible for seeing that the privacy procedures are adopted and followed.
- ◆ Securing patient records containing individually identifiable health information so that they are not readily available to those who do not need them.

Let us examine each of these points.

Privacy Policy

"The HIPAA Privacy Rule gives individuals a fundamental new right to be informed of the privacy practices of their health plans and of most of their healthcare providers, as well as to be informed of their privacy rights with respect to their personal health information. Health plans and covered healthcare providers are required to develop and distribute a notice that provides a clear explanation of these rights and practices. The notice is intended to focus individuals on privacy issues and concerns, and to prompt them to have discussions with their health plans and healthcare providers and exercise their rights.

"Covered entities are required to provide a notice in *plain language* that describes:

- ◆ How the covered entity may use and disclose protected health information about an individual.
- ◆ The individual's rights with respect to the information and how the individual may exercise these rights, including how the individual may complain to the covered entity.
- ◆ The covered entity's legal duties with respect to the information, including a statement that the covered entity is required by law to maintain the privacy of protected health information.
- ◆ Whom individuals can contact for further information about the covered entity's privacy policies."[4]

The privacy policy must meet the requirements of HIPAA law and the use or disclosure of PHI must be consistent with the privacy notice provided to the patient.

Consent

The term *consent* has multiple meanings in a medical setting. *Informed consent* refers to the patient's agreement to receive medical treatment having been provided sufficient information to make an informed decision. Consent for medical procedures must still be obtained by the practice.

---

[4]Ibid.

▶ Figure 10-1 The patient acknowledges receipt of the medical facility's privacy policy.

Under the Privacy Rule the term *consent* is only concerned with use of the patient's information, and *should not be confused with consent for the treatment itself*. The Privacy Rule originally required providers to obtain patient "consent" to use and disclose PHI except in emergencies. The rule was almost immediately revised to make it easier to use PHI for the purposes of treatment, payment, or operation of the healthcare practice.

Under the revised Privacy Rule, the patient gives consent to the use of their PHI for the purposes of treatment, payment, and operation of the healthcare practice. The patient does this by signing a consent form or signing an acknowledgment that he or she has received a copy of the office's privacy policy. Figure 10-1 shows a patient receiving a copy of the medical facility's privacy policy. The patient signs a form acknowledging receipt of the privacy policy.

Although most healthcare providers who see patients obtain HIPAA "consent" as part of the routine demographic and insurance forms that patients sign, the rule permits some uses of PHI without the individual's authorization:

◆ A healthcare entity may use or disclose PHI for its own treatment, payment, and healthcare operations activities. For example, a hospital may use PHI to provide healthcare to the individual and may consult with other healthcare providers about the individual's treatment.

◆ A healthcare provider may disclose PHI about an individual as part of a claim for payment to a health plan.

◆ A healthcare provider may disclose PHI related to the treatment or payment activities of any healthcare provider (including providers not covered by the Privacy Rule). Consider these examples:

   A doctor may send a copy of an individual's medical record to a specialist who needs the information to treat the individual.

   A hospital may send a patient's healthcare instructions to a nursing home to which the patient is transferred.

   A physician may send an individual's health plan coverage information to a laboratory that needs the information to bill for tests ordered by the physician.

A hospital emergency department may give a patient's payment information to an ambulance service that transported the patient to the hospital in order for the ambulance provider to bill for its treatment.

◆ A health plan may use protected health information to provide customer service to its enrollees.

Others within the office can use PHI also. For example, doctors and nurses can share the patient's chart to discuss what the best course of care might be. The doctor's administrative staff can access patient information to perform billing, transmit claims electronically, post payments, file the charts, type up the doctor's progress notes, and print and send out patient statements.

The office administrators can also use PHI for operation of the medical practice—for example, to determine how many staff they will need on a certain day, whether they should invest in a particular piece of equipment, what types of patients they are seeing the most of, where most of their patients live, and any other uses that will help make the office operate more efficiently.

The HHS *Guidance* document states: "A covered entity may voluntarily choose, but is not required, to obtain the individual's consent for it to use and disclose information about him or her for treatment, payment, and healthcare operations. A covered entity that chooses to have a consent process has complete discretion under the Privacy Rule to design a process that works best for its business and consumers."[5]

Modifying HIPAA Consent

"Individuals have the right to request restrictions on how a covered entity will use and disclose protected health information about them for treatment, payment, and healthcare operations. A covered entity is not required to agree to an individual's request for a restriction, but is bound by any restrictions to which it agrees.

"Individuals also may request to receive confidential communications from the covered entity, either at alternative locations or by alternative means. For example, an individual may request that her healthcare provider call her at her office, rather than her home. A healthcare provider must accommodate an individual's reasonable request for such confidential communications."[6]

Authorization

"A *consent* document is not a valid permission to use or disclose protected health information for a purpose that requires an *authorization* under the Privacy Rule."[7]

Authorization differs from consent in that it *does* require the patient's permission to disclose PHI.

Some instances that would require an authorization include sending the results of an employment physical to an employer and sending immunization records or the results of an athletic physical to the school.

---

[5]Ibid.
[6]Ibid.
[7]Ibid.

Authorization for Use or Disclosure of Protected Health Information

Health Information and Record Management Department

Medical Record Number

RI0001

Patient's Name: _____ Soc. Sec. #: _____
                Last   First   Middle
Telephone #: _____ Date of Birth: _____

Check if the patient is a: ☐ Shands at UF employee   ☐ University of Florida Physician

Send information to *(name of person, organization, or agency with full address):*

Name: _____
Attention: _____ Telephone #: _____
Address: _____
City: _____ State: _____ Zip: _____

Purpose of release *(For example: continued care, personal, etc.)*: _____
Specific items or dates needed: _____
☐ Cardiovascular Reports ☐ EKG Report ☐ Laboratory Results ☐ Pathology Report ☐ Radiology (X-ray) Reports
☐ History & Physical ☐ Operative Report ☐ Discharge Summary ☐ Emergency Room ☐ Other: _____

Needed for doctor's appointment on: _____
                                    (Date)   (Time)

This authorization is for release of medical records and information including diagnosis, treatment, and/or examination related to mental health (psychiatry or psychology), drug and/or alcohol abuse, HIV testing/AIDS, and sexually transmissible diseases.

As required by state and federal law, Shands at the University of Florida may not use or disclose your health information, except as provided in our Notice of Privacy Practices, without your authorization. Your signature on this form indicates that you are giving permission for the uses and disclosures of the protected health information described on this form.

I understand that state law prohibits the re-disclosure of the information disclosed to the persons/entities listed above without my further authorization, but that Shands at the University of Florida cannot guarantee that the recipient of the information will not re-disclose this information contrary to such prohibition.

I understand that this authorization will remain in effect for one (1) year or until I revoke it in writing. I understand that I may revoke this authorization at any time. I understand that if I revoke this authorization, I must do so in writing to Health Information and Record Management, Shands at the University of Florida, PO Box 100345, Gainesville, FL 32610-0345. I further understand that any such revocation does not apply to information already released in response to this authorization.

I understand that I am under no obligation to sign this authorization. I further understand that my ability to obtain treatment will not depend in any way on whether I sign this authorization.

I understand that I have a right to inspect and to obtain a copy of any information disclosed.

I hereby release Shands at the University of Florida and its employees from any and all liability that may arise from the release of information as I have directed.

I understand that I may be charged a fee of up to $1.00 per page (plus applicable tax and handling) for every page copied. This fee is waived for copies provided to a health care provider for continuing medical care. I understand that this fee is within the limits allowable by Florida law.

I hereby authorize Shands at the University of Florida to release health information as described above.

Patient's Signature: _____ Date: _____

Signature of Parent or Guardian: _____ Date: _____

Relationship to Patient: _____

After completing this release, please return it to:
   Medical Reports Section
   Health Information and Record Management
   Shands at the University of Florida
   PO Box 100345
   Gainesville, FL 32610-0345
Or fax it to: (352) 265-1098, telephone number: (352) 265-0131.

Rev.12/21/06   PS1985

For Department Use Only
Copied: _____ Initials: _____
Encounter: _____
AN ___ EM ___ OT ___
AU ___ EN ___ PF ___
CC ___ ER ___ PN ___
CH ___ FS ___ PO ___
CL ___ HP ___ PR ___
CO ___ IM ___ PS ___
DS ___ LA ___ PT ___
EC ___ LD ___ PX ___
EE ___ OP ___ XX ___
EK ___
Other: _____
Date: _____

▶ **Figure 10-2** Sample authorization form with elements required by HIPAA.

The appearance of an authorization form is up to the practice, but the Privacy Rule requires that it contain specific information. Specific elements required by HIPAA are highlighted in yellow on the sample form shown in Figure 10-2. The required elements are:

- Date signed
- Expiration date
- To whom the information may be disclosed
- What is permitted to be disclosed
- For what purpose the information may be used

Unlike the Privacy Rule concept of consent, authorizations are not global. A new authorization is signed each time there is a different purpose or need for the patient's information to be disclosed.

Research Authorizations are usually required for researchers to use PHI. The only difference in a research authorization form is that it is not required to have an expiration date. The authorization may be combined with consent to participate in a clinical trial study for example.

Research Exceptions To protect the patient's information while at the same time ensuring that researchers continue to have access to medical information necessary to conduct vital research, the Privacy Rule does allow some exceptions that permit researchers to access PHI without individual authorizations. Typically, these are cases where the patients are deceased; where the researcher is using PHI only to prepare a research protocol; or where a waiver has been issued by an internal review board, specifying that none of the information will be removed or used for any other purpose.

Marketing The Privacy Rule specifically defines marketing and *requires* individual authorization for all uses or disclosures of PHI for *marketing purposes* with limited exceptions. These exceptions are generally when information from the provider is sent to all patients in the practice about improvements or additions to the practice; or when the information is sent to the patient about their own treatments. For example, a reminder about an annual checkup is *not* marketing.

Government Agencies

One area that permits the disclosure of PHI without a patient's authorization or consent is when it is requested by an authorized government agency. Generally, such requests are for legal (law enforcement, subpoena, court orders, and so on) or public health purposes. A request by the FDA for information on patients who are having adverse reactions to a particular drug might be an example. Another example might be an audit of medical records by CMS to determine if sufficient documentation exists to justify Medicare claims.

The Privacy Rule also permits the disclosure of PHI, without authorization, to public health authorities for the purpose of preventing or controlling disease or injury as well as maintaining records of births and deaths. This would include, for example, the reporting of a contagious disease to the CDC or an adverse reaction to a regulated drug or product to the FDA.

Similarly, providers are also permitted to disclose PHI concerning on-the-job injuries to workers' compensation insurers, state administrators, and other entities to the extent required by state workers' compensation laws.

To ensure that covered entities protect patients' privacy as required, the Privacy Rule requires that health plans, hospitals, and other covered entities cooperate with efforts by the HHS Office for Civil Rights (OCR) to investigate complaints or otherwise ensure compliance.

Minimum Necessary

The Privacy Rule *minimum necessary* standard is intended to limit unnecessary or inappropriate access to and disclosure of PHI beyond what is necessary. For example, if an insurance plan requests the value of a patient's hematocrit test to justify a claim for administering a drug, then the minimum necessary disclosure would be to send only the hematocrit result, not the patient's entire panel of tests.

> ### No Restrictions on PHI for Treatment of the Patient
>
> The minimum necessary standard does not apply to disclosures to or requests by a healthcare provider for PHI used for treatment purposes.

"The Privacy Rule generally requires covered entities to take reasonable steps to limit the use or disclosure of, and requests for, protected health information to the minimum necessary to accomplish the intended purpose. The minimum necessary standard does not apply to the following:

- Disclosures to or requests by a healthcare provider for treatment purposes.
- Disclosures to the individual who is the subject of the information.
- Uses or disclosures made pursuant to an individual's authorization.
- Uses or disclosures required for compliance with the Health Insurance Portability and Accountability Act (HIPAA) Administrative Simplification Rules.
- Disclosures to the Department of Health and Human Services (HHS) when disclosure of information is required under the Privacy Rule for enforcement purposes.
- Uses or disclosures that are required by other law.

The implementation specifications for this provision require a covered entity to develop and implement policies and procedures appropriate for its own organization, reflecting the entity's business practices and workforce."[8]

Incidental Disclosures

"Many customary healthcare communications and practices play an important or even essential role in ensuring that individuals receive prompt and effective healthcare. Due to the nature of these communications, as well as the various

---

[8]Ibid.

environments in which individuals receive healthcare, the potential exists for an individual's health information to be disclosed incidentally.

For example, a hospital visitor may overhear a provider's confidential conversation with another provider or a patient, or may glimpse a patient's information on a sign-in sheet or nursing station whiteboard.

The HIPAA Privacy Rule is not intended to impede customary and essential communications and practices and, thus, does not require that *all* risk of incidental use or disclosure be eliminated to satisfy its standards. In fact the Privacy Rule permits certain incidental uses and disclosures of protected health information to occur where there is in place reasonable safeguards and minimum necessary policies and procedures that normally protect an individual's privacy"[9]

Incidental disclosure is one of the exceptions to the Breach Notification Requirements discussed later in the chapter.

Critical Thinking Exercise 60: What Is Required?

You are employed at a medical facility. One of your patients is being treated as a result of an accident. The doctor asks you to take the patient's x-rays to a colleague for an opinion on the best treatment.

1. What HIPAA form does the patient need to sign to permit you to do this?

The same patient is suing the company responsible for the accident. His attorney has asked for copies of the x-rays to prepare his case.

2. What HIPAA form does the patient need to sign to permit you to do this?

A Patient's Right to Know about Disclosures

Whether the practice has disclosed PHI based on a signed authorization or to comply with a government agency, the patient is entitled to know about it. Therefore, in most cases the medical facility must track the disclosure.

The Privacy Rule gives individuals the right to receive a report of all disclosures made for purposes *other than* treatment, payment, or operation of the healthcare facility. The report must include the date of the disclosure, to whom the information was provided, a description of the information, and the stated purpose for the disclosure. The patient can request the report at any time and the practice must keep the records for at least six years.

Furthermore, Breach Notification Requirements, discussed later in the chapter, require the patient to be notified in writing when a breach of his or her PHI has occurred.

Patient Access to Medical Records

In addition to protecting privacy, the law generally allows patients to be able to see and obtain copies of their medical records and request corrections if they identify errors and mistakes. Health plans, doctors, hospitals, clinics, nursing homes, and other covered entities generally must provide access to these

---

[9]Ibid.

records within 30 days of a patient request, but may charge patients for the cost of copying and sending the records.

Personal Representatives

"There may be times when individuals are legally or otherwise incapable of exercising their rights, or simply choose to designate another to act on their behalf with respect to these rights. Under the Rule, a person authorized to act on behalf of the individual in making healthcare related decisions is the individual's *personal representative.*

"The Privacy Rule requires covered entities to treat an individual's personal representative as the individual with respect to uses and disclosure of the individual's protected health information, as well as the individual's rights under the Rule.

"The personal representative stands in the shoes of the individual and has the ability to act for the individual and exercise the individual's rights. . . . In addition to exercising the individual's rights under the Rule, a personal representative may also authorize disclosures of the individual's protected health information."[10]

In general, the personal representative's authority over privacy matters parallels his or her authority to act on other healthcare decisions.

- Where the personal representative has broad authority in making healthcare decisions, the personal representative is treated as the individual for all purposes under the Privacy Rule.
- Examples include a parent with respect to a minor child or a legal guardian of a mentally incompetent adult.
- Where the representative's authority is limited to particular healthcare decisions, his or her authority concerning PHI is limited to the same area.
- For example, a person with limited healthcare power of attorney about artificial life support could not sign an authorization for the disclosure of protected health information for marketing purposes.

If the Individual Is:	The Personal Representative Is:	Examples:
An Adult or an Emancipated Minor	A person with legal authority to make health care decisions on behalf of the individual	Health care power of attorney Court appointed legal guardian General power of attorney
A Minor (not emancipated)	A parent, guardian, or other person acting in loco parentis with legal authority to make health care decisions on behalf of the minor child	Parent, guardian, or other person (with exceptions in state law)
Deceased	A person with legal authority to act on behalf of the decedent or the estate (not restricted to health care decisions)	Executor of the estate Next of kin or other family member Durable power of attorney

▶ **Figure 10-3** Persons automatically recognized as personal representatives for patients.

---

[10]Ibid.

♦ When the patient is deceased, a person who has authority to act on the behalf of the deceased or the deceased's estate is the personal representative for all purposes under the Privacy Rule.

Figure 10-3 provides a chart of who must be recognized as the personal representative for a category of individuals.

Minor Children

In most cases, the parent, guardian, or other person acting as parent is the personal representative and acts on behalf of the minor child with respect to PHI. Even if a parent is not the child's personal representative, the Privacy Rule permits a parent access to a minor child's PHI when and to the extent it is permitted or required by state or other laws.

Conversely, regardless of the parent's status as personal representative, the Privacy Rule prohibits providing access to or disclosing the child's PHI to the parent, when and to the extent it is expressly prohibited under state or other laws.

However, the Privacy Rule specifies three circumstances in which the parent is not the personal representative with respect to certain health information about the minor child. "The three exceptional circumstances when a parent is not the minor's personal representative are:

♦ When State or other law does not require the consent of a parent or other person before a minor can obtain a particular healthcare service, and the minor consents to the healthcare service;

Example: A State law provides an adolescent the right to obtain mental health treatment without the consent of his or her parent, and the adolescent consents to such treatment without the parent's consent.

♦ When a court determines or other law authorizes someone other than the parent to make treatment decisions for a minor;

Example: A court may grant authority to make healthcare decisions for the minor to an adult other than the parent, to the minor, or the court may make the decision(s) itself.

♦ When a parent agrees to a confidential relationship between the minor and the physician.

Example: A physician asks the parent of a 16-year-old if the physician can talk with the child confidentially about a medical condition and the parent agrees.

If state or other laws are silent or unclear about parental access to the minor's PHI, the Privacy Rule grants healthcare professionals the discretion to allow or deny a parent access to a minor's PHI based on their professional judgment."[11]

Critical Thinking Exercise 61: Comparison of Privacy Policy

The purpose of this exercise is let you compare what you have learned in this chapter to an example from the real world. Visit a medical office or other healthcare facility and ask for a copy of their HIPAA Privacy Policy. Some providers have their privacy policy on their web site as well. You may print a copy of that as an acceptable alternative for the purpose of this exercise.

---

[11]Ibid.

▶ **Figure 10-4** Patient Privacy Summary published by the U.S. Department of Health and Human Services Office for Civil Rights.

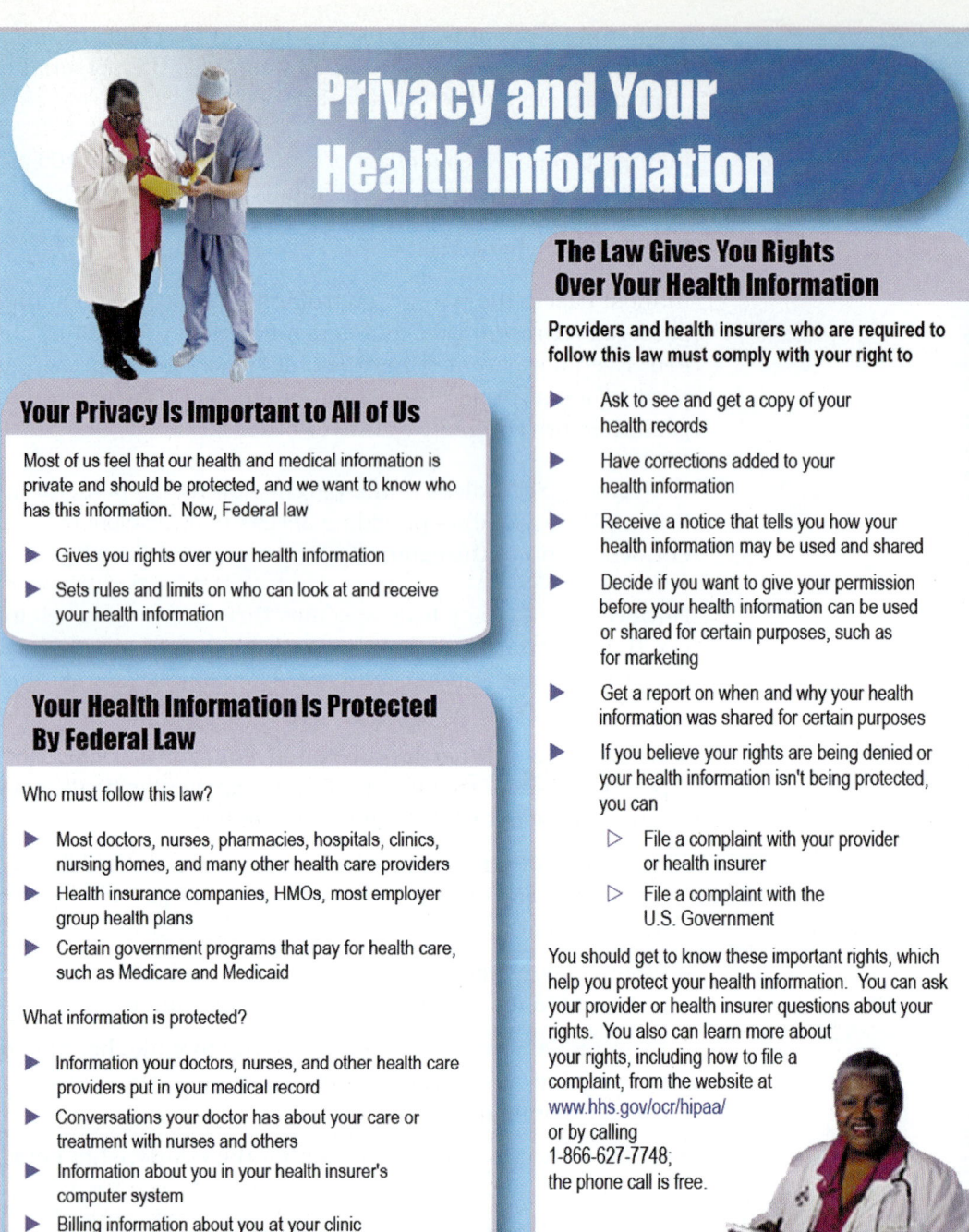

Figure 10-4 provides a summary of patient rights under the Privacy Rule. It is published by HHS Office of Civil Rights, which enforces the HIPAA Privacy Rule.

Compare the contents of the privacy policy you obtained with the points in the sample CMS brochure shown in Figure 10-4. Write a brief paper comparing the points of the government document with the copy of the privacy policy you obtained. Give your instructor a copy of the privacy policy you obtained along with your paper.

▶ Figure 10-4
(Continued)

PRIVACY

The Law Sets Rules and Limits on Who Can Look At and Receive Your Information

To make sure that your information is protected in a way that does not interfere with your health care, your information can be used and shared

- ▶ For your treatment and care coordination
- ▶ To pay doctors and hospitals for your health care and help run their businesses
- ▶ With your family, relatives, friends or others you identify who are involved with your health care or your health care bills, unless you object
- ▶ To make sure doctors give good care and nursing homes are clean and safe
- ▶ To protect the public's health, such as by reporting when the flu is in your area
- ▶ To make required reports to the police, such as reporting gunshot wounds

Your health information cannot be used or shared without your written permission unless this law allows it. For example, without your authorization, your provider generally cannot

- ▶ Give your information to your employer
- ▶ Use or share your information for marketing or advertising purposes
- ▶ Share private notes about your mental health counseling sessions

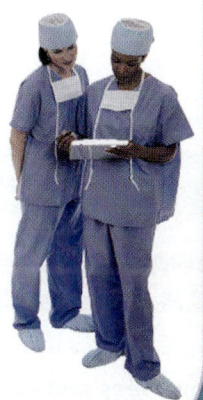

For More Information

This is a brief summary of your rights and protections under the federal health information privacy law. You can learn more about health information privacy and your rights in a fact sheet called *"Your Health Information Privacy Rights"*. You can get this from the website at www.hhs.gov/ocr/hipaa/. You can also call 1-866-627-7748; the phone call is free.

Other privacy rights
Another law provides additional privacy protections to patients of alcohol and drug treatment programs. For more information, go to the website at www.samhsa.gov.

Published by:

U.S. Department of Health & Human Services Office for Civil Rights

The Law Protects the Privacy of Your Health Information

Providers and health insurers who are required to follow this law must keep your information private by

- ▶ Teaching the people who work for them how your information may and may not be used and shared
- ▶ Taking appropriate and reasonable steps to keep your health information secure

Page 2

Business Associates

"The HIPAA Privacy Rule applies only to covered entities—healthcare providers, plans, and clearinghouses. However, most healthcare providers and health plans do not carry out all of their healthcare activities and functions by themselves. Instead, they often use the services of a variety of other persons or businesses. The Privacy Rule allows covered providers and health plans to disclose protected health information to these business associates if the providers or plans obtain written satisfactory assurances that the business associate will use the information only for the purposes for which it was engaged by the covered entity, will safeguard the information from misuse, and will help the covered entity comply with some of the covered entity's duties under the Privacy Rule.

"The covered entity's contract or other written arrangement with its business associate must contain the elements specified in the privacy rule. For example, the contract must:

- Describe the permitted and required uses of protected health information by the business associate;

- Provide that the business associate will not use or further disclose the protected health information other than as permitted or required by the contract or as required by law; and

- Require the business associate to use appropriate safeguards to prevent a use or disclosure of the protected health information other than as provided for by the contract."[12]

It will generally fall to the privacy officer (or in larger healthcare organizations, the legal department) to ensure that business associate agreements are on file for clearinghouses, transcription services, and other businesses with whom your employer will exchange PHI.

Civil and Criminal Penalties

"Congress provided civil and criminal penalties for covered entities that misuse personal health information. For civil violations of the standards, OCR may impose monetary penalties up to $100 per violation, up to $25,000 per year, for each requirement or prohibition violated. Criminal penalties apply for certain actions such as knowingly obtaining protected health information in violation of the law. Criminal penalties can range up to $50,000 and one year in prison for certain offenses; up to $100,000 and up to five years in prison if the offenses are committed under 'false pretenses'; and up to $250,000 and up to 10 years in prison if the offenses are committed with the intent to sell, transfer or use protected health information for commercial advantage, personal gain or malicious harm."[13]

The Health Information Technology and Economic Clinical Health (HITECH) Act, introduced in Chapter 1, also addressed privacy and security concerns associated with the electronic transmission of health information, in part through several provisions that strengthen the civil and criminal enforcement of the HIPAA rules. Subtitle D of the HITECH Act strengthens the civil and criminal enforcement of the HIPAA rules by establishing:

- Four categories of violations that reflect increasing levels of culpability

- Four corresponding tiers of penalty amounts that significantly increase the minimum penalty amount for each violation

- A maximum penalty amount of $1.5 million for all violations of an identical provision

> **Note**
>
> **HIPAA Duties of OCR versus CMS**
>
> OCR within HHS oversees and enforces the Privacy Rule, whereas CMS oversees and enforces all other Administrative Simplification requirements, including the Security Rule.

---

[12]Ibid.

[13]*Fact Sheet: Protecting the Privacy of Patients' Health Information* (Washington, DC: U.S. Department of Health and Human Services Press Office, April 14, 2003).

Real-Life Story

The First HIPAA Privacy Case

From the United States Attorney's Office, Western District of Washington[14]

The first legal case under the privacy rule concerned the theft of patient demographic information (name, address, date of birth, Social Security number) by an employee in a medical office.

The former employee of a cancer care facility pled guilty in federal court in Seattle, Washington, to wrongful disclosure of individually identifiable health information for economic gain. This is the first criminal conviction in the United States under the health information privacy provisions of the Health Insurance Portability and Accountability Act (HIPAA), which became effective in April 2003. Those provisions made it illegal to wrongfully disclose personally identifiable health information.

The former employee admitted that he obtained a cancer patient's name, date of birth, and Social Security number while employed at the medical facility, and that he disclosed that information to get four credit cards in the patient's name. He also admitted that he used several of those cards to rack up more than $9,000 in debt in the patient's name. He used the cards to purchase various items, including video games, home improvement supplies, apparel, jewelry, porcelain figurines, groceries, and gasoline for his personal use. He was fired shortly after the identity theft was discovered.

"Too many Americans have experienced identity theft and the nightmare of dealing with bills they never incurred. To be a vulnerable cancer patient, fighting for your life, and having to cope with identity theft is just unconscionable," stated United States Attorney John McKay. "This case should serve as a reminder that misuse of patient information may result in criminal prosecution."

The case was investigated by the Federal Bureau of Investigation (FBI) and prosecuted by the United States Attorney's Office. The man was sentenced to a term of 10 to 16 months. He also has agreed to pay restitution to the credit card companies, and to the patient for expenses he incurred as a result of the misuse of his identity.

Although identity theft is serious, the consequences are much greater in a medical setting than if the same information had been stolen from an ordinary business. Why? Because even the patient's name and date of birth are part of the PHI. Additionally, the disclosure of medical information for financial gain could have resulted in a sentence of 10 years for each violation. The case serves as a reminder for everyone in the healthcare field of the personal responsibility for protecting PHI.

Although the patient privacy rule under HIPAA does not restrict the internal use of health information by the staff for treatment, payment, and office operations, you should make every effort to protect your patients' privacy and always follow the privacy policy of the practice.

---

[14] Press release, United States Attorney's Office, Western District of Washington, August 19, 2004.

HIPAA Security Rule

To fully comply with the Privacy Rule, it is necessary to understand and implement the requirements of the Security Rule. There are clearly areas in which the two rules supplement each other because both the HIPAA Privacy and Security rules are designed to protect identifiable health information. However, the Privacy Rule covers PHI in all forms of communications, whereas the Security Rule covers only electronic information. Because of this difference, security discussions are assumed to be about the protection of electronic health records, but the Security Rule actually covers all PHI that is stored electronically. This is called EPHI.

> **Note**
>
> **PHI—EPHI**
>
> The Security Rule applies only to EPHI, whereas the Privacy Rule applies to PHI, which may be in electronic, oral, and paper form.

In this section, you will learn about the Security Rule. As with the previous section, much of the information provided is drawn directly from HHS documents. HHS regulates and enforces HIPAA using two different divisions for enforcement. OCR or Office of Civil Rights enforces the Privacy Rule whereas CMS enforces the Security Rule. As an employee of a covered entity, it is important that you participate in the security training and follow the security policy and procedures of your healthcare organization.

Why a Security Rule?

Before HIPAA, no generally accepted set of security standards or general requirements for protecting health information existed in the healthcare industry. At the same time, new technologies were evolving, and the healthcare industry began to move away from paper processes and rely more heavily on the use of computers to pay claims, answer eligibility questions, provide health information, and conduct a host of other administrative and clinically based functions.

In order to provide more efficient access to critical health information, covered entities are using web-based applications and other "portals" that give physicians, nurses, medical staff as well as administrative employees more access to electronic health information. Although this means that the medical workforce can be more mobile and efficient (i.e., physicians can check patient records and test results from wherever they are), the rise in the adoption rate of these technologies creates an increase in potential security risks. As the country moves towards its goal of a National Health Information Infrastructure (NHII), and greater use of electronic health records, protecting the confidentiality, integrity, and availability of EPHI becomes even more critical.

The security standards in HIPAA were developed for two primary purposes.

- First, and foremost, the implementation of appropriate security safeguards protects certain electronic healthcare information that may be at risk.

- Second, protecting an individual's health information, although permitting the appropriate access and use of that information, ultimately promotes the use of electronic health information in the industry.

The Privacy Rule and Security Rule Compared

The Privacy Rule sets the standards for, among other things, who may have access to PHI, while the Security Rule sets the standards for ensuring that only those who should have access to EPHI will actually have access. The primary distinctions between the two rules follow:

- **Electronic versus oral and paper:** The Privacy Rule applies to all forms of patients' protected health information, whether electronic, written, or oral. In contrast, the Security Rule covers only protected health information that is in electronic form. This includes EPHI that is created, received, maintained, or transmitted.

- ◆ **"Safeguard" requirement in Privacy Rule:** While the Privacy Rule contains provisions that currently require covered entities to adopt certain safeguards for PHI, the Security Rule provides for far more comprehensive security requirements and includes a level of detail not provided in the Privacy Rule section.

Security Standards

The security standards are divided into the categories of administrative, physical, and technical safeguards. Each category of the safeguards is comprised of a number of standards, which generally contain a number of implementation specifications.

- ◆ **Administrative safeguards:** In general, these are the administrative functions that should be implemented to meet the security standards. These include assignment or delegation of security responsibility to an individual and security training requirements.

- ◆ **Physical safeguards:** In general, these are the mechanisms required to protect electronic systems, equipment and the data they hold, from threats, environmental hazards and unauthorized intrusion. They include restricting access to EPHI and retaining off-site computer backups.

- ◆ **Technical safeguards:** In general, these are primarily the automated processes used to protect data and control access to data. They include using authentication controls to verify that the person signing onto a computer is authorized to access that EPHI, or encrypting and decrypting data as it is being stored and/or transmitted.

In addition to the safeguards (listed above), the Security Rule also contains several standards and implementation specifications that address organizational requirements, as well as policies and procedures and documentation requirements.[15]

Implementation Specifications

An implementation specification is an additional detailed instruction for implementing a particular standard. Implementation requirements and features within the categories were listed in the Security Rule by alphabetical order to convey that no one item was considered to be more important than another.

Implementation specifications in the Security Rule are either "Required" or "Addressable." Addressable does not mean optional.

To help you understand the organization of safeguards, security standards, and implementation specifications, a matrix of the HIPAA Security Rule is provided in Figure 10-5. The matrix is a part of the official rule and published as an appendix to the rule.[16] You may wish to refer to Figure 10-5 as we discuss each of the following sections.

---

[15]Adapted from *Security 101 for Covered Entities*, HIPAA Security Series (Baltimore, MD: Centers for Medicare and Medicaid Services, November 2004 and revised March 2007).

[16]Figure adapted from Appendix A to Subpart C of Part 164, Health Insurance Reform: Security Standards; Final Rule.

Security Standards Matrix

Administrative Safeguards

Standards	Section of Rule	Implementation Specifications	Required or Addressable
Security Management Process	§ 164.308Addressable(1)	Risk Analysis	Required
		Risk Management	Required
		Sanction Policy	Required
		Information System Activity Review	Required
Assigned Security Responsibility	§ 164.308Addressable(2)		Required
Workforce Security	§ 164.308Addressable(3)	Authorization and/or Supervision	Addressable
		Workforce Clearance Procedure	Addressable
		Termination Procedures	Addressable
Information Access Management	§ 164.308Addressable(4)	Isolating Health Care Clearinghouse Function	Required
		Access Authorization	Addressable
		Access Establishment and Modification	Addressable
Security Awareness and Training	§ 164.308Addressable(5)	Security Reminders	Addressable
		Protection from Malicious Software	Addressable
		Log-In Monitoring	Addressable
		Password Management	Addressable
Security Incident Procedures	§ 164.308Addressable(6)	Response and Reporting	Required
Contingency Plan	§ 164.308Addressable(7)	Data Backup Plan	Required
		Disaster Recovery Plan	Required
		Emergency Mode Operation Plan	Required
		Testing and Revision Procedure	Addressable
		Applications and Data Criticality Analysis	Addressable
Evaluation	§ 164.308Addressable(8)		Required
Business Associate Contracts and Other Arrangement	§ 164.308(b)(1)	Written Contract or Other Arrangement	Required

▶ **Figure 10-5** HIPAA Security Standards Matrix.

Administrative Safeguards[17]

The name *Security Rule* sounds like it might be very technical, but the largest category of the rule is Administrative Safeguards. The Administrative Safeguards comprise over half of the HIPAA security requirements.

Administrative Safeguards are the policies, procedures, and actions to manage the implementation and maintenance of security measures to protect EPHI. The Administrative Standards are as follows:

---

[17]Adapted from *Security Standards: Administrative Safeguards*, HIPAA Security Series #2 (Baltimore, MD: Centers for Medicare and Medicaid Services, May 2005 and revised March 2007).

Physical Safeguards

Standards	Section of Rule	Implementation Specifications	Required or Addressable
Facility Access Controls	§ 164.310Addressable(1))	Contingency Operations	Addressable
		Facility Security Plan	Addressable
		Access Control and Validation Procedures	Addressable
		Maintenance Records	Addressable
Workstation Use	§ 164.310(b)Required		Required
Workstation Security	§ 164.310(c)Required		Required
Device and Media Controls	§ 164.310(d)(1)	Disposal	Required
		Media Re-use	Required
		Accountability	Addressable
		Data Backup and Storage	Addressable

Technical Safeguards

Standards	Section of Rule	Implementation Specifications	Required or Addressable
Access Control	§ 164.312Addressable(1)	Unique User Identification	Required
		Emergency Access Procedure	Required
		Automatic Logoff	Addressable
		Encryption and Decryption	Addressable
Audit Controls	§ 164.312(b)		Required
Integrity	§ 164.312(c)(1)	Mechanism to Authenticate Electronic Protected Health Information	Addressable
Person or Entity Authentication	§ 164.312(d)		Required
Transmission Security	164.312(e)(1)	Integrity Controls	Addressable
		Encryption	Addressable

▶ Figure 10-5 (Continued)

Security Management Process

The Security Management Process is the first step. It is used to establish the administrative processes and procedures. There are four implementation specifications in the Security Management Process standard.

1. **Risk Analysis** Identify potential security risks and determine how likely they are to occur and how serious they would be.

2. **Risk Management** Make decisions about how to address security risks and vulnerabilities. The risk analysis and risk management decisions are used to develop a strategy to protect the confidentiality, integrity, and availability of EPHI.

3. **Sanction Policy** Define for employees what the consequences of failing to comply with security policies and procedures are.

4. **Information System Activity Review** Regularly review records such as audit logs, access reports, and security incident tracking reports. The information system activity review helps to determine if any EPHI has been used or disclosed in an inappropriate manner.

Assigned Security Responsibility

Similar to the Privacy Rule, which requires an individual be designated as the privacy official, the Security Rule requires one individual be designated the security official. The security official and privacy official can be the same person, but do not have to be. The security official has overall responsibility for security; however, specific security responsibilities may be assigned to other individuals. For example, the security official might designate the IT Director to be responsible for network security. Figure 10-6 shows a staff meeting at which security policy is being reviewed.

▶ **Figure 10-6** Medical office staff review security policy and appoint security officer.

Workforce Security

Within Workforce Security there are three addressable implementation specifications:

1. **Authorization or Supervision** Authorization is the process of determining whether a particular user (or a computer system) has the right to carry out a certain activity, such as reading a file or running a program.

2. **Workforce Clearance Procedure** Ensure members of the workforce with authorized access to EPHI receive appropriate clearances.

3. **Termination Procedures** Whether the employee leaves the organization voluntarily or involuntarily, termination procedures must be in place to

remove access privileges when an employee, contractor, or other individual previously entitled to access information no longer has these privileges.

Information Access Management

Restricting access to only those persons and entities with a need for access is a basic tenet of security. By managing information access, the risk of inappropriate disclosure, alteration, or destruction of EPHI is minimized. This safeguard supports the "minimum necessary standard" of the HIPAA Privacy Rule.

The Information Access Management standard has three implementation specifications.

1. **Access Authorization** In the Workforce Security standard (see preceding section) the healthcare organization determines who has access. This section requires the organization to identify who has authority to grant that access and the process for doing so.

2. **Access Establishment and Modification** Once a covered entity has clearly defined who should get access to what EPHI and under what circumstances, it must consider how access is established and modified.

3. **Isolating Healthcare Clearinghouse Functions** A clearinghouse is a unique HIPAA-covered entity whose function is to translate nonstandard transactions into HIPAA standards. In the very rare case that your healthcare organization also operates a clearinghouse, the rule requires the isolation of clearinghouse computers from other systems in the organization.

Security Awareness and Training

Security awareness and training for all new and existing members of the workforce is required. Figure 10-7 illustrates training an employee. In addition, periodic retraining should be given whenever environmental or operational changes affect the security of EPHI.

► Figure 10-7 Training a new employee on security policy and procedures.

Regardless of the Administrative Safeguards a covered entity implements, those safeguards will not protect the EPHI if the workforce is unaware of its role in adhering to and enforcing them. Many security risks and vulnerabilities within covered entities are internal. This is why the Security Awareness and Training standard is so important.

The Security Awareness and Training standard has four implementation specifications.

1. **Security Reminders** Security reminders might include notices in printed or electronic form, agenda items and specific discussion topics at monthly meetings, focused reminders posted in affected areas, as well as formal retraining on security policies and procedures.

2. **Protection from Malicious Software** One important security measure that employees need to be reminded of is that malicious software is frequently brought into an organization through email attachments and programs that are downloaded from the Internet. As a result of an unauthorized infiltration, EPHI and other data can be damaged or destroyed or, at a minimum, can require expensive and time-consuming repairs.

3. **Log-In Monitoring** Security awareness and training also should address how users log onto systems and how they are supposed to manage their passwords. Typically, an inappropriate or attempted login is when someone enters multiple combinations of user names or passwords to attempt to access an information system. Fortunately, many information systems can be set to identify multiple unsuccessful attempts to log in. Other systems might record the attempts in a log or audit trail. Still other systems might disable a password after a specified number of unsuccessful log in attempts. Once capabilities are established, the workforce must be made aware of how to use and monitor them.

4. **Password Management** In addition to providing a password for access, entities must ensure that workforce members are trained on how to safeguard the information. Train all users and establish guidelines for creating passwords and changing them during periodic change cycles.

Security Incident Procedures

Security incident procedures must address how to identify security incidents and provide that the incident be reported to the appropriate person or persons. Examples of possible incidents include:

- Stolen or otherwise inappropriately obtained passwords that are used to access EPHI

- Corrupted backup tapes that do not allow restoration of EPHI

- Virus attacks that interfere with the operations of information systems with EPHI

- Physical break-ins leading to the theft of media with EPHI

- Failure to terminate the account of a former employee that is then used by an unauthorized user to access information systems with EPHI

- Providing media with EPHI, such as a PC hard drive or laptop, to another user who is not authorized to access the EPHI before removing the EPHI stored on the media

There is one required implementation specification for this standard:

1. **Response and Reporting** Establish adequate response and reporting procedures for these and other types of events.

Contingency Plan

What happens if a healthcare facility experiences a power outage, a natural disaster, or other emergency that disrupts normal access to healthcare information? A contingency plan consists of strategies for recovering access to EPHI should the organization experience a disruption of critical business operations. The goal is to ensure that EPHI is available when it is needed.

The Contingency Plan standard includes five implementation specifications:

1. **Data Backup Plan** Data backup plans are an important safeguard and a required implementation specification. Most covered entities already have backup procedures as part of current business practices.
2. **Disaster Recovery Plan** These are procedures to restore any loss of data.
3. **Emergency Mode Operation Plan** When operating in emergency mode because of a technical failure or power outage, security processes to protect EPHI must be maintained.
4. **Testing and Revision Procedures** Periodically test and revise contingency plans.
5. **Application and Data Criticality Analysis** Analyze software applications that store, maintain, or transmit EPHI and determine how important each is to patient care or business needs. A prioritized list of specific applications and data will help determine which applications or information systems get restored first or that must be available at all times.

Evaluation

Ongoing evaluation of security measures is the best way to ensure all EPHI is adequately protected. Periodically evaluate strategy and systems to ensure that the security requirements continue to meet the organization's operating environments.

Business Associate Contracts and Other Arrangements

The Business Associate Contracts and Other Arrangements standard is comparable to the Business Associate Contract standard in the Privacy Rule, but is specific to business associates that create, receive, maintain, or transmit EPHI. The standard has one implementation specification:

1. **Written Contract or Other Arrangement** Covered entities should have a written agreement with business associates ensuring the security of EPHI. Government agencies that exchange EPHI should have a Memorandum of Understanding.

Real-Life Story

Contingency Plans Ensure Continued Ability to Deliver Care

By Tanya Townsend

Chief information Officer at HSHS—Eastern Division in Greenbay, Wisconsin.

Several years ago I had the opportunity to set up a new hospital that used all-digital health records—that is, there were no paper patient records, charts, or orders. As I talked to other hospitals and IT professionals about our accomplishments, one question I was frequently asked was, "What are your contingency plans in case of a power or system failure?"

Much of our plan was designed to avoid an outage in the first place. We had several redundancies in place to prevent that. For example, there are two WAN (wide-area network) connections—completely separate links going out different sides of the building to our core data center. The idea is that if one of those lines were to become disconnected for any reason, the other would seamlessly continue to function. In actual capacity they are balanced to make sure that can be accomplished. We also have redundancies on the LAN (local-area network) with wireless access points. As mobile as we are, we are very dependent on wireless.

For data protection we have multiple data centers. On the hospital side we have two different data centers that are redundant. On the ambulatory side there are three. In addition to these data centers, we also back up all the data in real time to another off-site location in Madison, which is a couple of hours away.

Should we lose connectivity because both links are down, we have a satellite antenna on the roof that can access the backup data in Madison. So as long as you can still power up your computer, you can get to the historical information. Electrical power can be supplied by an emergency generator that is designed to come online automatically in the event of a power loss.

Should the systems ever be completely down, we still need to take care of patients. In that event, we have downtime procedures for using paper forms that would allow us to continue to function. The necessary forms can be printed on demand but we have some preprinted copies on hand in case a power loss prevented us from printing. Once the system again becomes available, we have a policy and process for incorporating that paper documentation back into the system so we are not forced to carry that paper record forward.

The other area where we have built redundancy is our voice communications. We are using Voice-over-IP technology for our telecommunications, so a power or network outage would mean our phones would not work either. We plan for that by having cell phones and radios available. We also have certain phones that use traditional phone lines so we can continue to communicate.

We do a practice run, a mock downtime situation twice a year. One run is just simulated, but for the second one we actually take the systems down to make sure that we know how we are going to function. We also have planned outages, where we need to take the system down because we are upgrading it or doing maintenance on it. We continue to strive to keep those outages as brief as possible, but in those events we go to our downtime procedures and we continuously learn and improve on these.

Physical Safeguards[18]

The Security Rule defines physical safeguards as physical measures, policies, and procedures to protect a covered entity's electronic information systems and related buildings and equipment from natural and environmental hazards, and unauthorized intrusion.

---

[18]Adapted from *Security Standards: Physical Safeguards*, HIPAA Security Series #3 (Baltimore, MD: Centers for Medicare and Medicaid Services, February 2005 and revised March 2007).

▶ **Figure 10-8** Review facility security and emergency contingency plans periodically.

Facility Access Controls

Facility Access Controls are policies and procedures to limit physical access to electronic information systems and the facility or facilities in which they are housed. Figure 10-8 illustrates a staff meeting on facility security.

There are four implementation specifications.

1. **Access Control and Validation Procedures** Access Control and Validation are procedures to determine which persons should have access to certain locations within the facility based on their role or function.

2. **Contingency Operations** Contingency operations refer to physical security measures to be used in the event of the activation of contingency plans.

3. **Facility Security Plan** The Facility Security Plan defines and documents the safeguards used to protect the facility or facilities. Some examples include:

    ◆ Locked doors, signs warning of restricted areas, surveillance cameras, alarms

    ◆ Property controls such as property control tags, engraving on equipment

    ◆ Personnel controls such as identification badges, visitor badges, or escorts for large offices

    ◆ Private security service or patrol for the facility

    In addition, all staff or employees must know their roles in facility security.

4. **Maintenance Records** Document facility security repairs and modifications such as changing locks, making routine maintenance checks, or installing new security devices.

Workstation Use

Inappropriate use of computer workstations can expose a covered entity to risks, such as virus attacks, compromise of information systems, and breaches of confidentiality. Specify the proper functions to be performed by electronic computing devices.

Workstation use also applies to workforce members using off-site workstations that can access EPHI. This includes employees who work from home, in satellite offices, or in another facility.

Workstation Security

Although the Workstation Use standard addresses the policies and procedures for how workstations should be used and protected, the Workstation Security standard addresses how workstations are to be physically protected from unauthorized users.

Device and Media Controls

Device and Media Controls are policies and procedures that govern the receipt and removal of hardware and electronic media that contain EPHI, into and out of a facility, and the movement of these items within the facility.

The Device and Media Controls standard has four implementation specifications, two required and two addressable.

1. **Disposal** When disposing of any electronic media that contains EPHI, make sure it is unusable or inaccessible.

2. **Media Reuse** Instead of disposing of electronic media, covered entities may want to reuse it. The EPHI must be removed before the media can be reused.

3. **Accountability** When hardware and media containing EPHI are moved from one location to another, a record should be maintained of the move. Portable computers and media present a special challenge. Portable technology is getting smaller, is less expensive, and has an increased capacity to store large quantities of data, making accountability even more important and challenging.

4. **Data Backup and Storage** This specification protects the availability of EPHI and is similar to the Data Backup Plan for the contingency plan.

Technical Safeguards[19]

The Security Rule defines technical safeguards as "the technology and the policy and procedures for its use that protect electronic protected health information and control access to it."

Because security technologies are likely to evolve faster than legislative rules, specific technologies are not designated by the Security Rule. Where the CMS

---

[19]Adapted from *Security Standards: Technical Safeguards*, HIPAA Security Series #4 (Baltimore, MD: Centers for Medicare and Medicaid Services, May 2005 and revised March 2007).

guidance documents provide examples of security measures and technical solutions to illustrate the standards and implementation specifications, these are just examples. The Security Rule is *technology neutral*; healthcare organizations have the flexibility to use any solutions that help them meet the requirements of the rule.

Access Control

The Access Control standard outlines the procedures for limiting access to only those persons or software programs that have been granted access rights by the Information Access Management administrative standard (discussed earlier). Figure 10-9 shows one of the most common methods of access control.

Courtesy of Allscripts, LLC.

▶ **Figure 10-9** A clinician logs on Allscripts Enterprise using a unique user ID and secure password.

Four implementation specifications are associated with the Access Controls standard.

1. **Unique User Identification** Unique User Identification provides a way to identify a specific user, typically by name or number. This allows an entity to track specific user activity and to hold users accountable for functions performed when logged into those systems.

2. **Emergency Access Procedure** Emergency Access procedures are documented instructions and operational practices for obtaining access to necessary EPHI during an emergency situation. Access Controls are necessary

under emergency conditions, although they may be very different from those used in normal operational circumstances.

3. **Automatic Logoff** As a general practice, users should log off the system they are working on when their workstation is unattended. However, there will be times when workers may not have the time, or will not remember, to log off a workstation. Automatic logoff is an effective way to prevent unauthorized users from accessing EPHI on a workstation when it is left unattended for a period of time.

   Many applications have configuration settings for automatic logoff. After a predetermined period of inactivity, the application will automatically log off the user. Some systems that may have more limited capabilities may activate an operating system screen saver that is password protected after a period of system inactivity. In either case, the information that was displayed on the screen is no longer accessible to unauthorized users.

4. **Encryption and Decryption** Encryption is a method of converting regular text into code. The original message is encrypted by means of a mathematical formula called an *algorithm*. The receiving party uses a key to convert (decrypt) the coded message back into plain text. Encryption is part of access control because it prevents someone without the key from viewing or using the information.

Audit Controls

Audit Controls are "hardware, software, and/or procedural mechanisms that record and examine activity in information systems."

Most information systems provide some level of audit controls and audit reports. These are useful, especially when determining if a security violation occurred. This standard has no implementation specifications.

Integrity

Protecting the integrity of EPHI is a primary goal of the Security Rule. EPHI that is improperly altered or destroyed can result in clinical quality problems, including patient safety issues. The integrity of data can be compromised by both technical and nontechnical sources.

There is one addressable implementation specification in the Integrity standard.

1. **Mechanism to Authenticate Electronic Protected Health Information** Once risks to the integrity of EPHI data have been identified during the risk analysis, security measures are put in place to reduce the risks.

Person or Entity Authentication

The Person or Entity Authentication standard has no implementation specifications. This standard requires "procedures to verify that a person or entity seeking access to electronic protected health information is the one claimed."

There are several ways to provide proof of identity for authentication.

Courtesy of Digital Identification Solutions, LLC.

▶ **Figure 10-10** A staff ID card that uses smart card technology.

- Require something known only to that individual, such as a password or PIN.
- Require something that individuals possess, such as a smart card, a token, or a key. An example of a smart card is shown in Figure 10-10.
- Require something unique to the individual, such as a biometric. Examples of biometrics include fingerprints, voice patterns, facial patterns, or iris patterns.

Most covered entities use one of the first two methods of authentication. Many small provider offices rely on a password or PIN to authenticate the user.

Transmission Security

Transmission Security procedures are the "measures used to guard against unauthorized access to electronic protected health information that is being transmitted."

The Security Rule allows for EPHI to be sent over an electronic open network as long as it is adequately protected. This standard has two implementation specifications.

1. **Integrity Controls** Protecting the integrity of EPHI maintained in information systems was discussed previously in the Integrity standard. Integrity in this context is focused on making sure the EPHI is not improperly modified during transmission. A primary method for protecting the integrity of EPHI being transmitted is through the use of network communications protocols. Using these protocols, the computer verifies that the data sent is the same as the data received.

2. **Encryption** As previously described in the Access Control standard, encryption is a method of converting an original message of regular text into encoded or unreadable text that is eventually decrypted into plain comprehensible text.

   Encryption is necessary for transmitting EPHI over the Internet. There are various types of encryption technology available, but for encryption technologies to work properly both the sender and receiver must be using the same or compatible technology. Currently no single interoperable encryption solution for communicating over open networks exists.

Organizational, Policies and Procedures, and Documentation Requirements[20]

In addition to the standards in the Administrative, Physical, and Technical Safeguards categories of the Security Rule, there also are four other standards that must be implemented. These are not listed in the Security Standards Matrix (Figure 10-5), but they must not be overlooked.

---

[20]Adapted from *Security Standards: Organizational, Policies and Procedures*, HIPAA Security Series #5 (Baltimore, MD: Centers for Medicare and Medicaid Services, May 2005, and revised March 2007).

Organizational Requirements

There are two implementation specifications of this standard.

1. **Business Associate Contracts** The Business Associate Contracts are used if the business associate creates, receives, maintains, or transmits EPHI must meet the Security Rule requirements.

2. **Other Arrangements** The Other Arrangements implementation specifications apply when both parties are government entities. There are two alternative arrangements:

    ◆ A memorandum of understanding (MOU), which accomplishes the objectives of the Business Associate Contracts section of the Security Rule

    ◆ A law or regulations applicable to the business associate that accomplishes the objectives of the Business Associate Contracts section of the Security Rule

Policies and Procedures

Although this standard requires covered entities to implement policies and procedures, the Security Rule does not define either "policy" or "procedure." Generally, policies define an organization's approach. Procedures describe how the organization carries out that approach, setting forth explicit, step-by-step instructions that implement the organization's policies. Policies and procedures may be modified as necessary.

Documentation

The Documentation standard has three implementation specifications.

1. **Time Limit** Retain the documentation required by the rule for 6 years from the date of its creation or the date when it last was in effect, whichever is later.

2. **Availability** Make documentation available to those persons responsible for implementing the procedures to which the documentation pertains.

3. **Updates** Review documentation periodically, and update as needed, in response to environmental or operational changes affecting the security of the electronic protected health information.

The Security Rule also requires that a covered entity document the rationale for all security decisions.

Breach Notification Requirements[21]

The HITECH Act also added new requirements regarding the occurrence of a breach of unsecured protected health information. A *breach* is defined as an impermissible use or disclosure under the Privacy Rule that compromises the security or privacy of the PHI such that the use or disclosure poses a significant risk of financial, reputation, or other harm to the affected individual.

---

[21]Breach Notification Interim Final Regulation (45 CFR 164.408).

There are three exceptions to the definition of "breach":

- Unintentional acquisition, access, or use of PHI by an employee of a covered entity or business associate
- Inadvertent disclosure of PHI from an authorized person to another authorized person at the covered entity or business associate
- If the covered entity or business associate has a good faith belief that the unauthorized individual, to whom the impermissible disclosure was made, would not have been able to retain the information

Covered entities must notify affected individuals, the Secretary of Health and Human Services, and, in certain circumstances, the media following the discovery of a breach of unsecured PHI. Business associates must notify covered entities if a breach has occurred. The OCR must post a list of breaches that affect 500 or more individuals.

Individual Notice

Covered entities must provide affected individuals written notice by first-class mail, or alternatively, by e-mail if the affected individual has agreed to receive such notices electronically. If the covered entity has insufficient or out-of-date contact information for 10 or more individuals, the covered entity must provide substitute individual notice by either posting the notice on the home page of its web site or by providing the notice in major print or broadcast media where the affected individuals likely reside. If the covered entity has insufficient or out-of-date contact information for fewer than 10 individuals, the covered entity may provide substitute notice by an alternative form of written, telephone, or other means.

These individual notifications must be provided without unreasonable delay and in no case later than 60 days following the discovery of a breach and must include, to the extent possible, a description of the breach, a description of the types of information that were involved in the breach, the steps affected individuals should take to protect themselves from potential harm, a brief description of what the covered entity is doing to investigate the breach, mitigate the harm, and prevent further breaches, as well as contact information for the covered entity. Additionally, for substitute notice provided via web posting or major print or broadcast media, the notification must include a toll-free number for individuals to contact the covered entity to determine if their PHI was involved in the breach.

Media Notice

Covered entities that experience a breach affecting more than 500 residents of a State or jurisdiction are, in addition to notifying the affected individuals, required to provide notice to prominent media outlets serving the State or jurisdiction. Covered entities will likely provide this notification in the form of a press release to appropriate media outlets serving the affected area. Like individual notice, this media notification must be provided without unreasonable delay and in no case later than 60 days following the discovery of a breach and must include the same information required for the individual notice.

Notice to the Secretary

In addition to notifying affected individuals and the media (where appropriate), covered entities must notify the Secretary of Health and Human Services of breaches of unsecured PHI. Covered entities will notify the Secretary by visiting the HHS web site and filling out and electronically submitting a breach report form. If a breach affects 500 or more individuals, covered entities must notify the Secretary without unreasonable delay and in no case later than 60 days following a breach. If, however, a breach affects fewer than 500 individuals, the covered entity may notify the Secretary of such breaches on an annual basis. Reports of breaches affecting fewer than 500 individuals are due to the Secretary no later than 60 days after the end of the calendar year in which the breaches occurred.

Notification by a Business Associate

If a breach of unsecured PHI occurs at or by a business associate, the business associate must notify the covered entity following the discovery of the breach. A business associate must provide notice to the covered entity without unreasonable delay and no later than 60 days from the discovery of the breach. To the extent possible, the business associate should provide the covered entity with the identification of each individual affected by the breach as well as any information required to be provided by the covered entity in its notification to affected individuals.

Electronic Signatures for Health Records

The HIPAA Security Rule was originally titled "Security and Electronic Signature Standards." The original Security Rule also proposed a standard for electronic signatures. The final rule covered only security standards.

The Electronic Signatures in Global and National Commerce Act[22] made digital signatures as binding as their paper-based counterparts for commerce. However, HIPAA does not yet require the use of electronic signatures, because HIPAA does not yet have a Rule for Electronic Signature standards. Electronic Signature standards eventually will be necessary to achieve a completely paperless EHR. In this section, we will discuss electronic signatures and the criteria required for successful implementation.

What Is an Electronic Signature and What Is Not?

Compare Figure 10-11 and Figure 10-12. Which of these has an electronic signature? If you said Figure 10-12, you would be correct. An electronic signature is not a scanned image of someone's paper signature. Valid electronic signatures must meet three criteria.

1. **Message Integrity** Message Integrity means the recipient must be able to confirm that the document has not been altered since it was signed.

2. **Nonrepudiation** The signer must not be able to deny signing the document.

3. **User Authentication** The recipient must be able to confirm that the signature was in fact "signed" by the real person.

---

[22]Electronic Signatures in Global and National Commerce Act (ESIGN, Pub.L. 106-229, 14 Stat. 464, enacted June 30, 2000, 15 U.S.C. ch. 96.

▶ Figure 10-11 Scanned document with an image of signature.

> 5/1/2012 11:00AM
>
> **S.** Rosa Garcia is a 27 year old female complaining of chronic/recurring headaches for more than 5 days. Headaches are occurring daily, recently worse, inadequately controlled, and lasting 2-4 hours.
> Daily coffee consumption was 7-8 cups per day but she recently stopped all coffee consumption.
>
> **O.** Physical exam showed no evidence of a head injury. A mental status exam was normal.
> Vital Signs were WNL:
>
> | Vital Signs/Measurements | Value |
> |---|---|
> | Oral temperature | 98.6 F |
> | RR | 25 breaths/min |
> | PR | 75 bpm |
> | Blood pressure | 117/75 mmHg |
> | Weight | 140 lbs |
> | Height | 64 in |
>
> **A.** Vasoconstrictor withdrawal headache from caffeine
>
> **P.** Eat regular meals, get plenty of exercise, and limit intake of caffeine, and alcohol
>
> *Terry Jones, M.D*

▶ Figure 10-12 Electronically signed document with a PKI signature.

```
<Signed SigID=001>
```

> 5/1/2012 11:00AM
>
> **S.** Rosa Garcia is a 27 year old female complaining of chronic/recurring headaches for more than 5 days. Headaches are occurring daily, recently worse, inadequately controlled, and lasting 2-4 hours.
> Daily coffee consumption was 7-8 cups per day but she recently stopped all coffee consumption.
>
> **O.** Physical exam showed no evidence of a head injury. A mental status exam was normal.
> Vital Signs were WNL:
>
> | Vital Signs/Measurements | Value |
> |---|---|
> | Oral temperature | 98.6 F |
> | RR | 25 breaths/min |
> | PR | 75 bpm |
> | Blood pressure | 117/75 mmHg |
> | Weight | 140 lbs |
> | Height | 64 in |
>
> **A.** Vasoconstrictor withdrawal headache from caffeine
>
> **P.** Eat regular meals, get plenty of exercise, and limit intake of caffeine, and alcohol
>
> // Electronically Signed by Terry Jones, M.D. 201205011114EST

```
</Signed>
<Signature SigID=001 PsnID=jones001>
2AB3764578CB212990BA5C18A29870F40198B240C330249C9461D20774C1622D
39D2302B2349802DE002342
</Signature>
```

The electronic signature process involves the successful identification and authentication of the signer at the time of the signature, binding of the signature to the document, and nonalterability of the document after the signature has been affixed. Only "digital signatures" meet all three of these criteria.

How Digital Signatures Work

Digital signatures use a branch of mathematics called *cryptography and PKI*, which stands for Public Key Infrastructure. Each PKI user has two "keys," a private key for signing documents and a public key for verifying his or her signature. Only you know your private key, whereas your public key is available to all through a public directory.

Usually the directory for your public key is maintained by a certificate authority. The certificate authority is a trusted third party who has validated your identity and issued a certificate to that effect. A certificate is an electronic record of your public key, which has been digitally signed by the certificate authority. The certificate can be validated by its own key. This provides reasonable assurance that the signer and their public key are genuine.

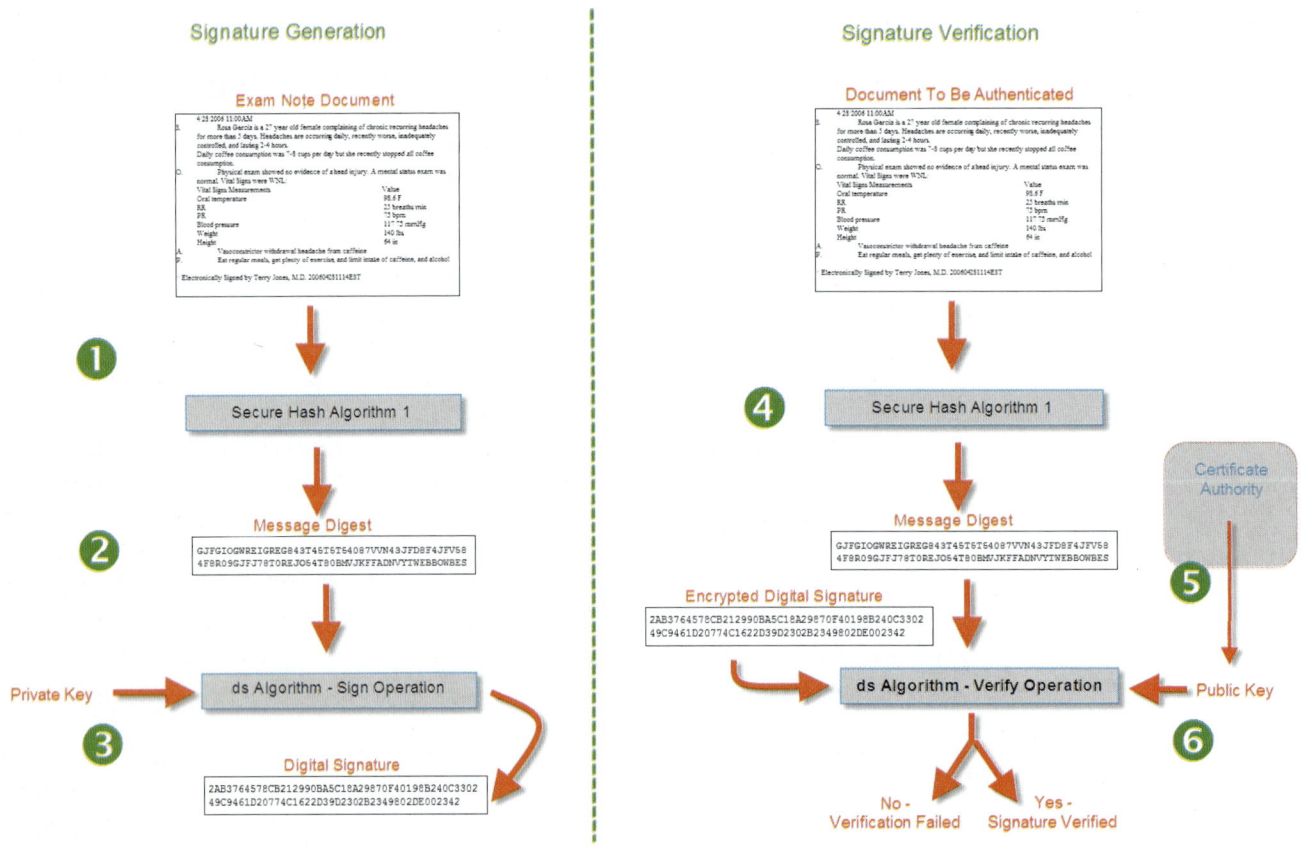

▶ Figure 10-13 How a digital signature works.

Figure 10-13 illustrates the electronic signature and verification process of PKI.[23] Compare Figure 10-13 with the following steps:

① A computer software program performs a mathematical calculation on the entire contents of the electronic document to be signed.

② The result is a unique code referred to as the "message digest."

---

[23]Figure adapted from Digital Signature Standard, published By U.S. Department of Commerce/National Institute of Standards and Technology, 2000.

❸ This code is encrypted using your "private" key. Your private key might be similar to a password, which you must keep secret so that no one else can "forge" your signature.

The digital signature is then typically attached to or sent with the document.

When the recipient wishes to validate your signature, that person uses a computer program that decodes the signature with your public key, and determines if the message digest is identical to that which was originally sent.

❹ The validation process uses the same algorithm as the original program to produce a "message digest" of the text of the document.

❺ The public key is retrieved from a public directory or certificate authority.

❻ The signature verification process decodes the digital signature using your public key and compares it to the message digest. If the results of the algorithm match, the signature is verified.

PKI digital signatures not only confirm that you are the signer but also that the document has not been altered since you signed it.

Some EHR Signatures Are Not True Electronic Signatures

Even though HIPAA has not adopted an official standard for electronic signatures, they are already necessary in the EHR. Prescriptions are sent to a pharmacy, dictation and electronic medical records are "signed," and orders are issued from EHR systems every day. However, most of the systems currently in use do not use the process described earlier to produce and store an electronic signature.

Many systems have a process to "sign" their records with a PIN, a password, or even a fingerprint, but the underlying software simply sets a field in the database indicating the provider "signed" the record. This is adequate to the particular EHR system, but it would not meet the criteria of an electronic signature if it were necessary to send a copy of the record to an outside entity. Partly this is the fault of HHS. Until there is a national infrastructure for issuing certificates and national standards for signing and validating digital signatures, EHR software cannot comply.

Whether electronic signatures in your office are true digital signatures or just mechanisms for locking and protecting EHR system records, it is important that you follow the policies and procedures of your facility. Most EHR systems have an internal audit trail detailing who has created each document and medical record.

◆ Always log on to the EHR as yourself.

◆ Always log off when you are through.

◆ Always keep your passwords or PIN numbers private.

This will prevent someone else from signing medical records under your ID.

The Future of Electronic Signatures

The Joint Commission (JCAHO) accepts the use of electronic signatures in hospital, ambulatory care, home care, long-term care, and mental health settings.

The Joint Commission requirement for electronic signatures and computer key signatures is simple: "The practitioner must sign a statement that he or she alone will use it."[24]

Currently, CMS permits the authentication of medical records by computer key but does not specify methods. The President of the United States directed the U.S. Department of Commerce, National Institute of Standards and Technology to develop a set of standards for Digital Signatures. HHS will likely adopt the same cryptographically based digital signature for the HIPAA standard.

State laws vary on electronic signatures for medical records and some do not address it at all. States will likely come into alignment only after HHS publication of HIPAA standards for electronic signatures. If you have any question about regulations in your state, check with the medical licensing authority in your state.

Critical Thinking Exercise 62: Your Electronic Signature

1. What is the legal status of the electronic signature in the EHR in your state?
2. How can you protect your own electronic signature?
3. Identify potential impacts of a failure to log off or exit from the patient record.

HIPAA Privacy, Security, and You

As someone who will work with patients' health records, it is especially important for you to understand the regulations regarding privacy and security. Follow the privacy policy and security rules at your place of work. Know who the privacy and security officials are. Ask them if you have any questions regarding policies at your practice or if you feel that you need additional training.

It is especially important not to give others your password and to always log out of a medical records computer when you are not using it. Remember to treat every medical record (paper or electronic) in a confidential manner.

Chapter Ten Summary

The Health Insurance Portability and Accountability Act, or HIPAA, was passed in 1996. The Administrative Simplification Subsection (Title 2, f) (hereafter just called HIPAA) has four distinct components:

1. Transactions and code sets
2. Uniform identifiers
3. Privacy
4. Security

HIPAA regulates health plans, clearinghouses, and healthcare providers as "covered entities" or a "covered entity" with regard to these four areas.

---

[24]*Comprehensive Accreditation Manual for Hospitals (CAMH),* Standard IM. 6.10, Joint Commission on Accreditation of Healthcare Organizations, 2004.

HIPAA standardized formats for EDI or Electronic Data Interchange by requiring specific Transaction Standards. These currently are used for eight types of transactions between covered entities. This was the first of the Administrative Simplification Subsection to be implemented. This section also requires standardized code sets such as HCPCS, CPT-4, ICD-9-CM, and others to be used.

HIPAA also established uniform identifier standards, which will be used on all claims and other data transmissions. These will include:

- National provider identifier for doctors, nurses, and other healthcare providers
- Federal employer identification number used to identify employer-sponsored health insurance
- National health plan identifier, a unique identification number that will be assigned to each insurance plan, and to the organizations that administer insurance plans, such as payers and third-party administrators

The privacy and security rules use two acronyms: PHI, which stands for Protected Health Information, and EPHI, which stands for Protected Health Information in an Electronic Format.

The HIPAA privacy standards are designed to protect a patient's identifiable health information from unauthorized disclosure or use in any form, while permitting the practice to deliver the best healthcare possible. To comply with the law, privacy activities in the average medical office might include:

- Providing a copy of the office privacy policy informing patients about their privacy rights and how their information can be used
- Asking the patient to acknowledge receiving a copy of the policy or signing a consent form
- Obtaining signed authorization forms and in some cases tracking the disclosures of patient health information when it is to be given to a person or organization outside the practice for purposes other than treatment, billing, or payment
- Adopting clear privacy procedures for its practice
- Training employees so that they understand the privacy procedures
- Designating an individual to be responsible for seeing that the privacy procedures are adopted and followed
- Securing patient records containing individually identifiable health information so that they are not readily available to those who do not need them

When the Privacy Rule initially was issued, it required providers to obtain patient "consent" to use and disclose PHI for the purposes of treatment, payment, and healthcare operations, except in emergencies. The rule was almost immediately revised to make consent optional. In general, the practice can use PHI for almost anything related to treating the patient, running the medical practice, and getting paid for services. This means doctors, nurses, and other staff can share the patient's chart within the practice.

Authorization differs from consent in that it does require the patient's permission to disclose PHI. Some examples of instances that would require an authorization would include sending the results of an employment physical to an employer, immunization records, or the results of an athletic physical to the school.

The authorization form must include a date signed, an expiration date, to whom the information may be disclosed, what is permitted to be disclosed, and for what purpose the information may be used. The authorization must be signed by the patient or a representative appointed by the patient. Unlike the open concept of consent, authorizations are not global. A new authorization is signed each time there is a different purpose or need for the patient's information to be disclosed.

Practices are permitted to disclose PHI without a patient's authorization or consent when it is requested by an authorized government agency. Generally, such requests are for legal (law enforcement, subpoena, court orders, and so on) public health purposes, or for enforcement of the Privacy Rule itself. Providers also are permitted to disclose PHI concerning on-the-job injuries to workers' compensation insurers, state administrators, and other entities to the extent required by state law.

Whether the practice has disclosed PHI based on a signed authorization or to comply with a government agency, the patient is entitled to know about it. The Privacy Rule gives the individuals the right to receive a report of all disclosures made for purposes other than treatment, payment, or operations. Therefore, in most cases the medical office must track the disclosure and keep the records for at least six years.

Most healthcare providers and health plans use the services of a variety of other persons or businesses. The Privacy Rule allows covered providers and health plans to disclose protected health information to these "business associates." The Privacy Rule requires that a covered entity obtain a written agreement from its business associate, which states the business associate will appropriately safeguard the protected health information it receives or creates on behalf of the covered entity.

Congress provided civil and criminal penalties for covered entities that misuse personal health information. The privacy rule is enforced by the HHS Office for Civil Rights (OCR).

The Privacy Rule sets the standards for, among other things, who may have access to PHI, whereas the Security Rule sets the standards for ensuring that only those who should have access to EPHI actually will have access. The Privacy Rule applies to all forms of patients' protected health information, whether electronic, written, or oral. In contrast, the Security Rule covers only protected health information that is in electronic form.

Security standards were designed to provide guidelines to all types of covered entities, while affording them flexibility regarding how to implement the standards. Covered entities may use appropriate security measures that enable them to reasonably implement a standard.

Security standards were designed to be "technology neutral." The rule does not prescribe the use of specific technologies, so that the healthcare community will not be bound by specific systems or software that may become obsolete.

The security standards are divided into the categories of administrative, physical, and technical safeguards.

Administrative safeguards. In general, these are the administrative functions that should be implemented to meet the security standards. These include assignment or delegation of security responsibility to an individual and security training requirements.

Physical safeguards. In general, these are the mechanisms required to protect electronic systems, equipment, and the data they hold, from threats, environmental hazards, and unauthorized intrusion. They include restricting access to EPHI and retaining off-site computer backups.

Technical safeguards. In general, these are primarily the automated processes used to protect data and control access to data. They include using authentication controls to verify that the person signing onto a computer is authorized to access that EPHI, or encrypting and decrypting data as it is being stored or transmitted.

Breach Notification Requirements require covered entities to notify affected individuals, the Secretary of Health and Human Services, and in certain circumstances the media, the occurrence of a breach of unsecured PHI. Business associates must notify covered entities if a breach has occurred. The OCR must post a list of breaches that affect 500 or more individuals.

The original Security Rule also proposed a standard for electronic signatures. The final rule covered only security standards.

The Electronic Signatures in Global and National Commerce Act made digital signatures as binding as their paper-based counterparts. Although the law made digital signatures valid for commerce, HIPAA does not require the use of electronic signatures. Electronic signature standards will eventually be necessary to achieve a completely paperless EHR. A Rule for Electronic Signature standards may be proposed at a later date.

A valid electronic signature must meet three criteria.

1. Message Integrity—the recipient must be able to confirm that the document has not been altered since it was signed.
2. Nonrepudiation—the signer must not be able to deny signing the document.
3. User Authentication—the recipient must be able to confirm that the signature was in fact "signed" by the real person.

Digital signatures meet all three of these criteria. Digital signatures use a branch of mathematics called *cryptography and PKI*, which stands for Public Key Infrastructure.

Each PKI user has two "keys," a private key for signing documents and a public key for verifying his or her signature. A computer software program performs a mathematical calculation on the entire contents of the electronic document to be signed. The result is a unique "message digest," which is then encrypted using the "private" key.

The digital signature is then attached to or sent with the document. When the recipient wishes to validate the signature, a similar computer program regenerates the "message digest" and decodes the digital signature with the public key. Comparing the two, the program determines if the message digest is identical to that which was originally sent. In this way digital signatures not only confirm that you are the signer but also that the document has not been altered since it was signed.

Testing Your Knowledge of Chapter 10

Answer the following questions:

1. What do the acronyms PHI and EPHI stand for?
2. List the three criteria of an electronic signature.
3. Compare the difference between consent and authorization.
4. Does a provider need the patient's consent to share PHI with an authorized government agency?
5. List the four components of the HIPAA Administrative Simplification Subsection.
6. Which part of the regulation went into effect first?
7. Which part of the regulation went into effect last?
8. Business Associate Agreements apply to which components of the Administrative Simplification Subsection?
9. What department of the U.S. government enforces HIPAA?
10. List the three categories of the Security Rule.
11. Name the covered entities under HIPAA.
12. Which components of the Administrative Simplification Subsection have employee training as one of the requirements?
13. List the requirements for the medical office privacy policy.
14. Name three of the technical safeguards.
15. Who may sign an authorization to release PHI?

Chapter Eleven

Using the Internet to Expedite Patient Care

Learning Outcomes

After completing this chapter, you should be able to:

- Discuss the effect of the impact of Internet technology on healthcare
- Explain how EHR systems use the Internet
- Describe decision support available on the web
- Understand how the Internet works
- Discuss methods of remote access and secure Internet communications
- Compare different types of telemedicine
- Describe the advantages and workflow of patient-entered data
- Contrast differences between provider-to-patient e-mail and secure messaging
- Understand the workflow of an E-visit
- Discuss patient access to electronic health records
- Explain the criteria for Patient-Centered Medical Home
- Understand and compare Personal Health Records

The Impact of Technology

In the book *The Electronic Physician*, the authors compare the adoption of the EHR to the automobile. Let us begin this chapter by expanding on that useful analogy.[1]

---

[1] Analogy paraphrased from Todd Stein, ed., *The Electronic Physician* (Chicago: Allscripts Healthcare Solutions, © 2005).

A hundred years ago, the most common means of transportation was the horse and carriage. As the first automobiles began to appear, people referred to them as "horseless carriages." The people of that era conceptualized this new invention in terms of the existing technology. Even the inventors of the technology were not immune to this viewpoint. Isn't the engine in the front of a car today because that's where the horse was yesteryear?

As the automobile began to appear across the country, many people did not rush to adopt it or understand the full potential of the change that society was about to undergo. The new vehicles seemed to some to be fancy toys, inferior to the horse and carriage in many ways.

- The supply chain of the period was built to feed and water the horse, not fuel the car.
- The condition of the roads, which were passable by horse, often caused cars to become stuck.

Viewed within the existing infrastructure of their time, the critics were right; driving an automobile instead of a horse seemed like a lot of work for very little gain.

People of our era use the term *electronic medical records* because they are thinking in terms of paper medical records. However, the opinion in a report by the IOM is that "Merely automating the form, content, and procedures of current patient records will perpetuate their deficiencies and will be insufficient to meet emerging user needs."[2]

Using the horseless carriage analogy, you can see that healthcare workflow has been designed around the infrastructure of a paper chart. Adapting the electronic chart to fit the old technology provides a level of comfort during the transition to the new system, but it also prevents us from seeing the full potential of the EHR. Similar to driving early automobiles on inadequate roads, implementing an EHR without considering the landscape can make it seem like a lot of work for very little gain.

In chapter 1, doctors Bachman and Wenner stated that adopting an EHR changes the way clinician's work. Implementation of an EHR enables the patient records to be used in ways that paper medical records cannot. To achieve these benefits clinicians must make it part of their workflow that is as natural as driving their car to the office.

Chapter 1 also listed the Internet as one of the social forces driving EHR adoption. If you are a college student today, the Internet as we know it did not exist when you were born. It is our newest technology. While we continue to evolve what we can do with it, the Internet changes the way we work.

The flexibility of the Internet and its ability to get information to and from almost any point in a worldwide network obviously has a lot of potential for healthcare. Providers can access their patients' charts, communicate with patients, transmit medical images, and work from anywhere. In this chapter we are going to discuss how the Internet and related technologies are changing

---

[2]R. S. Dick and E. B. Steen, *The Computer-based Patient Record: An Essential Technology for Health Care* (Washington, DC: Institute of Medicine, National Academy Press, 1991, revised 1997, 2000).

patient's expectations and changing the way healthcare is delivered. To conclude our analogy of the automobile, the Internet is the Information Highway and it is changing the 21st-century practice of medicine as surely as the interstate system changed the habits of 20th-century drivers.

The Internet and the EHR

The Internet is one of the key technologies impacting our society in general. It has changed the way that people communicate, research, shop, and conduct business. It also is influencing changes in healthcare.

People shop for doctors online, insurance companies provide online participating provider lists, physician specialty associations, and state and local medical societies all offer web sites that help patients locate a provider near them.

Patients also use the Internet for research. Many clinicians are finding their patients are coming to visits armed with printouts about their conditions gathered

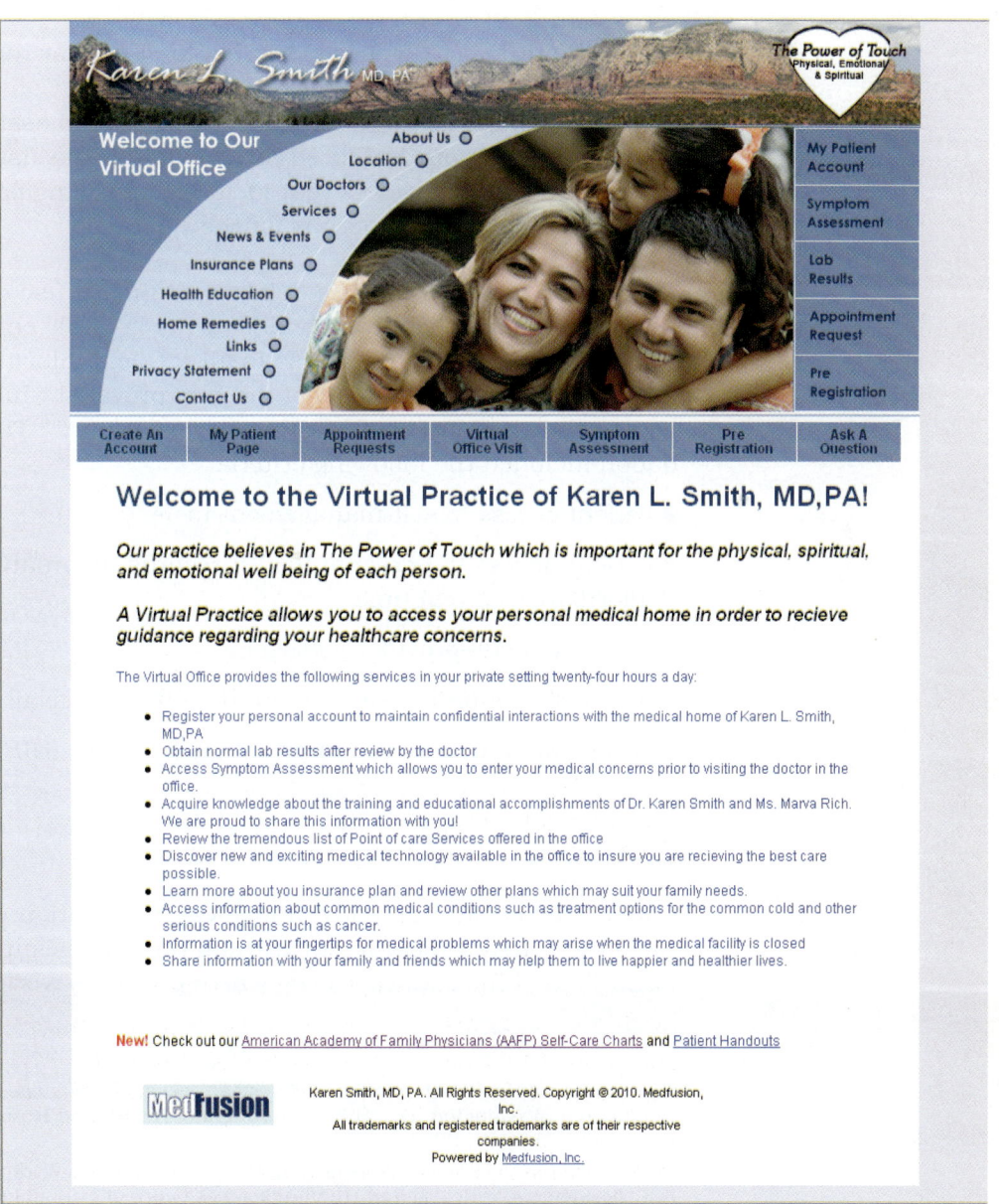

Courtesy of Medfusion, Inc.
▶ **Figure 11-1 Web site of Karen Smith, M.D., FAAFP**

Chapter 11 | Using the Internet to Expedite Patient Care   **419**

from web sites. Some of these web sites provide reliable information, some do not. One of the most trusted sources of consumer information on the web is webMD Health® (www.webmd.com). On the webMD Health consumer portal, patients can access health and wellness news, support communities, interactive health management tools, and more. Online communities and special events allow individuals to participate in real-time discussions with experts and with other people who share similar health conditions or concerns. By using sites such as webMD Health, patients can play an active role in managing their own healthcare.

Another reliable source of health information on the Internet is a web site set up by a hospital or medical practice. Many medical practices today have their own web sites. An example is shown in Figure 11-1. Although some of these sites are limited to information about the medical practice, clinicians, and office hours, the site shown in Figure 11-1 includes online information about preventative health measures, diseases, and conditions that the practice treats as well as other features we will discuss later. Patient educational information on a clinic's web site has the advantage of being consistent with the medical philosophy of the practice.

The ONC strategies discussed in Chapter 1 call for the use of technology to make health information available to the patient. "Consumer-centric information helps individuals manage their own wellness and assists with their personal health care decisions."[3] The HITECH Act, also discussed in Chapter 1, establishes criteria for providers that includes "engaging patients and families" through the use of web portals for their patients.

The ONC committee helping define meaningful use objectives stated: "The ultimate vision is one in which all patients are fully engaged in their health care, providers have real-time access to all medical information and tools to help ensure the quality and safety of the care provided while also affording improved access and elimination of health care disparities."[4] The committee recommendation included the following criteria:

◆ Patient access to self-management tools

◆ Patient access to personal health records, populated with patient health information in real time

◆ Secure patient–provider messaging

◆ Access to comprehensive patient data from all available sources

◆ Participation in a health information exchange (HIE)

Decision Support Via the Web

The rapidly expanding body of medical information challenges the clinician to continuously keep current with all the changes in healthcare practices. Regardless of the clinical setting where providers work, the need for up-to-date

---

[3]*The Decade of Health Information Technology: Delivering Consumer-centric and Information-rich Health Care* (Washington, DC: U.S. Department of Health and Human Services Office of National Coordinator, July 21, 2004).

[4]*Meaningful Use: A Definition* (Washington, DC: Meaningful Use Workgroup to the HIT Policy Committee, U.S. Department of Health and Human Services Office of National Coordinator, June 16, 2009).

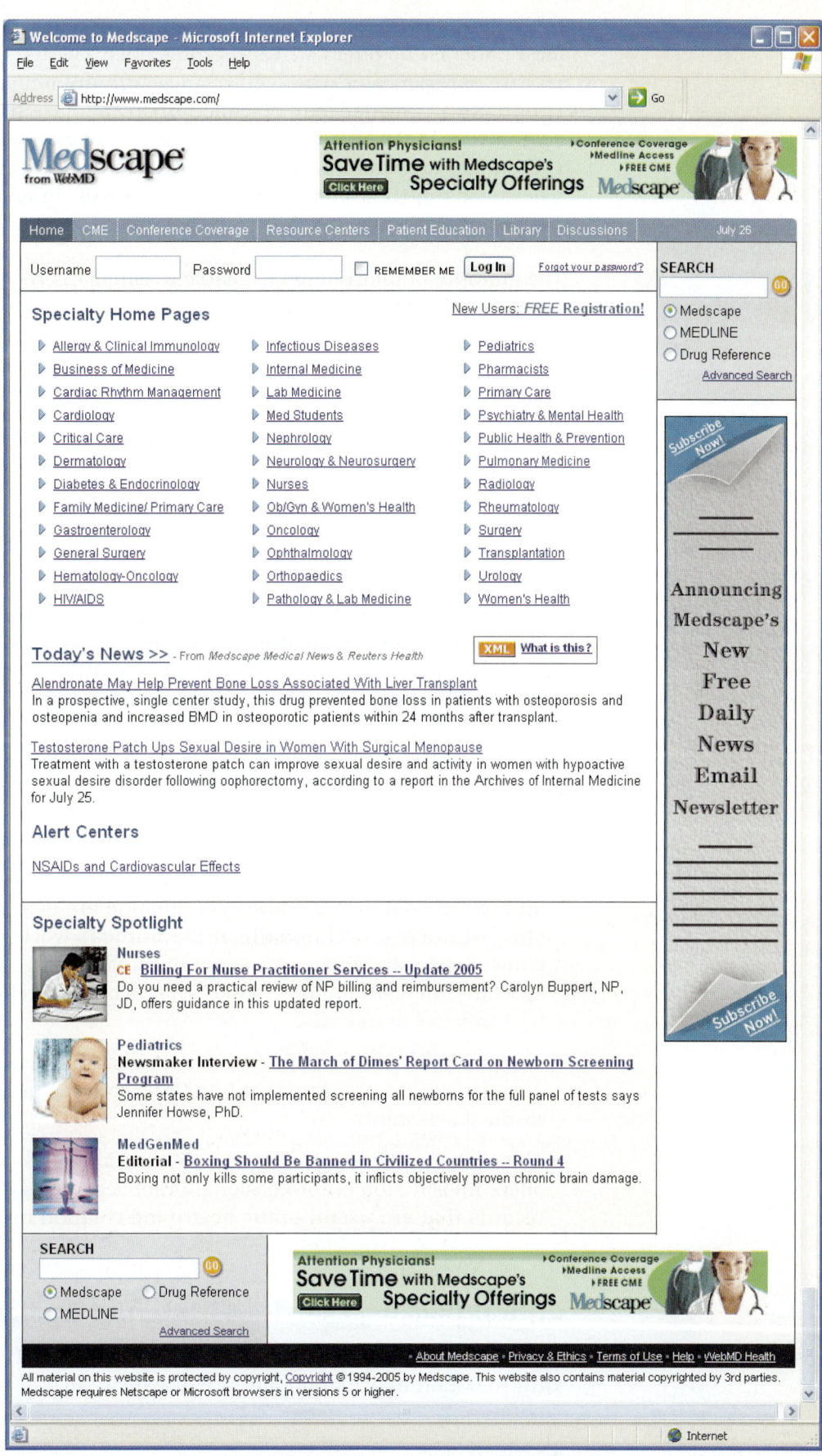

▶ Figure 11-2 Medscape web site used by thousands of clinicians.
Reprinted with permission from Medscape, http://www.medscape.com © 1994–2005, Medscape.

clinical support information is needed. Sometimes a provider may be caring for a patient who offers a health problem with which the provider has little or no care experience or who requires new and unfamiliar medications. In other situations a provider may be called upon to share his or her expertise with committees to develop new care protocols to support developing best practice guidelines. Providers may also be involved in new program development to meet needs in their community or to be involved in research to improve patient outcomes.

The quantity of information available to clinicians regarding conditions, disease management, protocols, case studies, and treatments far exceeds their available time to read it. No longer is it necessary for a physician to make a trip to the medical library or keep a vast library in the office.

Although the Internet offers easy access to a myriad of web sites that can quickly provide information to help support any knowledge deficit, it is important to obtain information from sites that can be depended on for accurate and quality information to guide their care. One such site is Medscape® (shown in Figure 11-2), the leading web site for providers, is a source of objective, credible, relevant clinical information and educational tools.

Medscape provides online continuing medical education (CME) as well as online coverage of medical conferences, access to over 100 medical journals, and specialty-specific daily medical news. Large numbers of research papers and nearly every medical journal is available on the site.

In addition to physician-oriented sites, professional organizations for other healthcare professionals are reliable sources of information on guidelines, practice standards, continuing education credits, upcoming conferences, and a variety of online networking opportunities. Here are several examples:

- Nursing professional organizations have many web sites offering information on professional practice and even include areas specifically designed for student nurses. Additionally, if the nurse is working within a particular clinical specialty, the professional nursing organization associated with the specialty will contain information that is clinical relevant and supportive of best practice standards.
- The American Association of Medical Assistants web site provides information on certification programs, online CME courses, and news useful to the medical assistant.
- The American Health Information Management Association (AHIMA) web site offers information on professional practices and issues regarding electronic records that are useful to the health information manager.

Critical Thinking Exercise 63: Internet Medical Research

In this exercise you will need access to the Internet. You will visit two web sites to obtain information for patient education.

Case Study

Arnie Greensher is a 66-year-old male who is beginning cancer treatment.

Step 1

Start your web browser.

Enter the following URL address: **www.careindividualized.com.**

Step 2

Locate and click on the link for **Patient**.

Step 3

Choose from any of the patient information documents, and click on it. When the document is displayed, review it and print only the first page. Give the printout to your instructor.

Case Study

Brenda Green is a 54-year-old established patient with a history of hypertension and possible peripheral arterial disease of the legs. She has been prescribed Coumadin, a drug which has specific dangers. Follow the steps below to locate the answers to the questions in step 6.

Step 4

Start your web browser, if it is not already running.

Enter the following URL address: **www.webmd.com.**

Step 5

When the web page is displayed, type **Coumadin** in the search field and click on the button labeled "Search."

A page of search results will be displayed. Locate and click on the link "Drug Information."

Locate and click on the link "Coumadin Oral."

Step 6

From the information displayed on the page answer the following questions:

What is the generic drug name for Coumadin?

What is a very serious (possibly fatal) effect of this drug?

What lab test is used to monitor the effect of this drug?

Integrated Decision Support

Although continuing education classes, medical journals, and web sites such as Medscape are available to a majority of clinicians, the information relevant to a particular case may not be easy to access during the patient encounter when it is most needed.

Decision support refers to the ability of EHR systems to store or quickly locate materials relevant to the findings of the current case. Clinics can imbed links in their forms that, when selected, display any type of helpful material. These might include defined protocols, results of case studies, or standard care guidelines prepared by specialists, medical societies, or government organizations.

In current EHR systems, the decision support documents are selected and linked to the system by each individual practice. (The author is not aware of any system that automatically installs standard decision support documents or links.) The selection of decision support items is generally one of the responsibilities of a practice setting up the EHR. Therefore, the support content of EHR systems will differ from one healthcare facility to another.

Understanding the Internet

Most people know the Internet because of the services they use on it such as e-mail, research, games, and web pages. However, before proceeding further it may be helpful to understand how it works.

Multiple computers can be connected together to exchange data in private networks that can be accessed only by the users in that network. These are called local-area networks (LAN) or wide-area networks (WAN). In a LAN, data flows to and from specific computers using cables in a wired building.

The Internet is a worldwide public network that can be accessed by any computer anywhere. The Internet was created by interconnecting millions of smaller business-, academic-, and government-run networks. It is really a very large network of networks. In a network schematic it is sometimes referred to as a "cloud" because data does not necessarily follow a consistent path.

To understand the difference between a private network and the Internet, let us compare the post office and the phone company. When you make a phone call, the wires and circuits must establish an electrical connection with the phone of the person you are calling before that person's phone rings and the call can go through. When you write a letter, you address the envelope and deposit it in the mailbox. You do not know how the post office will transport it or what roads the trucks will take, but in the end it is delivered to the address on the envelope.

The Internet Protocol encloses data in packets that have an address on them. The packets are sent through the various networks making up the Internet until they arrive at their address. The sending computer does not have to establish a wired connection with the receiving computer for this to occur.

Secure Internet Data

The problem is that the Internet is not secure. The packets of data pass through many computers and networks on their way to their destination. They can be copied, opened, and read by anyone with enough technical savvy.

How do we secure the information so we can use the accessibility of the Internet, but protect the information? As you learned in Chapter 10, encryption is necessary for transmitting EPHI over the Internet. Encryption uses a mathematical algorithm to convert readable data into encoded or scrambled data. The authorized recipient decrypts the message back to its original form using a mathematical key.

Secure transmission of data over the Internet usually relies on either of two methods. These are secured socket layer (SSL) or a virtual private network (VPN). Both of these rely on encrypting the transmission. There are additional secure transmission schemes not covered here.

SSL adds security by encrypting the content of web pages and automatically decrypting it when it is received to display the web page. This prevents anyone intercepting the transmitted packets from making sense of them. SSL, however, is limited to the type of things you can do on a web page. Some providers and organizations want to run software or view records that are on their office network computers from elsewhere. To do this, a VPN may be used.

The VPN uses the Internet to transport packets of data, but it has its own software that encrypts and decrypts the packets between the sending and receiving systems. The VPN also verifies the identity of the person signing on, ensuring access only to those who are permitted to use the system. A VPN is not limited to web pages and may be used to secure the data being transmitted for other application software, such as an electronic health record system.

Remote EHR Access for the Provider

As we discussed earlier, providers increasingly want access to their EHR when they are away from the office. Many medical facility networks are configured to allow providers to access their patients' medical records. This is often referred to as "remote access." Clinicians connect to their office network and sign on just as they would in the office.

The benefits to the provider and the patient are tremendous. Instead of staying late, the provider can go home, have dinner with the family, relax for a few hours, then sign on to the office computer system and complete any chart reviews or other work that would have previously meant staying late. Additionally, if the clinician receives an emergency call from or about a patient, the patient's records can be accessed from home, helping the clinician to make better decisions. Figure 11-3 shows Dr. Wenner accessing his EHR from his patio.

Courtesy of Primetime Medical Software & Instant Medical History.

▶ **Figure 11-3 Dr. Wenner cleaning up "paperwork" from home.**

There are several means by which remote access can be accomplished securely, to protect the patient's EPHI.

The most secure method of connecting is through direct dial. Small offices with only one or two doctors can set up phone lines with special modems that receive a call from the doctor's home, disconnect, and then redial the number for the home computer. This method prevents unauthorized persons from accessing the system. There are, however, several drawbacks to this method. First, it requires a modem and phone line for every user who needs remote access at the same time as someone else. This is the reason it is not usually used in clinics with more than a few doctors. The other drawback is that the clinicians can only access the EHR from phone numbers that have been preprogrammed for the modem to dial back.

Another means of getting remote access is by using the Internet. This allows the clinician to access the records from anywhere he or she can connect to the Internet. Security for direct access to the office computer on the Internet usually requires a VPN, which was described earlier. A VPN is ideal for medium to large practices because it is not limited by the number of phone lines at the practice. However, running programs over a VPN is usually somewhat slower. A VPN is also complicated to set up and maintain. A medical facility will need to have an IT professional to manage a VPN.

A third method of remote access is provided by the EHR system itself. Some EHR vendors have created special software within their system that allows the clinician to access and interact with the EHR through the Internet via a SSL secured web site. The features vary by vendor, but typically the clinician can retrieve patient records, review and sign charts and lab results, and look at anything else in the patient chart. The clinician in this case is not using the actual EHR software, but a special subset created just for the web. For most clinicians, this level of remote access is sufficient, although there maybe some things that can be done in the office EHR but not on the web. If this method of access is offered by the EHR vendor, its advantage is that it confines the remote access to an isolated web server instead of the facility's entire network. It therefore represents a lesser risk than a remote sign-on. This feature is equally desirable for smaller practices because it eliminates the need for a dial-back modem or a complicated VPN setup.

Practicing Medicine Online

Although the banking, brokerage/investing, and travel industries have made Internet-based transactions readily available to consumers, healthcare as a whole has not. That seems to be changing. An annual Survey of Health Care Consumers, conducted by the Deloitte Center for Health Solutions, found that "65 percent of consumers are interested in home monitoring devices that enable them to check their condition and send the results to their doctor" and "42 percent want access to an online personal health record connected to their doctor's office. E-visits with physicians, personal health records, self-monitoring devices, personalized physician referrals and customized insurance products are innovations that consumers support. They are willing to try new services, change providers and hospitals and use their money in different ways to obtain better value from the healthcare system. And they are highly receptive to technology-enabled care that eliminates redundant paperwork, replaces unnecessary tests and saves time and money."[5]

The leading organization in healthcare informatics, the Health Information Management Systems Society (HIMSS) has formed a Special Interest Group to study *e-health*, which they define as "The application of Internet and other related technologies in the healthcare industry to improve the access, efficiency, effectiveness, and quality of clinical and business processes utilized by healthcare organizations, practitioners, patients, and consumers to improve the health status of patients."[6]

Let us now examine several of the ways that providers and patients are using the Internet not only as a research tool, but as a tool for the actual process of patient care.

Telemedicine

Telemedicine uses communication technology to deliver medical care to a patient in another location. A consulting health professional studies the patient's case and offers advice or instructions to the requesting physician or directly to the patient, neither of whom are at the consultant's location.

Telemedicine can take many forms, ranging from a simple phone call between two doctors to a videoconference. Even examinations or surgical procedures have been conducted remotely.

Telemedicine can be practiced in real time or asynchronously (independent sessions not occurring at the same time). Before the Internet, early pioneers of telemedicine conceived of it terms of the technology of their time, television. They imagined a scenario in which the doctor and patient could see each other on television sets at each end. Satellites that carry television signals would securely transmit the bidirectional video sessions. There were several drawbacks to this approach.

- ◆ Real-time telemedicine requires the presence of all parties at the same time. When participants are located in different time zones, real-time telemedicine sessions can be difficult to schedule.
- ◆ Television cannot transmit or display at a sufficient resolution for diagnostic images, such as x-rays or CAT scans.
- ◆ State laws can prohibit treatment of patients by providers licensed in another state.

A better alternative was developed at Mayo Clinic in Rochester, Minnesota. Rather than trying to get participants on each end into respective television studios, they decided to conduct telemedicine asynchronously. Marvin Mitchell, division chair of Media Support Services at Mayo Clinic, calls this *store-and-forward telemedicine*. It allows a doctor requesting a consult to send case information that is saved and then reviewed and responded to later by a specialist at Mayo.

---

[5]Deloitte Center for Health Solutions, 2009 Survey of Health Care Consumers, Deloitte, LLP., Washington, DC, 2009.
[6]Richard Grehalva, *eHealth Patterns in the 21st Century* (Birmingham, AL: MEDSEEK, 2010).

If a video conference is an example of real-time telemedicine, voice mail would be a simple analogy of store-and-forward telemedicine. One doctor leaves a message stating the facts of the case; the other doctor listens to the message and then calls back, leaving a detailed response for the original doctor. In practice, however, telemedicine is not that simple.

In Mayo Clinic's practice, the patient's physician in a remote location does the necessary examinations and diagnostic tests he or she would normally do. Then the doctor creates an electronic package including high-resolution images, scanned paper documents, motion image capture, angiography, and anything else that the specialist at Mayo might need to review. The information is then transmitted with a consultation request to the Mayo telemedicine office via a secure Internet connection.

The Mayo telemedicine system follows the same workflow as if the patient were at the clinic. When the Mayo Clinic telemedicine office receives the electronic package, the patient is registered and given a Mayo Clinic patient number, then an electronic medical record is created. The diagnostic images from the package are stored in the Mayo PAC system and orders to the radiologist are created. Other records are imported into the EHR.

One of the principal advantages of this workflow is that it is as transparent to the Mayo physicians as possible. Specialists at Mayo see the remote patient's records in the same system they use everyday. A Mayo radiologist views the diagnostic images, interprets them, and dictates a report. Similarly, other specialties look at the imported EHR data and dictate their second opinion into Mayo's clinical notes system.

When all the subspecialists' reports have been completed, a comprehensive second-opinion document is compiled and sent back to the remote physician. That physician can use the second opinion to work up the diagnosis and treatment plan for the patient. In Mayo Clinic's case, real-time interactions between remote physicians are not necessary.

Although store-and-forward telemedicine works well for consults, it can involve delays when additional information or tests are needed and one must wait for the response to arrive. Also, it is not suitable to remote, robotic, or even guided surgery, all of which must be conducted in real time.

The benefit of telemedicine is that it makes high-level medical expertise available to remote and rural areas. Many communities do not have medical specialists. Even fewer places in the world have subspecialists, or sub-subspecialists who can recognize and treat rare or complex medical problems. Using telemedicine, it is possible for a local physician to get advice from a distant expert and guidance in treating the patient.

Teleradiology

One form of telemedicine that is specifically concerned with the transmission of diagnostic images from one location to another is teleradiology. Usually this is for the purpose of having the images "read" by a radiologist at the receiving end. This may be to obtain a second opinion or consult, or because the sending facility does not have sufficient radiologists on staff and has contracted to have radiology interpretations done by another facility. In the latter case, state laws may require the radiologist to be licensed by the state from which the images are sent.

Currently, most states require a physician to be licensed by that state to treat patients in that state. Mayo Clinic's method of telemedicine solves the problem of licensure that has hindered telemedicine in the United States. At Mayo, the telemedicine consultation is physician to physician as a resource for the patient's doctor. Because they are not giving advice directly to a patient in another state, no laws are broken. This method also has the additional advantage of keeping the patient's local physician in control of the patient care at all times.

Patient Entry of Symptoms and History

Contributed by Allen R. Wenner, M.D.[7]

A day in a medical clinic is a busy stream of patients ranging in age from newborn to geriatric. Their presenting complaints are as varied as their age range. Because patients may have a minor illness or a life-threatening condition, it is very hard to predict exactly how long each patient will take. As a result, the clinician falls behind schedule. Patients from the morning often spill over into lunch, which often becomes abbreviated.

In contrast to the hectic pace of the clinicians, time seems to drag for the patients who are waiting. A major challenge for the staff is keeping the patients from waiting too long in the waiting room or exam rooms.

In a traditional office, by the time the clinician enters the examination room and greets the patient, there is still little or no information about the patient except for vital signs and a few notes from the medical assistant or nurse. The clinician has to begin by asking why the patient has sought care. After briefly listening to the patient describe a complaint, the typical clinician interrupts the patient after 18 seconds to clarify the story, often cutting off the patient's natural flow of narration. Clinicians pressed for time need to get to the point quickly.

An experienced physician can make a preliminary assessment a few minutes into the interview. The bulk of the visit is spent confirming this hypothesis by querying the patient about symptoms and the history of present illness, by a review of systems, and then by performing the physical exam. Because of time pressures or fatigue as the day wears on, the clinician may forget to ask about vital pieces of data including essential symptoms, family or social history, or habits such as alcohol or drug use.

With the pressures of patients waiting, after completing the physical exam, assessment, and writing a prescription, the clinician may not have enough time to provide patient education. Instead of answering questions about the treatment and care plan, the clinician relies on a nurse or receptionist to educate the patient. In the traditional paper office, the clinician leaves the exam room and goes to a private area to complete the patient's chart by dictating or handwriting his or her recollection of the history as told by the patient, any other relevant data remembered from the encounter and the physical exam, as well as the diagnosis, prescription, and treatment plan.

---

[7]Courtesy of Primetime Medical Software and Instant Medical History, used by permission.

EHR systems facilitate documentation at the point of care, but only the patient has the information about what symptoms were present at the outset of the illness and what the outcome of medical treatment of those symptoms was. The patient is also typically the source of past medical, family, and social history. The clinician's time with the patient is spent entering the patient's symptom into the visit documentation.

In the late 1980s, Allen Wenner, M.D., a physician in Columbia, South Carolina, wondered if history couldn't be taken by a computer. The medical literature was replete with academic efforts at patient computer dialog, beginning with Warner Slack at Harvard[8] and John Meyne at Mayo Clinic.[9] If the patients entered their own data, it would free up clinical staff and allow more of the physician's time to be focused directly on the important issues identified by patient. Dr. Wenner confirmed the theories of the academics that given the opportunity to add information to their medical chart while waiting was readily accepted by most patients. Working with his colleagues at Primetime Medical Software, he developed Instant Medical History™, an automated patient data entry component for the EHR. It is available in many commercial EHR systems today.

Dr. Wenner decided that the computer could ask all the necessary questions intelligently if it was given a limited set of initial information. A nurse would start the interview by entering the patient's age and sex, and selecting the symptoms and organ systems for review. At that point, the computer could pose questions that simulated a live patient interview. The knowledge-based approach of the computer's artificial intelligence changed the questions based on the patient's answers, simulating a live clinical interview. The software sought to collect the necessary prerequisite data for the clinical interview.

Another important element of history taking is the depth to which a patient is asked questions. Dr. Wenner found the use of computer interviews improves the quality of the information presented by the patient because it is more complete. For example, an ideal interview about the upper respiratory tract and sinuses should include questions about unusual causes such as psittacosis, an infection acquired from raising birds, query about prevention such as use of tobacco, and consideration of the risk for pregnancy in determining treatment options. The clinician may forget or just not have enough time to ask these questions; the computer will not forget. Because the computer never forgets details, it allows a physician to converse casually with a patient while clarifying the objective information needed to make a confident diagnosis.

In the earliest days of computers, a study at Cornell University had patients answer questions on a punch card that was processed by a computer. The study found that "it collects for appraisal a large and comprehensive body of information about the patient's medical history at no expenditure of the physician's time; it facilitates interview by making available to the physician a preliminary survey of the patient's total medical problems; its data, being systematically arranged, are easier to review than those on conventional medical histories; and, by calling attention to the patient's symptoms and significant items of

---

[8]W.V. Slack, G. P. Hicks, C.E. Reed, et al., "A Computer-Based Medical-History System," *New England Journal of Medicine*, 274 (1966): 194–98.

[9]J. G. Mayne,. W. Weksel, and P. N. Sholtz, "Toward Automating the Medical History," *Mayo Clinic Proceedings*, 43 (1968): 1–25.

past history, it assures that their investigation will not be overlooked because the physician lacked time to elicit them."[10]

Because patients want their physicians to arrive at the best diagnosis, Dr. Wenner found they are willing to answer questions. Also, because the physician can review the information entered by the patient, more time is available for explaining the diagnosis and educating the patient; the patient's time and effort to enter the data are rewarded.

Workflow Using Patient-Entered Data

Instant Medical History can be administered on a kiosk or Tablet PC in the waiting room, in a subwaiting area, in the exam room, or at home via the web. Figure 11-4 illustrates one workflow of an office using Instant Medical History. As you will see in Exercise 64, it is also easily administered over the Internet.

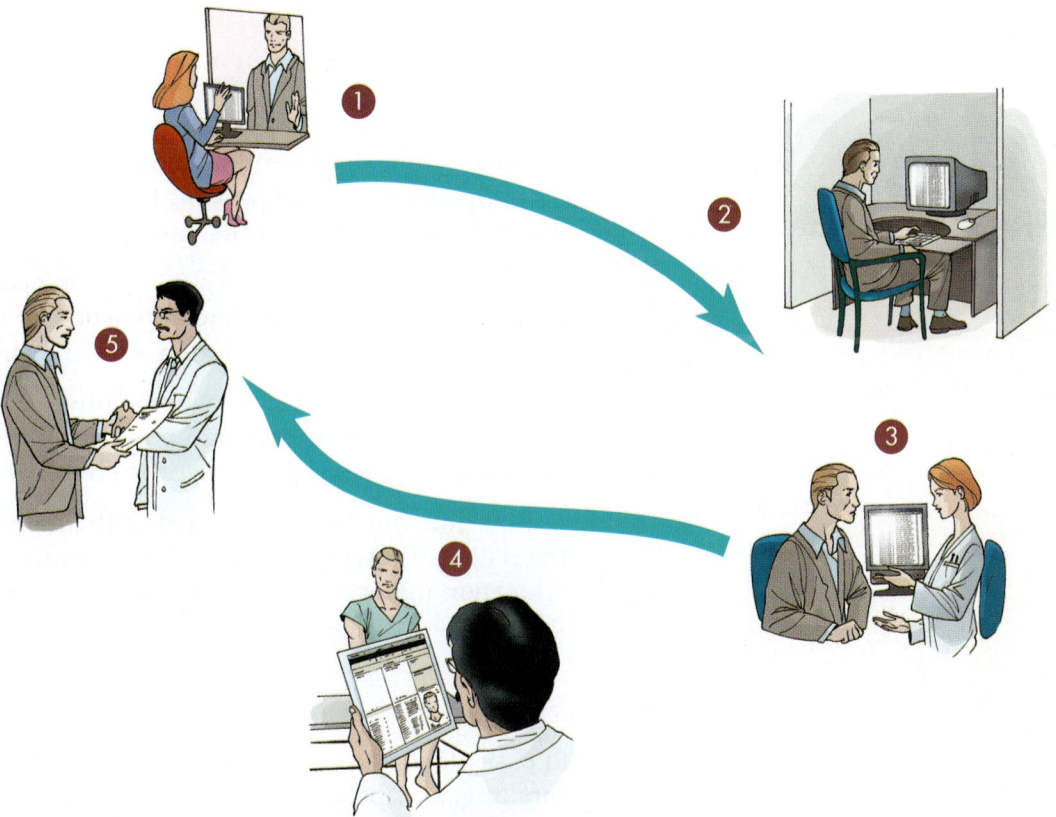

▶ Figure 11-4 Workflow of patient entering his own data.

❶ When the patient arrives, a receptionist, nurse, or medical assistant asks the patient to complete a medical history and reason for today's visit using a computer in a private area of the waiting room.

❷ The patient is given access to a kiosk or other computer to enter his or her own history and symptom information using a computer-guided

---

[10]K. Brodman, A. J. Erdmann, Jr., I. Lorge, et al., "The Cornell Medical Index: An Adjunct to Medical Interview," *Journal of the American Medical Association*, 140 (1949): 530–4.

Chapter 11 | Using the Internet to Expedite Patient Care   **431**

questionnaire. The questions are asked one at a time and can dynamically branch to other question sets based on the answers provided by the patient.

The patient completes the questions at his or her own pace and has an opportunity to change answers. Patients can review their histories and are better prepared to interact with the physician.

❸ When the patient has completed the questionnaire, the system alerts the nurse or medical assistant that the patient is ready to move to an exam room. The nurse and patient review the patient-entered symptoms and history together. Where necessary, the nurse edits the record if there is additional information.

The computer organizes the patient-entered information for the provider in a succinct and easy-to-read format that becomes the starting point for the encounter. After review of the data, the nurse or clinician can merge it into the EHR encounter note.

❹ The physician examines the patient and discusses the reason for the visit and reviews with the patient the HPI information now in the chart. Having a complete history in the EHR in advance of the exam provides the clinician with a great deal of useful information to begin making the proper diagnosis and considering appropriate treatment. It also allows the physician to spend less time documenting and more time with patient discussing the effects of the illness on the patient. It also allows the clinician time to discuss the treatment plan with the patient.

Because interview software records subjective information from the patient, the data represents a more complete and accurate reflection of a patient's complaints than a physician's dictation after the visit.

After asking a few confirmatory questions, physicians can complete the physical exam, assessment, and plan portions of the encounter note in the examination room while the patient is still present.

❺ The encounter note has been completed at the point of care. As the patient leaves, the patient is given a copy of the encounter note along with any patient education materials or prescriptions.

Internet Workflow

Providers and patients soon realized that it was possible to complete the symptom and history interview before the visit by using the Internet. Today many medical practices enable the patient to complete the Instant Medical History questionnaire online before the visit. This saves time during the office visit and allows the patient to give more thought to their answers when completing the interview from the comfort of their home. When the patient arrives for his or her appointment, the data will already be available to the clinician.

Improved Patient Information

Data from patient screening is useful for providing pertinent information that allows an immediate diagnosis. Not only does the physician have a reasonable idea of the patient's problems before any examination begins, but the data are also instantly ready to become part of the medical record.

Eliminating the bulk of transcription and dictation and replacing it with detailed, patient-entered data transforms the encounter from a data-gathering session into an opportunity to concentrate on the most important task at hand: caring for the patient.

The increased efficiency that computer screening allows makes office visits more enjoyable because the physician has more time to explain the diagnosis and educate the patient.

Dr. Wenner and his peers have found most patients willing and eager to answer a computer interview about their reason for the visit. The patient benefits because the time the doctor has saved from having to input the symptoms and history can be focused fully on the patient and used for counseling and education.

When the exam room is configured as shown in Figure 11-5, so that the patient and doctor or nurse can both see the screen, the patient is able to engage in the mutual process of documenting the visit. The patient benefits from this arrangement because when the patient and provider share information, the patient feels a part of the decisions and has a vested interest in following the plan of care.

Courtesy of Primetime Medical Software & Instant Medical History.

▶ **Figure 11-5 Exam room computer positioned so patient (on left) and doctor (on right) share information.**

John Mayne at the Mayo Clinic observed, "If the time physicians spend collecting, organizing, recording, and retrieving data could be reduced, at least in part, by information technology, more time would be available for actual delivery of medical care (and, thus, in effect increase the number of physicians) and at the same time the physician's capabilities for collecting information from patients would be extended."[11]

---

[11]J. G. Mayne, W. Weksel, and P. N. Sholtz, "Toward Automating the Medical History," *Mayo Clinic Proceedings*, 43 (1968): 1–25.

Guided Exercise 64: Experiencing Patient-Entered HPI

In this exercise you will have an opportunity to experience what we have been discussing, by taking on the role of a patient who is completing his "paperwork" for an upcoming appointment online. You will need access to the Internet for this exercise.

Case Study

Tomas Martiniz is a 24-year-old male who injured his knee when he jumped off a loading dock at work. He has an appointment at the Family Care medical clinic. He is going online to complete his medical questionnaire in advance.

▶ Figure 11-6 Simulated provider web page used for exercises in Chapter 11.

Step 1

Start your web browser program and follow the steps listed inside the cover of this textbook to select a discipline, click on the book cover that matches this *Electronic Health Records* textbook, and log in.

When the welcome page is displayed, click on the link "**Activities and Exercises**" or select "Activities" from the drop-down list and click on the button labeled "Go."

Step 2

A menu on the left of the screen will list various activities and exercises. Locate and click on the link **Exercise 64**.

Information about the exercise will be displayed.

Locate and click the link "Click here to start the web portal program."

Step 3

The sample provider web portal shown in Figure 11-6 will be displayed.

Locate the section of the web page labeled "Already have an appointment?" and click on the link "Medical Questionnaire."

The interview web page, "Get started preparing for your next doctor's visit," will be displayed.

Step 4

Locate and click on the button labeled "Start Interview."

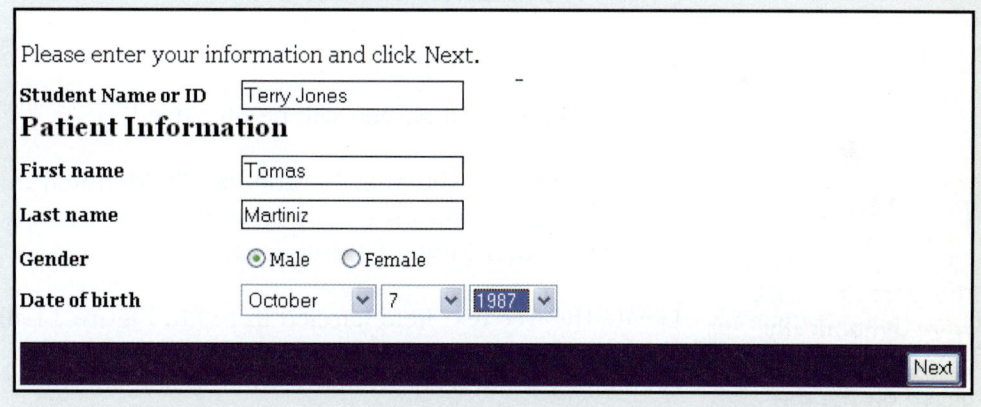

▶ Figure 11-7 Student ID and patient information portion of the interview.

Step 5

The center portion of the web page will display the Interview dialog as shown in Figure 11-7.

Enter the following:

Student Name or ID: Enter either your name or student ID as directed by your instructor.

Patient Information:

First Name: **Tomas**

Last Name: **Martiniz**

Click on the circle next to **Male**.

Click on the down arrow buttons in each of the Date of Birth fields and select from the drop-down lists: **October**, **7**, and **1987**.

Compare your screen to Figure 11-7. When everything has been entered correctly, locate and click on the button labeled "Next."

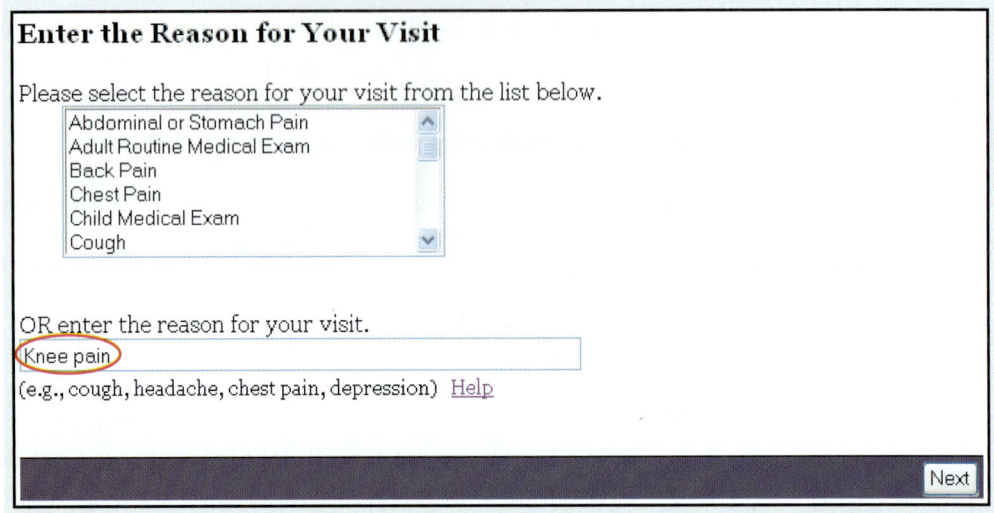

▶ Figure 11-8 Reason for visit: Knee pain.

Step 6

The reason for visit screen will be displayed.

The interview on web page is functionally identical to online questionnaires on the web sites of doctors such as Karen Smith, M.D. (shown in Figure 11-1), and many other forward-thinking doctors.

Locate the free text field (circled in red in Figure 11-8) and type: **Knee pain**.

Compare your screen to Figure 11-8. When you have finished typing, locate and click on the button labeled "Next."

Step 7

The software at the web site will conduct the interview by asking Mr. Martiniz the questions listed in the following table, one question at a time. For each question there will be buttons labeled with various answers to the question. Additional buttons allow you to skip a question or go back to the previous question.

For each question in the following table, locate click on the indicated button. If you make an error, click on the button labeled "Previous Question" and correct your error.

 **Alert**

The interview software dynamically changes questions based on the patient's input. If the order of questions deviates from the sequence listed in the table, click on the "Previous Question" button until you find your mistake and then resume.

Interview Question	Click on the button labeled
What kind of problem are you having with your knee (or knees)?	Pain
What were you doing when the problem or pain began?	Fell
How long ago did your knee symptoms begin?	3 to 4 days
How did your knee symptoms begin?	Suddenly or quickly
Please select the best answer which most closely describes the pace of your knee problem.	My symptoms seem to be getting better but improvement is slow
Has your knee symptoms caused you to stop or reduce work, exercise, or other activities?	Yes
On a scale of 0 (no pain) to 10 (severe), how severe is your knee problems?	5 to 6 moderate
What time of day does your knee problem occur?	No specific time of day
Do your knee problems improve with activity?	No
Are your knee problems made worse by walking, running or other movement?	Yes
Are your knee problems worse when at rest or not moved?	No
Does your knee swell?	Yes
Is your painful knee joint red?	No
Is the painful knee joint warm?	No
Is the painful knee joint tender when you touch it?	Yes
Is the skin of the knee draining or open?	No
Which best describes where your knee is tender?	On the outside of the knee
How long have you had knee pain?	1 to 3 days
Which knee is painful?	Left knee
Which part of your knee hurts?	The part towards the outside
Does your painful knee joint creak or make a grating noise when you move it?	No
Does your painful knee joint lock when it is moved in certain ways?	No
Does your knee give way?	No
Are you able to completely bend and extend your knee?	Yes
Is the skin around your knee red, warm, swollen, tender, or draining fluid?	No
Have you noticed any lumps under the skin around your knee along with the pain?	No
Does your knee(s) seem to be enlarged or larger on one or both sides?	Yes
When do you have knee pain?	Only during activity
Does your knee pain become worse when climbing up stairs?	Yes
Does your knee pain become worse when going down stairs?	No
Is your knee pain worse when you are bearing weight on your legs?	Yes
Is your knee pain worse when you are kneeling?	Yes
Is your knee pain worse when you turn or twist on your leg with your foot planted?	Yes
What happens to your painful knee joint when you are active?	Joint pain become worse during use
Does your knee pain become worse if you actively move the knee joint (that is if you make the knee joint move as you would during activity but without any stress or pressure on the knee joint)?	No

(continued)

(continued)

Interview Question	Click on the button labeled
Does your knee pain become worse if you move the knee joint passively (that is if you make the knee joint move by having someone else move it for you)?	No
Have you ever injured the knee joint that is now painful?	Yes
Have you ever had the knee joint that is now painful immobilized (motionless) for 3 days or more?	No
Did this episode of knee pain start at the same time as an injury to the knee?	Yes
Which best describes the way that you injured your knee?	I jumped or fell from a high place
Which best describes how quickly your knee pain has come on?	Suddenly and worsened quickly over hours
What time of day does your knee pain occur?	No specific time of day
How would you describe the pain you usually have in your knee?	Moderate
On a scale of 0 (no pain) to 10 (severe), how is your knee pain with walking on flat surfaces?	5 to 6 (moderate)
On a scale of 0 (no pain) to 10 (severe), how is your knee pain with walking up stairs?	7 to 8 (severe)
On a scale of 0 (no pain) to 10 (severe), how is your knee pain with walking up hills?	Skip this question
On a scale of 0 (no pain) to 10 (severe), how is your knee pain with walking down stairs?	5 to 6 (moderate)
On a scale of 0 (no pain) to 10 (severe), how is your knee pain with walking down hills?	Skip this question
On a scale of 0 (no pain) to 10 (severe), how is your knee pain while running?	Skip this question
On a scale of 0 (no pain) to 10 (severe), how is your knee pain while kneeling?	9 to 10 (unbearable)
On a scale of 0 (no pain) to 10 (severe), how is your knee pain sitting with knee straight?	3 to 4 (mild)
On a scale of 0 (no pain) to 10 (severe), how is your knee pain at night?	3 to 4 (mild)
Do you have a skin rash?	No
Have you had any fever in the past 4 weeks?	No
Do you have discolored blood vessels or varicose veins in your skin?	No
Do you have tenderness, swelling, redness, or pain anywhere on your leg in addition to around your knee?	No
Do you have a new hard lump or mass anywhere on your leg?	No
Do you have pain from your back shooting down your leg?	No
Have you tried any treatments for your knee problem?	No
Do you have rheumatoid arthritis?	No
Do you have osteoarthritis also known as degenerative arthritis?	No
Has a doctor ever diagnose you as having bursitis?	No
Has a doctor or other health professional ever told you that you had back problems?	No
Have you ever broken a bone of your lower extremity (thigh, knee, calf, ankle etc.)?	No
Have you ever dislocated a joint of your lower extremity (hip, knee, ankle, foot, etc.)?	No
Have you ever had a problem with phlebitis?	No
Have you had knee surgery?	No
Have you ever had an injury to your knee ligaments, knee tendons, or knee cartilage problem?	No
Have you ever had an infection in your knee?	No

Step 8

When you have reached the end of the interview, a free-text note box is displayed to allow the patient to enter additional comments in his or her own words.

Type: "**I jumped off a loading dock at work**."

Locate and click on the button labeled "Next."

Step 9

The final screen of the interview allows you to review your work.

Compare your screen to Figure 11-9 by scrolling the window as necessary. If there are any differences (other than the patient's age), repeat the exercise, making certain you answer each of the questions in steps 6 and 7 correctly.

Step 10

At the bottom of the interview report screen are two buttons labeled "Print" and "Save." The Save button will save the report to a file, similar to the Export button you have used in other exercises.

When everything in your report is correct, locate and click on the appropriate button to either print or save to a file, as directed by your instructor. Once you have your printout or file output in hand, close your browser and proceed to Exercise 65.

Critical Thinking Exercise 65: Reviewing Patient-Entered Data

It is important to note that a patient entering medical history either at the doctor's office or via the Internet is not accessing the actual EHR, but rather a separate application. This protects the security and integrity of the EHR.

Once the data is reviewed by the nurse, the data can be imported or merged directly into the EHR to become part of the encounter note. In this exercise you will take on the role of the nurse, to review the data Mr. Martiniz has entered.

Case Study

Tomas Martiniz is a 24-year-old male who has an appointment May 28, 2012, at 9:00 AM. He has used the Internet to complete his medical questionnaire in advance. The data has been merged into the EHR to initiate the encounter note for his visit.

Chief Complaint
    Tomas Martiniz is a 24 year old male. His reason for visit is "Knee Pain".
History of Present Illness
  #1. "Knee Pain"
    Location
      He reported: Left knee joint pain. Tenderness on the outside of the knee. Pain towards the outside of the knee.
    Quality
      He reported: Knee larger than normal.
      He denied: Knee unstable when stressed. Painful knee joint locks in certain positions. Back pain moves down the leg. Knee joint movement associated with grating noise. Lumps under the skin. Leg redness, swelling, or tenderness. New lump on leg. He reported: No limitation of range of motion of the knee.
    Severity
      He reported: Knee pain moderate. Knee pain moderate (5-6/10) walking on flat surfaces and walking down stairs. Knee pain mild (3-4/10) sitting with knee straight and at night. Knee problem slowly improving and moderate (5-6/10). Knee pain severe (7-8/10) walking up stairs. Knee pain unbearable (9-10/10) while kneeling.
    Duration
      He reported: Knee pain 1 to 3 days. Knee problem 3 to 4 days.
    Timing
      He reported: Knee pain occurs at no specific time of day. Knee problem started with a fall, started suddenly or quickly, and at no specific time of day. Knee pain began with injury. Knee pain starting suddenly and quickly worsening over hours.
    Context
      He reported: Knee pain only with movement.
      He denied: Previous immobilization of painful knee joint.
    Modifying Factors
      He reported: Knee pain becomes worse during use. Knee pain worse when climbing stairs, bearing weight, kneeling, and twisting.
      He denied: Knee pain worse when descending stairs. Knee problem improved with activity. Knee problem worsened by activity. Knee pain worsened by active motion. Knee pain worsened by passive motion.
    Associated Signs and Symptoms
      He reported: Knee swells and tender.
      He denied: Knee red and warm.
Past, Family, and Social History
  Past Medical History
    He denied: Bursitis. Rheumatoid arthritis. Back pain. Inflamed blood vessel. Internal derangement of knee. Knee infection.
  Surgical History
    He denied: Knee surgery.
  Accidents and Injuries
    History of: Previous injury to painful knee joint. Knee injured by jumping from a high place.
    He denied: Broken hip or leg. Lower extremity dislocation.
  Social History
    History of: Treatment for knee problem.
    Activities for Daily Living
      History of: Knee problem reduced activity.
Review of Systems
  Constitutional
    He denied: Fever in the last month.
  Cardiovascular
    He denied: Varicose veins.
  Skin
    He denied: Knee draining. Rash.
Additional Comments
  I jumped off a loading dock at work

▶ **Figure 11-9** Completed interview for Tomas Martiniz.

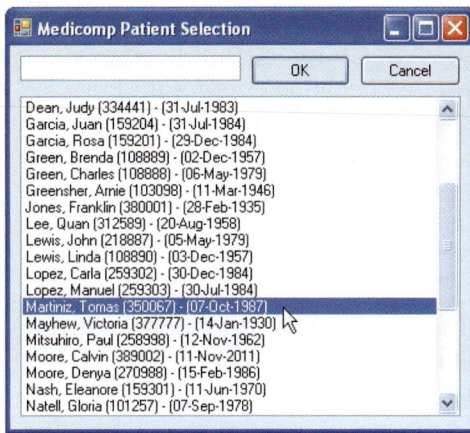

▶ Figure 11-10 Select patient Tomas Martiniz.

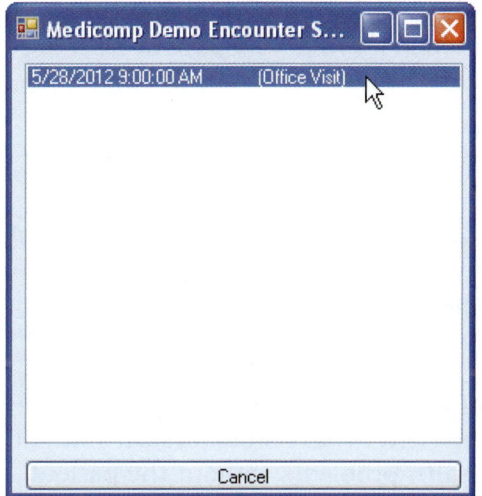

▶ Figure 11-11 Select existing encounter for May 28, 2012.

Step 1

If you have not already done so, start the Student Edition software.

Click Select on the Menu bar, and then click Patient.

In the Patient Selection window, locate and click on Tomas Martiniz as shown in Figure 11-10.

Step 2

Click Select on the Menu bar again, and then click **Existing Encounter**.

Select **5/28/2012 9:00 AM Office Visit** as shown in Figure 11-11.

The encounter note from that date will be displayed.

Step 3

Click on the Print button on the Toolbar at the top of your screen to invoke the Print Data window.

Be certain there is a check mark in the box next to "Current Encounter" and then click on the button labeled "Print and Close," even if you normally exported a file in previous exercises. You will need a printed copy for the next step.

Step 4

Compare the answers from the interview report you printed in the previous exercise with the encounter note you have just printed. On your printed encounter note identify and draw a circle around any instances where the terminology is different.

If there were any differences, why would the patient's terminology and the medical nomenclature be different?

When you are finished, give your interview report or output file to your instructor.

Provider-to-Patient E-Mail Communication

The HIPAA Security Rule does not expressly prohibit the use of e-mail for sending electronic protected health information (EPHI). The Security Rule allows for EPHI to be sent over an electronic open network as long as it is adequately protected. However, as you learned in Chapter 10, the security standard for transmission security includes addressable specifications for integrity controls and encryption.

The HIPAA Privacy Rule permits the patient to disclose information to anyone that the patient likes, but the covered entity cannot. This means a patient can e-mail a doctor or medical facility containing any information he or she wants about his or her medical condition, even if the e-mail is not encrypted. However, the clinician has to be very guarded in replying through unencrypted e-mail—that is, neither a copy of the patient's message should be included nor any specific information revealed. Most importantly, the patient should consider whether he or she should send private health information using unencrypted e-mail.

Although e-mail can be secured by encryption similar to the public/private keys discussed (as part of electronic signatures) in Chapter 10, it becomes unmanageable on the part of the medical practice because encryption keys would have to be kept on file for thousands of patients and the appropriate key used for e-mail from each. The preferred alternative is to use a secure web site for communication between the patient and provider.

Secure Messaging

Instead of sending an e-mail message from his or her usual e-mail system, the patient logs on to the clinician's web site and types the information in an e-mail screen on the web page. The web site handles all the security, protecting the EPHI as required by HIPAA.

Responses to the patient are handled similarly. The patient checks back to the site for messages, or receives a benign message via regular e-mail informing them that there is a reply from the medical office waiting. The patient then logs into the secure site to read the message and, if necessary, writes a reply.

E-Visits

Even when using secure messages, clinicians have concerns about the potential for medical liability, the lack of structure in the messages, and the difficulty of keeping the e-mail exchange as part of the patient's medical record. Also, the doctor does not receive payment for the e-mail exchange.

One solution that enhances the efficiency of providers and improves the accessibility of healthcare for the patients is the E-visit. An E-visit allows the patient to be treated by a clinician for nonurgent health problems without the patient having to come into the office.

An E-visit has all the advantages that e-mail lacks: not only are E-visits secure but the E-visit also gathers symptom and HPI information, creating a documented medical encounter. When the E-visit data is imported into the EHR, it becomes a part of the patient's chart, just like any other visit.

Equally as important to the clinician, e-visits are reimbursed as a legitimate E&M visit. At the time that this book was published, E-visits were being paid by Blue Cross/Blue Shield™ plans and other private insurance carriers in numerous states. A study by Price-Waterhouse-Coopers predicted that more than 20 percent of all office visits could be replaced by an online equivalent.[12]

Workflow of an E-Visit

The basic workflow of an E-visit begins with patient-entered symptom, history, and history of present illness information. Some E-visit web sites use Instant Medical History to gather HPI data from the patient. Other E-visit web sites use a combination of check boxes and free-text messages, similar to secure messaging discussed earlier. Some E-visit web sites such as one at the Mayo Clinic allow the patient to upload digital photos.

---

[12]PricewaterhouseCoopers Report, "HealthCast 2010: Smaller World, Bigger Expectations." November 1999.

The workflow begins when a patient accesses his or her physician's web site and signs on. The patient must already be an established patient with the practice and have medical records on file. E-visits are not generally permitted for a new patient who has never been seen at the practice.

The patient answers a few simple questions and selects the reason for the visit from a list. This allows the software to determine which question sets would be appropriate to ask. The patient also could just enter a free-text complaint.

The patient answers online interview questions related to his or her reported complaint, as shown later in Exercise 66. Answers to certain medically significant questions could cause the software to ask different sets of medically related questions automatically. The patient can add free-text clarification at various points in the interview.

E-visits are only used for nonurgent visits. If the software detects that the condition seems urgent, the patient is advised to seek immediate medical care and the provider is notified. If the software determines that although the condition is not urgent, it is one for which the patient should be seen in person, the patient is given a message to that effect and automatically offered a choice of available appointments.

When the interview is complete, the data entered by the patient is recorded in the EHR and the clinician is notified that an E-visit is ready to review. Even in the event that the patient must come in for the visit, the doctor is better prepared because the symptom and history information is already at hand.

Unlike e-mail, which is directed at a particular individual and therefore not likely to be accessible by another provider, E-visits can be directed to the "doctor on call," allowing practicing partners to share "E-visit" duty, just like they share other on-call services. Providers usually respond promptly after being notified. A study of E-visits that was done in California[13] found a majority of patients were happy if the provider responded by the next morning. Remember, E-visits are for nonurgent matters.

The clinician reviews the patient-entered data, reviews any relevant patient medical records, and replies to the patient. The system allows the provider and patient to continue to exchange messages, much as a question-and-answer session in the exam room, except for the factor of time, which is sometimes delayed by one or both parties' responses.

The clinician also can prescribe electronically during the E-visit, just as he or she would during an office visit. When the patient receives the clinician's reply to the E-visit, that patient is prompted to select a preferred pharmacy from a list (if it is not already known to the EHR) and the prescription is electronically transmitted to the pharmacy by the doctor's system.

The doctor's response also can include patient education material and comments or care instructions from the doctor, all of which are recorded in the care plan. The doctor's practice management system can verify the patient eligibility for the E-visit, and submit the claim electronically.

---

[13]Relay Health webVisit Study: Final Report, www.relayhealth.com © 2002–2003 RelayHealth Corporation.

Real-Life Story

Using the Internet to Build a Patient-Centered Practice

By Karen Smith, M.D., FAAFP

I practice medicine in Raeford, North Carolina, which is located in the second-most impoverished county in our state. We are close to a military base, so we have a culturally diverse mix of patients, those native to this area as well as people from all over who are stationed here.

After graduating from family medicine residency, my family relocated to Raeford. There were only three doctors in town caring for the whole population. The first two practices I worked at used paper medical records. When I set up my own practice I knew EHR was a necessary tool. That is when I met Dr. Alan Wenner. I went to his lecture symposium titled the "High-Performing Physician."

We simultaneously implemented both an EHR and a practice management system in place from day one. In 2008, the NCQA introduced the recognition process for the "medical home." We reviewed the criteria and the requirements for Patient-Centered Medical Home (PCMH) status; we already had most of it. The last component we needed was the virtual health office.

Our practice web site (shown in Figure 11-1) allows patients to register online, request an appointment, complete their Instant Medical History (IMH) symptom assessment before their appointment, review health insurance information, obtain their lab results, access medical information for common medical conditions, and have a virtual office visit with their doctor online.

Instant Medical History is readily accepted by our patients, especially military families. Because of a base realignment of the military, we have 30,000 new military personnel coming into our community and a lot of them already registered online and completed their IMH before they come into the office.

Workflow of Our Office

Our patients' have several ways of contacting us; some call on the telephone and some just walk in. Our preferred first point of contact, however, is our web site. We automate a lot of our pre-visit activity. I have already mentioned they can complete the IMH symptom assessment over the Internet. We also have an automated system that telephones patients to remind them of their appointments. Once the Televox system has confirmed their appointment, one of my staff reviews their chart to see if their immunizations are up to date, if they have a balance due, or need anything else before their visit. In addition, we have now introduced a live operator system via the practice portal and Athena communicator, which is a very important combination of the web with a person who is familiar with the office systems.

When a patient shows up, existing demographic information is verified as that person is checked in on the computer. Once the patient is checked into the system, the nurse is automatically notified on her computer that the patient is checked in. She then goes to the lobby and gets the patient. She takes the patient's vital signs and then brings the patient into the exam room. There she starts her nursing intake. She will start the Instant Medical History and then leave the patient in the room to do his or her own entry, unless the person did the entry from home via our web site before coming. About 15 percent of our patients do it in advance.

If the patient did it at home, the nurse would extract it and bring it into the HPI section of the note. If the patient does it in the office, the nurse will return when that person is finished and then paste it into the note. In either case, when that is done I will see a color change on my computer and know that the patient is ready for me.

I go into the exam room and log on to the EHR. I have computers in every exam room, so I do not have to carry anything around. I have the patient elaborate a little more on the purpose of the visit. I perform the exam and go over any issues the patient may have. Then I sit down with that person so that we are both on the same level and can both see the computer screen. The computer is positioned where we can both see it at the same time and yet I can maintain eye-to-eye contact. My exam room computers are set up the way Dr. Wenner recommends (as shown in Figure 11-5) and it works well.

Many of my patients have hypertension or hyperlipidemia. By sharing the screen, the patient can actually see the objective information: "Here is your cholesterol and what you have been doing is working well." To get the patient to be compliant with the treatment plan, we put it in together. I am literally entering the orders in front of the patient as a way of emphasizing "I am putting this in the way we mutually agreed." When I have everything ordered, I look at the patient and ask, "Did we cover everything today, or is there anything else we need to take care of?" When the person answers no, then I close the encounter note. I stand up and we walk out the room together.

All of our office systems are interfaced. For example, if I had ordered labs when I wrote the order, the lab system automatically printed the labels and if an ABN (advanced beneficiary notice) is necessary, it printed out as well. Many times I will walk the patient to the lab and the phlebotomist already has the tubes ready. Because I use a bidirectional interface, the lab orders have already gone to the lab company.

When the patient is finished, he or she is taken to the front desk where my instructions to the patient, follow-up visit information, and a summary of today's visit is already prepared—all of this from the click of a button on the exam room computer. By the time the patient gets to the front desk to check out, he or she already has an appointment card ready for the next appointment, the billing information for the claim has gone into the billing system, the charges have been posted, the patient due has been calculated and ready for the front desk to collect balance due, including any deductible that has not been met.

Even after the patient goes home, if he or she has a question about treatment, medication, or just forgot to ask something, the patient can go online to our web site and send me a secure message.

Virtual Office Visits

We also offer patients the ability to use our web portal to have their office visit online instead of coming into the office. What we had to do was make it clear to the patient that "using the virtual office means the doctor is going to see and take care of your problems online; you do not need to physically present to the office." Our virtual office visit uses an interview question format similar to the IMH symptom assessment.

- The patient logs in and chooses Virtual Office Visit. The normal E-visit workflow is to collect the payment on the web site at the time of service; however, we initially had an issue with the electronic payment process to be resolved.

- The patient confirms personal information and answers the health questions specific to the topic of the consultation, which normally takes about five minutes.

- Upon completion of their Virtual Office Visit, the system sends me a message.

- I log on and review the visit. I can see everything that the patient put in. I then create the response. I can reply with any further questions, but in most cases the online interview has gathered sufficient data. I also have access to my patient's medical history in the EHR. If I put in a prescription, it is sent to the pharmacy and adds information to the patient message that this is the patient's medication and the name of the drug store where it has been sent. Alternatively, I can say that the patient needs to come into the office in person.

- The patient then receives an e-mail notification from us. The confidential e-mail message does not disclose any information about the nature of the visit to our site. It simply asks the patient to return to our site for more information.

- Upon revisiting our site, the patient logs in and views the message from the physician. This message contains the treatment plan or a request for additional information. If the treatment plan involves prescription medications, the patient is given the pharmacy information.

In most cases, that completes the E-visit because these are very specific conditions and treatments that can be done this way. Also, because these are my patients, I know what their health conditions are. I usually do not have to ask patients for further information and can close out the E-visit.

The utility of the E-visit occurring is very useful for our group. We promote the use of our web site everywhere, including our practice policies and patient care information sheets, but using the web portal and virtual office visits has been a learning curve in our community. I think in part this is because of the impoverishment in our county; only 30 percent of the households have Internet access within the home. I have noticed our military patients and their families use E-visits more than my other patients, but the Army has given the families computers and Internet access, so that may be a factor.

Mayo Clinic Study of E-visits

The largest study of Internet use for online care (E-visits) using a structured history was conducted in the Department of Family Medicine at Mayo Clinic in Rochester, Minnesota. Here are excerpts from the study.[14]

"Patients in the department preregistered for the service and then were able to use the online portal for consultations with their primary care providers.

"After completing (data entry for) the e-visit, the patients received an e-mail stating that their clinician would review their consultation within 24 hours. Another e-mail was forwarded to the clinician informing him or her of an e-visit waiting in the secure portal. "The portal allowed the clinician to use templated encounter forms for many common illnesses so that information such as diagnostic codes, links to patient education, and treatment plans could be stored and reused. This standardization of treatment greatly speeded the process of reviewing an online visit. Medications were often prescribed during the process and faxed to the pharmacy. At the conclusion of the online visit, patients received an e-mail stating that the results of their encounter could be found on the portal. Patients would then log in and view the materials.

"Generally, online consultations were completed by clinicians within 24 hours of the e-visit submission; only 11 were not completed. E-visits were completed by the patient's primary provider 89% of the time; 11% of the consultations were provided by an on-call clinician for absent providers or if the patient selected 'first available doctor.'

"Because patients could enter any symptom or concern, ask questions, and add additional comments, the e-visits eliminated the need for clinicians to ask for further information in most instances. This was because the patient's history was organized and pertinent information including all medications, allergies, and vital signs such as weight were always obtained. The volume of exchanges could be decreased further by emphasizing the need to send pictures of rashes. . . .

"Some consultations for patients with chronic disease seemed to show promise. Patients with diabetes mellitus first had laboratory tests and then were asked to complete an online visit regarding their diabetes. If all was well according to the interview and laboratory results, the patients did not need to visit the office. Hypertension was also managed online; patients sent in their blood pressure responses and clinicians managed their medications and laboratory studies online.

"During the 2-year study, 4,282 patients were registered for the service. Patients made 2,531 online visits, and billings were made for 1,159 patients. E-visits were made primarily by working-aged women who completed e-visits for themselves, their dependents, and their older parents during office hours and involved 294 different conditions. Two percent of the visits included uploaded photographs, and 16% of the e-visits replaced nonbillable telephone protocols with billable

---

[14]Steven C. Adamson, MD, and John W. Bachman, MD, *Pilot Study of Providing Online Care in a Primary Care Setting* (Rochester, MN: Department of Family Medicine, Mayo Clinic, 2010).

encounters. The e-visits made office visits unnecessary in 40% of cases; in 12.8% of cases, the patient was asked to schedule an appointment for a face-to-face encounter.

"The study showed the feasibility of online visits to educate, treat, and bill patients. The extent of conditions possible for treatment by online care was far ranging and was managed with a minimum of message exchanges by using structured histories."

California Study

In an independent study sponsored by Blue Shield of California, most patients and doctors in the study preferred a web visit to an office visit for nonurgent medical needs. Providers found that the E-visit gathered the important details and eliminated multiple messages back and forth that occur when trying to provide patient care via e-mail. The patients found that the time spent scheduling, driving, parking, and waiting was saved with an E-visit.[15]

Guided Exercise 66: Patient Requests an E-Visit

Case Study

Jacob Silverstein is a 46-year-old male with a history of hypertension and diabetes. He is on medication and has regular check-ups at his family practice. He has an issue with his medication and is going to try an online E-visit instead of coming to the office.

Step 1

Start your web browser program and follow the steps listed inside the cover of this textbook to select a discipline, click on the book cover that matches this *Electronic Health Records* textbook, and log in.

When the welcome page is displayed, click on the link "**Activities and Exercises**" or select "Activities" from the drop-down list and click on the button labeled "Go."

Step 2

A menu on the left of the screen will list various activities and exercises. Locate and click on the link **Exercise 66**.

Information about the exercise will be displayed.

Locate and click the link "Click here to start the web portal program."

Step 3

The sample provider web page shown in Figure 11-6 will be displayed.

Locate the section labeled "E-visits for Established Patients" and click on the link "E-visit."

---

[15]Relay Health webVisit Study: Final Report, www.relayhealth.com © 2002–2003 RelayHealth Corporation.

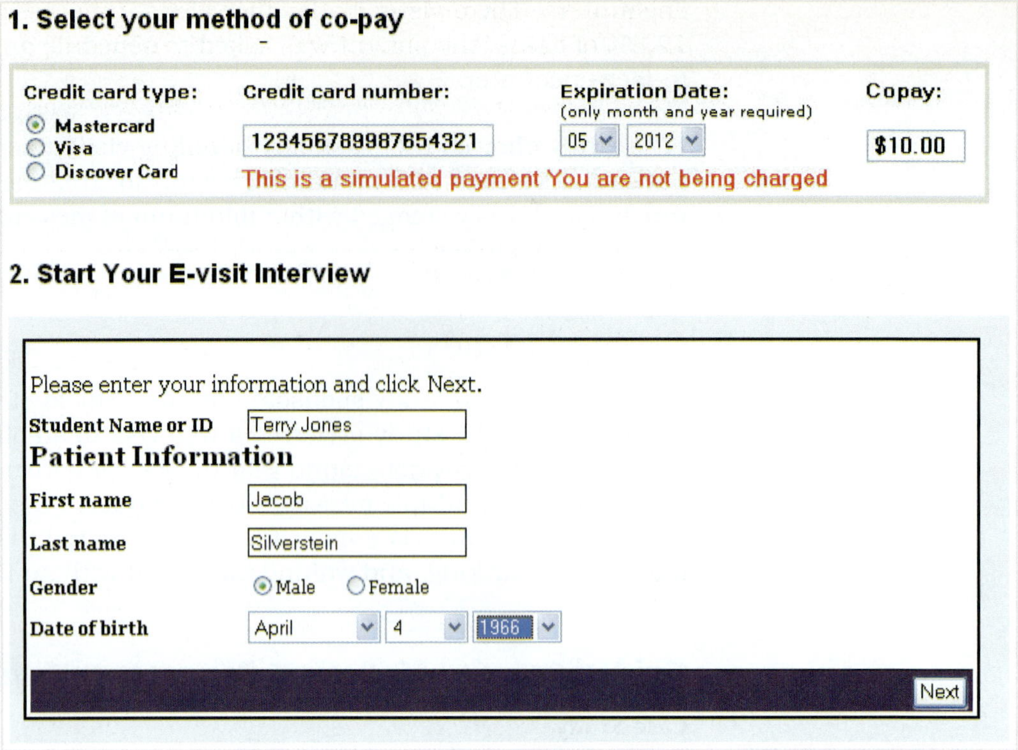

▶ Figure 11-12 Patient interview screen for an E-visit.

Step 4

The "Welcome to Family Care E-visit" web page is displayed. It includes simulated payment information as shown at the top of Figure 11-12. A key difference between an E-visit and a pre-visit questionnaire is that providers collect a copay at the time of the E-visit. It is not necessary to collect the copay on the pre-visit questionnaire page as the patient will be coming into the office, where the payment will be collected.

This is a student exercise; you will not be charged. Do not enter any personal credit card data; simply complete the student ID and patient information fields shown below.

Locate and click on the button labeled "Start Interview." The center portion of your web page will look similar to Figure 11-12.

Step 5

Enter the following:

Enter your name or student ID as you have in the previous exercise.

Enter the follow information about the patient:

First Name: **Jacob**

Last Name: **Silverstein**

Click the circle next to **Male**

Click on the down arrow buttons in each of the Date of Birth fields and select from the drop-down lists: **April**, **4**, and **1966**

Compare your screen to Figure 11-12. When everything has been entered correctly, locate and click on the button labeled "Next."

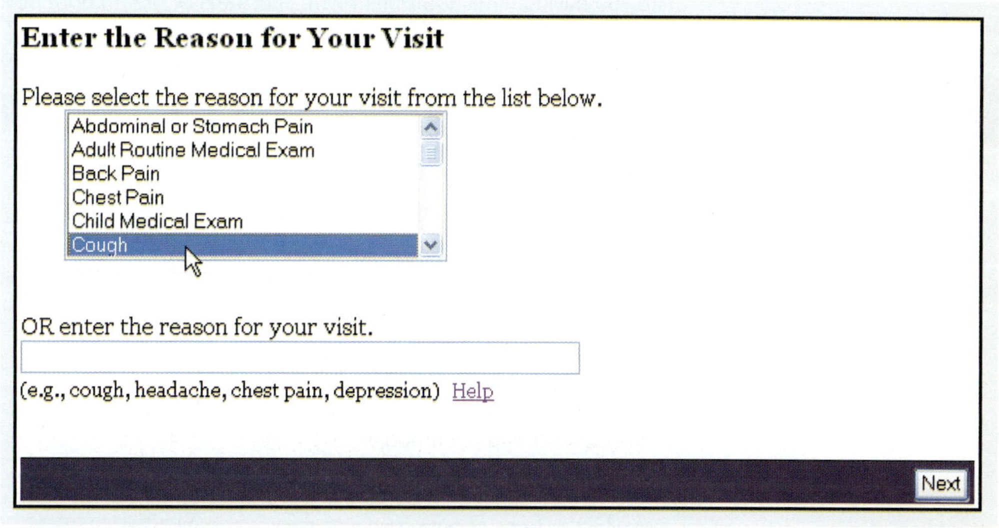

▶ Figure 11-13 Reason for visit "Cough" selected from list.

Step 6

The Reason for Visit screen will be displayed.

Locate and click on "Cough" in the list of reasons as shown in Figure 11-13.

Locate and click on the button labeled "Next."

Step 7

The interview process will start. For each question in the table below, locate and click on the indicated button. If you make an error, click on the button labeled "Previous Question," and correct your error.

Interview Question	Click on the following buttons
Do you have a cough?	Yes
How long have you had a cough?	16 - 20 days
Have you had a cold, flu, or cough within the last month that seemed to improve and then worsen?	No
Do you cough all day long?	Yes
Does your cough sometimes wake you up at night?	No
Does your cough seem to occur in spasms or episodes of multiple coughs?	No
When you cough, are you bringing up any sputum or phlegm from deep in your chest other than a small amount early in the morning?	No

(continued)

(continued)

Interview Question	Click on the following buttons
Is your cough worse after exercise?	No
Is your cough worse when you lie down?	No
Are you having a major problem with shortness of breath right now?	No
Do you have chest discomfort when you breathe?	No
Do you have any wheezing when you breathe?	No
Do you sound hoarse?	No
Do you have post-nasal drip or are you always clearing the back of your throat?	No
Have you had a fever in the past week?	No
Do you sometimes wake up with soaking sweats at night?	No
Did your cough begin after any change in your medications?	Yes
Do you have a cough at certain seasons of the year?	No
Have you ever had pneumonia?	No
Have you ever kept or raised birds?	No
Describe your use of tobacco	Never used

Step 8

When you have reached the end of the interview, a free-text note box is displayed to allow the patient to enter messages in their own words. Leave the box empty.

Locate and click on the button labeled "Next."

Step 9

The final screen of the interview allows you to review your work.

Compare your screen to Figure 11-14 by scrolling the window as necessary. If there are any differences (other than the patient's age), repeat the exercise, making certain you answer each of the questions in steps 6 through 8 correctly.

Step 10

At the bottom of the Interview Report screen are two buttons labeled "Print" and "Save."

When everything in your report is correct, locate and click on the appropriate button to either print or save to a file, as directed by your instructor. Once you have your print out or file output in hand, close your browser and proceed to Exercise 67.

Chief Complaint
  Jacob Silverstein is a 44 year old male. His reason for visit is "Cough".
History of Present Illness
  #1. "Cough"
    Severity
      He reported: Cough continuously throughout the day.
    Duration
      He reported: Cough 16 to 20 days.
    Timing
      He denied: Nocturnal cough. Seasonal cough.
    Context
      He reported: Cough nonproductive. Cough started after any medication change.
      He denied: Cough seems to occur in spasms or episodes, stopping in between. Deep breathing causes chest pain.
    Modifying Factors
      He denied: Cough after exercise. Cough worse lying down.
    Associated Signs and Symptoms
      He denied: Wheezing. Shortness of breath. Recent cold improved then worsened.
Past, Family, and Social History
  Past Medical History
    He denied: Pneumonia.
  Social History
    He denied: Cough associated with history of exposure to birds.
    Tobacco Use
      He reported: Never used tobacco.
Review of Systems
  Constitutional
    He denied: Cough associated with fever. Night sweats.
  Ear, Nose, and Throat
    He denied: Nasal drainage. Hoarseness.

▶ Figure 11-14 Completed interview for E-visit.

Guided Exercise 67: Clinician Completes the E-Visit

Step 1

If you have not already done so, start the Student Edition software.

Click Select on the Menu bar, and then click Patient.

In the Patient Selection window, locate and click on **Jacob Silverstein** as shown in Figure 11-15.

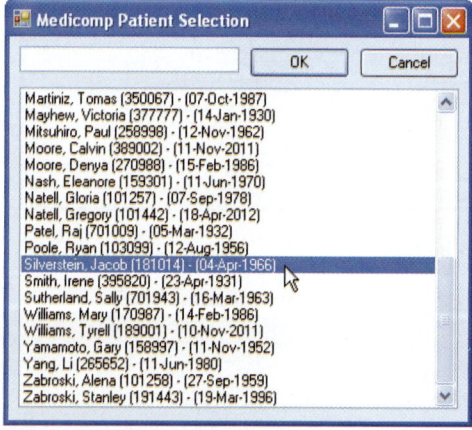

▶ Figure 11-15 Select patient Jacob Silverstein.

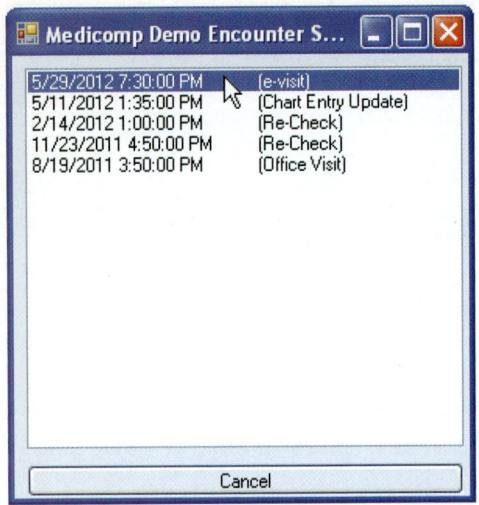

▶ Figure 11-16 Select the E-visit encounter for 5/29/2012.

Step 2

Click Select on the Menu bar again, and then click **Existing Encounter**.

Select **5/29/2012 7:30 PM e-Visit** as shown in Figure 11-16.

The encounter note containing the patient-entered data from the E-visit will be displayed.

Step 3

When the encounter is displayed, locate and click on the Manage tab at the bottom of your screen. Review the HPI data supplied by the patient displayed in the right pane and then locate and click on the tab labeled "Medications" in the left pane. Compare your screen to Figure 11-17. Review Mr. Silverstein's prescription history. Note that a new drug was prescribed on 5/11/2012.

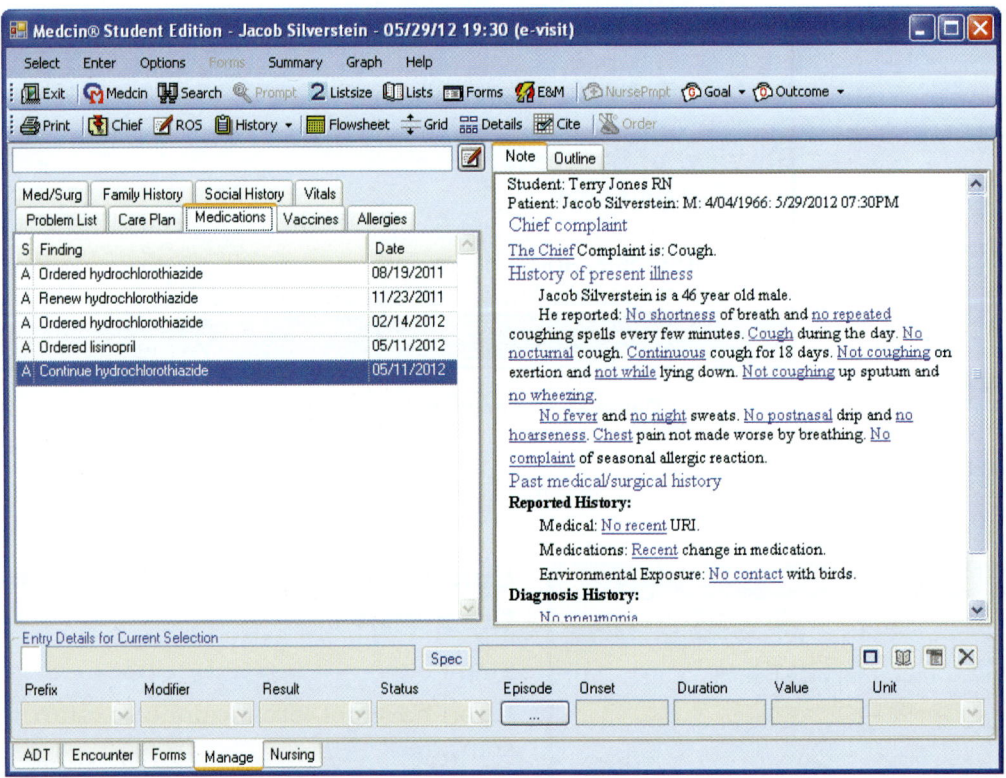

▶ Figure 11-17 Medications tab showing prescription history.

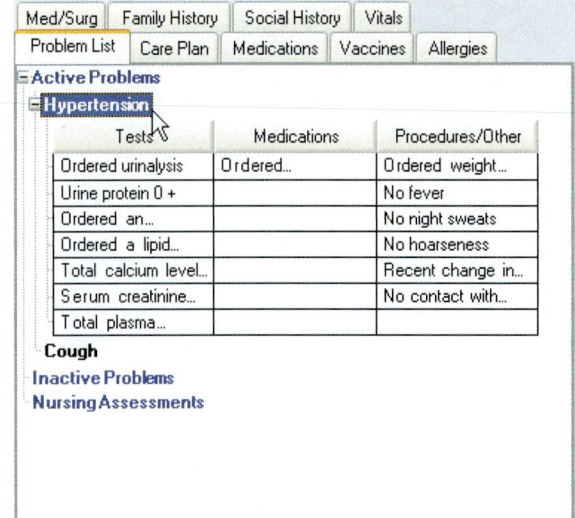

Step 4

Locate and click on the tab labeled "Problem List" and then click on "Hypertension" to highlight it, as shown in Figure 11-18.

Locate and click on the Flowsheet button on the Toolbar at the top of your screen (highlighted orange in Figure 11-19).

▶ Figure 11-18 Problem tab with Hypertension highlighted.

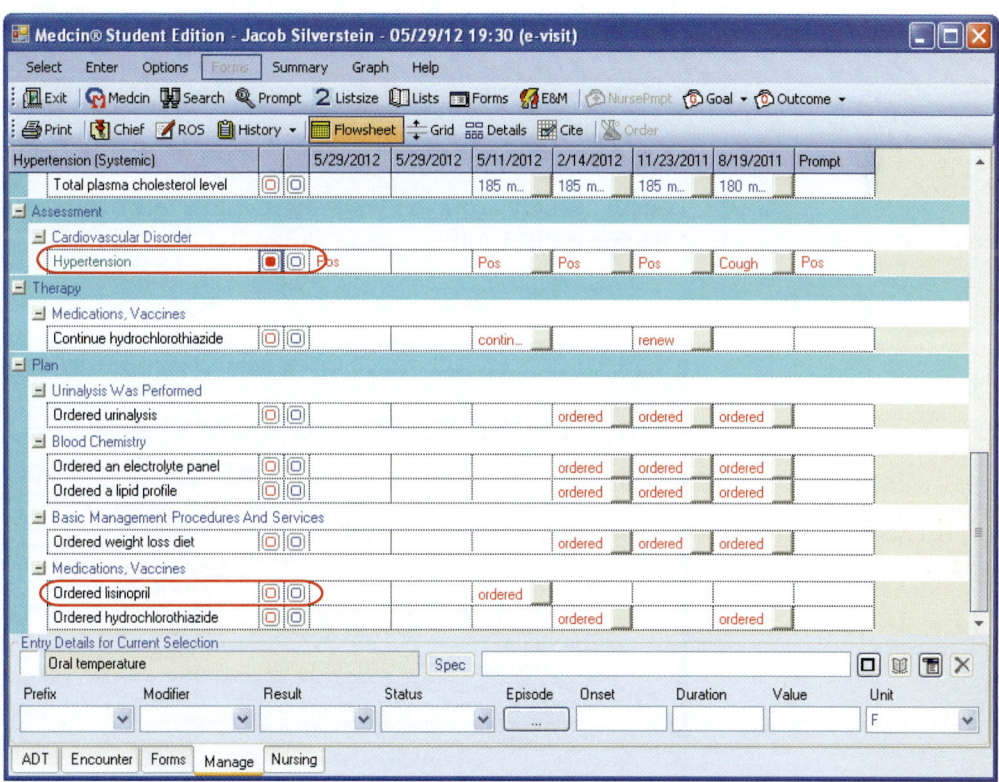

▶ Figure 11-19 Flowsheet with Hypertension and Lisinopril circled in red.

Step 5

Scroll the Flowsheet downward until your screen looks like Figure 11-19. Locate and click on the red button for the Assessment:

- (red button) Hypertension

Locate the Medications, Vaccines section near the bottom of the Flowsheet. Click on the description "Ordered Lisinopril" (circled in Figure 11-19). The entire row will become highlighted. Do not click the red or blue buttons.

Chapter 11 | Using the Internet to Expedite Patient Care 453

▶ Figure 11-20 Select "discontinue" from the Prefix drop-down list.

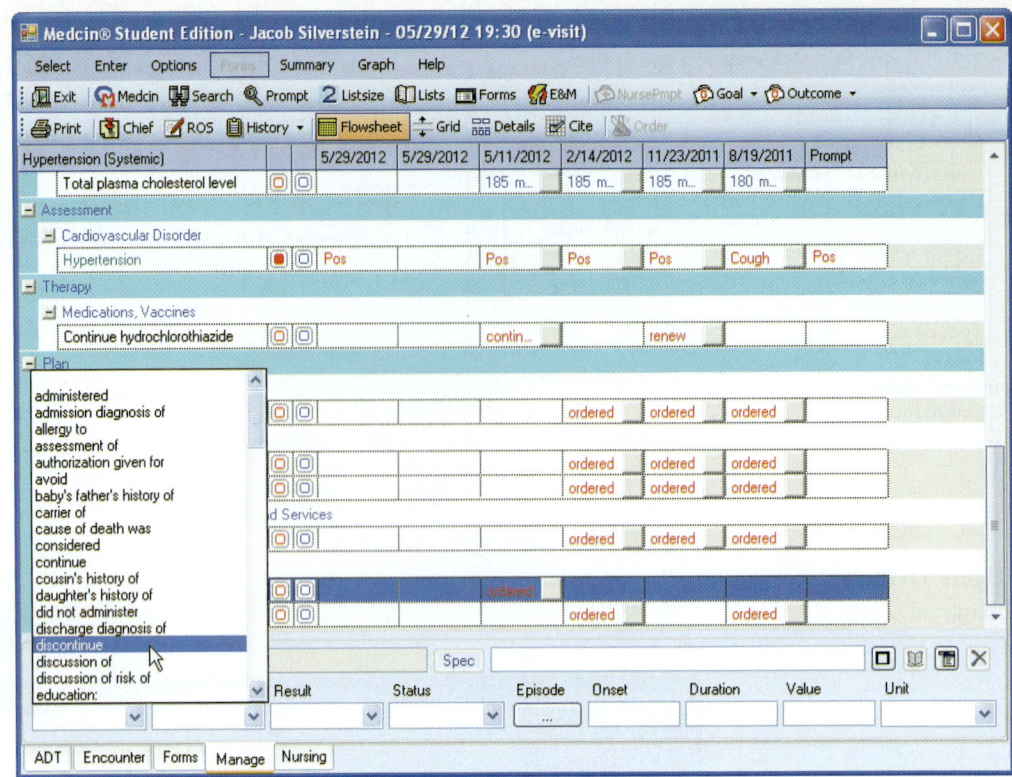

Step 6

Locate and click on the down arrow in the Entry Details "Prefix" field. Select "discontinue" from the drop-down list.

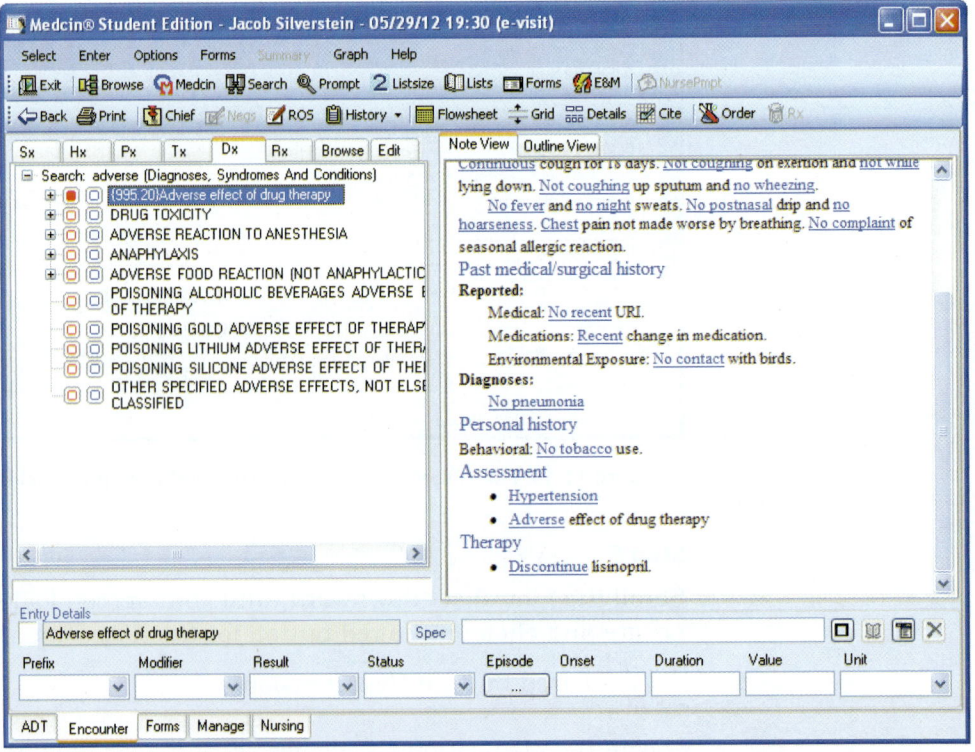

▶ Figure 11-21 Dx: Adverse effect of drug therapy.

Locate and click on the Flowsheet button on the Toolbar to close the Flowsheet.

Locate and click on the Encounter tab at the bottom of your screen.

Step 7

Click on the Dx tab in the left pane.

Locate and click on the Search button on the Toolbar at the top of your screen. When the search dialog window is displayed, type "**adverse**," and then click on the button in the dialog window labeled "Search." Compare your results to the left pane of Figure 11-21.

Locate and click on the red button for the following finding:

- (red button) Adverse effect of drug therapy

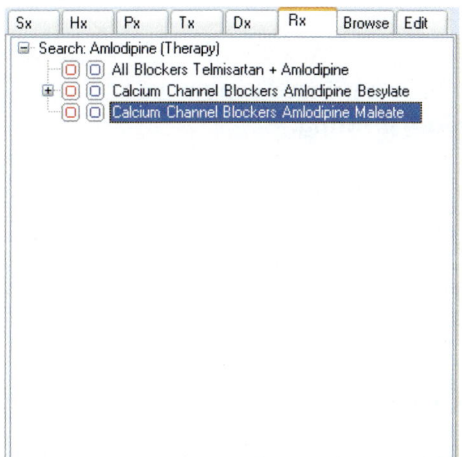

▶ Figure 11-22 Highlight Calcium Channel Blockers Amlodpine Maleate.

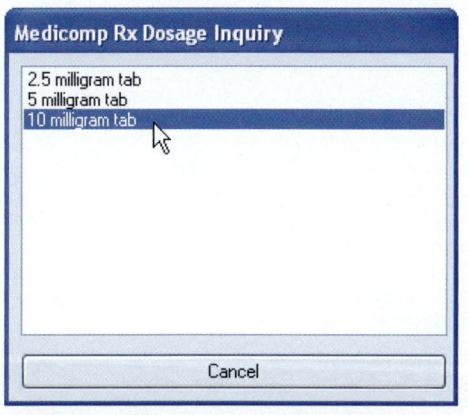

▶ Figure 11-23 Select the 10 milligram tablet in the Rx Dosage Inquiry window.

Step 8

Click on the Rx tab in the left pane.

Locate and click on the Search button on the Toolbar at the top of your screen. When the search dialog window is displayed, type "**Amlodipine**," and then click on the button in the dialog window labeled "Search." Compare your results in the left pane of your screen to Figure 11-22.

Highlight the finding "Calcium Channel Blockers Amlodipine Maleate," and then click the Rx button on the Toolbar at the top of your screen. This will invoke the Rx Writer.

Step 9

Select the dosage "10 milligram tab," as shown in Figure 11-23, and then double-click on it.

Step 10

The Rx Brand window will be displayed (not shown). There is only one brand, "Amvaz"; double-click on it.

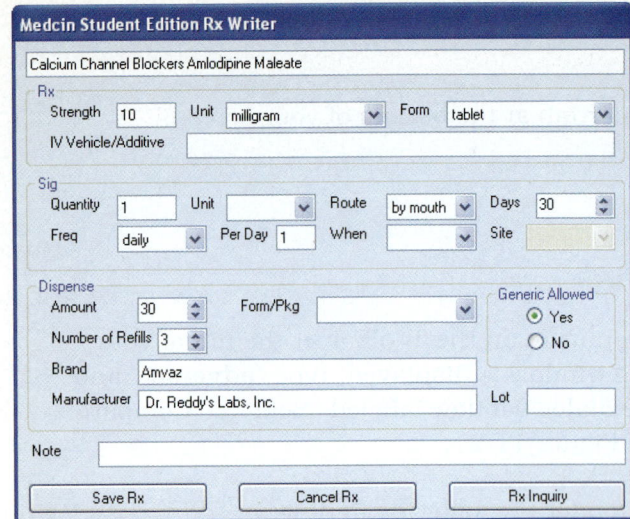

▶ Figure 11-24 Rx Writer prescription for Amlodipine.

Step 11

The Rx Writer will display the selected dosage and manufacturer. Complete the prescription by entering the remaining information in the following fields:

Quantity: **1**

Freq: **daily**

Per Day: **1**

Route: **by mouth**

Days: **30**

Amount: **30**

Refills: **3**

Generic: **Y**

Compare your screen to Figure 11-24. When everything is correct, locate and click the button labeled "Save Rx."

 **Alert** — Do not close or exit the Encounter until you have a printed copy in your hand. You will lose your work if you exit before printing.

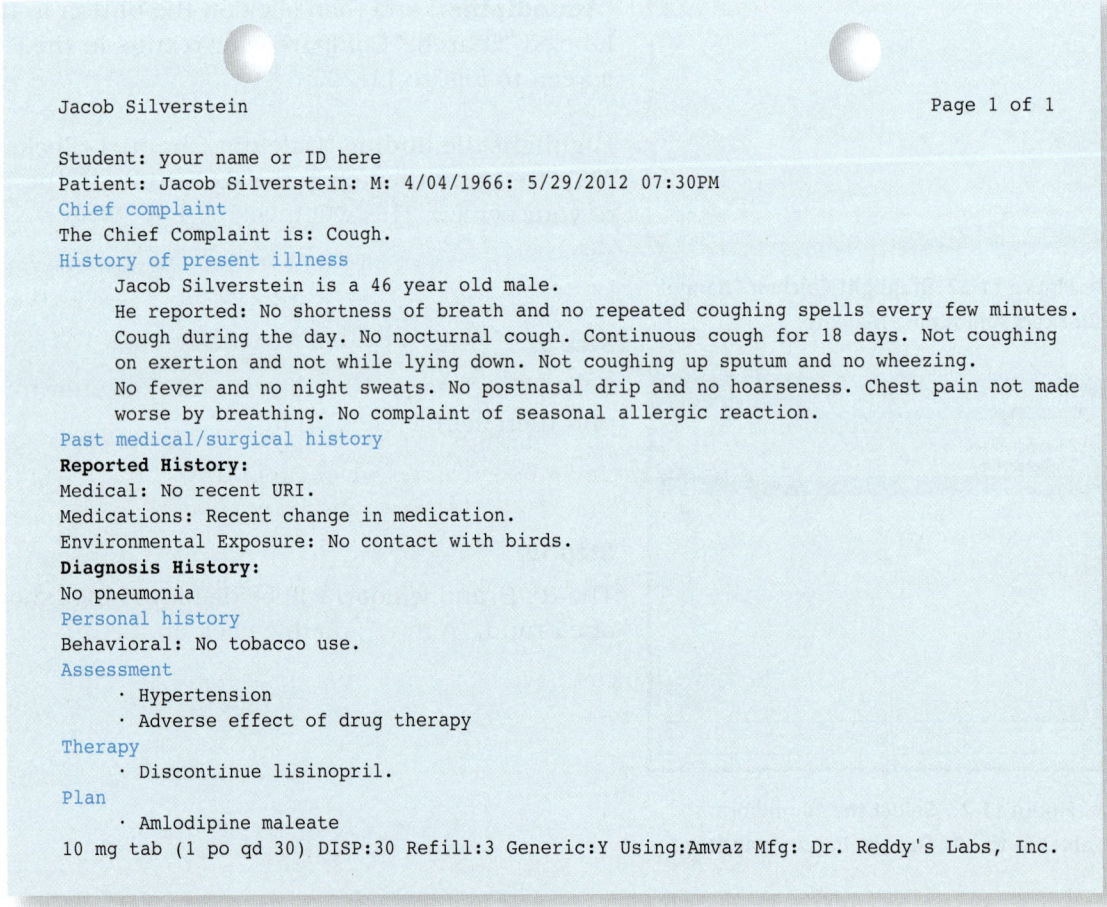

▶ Figure 11-25 Printout of E-visit encounter for Jacob Silverstein.

Step 12

Click on the Print button on the Toolbar at the top of your screen to invoke the Print Data window.

Be certain there is a check mark in the box next to "Current Encounter" and then click on the appropriate button to either print or export a file, as directed by your instructor.

Compare your printout or file output to Figure 11-25. If it is correct, hand it in to your instructor. If there are any differences, review the previous steps in the exercise and find your error.

Patient Access to Electronic Health Records

Although HIPAA guaranteed a patient's right to obtain copies of their health record, the HITECH Act went further. As we discussed in Chapter 1, CMS "meaningful use" criteria for EHR incentives included:

- Providing patients with timely electronic access to their health information (including lab results, problem list, medication lists, allergies, and so on) within 96 hours of the information being available to the provider.

- Providing patients with an electronic copy of their health information upon request.

- Providing inpatients with an electronic copy of their discharge instructions and procedures at time of discharge, upon request.

- Sending reminders to patients per patient preference for preventive/follow-up care.

The Agency for Healthcare Research and Quality (AHRQ) created the Hospital Consumer Assessment Healthcare Providers and Systems (HCAHPS) as a standardized survey instrument and data collection methodology for measuring patients' perspectives on care. In 2008 AHRQ reported that patients in the HCAHPS survey indicated that they preferred to go online to access records, results, and scheduling.[16]

The number of medical offices with interactive web sites is growing. Practice web sites provide a secure means of communication, as demonstrated in the earlier exercises. In addition, practice web sites allow the patient to request an appointment time or a prescription renewal, and provide secure access to results of recent lab tests and other information in the patient record.

Among primary care clinicians, much of this change is being fueled by the implementation of the Patient-Centered Medical Home.

The Patient-Centered Medical Home

"The Patient-Centered Medical Home (PCMH) is an approach to providing comprehensive primary care for children, youth and adults. The PCMH is

---

[16]Richard Grehalva, *eHealth Patterns in the 21st Century* (Birmingham, AL: MEDSEEK, 2010).

a healthcare setting that facilitates partnerships between individual patients, and their personal physicians, and when appropriate, the patient's family."[17]

Practices qualify for PCMH status by meeting the Physicians Practice Connections Patient-Centered Medical Home criteria, developed and owned by the National Committee for Quality Assurance (NCQA). There are three levels of recognition, with the higher levels achieved by increased use of electronic communication and web portals. The nine PCMH standards[18] are:

1. Access and Communication—processes for scheduling appointments, communicating with patients, and data showing that the practice meets this standard.

2. Patient Tracking and Registry Functions—organizes patient-population data using an electronic system that includes searchable patient clinical information used to manage patient care. The practice applies electronic or paper-based charting tools to organize and document clinical information consistently using standard data fields and uses the system to identify the following:
   - Most frequently seen diagnoses
   - Most important risk factors
   - Three clinically important conditions

   The practice uses electronic information to generate patient lists and remind patients or clinicians about necessary services, such as specific medications or tests, preventive services, pre-visit planning and follow-up visits.

3. Care Management—implement evidence-based guidelines for the three identified clinically important conditions, use guideline-based reminders to prompt physicians about a patient's preventive care needs at the time of the patient's visit. Maintain a team approach to managing patient care, use various components of care management for patients with one or more of the clinically important conditions and coordinate care with external organizations and other physicians.

4. Patient Self-Management Support—establish a system to identify patients with unique communication needs and facilitate self-management of care for patients with one of the three clinically important conditions.

5. Electronic Prescribing—eliminate handwritten prescriptions, use drug safety alerts when prescribing, and improve efficiency by using cost (drug formulary) information when prescribing.

6. Test Tracking—order and view lab test and imaging results electronically, with electronic alerts; manage the timely receipt of information on all tests and results.

7. Referral Tracking—coordination of care and following through critical consultations with other practitioners.

---

[17]American Academy of Pediatrics, American Academy of Family Physicians, American College of Physicians, and American Osteopathic Association, *Joint Principles of the Patient Centered Medical Home*, February 21, 2007: www.pcpcc.net/content/joint-principles-patient-centered-medical-home.

[18]Adapted from *PPC-PCMH Companion Guide* (Washington, DC: National Committee for Quality Assurance, 2010, www.ncqa.org/ppcpcmh.aspx).

8. Performance Reporting and Improvement—measures or receives performance data by physician or across the practice and reports on:
   - Clinical process
   - Clinical outcomes
   - Service data
   - Patient safety

   Collects data on patient experience with, and reports on:
   - Access to care
   - Quality of physician communication
   - Patient/family confidence in self-care
   - Patient/family satisfaction with care

   Uses performance data to set goals based on measurement results and, where necessary, act to improve performance. Produces reports using nationally approved clinical measures and electronically transmits them to external entities.

9. Advanced Electronic Communication—maximizes electronic communication with patients via the web to support patient access and self-management. Sends patients e-mail about specific needs and clinical alerts. Uses electronic communication among the care management team for patients with one of the three identified clinically important conditions.

The Personal Health Record

As we discussed in Chapter 1, even with growing adoption of EHR in many medical facilities, connectivity between the EHR systems of those entities is often lacking. Although the ONC strategies may eventually address this, there is one entity central to the record who can bring records from multiple sources together—that is the patient. The patient is also the person most likely to recognize discrepancies or differences in records from different providers.

Online services independent of any one medical group have sprung up to offer patients the ability to maintain their own medical records online. This is called a Personal Health Record (PHR). The ONC strategies discussed in Chapter 1 encourage the use of PHR.

A PHR is an online service that allows patients to log on to a secure web site, and to create and update their records. Patients control who has rights to access the information and can add or remove permission for clinicians they might visit to view the online record.

The clinicians, of course, retain their own records, but the doctor's EHR typically contains only the information gathered at that office. The record maintained online by a patient can contain data from patient visits at multiple practices. Another advantage of the online PHR is that it is available everywhere. Whether a patient is traveling and needs medical care, or is just being treated at a different medical practice, patients can retrieve their own records using the Internet and share them with the provider.

Early attempts to develop secure PHR solutions sometimes included stand-alone computer programs or flash drives that contained copies of the patient's records. The problem with these solutions is that if patients needs urgent care and do not have their computer or flash drive with them, then they do not have access to their PHR. The trend for most PHR systems today is to provide the PHR as an Internet service, making it almost universally available.

Kaiser-Permanente, one of the largest healthcare providers in the United States, has implemented what is perhaps the largest PHR to date. Their comprehensive web site securely connects more than 8.6 million members to a personal health record that includes timely access to lab results, medication information, summaries of their health conditions, and other important health information. Using the web site, Kaiser-Permanente patients can securely communicate with their physicians, nurses, and pharmacists, perhaps avoiding the need to make a trip to the clinic in person. The web site also provides access to the up-to-date medical knowledge and patient education information.

As Kaiser-Permanente has shown, the PHR can be more than just a repository of patient records. Sophisticated PHR services can present the patient with preventive health alerts, reminders to renew prescriptions, and links to evidence-based articles related to PHR data that can help the patient better manage their own health.

There are numerous organizations developing and sponsoring web-based PHR. While there may be differences between their offerings, there are some fundamental basics patients should look for in every PHR.

- Data is secure and private
- Data is managed by the patient
- Patient controls who can have access
- Universally accessible via the Internet
- PHR contains information for one's lifetime
- Patient can see who entered each data record and when
- (And ideally) the PHR should be able to exchange data with provider systems

Critical Thinking Exercise 68: Researching the PHR

You will need access to the Internet to complete this exercise.

Step 1

Start your web browser.

Listed below are six PHR web sites. Additionally, your local hospital, health insurance plan, or certain government programs may also offer PHR that you may use for this exercise. Select at least two sites to use for your will research.

www.google.com/health   www.myphr.com

www.healthvault.com   www.mymediconnect.net

www.ihealthrecord.org   www.webmd.com/phr

Step 2

Type the URL of your first choice in the address field of your web browser.

When the web site is displayed, read the information provided about that organization's PHR. Many of the sites offer a demonstration version, if one is available click on it.

Take notes or print pages of the web site. You will use these in step 4.

Step 3

Type the second URL you have chosen in the address field of your web browser. Study the information presented on the second site, taking notes or printing pages as you did in step 2.

Step 4

Write a comparative analysis of the web sites you have visited. Include the following information in your report:

What entity owns or operates the PHR web site?

Is the owner a nonprofit or for-profit corporation?

Compare the features offered by the two PHR.

Were there any significant advantages of one over the other?

Compare the two PHR for ease of use.

When you have finished, give your completed report to your instructor.

Chapter Eleven Summary

The Internet is one of the key technologies impacting healthcare. It not only facilitates remote access for the clinician, but gives the provider instant access to medical research and medical libraries for decision support.

Patients research their conditions using the Internet and bring the information with them to their office visits. Patients are also sending e-mail to their doctors asking medical questions about their conditions. However, the Internet is really a large network of networked computers, which is sometimes referred to as a "cloud." EPHI, which is sent over the Internet, needs to be secured.

Remote provider access to the EHR via the Internet usually involves setting up a VPN or using SSL encryption. Telemedicine provides specialist consultation to patients in remote locations. Similarly, teleradiology allows a radiologist to interpret diagnostic images from another location.

Providers are setting up secure web sites, where patients can see their medical information and consult with their doctor using secure messaging. One feature of these web sites is the ability for patients to use the Internet to enter information about their history and symptoms before arriving at a scheduled appointment.

Numerous studies have shown that patient data can become a significant contributor to the EHR, for some of the following reasons:

- Only the patient has the information about what symptoms were present at the outset of the illness.

- Only the patient knows the outcome of medical treatment of those symptoms.

- The patient is also the source of past medical, family, and social history.

- Patient-entered data is a more accurate reflection of a patient's complaints.

- Patients who can review their histories are better prepared for the visit.

- Up to 67% of the nurse or clinician's time with the patient is spent entering the patient's symptom into the visit documentation.

- A computer can be used by the patient over the Internet or in the waiting room to enter the same symptom and history information that the nurse or clinician would have entered.

- Patient-entered data is organized by the computer for the provider in a succinct and easy-to-read format that becomes the starting point for the encounter.

- Having a complete history in advance of the visit allows the clinician to ask fewer questions about the diagnosis and concentrate more on the effects of the illness on the patient. It also allows the clinician more time to discuss the treatment plan with the patient.

Other features found on practice web sites allow patients to request an appointment time or a prescription renewal, provide secure access to information from their medical record and securely communicate with their doctor. However, even using secure messaging, merging the e-mail threads into patients' EHR or filing an insurance claim for e-mail consults would be a challenge. A preferred alternative is the E-visit, which allows patients to be treated by their regular physician for nonurgent health problems without having to come into the office.

The E-visit gathers symptom and HPI information and creates a documented encounter. It can be integrated into the EHR to become part of patients' chart, and, equally important to the clinician, E-visits are reimbursed as a legitimate E&M visit in some states.

A Patient-Centered Medical Home is a model for providing primary care. PCMH standards encourage electronic orders, results, and communication with patients.

PHR, or Personal Health Records, enable patients to better manage their health by maintaining their own electronic copies of their health records. The PHR is secure, private, owned, and managed by the patient; patients control who can access their records. The most popular type of PHR is universally accessible by the Internet and many are able to exchange data with a provider's EHR system.

Testing Your Knowledge of Chapter 11

1. Name the two methods of securing information sent over the Internet described in this chapter.
2. List three examples of changes in healthcare related to the Internet.
3. What percentage of a clinician's time is spent entering patient symptoms and history into the chart?
4. What is an E-visit?
5. Name three criteria required to qualify for Patient-Centered Medical Home status.
6. Where was the largest study of using the internet for E-visits conducted?
7. Describe the differences between provider-to-patient e-mail and E-visits.
8. What were the two types of telemedicine described in this chapter?
9. What does HIPAA require when sending EPHI by e-mail?
10. Name two of the CMS criteria for EHR incentives related to patients' access of their health records.
11. What is a PHR?
12. Who controls access to the PHR?
13. Give three examples of decision support information available via the web.
14. Does the Internet function more like the telephone or the post office? Explain your answer.
15. You should have produced two Internet research documents, one printed encounter note, one printed interview report, and a report comparing PHR. If you have not already done so, give these to your instructor.

Chapter Twelve

12 EHR Coding and Reimbursement

Learning Outcomes

After completing this chapter, you should be able to:

- Explain why billing codes are important in an EHR system
- Show how Evaluation and Management (E&M) codes are determined
- Name and describe key components of E&M codes
- Read and understand the tables used in CMS guidelines
- Explain how the level of key components determines the level of the E&M code
- Use E&M calculator software
- Correctly use and document the time factor to change the level of an E&M code

The EHR and Reimbursement

There is no question that healthcare providers must be paid for their services and that the vast majority of those payments are from insurance plans, which require the use of standard codes. Some clinical workers ignore or resist a discussion of the relationship of the EHR to reimbursement, considering it the responsibility of the billing department. Unfortunately, that is not the case.

Whether the clinician is a doctor, nurse, or medical assistant, how and what that person documents in the patient chart has everything to do with what the medical facility is going to be paid for treating the patient.

Insurance plan audits follow this dictum: *If it isn't documented, it wasn't done.* This means no matter how long the medical assistant and patient discussed the patient's history and symptoms; no matter how thoroughly the nurse assessed the patient; no matter how brilliant the doctor's diagnosis; if those findings are not documented with sufficient detail in the chart, the auditor will assume that those portions of the encounter were never performed.

Knowing there is a direct relationship between the completeness of your clinical documentation and the financial well-being of your medical facility can help you understand the necessity of this chapter. If your interest is primarily clinical and not administrative, have no fear of this chapter. It is not intended to train you as a medical coder or billing specialist. A complete medical coding course could not be taught in one chapter anyway. The purpose of this chapter is to help you understand the guidelines used for calculating reimbursement by analyzing a patient encounter recorded in an EHR.

EHR Helps Meet Government Mandates

The U.S. government, Medicare, and insurance regulations financially affect all healthcare facilities. Adoption of an EHR system can not only improve patient care, as described in earlier chapters, but can also ensure reimbursement for services provided. In this chapter we are going to discuss three factors affected by an EHR:

1. Incentives and penalties
2. Proper coding of diagnoses
3. Factors of Evaluation and Management

Incentives and Penalties

In Chapter 1 we discussed the Health Information Technology for Economic and Clinical Health (HITECH) Act.[1] The government firmly believes in the benefits of using electronic health records. It is encouraging the widespread adoption of EHR by authorizing Medicare to make incentive payments to doctors and hospitals that use a certified EHR. This means that a practice adopting an EHR actually gets paid more than a practice continuing to use paper charts. Providers that implement and have a meaningful use of a certified EHR before 2015 are eligible for incentives. Here are some of the meaningful use requirements:

- Uses a certified EHR
- Submits most prescriptions electronically
- Reports clinical quality measures
- Has an EHR that interconnects electronically for healthcare delivery
- Reports billing codes indicating that patient encounters were recorded using an EHR.

After 2015, Medicare will begin to administer financial penalties for physicians and hospitals that do not use an EHR. These will involve reducing the provider's payments by 1 percent per year for up to five years. By 2020, a provider still using paper charts will have payments reduced by 5 percent.

---

[1]H.R. 1 American Recovery and Reinvestment Act of 2009, Title XIII Health Information Technology for Economic and Clinical Health, February 17, 2009.

HIPAA-Required Code Sets

HIPAA[2] law regulates many things, including the privacy and security of health records. It also standardized healthcare transactions and required the use of the ICD-9-CM, CPT-4, and HCPCS code sets.

Diagnoses Codes Justify Billing

Chapter 7 introduced ICD-9-CM codes and discussed their use for mortality and morbidity studies. The ICD-9-CM codes are also used daily by clinicians and the billing department because they are required for insurance claims.

Reimbursement for most inpatient hospitals is based entirely on the Diagnostic Related Group (DRG) determined from the primary and secondary diagnoses assigned by the attending physician.

For both inpatient and outpatient facilities, the use of the correct ICD-9-CM code on a claim serves to explain or justify the medical reason for the services being billed. Outpatient billing requires one or more ICD-9-CM codes be assigned to every procedure. Furthermore, the diagnosis must correspond to the procedure. For example, you cannot bill for an eye exam using the diagnosis for a broken toe.

ICD-9-CM codes are from three to five digits long. The first three digits, called the "rubric," are followed by a decimal point and up to two numerals, which serve to further specify or refine the description of the condition. Insurance billing rules require clinicians to code to the most specific level.

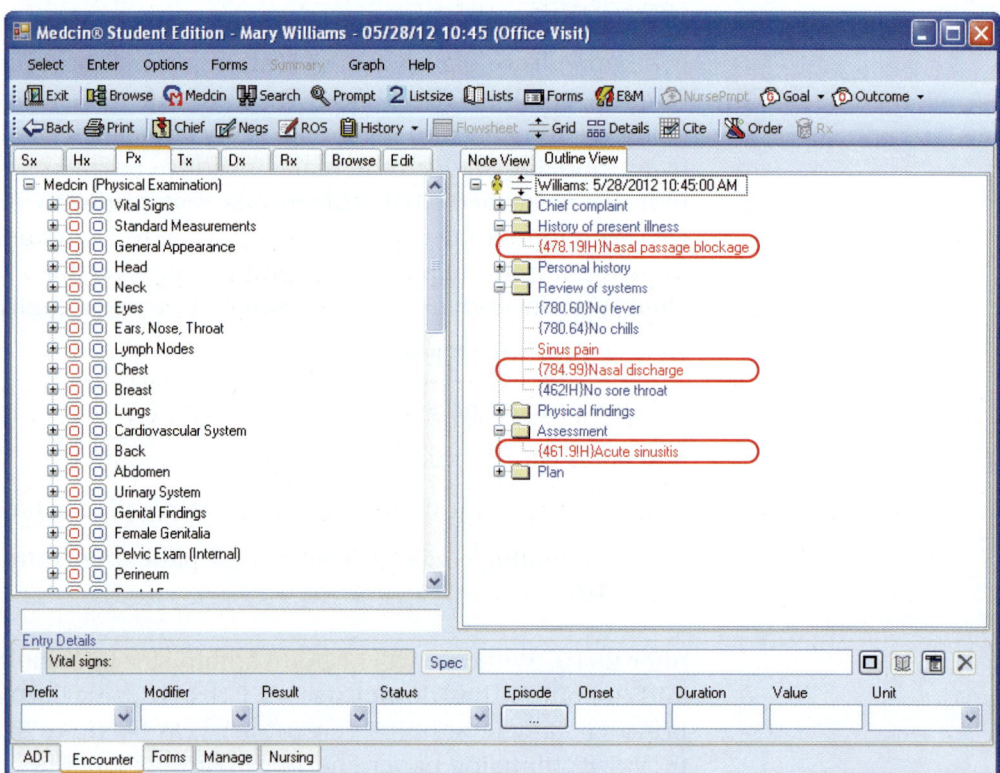

▶ Figure 12-1 ICD-9-CM codes displayed in Outline View tab.

---

[2]Health Insurance Portability and Accountability Act, Administrative Simplification Subsection, Title 2, subsection f.

466 Chapter 12 | EHR Coding and Reimbursement

Offices without an EHR print a list of diagnosis codes on the paper encounter form. The clinician indicates the diagnosis by checking or circling a code on the form. However, the preprinted codes on the form may not be as specific as the clinician's assessment. The clinician must also be careful to use the same terminology in the dictation as the ICD-9-CM description, or the billing for the visit may not match the transcribed encounter note.

Most EHR systems contain a "cross-walk" or internal reference table that can produce ICD-9-CM codes at the fourth or fifth digit specificity automatically. An example of this is shown in Figure 12-1. You can see this later in any exercise that has an assessment finding. To do so, click on the tab on the right pane labeled "Outline View." To return to the Note View, click on the tab on the right pane labeled "Note View."

The advantage of using an EHR with a codified nomenclature is that the codes billed will always be in sync with the note that is produced. Another advantage is that the EHR allows the clinician to record nuances that are beyond the scope of ICD-9-CM such as "mild" or "improving." The EHR software will automatically translate the assessment to the correct diagnosis code, which then may be used for billing.

CPT-4 and HCPCS Codes

In addition to standard codes for diagnoses, HIPAA requires the use of CPT-4 and HCPCS codes for procedures. CPT stands for Current Procedural Terminology, fourth edition. It was developed and is maintained by the American Medical Association (AMA). HCPCS stands for Healthcare Common Procedure Coding System. It was developed by the CMS to code for supplies, injectable medications, and blood products. CPT-4 is incorporated into the HCPCS standard even though it is separately maintained by the AMA.

Evaluation and Management (E&M) Codes

Although some CPT-4 codes represent a specific medical procedure, the most frequently used portion of the CPT-4 code set is the Evaluation and Management (E&M) codes. These CPT-4 codes are used to bill for nearly every kind of patient encounter, including medical office visits, inpatient hospital exams, nursing home visits, consults, emergency room (ER) doctors, and scores of other services. E&M codes are used by virtually all specialties.

At one time E&M billing was based on the provider's judgment of how complex the visit was. However, Medicare has developed strict guidelines for determining how the level of exam justified the level of E&M code. The time spent with the patient is no longer the controlling factor.

The E&M guidelines were published in 1995. Specialists, however, found fault with the 1995 guidelines. For example, an ophthalmologist performs an in-depth exam of the eyes but does not typically perform a complete head-to-toe review of systems. Under the 1995 guidelines, the ophthalmologist would never meet the criteria for higher level codes. In response, the guidelines were revamped in 1997. Today physicians are allowed to use either the 1995 or 1997 guideline, whichever best suits their practice. This chapter uses the 1997 guideline, because it is the most recent.

E&M guidelines determine the CPT-4 E&M code based almost exclusively on the findings documented in the encounter note. Gone are the days when a clinician might perform a very adequate physical but scribble only a few lines in the chart.

Four Levels of E&M Codes

There are four levels of E&M codes for each type of visit. The levels represent the least complicated exam (level 1) to the most complex exam (level 4). The level is important because a provider's "allowed payment" amount is proportionate to the level of the exam (with level 1 paying the least and level 4 paying the most).

Where the service is rendered is an important consideration as well. There are separate categories of E&M codes for different locations such as office visits, inpatient exams, ER exams, and so on. Each category of E&M codes has at least four codes representing the four levels of service. Some categories have more than four E&M codes because there are subcategories—for example, new patient versus established patient. The exercises in this chapter use the E&M codes for office visits.

How the Level of an E&M Code Is Determined

Seven components are evaluated to determine the level of E&M services:

◆ History

◆ Examination

◆ Medical decision making

◆ Counseling

◆ Coordination of care

◆ Nature of presenting problem

◆ Time

Three components—history, examination, and medical decision making—are the key components in determining the level of E&M services. The level of each key component is determined separately. The level of E&M code is derived from the highest level of two or three key components. There is one exception. For services such as psychiatry, which consist predominantly of counseling or coordination of care, time is the key or controlling factor determining the level of E&M service.

This chapter explains each of the components, the levels within the key components, and how they are combined to calculate the E&M code. A later exercise will also show how time can become an overriding factor, justifying a higher level code for visits that require more time for counseling the patient.

Undercoding

In an office using paper charts, clinicians often select the E&M code by circling a code on a paper encounter form. These clinicians are at risk. If they select a code that is at a higher level than the dictated note supports, they can be fined.

To avoid risk, many practices *undercode* (choosing a code one level below what they believe to be correct), taking the attitude "better safe than sorry." This is bad for the practice financially; they are losing payment for their work. When clinicians undercode by one level, it is the same as seeing 80 patients and getting paid for seeing 60.

Accurate Coding

The clinician using an EHR does not worry about the mandate "If it isn't documented, it wasn't done" because it is always documented. EHR systems that use standardized nomenclatures have a codified record of the encounter. This enables the software to use data in the encounter note to calculate the correct E&M code for billing.

EHR systems analyze the amount and type of data and accurately determine the correct E&M code at the correct level. Many EHR systems can show the provider how the calculation was determined, thus giving the provider confidence that the code can be substantiated. In addition to E&M codes, the EHR can suggest CPT-4 codes for other procedures performed during the encounter.

When the EHR is an integrated component of practice management software, or when it is interfaced to a practice management system, the ICD-9-CM, CPT-4, and HCPCS codes can transfer directly to the billing or charge posting module. Most practice management systems do not post the charges automatically, but transfer them as "pending" charges. The charges are reviewed by a billing or coding specialist before being "posted" to the patient's account or billed to insurance.

Using EHR Software to Understand E&M Codes

In the next few exercises, we are going to focus on understanding E&M codes. The Student Edition software contains an E&M code calculator. You are going to use that tool while learning how E&M codes are derived.

Guided Exercise 69: Calculating the E&M Code from an Encounter

In this exercise, you are going to learn how to use the E&M calculator by using a previously stored encounter that is already in your system. Using a previous encounter will allow you to focus on understanding the E&M codes themselves without worrying about creating the note.

Case Study

Mary Williams is a 26-year-old female who was seen for stuffy sinus. The healthcare provider who entered the encounter data has not yet recorded the history of present illness or vital signs.

Step 1

If you have not already done so, start the Student Edition software.

Click Select on the Menu bar, and then click Patient.

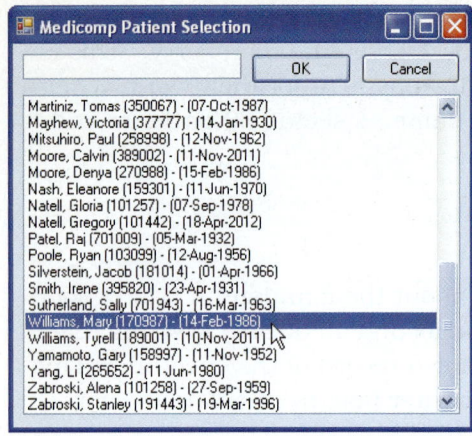

▶ Figure 12-2 Select patient Mary Williams.

In the Patient Selection window, locate and click on **Mary Williams** (as shown in Figure 12-2).

Step 2

Click Select on the Menu bar, and then click **Existing Encounter**.

A small window of previous encounters will be displayed. Compare your screen to the window showing in the center of Figure 12-3.

Select **5/28/2012 10:45 AM Office Visit**.

The encounter note from that date will be displayed.

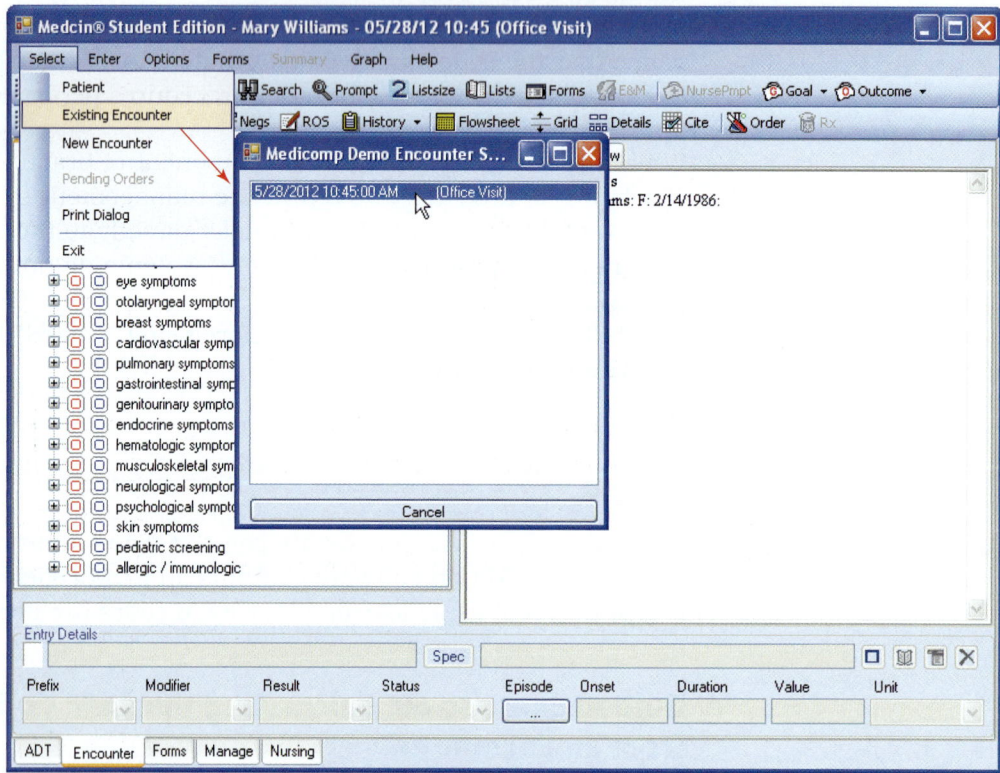

▶ Figure 12-3 Select existing encounter for May 28, 2012.

Step 3

Compare your screen to Figure 12-4. The exam was created using the Adult URI List and therefore should look familiar to you.

Because we are going to be using the information from the encounter note to calculate the E&M code, take a few minutes to look at the encounter note in the right pane of your screen.

Pay attention to the History section. It contains a Review of Systems, but no HPI or social history; this will be discussed later in this exercise.

▶ Figure 12-4 Patient encounter note for May 28, 2012, displayed in right pane.

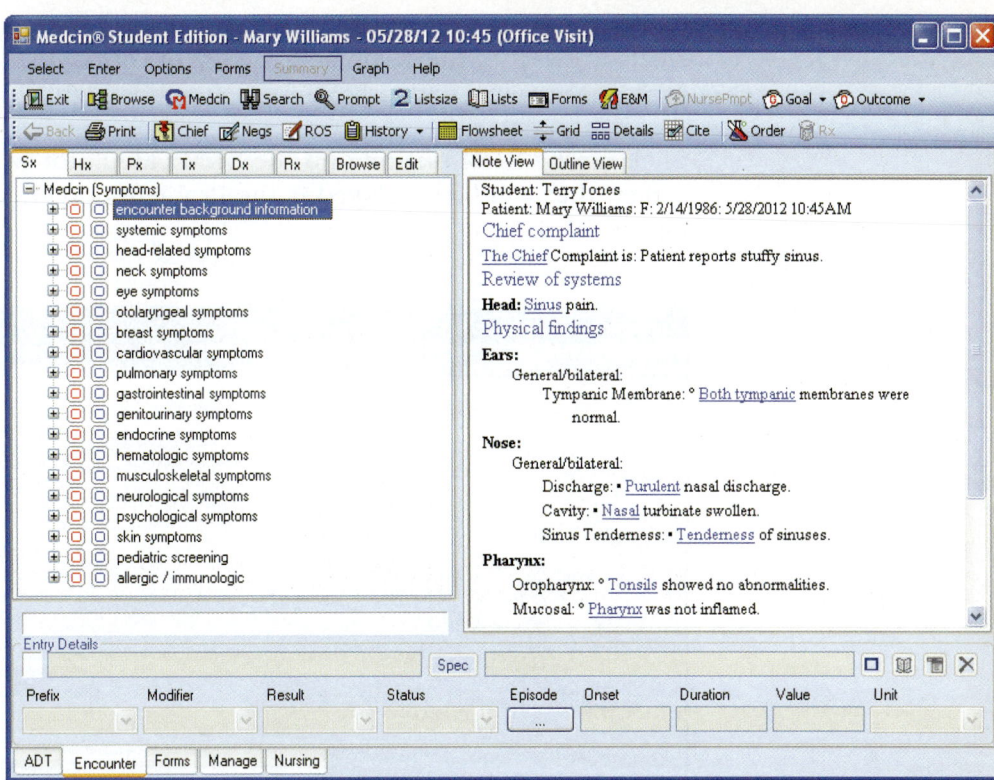

Not all of the note will fit in the pane, so you will need to use the scroll bar on the right to scroll downward to see the rest of the note, as shown in Figure 12-5.

Step 4

Compare the number of body systems in the Physical Findings section of the note with the number of body systems in the Review of Systems section.

▶ Figure 12-5 Scrolled portion of patient encounter note with E&M button highlighted.

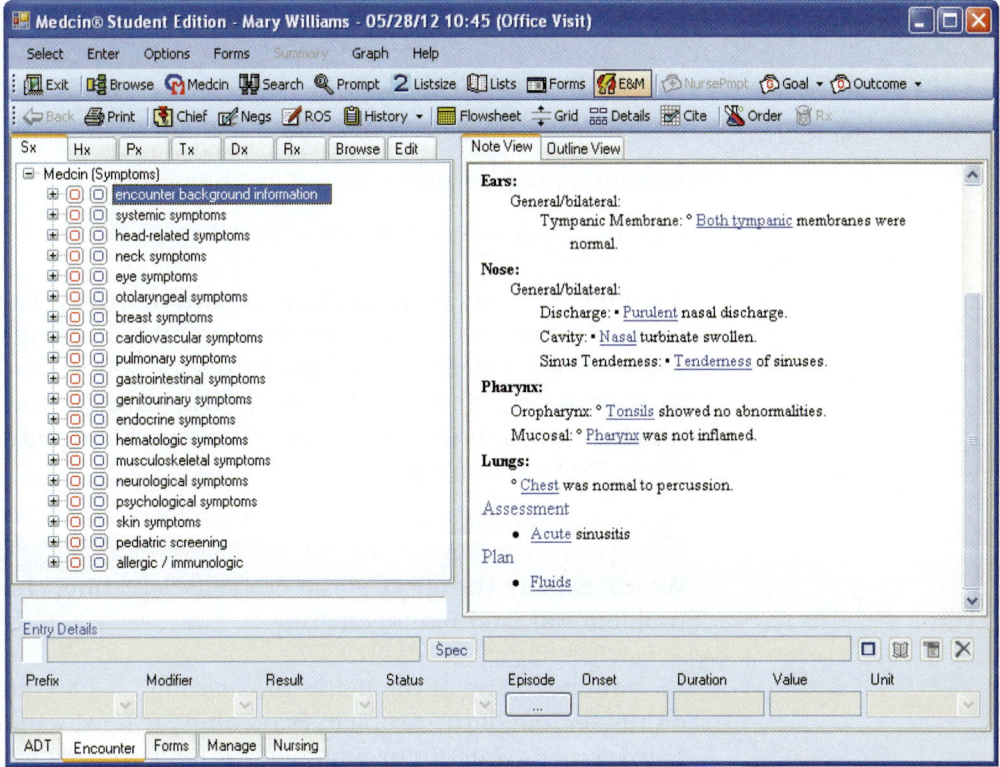

Chapter 12 | EHR Coding and Reimbursement 471

When you are sufficiently familiar with the encounter note, locate the button labeled "E&M" in the Toolbar at the top of your screen. The icon resembles a horseshoe magnet with a lightning bolt and is highlighted orange in Figure 12-5.

Click on the E&M button and the E&M calculator will be invoked. The first screen that will be displayed is the Problem Screening checklist shown in Figure 12-6.

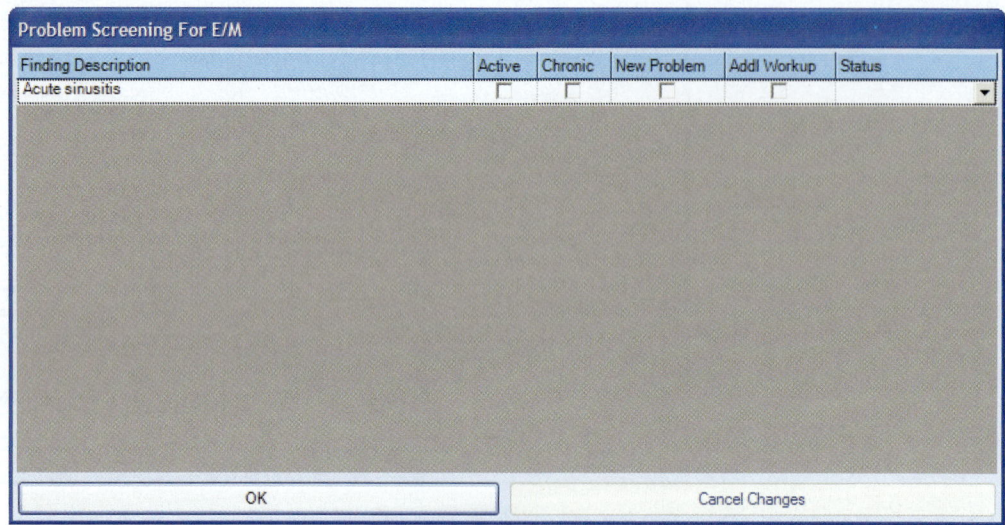

▶ Figure 12-6 Problem Screening checklist window.

Problem Screening Checklist Window

Certain E&M calculations are affected by factors of the problem assessment that may not be explicitly documented in the encounter note such as:

◆ Is the problem active or inactive?

◆ Is the problem chronic or not?

◆ Is the problem new to the examiner?

◆ Is additional workup planned for the problem?

◆ Is the problem stable or worsening?

The Problem Screening checklist (shown in Figure 12-6) displays assessments in the current encounter. Providers can add information for the E&M calculator about each problem by checking boxes for active, chronic, new, or additional workup. A drop-down list lets the provider inform the E&M calculator of the problem status, but this does not alter a problem status that has been recorded in the Entry Detail Status field.

Step 5

We will explore the effect of the Problem Screening checklist later as we discuss problem risk and management.

Do not check any of the boxes at this time. Locate and click on the OK button on the bottom of the Problem Screening for E/M window. The Evaluation and Management Calculator window will be displayed (as shown in Figure 12-7).

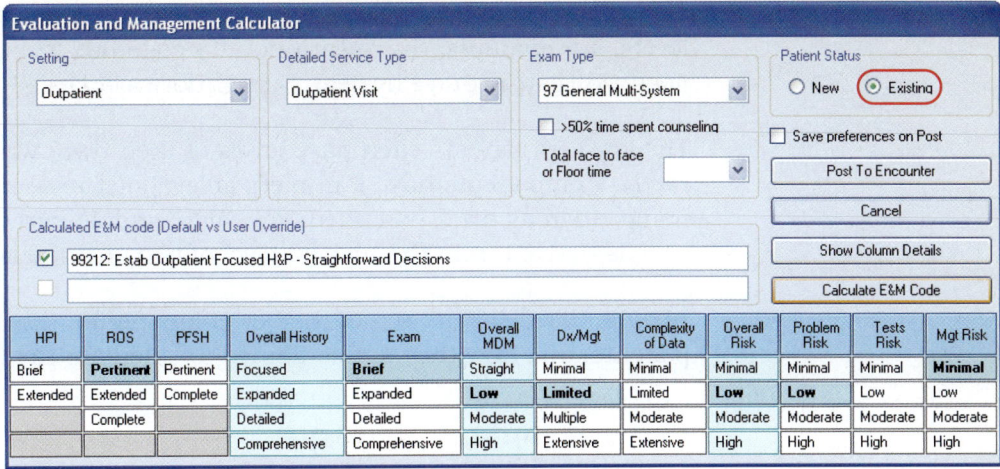

▶ Figure 12-7 E&M calculator for May 28, 2012, encounter.

Step 6

The fields in this screen will be explained in detail in Guided Exercise 70; for the moment, just calculate the E&M code. If the field labeled "Calculated E&M Code" displays "99212 Estab Outpatient Focused H&P—Straightforward Decisions," you are ready to proceed.

If it is blank or contains a different code, locate the area labeled "Patient Status" in the upper right corner. If the white circle next to "Existing" is empty, click it once with your mouse. It should then appear filled in the center as shown in Figure 12-7 (circled in red).

Locate the large button labeled "Calculate E&M Code" and click it.

Compare your screen to the Evaluation and Management Calculator window shown in Figure 12-7.

Step 7

You are going to use the E&M calculator window to help you understand the CMS Documentation Guidelines for Evaluation and Management Services.

Look at the bottom of the calculator window where there is a grid. The columns are labeled with terms you may recognize, such as HPI and ROS. There are four rows representing the four levels discussed earlier. Each of the columns lists the levels relevant to that particular type of finding. This will be further explained later in this chapter.

Leave your E&M calculator displayed as you read the following section. Do not click any more buttons until instructed to do so. If you cannot complete the reading in the allotted time, simply repeat steps 1, 2, and 5 to invoke the E&M calculator window again when you are ready to resume.

Levels of Key Components

You will recall from an earlier discussion that history, examination, and medical decision making are the key components that determine the level of E&M services.

The CPT-4 E&M code description lists the three key components and their levels. For example, the description for code 99212 is "Established Patient, Focused History and Physical, Straightforward Decision Making."

The key components each have levels of their own, which are determined separately. Components have a numerical level of 1 to 4; in addition, they have a name, such as brief, extended, low, high, simple, or complex. The level of E&M code is derived from the highest level of two or three key components.

We will now discuss each of the key components, the levels within the key components, and how they are combined to calculate the E&M code.

Key Component: History

The History component includes the following elements:

- **CC**, which is an acronym for Chief Complaint. A Chief Complaint is required for all levels of History.
- **HPI**, which is an acronym for History of Present Illness.
- **ROS**, which is an acronym for Review of Systems.
- **PFSH**, which is an acronym for Past History, Family History, and Social History.

The extent of history of present illness, review of systems, and past, family, or social history that is obtained and documented is dependent on clinical judgment and the nature of the presenting problems.

▶ Figure 12-8 E&M calculator with Show Column Details button highlighted.

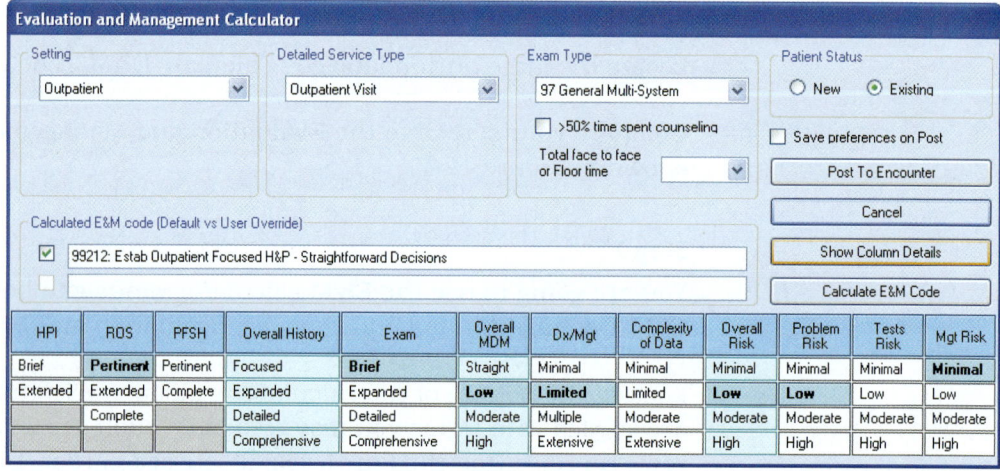

Step 8

Look at the grid section of the E&M calculator window shown in Figure 12-8. The History section consists of the four columns labeled HPI, ROS, PFSH, and Overall History.

Each of the history elements (HPI, ROS, PFSH) has levels that will determine the Overall History level. If the level in a column is shown in bold type, then the number of findings is sufficient to meet the guidelines for the level at which it appears. For example, look at the column labeled "ROS." The word "**Pertinent**" in the first row is bold, meaning ROS has enough findings for level 1 but not enough for level 2, "Extended."

474 Chapter 12 | EHR Coding and Reimbursement

We will now discuss the history elements and levels.

History of Present Illness (HPI) The HPI is a chronological description of the development of the patient's present illness from the first sign and/or symptom or from the previous encounter to the present. HPI includes the following characteristics:

- Location
- Quality
- Severity
- Duration
- Timing
- Context
- Modifying factors
- Associated signs and symptoms

HPI has two named levels, brief and extended. The levels are determined by the quantity of findings:

Brief (consists of one to three items in the HPI)

Extended (consists of at least four items in the HPI or the status of at least three chronic or inactive conditions)

In this encounter, there are no findings for HPI; therefore, none of the levels are in bold type.

Step 9

The E&M calculator will allow you to see which findings in the encounter note were used to determine the level. There are two ways to do this.

The first method is use the button labeled "Show Column Details" (highlighted in Figure 12-8).

Locate and click on the button labeled "Show Column Details." A drop-down list will appear.

Position your mouse over ROS details in the drop-down list, as shown in Figure 12-9, and click the mouse. A pane will open in the upper portion of the

▶ **Figure 12-9 Show Column Details drop-down list.**

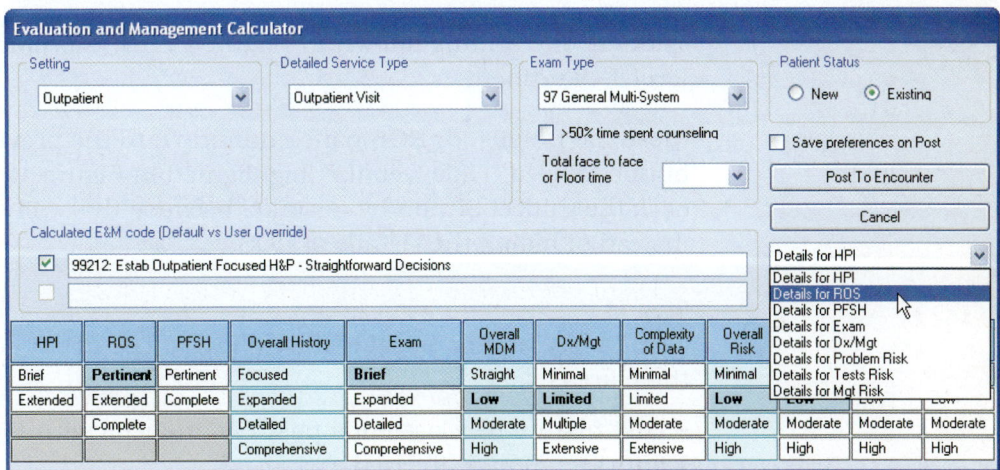

E&M calculator window to display the findings that were recorded in the encounter note for Review of Systems (ROS) (as shown in Figure 12-10).

▶ Figure 12-10 ROS details in E&M calculator with Hide Details button highlighted.

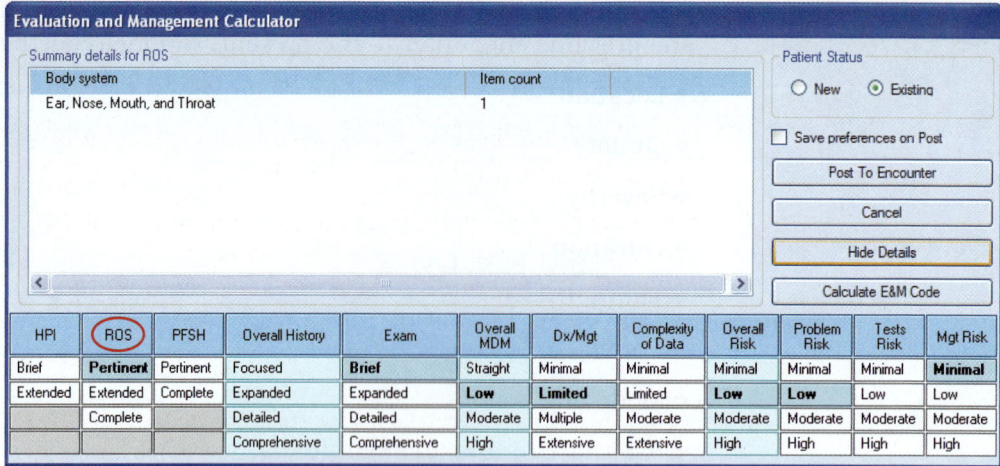

The second method of displaying column details is to click your mouse directly on the column label, for example, "ROS" (circled in red in Figure 12-10).

Using either method will change the button label to "Hide Details." Clicking the Hide Details button will close the detail pane and return to the previous view.

Step 10

Review of Systems (ROS) The ROS level is determined by the number of systems reviewed. You are familiar with ROS from previous exercises. ROS has three levels:

Problem Pertinent (ROS inquires about the system directly related to the problems identified in the HPI)

Extended (ROS inquires about the system directly related to the problems identified in the HPI and a number of additional systems. Extended level requires two to nine systems be documented)

Complete (ROS inquires about the systems directly related to the problems identified in the HPI plus all additional body systems. At least ten organ systems must be reviewed to meet the requirement for Complete.)

Compare your screen to Figure 12-10.

There is one finding shown in Figure 12-10; therefore, the ROS is level 1—Pertinent.

Close the Details for ROS pane and return to the previous view, by clicking the button labeled "Hide Details" (highlighted in Figure 12-10). Be careful not to click the Cancel button by mistake, because that will close the E&M calculator instead of hiding the Details of ROS.

Step 11
Past, Family, and/or Social History (PFSH) The PFSH consists of a review of three areas:

♦ Past history (the patient's past experiences with illnesses, operations, injuries, and treatments)

♦ Family history (a review of medical events in the patient's family, including diseases that may be hereditary or place the patient at risk)

♦ Social history (an age-appropriate review of past and current activities)

PFSH level is determined by the number of findings in these three history types. PFSH has two levels:

Pertinent (at least one item in any of PFSH area directly related to the problems identified in the HPI)

Complete (a review of two or all three of the PFSH history areas, depending on the category of the E&M service. Complete requires all three history areas for services that include a comprehensive assessment of a new patient or reassessment of an existing patient. A review of two of the three history areas is sufficient for other services)

Look at the column under PFSH on your screen. In this encounter, no PFSH was recorded.

Step 12

The key component History has four levels:

1. Problem Focused
2. Expanded Problem Focused
3. Detailed
4. Comprehensive

Figure 12-11 shows the elements required for each level of history.[3] The Level of History (shown in the first column of the table) is determined by the levels of the

▶ **Figure 12-11** Table of Elements Required for Each Level of History.

Table of Elements Required for Each Level of History

	Level of History	CC	History of Present Illness (HPI)	Review of Systems (ROS)	Past, Family, and/or Social History (PFSH)
1	Problem Focused	*	Brief (1–3 elements)	(No elements required)	(No elements required)
2	Expanded Problem Focused	*	Brief (1–3 elements)	Problem Pertinent (related to HPI)	(No elements required)
3	Detailed	*	Extended (4 or more)	Extended (2–9 body systems)	Pertinent (1 or more)
4	Comprehensive	*	Extended (4 or more)	Complete (10 or more body systems)	Complete (2 areas Past, Family, or Social)

* Chief Complaint is expected for all Types of History.

---

[3]Figure adapted from *1997 Documentation Guidelines for Evaluation and Management Services* (Washington, DC:U.S. Department of Health and Human Services, 1997).

HPI, ROS, and PSFH elements. The first column in Figure 12-11 Level of History is comparable to the column in the E&M calculator grid labeled "Overall History."

Compare Figure 12-11 to the HPI, ROS, and PFSH columns on your screen. Looking at the chart in Figure 12-11, do you see why the overall history is not level 1? It is because only the ROS has been recorded, and HPI is required for level 1.

Key Component: Examination

The second key component is the Physical Examination. Examination guidelines have been defined for a general multi-system exam and the following 10 single-organ systems:

- Cardiovascular
- Ears, Nose, and Throat
- Eyes
- Genitourinary (Female or Male)
- Hematologic/Lymphatic/Immunologic
- Musculoskeletal
- Neurological
- Psychiatric
- Respiratory
- Skin

A general multi-system examination or a single-organ system examination may be performed by any physician, regardless of specialty. The type and content of examination are selected by the examining physician and are based on clinical judgment, the patient's history, and the nature of the presenting problems.

There are four levels of any type of examination:

Problem Focused—a limited examination of the affected body area or organ system.

Expanded Problem Focused—a limited examination of the affected body area or organ system and any other symptomatic or related body areas or organ systems.

Detailed—an extended examination of the affected body areas or organ systems and any other symptomatic or related body areas or organ systems.

Comprehensive—a general multi-system examination, or complete examination of a single-organ system and other symptomatic or related body areas or organ systems.

The required elements for different levels of single-organ system exams and the general multi-system exam vary; therefore, separate tables are published for each type of system. An abridged example of the Elements of General Multisystem Examination table[4] has been reprinted in Figure 12-12.

Within the guideline tables, individual elements of the examination pertaining to a body area or organ system are identified by bullets. A bullet is a typographic

---

[4]Ibid.

▶ **Figure 12-12** Table of Elements of General Multisystem Examination (abridged sample).

Elements of General Multisystem Examination	
System/Body Area	**Exam Elements**
Constitutional	• Measurement of any three of the following seven vital signs: (1) sitting or standing blood pressure, (2) supine blood pressure, (3) pulse rate and regularity, (4) respiration, (5) temperature, (6) height, (7) weight (may be measured and recorded by ancillary staff) • General appearance of patient (e.g., development, nutrition, body habitus, deformities, attention to grooming)
Eyes	• Inspection of conjunctivae and lids • Examination of pupils and irises (e.g., reaction to light and accommodation, size and symmetry) • Ophthalmoscopic examination of optic discs (e.g., size, C/D ratio, appearance) and posterior segments (e.g., vessel changes, exudates, hemorrhages)
Ears, Nose, Mouth, and Throat	• External inspection of ears and nose (e.g., overall appearance, scars, lesions, masses) • Otoscopic examination of external auditory canals and tympanic membranes • Assessment of hearing (e.g., whispered voice, finger rub, tuning fork) • Inspection of nasal mucosa, septum, and turbinates • Inspection of lips, teeth, and gums • Examination of oropharynx: oral mucosa, salivary glands, hard and soft palates, tongue, tonsils, and posterior pharynx
Neck	• Examination of neck (e.g., masses, overall appearance, symmetry, tracheal position, crepitus) • Examination of thyroid (e.g., enlargement, tenderness, mass)
Respiratory	• Assessment of respiratory effort (e.g., intercostal retractions, use of accessory muscles, diaphragmatic movement) • Percussion of chest (e.g., dullness, flatness, hyperresonance) • Palpation of chest (e.g., tactile fremitus) • Auscultation of lungs (e.g., breath sounds, adventitious sounds, rubs)
Cardiovascular	• Palpation of heart (e.g., location, size, thrills) • Auscultation of heart with notation of abnormal sounds and murmurs Examination of: • carotid arteries (e.g., pulse amplitude, bruits) • abdominal aorta (e.g., size, bruits) • femoral arteries (e.g., pulse amplitude, bruits) • pedal pulses (e.g., pulse amplitude) • extremities for edema and/or varicosities
Chest (Breasts)	• Inspection of breasts (e.g., symmetry, nipple discharge) • Palpation of breasts and axillae (e.g., masses or lumps, tenderness)
Gastrointestinal (Abdomen)	• Examination of abdomen with notation of presence of masses or tenderness • Examination of liver and spleen • Examination for presence or absence of hernia • Examination (when indicated) of anus, perineum and rectum, including sphincter tone, presence of hemorrhoids, rectal masses • Obtain stool sample for occult blood test when indicated

character that looks like this: • (a solid black circle). Locate the bullets in the second column of Figure 12-12.

If you have taken a class in medical coding or read the CPT-4 book, you may be familiar with the concept of "the number of bullets required to meet a level of E&M coding." This simply means how many findings in the encounter note correspond to elements in the guideline table with bullet characters printed next to them.

Step 13

The grid in the E&M calculator window has only one column for the Exam component. Locate and click on the column labeled "Exam" (as shown in Figure 12-13). A pane displaying the exam details will open in the E&M calculator window.

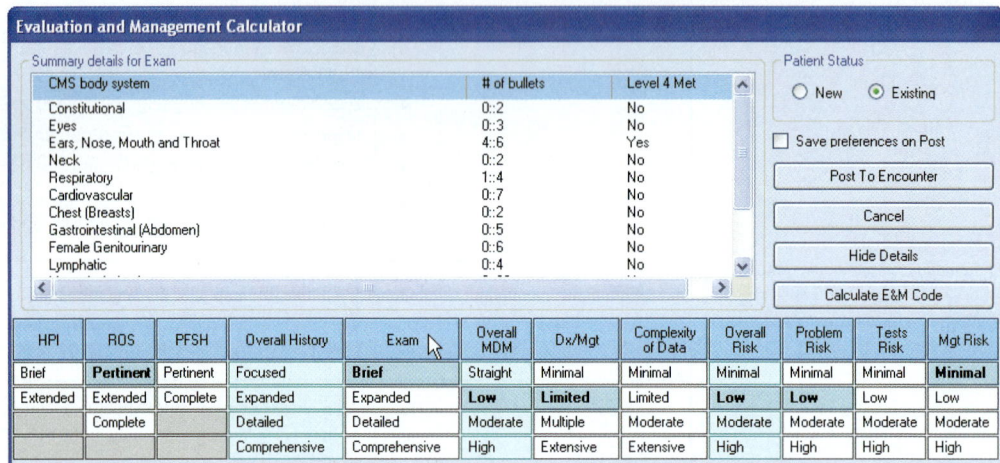

▶ Figure 12-13 Exam details of E&M calculator.

Look at the "Summary details for Exam" pane. It has three columns labeled "CMS body systems," "# of bullets," and "Level 4 Met."

Each row under the column labeled "# of bullets" has a pair of numbers. For example, locate the row for Ears, Nose, Mouth, and Throat; you will see the numbers 4:6. This means the clinician examined four of six elements in that system.

Step 14

Compare your screen with the table[5] in Figure 12-14. You will see your screen has five elements with bullets documented in the exam (four bullets in Ear, Nose, Mouth and Throat and 1 bullet in Respiratory). Therefore the examination is level 1, "Problem Focused Exam," because there are only five bullets.

The exam level is not determined by the number of findings but by the number of bullets satisfied within a system/body area.

Findings do not have to be abnormal; normal findings count as well. The guidelines state:

"A brief statement or notation indicating 'negative' or 'normal' is sufficient to document normal findings related to unaffected areas or asymptomatic organ

---

[5]Ibid.

▶ **Figure 12-14** Table of Elements Required for Each Level of Examination.

Table of Elements Required for Each Level of Examination

Level of Examination		General Multisystem Examinations	Single Organ System Examinations
		Examination Elements by Type of Exam	
1	Problem Focused (Brief)	1 to 5 elements identified by a bullet (•) in one or more organ systems or body areas.	1 to 5 elements identified by a bullet (•), whether in a box with a shaded or unshaded border.*
2	Expanded Problem Focused	At least 6 elements identified by a bullet (•) in one or more organ systems or body areas.	At least 6 elements identified by a bullet (•), whether in a box with a shaded or unshaded border.*
3	Detailed Examination	At least 6 organ systems or body areas; for each system/area selected at least 2 elements identified by a bullet (•). Alternatively, at least 12 elements identified by a bullet (•) in 2 or more organ systems or body areas.	At least 12 elements identified by a bullet (•), whether in a box with a shaded or unshaded border.* Exception: requirement reduced to 9 elements for Eye and psychiatric examinations.
4	Comprehensive Examination	At least 9 organ systems or body areas; for each system/area selected all elements identified by a bullet (•).	Every element in each box with a shaded border and at least 1 element in each box with an unshaded border; Plus all elements identified by a bullet (•) whether in a box with a shaded or unshaded border.*

* This refers to sections of the printed tables for Single Organ System Exams, which are outlined with a shaded border.

systems."[6] Think about the Auto Negatives feature you used in previous exercises in the context of this document guideline.

Key Component: Medical Decision Making

The third key component is Medical Decision Making (MDM). The remaining columns in the E&M calculator window grid are all concerned with medical decision making. Medical decision making refers to the complexity of establishing a diagnosis or selecting a management option as measured by these elements:

♦ **Number of possible diagnoses or management options** that must be considered. This element has four levels. The level is determined by the number and types of problems addressed during the encounter, the complexity of establishing a diagnosis, and the management decisions that are made by the clinician. The levels include:

    Level 1: Minimal

    Level 2: Limited

    Level 3: Multiple

    Level 4: Extensive

In addition to the actual number of diagnoses codes selected, the number and type of diagnostic tests employed may be an indicator of the number of

---

[6] *1997 Documentation Guidelines for Evaluation and Management Services* (Washington, DC: U.S. Department of Health and Human Services, 1997).

possible diagnoses. Problems that were reviewed also are counted. Consulting or seeking advice from others is another indicator of complexity of diagnostic or management problems.

- **Amount or complexity of medical records, diagnostic tests, or other information that must be obtained, reviewed, and analyzed.** There are four levels for this element as well, including:

    Level 1: Minimal or None

    Level 2: Limited

    Level 3: Moderate

    Level 4: Extensive

- **Risk of significant complications, morbidity or mortality, as well as comorbidities**, associated with the patient's presenting problems, the diagnostic procedures, or the possible management options. Risk also has four levels:

    Level 1: Minimal

    Level 2: Low

    Level 3: Moderate

    Level 4: High

As you can see, each of the elements of medical decision making has four levels. The overall level of the MDM component is derived from the highest level of two of the three elements. This is shown in the column labeled "Overall MDM" in the E&M calculator window. Let us look at how it was determined.

Step 15

Locate and click on the column labeled "Dx/Mgt (as shown in Figure 12-15). Dx/Mgt stands for Diagnosis and/or Management Options. The pane in the E&M calculator window will display the Details for Dx/Mgt pane.

▶ Figure 12-15 Medical decision making—Details for Dx/Mgt.

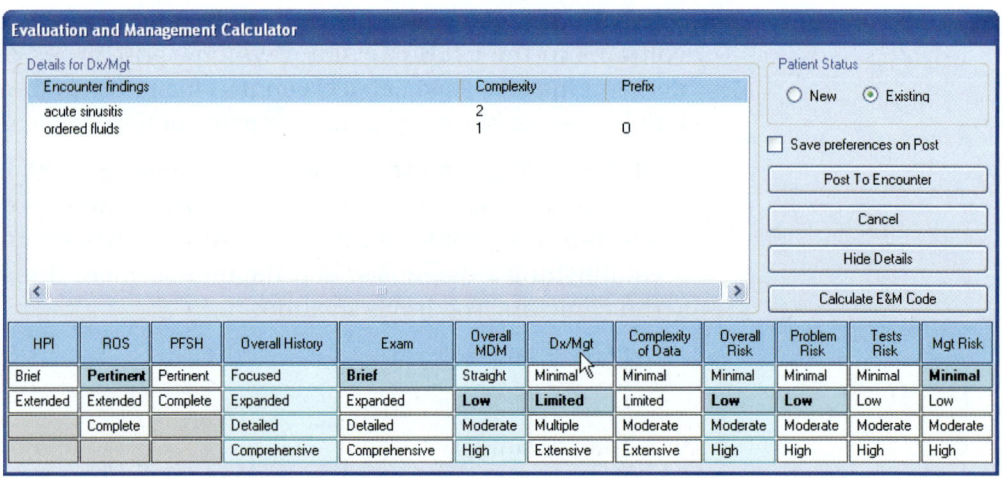

The details pane has three columns labeled "Encounter findings," "Complexity," and "Prefix." The Complexity column displays a level of complexity associated with the finding. The Prefix column contains a code or abbreviation if the finding has a prefix. In this example, the finding "ordered fluids" displays the letter "O," which stands for ordered.

Step 16

The remaining columns in the E&M calculator window grid are concerned with the MDM element of risk. Risk has its own table for calculating the level of risk (shown later in Figure 12-18).

Locate and click on the column labeled "Problem Risk" (as shown in Figure 12-16). The E&M calculator window will display the "Details for Problem Risk" pane. The details pane has three columns, labeled "Encounter findings," "Risk," and "Prefix," which were explained in the previous step.

▶ Figure 12-16 Medical decision making—Details for Problem Risk.

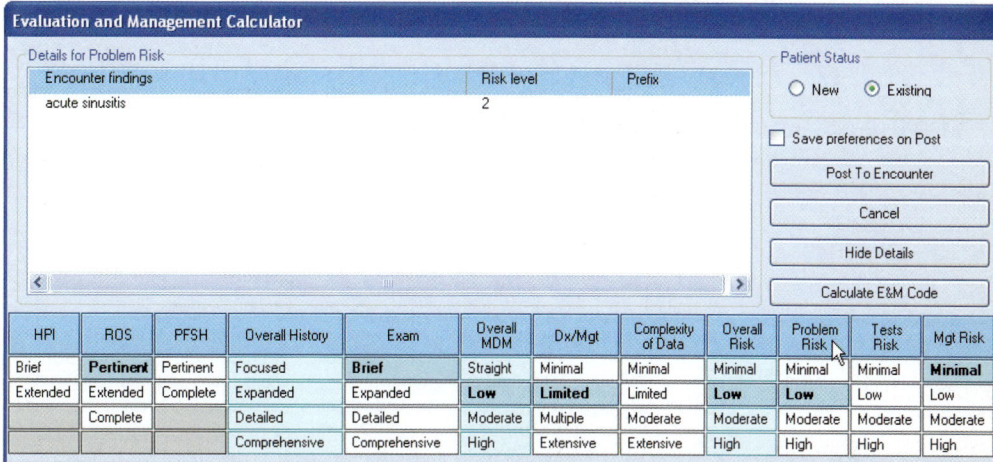

Note that the E&M calculator also includes a column measuring the risk of tests, but none were ordered during this exam.

Step 17

Locate and click on the column labeled "Mgt Risk" (as shown in Figure 12-17). Mgt is the software abbreviation for management. The E&M calculator window will display the "Details for Mgt Risk" pane. The details pane has three columns, labeled "Encounter findings," "Risk," and "Prefix," which were explained in step 15.

▶ Figure 12-17 Medical decision making—Details for Mgt Risk.

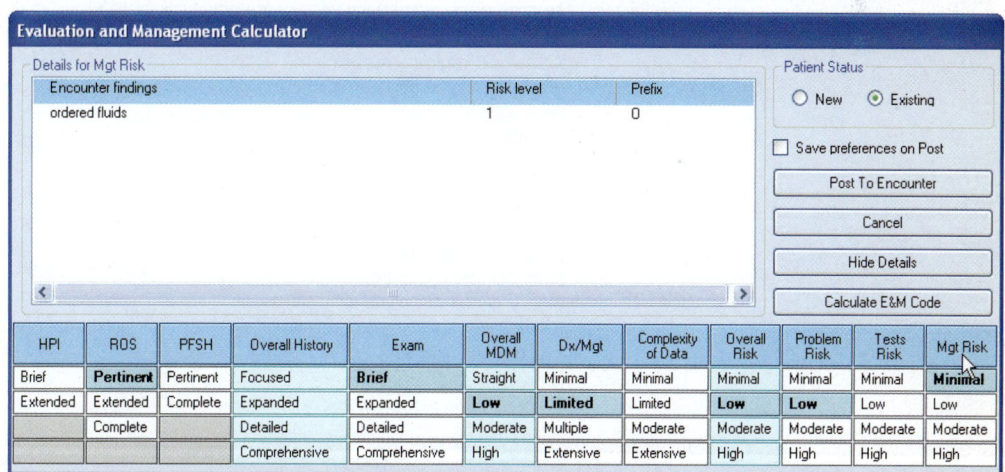

The risk level in this column is "minimal" because there is little risk involved when ordering fluids.

Locate and click on the button labeled "Hide Details" to return to the E&M calculator screen. (If you have difficulty locating the button, refer to Figure 12-10.)

Table of Risk

Level of Risk	Presenting Problem(s)	Diagnostic Procedure(s) Ordered	Management Options Selected
1 Minimal	• One self-limited or minor problem, e.g., cold, insect bite, tinea corporis	• Laboratory tests requiring venipuncture • Chest x-rays • EKG/EEG • Urinalysis • Ultrasound, e.g., echocardiography • KOH prep	• Rest • Gargles • Elastic bandages • Superficial dressings
2 Low	• Two or more self-limited or minor problems • One stable chronic illness, e.g., well-controlled hypertension, non–insulin dependent diabetes, cataract, BPH • Acute uncomplicated illness or injury, e.g., cystitis, allergic rhinitis, simple sprain	• Physiologic tests not under stress, e.g., pulmonary function tests • Non-cardiovascular imaging studies with contrast, e.g., barium enema • Superficial needle biopsies • Clinical laboratory tests requiring arterial puncture • Skin biopsies	• Over-the-counter drugs • Minor surgery with no identified risk factors • Physical therapy • Occupational therapy • IV fluids without additives
3 Moderate	• One or more chronic illnesses with mild exacerbation, progression, or side effects of treatment • Two or more stable chronic illnesses • Undiagnosed new problem with uncertain prognosis, e.g., lump in breast • Acute illness with systemic symptoms, e.g., pyelonephritis, pneumonitis, colitis • Acute complicated injury, e.g., head injury with brief loss of consciousness	• Physiologic tests under stress, e.g., cardiac stress test, fetal contraction stress test • Diagnostic endoscopies with no identified risk factors • Deep needle or incisional biopsy • Cardiovascular imaging studies with contrast and no identified risk factors, e.g., arteriogram, cardiac catheterization • Obtain fluid from body cavity, e.g., lumbar puncture, thoracentesis, culdocentesis	• Minor surgery with identified risk factors • Elective major surgery (open, percutaneous, or endoscopic) with no identified risk factors • Prescription drug management • Therapeutic nuclear medicine • IV fluids with additives • Closed treatment of fracture or dislocation without manipulation
4 High	• One or more chronic illnesses with severe exacerbation, progression, or side effects of treatment • Acute or chronic illnesses or injuries that pose a threat to life or bodily function, e.g., multiple trauma, acute MI, pulmonary embolus, severe respiratory distress, progressive severe rheumatoid arthritis, psychiatric illness with potential threat to self or others, peritonitis, acute renal failure • An abrupt change in neurologic status, e.g., seizure, TIA, weakness, sensory loss	• Cardiovascular imaging studies with contrast with identified risk factors • Cardiac electrophysiological tests • Diagnostic endoscopies with identified risk factors • Discography	• Elective major surgery (open, percutaneous, or endoscopic) with identified risk factors • Emergency major surgery (open, percutaneous, or endoscopic) • Parenteral controlled substances • Drug therapy requiring intensive monitoring for toxicity • Decision not to resuscitate or to deescalate care because of poor prognosis

▶ Figure 12-18 Table for determining level of risk.

Step 18

The E&M guidelines use a special table for calculating the overall level of risk[7] (shown in Figure 12-18). However, risk differs from the other two MDM elements in that risk level is the highest level of any *one* column in the table.

The table in Figure 12-18 is used to help determine whether the risk of significant complications, morbidity, or mortality is minimal, low, moderate, or high. Because the determination of risk is complex and not readily quantifiable, the table includes common clinical examples rather than absolute measures of risk.

Locate the column in the E&M calculator window labeled "Overall Risk." Notice that the level of the overall risk column is "low," because that was the level of the highest of the three risk elements, Problem Risk. You will see another example of this aspect of risk in Guided Exercise 70.

Determining the Level of Medical Decision Making

There are four levels of Medical Decision Making:

Level 1: **Straight** forward

Level 2: **Low** Complexity

Level 3: **Moderate** Complexity

Level 4: **High** Complexity

The individual levels from each of the elements we have discussed, number of diagnoses, amount or complexity of data, and the level of risk are used to determine the level for Medical Decision Making.

The chart in Figure 12-19 shows the level of elements required for each level of medical decision making.[8] The level of MDM (shown in the first column of Figure 12-19) is determined by the highest levels of any two of the three elements.

▶ **Figure 12-19** Table of elements required for each level of medical decision making.

Table of Levels of Medical Decision Making

Level of MDM	Medical Decision Making	Number of diagnoses or management options	Amount and/or complexity of data to be reviewed	Risk of complications and/or morbidity or mortality
1	Straightforward	Minimal	Minimal or None	Minimal
2	Low Complexity	Limited	Limited	Low
3	Moderate Complexity	Multiple	Moderate	Moderate
4	High Complexity	Extensive	Extensive	High

Step 19

Compare the chart in Figure 12-19 to the E&M calculator window.

Locate the column labeled "Overall MDM," which is "low" or level 2.

---

[7]Figure adapted from *1997 Documentation Guidelines for Evaluation and Management Services*, (Washington, DC: U.S. Department of Health and Human Services, 1997).
[8]Ibid.

Looking at the columns for the individual elements, note that those labeled "Dx/Mgt Options" and "Overall Risk" are also level 2. Even though there is no report for "Complexity of Data," the MDM level is set to the highest of two out of three elements.

Other Components: Counseling, Coordination of Care, and Time

Time is considered the key or controlling factor to qualify for a particular level of E&M services only when counseling or coordination of care dominates more than 50% of the encounter (face-to-face time in the office or other outpatient setting, floor/unit time in the hospital or nursing facility).

Step 20

In the center of the E&M calculator window (beneath the exam type field) are two fields related to time. First is a check box used to indicate that counseling (or coordination of care) exceeded 50% of the face-to-face time for the visit. The second field is used to enter the total face-to-face time.

Face-to-face time incorporates the total time both before and after the visit, such as taking patient history, performing the exam, reviewing lab results, planning for follow-up care, and communicating with other providers about the patient's case.

The E&M calculator allows you to record the amount of face-to-face time even when you are not using counseling time as a factor. It is a good practice to record the face-to-face time for each encounter.

Click on the down arrow button in the field labeled "Total face-to-face or Floor time" and select 15 minutes from the drop-down list (as shown in Figure 12-20).

▶ Figure 12-20 Counseling and face-to-face time drop-down list.

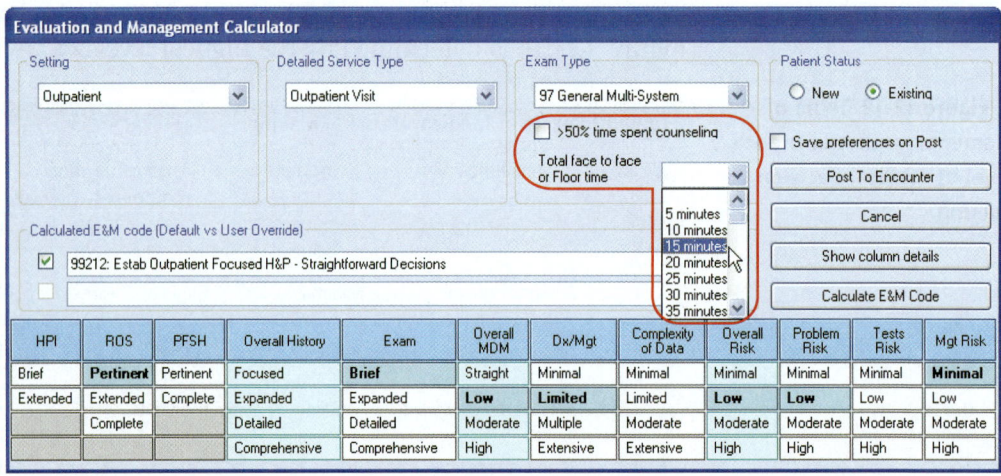

This will not change the E&M code because time does not become a factor until it is more than half of the face-to-face time. In Guided Exercise 72 you will learn to use both of these time-related fields to change the E&M code and to document the results in your encounter note.

Putting It All Together

Momentarily leaving the element of time aside, you will see that the levels of each of the three *key components* combine to determine the level of the E&M code.

▶ **Figure 12-21** Relationship of key component levels determines E&M code.

Relationship of Key Elements to E&M Codes for Outpatient Visits

E&M Code	Type of Patient	# of Key Elements Met	History Level	Exam Level	Medical Decision Making	Face-to-face Time
99201	New	All 3	1	1	1	10 min
99202	New	All 3	2	2	1	20 min
99203	New	All 3	3	3	2	30 min
99204	New	All 3	4	4	3	45 min
99205	New	All 3	4	4	4	60 min
99211	Established	2 of 3	Presentation of Problem Minimal Documentation Req.			5 min
99212	Established	2 of 3	1	1	1	10 min
99213	Established	2 of 3	2	2	2	15 min
99214	Established	2 of 3	3	3	3	25 min
99215	Established	2 of 3	4	4	4	40 min

Step 21

The chart in Figure 12-21 shows the E&M codes used for the category of outpatient office visits. It will help you to visualize how the relationship of the key components determines the E&M code.

The first column in Figure 12-21 is the CPT-4 code. The second column indicates if the code is for a new or established patient. Note that there are two groups of codes listed. The first five codes are for new patients, and then five different codes are listed for established patients.

The third column labeled "# of Key Elements Met" indicates how many key components determine the E&M code.

The blue, green, and lavender columns list the levels of the three key components: History, Exam, and Medical Decision Making. The level numbers under each key component are derived from the individual tables in the sections you have just completed. The tables are:

History—Figure 12-11

Exam—Figure 12-14

MDM—Figure 12-19

The final column lists the number of minutes per type of visit used by the E&M calculator. Time will be discussed further in Guided Exercise 72.

Evaluating Key Components

Once the level of each of the key components has been determined, calculating the level of the E&M code is fairly straightforward. The E&M code level is determined by the lowest level of the key components considered. However, different requirements apply when determining the E&M code for new versus established patients.

Scan down the third column of Figure 12-21. Note that the number of key components for a new patient is "All 3." Notice that for established patients

Chapter 12 | EHR Coding and Reimbursement   487

it is "2 of 3." This does not mean that an encounter will not have findings for all three components—in most cases it will. It means that, for an established patient, the two key components with the highest levels are considered and the lowest level of the two determines the E&M code.

For example, consider an encounter that has:

History Level 1 (Problem Focused)

Exam Level 2 (Expanded Problem Focused)

MDM Level 3 (Moderate Complexity)

The E&M code for an established patient will be level 2 because the elements with the highest levels (Exam and MDM) are the relevant elements and Exam has the lower level of the two.

Now compare the E&M codes for a new patient. Locate the section of the table in Figure 12-21 for new patients. What E&M code would be used when History is level 1 (Problem Focused), Exam is level 2 (Expanded Problem Focused), and MDM is level 2 (Low Complexity)?

If you answered 99201, you are correct. The E&M code for new patients is determined by all three elements. Even though the Exam and MDM components are level 2, if the History level is not 2, then the lower code must be used.

Having tried to determine a code manually, you can appreciate the value that an E&M calculator brings to an EHR system. Remember that the level of each of the key components is a combination of elements:

- To qualify for a given level of history, the quantity and types of HPI, ROS, and PFSH must be met.
- To qualify for a given level of exam, the number of "bulleted" items in the appropriate number of body systems must be met.
- To qualify for a given level of medical decision making, two of the three elements (the number of diagnosis, the amount of data, and the risk assessment) must be either met or exceeded.

If you can imagine trying to count bullets from your encounter notes, calculate the amount of and types of history, and determine the level of decision making in your head, all while you are seeing the patient, you can understand why so many doctors code at the wrong level, just to be safe. You also can appreciate the skill required of medical coders who do this manually.

Step 22

Click the Cancel button to close the E&M calculator window. You may exit the Student Edition software **without printing** an encounter this time because you have not made any changes to the note.

How Changes in Key Components Affect the E&M Code

At this point, you should have a good understanding on how an E&M code is determined from the key components of the encounter. However, what raises the E&M code for an encounter to the next level is not always apparent.

The level of E&M code for an established patient is dependent on two of three of the key components. Merely adding more findings to any one component may bring that component to a higher level, but that does not necessarily mean that the visit as a whole will qualify for the higher level E&M code.

For example, in Guided Exercise 69 an established patient had:

History Level 1 (Problem Focused)

Exam Level 1 (Problem Focused)

MDM Level 2 (Low Complexity)

The E&M code was level 1 (99212) because one of the two highest key components was a level 1. Even if the level of MDM was raised to three, the E&M code would still be level 1 because the exam component was only level 1.

Work must be performed and documented in the appropriate areas to result in a higher E&M code. The next exercise demonstrates how changes to key components affect an increase to the level of an E&M code.

In the next exercise, you are going to add findings to an existing encounter to study the effects on E&M coding.

Fraud and Abuse

The goal of these exercises is to provide an experiential understanding of concepts discussed in this chapter. They should not be construed as having any other purpose.

It is unethical and illegal to maximize payment by means that contradict regulatory guidelines. The HHS Office of Inspector General (OIG) investigates allegations of medical billing fraud and abuse. It does not matter if coding errors are made deliberately or inadvertently; OIG still treats it as fraud and abuse.

The student should not get the impression that it is okay to up-code to maximize reimbursement unless legally entitled by documentation and service provided. Similarly, a clinician cannot adjust the time factor unless it is substantiated in the documentation. Diagnoses or procedures should not be inappropriately included or excluded to affect or alter payment or insurance policy coverage requirements.

EHR systems support accurate, complete, and consistent coding practices by documenting the encounter with codified nomenclature that can be analyzed and used to determine the levels of billing justified. Medical coders must adhere to the coding conventions, official coding guidelines, and official rules, and assign codes that are clearly and consistently supported by clinical documentation in the health record.

Guided Exercise 70: Calculating E&M for a More Complex Visit

In this exercise, you are going to add findings to an existing encounter to study the effects on E&M coding.

Step 1

If the patient encounter used in the previous exercise is currently displayed on your screen, proceed to step 2. If it is not, start the Student Edition software.

From the Select menu, click Patient, and from the Patient Selector window select **Mary Williams**. If you have difficulty, refer to Figure 12-2 at the beginning of this chapter.

From the Select menu, click Existing Encounter, and from the Encounter Selector window select **5/28/2012 10:45 AM Office Visit**. If you have difficulty, refer to Figure 12-3 at the beginning of this chapter.

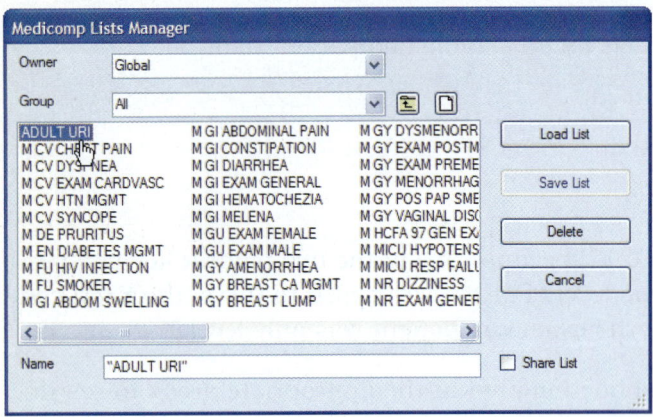

▶ Figure 12-22 Select the Adult URI list from the Lists Manager window.

Step 2

You will recall from Guided Exercise 69 that this patient encounter note produces a calculated E&M code of "99212 Established Outpatient Focused H&P—Straightforward Decisions." You do not need to run the E&M calculator yet.

Because this encounter note was for an URI, and was created using the List feature, You are going to load the Adult URI list.

Locate and click on the button labeled "List" on the Toolbar at the top your screen. When the Lists Manager window shown in Figure 12-22 is displayed, select **Adult URI** and click the button labeled "Load List."

In the following steps, you are going to use the list to add findings and study their effect on the levels of E&M codes.

History The History level is determined by the relationship between HPI, ROS, and PFSH. If you refer back to the table in Figure 12-11, you will see the following:

◆ An increase in the number of findings for HPI will only affect the level of history if ROS and PFSH contain data as well.

▶ Figure 12-23 Upper portion of encounter note with Review of Systems section circled in red.

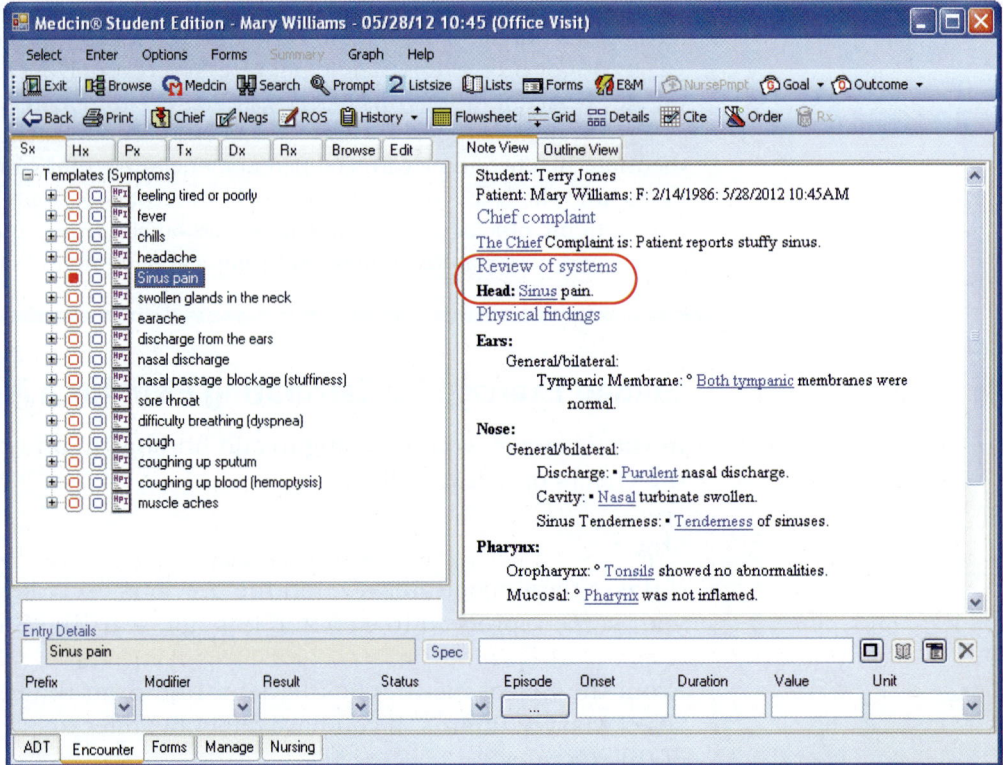

490 Chapter 12 | EHR Coding and Reimbursement

◆ An increase in the number of body systems in ROS will only affect the level of history if HPI contains at least four findings and PFSH contains at least one.

◆ Adding even one finding for PFSH will only affect the level of history if HPI contains at least four findings and ROS contains at least two body systems.

◆ A "Complete" level of PFSH will only affect the overall history level when HPI contains at least four findings and ROS has at least 10 systems.

Step 3

Scroll the encounter note, displayed in the pane on the right, upward to view the History section (circled in red in Figure 12-23). Note that there is only one type of History, Review of Systems; HPI or PFSH findings are not present in the encounter. This means that there is only one of the three History elements in the current E&M calculation.

Locate and click on the following symptom finding:

● (red button) Nasal passage blockage (stuffiness)

This symptom describes the presenting problem.

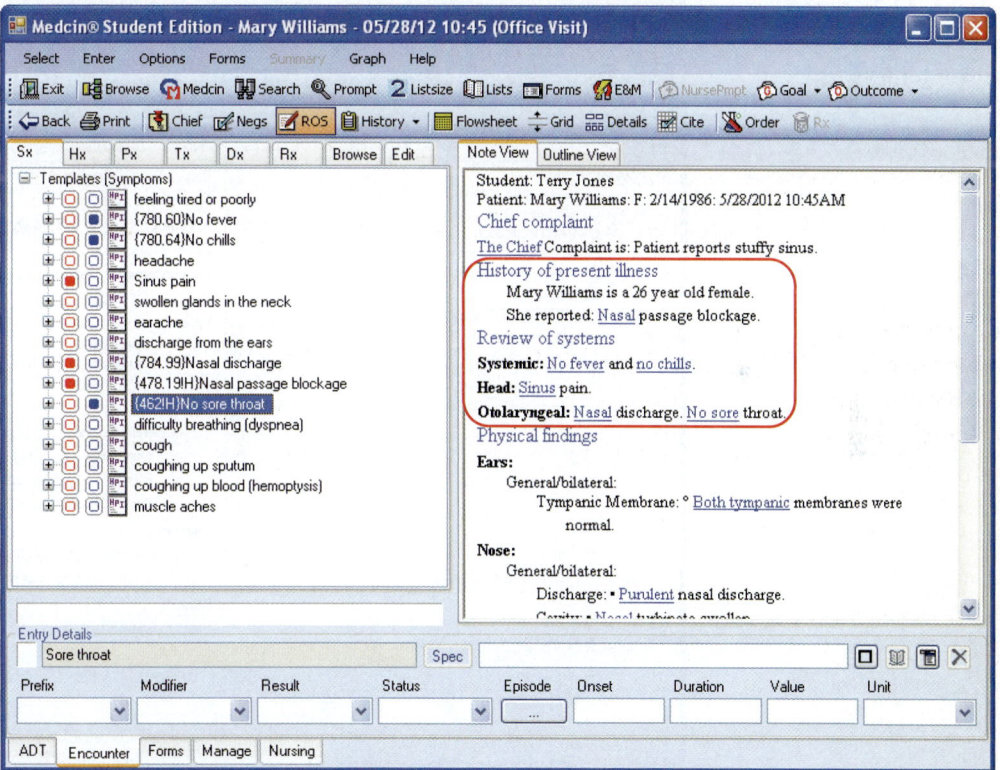

▶ Figure 12-24 Encounter with both History of Present Illness and Review of Systems sections.

Step 4

Locate and click on the button labeled "ROS" on the Toolbar at the top of the screen. Verify it is "on" (orange).

Locate and click on the following symptom findings:

● (blue button) Fever
● (blue button) Chills

Chapter 12 | EHR Coding and Reimbursement

- (red button) Nasal discharge
- (blue button) sore throat

Compare your screen to Figure 12-24 (scroll the right pane upward if necessary to see the full history).

These symptoms are in systems related to the presenting problem. Figure 12-24 shows, circled in red, that two types of history are now in the encounter note.

Step 5

Click on the Hx tab to add PSFH.

Locate and click on the following History finding:

- (red button) current smoker

In the Entry Details section at the bottom of your screen, type "6 years" in the field labeled "Duration" (circled in red in Figure 12-25).

Compare your screen to Figure 12-25. Note that you now have findings in all three History sections: HPI, ROS, and behavioral history (PFSH).

▶ Figure 12-25 Social (behavioral) history—smoker for 6 years.

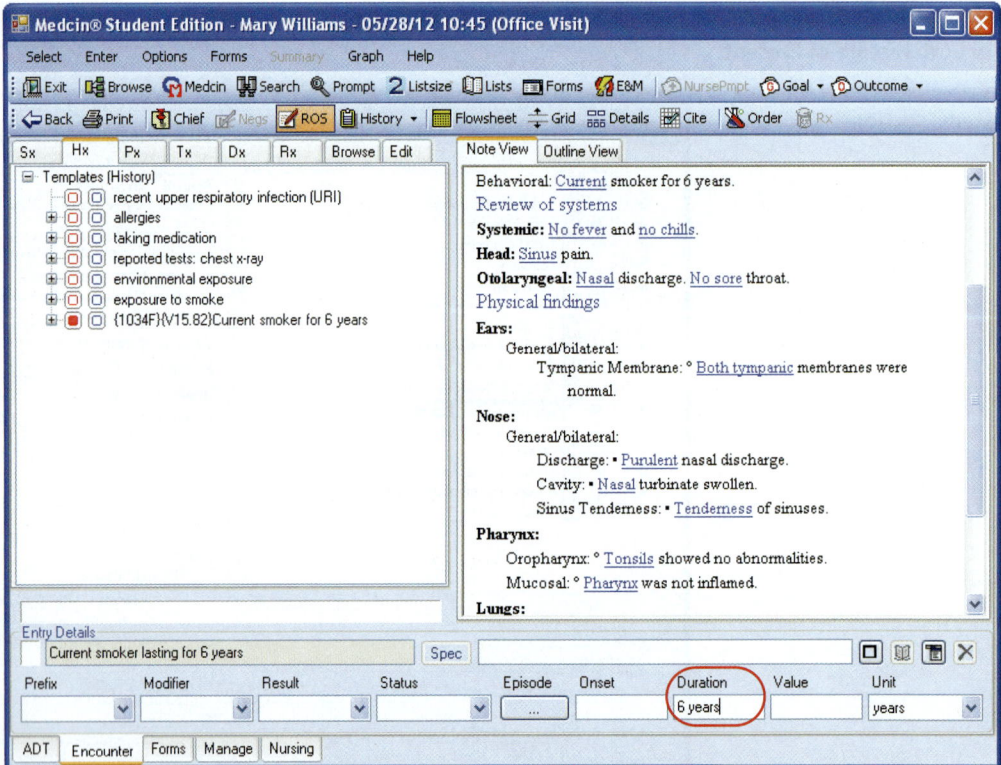

Examination Exams provide the most direct, but not the easiest means to reach a higher level code. The more systems examined, the more bullet points that are met, represent more work has been done and therefore a higher level of code should be justified. However, consider the following:

◆ In a general multi-system examination, six or more elements with a bullet are required to reach the second level.

- The third level is reached when you have at least two elements in six or more systems/body areas.
- The fourth level requires all of the bulleted items in at least nine systems/body areas.

▶ Figure 12-26 Added findings on physical exam.

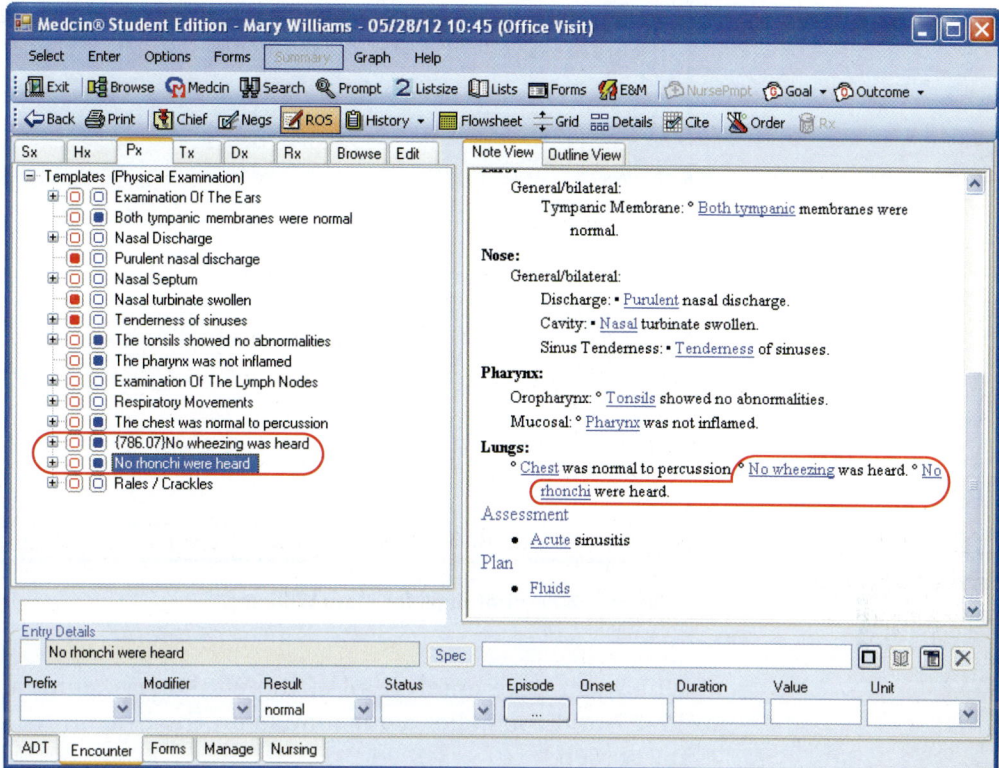

Step 6

Click on the Px tab.

Locate and click on the following Physical Exam findings:
- (blue button) Wheezing
- (blue button) Rhonchi

Compare your screen to Figure 12-26.

Step 7

Enter the patient's vital signs using the Vitals form.

Ms. Williams's vital signs are as follows:

Temperature:	97.7
Respiration:	25
Pulse:	65
BP:	128/90
Height:	64
Weight:	155

Chapter 12 | EHR Coding and Reimbursement 493

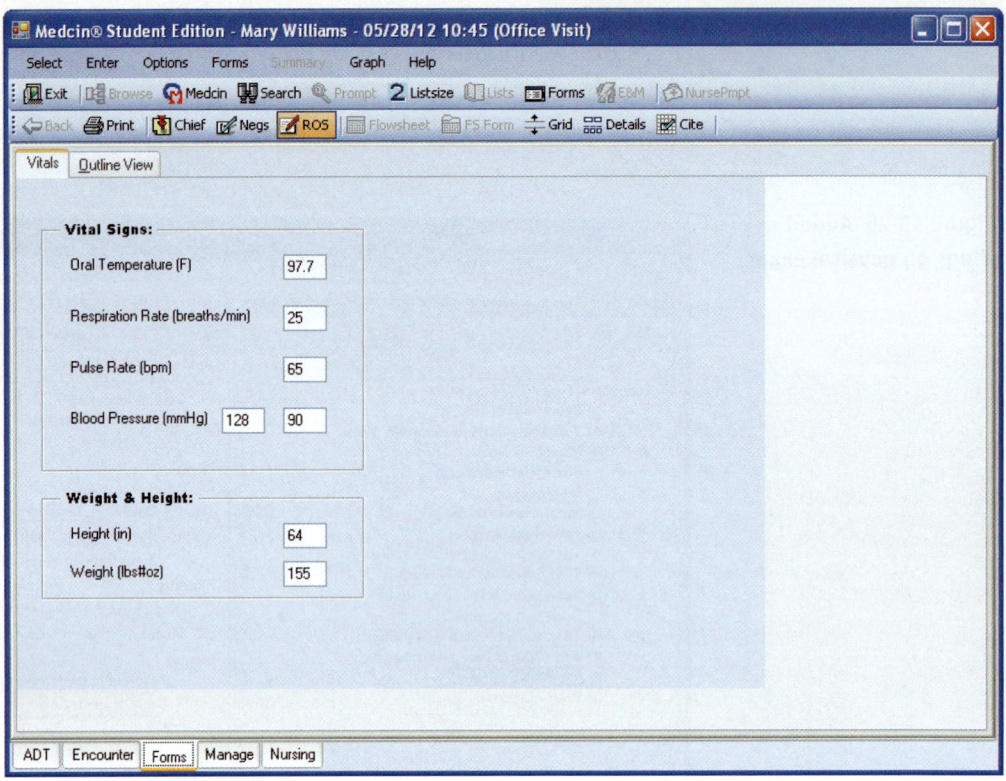

▶ **Figure 12-27** Vital signs for Mary Williams.

When you have entered all of the vital signs, compare your screen to Figure 12-27 and then click your mouse on the Encounter tab at the bottom of the screen.

Step 8

Click on the E&M button in the Toolbar at the top of your screen. When the Problem Screening checklist window appears, click the OK button without checking any of the boxes. The Evaluation and Management Calculator window should now display the code 99213. If it does not, locate the section labeled

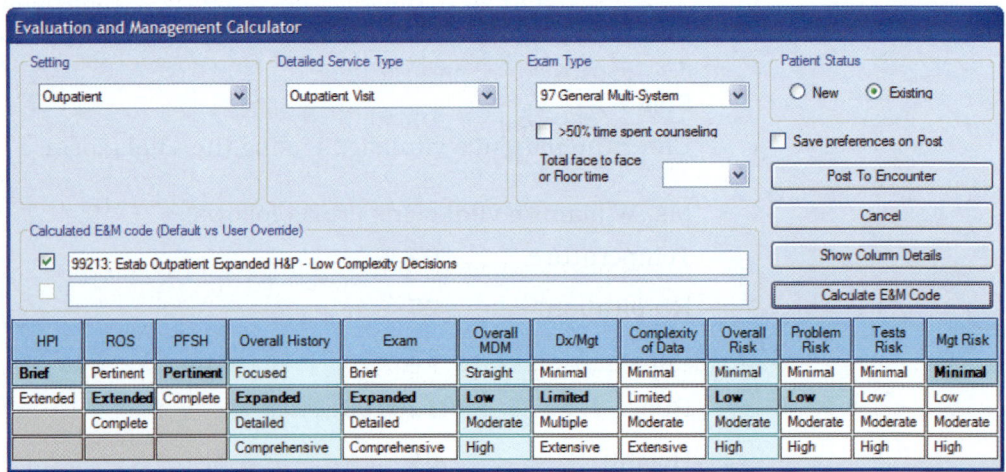

▶ **Figure 12-28** Recalculated E&M code.

494   Chapter 12 | EHR Coding and Reimbursement

Patient Status in the upper right corner of the calculator window. Click on the circle next to the label "Existing" and then click on the button labeled "Calculate E&M Code."

Figure 12-28 shows the E&M code generated as a result of the additional findings you have added. The new code is "99213: Estab Outpatient Expanded H&P - Low Complexity Decisions." Refer back to Figure 12-7 which shows the previously calculated E&M code of 99212. Compare the grid at the bottom of your E&M calculator window to Figure 12-7.

Note that the History sections HPI and PFSH now have bold levels listed in them. Although only the ROS history element moved to level 2, the Overall History level changed from 1–Problem Focused to 2–Expanded Problem Focused. This is because of the presence of the HPI finding and six ROS findings related to the problem. The addition of the PFSH did not, however, affect the Overall History level. Refer to Figure 12-11, Table of Elements Required for Each Level of History.

Look again at the grid at the bottom of your E&M calculator window. Notice that the level of Exam has also increased to level 2, Expanded. This was a result of the addition of vital signs and two Physical Exam findings.

Why, if none of the key components changed to level 3, did the E&M code change from a level 2 code (99212) to a level 3 code (99213)?

Refer back to the chart in Figure 12-21; you will notice that for an established patient, the CPT-4 requirement for 99213 is that two of the three key components are at least level 2. Because Overall History and Exam are now level 2 (Expanded), the encounter justifies a higher level E&M code.

At this point, the medical decision-making components did not change levels.

Medical Decision Making   The level of MDM is determined by two out of three elements in the table shown in Figure 12-19. However, the risk table in Figure 12-18 indicates that managing prescribed medications raises the risk to Level 3. Therefore, the MDM level for any patient on medications will usually be determined by the number of diagnosis and the amount or complexity of data reviewed during the visit.

Step 9

Click on the button labeled "Cancel" to close the E&M calculator window.

Click on the E&M button in the Toolbar at the top of your screen to restart the E&M calculator.

This time you are going to enter data in the Problem Screening checklist window before proceeding to the E&M calculator.

When you click your mouse on the check boxes in the Problem Screening For E/M window, a check mark appears.

▶ **Figure 12-29** Problem Screening window with Active and New Problem checked.

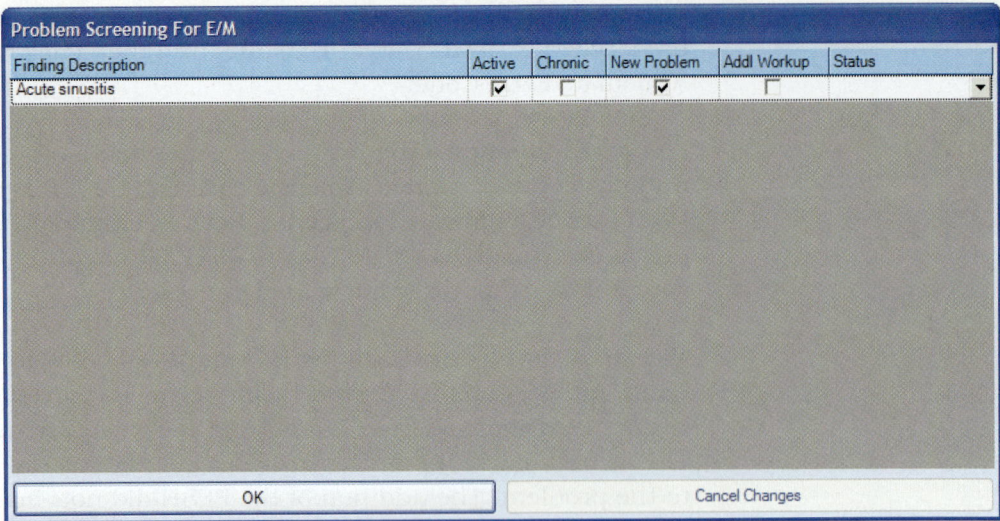

Locate and click the boxes for the following:

✓ Active

✓ New Problem

Compare your screen to Figure 12-29.

Click the OK button at the bottom of the checklist window.

▶ **Figure 12-30** Dx/Mgt level changed to Multiple.

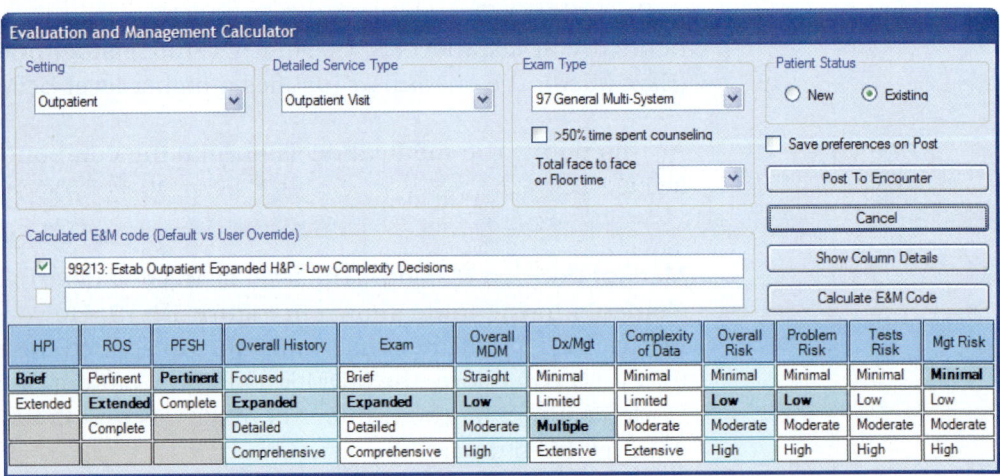

Step 10

Locate the column labeled "Dx/Mgt." You will recall that Dx/Mgt stands for Diagnosis and/or Management. Compare Figure 12-28 and Figure 12-30.

Notice that the Dx/Mgt column has changed from level 2, Limited, to level 3, Multiple. This change in level was caused by the addition of data from the Problem Screening checklist window concerning the diagnoses.

Time As you learned earlier, time can be a factor when more than 50% of the face-to-face time is spent counseling the patient. Both the face-to-face time and the counseling time must be documented. This will be covered in Guided Exercise 72.

▶ Figure 12-31 Setting the face-to-face time.

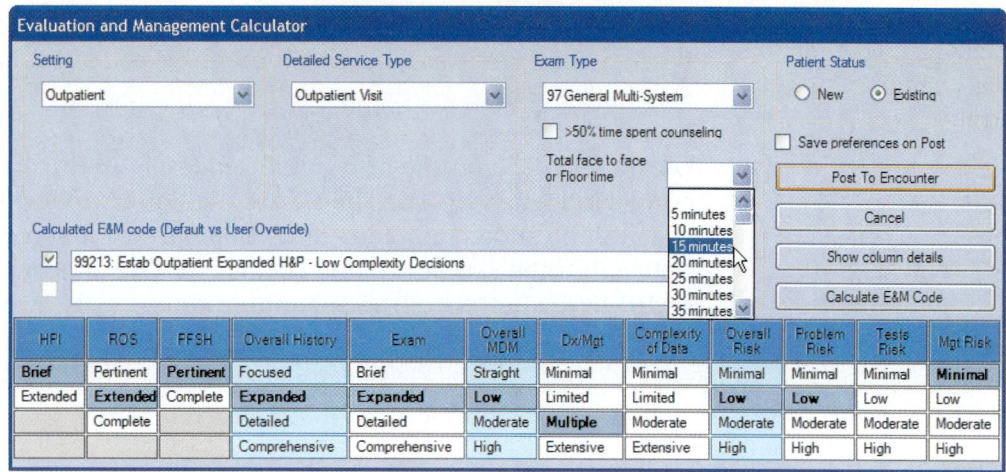

Step 11

Because it is always a good idea to record the face-to-face time in the encounter note, the software allows you to do this when you record the E&M code even if you are not using time as a factor in E&M calculation. Remember, face-to-face time is the total time you spent on the visit before, during, and after the patient exam. It is not just the time spent counseling the patient.

Click on the button with the down arrow in the field labeled "Total Face-to-face or Floor time" and select **15 minutes** (as shown in Figure 12-31).

Recalculate the E&M code by clicking on the button labeled "Calculate E&M Code" again. Note that the time did not change the calculated code, which is still 99213.

▶ Figure 12-32 Encounter note with E&M code and face-to-face time circled in red.

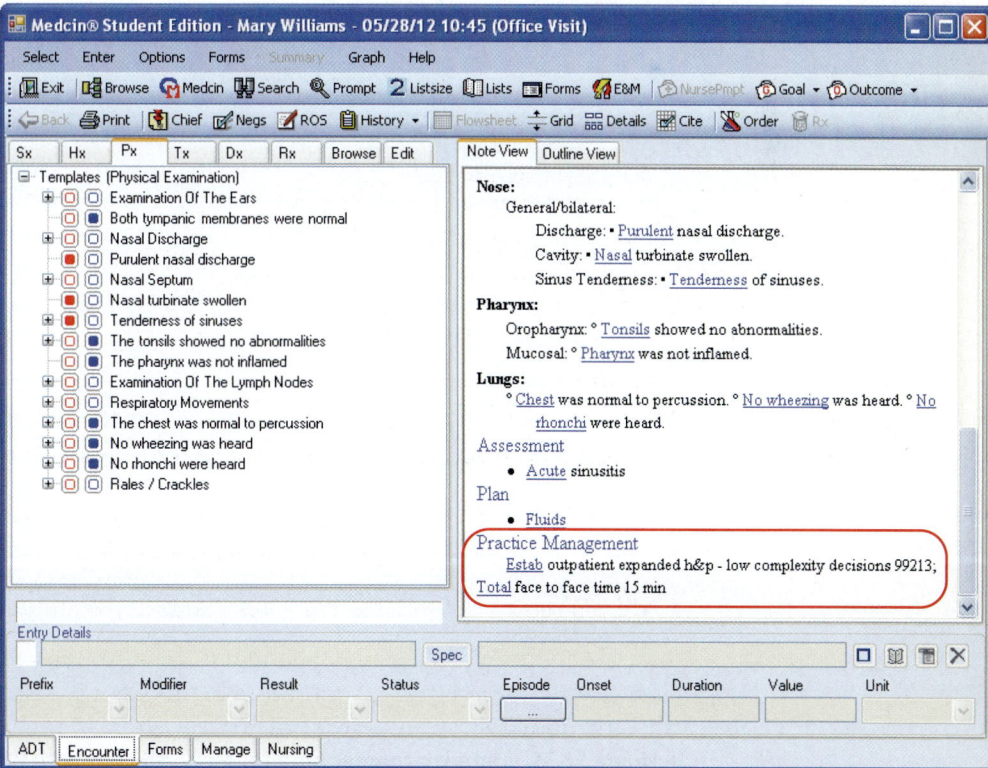

Chapter 12 | EHR Coding and Reimbursement 497

Step 12

When a clinician is satisfied with the E&M code that has been calculated, it is posted to the note.

Locate and click on the button labeled "Post To Encounter" (highlighted with orange in Figure 12-31). The E&M Calculator window will close and the E&M code will be added into your note. Compare your screen with Figure 12-32. Notice that the procedure and the face-to-face time (circled in red) have been added to the bottom of the encounter note.

```
Mary Williams                                                    Page 1 of 1

Student: your name or ID here
Patient: Mary Williams: F: 2/14/1986: 5/28/2012 10:45AM
Chief complaint
The Chief Complaint is: Patient reports stuffy sinus.
History of present illness
    Mary Williams is a 26 year old female.
    She reported: Nasal passage blockage.
Personal history
    Behavioral: Current smoker for 6 years.
Review of systems
    Systemic: No fever and no chills.
    Head: Sinus pain.
    Otolaryngeal: Nasal discharge. No sore throat.
Physical findings
Vital Signs:
Vital Signs/Measurements         Value                 Normal Range
Oral temperature                 97.7 F                97.6 - 99.6
RR                               25 breaths/min        18 - 26
PR                               65 bpm                50 - 100
Blood pressure                   128/90 mmHg           100-120/56-80
Weight                           155 lbs               98 - 183
Height                           64 in                 60.24 - 68.5
Ears:
    General/bilateral:
    Tympanic Membrane: ° Both tympanic membranes were normal.
Nose:
    General/bilateral:
    Discharge: • Purulent nasal discharge.
    Cavity: • Nasal turbinate swollen.
    Sinus Tenderness: • Tenderness of sinuses.
Pharynx:
    Oropharynx: ° Tonsils showed no abnormalities.
    Mucosal: ° Pharynx was not inflamed.
Lungs:
    ° Chest was normal to percussion. ° No wheezing was heard. ° No rhonchi were heard.
Assessment
    • Acute sinusitis
Plan
    • Fluids
Practice Management
    • Estab outpatient expanded h&p - low complexity decisions 99213; Total face to face
      time 15 min.
```

▶ Figure 12-33 Printed encounter note for Mary Williams with HPI, PFSH, and Vitals added.

Step 13

Click on the Print button on the Toolbar at the top of your screen to invoke the Print Data window.

Be certain there is a check mark in the box next to "Current Encounter" and then click on the appropriate button to either print or export a file, as directed by your instructor.

Compare your printout or file output to Figure 12-33. If it is correct, hand it in to your instructor. If there are any differences, review the previous steps in the exercise and find your error.

Alert

Do not exit. Proceed to step 14.
Do not close or exit the encounter until you have completed step 14.

Critical Thinking Exercise 71: Understanding How Procedures Are Posted to the Billing System

EHR systems that are integrated with practice management or billing software can transfer the Procedure and Diagnosis (CPT-4, HCPCS, and ICD-9-CM) codes from the EHR directly into the practice management billing system.

In most healthcare facilities the codes that are transferred from the EHR do not post automatically to the billing system. Most systems hold these as "pending" charges until they are reviewed by a billing or coding expert, who may make modifications to the codes before posting them as charges. Here are few examples of why this is necessary:

◆ Certain procedures are considered part of another procedure (bundled).

◆ Under certain conditions a coding specialist may need to add procedure modifier codes.

◆ Certain codes may represent a supply or sample for which the doctor does not wish to charge the patient.

Step 14

Locate and click on the tab on the top of the right pane labeled "Outline View."

Locate and click the small plus signs next to the folders "Assessment" and "Practice Management." Compare your screen with Figure 12-34. Notice that the Assessment Acute Sinusitis displays an ICD-9-CM code in this view.

Notice that the text beneath the Practice Management folder not only displays the description information of the calculated E&M code, but the CPT-4 code as well.

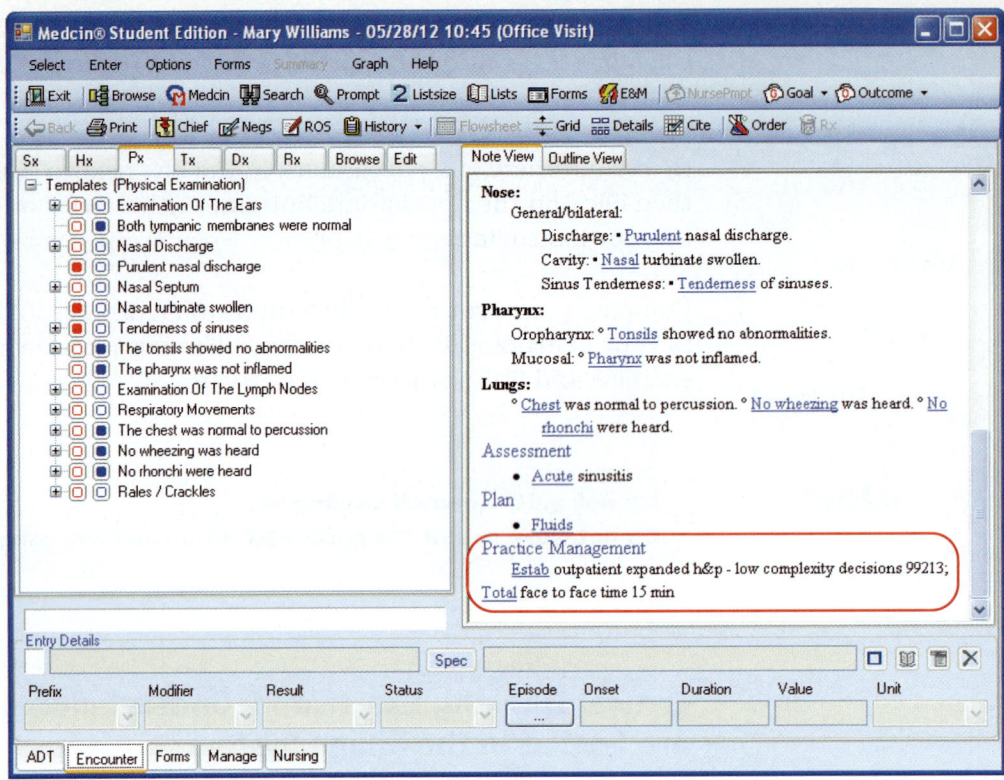

▶ Figure 12-34 Outline View with E&M code and description circled in red.

Your version of the Student Edition is not interfaced to a billing system and therefore does not transfer the codes automatically. However, it does post codes to the patient encounter. You can view the codes that would be transferred in Figure 12-34.

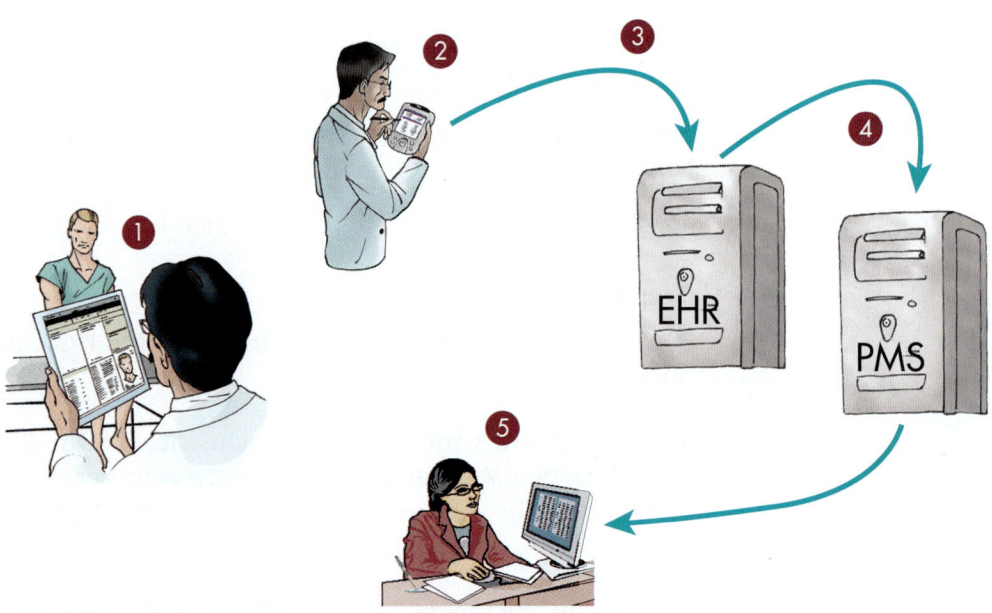

▶ Figure 12-35 Flow of procedures posted from EHR to billing.

500   Chapter 12 | EHR Coding and Reimbursement

Figure 12-35 illustrates the typical method of posting charges from an EHR to a practice management billing module. These steps include the following:

① Clinician documents encounter at point of care.

② EHR calculates E&M code.

③ Clinician clicks button labeled "Post To Encounter."

④ EHR adds procedure codes to encounter note and transfers CPT-4 and ICD-9-CM codes to the practice management system.

⑤ A billing or coding specialist reviews the "pending" charges, adds modifiers or other information, and posts them.

Figure 12-36 shows a practice management billing screen used to post charges transferred from the EHR after being reviewed by a billing or coding specialist.

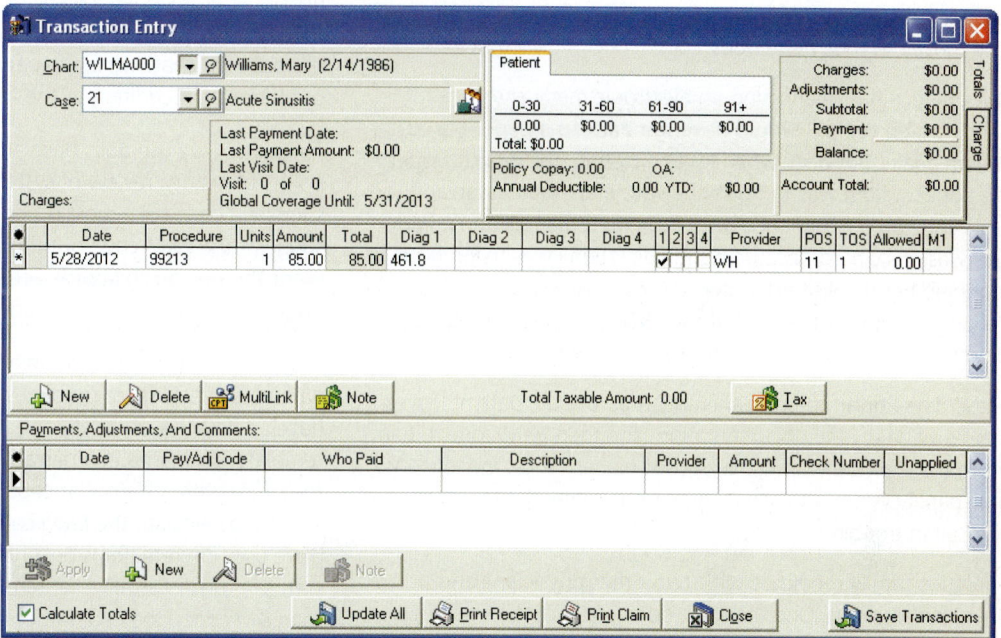

Courtesy of Medisoft

▶ **Figure 12-36** Practice management system posting E&M code from EHR.

Real-Life Story

A New Level of Efficiency in Addition to Improved E&M Coding

Philip C. Yount, M.D.

Ashe Medical Associates

Every medical doctor in America reviews the patient's past medical problems, medication list, social history, and so on, but does each one always document that? I think it is safe to say that doctors, who dictate after the visit, actually get more information, examine more of the patient, and say things to the patient that they do not recall when they dictate later. Certainly when I was dictating or writing notes I did not always remember to document all that I did. To be safe, I tended to undercode; I am sure most everybody else does, too.

Our practice has been using an electronic medical record for almost three years. I would never go back to a paper-based system again. But back when I was dictating, the workflow with the paper system was to finish the visit, mark the charge and the E&M code on a paper encounter form, and then dictate it later. This was really hard because during dictation I was trying both to remember the visit accurately and to make sure I dictated enough to support the level of the E&M code already selected. Now that we use an EMR, both things are done simultaneously.

These days I finish the documentation before the patient leaves. I review it, verify my documentation, and then E&M code it. I am much more accurate and I think I code higher. I think the tendency on a paper system is to always downcode rather than risk getting yourself in trouble.

I practice family medicine with two other physicians and a physician assistant. One thing we do in our quarterly meetings is to review each other's charts to see if we agree with the level of E&M coding that the other provider has charged. Our office manager randomly selects three patients' charges for each of us and prints out the exam notes for peer review. Since we have been on the electronic system, we have had very few discrepancies. Not only is the coding very accurate with the EMR, but the quarterly review itself is facilitated by the electronic records. If you had to dig up charges and pull records from a paper file system . . . well, with electronic medical records it is a lot simpler.

Did switching to electronic records increase our level of coding? I think we are all doing a much better job of coding than we were in the past and we have definitely stopped downcoding, but it is difficult to compare the coding of visits before the EMR because you would have to analyze all those old charts. I have a sense that our documentation went up 15%–20% in terms of levels, but we actually chose to measure something else. We wanted something easy to track, so we tracked the number of patient encounters instead of the coding levels.

In the first year of using the EMR, compared to the previous year, we went up 15% in number of visits, so it really improved our efficiency to that extent. The second year we were up 17% and this year we are up 5% above that—with no additional providers, no longer hours open, or anything else. In addition, we get done on time. I am rarely at the office after 5:00 P.M. anymore. I finish the patient's chart while the patient is still there. So there is a lot of efficiency in addition to the improved E&M coding.

The system we use does have an E&M coder that will count the points of history, review of systems, exam, and so on, and then suggest a code. Like most other EMR systems, it calculates and suggests the E&M code but the software developer does not want the responsibility for actually posting it. It is up to the doctor to decide to use the code.

Most EMR systems have templates, but there are two types. One type uses checklists of problems: "You're here for a cold; you have an earache, a cough, and a sore throat." The other type of template fills blanks in a narrative: "30-year-old male presents to the office with a history of cough, cold, fever." The ability of the system to calculate the E&M code depends on whether the template uses discrete items or sentences, because it can't count the status in those narrative sentences. However, even without using the E&M coder, the coding becomes more accurate because the electronic record is capturing the exam more accurately. A doctor can look at a finished EMR note and see the data points.

Our software uses templates and I designed the history items right into them. We don't miss documenting them now and that lends significant points to the E&M coding. But there is something else our templates do that is perhaps more toward the issue of quality of care than just coding, and that is in the plan. By building templates for certain diagnoses we include all the things we might choose in the plan. This not only helps document simple things that might have been overlooked in the old dictation method, like telling the patient to take Tylenol, but it also gives us a complete checklist of things to consider when concluding the visit.

During the first year, we built templates and customized the software to suit our practice's needs. We worked evenings at the office to overcome a steep learning curve and technological obstacles. With the system finally in place and reaching comfortable levels of proficiency, we have now come to realize a new level of efficiency in our practice.

Our workflow has improved markedly since the implementation of an electronic medical record system, allowing us to do more work in less time with the same sized staff. We are now able to accommodate more patients in a day; able to access our system from home; fax prescriptions to pharmacies from our computers; scan and add outside reports to our records; and we have reduced paperwork and increased staff efficiency. Our medical recordkeeping has improved exponentially and we have added at least 20 percent to our bottom line.

Guided Exercise 72: Counseling Over 50% of Face-to-Face Time

When counseling or coordination of care represent over 50% of the face-to-face time of the visit, time becomes a key or controlling factor to the level of E&M services. The guideline states, "If the physician elects to report the level of service based on counseling and/or coordination of care, the total length of time of the encounter (face-to-face or floor time, as appropriate) should be documented and the record should describe the counseling and/or activities to coordinate care."[9]

In this exercise, you are going to reload the encounter, re-enter the history, and recalculate the code using time as a factor.

Case Study

You will recall from the previous exercise that the patient has been smoking since she was 20. The clinician spent about 15 minutes of time counseling the patient on the need to stop using tobacco and discussing possible strategies she might use to quit. This extra time spent counseling caused the visit to take longer.

Step 1

If the Student Edition software is not currently running on your system, start it at this time.

Perform the following tasks even if the patient encounter used in the previous exercise is still displayed on your screen. This will refresh the encounter and eliminate the changes you made in the previous exercise.

From the Select menu, click Patient, and from the Patient Selector window select **Mary Williams**. If you have difficulty, refer to Figure 12-2 at the beginning of this chapter.

From the Select menu, click Existing Encounter, and from the Encounter Selector window select **5/28/2012 10:45 AM Office Visit**. If you have difficulty, refer to Figure 12-3 at the beginning of this chapter.

Do not run the E&M calculator yet.

Step 2

From the Toolbar at the top of your screen, click on the button labeled "List." When the Lists Manager window shown in Figure 12-22 is displayed, select **Adult URI** and click the button labeled "Load List."

---

[9] *1997 Documentation Guidelines for Evaluation and Management Services* (Washington, DC: U.S. Department of Health and Human Services, 1997).

Step 3

Click on the Hx tab.

Locate and click on the following History finding:

- (red button) current smoker

In the Entry Details section at the bottom of your screen, type "**6 years**" in the field labeled "Duration."

If you have difficulty, refer to Figure 12-25 in the previous exercise.

In the next three steps, you are going to experiment with the factor of Time, by calculating the E&M code three times.

Step 4

Locate and click on the E&M button in the Toolbar at the top of your screen to invoke the Evaluation and Management Calculator window.

The Problem Screening checklist window is displayed.

Locate and click the boxes for the following:

✓ Active

✓ New Problem

The Evaluation and Management Calculator window is displayed.

Locate the Patient Status field and click on the circle labeled "Existing."

Locate and click the button labeled "Calculate E&M Code." Note that the Calculated E&M Code is 99212, the same as it was in the beginning of the previous exercise.

▶ Figure 12-37 E&M code recalculated using time as a factor.

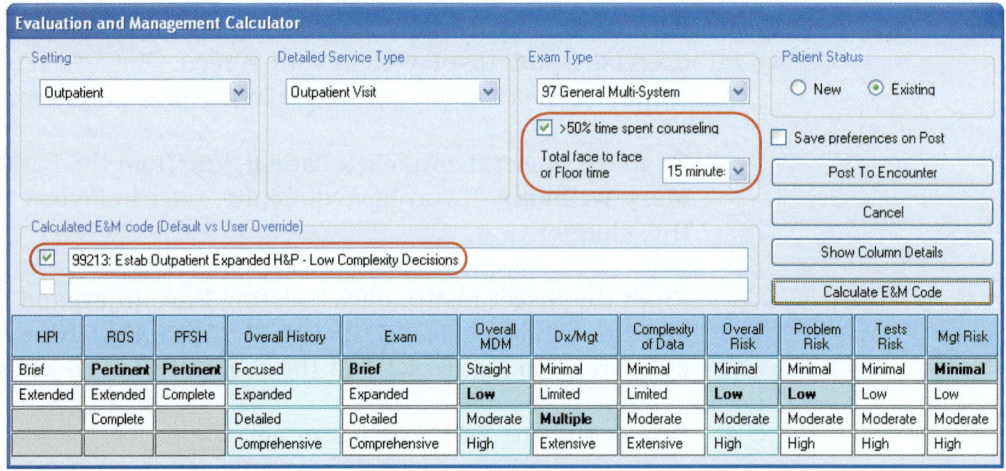

Step 5

Locate the check box used to indicate that counseling (or coordination of care) exceeded 50% of the face-to-face time for the visit. The box is circled in red in Figure 12-37. Click your mouse on the field and a check mark will appear.

Click your mouse on the down arrow button in the field labeled "Face-to-face or Floor time," and select **10 minutes** from the drop-down list.

Click the button labeled "Calculate E&M Code." The code should still calculate as 99212. Notice that the code did *not* change, even though the box labeled ">50%" was checked.

Step 6

Click your mouse on the down arrow button in the field labeled "Face-to-face or Floor time," and this time select **15 minutes** from the drop-down list.

Click the button labeled "Calculate E&M Code." Compare your screen to Figure 12-37. The newly calculated code on your screen should be 99213.

In step 5, the code did not increase to a higher level because there is a minimum amount of time expected to complete each level of exam. Refer back to the table in Figure 12-21. In the right column, the standard amount of time is shown for each code. The E&M code 99212 has a minimum face-to-face time of 10 minutes, whereas the next higher level E&M code 99213 has a minimum face-to-face time of 15 minutes.

When the face-to-face time for this exam was set at less than 15 minutes, the E&M calculator did not increase the code to the next level. Once you increased the amount of time and checked the box labeled ">50% time spent counseling," time became the controlling or key component.

Locate and click on the button labeled "Post To Encounter."

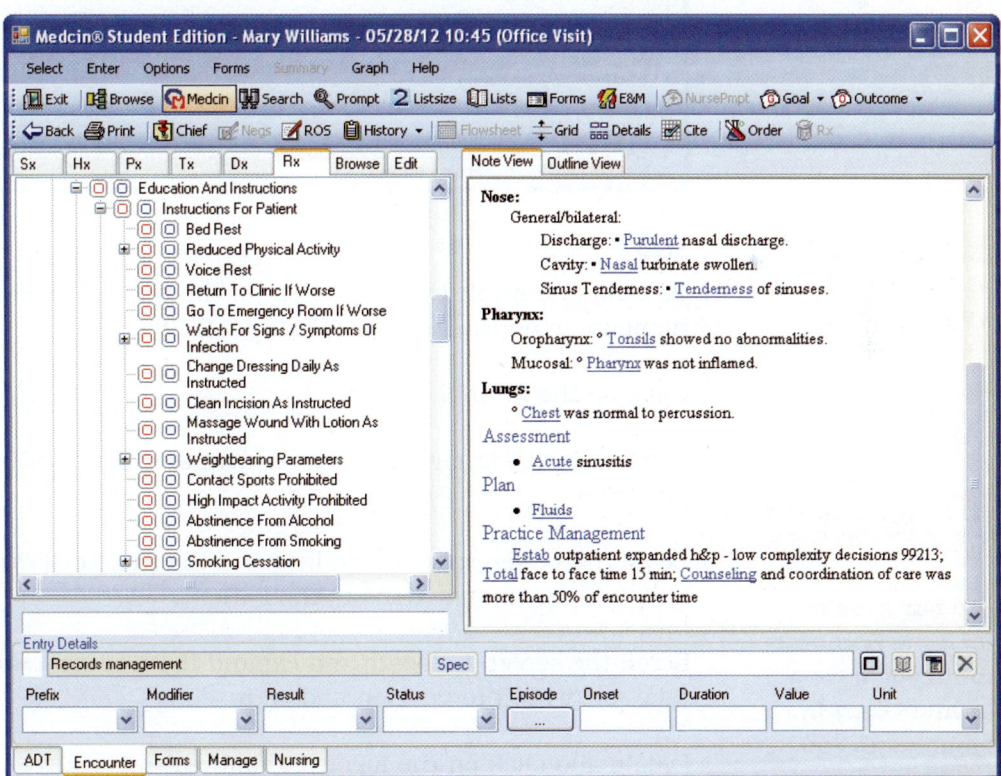

▶ Figure 12-38 Encounter note showing counseling time >50% with Medcin button highlighted.

Step 7

The E&M description, code, time, and justification are posted to your encounter, as shown in Figure 12-38. Remember you can only use time to increase the level of E&M code when the clinician has spent more than 50% of the face-to-face time in counseling or coordination of care. In Mary's case, the clinician spent 10 minutes of the total 15 minutes in counseling.

Remember that the guideline also states "the record should describe the counseling and/or activities to coordinate care."[10] This means that whenever you use this feature in a medical office, you must add a finding or free text to describe the counseling.

▶ Figure 12-39 Rx tab—time counseling on cessation of smoking was greater than 10 minutes.

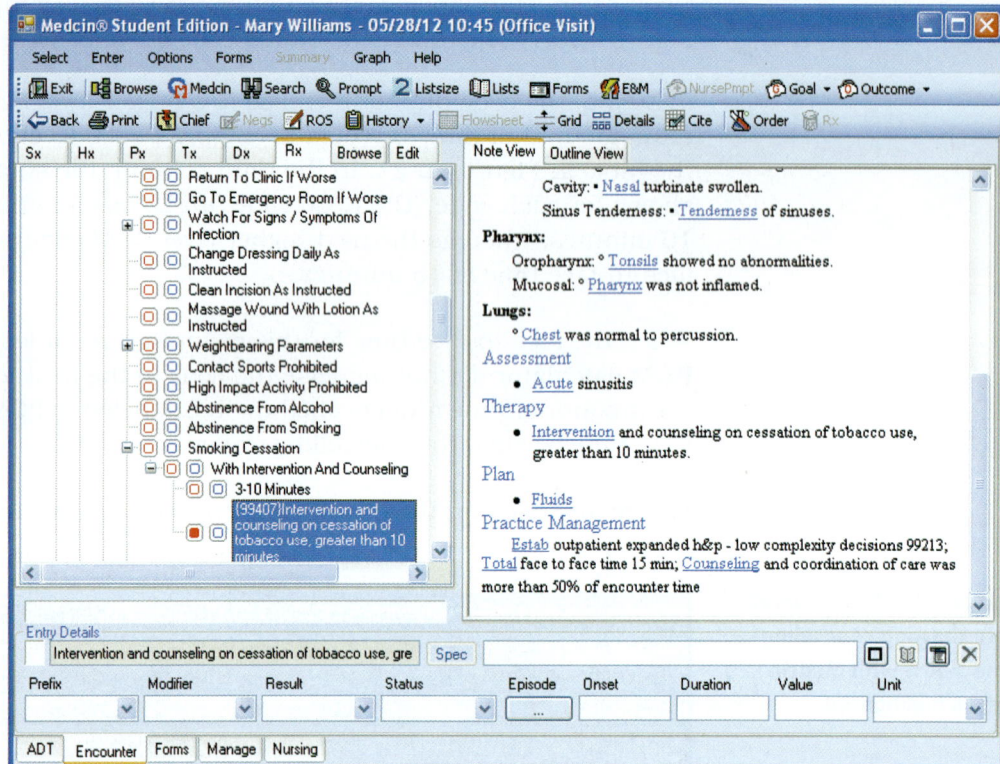

Step 8

To clear the Adult URI list, click on the button labeled "Medcin," which is highlighted on the toolbar in Figure 12-38.

Click on the Rx tab.

Locate "Basic Management Procedures and Services" and click on the small plus sign.

Scroll the screen to locate and expand the tree for "Education and Instructions" and then for "Instructions to the Patient."

Scroll the screen to locate and expand the tree for "Smoking cessation" and then for "with intervention and counseling."

Locate and click on the following finding:

● (red button) Greater than 10 minutes

Compare your screen to Figure 12-39.

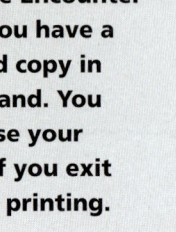

Alert

Do not close or exit the Encounter until you have a printed copy in your hand. You will lose your work if you exit before printing.

---

[10]Ibid.

```
Mary Williams                                                    Page 1 of 1
Student: Your name or ID here
Patient: Mary Williams: F: 2/14/1986: 5/28/2012 10:45AM
Chief complaint
The Chief Complaint is: Patient reports stuffy sinus.
Personal history
     Behavioral: Current smoker for 6 years.
Review of systems
     Head: Sinus pain.
Physical findings
Ears:
     General/bilateral:
     Tympanic Membrane: ° Both tympanic membranes were normal.
Nose:
     General/bilateral:
     Discharge: • Purulent nasal discharge.
     Cavity: • Nasal turbinate swollen.
     Sinus Tenderness: • Tenderness of sinuses.
Pharynx:
     Oropharynx: ° Tonsils showed not abnormalities.
     Mucosal: ° Pharynx was not inflamed.
Lungs:
     ° Chest was normal to percussion.
Assessment
     • Acute sinusitis
Therapy
     • Intervention and counseling on cessation of tobacco use, greater than 10 minutes.
Plan
     • Fluids
Practice Management
     • Estab outpatient expanded h&p - low complexity decisions 99213; Total face to face
       time 15 min; Counseling and coordination of care was more than 50% of
       encounter time.
```

▶ **Figure 12-40** Printed encounter note for Mary Williams with counseling finding and time added.

Step 9

Click on the Print button on the Toolbar at the top of your screen to invoke the Print Data window.

Be certain there is a check mark in the box next to "Current Encounter" and then click on the appropriate button to either print or export a file, as directed by your instructor.

Compare your printout or file output to Figure 12-40. If it is correct, hand it in to your instructor. If there are any differences, review the previous steps in the exercise and find your error.

Factors That Affect the E&M Code Set

Thus far you have seen the effects of key components and time on determining the E&M code. However, you will recall that earlier in this chapter it was mentioned that there are different sets of E&M codes used for new versus established patients as well as for location of service. It was also mentioned that a provider may choose to use the 1995 or 1997 E&M guidelines (or a single-organ guideline).

Guided Exercise 73: Exploring Other Factors of E&M Codes

In this exercise you are going to use the E&M calculator window to see examples of different sets of E&M codes, by changing the settings of several fields that you have not yet worked with. The first four steps should be familiar to you, as you performed them in the previous exercises.

Step 1

If the Student Edition software is not currently running on your system, start it at this time.

Perform the following tasks even if the patient encounter used in the previous exercise is still displayed on your screen. This will refresh the encounter and eliminate the changes you made in the previous exercise.

From the Select menu, click Patient, and from the Patient Selector window select **Mary Williams**. If you have difficulty, refer to Figure 12-2 at the beginning of this chapter.

From the Select menu, click Existing Encounter, and from the Encounter Selector window select **5/28/2012 10:45 AM Office Visit**. If you have difficulty, refer to Figure 12-3 at the beginning of this chapter.

Do not run the E&M calculator yet.

Step 2

From the Toolbar at the top of your screen, click on the button labeled "List." When the Lists Manager window shown in Figure 12-22 is displayed, select **Adult URI** and click the button labeled "Load List."

Step 3

Verify you are on the Sx tab.

Locate and click on the following symptom findings:

- (red button) Nasal passage blockage (stuffiness)

Step 4

Locate and click on the E&M button in the Toolbar at the top of your screen to invoke the Evaluation and Management Calculator window.

The Problem Screening checklist window is displayed.

Locate and click the boxes for the following:

✓ Active

✓ New Problem

The Evaluation and Management Calculator window is displayed. The calculated E&M code field should display "99213 Estab Outpatient Expanded H&P - Low Complexity Decisions," as it did in Exercise 70.

▶ **Figure 12-41** New Patient (circled in red) uses a different E&M code set.

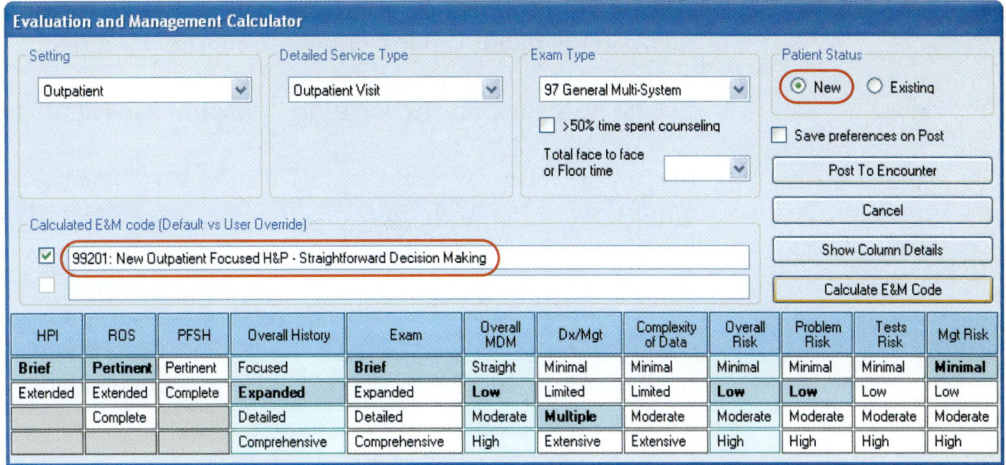

Step 5

Some E&M categories, such as outpatient, provide two sets of codes, one for new patients and one for established patients. The Patient Status field allows the E&M calculator to select the appropriate code set for categories that make this distinction. You have used this field in previous exercises and should be familiar with it. In this step, you will see its effect on coding.

Locate the section labeled "Patient Status" in the upper right corner of the calculator window. Click on the circle next to the label "New" (circled in red). Then click on the button labeled "Calculate E&M code." Compare your screen to Figure 12-41.

Notice the code and description "99201: New Outpatient Focused H&P - Straightforward Decision Making" (circled in red) are different from the code and description generated in step 4.

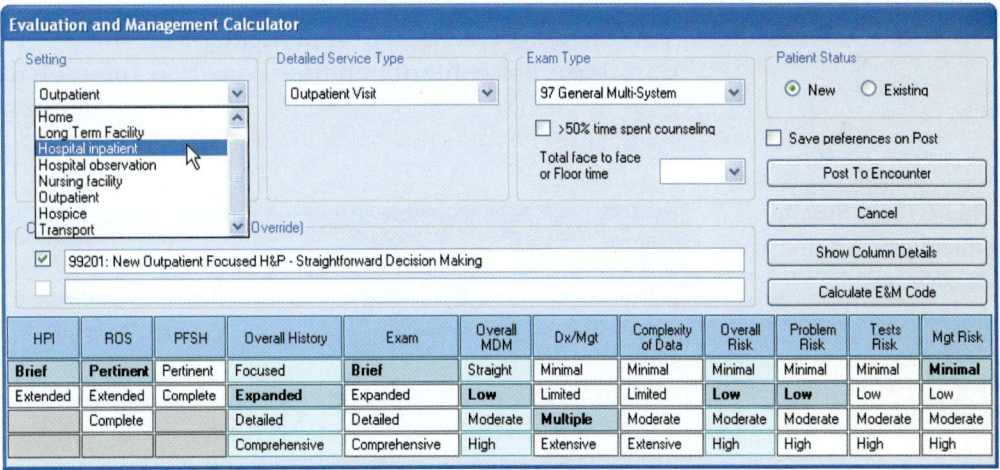

▶ **Figure 12-42** Drop-down list for the field labeled "Setting."

Step 6

Locate the field labeled "Setting" in the upper left corner of the E&M calculator window. This field allows you to set the location where the service was rendered. The field should already be set to Outpatient.

Click on the down arrow button within the field. A drop-down list of service locations is displayed (as shown in Figure 12-42).

Locate and click on the location "Hospital inpatient" in the drop-down list.

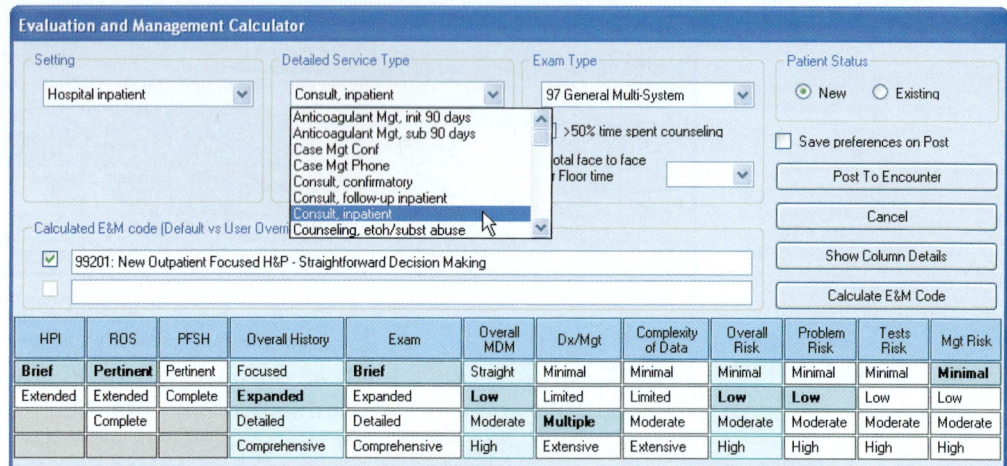

▶ Figure 12-43 Drop-down list for Detailed Service Type when inpatient is set.

Step 7

You will recall from earlier in this chapter that within categories of E&M codes for different locations there were also subcategories of the types of services that might be rendered. The Detailed Service Type field is used to indicate the type of service that was performed in a given setting.

Locate the field labeled "Detailed Service Type" in the center of the E&M calculator window. Click on the down arrow button within the field. A drop-down list of service types is displayed (as shown in Figure 12-43).

Locate and click on the service type "Consult inpatient." The "Detailed Service Type" field is related to and dependent on the "Setting" field—that is, the drop-down list contents change based on the type of facility selected in the "Setting" field.

▶ Figure 12-44 Hospital inpatient uses a different E&M code set.

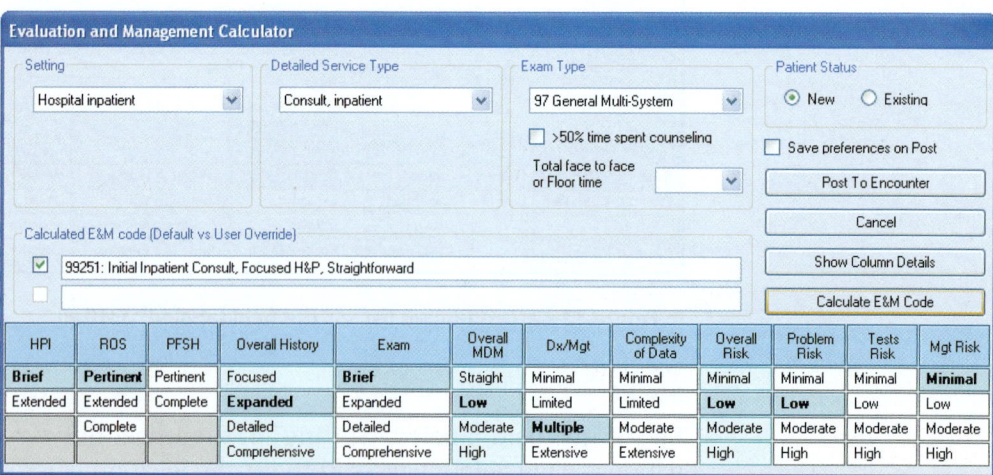

510   Chapter 12 | EHR Coding and Reimbursement

Step 8

Locate and click on the button labeled "Calculate E&M code." Compare your screen to Figure 12-44. Notice that inpatient services generate an entirely different E&M code, even though the encounter data has not been changed.

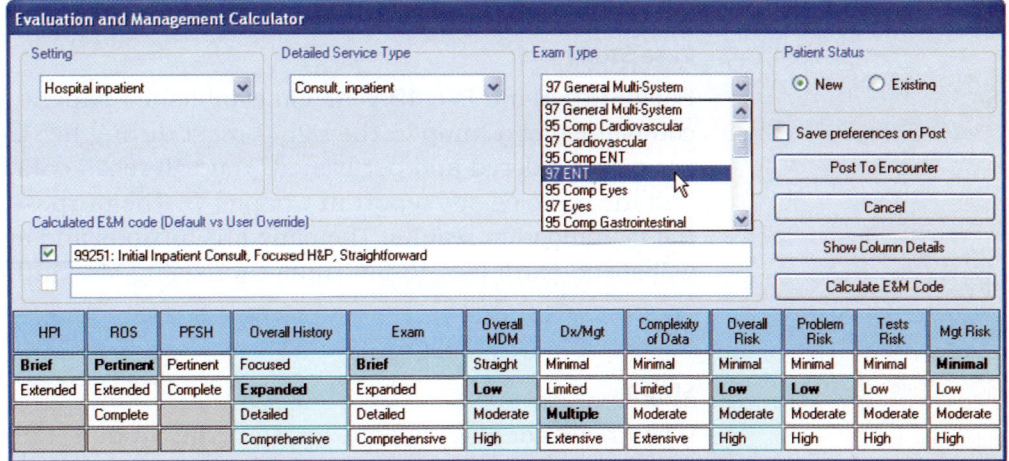

▶ Figure 12-45 Drop-down list of different exam types in E&M calculator.

Step 9

You will recall that in addition to the general multisystem exam, there are guidelines for 10 different specialty exams. Also, clinicians are permitted to use either the 1995 or 1997 guideline, whichever best suits their practice. The field labeled "Exam Type" allows the clinician to select the appropriate guideline for the E&M calculator to use.

Locate the field labeled "Exam Type" in the upper center of the E&M calculator window. Click on the down arrow button in the field. The drop-down list not only displays the various exam types, but indicates for each name if it is from the 1995 or 1997 guidelines.

Locate and click on the guideline labeled "97 ENT" as shown in Figure 12-45.

Locate and click on the button labeled "Calculate E&M code."

Compare the grid at the bottom of your E&M calculator window to Figure 12-44. Notice that changing the guideline from "97 general multisystem" to "97 ENT" changed the Exam column from "Brief" to "Expanded."

Step 10

Locate and click on the button labeled "Cancel" to close the E&M calculator window.

This completes Exercise 73. You may exit and close your program without printing.

Critical Thinking Exercise 74: Counseling an Established Patient

In this exercise you will use features of the software with which you are already familiar to document an encounter. You will then calculate the E&M code and post it to the encounter.

Case Study

Sally Sutherland is a 49-year-old established patient with Type II diabetes who complained of a lump in the right breast during her last checkup. A mammogram was ordered and performed. You will recall cataloging her mammogram and the radiologist's report in Chapter 2. The purpose of this visit is to discuss the mammogram results. The patient is anxious and apprehensive. The clinician will spend extra face-to-face time counseling Ms. Sutherland.

Step 1

If you have not already done so, start the Student Edition software.

Click Select on the Menu bar, and then click Patient.

In the Patient Selection window, locate and click on **Sally Sutherland**.

Step 2

Click Select on the Menu bar, and then click New Encounter.

Select the date **May 30, 2012**, the time **1:00 PM**, and the reason **Follow-Up**.

Make certain that you set the date and reason correctly. Compare your screen to the date, time, and reason printed in bold type before clicking on the OK button.

Step 3

Enter the chief complaint by locating the button in the toolbar labeled "Chief" and clicking on it.

In the dialog window that will open, type "**Review mammogram results**."

When you have finished typing, click on the button labeled "Close the note form."

Step 4

Begin the visit by taking Sally's vital signs and medical history using the "Diabetes" form. Locate and click on the button labeled "Forms" in the Toolbar at the top of your screen.

Locate and click on the form labeled "Diabetes" as you have done in previous exercises. Enter Sally's vital signs in the corresponding fields on the form as follows:

Temperature:	**98.6**
Respiration:	**28**
Pulse:	**83**
BP:	**150/90**
Weight:	**168**

Step 5

Locate and check the following diagnosis:

✓ Diabetes Mellitus Type II

Locate and click on the button labeled "Negs" in the Toolbar at the top of your screen.

When you have finished, check your work. If it is correct, proceed to step 6.

Step 6

Locate and click on the button labeled "Forms" in the Toolbar at the top of your screen to invoke the Forms Manager window again.

Locate and click on the form labeled "Hypertension."

When the Hypertension form is displayed, locate and click on the **Y** box for the diagnosis:

✓ Hypertension

Locate and click on the button labeled "Negs" in the Toolbar at the top of your screen.

When you have finished, check your work. If it is correct, click on the Encounter tab at the bottom of the screen.

Step 7

Verify that you are on the Sx tab.

Locate and click the small plus signs next to "Psychological symptoms" and "mood."

Locate and click on the following findings:

- (red button) nervous
- (red button) anxiety
- (red button) depression

When you have finished, check your work. If it is correct, proceed to step 8.

Step 8

Locate and click on the button labeled "Lists" in the Toolbar at the top of your screen to invoke the Lists Manager window.

Locate and click on the list labeled "M GY BREAST CA MGMT" (it is located near the bottom of the second column). Click on the button labeled "Load List."

Step 9

Click on the Sx tab, if you are not already there.

Locate and click the small plus sign next to "Breast lump."

Locate and click on the following symptom findings:

- ● (red button) in the right breast

The description will change to "Lump in the right breast."

Step 10

Click on the Hx tab.

Locate and click the small plus sign next to "reported mammogram."

Locate and click on the following finding:

- ● (red button) abnormal

The description will change to "A mammogram was abnormal."

Step 11

Click on Tx tab.

Locate and click the small plus signs next to "Tests" and "Pathology."

Locate and highlight the description, then click the Order button for the following test:

- 🧪 (order button) Fine Needle Aspiration

Verify that the test appears in the Plan section of the note before proceeding.

Step 12

Locate and click on the button labeled "Search" in the Toolbar at the top of your screen to invoke the "Search String" window. Position your mouse in the Search String field and enter the medical term "**mammogram**." Verify that you have spelled this correctly, and then click the button in the Search String window labeled "Search."

Step 13

Click on the Rx tab.

Locate and click on the small plus sign next to "Prev Medicine Results Document/Review Screening Mammography."

Locate and click on the small plus sign next to "Assessment Category."

Locate and click on the following findings:

- (red button) Highly Suggestive of Malignancy
- (red button) Communicated Mammogram Results to Patient Within 5 Days of Interpretation

Step 14

Locate and click on the button labeled "E&M" in the Toolbar at the top of your screen.

When the Problem Screening window is displayed, click the check boxes next to "chronic" for each of the diagnoses and then click on the button labeled "OK."

The E&M calculator window should be invoked.

Step 15

Verify that the Patient Status section in the upper right corner of the E&M calculator is set to "Existing." If it is not, click on the white circle next to "Existing" and then click on the button labeled "Calculate E&M Code."

Notice that the calculated E&M code is 99213.

Step 16

Locate and click on the checkbox next to ">50% time spent counseling."

Locate and click your mouse on the down arrow button in the field labeled "Face-to-face or Floor time." Select **30 minutes** from the drop-down list.

Locate and click on the button labeled "Calculate E&M Code."

Step 17

The Calculated E&M Code field should display "99214: Estab Outpatient Detailed H&P - Moderate Complexity Decisions." If this is the code displayed in your window, locate and click on the button labeled "Post To Encounter." If this is not the code calculated, click on the Cancel button, and review the previous steps to find your error.

 **Alert** — Do not close or exit the encounter until you have a printed copy in your hand. You will lose your work if you exit before printing.

Sally Sutherland   Page 1 of 1

Student: *your name or ID here*
Patient: Sally Sutherland: F: 3/16/1963: 5/30/2012 01:00PM

Chief complaint
The Chief Complaint is: Review mammogram resuts.

History of present illness
    Sally Sutherland is a 49 year old female.
    She reported: Lump in the right breast.
    Feeling nervous, anxiety, and depression.
    Not feeling tired or poorly and no recent weight change. No worsening vision.
    No increase in urinary frequency.
    No polydipsia. No tingling of the limbs and no numbness of the limbs.

Past Medical/Surgical history
Reported Hisotry:
    Tests: A mammogram was abnormal.

Physical findings
Vital Signs:

Vital Signs/Measurements	Value	Normal Range
Oral temperature	98.6 F	97.6 - 99.6
RR	28 breaths/min	18 - 26
PR	83 bpm	50 - 100
Blood pressure	150/90 mmHg	100-120/56-80
Weight	168 lbs	98 - 183

Eyes:
    General/bilateral:
    Optic Disc: º Normal.
    Retina: º Normal.

Cardiovascular:
    Heart Rate and Rhythm: º Normal.
    Heart Sounds: º S1 normal. º S2 normal.º No S3 heard. º No S4 heard.
    Murmurs: º No murmurs were heard.
    Heart Borders: º By percussion, heart size and position were normal.

Assessment
- Hypertesnion
- Type 2 diabetes mellitus

Plan
- Fine needle aspiration

Practice Management
- Mammography assessment category: highly suggestive of malignancy; Documented: mammogram findings communicated to patient within 5 days of interpretation; Estab outpatient detailed h&p - moderate complexity decision 99214; Total face to face time 30 min; Counseling and coordination of care was more than 50% of encounter time.

▶ Figure 12-46 Printed encounter note for Sally Sutherland.

Step 18

Click on the Print button on the Toolbar at the top of your screen to invoke the Print Data window.

Be certain there is a check mark in the box next to "Current Encounter" and then click on the appropriate button to either print or export a file, as directed by your instructor.

Compare your printout to Figure 12-46 if anything is missing, review the previous steps and correct your mistake.

Chapter Twelve Summary

CPT-4 and ICD-9-CM codes are national standards that are required on insurance claims for outpatient and other services.

ICD-9-CM codes (introduced in Chapter 7) are also used for billing. For both inpatient and outpatient facilities, the use of the correct ICD-9-CM code on a claim serves to explain or justify the medical reason for the services being billed.

Reimbursement for most inpatient hospitals is based entirely on the Diagnostic Related Group (DRG) determined from the primary and secondary diagnoses assigned by the attending physician.

Outpatient billing requires one or more ICD-9-CM codes be assigned to every procedure and the diagnosis must be appropriate to the procedure.

The use of HCPCS and CPT-4 codes for procedures is also required. CPT stands for Current Procedural Terminology. It was developed and is maintained by the AMA.

A group of the CPT-4 codes called Evaluation and Management (E&M) codes is used to bill for nearly every kind of patient encounter.

There are separate categories of E&M codes for different locations such as outpatient, inpatient hospital exams, nursing home visits, consults, emergency room doctors, and so on.

There are four levels of E&M codes within each category. The levels represent the least complicated exam (level 1) to the most complex exam (level 4), with higher levels paying the provider more.

The medical record for the encounter must support the level of E&M code billed with documented findings. An EHR can accurately calculate the correct level of E&M code from the findings that are documented.

There are seven components that are used in defining the level of E&M services. These components are:

- History
- Examination
- Medical Decision Making
- Counseling
- Coordination Of Care
- Nature Of Presenting Problem
- Time

The first three of these components, History, Examination, and Medical Decision Making, are called key components. Each of the key components has subcomponents called elements that determine the level of the component. Once the level of each of the key components is determined, the results are evaluated to calculate the correct level of E&M code.

Time is used to adjust the level of the E&M code only when counseling/coordination of care exceeds 50% of the face-to-face time.

Because the level of E&M code is dependent on the levels of multiple key components, merely adding more findings to only one key component may bring that component to a higher level, but that does not necessarily mean that the visit as a whole will qualify for the higher level E&M code.

Testing Your Knowledge of Chapter 12

1. What does the acronym E&M stand for?
2. How many levels are there for a category of E&M code?
3. Name the three key components of an E&M code.
4. How many levels are there for each key component?
5. How many key components determine the level of E&M code for an established patient?

Write the definitions for the following History acronyms:

6. HPI   _____
7. ROS   _____
8. PFSH   _____
9. Explain how the level of a general multisystem exam is determined.
10. What determines the level of risk?
11. What makes up face-to-face time?
12. When does time become a factor in determining the level of E&M code?
13. What does the E&M button on the Toolbar do?
14. How do you record an E&M code in the patient encounter note?
15. You should have produced three narrative documents of patient encounters. If you have not already done so, hand these in to your instructor with this test. The printed encounter notes will count as a portion of your grade.

Comprehensive Evaluation of Chapters 7–12

This comprehensive evaluation will enable you and your instructor to determine your understanding of the material covered in the second half of this book. Complete both the written test and the hands-on exercises provided below. Depending on the time provided, it may be necessary to do this in two separate sessions. Your instructor will advise you. Do not begin Part II if there will not be enough class time to complete it. You will need access to the Internet for Part III.

Part I—Written Exam

1. Where does the data that appears in the patient management tab come from?
2. Why would clinicians use trending of lab results and what type of results can be graphed?
3. Describe the benefits of having patients entering their own symptoms and history.
4. Why are childhood immunizations important?
5. List at least three ways that codified data in the EHR can be used to manage and prevent disease.
6. Describe a problem list and provide at least two reasons why clinicians use a problem list.
7. Describe how to create a flow sheet from a form.
8. What does it mean to cite a finding and how would you do it from a flow sheet?
9. How does an E-visit differ from provider-to-patient e-mails?
10. What are "evidence-based" guidelines?
11. Name at least three external sources of data for populating the EHR?
12. What is a growth chart percentile?
13. List the four components of the HIPAA Administrative Simplification Subsection.
14. Compare the difference between HIPAA Consent and HIPAA Authorization.
15. Does a provider need the patient's consent to share PHI with an authorized government agency?
16. Name the Covered Entities under HIPAA.
17. Name some advantages of a PHR.
18. Give an example of a specialty that might use annotated drawings in an encounter note.
19. How is the Internet changing healthcare? Give examples of changes.
20. List the three criteria of an Electronic Signature.

21. Name the key components of an E&M code.

22. Where are "bullets" used in E&M calculation?

For questions 23–30, select the acronym from the list below that best matches the description, and write it next to the number.

BMI	HPI	PDA
EPHI	MMR	PKI
HCPCS	OCR	VPN

23. _____ Information protected by the Security Rule

24. _____ Electronic Signature standard

25. _____ Calculation for height/weight ratio

26. _____ Procedure code set

27. _____ Three vaccines

28. _____ Enforces HIPAA Privacy Rule

29. _____ Element of a patient exam

30. _____ Method of Internet Security

Part II—Hands-On Exercise

The following exercise will require use of the Student Edition software and it may require a full class period to complete the exercise. Do not start the exercise unless there is sufficient time remaining to complete it.

Critical Thinking Exercise 75: Examination of a Patient with Arterial Disease

In this exercise, you will use all of the skills you have acquired to document this patient encounter. Complete each step in sequential order using the instructions and other information provided.

Case Study

Brenda Green is a 54-year-old female with a history of hypertension and possible peripheral arterial disease of the legs. During her last visit, she complained of pain in the legs and cold feet following exercise. After performing an ankle-brachial index test in the office, the clinician ordered an angiogram. Brenda is coming today for the results of her test and a follow-up exam.

Alert

Make certain you set the date and time correctly for this exercise.

Step 1

Start the Student Edition software and log in.

Click Select on the Menu bar, and then click Patient.

In the Patient Selection window, locate and click on **Brenda Green**.

Step 2

Click Select on the Menu bar, and then click New Encounter.

Select the date **May 31, 2012**, the time **10:15 AM**, and the reason **Office Visit**.

Compare your screen to the date, time, and reason printed in bold type before clicking on the OK button.

Step 3

Enter the Chief complaint: "**Patient reports leg pain after exercise**."

When you have finished typing, click on the button labeled "Close the Note Dialog."

Step 4

Begin the visit by recording Brenda's vital signs and Quick Screening Exam using a form.

Locate the Forms button on the Toolbar and select the form labeled "**Hypertension**." Enter Brenda's vital signs in the corresponding fields on the form as follows:

Temperature:	**98.6**
Respiration:	**22**
Pulse:	**78**
BP:	**130/90**
Weight:	**210**

When you have finished, check your work; if it is correct, proceed to step 5.

Step 5

Remain on the Forms tab.

Locate and click on checkbox for hypertension. The small circle will turn red.

● Hypertension ✓ Y

Enter the Quick Screening Exam portion by using the Negs button in the Toolbar at the top of your screen. The Quick Screening Exam items should be checked as follows:

Retina	✓ N
Optic Disc	✓ N
Heart Rate and Rhythm	✓ N
Heart Borders	✓ N
Murmurs	✓ N
Heart Sounds S1	✓ N
Heart Sounds S2	✓ N
Heart Sounds S3	✓ N
Heart Sounds S4	✓ N

Step 6

Locate and click on the button labeled "FS Form" in the Toolbar at the top of your screen to invoke the Flow Sheet view.

Locate and click on the button labeled "Cite" in the Toolbar at the top of your screen.

Move your mouse pointer over the column date "**5/17/2012**." The pointer should change to include a large question mark. Click on the column date. A window of findings from that encounter will be displayed.

Review the findings and then click the button labeled "Post To Encounter."

Locate and click on the button labeled "Cite" in the Toolbar at the top of your screen to turn off the Cite feature. Then locate and click on the button labeled "FS Form" in the Toolbar at the top of your screen to return to the Hypertension form.

Step 7

Locate the section of the Hypertension form labeled "Standard Orders."

Click on the checked boxes to remove the orders for the tests:

- ☐ Hematocrit
- ☐ Hemoglobin

Confirm each deletion by clicking on the OK button in the confirmation dialog box that will appear.

Step 8

Locate and click on the Manage tab at the bottom of the screen.

Review the patient's problem list. Locate and click on the problem "Atherosclerosis of the femoral artery" to highlight it.

Locate and click on the button labeled "Flowsheet" in the Toolbar at the top of your screen. The Flowsheet view will be invoked for the specific problem.

Locate and click on the button labeled "Cite" in the Toolbar at the top of your screen.

Locate the section of the Flowsheet with the label "Tests" (in a teal divider) by scrolling the window.

Cite an individual test result by moving your mouse pointer over the column "**5/18/2012**." The pointer should change to include a large question mark.

Locate the finding of Bilateral Angiography and click on the column with the abbreviation "72% blockage" (in red). The finding will be recorded in the current encounter.

Cite the findings from the previous exam by moving your mouse pointer over the date "**5/17/2012**" at the top of the column, and click on the date.

A window of findings from that encounter will be displayed.

Locate and click on the red button (in the Review Cite of Flowsheet window) for the finding:

- (red button) ordered bilateral angiography of the extremity

This will prevent a reorder of that test.

Locate and then click the button labeled "Post To Encounter."

> **Note**
>
> If you have difficulty locating the test finding of Bilateral Angiography in the problem-oriented flow sheet because it does not appear on the problem flow sheet, the most likely cause is a misstep with the Flowsheet and Cite buttons earlier in the exercise. Do the following to remedy the situation:
>
> Before citing anything in step 8, locate and click on the button labeled "Cite" in the Toolbar at the top of the screen to turn off the Cite feature.
> Then locate and click on the button labeled "Flowsheet" in the Toolbar at the top of the screen to close the flow sheet and return to the Patient Management Problem tab.
> Locate and click on the Encounter tab to return to the Encounter note view.
> Start Step 8 over again from the beginning. "Bilateral Angiography" should then appear in the flow sheet as indicated in the directions.

Step 9

Locate and click on the button labeled "Cite" in the Toolbar at the top of your screen to turn off the Cite feature. Then locate and click on the button labeled "Flowsheet" in the Toolbar at the top of your screen to return to Patient Management.

Locate and click on the Manage tab labeled "Medications." Review the patient's current medications.

When you have reviewed her medications, locate and click on the tab labeled "Encounter" at the bottom of the window to return to the encounter note view.

Step 10

Locate and click the assessment "Atherosclerosis of the femoral artery" in the encounter note (right pane). The finding will then be displayed in the left pane on the Edit tab.

Highlight the diagnosis description, then locate and click on the button labeled "Prompt" in the Toolbar at the top of your screen.

Locate and click on the Rx tab in the left pane. Locate and highlight **"Anticoagulants Warfarin sodium (Coumadin)**," and then click the Rx button on the Toolbar.

This will invoke the prescription writer.

Step 11

Enter the following prescription by selecting the following options as they are presented:

Rx Dosage: **2 mg**

Rx Brand: **Coumadin**

Enter the following data in the prescription fields:

Sig

Quantity: **1**

Frequency: **daily**

Per Day: **1**

Days: **30**

Dispense

Amount: **30**

Refill: **3**

Generic: **Y**

Verify that you have entered the information correctly, and then click the button labeled "Save Rx."

Step 12

Locate and click the button labeled "Search" in the Toolbar at the top of your screen. The Search window will be invoked. Type "**Low fat diet**" and click the Search button.

Locate and select the following findings from the list displayed in the Rx tab:

- (red button) Low Fat Diet
- (red button) Patient Education Dietary Low Fat Cooking
- (red button) Patient Education Dietary Changing Eating Habits

Step 13

Click on the button labeled "Search" on the Toolbar at the top of your screen. The Search String window will be invoked.

Type the search string "**INR**" and click on the Search button in the window.

If the left pane is not on the Rx tab, click on the Rx tab.

Locate and highlight the finding "**Anticoagulants management**."

Locate and click on the down arrow in the Entry Details Prefix field. Select "**Follow-up with**" from the drop-down list.

In the Entry Details Duration field, type "**2 weeks**" and press the Enter key on your keyboard.

Step 14

Create an annotated drawing to explain the angiography results to the patient.

Scroll the encounter note in the right pane to locate the imaging study finding "Bilateral Angiography." Click on the word "Bilateral." The left pane should change to the Edit tab.

Locate the context button (the second button from the right in the lower right corner of your window) and click on it. From the drop-down list displayed, choose "Add Object to Finding."

The drawing window will be invoked in the right pane.

If the cardiovascular drawing is not displayed, use the fields at the top of the drawing to select the Cardiovascular, Full Body, Front view from the drop-down lists.

Step 15

Once the correct illustration template is displayed, use the Toolbar in the drawing tool to set up the tool.

Locate and click on the down arrow next to the first button; then select "Circle" from the drop-down list.

Locate and click on the Lock button (with the padlock). It should have a white background.

Locate and click on the Color pallet button. When the window is displayed, select Blue. Click OK to close the Color pallet window.

Step 16

As closely as possible, replicate the drawing in Figure C-1.

Draw a blue circle over the femoral artery midway between the groin and the knee (as shown in Figure C-1).

Change the drawing tool.

Locate and click on the down arrow next to the first button, then select "Line" from the drop-down list.

Draw a horizontal line from the circle to the blank area of the drawing on the right.

Next, change the color to red by selecting the Color pallet button.

In the blank area of the drawing, draw two vertical, parallel lines to represent an enlarged view of the artery.

Change the drawing tool.

Locate and click on the down arrow next to the first button, then select "Brush" from the drop-down list.

Using the Brush, make a thick line on the interior of each of the parallel lines to represent the blockage in the artery (similar to Figure C-1).

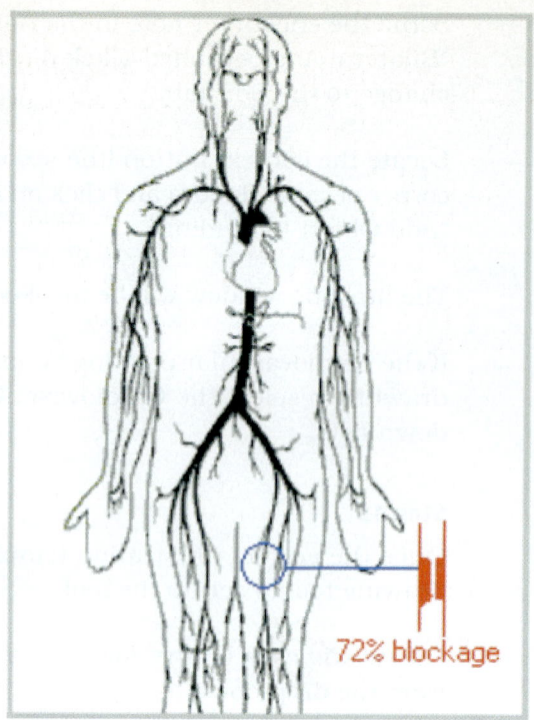

Anatomical Figure © MediComp Systems, Inc.

▶ **Figure C-1** Drawing of annotations to be performed in Exercise 75.

Annotate the drawing.

Locate and click on the down arrow next to the first button, then select "Text" from the drop-down list.

Click your mouse in the image to the right of the knee and a text field will open. Type "**72% blockage**."

Right click anywhere on the drawing except in the text box to display a list of options; click on "Complete Text" from the list displayed.

Compare your drawing to Figure C-1. If you need to correct the line or circle, change the tool button to "Select" and click on the object. Use the Delete button in the Toolbar and then redraw the correct element.

Step 17

Click the Print button on the *drawing toolbar*, **not** the Print button on the main Toolbar. The familiar Print Data window will be invoked.

Be certain there is a check mark in the box next to "Imager Drawing" and then click on the appropriate button to either print or export a file, as directed by your instructor.

Compare your printout or file output to Figure C-1.

When you have a printout of your annotated drawing in hand, close the Print Data window.

> **! Alert**
>
> **Do not exit the drawing or change tabs until you have a printed copy in your hand. You will lose your work if you exit before printing.**

Step 18

Locate and click on the Exit button in the *drawing toolbar* to close the drawing tool and redisplay the encounter note.

Step 19

Locate and click on the button labeled "Search" in the Toolbar at the top of your screen. The Search String window will be invoked.

Type the search string "Total cholesterol" and click on the Search button in the window.

Click on the Tx tab.

The left pane should display several findings with the words "Total Cholesterol" in them.

Locate and highlight the finding "Total plasma cholesterol" (the finding with the red button selected).

Click Graph on the Menu bar, and then click "Current Finding" from the drop-down list. The Graph window will be invoked with a graph of Brenda's recent cholesterol results.

Locate and click on the Print button in the upper left corner of the graph window to invoke the Print Data window.

Locate the check box for Total Cholesterol in the left column and click on it.

Locate and click on the appropriate button to either print or export a file, as directed by your instructor. When your graph has printed successfully, click on the Exit button in the window displaying the Total Cholesterol graph.

Step 20

Print a chart of Brenda's weight.

Click Graph on the Menu bar, and then click "Weight" from the drop-down list. The Graph window will be invoked with a graph of Brenda's weight measurements.

Locate and click on the Print button in the upper left corner of the graph window to invoke the Print Data window.

Locate the check box for Weight in the left column and click on it.

Locate and click on the appropriate button to either print or export a file, as directed by your instructor. When your graph has printed successfully, click on the Exit button in the window displaying the Total Cholesterol graph.

Step 21

Locate and click on the button labeled "E&M" in the Toolbar at the top of the screen to invoke the E&M calculator.

When the Problem Screening Checklist window is displayed, check the box next to "Chronic" for the diagnosis "Hypertension" and check the boxes next to

"Active" and "New Problem" for the diagnosis "Atherosclerosis of the femoral artery," and then click on the OK button.

Step 22

The E&M calculator window will be displayed.

Click on the Check box labeled ">**50% time spent counseling**."

Click the down arrow in the Face to face/Floor time field and select **50 minutes** from the drop-down list.

Click on the circle next to "Existing Patient."

Click on the button labeled "Calculate E&M Code."

The Code field should display "99215: Estab Outpatient Comprehensive H&P—High Complex Decisions."

If this is the code displayed in your window, locate and click on the button labeled "Post To Encounter."

> **Note**
>
> If the calculated E&M code is not 99215, verify that you have set the time fields in step 22. If the code is still not correct, click on the Cancel button, and review steps 4 to 13 to find your error and correct it, then repeat steps 21 and 22.

Step 23

Locate and click on the finding "Counseling" in the right pane (in the Practice Management section of the encounter note). The finding should appear on the Edit tab in the left pane.

Locate and click on the Finding Note button (in the lower right corner of your screen).

Type the following text into the Finding Note window: "**30 minutes of visit spent on dietary and Coumadin counseling.**"

When you have finished, click your mouse on the button labeled "Close the note form."

> **Alert**
>
> Do not close or exit the encounter until you have a printed copy in your hand. You will lose your work if you exit before printing.

Step 24

Click on the Print button on the Toolbar at the top of your screen to invoke the Print Data window.

Be certain there is a check mark in the box next to "Current Encounter" and then click on the appropriate button to either print or export a file, as directed by your instructor.

Part III—Internet Exercise

You will need access to the Internet for this portion of your evaluation.

Critical Thinking Exercise 76: Patient Researches Medication

Case Study

Brenda Green has been prescribed a new drug. Upon returning home from the doctor's office, she uses the Internet to look up information about it.

Step 1

Start your web browser. In the address bar type the URL: **www.webmd.com.**

Step 2

When the web site is displayed, locate the search field and type: **warfarin**.

Click on the Search button.

Step 3

A list of search results will be displayed.

Locate and click on the link for "**Warfarin for arterial fibrillation**."

Step 4

When the article is displayed, locate and click on the link "**Print Article**."

If your instructor normally requires printouts of your work, click the Print button.

If you normally submit your work as a file, copy the URL displayed in the print window, and paste it into an e-mail or text file. Consult your instructor as to his or her preference for this step.

Give your instructor the following printouts or files along with your written exam:

1. Annotated drawing of femoral artery
2. Graph of Total Cholesterol
3. Graph of Brenda Green's Weight
4. Encounter note for May 31, 2012, for Brenda Green
5. Printed WebMD article or file containing URL of print window.

Glossary

ABC An acronym for Alternative Billing Codes, which are used to bill for alternative medicine such as acupuncture, behavioral health, homeopathy, and others.

ABG A medical abbreviation for arterial blood gas.

ABN An acronym for Advance Beneficiary Notice—information presented to the patient in advance that the test or procedure will not be covered by Medicare or insurance. The same acronym is sometimes uses as the abbreviation for Abnormal.

Access Control (HIPAA) Technical policies and procedures to allow access only to those persons or software programs that have been granted rights to access EPHI.

Acetaminophen A medicine used as an alternative to aspirin to relieve pain and fever. The active ingredient in Tylenol.

Acute Severe, but of short duration.

Acute Self-Limiting Problems that normally resolve themselves over a short period of time.

Administrative Safeguards (HIPAA) These are the administrative functions that should be implemented to meet the standards of the HIPAA Security Rule. These include assigning security responsibility to an individual and security training requirements.

Administrative Simplification (HIPAA) The Administrative Simplification Subsection of HIPAA covers providers, health plans, and clearinghouses. It has four distinct components: Transactions and Code Sets, Uniform Identifiers, Privacy, and Security.

AHIMA An acronym for American Health Information Management Association, the leading organization of health information professionals.

AHRQ An acronym for Agency for Healthcare Research and Quality, a Public Health Service agency in the Department of Health and Human Services to support research designed to improve the quality, safety, efficiency, and effectiveness of healthcare for all Americans.

Alert A warning, message, or reminder automatically generated by EHR systems based on logical rules.

Allergy (tab) A feature on the Patient Management tab that provides a list of the patient's allergies, or the fact that the patient has no known allergies. This information is reviewed before writing a prescription.

AMA An acronym for American Medical Association; also an acronym for Against Medical Advice.

Ambulatory Setting Outpatient setting.

Amoxicillin An oral antibiotic; a synthetic penicillin derived from ampicillin.

ANA An acronym for the American Nurses Association.

Angina Pectoris A disease marked by brief, recurrent pain, usually in the chest and left arm, caused by a sudden decrease of the blood supply to the heart muscle.

Angiogram An x-ray (roentgenogram) of the flow of blood after injecting a contrast material.

Angiography *See* Angiogram.

Annotated Drawing Anatomical drawings of the body and body systems on which the clinician has marked observations and text notes. Medcin-based software is capable of linking an annotated drawing to a relevant finding.

ANSI An acronym for American National Standards Institute, a private, nonprofit organization that administers and creates product and communication standards in the United States. ANSI uses a voluntary consensus process to arrive at and maintain standards not only in healthcare but also in many diverse areas of industry and manufacturing.

ARRA An acronym for American Recovery and Reinvestment Act, federal legislation that included the HITECH Act. *See* HITECH Act.

Assessment (chart) The diagnosis or determination arrived at by the clinician from the medical examination, subjective and objective findings, and test results.

Asthma A generally chronic disorder often caused by an allergic origin, characterized by wheezing, coughing, labored breathing, and a suffocating feeling.

Auscultation Listening (in this text, listening with a stethoscope).

Authorization (HIPAA) Authorization differs from consent in that it does require the patient's permission to disclose PHI. Under the HIPAA Privacy Rule, authorization is required for most disclosures of PHI other than for treatment of the patient, seeking payment, or operation of the healthcare facility.

Auto Negative *See* Negs (button).

BID A medical abbreviation for "twice daily."

BIPAP A medical abbreviation for Bilevel Positive Airway Pressure.

Blood Glucose Level The amount of glucose (a type of sugar) in the blood at the time the specimen is taken. A random blood glucose test is done without regard to when the patient last ate. A fasting blood glucose test is done after a patient has not had food or drink (except water) for 12 hours.

BMI An acronym for Body Mass Index, a number that shows body weight adjusted for height.

BMP A medical abbreviation for basic metabolic panel.

Bradycardia Abnormally slow heart rate (less than 60 beats per minute).

Bronchitis A disease marked by inflammation of the bronchial tubes.

Browse (button) Displays the current finding's position in the Medcin nomenclature hierarchy. Also a tab in the software.

Bullets (for E&M) A bullet is a typographic character that looks like this: • (a solid black circle). Bullets are printed in the E&M guideline tables next to certain individual elements of the examination pertaining to a body area or organ system. The level of the examination component when calculating E&M code is determined by the number of findings in the exam that corresponded to elements in the guideline table with bullet characters printed next to them.

Business Associate Agreement The HIPAA Privacy Rule requires covered entities that use the services of other persons or businesses to obtain a written agreement that the business associate will comply with the protection of PHI under the Privacy Rule.

Button (software) A raised or indented object in the software used to invoke an action or change of state when clicked on with a mouse. Found in most Windows software programs, buttons usually contain a word or icon representing their function.

Bypass Surgery See Cardiac Bypass.

Cardiac Bypass A surgical shunt to divert blood supply from one circulatory path to another.

Cardiac Catheterization A test to evaluate the heart and arteries. A thin flexible tube is threaded through a blood vessel into the heart, then a contrast material is injected to trace the movement of blood through the coronary arteries.

Cardiovascular The heart and the system of blood vessels.

Care Plan (tab) A feature on the Patient Management tab that provides a view of the plan from each previous encounter in a problem-oriented view. It is organized by problem and encounter date for which the patient was seen for that problem.

CAT scan Computerized Axial Tomography uses multiple x-rays and a computer to generate images of cross sections of the body.

CBC An acronym for Complete Blood Count, which is a lab test that includes separate counts for both white and red blood cells.

CC See Chief complaint.

CCC An acronym for Clinical Care Classification system used by nurses to codify documentation of patient care in any setting. It is an evolution of the HHCC nursing codes.

CCHIT An acronym for Certification Commission for Healthcare Information Technology, a nonprofit organization that certifies EHR systems.

CDA An acronym for Clinical Document Architecture, an HL7 standard for incorporating clinical text reports or other information in a Claim Attachment.

CDC An acronym for the Centers for Disease Control, an agency of the U.S. Department of Health and Human Services.

CDISC An acronym for Clinical Data Interchange Standards Consortium, an organization that has created standards that enable sponsors, vendors, and clinicians to acquire and exchange data used in clinical drug trials. CDISC has become part of HL7.

CDR An acronym for Clinical Data Repository, a database used to aggregate EHR data from several disparate systems.

CHCS II An acronym for Composite Health Care System II, the U.S. Department of Defense Electronic Health Record System.

CHF A medical abbreviation for Congestive Heart Failure.

Chief Complaint A concise statement describing the symptom, problem, condition, diagnosis, physician-recommended return, or other factor that is the reason for the encounter, usually stated in the patient's words.

Chronic Disease or problem that lasts a long time or recurs often.

Cite (software) A feature of the software that allows follow-up visits to be quickly documented by bringing forward findings from previous exams into the current encounter. While doing so, the clinician can update or make any changes to the finding without affecting the previous encounter.

Clearinghouse See Healthcare Clearinghouse.

Clinical Terminology An organized list of medical phrases and codes. See Nomenclature.

Clinical Vocabulary An organized list of medical phrases and codes. See Nomenclature.

CME An acronym for Continuing Medical Education, courses required to maintain licenses for licensed healthcare professionals.

CMS An acronym for the Centers for Medicare and Medicaid Services, an agency of the U.S. Department of Health and Human Services (formerly HCFA).

COB Coordination of Benefits; when a patient is covered by more than one health insurance plan, the plans involved determine how much each plan is to pay. A HIPAA transaction permits the plans to do this electronically.

Codified Data (chart) EHR data with each finding assigned a standard code assures uniformity of the medical records, eliminates ambiguities about the clinician's meaning, and facilitates communication between multiple systems.

Comprehensive Metabolic Chem Panel A blood test to determine blood sugar level, electrolytes, fluid balance, kidney function, and liver function. The panel measures (in blood) the sodium, potassium, calcium, chloride, carbon dioxide, glucose, blood urea nitrogen (BUN), creatinine, total protein, albumin, bilirubin, alkaline phosphatase transferase (ALP), aspartate amino transferase (AST), and alamine amino transferase (ALT).

Consent (HIPAA) Under the revised HIPAA Privacy Rule, a patient gives consent to the use of their PHI for purposes of treatment, payment, and operation of the healthcare practice by acknowledging that they have received a copy of the office's privacy policy. HIPAA privacy consent should not be confused with consent to perform a medical procedure.

Contingency Plan Strategies for recovering access to EPHI should a medical facility experience an emergency, such as a power outage or disruption of critical business operations. The goal is to ensure that EPHI is available when it is needed.

Covered Entity (HIPAA) HIPAA refers to healthcare providers, plans, and clearinghouses as Covered Entities. In the context of this book, think of covered entity as the medical practice and all of its employees.

CPOE An acronym for Computerized Physician Order Entry; also for Computerized Provider Order Entry.

CPR A medical abbreviation for cardio-pulmonary resuscitation.

CPRI An acronym for Computer-Based Patient Record Institute, formed to promote the universal and effective use of electronic healthcare information systems to improve health and the delivery of healthcare was merged into HIMSS in 2002.

CPT-4 An acronym for Current Procedural Terminology, fourth edition. CPT-4 are standardized codes for reporting medical services, procedures, and treatments performed for patients by the medical staff. CPT-4 is owned by the American Medical Association.

CQM An acronym for Clinical Quality Measures, data reported to CMS by a provider which indicates the quality of care provided by measuring the quantity of patients assessed or successfully treated according to evidence-based best practices.

Cross-walk (codes) A reference table for translating a code from one set to a code with the same meaning in another code set. For example, the Medcin and SNOMED-CT nomenclatures each have tables for translating a finding code to an ICD-9-CM code.

Cruciate Ligament (of the knee) Two ligaments in the knee joint that cross each other from the femur to the tibia. The anterior one limits extension and rotation.

CT (codes) An acronym for Clinical Terms. *See* Read codes.

CT Scan Computerized Tomography (*see* CAT scan).

CVP A medical abbreviation for cerebral vascular pressure.

DAW The acronym for Dispensed As Written is used on a prescription as an instruction to dispense the exact brand of medication specified. Do not substitute a generic equivalent drug.

Decision Support *See* Medical Decision Support.

Decryption A method of converting an encrypted message back into regular text using a mathematical algorithm and a string of characters called a "key." *See also* Encryption.

Description (entry detail) The Description field (in entry details) presents the text of the currently selected finding exclusive of any attached free text. The user cannot enter or modify the description in this field.

Diabetes Mellitus A chronic form of diabetes; characterized by an insulin deficiency, an excess of sugar in the blood and urine, and by hunger, thirst, and gradual loss of weight.

Diagnosis A disease or condition; or the process of identifying the diseased condition. Generally codified using ICD-9CM.

DICOM An acronym for Digital Imaging and Communication. It is a standard for communication and file structure for transfer of digital images between equipment and computer systems.

Digital Images (chart) EHR data in image format. This includes diagnostic images, digital x-rays, as well as documents scanned into the EHR. *See also* Scanned Images. Image data usually requires specific software to view the image.

Discrete Data (chart) EHR data in computer format. Discrete data is typically either Fielded or Codified. Fielded data identifies the type of information by its position in the EHR record. Codified data pairs each piece of information with a code that identifies the information in uniform way.

DOQ-IT An acronym for Doctors' Office Quality Information Technology, a demonstration project that aims to provide implementation, education, and quality improvement assistance for small- to medium-sized physician offices migrating from paper charts to an EHR.

Drop-down List A standard feature in most Windows software, which displays a list of items the user may select when a mouse is clicked in the field or on a down-arrow button next to the field.

Drug Formulary Drug formularies are used to look up drugs by names or therapeutic class, provide an updated list of the drugs that are available in the inventory, provide information on costs, indications for use, treatment recommendations, dosage, guidelines, andprescribing information. Health insurance programs use the term *formulary* for plan-specific drug lists.

DTaP An acronym for Diphtheria, Tetanus, acellular Pertussis (whooping cough); a combination vaccine.

DUR An acronym for Drug Utilization Review, which is the process of comparing a prescription drug to a patient's history and recent medications for contraindications, overdosing, underdosing, allergic reactions, drug-to-drug interactions, and drug/food interactions.

Duration (entry detail) The Duration field is used to enter a number and a unit of time related to the duration of the currently selected finding. The time unit can be "second," "minute," "hour," "day," "week," "month," "year," or their plurals. A window with keypad for entering duration can be invoked by double-clicking the mouse in the Duration field.

Dx An abbreviation for Diagnosis (also Diagnosis tab in the software).

Dx/Mgt Options An abbreviation used in the E&M calculator for Diagnosis and/or Management Options. The number of possible diagnoses and management options are factors in the Medical Decision Making component when determining the E&M code.

Dysplasic Polyp Abnormal growth, a tumor.

E&M (codes) An acronym for Evaluation and Management codes, which are a subset of CPT-4 codes used to bill for nearly every kind of patient encounter, such as physician office visits, inpatient hospital exams, nursing home visits, consults, emergency room doctors, and scores of other services. *See also* Key Components.

E&M Calculator A pop-up window in EHR software, which calculates then displays Evaluation and Management codes by analyzing the findings in the current encounter note.

ECG An acronym for Electrocardiogram.

EDI An acronym for Electronic Data Interchange. Information exchanged electronically as data in codified transactions.

EHR An acronym for Electronic Health Records—the portions of a patient's medical records that are stored in a computer system as well as the functional benefits derived from having an electronic health record. Also known as Electronic Medical Records, Computerized Patient Records, or Electronic Chart.

Electrolyte Panel A blood test that measures the levels of the minerals sodium, potassium, and chloride in the blood. The test also measures the level of carbon dioxide, which takes the form bicarbonate when dissolved in the blood. Certain medications can create in electrolyte imbalance, which is often the reason an Electrolyte Panel is ordered for patients on those medications.

Electronic Signature A method of marking an electronic record as "signed" having the same legal authority as a written signature. The electronic signature process involves the successful identification and authentication of the signer at the time of the signature, binding of the signature to the document, and nonalterability of the document after the signature has been affixed. *See also* How Electronic Signatures Work in Chapter 10.

Eligible Professionals Providers designated as eligible to receive incentive payments under the HITECH Act.

EMR An acronym for Electronic Medical Record.

Encounter The medical record of an interaction between a patient and a healthcare provider.

Encryption A method of converting an original message of regular text into encoded text, which is unreadable in its encrypted form. The text is encrypted by means of an algorithm using a private "key." *See also* Decryption.

Endoscopy Examination of the digestive tract using a flexible tube with a light and camera.

ENT An acronym for Ears, Nose, and Throat.

Entry Details The bottom portion of the Student Edition software window contains 10 fields that can be used to enter additional information about, or modify the meaning of, the finding that is selected at that time. *See* Description, Prefix, Modifier, Results, Status,Episode, Onset, Duration, Value, Units, or Note Textbox.

EPHI (HIPAA) Protected Health Information in electronic form.

Episode (entry detail) The Episode button is used to display the episode dialog window. This window is used to enter or edit data regarding the frequency or interval of occurrence of the currently selected finding.

ER An abbreviation for Emergency Room or emergency department.

E-Visit An E-visit is a patient encounter conducted over the Internet, without an office visit. The patient enters symptom, history, and HPI information, which is then reviewed by a clinician, who communicates via the Internet to ask additional questions, and provides a diagnosis, treatment orders, and patient education. E-visits are used only for nonurgent visits and are reimbursed by a growing number of insurance plans.

Exacerbate To cause a disease or its symptoms to become more severe; to aggravate the condition.

Face-to-Face Time The total time both before and after a patient visit (in the office or other or outpatient setting) such as taking patient history, performing the exam, reviewing lab results, planning for follow-up care, and communicating with other providers about the patient's case.

Family History (tab) A feature on the Patient Management tab that provides a list of the patient's family history items recorded in the EHR during all previous encounters.

FDA An acronym for Food and Drug Administration, an agency of the U.S. Department of Health and Human Services. This federal agency regulates prescription and nonprescription drugs.

FEIN Federal Employer Identification Number—a number assigned by the U.S. Internal Revenue Service, also known as a business tax ID.

FEV$_1$ Forced Expired Volume in one second; the volume of air expired in the first second of maximal exhalation after a full inhalation. This can be used to measure of how quickly full lungs can be emptied.

Finding A precorrelated combination of terms from a nomenclature or clinical terminology into a clinically relevant phrase.

Floor/Unit Time The total time both before and after a patient visit (in the hospital or nursing facility) such as taking patient history, performing the exam, reviewing lab results, planning for follow-up care, and communicating with other providers about the patient's case.

Flow Sheet (software) A feature of the software that presents data from multiple encounters in column format resembling a spreadsheet. Flow sheets allow findings from any previous encounter to be cited into the current note. Flow sheets can be created based on a list, a form, or a problem.

Forms (software) Forms are used to consistently display a desired group of findings in a presentation that allows for quick entry of not only the selected findings but of any entry details as well. Forms are selected from the Forms Manager on the Forms tab. Multiple forms may be used to document an encounter.

Forms Manager A window in the EHR software used to organize and select Forms. See Forms.

Formulary See Drug Formulary.

Free text EHR data that is not codified; may be attached to a codified finding as supplemental notes.

FVC An acronym for Forced Vital Capacity.

Gallop An abnormal heartbeat marked by three distinct sounds, like the gallop of a horse.

Gastrointestinal The stomach and the intestines.

Generalized Pallor An unusual paleness, a lack of color especially in the face.

Genitourinary The genital and urinary organs.

GI/GU An acronym for Gastrointestinal/Genitourinary body systems.

Glucose Monitors Home device used by diabetes patients to monitor glucose levels.

GMDN An acronym for Global Medical Device Nomenclature, used to identify the medical devices for ordering, inventory, or regulatory purposes, but does not provide for the codification of data from the devices.

Google™ An Internet web site that provides a free, high-speed index of nearly every piece of information on the World Wide Web. The name is derived from Googol, the mathematical term for the number 1 followed by 100 zeros. Access Google by typing the address www.google.com in an Internet browser.

H&P An acronym for History and Physical.

HAC An acronym for Hospital acquired condition, an infection or other medical problem occurring after admission.

HCAHPS is an acronym for Hospital Consumer Assessment Healthcare Providers and Systems, a standardized survey instrument and data collection methodology developed by NCQA for measuring patients' perspectives on care.

HCFA An acronym for the Health Care Financing Administration, which has since been renamed CMS. See CMS.

HCPCS An acronym for Healthcare Common Procedure Coding System. HCPCS is an extended set of billing codes for reporting medical services, procedures, and treatments including codes not listed in CPT-4 codes.

HDL High Density Lipoprotein cholesterol in blood plasma, sometimes referred to as good cholesterol because of its tendency to pull LDL cholesterol out of the artery wall.

Health Maintenance EHR system component to provide preventative health recommendations.

Healthcare Clearinghouse A computer system or covered entity that performs the specific function of translating non-standard EDI transactions into HIPAA-compliant transactions.

HEENT An acronym for Head, Eyes, Ears, Nose, Mouth, Throat (body system).

Hematocrit A blood test to determine the ratio of packed red blood cells to the volume of whole blood; also the result of the test.

Hematologic Blood and blood forming organs (discussed in the text as a component of a physical exam).

Hemoglobin A1c A test that measures the average amount of sugar in the patient's blood over the past three months.

Hepatic Function Panel A blood test used to determine liver function and liver disease. The panel measures total protein, albumin, bilirubin, alkaline phosphatase transferase (ALP), aspartate amino transferase (AST), and alamine amino transferase (ALT).

HepB An acronym for Hepatitis B (vaccine).

HHCC An acronym for Home Health Care Classification nursing codes developed to codify documentation by home care nurses, the code set has evolved for use in all clinical settings and is now referred to as CCC.

HHS An acronym for U.S. Department of Health and Human Services.

Hib An acronym for Haemophilus Influenza Type B (vaccine).

HIMSS An acronym for Healthcare Information and Management Systems

Glossary 533

Society, which is an organization that provides leadership in healthcare for the management of technology, information, and change through member services, education and networking opportunities, and publications. Members include healthcare professionals, hospitals, corporate healthcare systems, clinical practice groups, HIT supplier organizations, healthcare consulting firms, and government agencies.

HIPAA An acronym for Health Insurance Portability and Accountability Act (of 1996). HIPAA law regulates many things; however, healthcare workers often use the term HIPAA when they actually mean only the Administrative Simplification Subsection of HIPAA. *See* Administrative Simplification (HIPAA).

HIT An acronym for Health Information Technology; also Healthcare Information Technology.

HITECH Act An acronym for the Health Information Technology for Economic and Clinical Health Act, federal legislation which promotes the widespread adoption of EHR systems by authorizing incentive payments for providers that use EHR and financial penalties for those who continue using paper charts.

HIV An acronym for Human Immunodeficiency Virus (disease).

HL7 An acronym for Health Level Seven, the leading messaging standard used to exchange clinical and administrative data between different healthcare computer systems.

Holter Monitor A device worn by the patient to record the heart rhythm continuously for 24 hours. This provides a record that can be analyzed by a cardiologist to determine any irregular or abnormal activity of the heart. Named for Dr. Norman Holter, its inventor.

HPI An acronym for History of Present Illness, which is a chronological description of the development of the patient's present illness from the first sign or symptom or from the previous encounter to the present.

Hx An abbreviation for History. (Also the History tab in the software.)

Hyperlipidemia High levels of fat in the blood, such as cholesterol and triglycerides.

Hypertension A disease of abnormally high blood pressure.

Hypotension Abnormally low blood pressure.

ICD-9-CM An acronym for International Classification of Diseases, Ninth Revision, Clinical Modifications, a system of standardized codes to classify mortality and morbidity. ICD-9-CM is currently published in three volumes. The first two volumes provide a listing and an index of diagnosis codes. The third volume, however, lists codes for hospital inpatient procedures.

ICD-10 An acronym for International Classification of Diseases, Tenth Revision, a revision of the ICD-9 codes; scheduled to replace ICD-9-CM as the standard diagnoses codes for the United States in October 2013.

ICD-10-PCS International Classification of Diseases, Tenth Revision, Procedure Coding System (but not derived from the ICD-10 codes). PCS stands for Procedure Coding System, and it is intended to replace inpatient procedure codes in ICD-9-CM volume 3. The ICD-10-PCS is not used for billing at this time.

ICNP An acronym for International Classification for Nursing Practice, which is intended as an organizing structure for mapping other nursing terminologies.

Icon (software) In computer software, a small image usually used on a button to represent the purpose of the button—for example, a picture of a printer on the Print button.

ICU An acronym for Intensive Care Unit, a special section of the hospital with monitoring equipment and staff for seriously ill patients.

IHS An acronym for Indian Health Service, an agency of the U.S. Department of Health and Human Services responsible for providing federal health services to American Indians and Alaska natives.

Immunologic The immune system; discussed as a component of evaluation during a physical exam.

Implementation Specifications An additional detailed instruction for implementing a specific security standard under the HIPAA Security Rule.

Incidental Disclosures (HIPAA) HIPAA Privacy Rule permits incidental uses and disclosures of protected health information when the covered entity has in place reasonable safeguards and minimum necessary policies and procedures to protect an individual's privacy.

Information System Activity Review (HIPAA) A regular review of records such as audit logs, access reports, and security incident tracking reports. The information system activity review helps to determine if any EPHI is used or disclosed in an inappropriate manner.

Inpatient A hospital patient who stays overnight.

IOM An acronym for Institute of Medicine of the National Academies, a nonprofit organization created to provide unbiased, evidence-based, and authoritative information and advice concerning health and science policy.

IPV Inactivated Polio Virus (Salk vaccine).

JCAHO Joint Commission on Accreditation of Healthcare Organizations.

Key Components There are seven components that are evaluated to calculate the CPT-4 code for E&M services. Three of the components—history, examination, and medical decision making—are called the key components because they are used to determine the level of E&M services. *See also* E&M Codes.

Kiosk An unattended computer terminal for use by the patients in the waiting area.

LAN An acronym for Local Area Network, a network of computers that share data and programs located on a central computer called a server.

Laparoscopy Examination of the abdominal cavity through a small incision using a fiber optic instrument.

Laptop Computer A self-contained, battery-operated computer, which typically includes the screen, keyboard, mouse, and speakers, in a package about the size of a standard notebook.

LDL Low Density Lipoprotein cholesterol in blood plasma; sometimes referred to as bad cholesterol, it is often associated with clogged arteries.

Leapfrog Group A coalition of 150 of the largest employers who created a strategy that tied purchase of group health insurance benefits to quality care standards, promoted Computerized Physician Order Entry, and the use of an EHR.

Lipids Test Panel A blood test that measures the levels of lipids (fats) in the bloodstream. A lipids profile measures total cholesterol, triglycerides, HDL (high-density lipoprotein), and LDL (low-density lipoprotein).

LIS An acronym for Laboratory Information System, a computer system that connects to and collects data from lab test instruments.

List A subset of findings (typically) used for a particular condition or type of exam, making it easier to read and navigate.

List (button) A button on the Student Edition software Toolbar that invokes the List Manager. *See* List Manager.

List Manager A window from which the user may select and load a List.

List Size (button) A feature of the software that controls how many findings are displayed in the nomenclature tree. List Size 1 displays the least number of findings; List Size 3 displays the most.

Login A computer screen requiring the user to enter their name or ID (and password) before gaining access to the programs; or the action of entering a program through such a screen. EHR software typically requires the user to "log in." Note that some systems use the term "log on" for this function.

LOINC An acronym for Logical Observation Identifier Names and Codes. LOINC was created and is maintained by the Regenstrief Institute, affiliated with the Indiana University School of Medicine, and is an important clinical terminology for laboratory test orders and results.

Lymphatic System A network of lymph nodes and small vessels that collects lymph and returns it to the bloodstream.

Macular Degeneration A disease marked by the loss of central vision in both eyes.

Malicious Software Software such as viruses, Trojans, and worms create an unauthorized infiltration to computer networks that can damage or destroy data or cause expensive and time-consuming repairs. Malicious software is frequently brought into an organization through e-mail attachments and programs that are downloaded from the Internet. One requirement of the HIPAA Security Rule is to protect against malicious software.

Mammogram An x-ray of the breast that can be used to detect tumors before they can be seen or felt.

Mammography *See* Mammogram.

MDM An acronym for Medical Decision Making (an E&M key component).

Meaningful Use Criteria providers must meet to qualify for incentive payments under the HITECH Act.

Med/Surg Med/Surg is an abbreviation for Medical/Surgical History on a tab in the Patient Management feature. It provides a list of the patient's past medical or surgical history items recorded in the EHR during all previous encounters.

MEDCIN A medical nomenclature and knowledge base developed by Medicomp Systems, Inc. Recognized as a national standard, it is incorporated in many commercial EHR systems as well as the U.S. Department of Defense CHCS II system.

Medical Decision Making A key component in calculating the level of E&M code; the level of complexity in Medical Decision Making is determined by the number of diagnoses and management options, the amount or complexity of data to be reviewed, and the risk of complications or morbidity or mortality.

Medical Decision Support Computer- or Internet-based systems used to improve the process and outcome of medical decisions by delivering evidence-based information to the clinician who is determining the diagnosis or treatment orders.

Medication List (tab) A feature on the Patient Management tab that provides a list of the medications that the patient currently is taking. The Medication list is always reviewed before writing new prescriptions.

Menu Bar The Menu Bar consists of a row of words across the top of the Student Edition software screen: File, Select, Enter, Options, Forms, Summary, Graph, and Help. Clicking the mouse on any of the words on the Menu Bar will display list of related software functions. Clicking the mouse on an item in the list will invoke that function.

Metformin An oral medication used along with a diet and exercise program to control high blood sugar in diabetic patients.

Microscopy Studies or images of studies performed using a microscope.

Minimum Necessary Standard (HIPAA) A standard in the HIPAA Privacy Rule intended to limit unnecessary or inappropriate access to and disclosure of PHI beyond what is necessary. The minimum necessary standard does not apply to disclosures to or requests for information used by a healthcare provider for treatment of the patient.

MMR An acronym for a combination of vaccines to immunize against Measles, Mumps, Rubella (German measles).

MODEM An acronym for Modulate-Demodulate. It is a device that converts computer data into signals that can be sent over a standard telephone connection. A second modem on the receiving end converts the signals back to data for the receiving computer.

Modifier (entry detail) The Modifier field (in entry details) is used to modify a selected finding. For example, the finding "Pain" may be qualified as mild, severe, and such.

Morbidity A diseased state or symptom.

MOU An acronym for Memorandum of Understanding (between government entities). It can be used between government agencies to meet the HIPAA Security Rule requirement in lieu of Business Associate agreements.

Mouse (computer) A computer device for moving the pointer or cursor on the screen, selecting items, and invoking actions in Windows software.

Mouse Button A button on the mouse that when pressed causes a Windows software program to invoke some action. The Student Edition software requires a mouse that has at least two buttons (left and right click). The left button is most frequently used to highlight items (single-click) or select items. Some programs require a double-click of the left mouse button to invoke an action. (Double-click is to press the left button twice in quick succession.) The right button generally invokes a small drop-down list or menu of options related to a particular item or area of the Window program. In most software, the right-click option is only available for selected areas of the program.

Mouse Pointer Typically an arrow shape that moves over the Window program in relationship to the movements of the mouse by the user. It also is sometimes referred to as a "cursor." When using flow sheets or forms, the Student Edition software may change the shape of the mouse pointer to a large question mark or the shape of a hand, indicating a different mode of functionality is temporarily in effect.

MPI An acronym for Master Person Index, a central database of demographic information for persons registered in a healthcare facility or organization.

MRI An acronym for Magnetic Resonance Imaging, which uses magnetic fields and pulses of energy to create images of organs and structures inside the body that cannot be seen by x-ray or CAT scan.

Musculoskeletal Components of the physical exam involving both the musculature and the skeleton.

MVV An acronym for Maximal Voluntary Ventilation, which is a measurement of the total volume of air that a person can breathe in and out of the lungs in 1 minute.

NANDA An acronym for the North American Nursing Diagnosis Association, which has developed the Taxonomy II Nursing Diagnosis code set. It can be used to identify and code a patient's responses to health problems and life processes.

NASA An acronym for National Aeronautics and Space Administration.

Nasal Turbinate Spongy, spiral-shaped bones in the nose passages.

NCQA An acronym for the National Committee for Quality Assurance, a not-for-profit organization dedicated to improving healthcare quality by measuring the performance of providers and health plans. NCQA is the developer of the HEDIS and PCMH standards.

NCVHS An acronym for National Committee on Vital and Health Statistics, an advisory panel within the U.S. Department of Health and Human Services, which selects national standards for HIPAA and recommends standards for the federal government initiatives on Electronic Health Records.

NDC An acronym for National Drug Code. The NDC is the standard identifier for human drugs. It is assigned and used by the pharmaceutical industry.

NDF-RT A nonproprietary terminology being developed by the Veterans Administration that classifies drugs by mechanism of action and physiologic effect.

NEC An acronym for Not Elsewhere Classified (diagnosis codes).

Negs (button) Auto Negative; a button that will automatically set all the findings (that are not already set) to "normal." The Negs button is operative only on Symptom or Physical Exam findings.

Neurological Disorders Disorders of the nervous system.

Nevi Moles on the skin; plural of nevus.

NHII An acronym for National Health Information Infrastructure, a plan to make EHR records available wherever the patient is treated.

NHS An acronym for National Health Service, the national medical system in the United Kingdom.

NIC An acronym for Nursing Interventions Classification, which is a code set designed for codifying nursing interventions in any clinical setting.

NLM An acronym for the United States National Library of Medicine; a unit of the National Institute of Health, it is the world's largest medical library.

NMDS An acronym for Nursing Minimum Data Set, which defines the minimum set of basic data elements for nursing in a computerized patient record.

NOC An acronym for Nursing Outcomes Classification, which is a code set used in conjunction with NIC for codifying the outcome of nursing interventions.

Nomenclature A system of names created by a recognized group or authority and used in a field of science. An EHR nomenclature is an organized list of medical phrases and codes that helps to standardize the way clinicians record information. These are also referred to as clinical vocabularies or clinical terminologies.

NOS An acronym for Not Otherwise Specified (diagnosis codes).

Note Textbox (entry detail) The Note textbox (in entry details) is used to enter or view a free-text note attached to the currently selected finding. Free text also may be added through a Note window, allowing easier entry of a longer note. The note dialog window can be invoked by clicking the Note button located beneath the right pane in the Student Edition software. (See also Free Text.)

NPI An acronym for National Provider Identifier for doctors, nurses, and other healthcare providers. Established under HIPAA Uniform Identifier Standards.

OB Obstetrics is the field of specialty concerned with pregnancy, childbirth, and the period following.

Objective (chart) The clinician's observations and findings from the physical exam.

OCR (computer) An acronym for Optical Character Recognition, which is software that can analyze scanned document images, identify typed characters, and convert them into computer text.

OCR (HIPAA) An acronym for Office for Civil Rights, an agency of the Department of Health and Human Services that enforces the HIPAA Privacy Rule, in addition to other federal laws.

OIG An acronym for Office of Inspector General (Department of Health and Human Services).

Omaha System (codes) The Omaha System is the oldest standardized terminology for nursing documentation.

ONC An acronym for the Office of National Coordinator for Health Information Technology, an agency of the U.S. Department of Health and Human Services responsible for creating a national health information network and encouraging the use of EHR systems.

ONC-ATCB An acronym for organizations designated by the Office of the National Coordinator as Authorized Testing and Certification Body for purposes of certifying EHR systems.

Onset (entry detail) The Onset field (in entry details) is used to enter a number and a unit of time related to the onset of the currently selected finding. The time unit can be "second," "minute," "hour," "day" "week," "month," "year," or their plurals. A window with keypad for entering onset can be invoked by double-clicking the mouse in the onset field. Alternatively, a calendar in the window can be used to record a specific date of onset.

Order (button) Prefaces the highlighted finding with the prefix "Ordered" and records the finding in the Plan section. The button is enabled only when a finding is "orderable" but not a medication.

Otitus Media Inflammation of the middle ear, often accompanied by pain, fever, dizziness, or hearing abnormalities.

Otolaryngeal Ears, Nose, and Throat.

Outpatient A patient who is examined or treated at a healthcare facility but is not hospitalized overnight. In this textbook, outpatient applies to all medical offices and clinics without overnight accommodation.

PAC(s) An acronym for Picture Archive and Communication System, a computer system that stores diagnostic images such as x-rays and CAT scans.

Pane (software) Two smaller windows within the Student Edition software, each capable of displaying and updating information. The left pane generally displays the nomenclature, or patient management tabs. The right pane generally displays the encounter note, outline view, or drawing tools; however, when using forms or flow sheets, the nomenclature tree may temporarily appear on the right to avoid covering a portion of the form or flow sheet.

Patient-Centered Medical Home An approach to providing comprehensive primary care in a healthcare setting that facilitates partnerships between individual patients, their personal physicians, and when appropriate, the patient's family.

PC An acronym for Personal Computer, any computer capable of running applications without requiring connection to a server.

PCDS An acronym for Patient Care Data Set, which is a comprehensive set of nursing codes gathered from use in nine hospitals.

PDA An acronym for Personal Digital Assistant, a small handheld computer of a size that will fit in the palm of your hand.

PDF An acronym for Portable Document Format, a file format that retains the layout and fonts of the original document.

PE An abbreviation for Physical Exam. (*See also* Px.)

PEA A medical abbreviation for Pulseless Electrical Activity.

PEFR An acronym for Peak Expiratory Flow Rate of air exhaled from the lungs.

Pending Order A lab test or diagnostic procedure that has been ordered but for which no results have been received.

Personal Representative (HIPAA) The HIPAA Privacy Rule allows a patient to appoint a personal representative and requires covered entities to treat an individual's personal representative as the individual with respect to uses and disclosures of the individual's protected health information and the individual's rights under the Privacy Rule.

Pertussis Whooping cough (vaccine).

PET Positron Emission Tomography combines CT (Computer Tomography) and nuclear scanning using a radioactive substance called a tracer, which is injected into a vein. A computer records the tracer as it collects in certain organs, then converts the data into a three-dimensional images of the organ, which can be used to detect or evaluate cancer.

PFSH An acronym for Past History, Family History, and Social History, obtained from patient or other family member.

Pharynx The muscular and membranous cavity leading from the mouth and nasal passages to the larynx and esophagus.

PHI (HIPAA) An acronym for Protected Health Information; a patient's personally identifiable health information (in any form) is protected by the HIPAA Privacy Rule.

Phlebotomist A medical technician who draws blood specimens.

Physical Safeguards (HIPAA) The HIPAA Security Rule requirements to implement physical mechanisms to protect electronic systems, equipment, and EPHI from threats, environmental hazards, and unauthorized intrusion. They include restricting access to EPHI and retaining off-site computer backups.

PHR An acronym for Personal Health Record, an electronic health record owned and maintained by the patient.

PIN An acronym for Personal Identification Number, a secret number used like a password.

PKI An acronym for Public Key Infrastructure, which is used to secure messages or electronically sign documents.

Plan of Treatment Prescribed therapy, medication, orders, and patient instructions for treatment or management of the diagnosed condition.

PMRI An acronym for Patient Medical Record Information.

PMS A medical abbreviation for Premenstrual Syndrome.

PNDS An acronym for Perioperative Nursing Data Set nursing codes.

POA Acronym for "present on admission," which is an indicator that a condition was present at the time of the order for inpatient admission. The POA indicator is required for each primary and secondary diagnosis on an inpatient claim.

Polydipsia Excessive, abnormal thirst.

Posting A term used for the act of entering data into the practice management or hospital system—for example, entering charges and payments into the patient accounting system.

Prefix (entry detail) The Prefix field (in entry details) is used to qualify a selected finding. The prefix will sometimes change the section of the note to which the finding is assigned. For example, penicillin normally appears under Medications. When the prefix "Ordered" is used, it will appear under Plan. If the prefix "Allergy to" is used, it will appear under Allergies.

Privacy Official (HIPAA) One individual designated by the medical practice as having overall responsibility for the HIPAA Privacy Rule.

Privacy Policy Covered entities are required to adopt a privacy policy, which meets the requirements of the HIPAA Privacy Rule, and to provide a copy of it to patients.

Privacy Rule (HIPAA) Federal privacy protections for individually identifiable health information.

PRN A medical abbreviation for "as needed."

Problem List Acute conditions for which the patient was recently seen as well as chronic conditions such as high blood pressure, diabetes, and so on, which are monitored at nearly every visit, and can affect decisions about medications and treatments for even unrelated illness.

Problem-Oriented Chart A method of documenting or viewing a patient's chart by listing each problem or condition with the correlating symptoms, observations, and treatments related to that assessment.

Proctosigmoidoscopy *See* Sigmoidoscopy.

Prompt (button) Prompt stands for "prompt with current finding." Prompt is a software feature that generates a list of findings that are clinically related to the finding currently highlighted when the prompt button is clicked.

Protocol Standard plans of therapy used to treat a disease or condition.

PSA An acronym for Prostate-Specific Antigen, a test used to detect possible cancer of the prostate gland in men.

Psittacosis An infection acquired from raising birds.

Pulmonary Embolism Obstruction of the pulmonary artery or one of its branches by an abnormal particle such as a blood clot.

Purulent Discharge Pus or puslike discharge.

PVC An acronym for Pneumococcal Conjugate (vaccine).

Px An acronym for Physical Exam (same as PE). Also the Physical Exam tab in the software.

Radiologists Specialists who interpret x-rays, CAT scans, and other diagnostic tests.

RAM An acronym for Random Access Memory, a measure of the quantity of computer memory.

Read Codes A nomenclature developed by Dr. James Read, later renamed Clinical Terms and merged into SNOMED-CT.

RELMA A free software program provided by Regenstrief Institute to assist with LOINC coding. *See also* LOINC.

Remote Access The ability to access the EHR from outside the medical facility

Glossary 537

network by using a direct-dial connection or a secure connection through the Internet.

Resectable Surgically removable.

Result (entry detail) The Result field (in entry details) is used to enter a result qualifier associated with the current finding. Examples include normal, abnormal, high, or low.

Review of Systems An inventory of body systems starting from the head down, often referred to as ROS. The body systems in a standard ROS are Constitutional symptoms, HEENT (Head, Eyes, Ears, Nose, Mouth, Throat), Cardiovascular, Respiratory, Gastrointestinal, Genitourinary, Musculoskeletal, Integumentary (skin and/or breast), Neurological, Psychiatric, Endocrine, Hematologic/Lymphatic, and Allergic/Immunologic.

Rhinitis Inflammation of the mucus membrane of the nose.

RHIO An acronym for Regional Health Information Organizations, entities formed to facilitate data exchange of patient medical information in a region or state.

Rhonchi Rattling or snoring sounds heard in the chest when there is a partial bronchial obstruction.

RIS An acronym for Radiology Information System.

Risk Analysis (HIPAA) Identify potential security risks, and determine the probability of occurrence and magnitude of risks.

Risk Management (HIPAA) Making decisions about how to address security risks and vulnerabilities.

ROS An acronym for Review of Systems. *See* Review of Systems.

ROS (button) A button that toggles On and Off with each click of the mouse. When On, the button is orange and symptom findings are recorded in the Review of Systems section; when Off, symptom findings are recorded in the History of Present Illness section.

RT An acronym for Respiratory Therapist.

Rx An abbreviation for Therapy (including prescriptions). Also the therapy tab in the software.

Rx (button) Invokes the prescription writer. The button is enabled only if the highlighted finding is a medication.

Rx Norm A nonproprietary vocabulary being developed by the NLM to codify drugs at the level of granularity needed in clinical practice.

Sanction Policy (HIPAA) An office policy to deter noncompliance so that workforce members understand the consequences of failing to comply with security policies and procedures.

Scanned Data (chart) Exam Notes, Letters, Reports, and other documents that have been converted to an image by use of a scanner, then stored in the EHR. The data is accessible by a person viewing the chart, but the image contents cannot be used as data by the system for trend analysis, health maintenance, or similar purposes.

Scroll bar (software) A scroll bar is a feature of most Windows software that automatically appears on the right of a list or text that is too long to fit in the window. The scroll bar has a button that can be moved by pressing the mouse button when dragging the mouse. The information in the window (or window pane) scrolls respective to the movement of the mouse.

Search (button) A word search used to quickly locate all findings in the nomenclature containing either matching words or synonyms of the search word.

Secure Messaging A recommended alternative to sending PHI in e-mail messages; secure messaging uses a secure Web page to read and write messages. The only message sent as e-mail is an alert to the receiving party that the actual message is waiting on the secure site. The contents of secure messages are stored in a secure server not in an e-mail system.

Security Official (HIPAA) One individual designated by the medical practice as having overall responsibility for the HIPAA Security Rule; however, specific security responsibilities may be assigned to other individuals.

Security Reminders (HIPAA) One of the implementation requirements in the HIPAA Security Rule, includes notices, agenda items, and specific discussion topics at monthly meetings, as well as formal retraining about office security policies and procedures.

Security Rule (HIPAA) HIPAA security standards requiring implementation of appropriate security safeguards to protect health information stored in electronic form.

Sig Instructions for labeling a prescription (from Latin *signa*).

Sigmoidoscopy Examination of the rectum, colon, and sigmoid flexure using an illuminated, tubular instrument.

Sinusitis Inflammation of the sinus of the skull.

SNOMED An acronym for Systemized Nomenclature of Medicine had its origins in 1965 as Systemized Nomenclature of Pathology.

SNOMED-CT A medical nomenclature developed by the College of American Pathologists and United Kingdom's National Health Service. It is a merger of two previous coding systems, SNOMED and the Read codes, and has been recommended to become the core terminology for codified EHR in the United States.

SOAP A defined structure for documenting a patient encounter by organizing the information into four sections. The acronym SOAP represents the first letter of each of the section titles: subjective, objective, assessment, and plan.

Social History (tab) A feature on the Patient Management tab that provides a list of the patient's social and behavioral history items recorded in the EHR during all previous encounters.

Speech Recognition software Software that recognizes the patterns in human speech as words and turns them into computer text.

Spirometer An instrument that measures how much and how quickly air can enter and leave the lungs. Measurements may include VC (Vital Capacity), FVC (Forced Vital Capacity), PEFR (Peak Expiratory Flow Rate), MVV (Maximal Voluntary Ventilation), and FEV (Forced Expired Volume).

Spirometry An objective measurement useful in the diagnosis and management of asthma and other lung conditions. (*See* Spirometer.)

SSL An acronym for Secure Socket Layer that transparently encrypts and decrypts Web pages over the Internet.

Status (entry detail) The Status field (in entry details) is used to add the status of the currently selected finding. Examples include worsening, improving, resolved, and similar designations.

Stress Test An electrocardiogram performed before, during, and after strenuous exercise, to measure heart function.

Subjective (chart) The patient describes in his or her own words what the problem is, what the symptoms are, and what he or she is experiencing.

Sx An abbreviation for Symptoms—subjective evidence of disease or physical disturbance. Also the Symptom tab in the software.

Tablet PC A self-contained battery-operated computer similar to a laptop computer but using a special stylus and screen to replace the mouse, thus allowing the computer to be used as though the user was writing on a tablet.

Td An abbreviation for Tetanus and Diphtheria toxoids vaccine.

Technical Safeguards (HIPAA) Primarily automated processes used to protect EPHI data and control access to data. They include using authentication controls to verify that the person signing onto a computer is authorized to access that EPHI, or encrypting and decrypting data as it is being stored or transmitted.

Telemonitors Biomedical devices worn by the patient to capture vital signs or other data during the course of normal activity. The data is then downloaded or transmitted to the EHR.

Telemedicine Uses communication technology to deliver medical care to a patient in another location, usually through online consultation with that person's physician.

Teleradiology Uses communication technology to enable a radiologist in another location to interpret diagnostic images remotely.

Text Data (chart) Information stored in the EHR as word processing, blocks of text, or text reports. The data is searchable but neither codified nor standardized and is generally not indexed.

Toolbar A "Toolbar" is row of icon buttons, the purpose of which is to allow quick access to commonly used functions. The Student Edition software has dynamic toolbars that change the selection of icons depending on the tab the user has selected, as well as special toolbars for functions such as annotated drawings and printing graphs.

Total Cholesterol A blood test that measures the total of all cholesterol in the blood, including both HDL (high-density lipoprotein) and LDL (low-density lipoprotein).

Transactions and Code Sets(HIPAA) HIPAA regulations requiring all covered entities to use standard EDI transaction formats and standard codes within those transactions for claims, remittance advice and payments, claim status, eligibility, referrals, enrollment, premium payments, claim attachments, report of injury, and retail drug claims.

Tree (software) A standard Windows software method of displaying hierarchical lists using small plus and minus symbols to indicate where additional hierarchical levels are hidden from view. The tree structure is used in the Student Edition nomenclature pane. Clicking the mouse on the plus sign next to a finding will "expand the tree" to display additional related findings in an indented list. Clicking on the minus sign next to a finding will "collapse the tree," hiding all findings in the indented list below the selected finding. The purpose of the tree structure is to allow the user to quickly navigate extremely long lists by viewing only the level of hierarchy necessary.

Trend Analysis Comparing data from different dates, tests, or events to correlate the changes in the results with changes in the patient's health.

Triage The screening of patients for allocation of treatment based on the urgency of their need for care. ER triage is often a simplified, organ-specific review of systems conducted by the triage nurse, based on the presenting complaint.

Tx An abbreviation for Tests (performed). Also a tab in the software.

URL An acronym for Universal Resource Locator, the address of a web site—for example: www.myhealthprofessionskit.com.

U.S. Preventive Services Task Force An independent panel of experts in primary care and prevention sponsored by AHRQ that systematically reviews the evidence of effectiveness and develops recommendations for clinical preventive services based on the patient's age, sex, and risk factors for disease. These recommendations are published by the AHRQ and also are incorporated in EHR systems from several vendors.

UMDNS An acronym for Universal Medical Device Nomenclature System, which is used to identify the medical devices for ordering, inventory, or regulatory purposes, but does not provide for the codification of data from the devices.

UMLS An acronym for Unified Medical Language System from the National Library of Medicine. UMLS is not itself a medical terminology but, rather, a resource of software tools and data created from many medical nomenclatures to facilitate the development of EHR.

Uniform Identifiers (HIPAA) HIPAA regulations require all covered entities to adopt and use standard identification numbers for plans, providers, and employers in all HIPAA EDI transactions.

Unit (entry detail) The Unit field (in entry details) shows the currently selected unit for the currently selected finding, provided a standard unit exists. If more than one unit is available for selection, the selection will be shown in blue; otherwise, the selection will be shown in black.

URI An acronym for Upper Respiratory Infection. An infection affecting the nose, nasal passages, or upper part of the pharynx.

UTI A medical abbreviation for Urinary Tract Infection.

VA A common abbreviation for U.S. Department of Veteran Affairs.

Vaccine (tab) A feature on the Patient Management tab that provides a list of the patient's immunizations that have been administered at the clinic.

Value (entry detail) The Value field (in entry details) is used to enter a numerical value for those findings that have a numeric value. (For example: blood pressure, weight, test results, and similar designations.) A window with keypad for entering numeric values can be invoked by double-clicking the mouse in the Value field.

Varicella Chicken pox (vaccine).

Vasoconstrictor An agent or drug that initiates or induces narrowing of the lumen (cavity) of blood vessels.

VC An acronym for Vital Capacity, a measure of the amount of air that can be forcibly exhaled after a full inhalation. An indicator of the breathing capacity of the lungs.

Vital Signs Functional measurements recorded at nearly every visit, temperature, respiration rate, pulse rate, and blood pressure; most clinics measure height and weight as well.

Vital Statistics Statistics of birth, death, disease, and health of a population.

VPN An acronym for Virtual Private Network. Data sent over a public network is encrypted and decrypted without user intervention to attain a level of security similar to a private network.

Wellness Conditions Findings that are not disease-related but, rather, used in health maintenance and preventative screening programs to keep healthy patients healthy. Wellness conditions are based on the age, sex, and history of the patient. Examples of preventative recommendations based on wellness conditions include a mammogram for a healthy woman over 35; immunization vaccines at certain ages in children; and a colonoscopy for a healthy person with a family history of colorectal cancer.

WEP An acronym for Wired Equivalent Privacy, a protocol for securing the content of signals sent over a wireless network.

WHO An acronym for World Health Organization.

Wi-Fi An abbreviation for Wireless Fidelity, a type of fast wireless computer networking. *See also* Wireless Network.

Wireless Network A local area computer network using radio signals in place of wired network cables.

WNL (chart) An acronym for Within Normal Limits in medical charts.

Workstation A personal computer, usually connected to a main computer (server) via a network.

XML An acronym for eXtensible Mark-up Language, a file format similar to the hypertext mark-up language files, which contain fielded data with "tags" or names for the fields.

XPS An acronym for XML Paper Specification, a file format that retains the layout and fonts of the original document yet viewable with a web browser.

X-Ray Traditionally an image made by the passage of short wave radiation through the body onto photographic film. Digital receptors are now able to replace film, allowing the image to be captured and stored in a computer form without photo processing.

Index

Access
- control, 403–404
- patient, to electronic health records, 457–459
- remote, 425–426

Administrative Safeguards, 393, 394–399
Advance Beneficiary Notice (ABN), 70, 71, 200
Agency for Healthcare Research and Quality (AHRQ), 6, 457
Alerts, 68–72
American Academy of Family Physicians, 363
American Academy of Pediatrics, 363
American Association of Medical Assistants, 422
American Health Information Management Association (AHIMA), 422
American Medical Association (AMA), 467
American Nurses Association, 43, 44, 45
American Recovery and Reinvestment Act (ARRA), 7
Anatomical drawings, using, 320–339
Association of Perioperative Registered Nurses, 45
Audit controls, 404
Authentication
- electronic signatures and user, 408–409
- person or entity, 404–405

Auto Negative, 160–161, 194

Bachman, John, 25–26, 368, 418
Bachman's Law and Bachman's Rule, 26
Billing, 499
Biomedical devices, 61
Body mass index (BMI), 358–360
Brailer, David J., 7
Breach notification requirements, 406–408
Browse, 195
Bush, George W., 6
Business associates
- privacy issues and, 389–390
- security issues and, 399, 406, 408

Buttons, 85, 91
- Alternative button styles, 112
- Cite, 307–308, 310
- Color, 325
- Delete, 326
- Ellipsis, 308
- Encounter, 111
- Exit, 326
- Flowsheet, 319
- Font, 325
- Forms, 111
- FS Flow, 310
- List, 194
- Lock, 324–325
- Order, 213
- Print, 134
- Rx, 226–228, 251
- Style, 325
- Undelete, 326

Cataloging images, 45, 51–57
Catalog Pane, 48–50
CDISC (Clinical Data Interchange Standards Consortium), 61
Centers for Disease Control and Prevention, 352, 354, 358
- immunization schedules, 362–363

Certification Commission for Healthcare Information Technology (CCHIT), history of, 13–14
Certified EHR, 13–14
Charts
- *See also* Paper charts
- inpatient versus outpatient, 22–24

Chief complaint, 108–109, 474
Children, privacy issues for minor, 387
Citing, 340
Clinical Care Classification System (CCC), 43
Clinical quality measures (CQM), 14
Clinician's notes, documentation of, 16
Clinton, Bill, 6
CMS (Centers for Medicare & Medicaid Services), 11, 13, 14, 33, 70, 392, 412, 467
Coded data, 36, 37

Codified observations. *See* Findings
Coding systems/nomenclatures
  benefits of, 38–39, 65
  CPT-4 (Current Procedural Terminology), 467
  government mandates, 465
  HCPCS (Healthcare Common Procedure Coding System), 467
  HIPPA code sets, 376–377
  ICD-9-CM (International Classification of Diseases), 235–239, 466–467
  ICD-10, 235, 237–238
  LOINC®, 37, 42
  MEDCIN®, 37, 40–42
  nursing code sets, 43–45
  SNOMED-CT®, 37, 39–41
  standard, 37–45
  UMLS, 43
  undercoding, 186
College of American Pathologists, 39
Color button, 325
Comorbidity, 238
Computer-based Patient Record Institute (CPRI), 4
Computer-based patient records, 2
Computerized axial tomography (CAT), 217
Computerized medical records, 2
Computerized provider order entry (CPOE) systems, 2, 5, 217, 221, 223
  importance of, 196–197
  workflow of, 203–204
Computers
  laptops, 29–30
  Tablet PCs, 30–31
  workstations, 28–29
Consent and informed consent, 379–381
Costs, 5
Counseling and coordination of time component, 486, 503–507, 512–516
CPT-4 (Current Procedural Terminology), 467

Data
  adding, 45–51
  capturing and recording, 45–51
  cataloging, 45, 51–57
  coded, 36, 37
  digital, 36, 37
  discrete, 36
  fielded, 36, 37
  formats, 36
  importance of speed when entering, 152–153
  importing, 58–63
  limitations of, 36–37
  patient-entered, 63–64

  provider-entered, 64
  text, 36, 37
Decision making, medical, 481–486
Decision support, 73–74
  Internet and, 420–424
Delete button, 326
Device and Media Controls, 402
Diagnoses
  multiple, 238–250
  primary and secondary, 238
  rule-out, 239
Diagnosis codes. *See* Coding systems/nomenclatures
Diagnostic tests, ordering, 212–216
DICOM (Digital Imaging and Communications in Medicine), 61, 218
Digital images, 36, 37
  adding, 45–51
  cataloging, 45, 51–57
Disclosures
  incidental, 384–385
  minimum necessary, 384
  patient's right to know about, 385
Discrete data, 36
Documentation, security, 406
Documentation Guidelines for Evaluation and Management (CMS), 473
Document/Image System, 46
Documenting office visits, 119–129, 134–143
Drug Information Association, 61
Drug utilization review (DUR), 69–70, 221–222
Dx. *See* Diagnosis codes

E-health, 427
EHR. *See* Electronic health records
Electronic charts, 2
Electronic Data Interchange (EDI), 376, 377
Electronic health records (EHR)
  certified, 13–14
  defined, 4–5
  evolution of, 1–2
  functions of, 2–4
  importance of, 14–16
  incentives, 465
  Internet and, 419–420
  other names for, 2
  penalties for not using, 465
  reimbursement, 464–465
  stages of change in adopting, 27
  workflow of, 18–21, 203–205
Electronic lab orders, 215
Electronic medical records, 2, 418

Electronic personal health information (EPHI), 392
  See also Privacy issues; Security issues
Electronic Physician, The, 417
Electronic signatures, 408–412
Electronic Signatures in Global and National Commerce Act, 408
Elsevier Science, 44
E-mail, use of, 441–442
Encounter
  creating an, 88–90, 119–129
  date and time, 261
  other terms for, 88
  printing, 130–134
  tab, 111
  view pane, 81
Encryption, 404, 405, 424
Episode details, 104
Evaluation and Management (E&M) codes
  accuracy with, 469
  calculating, 469–473, 489–499
  counseling and coordination of time component, 486, 503–507, 512–516
  determination of levels, 468
  evaluating components, 487–488
  examination component, 478–481
  factors that affect, 488–489, 507–511
  guidelines, 1995 versus 1997, 467
  history component, 474–478
  levels of, 468
  medical decision making component, 481–486
  posting to billing system, 499–501
  problem screening checklist window, 472
  relationship of components, 486–487
  role of, 467–468
  undercoding, 468–469
E-visits, 6
  advantages of, 442
  Blue Shield of California study of, 447
  exercises on, 447–457
  Mayo Clinic study of, 446–447
  workflow, 442–443
Examination component, 478–481
Exit button, 326
Exporting print files, 131

Facility access controls, 401
Federal Health IT Strategic Plan, 8–10
Fielded data, 36, 37
Files, exporting, 131
Findings
  adding details to, 103–104
  navigating, 84–86
  recording, 91–93
  recording history, 96–97
  recording more specific, 95–96
  recording objective, 101
  removing, 94–95
  use of term, 38
Flow sheets
  Cite button, 307–308, 310
  creating problem-oriented, 316–320
  Ellipsis button, 308
  FS Flow buttons, 310
  how to use, 302–316
  purpose of, 301–302
  summary of, 340
  views of, 305
Font button, 325
Forms and Forms Manager
  button, 111
  chief complaint, 108–109
  customizing, 184–187
  differences between lists and, 171
  how to use, 108–112, 171–193
  summary, 194
  vital signs, 109–112
Formulary alerts, 70, 221
Fraud, 489

Glucose monitor, 199
Government agencies, authorizations and, 383–384
Government mandates, 465
Granularity, 38
Graphing
  patient-entered data, 368–369
  to view total cholesterol and weight, 297–298
  to view trends of lab results, 290–294
  to view vital signs in chart, 294–297
Growth charts, 343, 352, 354–357

Hanging protocol, 217
HCPCS (Healthcare Common Procedure Coding System), 467
Health Information Management Systems Society (HIMSS), 62, 427
Health Information Technology for Economic and Clinical Health (HITECH) Act, 7, 9, 390
  requirements of, 10
Health Insurance Portability and Accountability Act. *See* HIPAA
Health Level 7 (HL7), 42, 43, 44, 59–61, 218
Health maintenance, 72–73, 361, 370
HEENT, 175

HIPAA (Health Insurance Portability and
    Accountability Act), 4
  covered entities, 376
  identifiers, uniform, 377–378
  privacy issues, 378–391, 392–393
  purpose of, 375–376, 466
  security issues, 391–412
  transaction and code sets, 376–377
History component, 474–478
History of present illness (HPI), 474, 475–476
Holter monitor, 62
Home Health Care Classification, 43
Hospital Consumer Assessment Healthcare
    Providers and Systems (HCAHPS), 457

ICD-9-CM (International Classification of
    Diseases), 235–239, 466–467
ICD-10, 235, 237–238
ICNP (International Classification for Nursing
    Practice), 44
Identifiers, HIPAA uniform, 377–378
Image Tools, 51
Image Viewer Pane, 51
Immunizations, 73
  adult, 368
  CDC immunization schedules, 362–363
  pediatric, 360–367
Importing data, 58–63
Incentives, 465
Incidental disclosures, 384
Information Access Management, 397
Informed consent, 379–381
Inpatient charts versus outpatient charts, 22–24
Instant Medical History, 63, 430, 442
Institute of Medicine (IOM), 2, 196, 197
Integrity of EPHI, 404
International Council of Nurses, 44
Internet, 6
  access control, 403–404
  decision support, 420–424
  EHR and, 419–420
  electronic signatures, 408–412
  how it works, 428
  patient-entered data, 429–441
  remote access, 425–426
  security, 398, 402–405, 424–425
  telemedicine, 427–429
  teleradiology, 428–429
  workflow, 432
Item Details, 51

Joint Commission, 262, 411–412

Kaiser-Permanente, 460

Laboratory Information System (LIS), 199
Lab orders and reports, 197–201
  using graphs to view trends of lab results,
    66–67, 290–294
Laptops, 29–30
Lists and Lists Manager
  differences between forms and, 171
  how to use, 154–170
  summary, 194
List size function, 194, 209–210
Lock button, 324–325
LOINC® (Logical Observation Identifiers Names
    and Codes), 37, 42
Longitudinal patient records, 2

Magnetic resonance imaging (MRI), 217
Marketing, authorizations and, 383
Mayne, John, 430, 433
Mayo Clinic, 427–428, 446–447
Meaningful use, 10–12, 457, 465
MEDCIN® nomenclature, 37, 40–42
MEDCIN® Student Edition
  anatomical drawings, using, 320–339
  assessment, recording, 105
  buttons, 85, 91, 112
  calculating E&M code, 469–473, 489–499
  chief complaint, 108–109
  data entry, 87–88
  documenting office visits, 119–129, 134–143
  encounter, creating an, 88–90, 119–129
  encounter note, printing, 130–134
  encounter tab, 111
  encounter view pane, 81
  episode details, 104
  exiting and restarting, 81–82
  exporting print files, 131
  findings, adding details to, 103–104
  findings, navigating, 84–86
  findings, recording, 91–93
  findings, recording history, 96–97
  findings, recording more specific, 95–96
  findings, recording objective, 101
  findings, removing, 94–95
  forms, 108–112, 171–193
  free text, 99–100
  list size function, 194, 209–210
  Lists Manager, 154–170
  menu bar and toolbar, 80–81
  navigating the screen, 80–87
  nomenclature pane, 81
  nomenclature pane tabs, 81, 87

patient management, 263–269, 299–300
patient selection, 82–84
printing, 130–134
prompt feature, 206–212, 251
recording prescriptions, 221–230
recording tests and orders, 197–201
result field, setting, 101–103
search feature, 205–212, 251
starting up, 78–80
Status field, setting, 103
toolbar, 48, 80–81
treatment plan and physician orders, recording, 105–107
values, recording, 98–99
vital signs, 109–112

Medical decision making (MDM)
component, 481–486
levels of, 485

Medical errors, 5, 6
alerts, 68–72

Medication administration
electronic, 222, 224–230
Five Rights, 224
quick-pick list to frequent orders, 230–235
recording, 221–230
safety issues, 223–224
written, 221–222

Medicomp Systems, Inc., 40
Medscape, 421, 422
Menu bar, 47
Minimum necessary, 384
Mitchell, Marvin, 427
Mobility issues, 27
Mouse buttons, 176–177

NANDA-1 (North American Nursing Diagnosis Association International), 43
National Center for Health Statistics (NCHS), 352
National Electrical Manufacturers Association, 61
National Health Information Infrastructure (NHII), 392
National health information network (NHIN), 62
National Library of Medicine (NLM), 43
Negs (Auto Negative), 160–161, 194
NIC (Nursing Interventions Classification, 43–44
NMDS (Nursing Minimum Data Set, 44
NOC (Nursing Outcomes Classification), 44

Nomenclatures
See also Coding systems/nomenclatures
pane, 81
pane tabs, 81, 87

Nursing code sets, 43–45

Obama, Barack, 7
Office of Civil Rights (OCR), 390, 392, 407
Office of the National Coordinator (ONC) for Health Information Technology, 7, 62, 420
Office visits, documenting, 119–129, 134–143
Omaha System, 44
Optical Character Recognition (OCR), 53
Order button, 251

Orders
recording, 197–201
view pending, 279–288

Organizational requirements, security and, 406
Outline View tab, 178–180, 194
Outpatient charts versus inpatient charts, 22–24
Ozbolt, Judy, 45

Paper charts, workflow of, 16–18, 201–203
Past, family, and social history (PFSH), 474, 476–477
Patient access to electronic health records, 457–459
Patient-Centered Medical Home (PCMH), 457–459
Patient-entered data, 63–64
graphs, 368–369
Internet use, 429–441

Patient management
following up on problems using, 269–278
how to use, 263–269
summary of, 299–300

Patients' rights
access to medical records, 385–386
to know about disclosures, 385

Patient selection, 82–84
PCDS (Patient Care Data Set), 45

Pediatric wellness visits
body mass index, 358
documenting, 343–352
growth charts, 343, 352, 354–357
immunizations, 360–367

Penalties
for misuse of personal health information, 390–391
for not using EHR, 465

Pending orders, viewing, 279–288
Percentiles, 355–356

Personal health records (PHR)
availability of, 6, 385–386
basics to look for in, 460
development of, 459–460
researching, 460–461

Personal representatives, 386–387
Pharmacy benefit manager, 221

INDEX 545

PHI (Protected Health Information). *See* Privacy issues; Security issues
PHR. *See* Personal health records
Physical Safeguards, 393, 395, 400–402
Picture Archival and Communication (PAC) System, 58, 217
PNDS (Perioperative Nursing Data Set), 45
Point-of-care documentation, 24–27
Point-of-care testing, 199
Policies and procedures, security and, 406
Positron emission tomography (PET), 217
Prescriptions
  electronic, 222, 224–230
  recording, 221–230
  safety issues, 223–224
  written, 221–222
Preventive care, 72–73
  body mass index, 358–360
  growth charts, 343, 352, 354–357
  immunizations, 360–368
  pediatric wellness visits, 343–352
  screening, 370
Printing encounters, 130–134
Privacy issues
  access to medical records, 385–386
  authorization, 381–383
  business associates, 389–390
  compared to security rule, 392–393
  compliance issues, 378–379
  consent and informed consent, 379–381
  disclosures, incidental, 384–385
  disclosures, patient's right to know about, 385
  government agencies, 383–384
  HIPAA, 378–391, 392–393
  minimum necessary, 384
  minor children, 387
  penalties for misuse, 390–391
  personal representatives, 386–387
  plain language, 379
Problem Lists
  following up on problems, 269–278
  how to use, 262–263
  Patient Management, 263–269
  summary of, 298–299
Problem screening checklist window, 472
Prompt feature, 206–212, 251
Protected Health Information (PHI). *See* Privacy issues; Security issues
Provider-entered data, 64
Providers, use of term, 262
Public Key Infrastructure (PKI), 410–411

Radiology Information System (RIS), 217
Radiology orders and reports, 217–221
Read, James, 39
Recording
  prescriptions, 221–230
  tests and orders, 197–201
Reference terminologies, 38
Regenstrief Institute, 42
Regional Health Information Organizations (RHIOs), 33, 62–63
Reimbursement. *See* Coding systems/nomenclatures
Research
  authorizations and, 383
  Internet, 422–423
Results management, 278
  pending orders, viewing, 279–288
Retrieving information, 65–68
Review of systems (ROS), 159–160, 194, 474, 476
Rule-out diagnosis, 239
Rx button, 226–228, 251

Saba, Virginia, 43
Safeguards, 393
  Administrative, 393, 394–399
  Physical, 393, 395, 400–402
  Technical, 393, 395, 402–405
Safety issues. *See* Security issues
Safety Management Process, 395–396
Search feature, 205–212, 251
Secured socket layer (SSL), 425
Security issues, 5
  Administrative Safeguards, 393, 394–399
  assigned responsibility, 396
  breach notification requirements, 406–408
  business associates, 399, 406, 408
  compared to privacy rule, 392–393
  contingency plans, 399
  electronic signatures, 408–412
  evaluation, ongoing, 399
  HIPAA and, 391–412
  implementation specifications, 393
  incident procedures, 398–399
  Internet, 398, 402–405, 424–425
  Physical Safeguards, 393, 395, 400–402
  standards, 393, 394
  Technical Safeguards, 393, 395, 402–405
  training, 397–398
  transmission, 405
  workforce, 396–397
Sig, 69, 227
Slack, W. V., 430

SNOMED-CT® (Systematized Nomenclature of Medicine-Clinical Terms), 37, 39–41
SOAP format, 16, 24
Specimens, 199
Speech recognition systems, 31–32, 218
Student Edition software. *See* Medcin Student Edition
Study (radiology), 217
Style button, 325

Tablet PCs, 30–31
Technical Safeguards, 393, 395, 402–405
Technology
　See also Internet; *type of*
　effects of, 27–28
　impact of, 417–419
　security, 398, 402–405
Telemedicine, 427–429
Telemonitors, 62
Teleradiology, 428–429
Tests, recording, 197–201
Text files, 36, 37
　importing, 58
Toolbar, 48, 80–81
　print dialog window from, 134
Training, security, 397–398
Transactions, HIPPA, 376–377
Transmission security, 405
Trending, 65, 201
　using graphs to view trends of lab results, 290–294
　using graphs to view vital signs in chart, 294–297

UMLS (Unified Medical Language System), 43
Undelete button, 326

Undercoding, 468–469
U.S. Preventive Services Task Force, 370
University of Illinois, College of Nursing, 44
University of Iowa, College of Nursing, 44
University of Wisconsin, Milwaukee School of Nursing, 44

Values, recording, 98–99
Virtual private network (VPN), 425
Vital signs, 109–112
　pediatric vital signs, 349
　using graphs to view vital signs in chart, 294–297

webMD Health, 420
Web sites, 420, 421, 422
Wenner, Allen R., 25–26, 27, 63, 368–369, 418, 429, 430–431, 433
Workflow
　comparison of paper versus EHR orders, 201–205
　EHR, 18–21
　e-visit, 442–443
　from EHR to billing, 500–501
　Internet, 432
　paper charts, 16–18
　patient-entered data and, 431–432
　safe medication administration, 223–224
Workforce Security, 396–397
Workstations, computer, 28–29, 402
World Health Organization (WHO), 236, 237, 352

XPS file, 131
X-rays, 217
　ordering, 218–221

Acronyms Used in This Book

ABG	Arterial Blood Gas	ENT	Ears, Nose, Throat
ABN	Advance Beneficiary Notice	EPHI	Protected Health Information in Electronic form
ABN	Abnormal		
AHIMA	American Health Information Management Association	EPs	Eligible Professionals
		ER	Emergency Department or Emergency Room
AHRQ	Agency for Healthcare Research and Quality	FDA	Food and Drug Administration
AMA	Against Medical Advice	FEIN	Federal Employer Identification Number
ARRA	American Recovery and Reinvestment Act	FS Form	Flow Sheet (based on a) Form
BID	Twice Daily	FS Hx	Family and Social History
BIPAP	Bilevel Positive Airway Pressure	GI	Gastrointestinal
BMI	Body Mass Index	H&P	History and Physical
BMP	Basic Metabolic Panel	HAC	Hospital Acquired Condition
CAT	Computerized Axial Tomography	HCAHPS	Hospital Consumer Assessment Healthcare Providers and Systems
CBC	Complete Blood Count		
CC	Chief Complaint	HCPCS	Healthcare Common Procedure Coding System
CCC	Clinical Care Classification system		
CCHIT	Certification Commission for Healthcare Information Technology	HDL-C	High-Density Lipoprotein (cholesterol test)
		HEENT	Head, Eyes, Ears, Nose, (Mouth), and Throat
CCU	Critical Care Unit	HepB	Hepatitis B (vaccine)
CDC	Centers for Disease Control and Prevention	HHS	U.S. Department of Health and Human Services
CDISC	Clinical Data Interchange Standards Consortium	Hib	Haemophilus influenzae type B (vaccine)
		HIM	Health Information Management
CDR	Clinical Data Repository	HIMSS	Health Information Management Systems Society
CHF	Congestive Heart Failure		
CIR	Citywide Immunization Registry (New York City)	HIPAA	Health Insurance Portability and Accountability Act
CME	Continuing Medical Education	HITECH	Health Information Technology for Economic and Clinical Health
CMS	Centers for Medicare and Medicaid Services		
COB	Coordination of Benefits	HIV	Human Immunodeficiency Virus
CPOE	Computerized Provider Order Entry	HL7	Health Level 7
CPR	Cardio-Pulmonary Resuscitation	HPI	History of Present Illness
CPRI	Computer Based Patient Record Institute	Hx	History
CPT-4	Current Procedural Terminology, 4th Revision	ICD-9-CM	International Classification of Diseases, ninth revision, with clinical modifications
CRNA	Certified Registered Nurse Anesthesiologist	ICD-10	International Classification of Diseases, tenth revision
CT	Computed Tomography		
CVP	Cerebral Vascular Pressure	ICNP	International Classification for Nursing Practice
DAW	Dispense As Written		
DICOM	Digital Imaging and Communications in Medicine	IMH	Instant Medical History
		IOM	Institute of Medicine
DTaP	Diphtheria, Tetanus, Pertussis (vaccine)	IPV	Inactivated Polio Virus (vaccine)
DUR	Drug Utilization Review	IT	Information Technology
Dx	Diagnosis	JCAHO	The Joint Commission
E&M	Evaluation and Management codes	LAN	Local Area Networks
ECG or EKG	Electrocardiogram	LIS	Laboratory Information System
EDI	Electronic Data Interchange	LOINC	Logical Observation Identifiers Names and Codes
EMR	Electronic Medical Record		